W9-BLP-472

Positive Psychology

The Science of Happiness and Flourishing

Second Edition

WILLIAM C. COMPTON

EDWARD HOFFMAN

WADSWORTH
CENGAGE Learning·

Australia • Brazil • Japan • Korea • Mexico • Singapore • Spain • United Kingdom • United States

WADSWORTH
CENGAGE Learning·

Positive Psychology: The Science of Happiness and Flourishing, Second edition
William C. Compton and Edward Hoffman

Publisher: Jon-David Hague

Editorial Assistant: Travis Holland

Marketing Manager: Janay Pryor

Production Management, and Composition: PreMediaGlobal

Manufacturing Planner: Karen Hunt

Rights Acquisitions Specialist: Don Schlotman

Art Editor: Vernon T. Boes

Photo Researcher: Kathleen Olson

Cover Designer: Andy Norris

Cover Image: Masterfile

© 2013, 2005 Wadsworth, Cengage Learning

ALL RIGHTS RESERVED. No part of this work covered by the copyright herein may be reproduced, transmitted, stored, or used in any form or by any means graphic, electronic, or mechanical, including but not limited to photocopying, recording, scanning, digitizing, taping, Web distribution, information networks, or information storage and retrieval systems, except as permitted under Section 107 or 108 of the 1976 United States Copyright Act, without the prior written permission of the publisher.

For product information and technology assistance, contact us at
Cengage Learning Customer & Sales Support, 1-800-354-9706.
For permission to use material from this text or product,
submit all requests online at **www.cengage.com/permissions.**
Further permissions questions can be e-mailed to
permissionrequest@cengage.com

Library of Congress Control Number: 2011942963

Student Edition:

ISBN-13: 978-1-111-83412-8

ISBN-10: 1-111-83412-1

Wadsworth
20 Davis Drive
Belmont, CA 94002-3098
USA

Cengage Learning is a leading provider of customized learning solutions with office locations around the globe, including Singapore, the United Kingdom, Australia, Mexico, Brazil, and Japan. Locate your local office at **www.cengage.com/global**.

Cengage Learning products are represented in Canada by Nelson Education, Ltd.

To learn more about Wadsworth, visit **www.cengage.com/wadsworth**
Purchase any of our products at your local college store or at our preferred online store **www.cengagebrain.com**.

Printed in the United States of America
4 5 6 7 15 14

Dedication

To Barbara, once again. Her laughter continues to be the music of my life
—(W.C.)

To Elaine, who has quietly taught me about flourishing.
—(E.H.)

Brief Contents

PREFACE TO THE SECOND EDITION   xiv

ACKNOWLEDGMENTS   xvi

ABOUT THE AUTHORS   xvii

1   An Introduction to Positive Psychology   1

2   Foundations: Emotion, Motivation, and the Nature of Well-Being   23

3   Subjective Well-Being   51

4   Leisure, Flow, Mindfulness and Peak Performance   79

5   Love and Well-Being   101

6   Positive Health   127

7   Excellence, Aesthetics, Creativity, and Genius   153

8   Well-Being Across the Lifespan   177

9   Optimal Well-Being   199

10   Religion, Spirituality, and Well-Being   229

11   Positive Institutions and Cultural Well-Being   259

12   A Look Toward the Future of Positive Psychology   283

REFERENCES   297

NAME INDEX   361

SUBJECT INDEX   375

Contents

PREFACE TO THE SECOND EDITION   xiv
ACKNOWLEDGMENTS   xvi
ABOUT THE AUTHORS   xvii

Chapter 1   An Introduction to Positive Psychology   1

Welcome to Positive Psychology   1

The Dimensions of Positive Psychology   2

The Scope of Positive Psychology   2

Basic Themes of Positive Psychology   3

The Good Life   3

Positive Emotions Are Important   3

People Can Flourish and Thrive   5

Compassion and Empathy Are Important   6

People Need Positive Social Relationships   7

Strengths and Virtues Are Important   7

Independence of Positive and Negative Emotions   8

Negative Emotions Are Still Important   8

The Science of Well-Being   9

A Short History of Well-Being in the Western World   9

Hedonism   10

The Early Hebrews   10

The Greeks   10

Early Christianity and the Middle Ages   13

The Renaissance to the Age of Enlightenment   15

Romanticism and the Nineteenth Century   16

The Twentieth Century   17

Lessons on Well-Being from History   19

Positive Psychology Today   20

Summary   21

Chapter 2   Foundations: Emotion, Motivation, and the Nature of Well-Being   23

The Basic Emotions   23

The Components of Emotion   25

The Biology of Emotions   25

Cognition: How We Think Impacts How We Feel   28

Behavior: How We Act Influences How We Feel   28

Social and Cultural Influences on Emotions   31

Moods and Well-Being   32

Positive Psychology and Motivation   33

Early Theories of Motivation   33

Intrinsic and Extrinsic Motivation   33

Motivation and the Pursuit of Goals   34

Well-Being and Positive Emotion   37

The Broaden-and-Build Model   37

Emotional Intelligence   40

Definitions of Happiness and Well-Being   42

One-Dimensional Theories   42

Multidimensional Theories   44

Summary   48

Chapter 3   Subjective Well-Being   51

The Measurement of Subjective Well-Being   51

Self-Report Measures of Subjective Well-Being   52

The Stability of Subjective Well-Being   53

Why Is Happiness Important?   53

Top-Down and Bottom-Up Theories   54

Top-Down Predictors of Subjective Well-Being   55

Cognition: Is the Glass Half Full or Half Empty?   55

Positive Relationships with Other People   60

Personality Traits   60

Bottom-Up Predictors of Subjective Well-Being   62

Money, Income, and Wealth   62

Gender: Are Men or Women Happier?   65

Age: Is One Age Group Happier than Another?   66

Race, Education, Climate, and Politics   67

Bottom-Up Predictors and the "Happiest Man in America"   68

Cautionary Tales: The Down Side of Feeling Up   69

Increasing Happiness and Life Satisfaction   69

   Intensity and Frequency of Positive Emotion   *70*

   Strategies for Creating a Good Mood   *71*

   Fordyce's Happiness Training Program   *71*

   Sustainable Happiness   *72*

   Barbara Fredrickson's Positivity   *73*

   Hope Training   *73*

   Comparing Interventions: Which Ones Work Better?   *73*

   Maintaining Happiness   *74*

   General Comments on Increasing Happiness   *74*

Summary   76

Chapter 4   Leisure, Flow, Mindfulness and Peak Performance   79

Leisure   79

   Leisure and Well-Being   *79*

   What Turns an Activity into "Leisure"?   *81*

Flow and Optimal Experience   82

   Definition of Flow   *82*

   Characteristics of Flow   *83*

   Contexts and Situations of Flow   *85*

   Unique Qualities of Flow   *86*

   Flow and Subjective Well-Being   *86*

   Absorption and Curiosity   *88*

   Comments on the Theory of Flow   *89*

Mindfulness   90

   Ellen Langer's Approach to Mindfulness   *90*

   The Buddhist Approach to Mindfulness   *91*

   Comparison Between Ellen Langer's and Buddhist Styles of Mindfulness   *93*

Savoring   94

Peak Performance   94

   Peak Performance in Sports   *96*

Comments on Flow, Mindfulness, Savoring, and Peak Performance   97

Summary   98

Chapter 5   Love and Well-Being   101

Genes, Hormones, and Marriage   101

Evolution and Love   101

The Biochemistry of Love   102

Marriage and Well-Being   102

The Varieties of Love   104

A Two-Factor Theory of Love   104

The Love Styles   104

Sternberg's Love Triangle   105

Love as a Prototype or an Ideal   106

The Love Hierarchy   106

Finding Romance and Love   107

What Attracts Us to Someone?   107

Relationship Satisfaction: Why Do Caring Relationships Make Us Feel Good?   108

Personality Traits   108

Communication   109

Relationship Stability: What Makes It Last?   111

What Does the Research Say about Stability?   112

Minding Relationships   112

Knowing and Being Known   113

Attributions   113

Acceptance and Respect   115

Reciprocity   115

Continuity   116

Positive Families   117

What Makes a Flourishing Family?   118

The Family Life Cycle   120

Social and Cultural Influences   121

What Hurts Relationships?   122

Conflict   122

The Demand-Withdraw Pattern and Stonewalling   123

How to Nurture Positive Relationships that Last   123

Summary   124

Chapter 6   Positive Health   127

Wellness   127

Positive Health   128

Vitality and Positive Health   128

Exercise and Positive Health   128

Vagal Tone and Heart Rate Variability (HRV)   129

Health Psychology and PNI   129

Psychological Factors Important to Health   130

Positive Emotionality   130

Social Support   131

Love and Positive Health   134

Humor and Positive Health   136

Music and Health   137

Emotional Expression and Health   137

Cognition and Thinking: Optimism, Hope and Control   140

Hardiness and Mindfulness Meditation   142

Hardiness   143

Mindfulness Meditation   143

Positive Aging   145

Zestful Old Age   145

Longevity   145

Positive Coping   147

A Definition of Positive Coping   147

The Importance of Daily Hassles   147

Dimensions of Positive Coping   148

Coping Styles   148

Comments on Positive Coping and Health   149

Summary   149

Chapter 7   Excellence, Aesthetics, Creativity, and Genius   153

The Pursuit of Excellence   153

The Foundations of Excellence   153

The Development of Excellence   154

Resonance   156

Passion   157

Grit   157

Aesthetics and the Good Life   158

Why Is the Aesthetic Sense Important?   159

Four Attributes of the Aesthetic Experience   159

Music and the Brain   161

Art, Music, and Dance Therapy   161

Finding Beauty Outside the Arts   162

Origins of the Aesthetic Sense   163

Can Tragedy and Sadness Be Beautiful?   163

Creativity   164

What is Creativity?   164

"Little c" and "Big C" Creativity   164

Research Perspectives on Creativity   164

How to Enhance the Potential for Creativity   170

Genius   172

Genius and "Madness"   172

Summary   173

Chapter 8   Well-Being Across the Lifespan   177

Well-Being Over the Lifespan   178

Stage Models and Well-Being   178

Lifespan and Life-Course Models and Well-Being   180

Different Paths to Maturity: Individual Differences in Lifespan
Development   185

*Narrative Approaches to the Lifespan: Telling Stories to Make Sense
of Our Lives*   187

Adjusting to Difficult Life Events   189

Resilience: In Children   190

Resilience in Adulthood   192

Healthy and Adaptive Defense Mechanisms   196

Summary   197

Chapter 9   Optimal Well-Being   199

What Wisdom Did King Solomon Have?   200

Preliminary Wisdom About Wisdom   200

Wisdom and Well-Being   201

Wisdom as a Stage of Life   201

Wisdom as Post-Formal Cognitive Development   202

Wisdom as a Form of Excellence   202

A Balance Theory of Wisdom   203

Wisdom as the "Master" Virtue   205

How to Cultivate Wisdom   205

Early Psychodynamic Ideas of Optimal Personality   206

Alfred Adler   206

Carl G. Jung   206

Erich Fromm   207

Existentialism and Authenticity   209

Rollo May   210

Viktor Frankl   210

Authenticity: Finding One's True Self   211

Humanistic Perspectives   214

Carl Rogers and the Fully Functioning Person   214

Abraham Maslow and Self-Actualization   215

Julius Seeman and Personality Integration   221

Personal Growth Initiative   222

Personal Growth and Human Potential   222

The Optimal Personality: Common Themes   223

Marie Jahoda and Positive Mental Health   223

Personality Traits Important for Optimal Well-Being   224

Your Own Inner Hero   225

Summary   226

Chapter 10   Religion, Spirituality, and Well-Being   229

Religion and Subjective Well-Being   229

Religion and Health   230

Prayer and Well-Being   231

Why is Religion Related to Well-Being?   233

A Sense of Meaning and Purpose in Life   234

Ways to Create Meaning   234

The Sacred Emotions   236

Gratitude and Appreciation   236

Forgiveness   238

Compassion and Empathy   239

Humility   240

Religious Experiences   241

Elation and Awe   241

Wonder   242

Peak Experiences   244

Numinous Experiences   245

Conversion   245

Contemplative Spirituality   246
   Transpersonal Psychology   246
   Mysticism   247
Contemplative Religious Traditions   248
   Monastic Christianity   248
   Kabbalah   248
   Buddhism   249
   Mindfulness Meditation   250
Mysticism and the Brain   251
   Neurotheology   253
   An Unusual Route to Transcendent Experiences   254
   Entheogens and Religious Experiences   254
Psychological Theories of Religious Maturity   255
   Intrinsic and Extrinsic Religiousness   255
   Stages of Religious Cognition   255
   Psychodynamic Perspectives on Religion   256
   Perspectives on Morality and Ethics   256
Summary   257

Chapter 11   Positive Institutions and Cultural Well-Being   259

Employee Engagement and Job Satisfaction   259
   A Definition of Employee Engagement   259
   What Promotes Employee Engagement?   260
   A Strength-Based Approach to Engagement   263
   Employee Engagement: A Positive Work Environment   264
   Leadership   265
   Conclusions about Employee Engagement   266
Careers That Use Positive Psychology   267
   Positive Psychotherapy   267
   Positive Psychology in Schools   269
Positive Communities   270
   Social Well-Being   270
   Flourishing Communities   270
   Social Contagion: The Power of Social Networks   271
   Community Psychology   272
   Volunteerism   273

Cross-Cultural Subjective Well-Being   273

    Why Do Cultures Differ in Subjective Well-Being?   *275*

    Comments on Culture and Well-Being   *279*

Summary   280

Chapter 12   A Look Toward the Future of Positive Psychology   283

How Do We Recognize a Life Well-Lived?   284

Positive Psychology Needs Both Positive and Negative Emotions   285

    Theories That Integrate Positive and Negative Emotion   *286*

Alternatives to Happiness   287

    Meaning in Life   *287*

    Purpose in Life   *288*

New Research Methods   288

    Systems Theory   *289*

Integrate Positive Psychology with General Psychology   291

The Question of Values   291

Cross-Cultural Considerations   292

    Cross-Cultural Well-Being   *292*

    Post-Modern Considerations   *293*

Toward the Future with Optimism   295

Summary   295

REFERENCES   297
NAME INDEX   361
SUBJECT INDEX   375

Preface to the Second Edition

Around the world today, the field of positive psychology is booming. Since being launched over a dozen years ago, it has gained thousands of professional adherents in diverse countries, inspired countless college students, and achieved widespread media attention. Initially dubbed rather simplistically as the *science of happiness*, positive psychology is increasingly recognized as both more encompassing—and more important—than merely helping people put a daily grin on their faces. For example, topics like forgiveness, gratitude, flow, resilience, positive families, zestful work, and wellness have all gained increased interest. Even newer topics, like the role of social contagion in the spread of happiness and the importance of mindfulness to well-being are creating fresh concepts and possible interventions.

When the first edition of this book was released in July of 2004, positive psychology had been rapidly gaining momentum since it was created in 1998. Since the initial release of the book, the field of positive psychology has grown tremendously—so much so that a new edition of this textbook was clearly necessary. Therefore, not only have we expanded many sections of the first edition to represent the newest research, but added dozens of new sections reflecting the rapid progress of positive psychology.

Chapter 1: The introduction has been updated and revised to reflect the latest research in positive psychology. The section on history has been expanded to include developments in the 20th Century and clarifications of what history can teach us about well-being today.

Chapter 2: Considerable revision of this chapter has emphasized the basic research foundations of positive psychology and how people create their emotional lives. Topics now include: an updated review of the role of positive emotions and the broaden-and-build model, cognitive perspectives such as learned optimism and how our perspective on time may impact well-being, how strengths and virtues foster well-being, as well as the social and cultural influences on emotion. In addition, the research on motivation has been updated and a new section has been added on theoretical perspectives of well-being influential in positive psychology research.

Chapter 3: The research on subjective well-being has been updated including the newest research on how money may influence happiness. A new section has been added that discusses how many emotions, such as nostalgia, may be difficult to categorize as purely positive or negative. A new section has been added on interventions to enhance happiness and life satisfaction.

Chapter 4: Research on leisure, flow, savoring, and peak performance has been updated. In addition, the section on mindfulness has been expanded considerably to reflect recent research. A section on curiosity and absorption has been added.

Chapter 5: The research on positive intimate relationships has been updated considerably to include new topics such as minding relationships, capitalization, and the Michelangelo phenomenon. In addition, a new section on positive families has been added. A new section on self-disclosure has also been added— a topic not often found in positive psychology textbooks.

Chapter 6: The research on positive health and positive coping has been updated along with expanded sections on mindfulness-based stress reduction and longevity. A new section has been added on regrets and well-being, again, a topic not often found in other positive psychology textbooks.

Chapter 7: The research on excellence, creativity and genius has been updated. The section on aesthetics and the arts has been expanded. New research on the importance of passion and grit has been added.

Chapter 8: This chapter has been considerably rewritten. It now covers well-being across the lifespan and positive aging. Research on resilience is still included in the chapter. It has, however, been updated to reflect both resilience in children and adults.

Chapter 9: This chapter has also been extensively rewritten. It now reflects different perspectives on optimal well-being or high-level flourishing. The chapter includes expanded sections on wisdom, theories of optimal well-being, authenticity, and self-actualization. A new section has been added that covers personality traits important to optimal well-being (such as openness to experience and courage) and how to create your own "inner hero".

Chapter 10: Newer research on religion and meaning has been incorporated. A new section on the "sacred emotions" has been added (i.e. gratitude, forgiveness, compassion, and humility). The sections on religious experiences and contemplative spirituality have been updated and expanded along with newer research on cross-cultural studies of peak experiences. The newest research on neurological and physiological correlates of religious experiences has been added.

Chapter 11: The research on employee engagement and work satisfaction has been updated. A section on careers that use positive psychology has been added. The sections on positive communities and cross-cultural perspectives have been updated to reflect newer topics such as the social contagion of happiness and the importance of need satisfaction to cross-cultural comparisons of well-being. In fact, throughout the new edition we have tried to broaden the cultural base of positive psychology by discussing cross-cultural research.

Chapter 12: The final chapter has been updated to reflect changing perspectives for the future of positive psychology. We both have been active in our field for more than 30 years as educators and researchers, and are convinced that positive psychology is among the most exciting scientific developments of today. For science is not only about understanding the mechanistic aspects of the universe, but human emotions, hopes, aspirations, skills, talents, and creative impulses as well. The more precise and articulate that psychologists can be in delineating these aspects of personal and social life, the greater the likelihood of creating a more harmonious and peaceful world.

Acknowledgments

We would also like to thank the researchers who generously shared their photographs with us for this edition and Dr. David G. Myers for allowing us to use tables and graphs that appear in the book. We extend our appreciation to a number of students who helped with various research tasks for the second edition: Tori Counts, Courtney Allison, and Richard ("Ranger") Tillman (good luck in your doctoral program Ranger—you will be a great psychologist), Melani Landerfeldt, and Megan Williams. Thanks are also extended to Ranger and George Oeser for putting Figure 2.1 into a computer-friendly format. We would also like to extend our deep appreciation to the students who have taken our courses in positive psychology over the years. We thank them for their interest, questions, and enthusiasm for a positive approach to psychology.

Finally, for their help and careful attention to the quality of this book, we are grateful to Jon-David Hague, Ph.D., our publisher at Cengage Learning, to the project manager Arul Joseph Raj, and to the many others who worked on the production of this book.

About the Authors

William Compton has nurtured a fascination with and enthusiasm for ideas about psychological well-being for over 45 years. He began his search in a somewhat unusual place for a future psychologist—as a Far Eastern Studies major at the University of Wisconsin–Madison studying Eastern religions. Seeking a more applied and practical approach to well-being, he entered psychology and received his doctorate in clinical psychology from George Peabody College of Vanderbilt University in 1987. He worked as a psychotherapist until joining the psychology faculty at Middle Tennessee State University in 1989. In 1992, he created a course on the psychology of well-being. At that time, it was one of the only courses on well-being offered in any university. Six years later, positive psychology was created by Martin E. P. Seligman and colleagues. Finally, there was a way to bring all the various elements of well-being together under one banner. Compton is extremely grateful to Seligman and the other founders of positive psychology for fostering a new recognition of well-being in psychology. Throughout his career as an academic psychologist, Compton has published papers that focused on various aspects of positive mental health, particularly on meditation, eastern psychology, and the dimensions of well-being. He is also the author of *Eastern Psychology: Buddhism, Hinduism, and Taoism* (2012). Dr. Compton lives in Nashville, Tennessee with his wife. He enjoys playing music, gardening, and travel.

Edward Hoffman is a leading scholar in humanistic psychology, and has been writing and lecturing on topics related to emotional well-being, higher motivation, and spirituality for more than 30 years. He is an adjunct associate psychology professor at Yeshiva University in New York City, where he created its popular course on positive psychology. For more than 25 years, he has maintained a private practice as a licensed clinical psychologist. He is the author of more than a dozen books in psychology and related fields, including award-winning biographies of Alfred

Adler and Abraham Maslow, and an anthology of Maslow's major unpublished papers entitled *Future Visions* (Sage Publications). Dr. Hoffman has also written/edited several books relating classic Jewish thought to contemporary interests in psychology, such as personality growth, mindfulness, and altruism. These works include *The Wisdom of Maimonides* and *The Kabbalah Reader* (both by Shambhala/Trumpeter). A senior editor of the Journal of Humanistic Psychology, Dr. Hoffman received his degrees from Cornell University and the University of Michigan-Ann Arbor. He lectures widely throughout the United States and abroad, and in 2009, served as a visiting scholar at the University of Tokyo. Dr. Hoffman lives in New York City with his wife and their two children. His hobbies include travel, swimming, and playing the flute.

An Introduction to Positive Psychology

Psychology is not just the study of weakness and damage; it is also
the study of strength and virtue. Treatment is not just fixing what is broken;
it is nurturing what is best within us.
MARTIN E. P. SELIGMAN

WELCOME TO POSITIVE PSYCHOLOGY

In 1998 Martin E. P. Seligman, then-president of
the American Psychological Association, urged
psychologists to remember psychology's forgotten
mission: to build human strength and to nurture
genius. In order to remedy this omission in the
field of psychology, Seligman set out, quite
deliberately, to create a new direction and a new
orientation for psychology. The name for this
new discipline is **positive psychology**. Its challenge to increase research on psychological
well-being and areas of human strength has been
heralded as a welcome development by many
psychologists.

In the most general terms, positive psychology is concerned with the use of psychological
theory, research, and intervention techniques to
understand the positive, adaptive, creative, and
emotionally fulfilling aspects of human behavior.

In their introduction to a special edition of the
American Psychologist on positive psychology, Kennon
Sheldon and Laura King (2001) described the new
area as follows:

> What is positive psychology? It is nothing
> more than the scientific study of ordinary
> human strengths and virtues. Positive
> psychology revisits "the average person"
> with an interest in finding out what works,
> what's right, and what's improving. It asks,
> "What is the nature of the efficiently
> functioning human being, successfully
> applying evolved adaptations and learned
> skills? And how can psychologists explain
> the fact that despite all the difficulties, the
> majority of people manage to live lives of
> dignity and purpose?" ... Positive psy-
> chology is thus an attempt to urge psy-
> chologists to adopt a more open and
> appreciative perspective regarding human
> potentials, motives, and capacities (p. 216).

In sum, positive psychology investigates the potential for doing what is right that people have access to and that, with a little help, they can actualize in their lives. "Positive psychology is the scientific study of what enables individuals and communities to thrive" (International Positive Psychology Association, 2009), according to the mission statement of the International Positive Psychology Association. In studying what people do right and how it is that they manage to do it, positive psychology underscores what they do for themselves, for their families, and for their communities.

THE DIMENSIONS OF POSITIVE PSYCHOLOGY

Although the range of interests in positive psychology is quite large, its dimensions encompass human life in its positive aspects. In order to nurture talent and make life more fulfilling, it focuses on three broad areas of human experience (Seligman & Csikszentmihalyi, 2000) that reflect its positive perspective.

Courtesy of Martin E. P. Seligman

Martin E. P. Seligman

1. At the subjective level, positive psychology looks at POSITIVE SUBJECTIVE STATES, or positive emotions such as happiness, joy, satisfaction with life, relaxation, love, intimacy, and contentment. Positive subjective states also include constructive thoughts about the self and the future, such as optimism and hope, as well as feelings of energy, vitality, and confidence and the effects of positive emotions such as laughter.

2. At the individual level, positive psychology focuses on POSITIVE INDIVIDUAL TRAITS, or the more positive behavioral patterns seen in people over time, such as manifestations of courage, persistence, honesty, and wisdom. It can also include the ability to develop aesthetic sensibility or to tap into creative potential as well as the drive to pursue excellence. That is, positive psychology includes the study of positive behaviors and traits that in the past were understood in the language of *character strengths* and *virtues*.

3. Last, at the group or societal level, positive psychology focuses on the development, creation, and maintenance of POSITIVE INSTITUTIONS. In this regard, it addresses issues such as the development of civic virtues, the creation of healthy families, and the study of healthy work environments. It investigates how institutions can work better to support and nurture all of the citizens they impact.

Positive psychology, then, is the scientific study of positive human functioning and flourishing on multiple levels that include the biological, personal, relational, institutional, cultural, and global dimensions of life (Seligman & Csikszentmihalyi, 2000).

THE SCOPE OF POSITIVE PSYCHOLOGY

A comprehensive list of topics that may be studied by a positive psychologist would, of course, be quite exhaustive. Evidently, people seem to be quite good at doing things well. In fact, the ways in which persons excel is much more extensive than has been recognized in psychology.

Even a partial list of areas of interest for positive psychology runs the gamut from *A* to *Z*: altruism, empathy, the building of enriching communities, creativity, forgiveness, compassion, the study of positive emotions in job satisfaction, the enhancement of our immune system functioning, models of positive personality development throughout the lifespan, psychotherapeutic emphasis on accomplishments and positive traits, the savoring of each fleeting moment of life, the strengthening of virtues as way to increase authentic happiness, and the psychological benefits of Zen meditation (Lopez & Snyder,

2009). Encouraging psychologists to pay attention to what people do right was an early accomplishment of positive psychology. Once psychologists began to notice the many ways that human beings succeed in life, these neglected characteristics and behaviors became the focus of theory, research, and psychological intervention strategies.

A discussion of why the perspective of positive psychology is relevant today follows. This will entail a deeper examination of just what we consider to be *the good life*.

BASIC THEMES OF POSITIVE PSYCHOLOGY

The Good Life

Positive psychology is concerned essentially with the elements of and predictors of *the good life*. This term might be only somewhat familiar to students of psychology, having popular associations with the possession of extreme wealth, power, prestige, and beauty. Such popular usage is quite loose, for in fact the term comes to us from philosophy.

The idea of the good life derives from speculation about what holds the greatest value in life—that is, what is the nature of the highest or most important *good*. When this idea is applied to human life, *the good* refers to the factors that contribute most to a well-lived and fulfilling life. Honderich (1995) stated:

> Things that are good may also be considered from the point of view of how they will contribute to a well-spent or happy human life. The idea of a complete good is that which will wholly satisfy the complete need and destiny of humans, the *summum bonum* (p. 322).

Qualities that help define the good life are those that enrich our lives, make life worth living, and foster strong character. Martin Seligman (2002), the founder of positive psychology, defined the good life as "using your signature strengths every day to produce authentic happiness and abundant gratification" (p. 13).

In positive psychology, the good life is seen as involving a combination of three elements: connections to others, positive individual traits, and life regulation qualities. Aspects of our behavior that contribute to forging *positive connections to others* include the ability to love, the presence of altruistic concerns, the ability to forgive, and the presence of spiritual connections to help create a sense of deeper meaning and purpose in life. *Positive individual traits* include such elements as a sense of integrity; the ability to play and to be creative; and the presence of virtues like courage and humility. Finally, *life regulation qualities* allow us to regulate our day-to-day behavior so that we can accomplish our goals while helping to enrich the people and institutions we encounter along the way. These qualities include a sense of individuality or autonomy; a high degree of healthy self-control; and the presence of wisdom as a guide to behavior.

In short, positive psychology's concern with living the good life entails the consideration of factors that lead to the greatest sense of well-being, satisfaction, or contentment. Note, however, that the good life is not to be understood here in the sense of individual achievement removed from its social context. On the contrary, if it is to be a worthwhile determination, the good life must include relationships with other people and with society as a whole.

Although the definition of the good life has so far been rather broad and abstract, future chapters will address the finer points involved.

Positive Emotions Are Important

In the past 30 years, scientific research has revealed how important positive emotions and adaptive behaviors are to living a satisfying and productive life. For much of the twentieth century, many scientists assumed that the study of positive emotions was somewhat frivolous at best, and probably unnecessary. Many assumed that psychology should focus on more pressing social problems, such as drug abuse, criminal behavior, and the treatment of serious psychological disorders like depression. This assumption is only partially correct. It is quite true that psychology does need to study serious social and psychological problems. In fact, positive psychologists do not reject the need to study and attempt to eliminate the terrible social and personal costs of such problems. Recent research, however, suggests that the study of positive emotions can actually help to fight these problems.

For instance, an awareness of their psychological strengths can help people recover from psychological problems (Huta & Hawley, 2010). In addition, a lack of well-being in the present can set the stage for the development of depression up to 10 years later (Joseph & Wood, 2010). Newer forms of psychotherapy focus on the development of positive emotions and adaptive coping strategies rather than on negative emotions, internal conflicts, and anxieties formed in childhood. Positive psychology researchers have found that positive forms of therapy can be as useful as older therapies that focus on eliminating negative emotions (Duckworth, Steen, & Seligman, 2005; Seligman, Rashid, & Parks, 2006; Rashid, 2009). In an interesting twist, psychoanalyst Volney Gay (2001) argued that adult distress actually occurs

because people cannot recollect joy, which in turn leads to a retreat from active participation in life. In practice, positive forms of psychotherapy can be useful adjuncts to more traditional forms of psychotherapy and even quite successful in helping people emerge from debilitating psychological problems (Stalikas & Fitzpatrick, 2008).

Recent studies also support the important influence that positive emotions and adaptive behavior have on several positive outcomes in life. Sonja Lyubomirsky, Laura King, and Ed Diener (2005) completed a somewhat voluminous review of 225 studies on happiness and well-being. They concluded that people who experience more positive emotions tend to have greater success in numerous areas of life than those more negatively oriented. For instance, people who experience and express positive emotions more often than those who do not are more likely to be satisfied with their lives, have more rewarding interpersonal relationships, be more productive and satisfied at their job, be more helpful to other people, and be more likely to reach desired goals in life. Interestingly,

"Do I get partial credit for simply having the courage to get out of bed and face the world again today?"

people who experience and express positive emotions more often than those less positive are also more likely to be physically healthier, be more resistant to illness, and even live longer. The authors also conclude that while being successful can make one feel happier, the converse is also true: being happier can lead to greater success later in life! By helping people both to reach their potential and to eliminate negative emotions and problematic behaviors, the study of positive emotions and adaptive behavior can thereby offer beneficiaries more fulfilling lives.

People Can Flourish and Thrive

Positive psychology investigates what people do correctly in life. As Sheldon and King (2001) noted earlier, positive psychology recognizes that many people adapt and adjust to life in highly creative ways that allow them, and those they come in contact with, to feel good about life. All too often psychological research has displayed a blatant bias toward assumptions that people are unwitting pawns of their biology, their childhood, and their unconscious. Previous psychological theories have often argued that human beings are determined by their past; by their biology, their cultural conditioning and unconscious motives. Positive psychology takes the position that despite the very real difficulties of life, it must be acknowledged that most people adjust quite well to life's ups and downs. Most people at least try to be good parents, to treat others with some degree of respect, to love those close to them, to find ways to contribute to society and the welfare of others, and to live their lives with integrity and honesty. These achievements should be celebrated rather than explained away as "nothing but" biological urges or unconscious attempts to ward off anxiety and fear. Therefore, a basic premise of positive psychology is that "human beings are often, perhaps more often, drawn by the future than they are driven by the past" (Seligman, 2011, p. 106).

In addition, in the past psychology has paid even less attention to how people move beyond basic adjustment to life to actually flourish and thrive in the face of change. That is, some people don't just adapt to life—they adapt extraordinarily well. Some adapt so well that they serve as role models of incredible resiliency, perseverance, and fortitude. One of the goals of positive psychology is to understand how those people manage to accomplish such high levels of thriving.

Corey L. M. Keyes and Shane Lopez (2002) created a classification system that has yielded some basic terms in positive psychology. In their fourfold typology of mental health functioning, people who score high on well-being and low on mental illness are *flourishing*. As we will see, the term **flourishing** is used in many areas of positive psychology to describe high levels of well-being. In contrast, someone who exhibits both high well-being and high mental illness is *struggling*. This refers to a person who is generally doing quite well in life but is currently experiencing significant distress about some issue. People who register low on well-being but high on mental illness symptoms are *floundering*. Obviously, floundering describes a difficult situation. When someone shows signs of low well-being but also scores low on mental illness, they are *languishing*. This would describe someone who has no significant mental health issues but is nevertheless very dissatisfied or unfulfilled in life.

Keyes and Lopez take their system a bit farther to look at how well-being has been defined in the past. They believe that other systems of classifying mental health and well-being are incomplete because they focus on only a portion of what it means to be mentally healthy. Instead, they suggest that **complete mental health** is a combination of high emotional well-being, high psychological well-being, and high social well-being, along with low mental illness.

High *emotional well-being* or emotional vitality is present when people are happy and satisfied with their lives. High *psychological well-being* is found when people feel competent, autonomous, self-accepting, have a purpose in life, exhibit personal growth, and have positive relationships with others. High *social well-being* is found when people have positive attitudes toward others, believe that social change is possible, try to make a contribution to society, believe the social world is understandable, and feel part of a larger social community (see chapter 11). High social well-being is further measured in five dimensions: social acceptance; social actualization; social contribution; social coherence; and social integration.

When the psychological assessments of flourishing, struggling, languishing, and floundering are applied across each of the three levels of well-being—emotional, psychological, and social—twelve classifications of mental health result. Figure 1.1 below depicts the complete mental health model of Keyes and Lopez.

Keyes (2005, 2009) investigated certain parts of this model in a large sample of U.S. residents aged 25–74 years. First, he found that high mental illness tended to decrease mental health, as would be expected. However, it was also possible to be relatively high in both mental illness and mental health at the same time (that is, to be struggling). Second, he found that 18% of the sample was flourishing since they scored high on at least one measure of well-being and at least six measures of positive functioning. Because Keyes required increasing measures of positive well-being to indicate flourishing, the percentage in this category dropped until less than 10% of the sample showed high-level mental health (that is, by scoring high on almost all measures of well-being and positive functioning). One conclusion of the study is that therapeutic interventions to

eliminate mental illness do not automatically enhance well-being. Efforts to improve well-being may need different types of interventions.

Compassion and Empathy Are Important

For several years much research in psychology was based on the assumption that human beings are driven by base motivations such as aggression, egoistic self-interest, and the pursuit of simple pleasures. Since many psychologists began with that assumption, they inadvertently designed research studies that supported their own presuppositions. Consequently, the view of humanity that prevailed in psychology was that of a species barely keeping its aggressive tendencies in check and managing to live in social groups more out of motivated self-interest than out of a genuine affinity for others or a true sense of community. Both Sigmund Freud and the early behaviorists led by John B. Watson believed that humans were motivated primarily by selfish drives. From that perspective, social interaction is possible only by exerting control over those baser emotions and, therefore, it is always vulnerable to eruptions of violence, greed, and selfishness. The fact that humans actually live together in social groups has traditionally been seen as a tenuous arrangement that is always just one step away from violence.

It should be noted, however, that some early theorists did see potentials in human beings for cooperation, caring, and empathy. Two of Freud's earliest colleagues, Alfred Adler and Carl Jung, both believed that certain positive traits were innate. Other researchers also saw potential for prosocial behaviors in people. Nonetheless, a distinct trend in much psychological research was toward a fairly negative view of why people behave the way they do. Even positive behaviors, such as altruism, were seen as essentially the result of self-centered motives.

In contrast, a new vision of human beings has been emerging from recent psychological research that sees human socialization and the ability to live in groups as a highly adaptable trait (Buss, 2000).

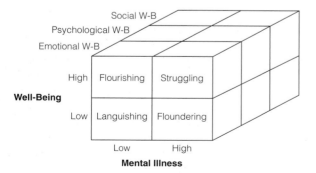

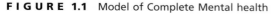

FIGURE 1.1 Model of Complete Mental health

In fact, a newer perspective holds that the need to cooperate and the desire to help others may be biologically based and innate (Keltner, 2009; Tomasello, 2009). We now know that animals demonstrate empathy for others and compassion for those in pain as well as show cooperation and a sense of social connectedness. Studies have also found that across the lifespan a greater capacity for empathy is associated with higher life satisfaction and more positive relationships (Gruhn, Diehl, Rebucal, Lumley, & Labouvie-Vief, 2008). Another study has discovered that people can be motivated to overcome their low self-esteem if they feel their efforts would also help others (Grant & Sannentag, 2010). It may be that doing good can buffer the effects of feeling bad. Even 21-month-old toddlers were found to appreciate when someone was helpful to them (Kuhlmeier & Dunfield, 2010). The toddlers studied were also more likely to help someone who made an effort to help them by returning the favor.

People Need Positive Social Relationships

A corollary to the assumption above is that people exist in social contexts and that well-being is not just an individual pursuit. As Christopher Peterson (2006) put it, "Other people matter." Of course, positive psychology is not alone in recognizing the importance of the social context for human behavior. What positive psychology has done is to embrace ideas about positive social environments, such as social well-being and empowerment. Many of these ideas were initiated by community psychologists (see chapter 11), but many positive psychologists have welcomed them.

Related to this idea is a recognition that differences exist in how cultures conceptualize, encourage, and teach their children about the nature of happiness and the good life (see Matsumoto, 1994). In general, the search for happiness appears to be a universal quest. Nonetheless, there is a fascinating variety of ideas among cultures of the world about the specific nature of happiness. One of the more prominent distinctions is between cultures that view happiness as an emotion achieved by individuals through their own unique efforts and those that consider happiness a more collective experience—that is, as a joint product of persons and their immediate family environments. (These distinctions will be covered in more detail later in chapter 11.) Positive psychology, like other schools of psychology, is beginning to explore cross-cultural comparisons that enhance our understanding of how people throughout the world experience psychological well-being.

Strengths and Virtues Are Important

In positive psychology any discussion of what constitutes the good life must inevitably touch on virtues, values, and character development (Fowers, 2005). It is not possible to consider the dimensions of an admirable and fulfilling life without introducing discussions of virtues such as honesty, fidelity, or courage. This is not to say that positive psychologists advocate certain virtues and values simply because they personally admire them. Science cannot address in any ultimate or absolute sense which values a person *must* believe in or practice in her or his life. Science will never be able to declare, for instance, that everyone *should* value happiness as the ultimate goal of life. However, a science of positive psychology does have a role in any investigation of values.

Over 40 years ago, M. Brewster Smith (1969) cautioned that the science of psychology can never dictate which values are "best." What psychology can do is use scientific methods to investigate the consequences of living a life based on the values of honesty, integrity, tolerance, and self-control. Likewise, Maslow (1970, p. 20) argued that psychology had gained the ability to indicate "what makes [people] healthier, wiser, more virtuous, happier, more fulfilled." In addition, scientific methods can be applied in any cultural setting or in any society around the world to discover which values tend to enhance the quality of life for everyone in a community. Therefore, the consequences of holding certain social values can be investigated within that specific culture. Scientific methods can be used to investigate the possibility that certain values are found almost universally and, as such, represent a common core of virtues that have grounded many cultures over time.

Independence of Positive and Negative Emotions

Another basic theme in positive psychology concerns the relationship between positive emotional states and well-being. For some time, psychologists assumed that if a person could eliminate his or her negative emotions, then positive emotions would automatically take their place. For instance, many people who hope to win large sums of money in the lottery are driven by this assumption. They assume that money will eliminate negative emotions such as worry and then they will be happy. That is, these people assume that positive and negative emotions exist in a dependent relationship such that if negative emotions go down, then positive emotions must go up.

However, Ulrich Schimmack (2008) reviewed several research studies that examined this notion and found that positive and negative emotions are relatively independent. He discovered that they tend to have distinct causes and can even occur together at the same time. For instance, a mother can easily feel both some degree of sadness and considerable joy at the wedding of her only daughter. Physiological studies have also found that positive and negative emotions are associated with different biological markers (Ryff, Love, Urry, et al., 2006). Of interest to applied positive psychologists is Schimmack's additional conclusion that interventions to influence one type of emotionality may have no effect or even an opposing impact on another type of emotionality. Therefore, efforts to increase positive emotionality need not impact negative emotionality. Corey Keyes (2007) has argued for a *two-continua model* of mental health and illness that recognizes that the predictors of mental health and illness are often unique and somewhat independent.

To illustrate this point, Argyle (1987) noted that the probability of experiencing negative emotionality is predicted by several factors, such as unemployment, high stress, and low-economic status. It should be quite apparent to most people, however, that happiness and psychological well-being are not automatically achieved when a person has a job, is subject to normal stress levels, and is middle-class. By comparison with someone undergoing greater stresses, a person feels better but is not necessarily as happy as he or she could be. Just eliminating one's negative feelings does not automatically create human strengths, virtues, and the capacity to thrive and flourish. Just because someone is relatively free of anxiety, depression, and worry doesn't mean that he or she automatically exhibits inspiring instances of courage, self-sacrifice, honesty, and integrity. Similarly, Peterson and Steen (2002) found that optimism and pessimism had differential effects on a person's self-reported well-being.

So while some of the predictors of positive emotionality and negative emotions are similar, they are not identical. There are unique psychological processes that help a person move from feeling negative emotions such as anxiety and depression to a position of neutral emotionality (for example, decreasing the amount of negative self-talk). At the same time, there are other equally unique psychological processes that help someone move from neutral emotionality to greater happiness, life satisfaction, and joy in life (for example, creating a sense of vibrant engagement in life). Many of these positive psychological processes will be the subjects of the chapters to follow.

Negative Emotions Are Still Important

At this point, it should be emphasized again that positive psychologists do not wish to limit the topics of study but rather to expand them to include aspects of human flourishing. Positive psychology does not deny that there are many problems in the world that need attention. It is also obvious that negative emotions can be necessary for survival at times. We would be far too vulnerable if we completely eliminated fear, anxiety, or skepticism from our lives. The recognition of and expression of negative emotions are also vital to self-understanding and personal growth (Algoe, Fredrickson, & Chow, 2011; Lambert & Erekson, 2008; Shmotkin, 2005). Positive psychology is not simply "happiology" (Seligman, 2011). In addition, positive psychology also recognizes that the tragic elements in life can enrich our experience of being human (Woolfolk, 2002). Kirk Warren Brown and Melissa Holt (2011) argued that positive psychology should be "founded upon an accounting of the full range of human cognitive and emotional experience" (p. 147). There must be a reason why people throughout history have been drawn to plays, paintings, poetry, and even music that express sadness, tragedy, and defeat. It may be that in order to appreciate the positive in life we must also know something of the negative. Further, positive psychology does not deny that every effort should be made to help eliminate problems associated with social injustice and social inequality.

Having recognized a place for negative emotions, however, it also may be true that the desire to be happier and more satisfied with life is universally human. In most cases, people simply operate better within the world, whatever world they live in, if they are more optimistic, hopeful, and can rely on solid supportive relationships. Interestingly, some of the findings of positive psychology may approach universal applicability. For instance, Ed Diener (2000, October), a leading researcher of well-being, said that the closest thing psychology has to a "general tonic" for well-being is to improve happiness. One of the best things a person can do to increase one's quality of life is to help others increase their level of happiness and life satisfaction. This applies to people at all levels of income and psychosocial adjustment.

The Science of Well-Being

One of the most distinguishing features of positive psychology is an insistence that research must follow the standards of traditional scientific investigation (Seligman & Csikszentmihalyi, 2000). Positive psychology is certainly not the first attempt by psychologists to study well-being and the good life. From the very beginnings of psychology, there has been an interest in studying healthy personality development and optimal states of well-being. For example, in the early part of the twentieth century many investigations into psychological well-being and the nature of the good life began first as scholarly analyses or as in-depth case studies of clients in psychotherapy. Attempts were then made to move the results of those studies into psychological laboratories for further experimental research or into real-life situations to help people increase well-being. Unfortunately, many attempts to move results into the laboratory were difficult or even impossible.

In light of such past difficulties, positive psychologists have seen a need to reverse the direction of information flow. That is, they hope to build an experimental knowledge base in the psychological laboratory and then move those results out into real-world arenas such as schools, clinics, and the workplace. Toward this end, many of the founders of positive psychology have placed considerable emphasis on promoting and developing opportunities for experimental research on psychological well-being and on the potential for greater fulfillment in life.

A SHORT HISTORY OF WELL-BEING IN THE WESTERN WORLD

In order to understand any field, it is important to examine the history of how ideas in that field developed over time. Positive psychology is the latest effort by human beings to understand the nature of happiness and well-being, but it is by no means the first attempt to solve that particular puzzle. Therefore, this section offers a brief history of how Westerners have answered the question *What is happiness?*

For students of psychology, the study of history often seems like an intellectual abstraction with little relevance to the present. However, it is our strong belief that an exploration of history can teach valuable lessons for the study of psychological well-being. For contemporary theories of happiness, life satisfaction, and well-being actually derive from older ideas on the good life and in fact remain relatively unchanged since at least the time of the ancient Greek philosophers.

It should be noted that non-European cultures have different histories of well-being, although space limitations do not permit a cross-cultural review. Nevertheless, a short section on how Buddhism views well-being is presented in chapter 10 and a brief exploration of cross-cultural ideas on happiness is covered in chapter 11.

Hedonism

Without question, the oldest approach to well-being and happiness can be traced to that of hedonism. The perspective of **hedonism** focuses on pleasure as the basic component of the good life. Hedonism in its basic form considers the pursuit of well-being to be fundamentally the pursuit of individual sensual pleasure and the avoidance of harm, pain, and suffering.

However, although the single-minded pursuit of pleasure is one the oldest ideas of the good life, this form of hedonism has been seen as self-defeating and unworkable by most societies throughout history. Nearly everyone realizes that sensual pleasures are short-lived, that they require a constant struggle to sustain them, and that when focused on too exclusively the hedonistic drive produces no lasting changes in personality and no personal growth. In general, the simple proposition that we behave in order to increase physiological pleasure and to avoid physiological pain is violated frequently enough that it cannot serve universally as the ultimate basis for the good life or of psychological well-being (Larsen, Hemenover, Norris, & Cacioppo, 2003; Parrott, 1993).

The Early Hebrews

One of the most influential factors in the development of and proliferation of the Western worldview has been Judaism. The religion and culture of the ancient Hebrews represents one of three pillars—along with Greek civilization and Christianity—that have sustained Western culture. The ancient Hebrews forged a new social identity by developing a relationship with their own personal God. For the Hebrews, many of the rules that governed their relationship to God were expressed as prohibitions, particularly in the form of the Ten Commandments. In general, these are prohibitions against self-centeredness, greed, and irrational anger as well as a commandment to accept the God of the ancient Hebrews as the only true God.

Philosophically, this approach to the search for happiness has been called a **divine command theory** of happiness. The idea here is that happiness is found by living in accord with the commands or rules set down by a Supreme Being (Honderich, 1995). In its most basic form, this theory holds that if one follows the commands, there will be rewards, and conversely if one doesn't follow the commands, there will be punishments. Therefore, for the Hebrew patriarchs, as later for many Christians, true happiness was related to a religious piety based on submission to God's supreme authority and a rejection of self-centered hedonistic behavior. The influence of this worldview on Western culture for the next 2,500 years cannot be overemphasized. Obviously, the divine command theory continues to be one of the dominant orientations people follow in their pursuit of happiness (see chapter 10).

The Greeks

As noted, the second pillar to sustain Western intellectual and moral development is the legacy of ancient Greek culture. Although the Jewish tradition was largely influential in the development of ethical, moral, and religious beliefs, Greek culture set the stage for developments in philosophy, science, art, and psychology for the next 2,500 years. In fact, the core philosophical ideas of the Western tradition are rooted in Greek philosophy. It was the Golden Age of Greece that introduced the fundamental idea that the good life and the proper path to happiness could be discovered through logic and rational analysis. That is, neither the gods nor societal traditions were the ultimate arbitrator of individual values and goals. The general answer to the happiness question was that rational human beings could decide for themselves which paths most reliably lead to well-being.

Socrates The person most responsible for the new direction in Greek intellectual life was Socrates (c. 469–399 BCE). Socrates directed reason to ultimate questions of human knowledge and especially to ideas on the nature of the good life and on what we need to be truly happy. In his method Socrates affirmed the Delphic motto *Know Thyself*. The search for truth was thus centered on an exploration of the unchanging truths of the human psyche (Robinson, 1990). He believed that true happiness could only be achieved through self-knowledge and that only this examination of one's universal soul was true wisdom.

Yet to know what is truly good—and not just what is self-indulgent or socially expected—a person must know the essence or the nature of virtue. One must know *the good*, meaning the core elements of the good life. Socrates believed that once the true nature of *the good* is known, it will automatically be desired and so will rationally motivate virtuous behavior. However, Socrates distrusted perceptual forms of knowledge. For him, true wisdom must be found in a reality that expresses timeless and unchanging truths. Any conclusions based on sensory experience or on the emotions cannot reveal that truth insofar as they are constantly changing in response to ephemeral external circumstances.

Plato Following in Socrates' footsteps was his most important student, Plato (427–347 BCE). Plato also believed that changeable sensory experience could not be the basis of true wisdom. True wisdom must be found in an unchanging realm that transcends the sensory world. The search for wisdom involves a passionate and difficult quest that looks beneath surface appearances and challenges preconceived notions. The method of this search consists of both reason and formal intuition. The person who undertakes this quest must have the courage to find the truth hidden beneath the world of appearances that we experience by means of the senses.

In his famous analogy of the cave, Plato compared most men and women to people chained inside a cave who can only look at the back wall in front of them. As figures pass by outside the cave, the bright sun projects their shadows onto the back wall of the cave. For Plato, those inside the cave mistake the passing shadows for reality since they know nothing other than copies of reality. The philosopher, however, is someone able to loosen the chains and turn around to see directly the sources of the shadows in the brightness of the sun, that is, to attain true knowledge beyond the illusory cave.

In the contemporary world, Plato's influence can be traced in any search for happiness or the good life that involves looking beyond sensory experience toward a deeper meaning to life. This can take such forms as a spiritual quest for deeper meaning, a search for one's true self, and an examination of the unconscious motivations that keep one from experiencing well-being.

Aristotle With Aristotle (384–322 BCE), who was Plato's student, the intellectual tradition of the West took a significantly different turn. Universal truth was to be found in the intellectual discovery of order in the world. The vehicle for this search was the senses and the tools were logic, classification, and

Aristotle

conceptual definition. Unlike his teacher Plato, Aristotle did not favor the intuition of eternal forms in the search for higher truth and well-being. The Aristotelian ideal valued poise, harmony, and the avoidance of emotional extremes. Aristotle believed that "the emotions were to be tamed, by rigorous self-discipline, to accept the dictates of reason" (Kiefer, 1988, p. 43).

© Bettmann/Corbis

One of Aristotle's goals was to find the *golden mean* that existed between the extremes of life. This was a state of balance, harmony, and equilibrium, which leads to a life lived in accordance with the principle of *eudaimonia*. Robinson (1990) explained **eudaimonia** as

> that condition of flourishing and completeness that constitutes true and enduring joy.... Eudaimonia is not merely a set of pleasures or creature comforts or Epicurean delights. It is a life lived in a certain way, where life here refers to life-on-the-whole, not some number of moments strung together. Progress toward this end calls for the recognition that the better course of action is not the one that invariably satisfies the current desire or even an abiding desire.... To be wise is to strive for a condition of moral perfection or virtue (*arete*) by which the "golden mean" is found and adopted in all of the significant affairs of life (pp. 16–17).

The good life, then, is found in the total context of a person's life. It is not just a momentary emotional state or even one specific emotion.

Although eudaimonia is usually translated as *happiness*, it can also be translated as *truly fortunate*, *possessed of true well-being*, or *flourishing* (Telfer, 1980). The central idea is that the person who is truly happy has what is *worth* desiring and *worth* having in life. Implicit here is the notion that though certain goals or objectives in life may produce positive emotions, they do not necessarily lead to eudaimonia. In many ways, eudaimonia is a telos or goal that exists as a future possibility. The search for eudaimonia is an ideal toward which one strives. For Aristotle, eudaimonia was associated with a life of character, albeit a specific type of good character.

Aristotle considered certain virtues to be dispositions of character that lead a person toward eudaimonia (Schimmel, 2000). In his *Nicomachean Ethics* (trans. 1908) he wrote, "We are what we repeatedly do. Excellence, then, is not an act, but a habit" (p. 61). He proposed 12 basic virtues that when cultivated allow us to approach a state of eudaimonia. These are: courage, liberality, pride (as self-respect), friendliness, wit, justice, temperance, magnificence, good temper, truthfulness, shame (or appropriate guilt for our transgressions), and honor (see Aristotle, 1908). These virtues are examples of the *golden mean* between extremes. For instance, courage lies between the excess of rashness and the deficiency of cowardice. Since these virtues are considered to be innate in every person, Aristotle's theory represents a naturalistic conception of happiness. Recognizing and cultivating our innate potential can lead to happiness.

This **virtue theory** of happiness (see Honderich, 1995) holds that the cultivation and development of certain virtues lead a person toward the greatest well-being and therefore toward the good life. Unlike the divine command theory, Aristotle did not list specific behaviors that must be avoided. Rather, whether any single behavior is a virtue or a vice depends upon the specific situation in which it occurs. Aristotle's perspective on well-being is termed the *Aristotelian circle* because well-being, virtue, and practical wisdom are all interrelated such that each continuously influences the other (Honderich, 1995). Today many theories of mental health postulate a set of admirable or virtuous traits associated with healthy personality development. As seen earlier, positive psychology is in part defined as the search for human strengths and virtues. In fact, such research can be seen as a contemporary adaptation of Aristotle's virtue theory.

The Epicureans   Toward the end of the fourth century BCE, Epicurus founded the school of Epicureanism, which asserts that happiness is best achieved by withdrawing from the world of politics to cultivate a quiet existence of simple pleasures. The ancient Epicureans, however, were not hedonists. In fact, Epicurus lived a quite simple lifestyle that would seem overly Spartan to most people today. Actually, the Epicureans sought a secure and comfortable existence by avoiding unnecessary pain and cultivating moderate pleasure. The image of the good life as involving a combination of relaxation, moderate pleasure, and freedom from pain or worry is in fact a popular ideal of happiness today. Many people in today's world, including many psychologists, can be considered modern-day epicureans.

The Stoics   Concurrent with the Epicureans was the founding of the Stoic school by Zeno. The ancient Stoics believed that material wealth, happiness, love, and admiration all were subject to change and that therefore a person must not base his or her well-being on such ephemera (Robinson, 1997). The only choice is to perform one's duties without complaining and to accept one's place in the divine plan. Stoicism ultimately became one of the major philosophical schools in the Roman world where it was cultivated and promoted by Epictetus and others (Robinson & Groves, 1998). Today there are few approaches to happiness based on purely stoic ideas. However, several religious viewpoints focus on accepting "God's plan" for one's life. In addition, certain existential schools of thought advise us to accept that we are thrown into a life we did not choose and so must work within its limits.

Summary of Greek Ideas on the Good Life   Only somewhat facetiously, Kiefer (1988) summarized the Greek approach to knowledge as follows: "Once its straightforward principles were grasped, anyone who could stand several hours a day of brutal self-criticism could be a philosopher" (p. 38). Although one might argue with Kiefer's understanding of Greek philosophy, there is no denying that the Greeks provided the search for well-being with a democratic structure based on self-awareness, rationality, and logic. The legacy left to Western civilization by the ancient Greeks cannot be overestimated.

Daniel Robinson (1997) believed that the Greek (particularly Socrates, Plato, and Aristotle) and Roman philosophers bequeathed us four major theories of the good life: the contemplative life, the active life, the fatalistic life, and hedonism.

In the *contemplative life* one pursues higher knowledge; understanding; self-reflection; and wisdom. The contemplative view of the good life is guided by Socrates' contention that "the unexamined life is not worth living." The *active life* is based on a sense of duty, social responsibility, and

engagement in the world. It centers on involvement in civic, political, or commercial activity in an effort to influence society. The *fatalistic life* recognizes that life brings difficulties and that consequently some measure of well-being must come from an acceptance without unnecessary complaint or struggle of these unwelcome inevitabilities. The first three perspectives can each be seen in the famous prayer by Reinhold Niebuhr: "God grant me the serenity to accept the things I cannot change *[the fatalistic life]*, the courage to change the things I can *[the active life]*, and the wisdom to know the difference *[the contemplative life]*." And last, a life of hedonism is also an option for the good life, although the limitations of this approach have been addressed earlier.

Robinson also mentioned two additional perspectives on the good life: the *heroic life* and the *saintly life*. These paths to well-being are generally taken by only a small number of people since they require considerable sacrifice and renunciation—at least it seems that way to an outside observer.

In sum, most contemporary views on how to achieve well-being and contentment were expressed by the ancient Greeks. Moreover, the considerable variety of options available to the ancient Greeks in the search for well-being was unique in the ancient world. Unfortunately, the emphasis the Greeks placed on rational analysis, the freedom to choose one's own beliefs, and an honest and thorough search for wisdom and truth was lost during the Middle Ages. These qualities would not be central again to the search for well-being in Western civilization until the late nineteenth century.

Early Christianity and the Middle Ages

The rise of Christianity represented one of the most significant developments in Western civilization and constituted the third pillar that has sustained it for two millennia. Christianity also transformed the meaning of religious devotion in Western society by viewing God not as an awesome and powerful deity to be feared but as a loving presence who deeply cares for humanity. The way to find true happiness is believed to be found in the message and life of Jesus, which is one of love and compassion. People should love others as God loves the world and even "love thy neighbor as thyself." Christians are therefore encouraged to emulate the love of Jesus. By expressing God's love and sharing it with other people, a person may find peace, happiness, and salvation.

During the early Middle Ages (approximately 500–1200 CE), the Christian Church and its monasteries were the center of spiritual, intellectual, and often political life. Conceptions of the good life were therefore based on the religious perspective of the time that true happiness—as opposed to secular and temporary pleasures—was delayed until after death and the resurrection into heaven. In official Church doctrine, the pleasures of the flesh and of the spirit were rigidly separated and enjoyment of even the simple pleasures was considered a distraction from more spiritual concerns. It may be helpful to cite Lowry's (1982) summary of the medieval conception of human nature:

> In the Middle Ages, man[1] was regarded as a creature of conflict and contradictions…. He had a spiritual nature and a carnal nature, and so long as the spirit inhabited the flesh, the two were constantly at odds…. In short, human nature was held to be the scene of a constantly raging battle between the demands of the spirit and the demands of the flesh (p. 59).

This idea of an internal battle between the physical appetites and the more rational intellectual aspects is still quite common today. The most familiar example is found in Freud's psychoanalytic theory in which the irrational pleasure principle of the id must be moderated by the ego, driven by the reality principal.

The Virtue Theory in the Middle Ages   Given the pervasiveness of this struggle between spirit and flesh, the Church deemed it necessary to warn people about worldly dangers and how these could ensnare the careless. The Church's doctrine of the *Seven Deadly Sins* is a list of basic evils that destroy character and can lead to a host of other sins. These are anger, envy, sloth, pride, lust, intemperance, and greed (Schimmel, 1997). In general, this list of core sins condemns behaviors of self-indulgent hedonism and narcissism.

Less well known is the alternate list called the Four Cardinal Virtues (or the Natural Virtues) and the addition of the Three Theological Virtues. As might be expected, this is a list of behaviors that lead to virtuous behavior and the abandonment of sins. The *Four Cardinal Virtues* are those on which all other virtues depend. These are justice; prudence; fortitude; and temperance. They appear to have been derived by St. Ambrose in the fourth century from the four basic virtues of the Greeks (Bowker, 2006). The medieval scholastics added the *Three Theological Virtues* of faith; hope; and charity. Again, many contemporary conceptualizations of psychological well-being rely on this list of core traits. The basic foundations of ethical behavior and humanitarianism in the Western world appear to be based on this list of seven positive virtues.

Moses Maimonides   Among the major historical figures relevant to positive psychology is Moses Maimonides (1138–1204). He was a renowned Jewish religious leader, philosopher, and physician in Egypt, admired as well by Christians and Muslims for his medical ability and wisdom. As related by Hoffman (2009), Maimonides emphasized the role of both positive and negative emotions in affecting health, and especially warned about the harmfulness of chronic anger and sadness. He also regarded aesthetic experience, such as listening to music or gazing at beautiful architecture, as beneficial. In addition, Maimonides advocated the practice of mindfulness as vital to healthy functioning: that is, of staying focused on the present moment instead of dwelling on the past or worrying about the future. In keeping with earlier Jewish teachings from the Talmud, Maimonides encouraged the development of positive character traits, such as cheerfulness, friendliness, and generosity, in leading a worthy life.

Mysticism The Middle Ages was also a time when the personal pursuit of a profound relationship with God was institutionalized. Within the walls of the monasteries could be found monks involved in the intense practice of contemplative spirituality, or *mysticism*. For these men and women the passionate pursuit of a spiritual relationship with God was so satisfying that most worldly concerns were secondary. The monastic tradition and mysticism continue today, although as disciplines they are undertaken by relatively few individuals.

The Renaissance to the Age of Enlightenment

In Europe, the years between 1400–1600 produced a steady transformation in how people understood personhood. Originating in the Italian Renaissance, this shift to humanism involved a liberation from Church dogma to explore classical teachings; Judaic Kabbalah; critical inquiry; and the study of the humanities. Some of the most important thinkers associated with humanism included Francis Bacon and Sir Thomas More in England, Desiderius Erasmus in Holland, Francisco Petrarch in Italy, and Michel Montaigne in France. Though presenting differing philosophies, all valued independent thought over Church-imposed religious doctrine. In this respect, they laid the groundwork for the later emergence of science.

Creativity and the Rise of the Artist During this epoch, two notions contributed vitally to this intellectual transformation: the idea that artists possessed a special gift and the rise of individualism. One of the lasting changes that appeared during the Renaissance was the elevation of the social status of artists and the belief that they possessed a special gift that other people did not have. Certainly persons throughout history had been recognized in their societies as creative. However, they were regarded as craftsmen. By contrast, the concept of the creative artist involves an element of *personal vision* as expressed through arts such as painting, sculpture, music, and architecture. This idea of

personal vision implies an individual uniqueness that was not afforded artists of the Middle Ages. The rise of individualism eventually changed the image of a person in ways that significantly altered how people search for happiness (Baumeister, 1987).

The Rise of Science The end of the seventeenth century brought a new conception of human nature that was increasingly founded on the rise of modern science. As Lowry (1982) stated, "The historical significance of the seventeenth century can scarcely be exaggerated. For it was during this century that Western intellectual life first became recognizably *modern* in mood, temper, purpose, and presupposition" (p. 6).

The new worldview advocated by enthusiastic thinkers of the seventeenth century was based on two general ideas. The first was that rational persons could decide for themselves what was true and of ultimate value. The method to be used in the search for truth was a rationality based on dispassionate and objective observation of the events in the world. The tools were logic, objectivity, and empiricism. *Empiricism* is the belief that valid knowledge is constructed from experience derived from the five senses (Honderich, 1995). Note the difference between this idea and the rationalism of Socrates and Plato.

The second idea was that the "universe as a whole is one vast machine, a kind of cosmic clockwork, and that all its parts and processes are likewise governed by the inexorable laws of mechanical causation" (Lowry, 1982, p. 4). This philosophy became known as *mechanism*, and it was applied equally to events in nature and to human psychology.

The Rising Importance of the Social World
The focus on empiricism, rationalism, and mechanism created an image of human nature that appeared to be simple, understandable, and clear. Eighteenth and nineteenth century social reformers such as Jeremy Bentham and John Stuart Mill believed that the basic need of people to seek pleasure and avoid pain could be used to create a more

stable and enlightened society. If you want to know whether a certain behavior is right, ethical, or fosters the good life, then you must show that it leads to the enhancement of happiness for the greatest number of people. Early adherents called this idea **utilitarianism**. According to utilitarianism, happiness for all people is the ultimate aim of all human actions and the standard by which actions should be evaluated as right or wrong.

Jeremy Bentham believed that it was possible to quantify happiness by examining the ratio of positive to negative experiences in one's life. This principle was called the **hedonic calculus** (Viney & King, 1998). John Stuart Mill agreed with many ideas in utilitarianism but disagreed with Bentham's belief that all pleasures should be given equal value—a notion central to the hedonic calculus. He believed there are important differences among pleasures in terms of their quality. Specifically, Mill believed the intellectual pleasures to be far more important to human happiness than the biological pleasures, which humans share with other animals. Mill famously summed up his critique of utilitarianism by saying, "It is better to be a human dissatisfied than a pig satisfied; better to be Socrates dissatisfied than a fool satisfied" (Hergenhahn, 2009, p. 158).

The Rise of Democracy   By the mid-1700s some people believed that the prevailing political power structure could be at odds with the welfare of the individual and that when these two were in conflict, members of society had the right to overthrow the state and put in its place a system more conducive to individual liberty. Thomas Jefferson made these principles the founding assumptions of a new government when he wrote in the United States Declaration of Independence, "We hold these truths to be self-evident, that all men are created equal, that they are endowed by their Creator with certain inalienable Rights, that among these are Life, Liberty, and the pursuit of Happiness." A form of government was instituted for an entire country that elevated the individual to a status above royalty and that gave to ordinary persons the power to make decisions about their own life

that had previously resided only in a ruling elite. The pursuit of happiness became a right as well as a personal choice. Democracy joined with utilitarianism to create a new system of government that, in theory, would result in the greatest happiness for everyone. Now the search for happiness also involves a search for the social environments that best promote well-being.

Romanticism and the Nineteenth Century

Emotion and the Romantics   In the early 1800s the growth of Western individualism began to turn toward the emotional expressionism that made each person unique. In fact, the word *individualism* first appeared in 1835 when de Tocqueville used it to describe the emerging American perspective. People began to believe that the best way to express their individualism was to explore their own unique emotional experience of the world. The Romantic movement captured the intelligentsia as they pursued the full range of their emotional life from the spiritual to the mundane. At times it was the intensity of emotions that was important rather than the emotion itself. For instance, Hunt (1959) noted that "the typical romantic prided himself on the ability to fall tumultuously and passionately in love … [However] in place of sexuality, the romantics delighted in being demonstratively sentimental, melancholic, tempestuous, or tearful, according to the occasion" (p. 309). The ability to feel emotions intensely was considered important to living a full and significant life.

It was during this period that the focus on personal emotional expression combined with the notion that social environments can inhibit individualism. The result was the idea that a "true self" exists beneath the social exterior or the social masks that people wear. Today numerous perspectives on well-being urge people to find and express their true selves. For example, the existentialist perspective in psychology and philosophy has long held that a hallmark of optimal mental health is *authenticity* or the recognition of our genuine self-identity and the honest expression of one's "true voice" (chapter 9).

Love in the Romantic Period   Another conse-quence of rising individualism was the idea that marriage should be based on affection between two people coupled with the unique emotional bond they create together. Marriage based on romantic love presupposes that two people volun-tarily enter into an emotional, legal, and religious commitment. This requires choice and a certain degree of personal autonomy from family, friends, and institutions. It also assumes that individual sen-timents and emotions should be more important to the decision to marry than any social authority (Taylor, 1989). With the rise of individualism comes the view that love is the major avenue to soothe the sense of being alone in the world. As Singer (1987) noted, from this point forward

> romantic love … involved oneness with an alter ego, one's other self, a man or woman who would make up one's deficiencies, respond to one's deepest inclinations, and serve as possibly the only person with whom one could communicate fully.… This would be the person one would marry,… establishing a bond that was permanent as well as ecstatically consum-matory (quoted in Hendrick & Hendrick, 1983, p. 4).

By the 1920s in the United States and other industrialized Western countries, romantic love was considered the most important basis for mar-riage. The institution of dating—in which unchap-eroned young men and women joined in fun activities like going to a movie, restaurant, or sport-ing event—therefore began to be favored, and that over time a couple might see whether they had mutually fallen in love and then decide to marry. Nevertheless, in many Asian countries, such as China, Japan and India, marriages were still mainly arranged by parents for their offspring. Despite knowing about romantic love as depicted in Hollywood movies, many Asians rejected it as a silly, unrealistic basis for the serious financial and social realities of marriage. Only recently have arranged marriages begun to disappear decisively from the world.

Of course, today in Western industrialized countries it is assumed that love should be the only real motivation for marriage. Today, the ulti-mate test of whether two people should commit themselves to each other is found in their answer to a simple question, "Are you in love?". If the answer to this question is a resounding yes, then many people assume that the couple should commit themselves to each other for the rest of their lives. Today, for many people the search for intimacy and love is the major activity of their lives and the ulti-mate emotion for true happiness.

Celebrating Childhood Experience   A lasting influence of the Romantics has been an adoration of childhood experience. In particular, the English poets William Wordsworth (1770–1850) and his friend Samuel Coleridge (1772–1834) viewed childhood as a special time of joy, when our senses are most open to the world and we are filled with exuberance and delight. They extolled the child's sense of wonder as a true basis for enjoying life to the fullest. As Wordsworth (1807/1998) famously wrote, "The world is too much with us, late and soon, getting and spending, we lay waste our powers" (p. 307). Later in the United States philosophers and friends Ralph Waldo Emerson (1803–1882) and Henry David Thoreau (1817–1862) emphasized the importance of exposing children to nature and encouraging their individual self-expression. For all these thinkers, children were viewed neither as miniature adults nor as adults-in-waiting but as persons with their own valid ways of perceiving the world.

The Twentieth Century

The first significant development in the search for well-being extending into the early twentieth cen-tury came from William James (1842–1910). Acclaimed as among America's greatest philosophers, he was also the founder of American psychology and authored its first textbook. James was initially trained as a physician at Harvard, where he taught psychol-ogy and philosophy for more than 30 years. He became increasingly interested in how to awaken

William James

human potential, for he was convinced that we use only a tiny fraction of our full range of emotional and cognitive capabilities in daily life. To this end, he explored unusual mental phenomena such as hypnotism, altered states of consciousness, and trance mediumship. In James' most influential book, *The Varieties of Religious Experience* (1902/1958), he affirmed spiritual and mystical experiences as providing important clues to the heights of human personality. This viewpoint influenced Abraham Maslow and the founding of humanistic psychology during the 1950s and early 1960s. More broadly, James' abiding interest in the psychology of religion has expanded the purview of positive psychology today.

At the beginning of the twentieth century, Freud and his followers added another significant perspective to the search for well-being with the theory of the unconscious, which wasn't completely new. Today many different ideas exist on what constitutes the unconscious and how the unconscious affects behavior. Most psychologists agree that at least some motivations for behavior and some emotions are hidden from conscious awareness. In fact, we know that the search for happiness may be either helped or hindered by unconscious forces such as defense mechanisms.

Early attempts to heal mental illness and eliminate debilitating neurosis also led to the development of perspectives on optimal mental health. Beginning with Alfred Adler (1870–1937) and Carl Jung (1875–1961), two of Sigmund Freud's most influential early associates, psychologists throughout the twentieth century created theories of well-being and of human flourishing. Adler called his system *Individual Psychology* and stressed the importance of social feeling in healthy child development and adult functioning. He had an optimistic view of human capability, and his slogan—"Any child can learn anything"—inspired generations of teachers, social workers, and child

guidance workers in Europe and the United States. In Adler's (1930, 1938) view, such traits as friendship, love, compassion, and altruism are innate in every child but are invariably affected by social support and discouragement. In this regard, Adler strongly influenced Maslow, who studied with him personally in the 1930s. Adlerians have remained active in fostering positive social skills in classroom and home environments and, more recently, among romantic partners as well as organizational workers.

Jung's system is known as *Analytic Psychology*. More than either Freud or Adler, Jung emphasized our capacity for personality growth in the second half of the lifespan. He regarded the healthy personality as one that integrates the different components of the self, such as the *persona* (social self), with one's striving for meaning. Late in life, Jung (1965, 1976) argued that modern civilization bred too much conformity and empty busyness, and needed to allow individuals more freedom for inner exploration, such as through creative artistic activity.

Humanistic Psychology   As mentioned earlier, positive psychology is not the first attempt by psychologists to focus research on positive emotions, healthy adaptation, and the development of human potential. In the mid-twentieth century, the humanistic school of psychology focused on many of the same goals as current positive psychology. Abraham Maslow, one of the founders of humanistic psychology, titled a chapter in his seminal book, *Motivation and Personality* (1954), as "Toward a Positive Psychology." Even today humanistic psychologists study what is healthy, adaptive, creative, and addresses the full range of human potential.

The differences between humanistic psychology and positive psychology are found in the focus of investigations and the greater emphasis on traditional empirical research in the latter school. Much of the emphasis in humanistic psychology—particularly early humanistic psychology—has been on theories of optimal personality development such as self-actualization. Although positive psychology also investigates the potential for greater psychological development, it tends to place greater emphasis on the well-being and satisfaction of the "average" person on the street (see the quote by Sheldon and King early in this chapter). In general, positive psychologists focus more on the benefits of happiness and satisfaction with life than do humanistic psychologists.

Further, in terms of empirical research, positive psychologists place a much greater emphasis on the use of traditional scientific methods to study well-being and positive adaptation (Lopez & Snyder, 2009). Of course, over the years many humanistic psychologists have been actively involved in empirical research (for example, Bohart & Greenberg, 2001; Cain & Seeman, 2002). However, humanistic psychologists tend to be more comfortable with types of research based not on statistical analyses but on individual case studies and introspective, phenomenological analyses.

The twentieth century also saw a new approach to understanding complex psychological and biological processes. Systems theory was created as a way to understand how complex, dynamic, interacting elements combine to form stable systems. Probably the most obvious application of systems theory is in work in ecology, where complex elements combine in intricate ways to maintain stable and healthy environments. In complex systems the organization among various elements is often more important than the individual elements themselves. The concept of wellness is also a case in which biological, psychological, emotional, and social elements form a dynamic yet balanced and stable pattern of physical and mental health. In psychology, a systems perspective has been used in family therapy and in analyses of group and community interactions. A systems perspective on well-being, however, is fairly rare.

Jules Seeman provided an early example of a systems perspective on well-being with his theory of personality integration (1959, 2008). He argued (1983) that the holistic organization of a psychological system can be more important than the individual parts:

> Holism in a system means that a system cannot be understood adequately by examining its parts as entities, for the parts

take their meaning not as entities at all but as sub-organizations in the *unitas* [unity] … What is fundamental about the components of a system is not relationship but organization" (p. 215).

More contemporary versions of systems perspectives can be found in Kennon Sheldon's (2004) theory of the optimal human being and in elements of Barbara Fredickson's work on flourishing (Fredrickson & Losada, 2005).

Finally, the twentieth century also saw a recognition by Western psychology that cross-cultural perspectives on well-being are also important (see chapter 11). Influential contributions have come from Eastern psychology in the form of research on meditation, yoga, acupuncture, and tai chi chuan. In particular, ideas from Buddhist mindfulness meditation have recently become very important in positive psychology (see chapter 4).

Lessons on Well-Being from History

Philosopher Joel Kupperman (2006) offered six myths about the good life that we can learn from history. In the spirit of positive psychology, Kupperman's myths can be switched into intriguing hypotheses for the study of well-being:

1. Simple hedonism is not an adequate path to well-being.
2. Happiness should not be the sole criteria for well-being.
3. Trying to suppress emotions doesn't eliminate them.
4. A stress-free life—one devoid of any challenges—is not the most desirable life.
5. Virtues and good character are important to the good life.
6. It is not necessary to be perfect to be an admirable and a good person.

Jonathon Haidt (2006) also provided several lessons on well-being that can be learned from a study of history. His list indicates considerable overlap with Kupperman's but shows the influence of a psychological perspective:

1. The human mind is divided into parts that can be in conflict.

2. Therefore, training the mind is important to well-being.

3. Pleasure comes more from making progress toward goals than in goal attainment.

4. It is possible for adversity to make you stronger.

5. We need to rise above our tendencies to be self-centered, egocentric, judgmental, and biased.

6. Positive social relationships are important to well-being.

7. In particular, love and emotional attachment are important to well-being.

8. Virtues are important to well-being.

9. Spirituality and self-transcendence are important to well-being.

10. Having a sense of meaning and purpose in life is important. It comes from vital engagement in life and a sense of coherence or integration among various parts of your life.

POSITIVE PSYCHOLOGY TODAY

People of Western industrialized nations entered the twenty-first century with a range of freedoms unprecedented in history. The ideals of freedom, democracy, and self-reliance have allowed people to choose their professions, spouses, systems of religious belief, systems of government, and locales, as well as make endless other choices important to their pursuit of the good life. In fact, citizens of democratic countries are expected to exercise those freedoms and make individual choices that affect their daily lives.

When these choices are brought to bear on the question of the good life or happiness, people today find a veritable cornucopia of different philosophies, beliefs, theories, ideas, and pronouncements all laying claim to authority. The freedom of full inquiry opens up a stunning array of possible answers. In fact, the number of definitions of the good life seems to expand to fit the growing complexity of the world. One of the goals of positive psychology, therefore, is to bring some understanding to these various perspectives on the good life and well-being.

Throughout the twentieth century, many researchers were involved in studying topics relevant to positive human functioning. In fact, all the topics covered in this book were studied prior to the creation of positive psychology. Topics such as happiness and life satisfaction, optimal experiencing, love, wellness, wisdom, creativity, healthy lifespan development, and self-actualization have all been the focus of significant research studies. One of the advantages of positive psychology is that it allows all these topics to be assembled under one heading. Positive psychology enables researchers from diverse areas to come together and share ideas on the adaptive and creative abilities of people.

Despite the fact that positive psychology is a very new field, its popularity is growing rapidly. Seligman and others have worked extensively to provide awareness of the new area and to provide opportunities for interested researchers. The first Positive Psychology Summit was held in 1999. In February 2000 the first recipients of the Templeton Prize in Positive Psychology were announced. In October 2002, the First International Conference on Positive Psychology took place. In June 2009, the International Positive Psychology Association sponsored the First World Congress on Positive Psychology, during which people from all corners of the globe filled the meetings and seminars to capacity. (For more details of the early years, see Csikszentmihalyi & Nakamura, 2011.)

The January 2000 and March 2001 special issues of the *American Psychologist* (the official journal of the American Psychological Association) were devoted to articles on positive psychology. Special issues on positive psychology have followed in professional journals such as the *Journal of Community Psychology* (2002, 30(4)); the *Review of General Psychology* (2005, 9(2)); the *Journal of Cognitive Psychotherapy* (2006, 20(2)); and the *Journal of Organizational Behavior* (2008, 29(2)).[2] The field of positive psychology has also spawned several well-regarded academic journals. These include the *Journal of Positive Psychology*; the *Journal of Happiness Studies*; *Health and Well-Being*; and *The International Journal of Well-Being*.

Although the editorial boards of these and other academic venues draw international expertise, the field of positive psychology today is most advanced in the United States and Western Europe. For example, comparatively few university courses on positive psychology have yet emerged in South America, Eastern Europe, or Asia. However, interest is growing throughout these diverse regions, led mainly by younger scholars and researchers. The research focus of positive psychology is also becoming increasingly global in scope, with empirical studies, for example, in rural China (Nielsen, Smyth & Zhai, 20 Kong (Kwan, 2010), Japan (Asakawa, 2010), Mexico (Rojas, 2010), Bangladesh, and Thailand (Canfield, Guillen-Royo, & Velazsco, 2010).

Although the field of positive psychology offers a new approach to the study of positive emotions and behavior, as this chapter has demonstrated, the ideas, theories, research, and motivation to study the positive side of human behavior is as old as humanity. Positive psychology appears to be well on its way to gaining a permanent place in general psychology. Findings from research that takes a positive psychology approach are already influencing interventions that help people enhance their strengths and develop their potential for greater happiness and satisfaction with life.

SUMMARY

This chapter has introduced positive psychology as the scientific study of optimal human functioning. This new field searches for those qualities that allow individuals, communities, and societies to thrive and flourish, focusing on three major dimensions: positive subjective states, positive traits, and positive institutions. As has been discussed, several basic themes differentiate positive psychology from other schools of psychological research. This chapter has also reviewed the historical understanding of happiness, well-being and the good life in Western intellectual and spiritual traditions. The chapter has ended on an appropriately hopeful note that speculates about the future of positive psychology. On the basis of evidence of a rapidly growing interest in this field, we predict that positive psychology will be a thriving discipline for many years to come.

NOTES

1. Throughout this book the gender-specific term "man" will be used only in a direct quote or when its use accurately reflects the cultural understanding of the time or place.

2. Other special issues in journals have included: the *Humanistic Psychologist* (2008, 36(1)); the *International Coaching Psychology Review* (2007, 2(1)); *Mental Health, Religion, & Culture* (2006, 9(3)); *Psychology in the Schools* (2004, 41(1)); *Journal of Psychology in Chinese Societies* (2004, 5(1)); *Organizational Dynamics* (2004, 33(4)); and *School Psychology Quarterly* (2003, 18(2)). However, not all articles in the special issues have shown unswerving support for positive psychology. A special issue of *Theory and Psychology* (2008, 18(5)) was critical of many underlying assumptions of positive psychology.

LEARNING TOOLS

Key Terms and Ideas

the good life

flourishing

hedonism

divine command
theory

eudaimonia

virtue theory

utilitarianism

hedonic calculus

Books

Fowers, B. (2005). *Virtue and psychology: Pursuing excellence in ordinary practices.* Washington, D.C.: American Psychological Association. A compelling argument for Aristotle's approach to virtue in contemporary psychology. *(professional/popular)*

Haidt, J. (2006). *The happiness hypothesis: Finding modern truth in ancient wisdom.* NY: Basic Books. *(professional/popular)*

Keltner, D. (Ed.). *Greater Good Magazine.* A popular magazine that explores what people do right and how positive ideas are changing the world.

Lopez, S. J., & Snyder, C. R (Eds.). (2009). *The Oxford handbook of positive psychology* (2nd ed.). New York: Oxford University Press. An impressive collection of research articles on the wide variety of topics studied in positive psychology. *(professional, but can be read by interested students)*

Tarnas, R. (1991). *The passion of the Western mind: Understanding the ideas that have shaped our world view.* New York: Ballantine. A beautifully written book that makes reading about history a real pleasure. *(popular/professional)*

On the Web

http://www.ppc.sas.upenn.edu/ Positive psychology on the University of Pennsylvania Web site. Links for researchers, teachers, and others.

http://positivepsychologynews.com Online newsletter for those interested in positive psychology.

http://www.apa.org The Web page for the American Psychological Association with links to positive psychology articles and books.

http://www.goodnewsnetwork.org The Web site for the Good News Network that publishes a newsletter covering good news from around the world.

Personal Explorations

In a famous essay called "The Energies of Men," William James wrote that people often give up on tasks and projects too soon—that is, before they get their "second wind" to propel them across the finish line. "Our organism has stored-up reserves of energy that are ordinarily not called upon" but that exist and can be drawn up effectively, James insisted. Usually, the process happens without our conscious planning or effort, but James believed that psychology might someday discover ways to help each of us tap our stored-up energy, whether we engage in "physical work, intellectual work, moral work, or spiritual work."

1. *Describe an experience in your life when you were feeling exhausted or drained—either mentally or physically—and then you suddenly possessed renewed vitality and enthusiasm.* (a) What do you think caused your "second wind" to kick in? Might it have involved encouragement from

another person, a powerful moment of self-motivation, both of these causes, or something else entirely? (b) If you were teaching a skill or sport to elementary-school children, what advice would you give to help them tap into their "second wind"? (c) Over the next week, record any experiences in which you felt tired or discouraged but then caught your "second wind" of energy and enthusiasm. See if you can identify what caused it to arise.

2. *Have a beautiful day: Applying principles of positive psychology.* This exercise is designed to help you explore qualities of the good life that exist in your life right now. It requires no special materials or equipment. For instructions go to the following Web site: www.ppc.sas.upenn.edu/teachinghigh school.htm

Chapter 2

Foundations: Emotion, Motivation, and the Nature of Well-Being

> The latest scientific research tells us that positivity doesn't simply *reflect*
> success and health, it can also *produce* success and health ... positivity spells
> the difference between whether you languish or flourish.
> BARBARA FREDRICKSON (2009)

It may come as no surprise that a book on positive psychology focuses significantly on our emotional responses to life. Our emotional reactions can range from simple impulsive reactions toward unexpected events, such as the fight–or–flight reaction, to complex combinations of experiences that create our feelings of love, devotion, gratitude, and sense of meaningfulness. In addition, emotions can be temporary or they can extend over time. In the later case, we generally refer to them as moods.

The first question to consider concerns the nature of emotion, for just what is an emotion? Although many people feel it is all too obvious what constitutes an emotion, researchers take a more complex view. In fact, our emotions result from a complex interplay of biological, cognitive, behavioral, and sociocultural processes (Frijda, 2008). This chapter therefore explores how all these components contribute to our experience of emotions, particularly of positive emotions. We also discuss theories of motivation and new perspectives on positive emotion. Finally, we examine how well-being has been defined by various researchers in positive psychology and other disciplines.

THE BASIC EMOTIONS

Throughout the history of psychology, investigators have sought to focus on our most basic human emotions, that is, those innate emotions that provide the foundation for all other emotions. The exact number of basic emotions varies from seven to ten, depending on the theory. Nevertheless, various lists of basic emotions show a fair amount of agreement (see Weitan, 2005). Of relevance for positive psychology is the fact that research concurs that enjoyment, or happiness, or joy is a basic emotion. However, the number of basic positive emotions is less than the total number of basic emotions. This observation is important for a new theory of emotion discussed later in this chapter.

The basic emotions can be combined in many ways to create more subtle variations of emotional experience. For example, Robert Plutchick (1980) pointed out that the emotion of awe is a combination of surprise and fear. This means that a positive emotion often related to religious experience arises from the somewhat positive emotion of surprise in conjunction with the basic negative emotion of fear. This suggests that any attempt to wholly eliminate negative emotions from our life would have the unintended consequence of losing the variety and subtlety of our most profound emotional experiences.

Interestingly, substantial research has supported the consideration of positive emotions and negative emotions as relatively independent (for example, Ryff, Love, Urry, Muller, Rosenkranz et al., 2006). That is, how often a person feels positive emotions may have very little to do with how often that person feels negative emotions (Schimmack, 2008). This means that efforts to increase positive emotions will not automatically result in decreased negative emotions, nor will decreased negative emotions necessarily result in increased positive emotions. This finding is relevant to positive psychology intervention.

It is also possible to classify emotions by how central they are to our daily experience. James Russell and Feldman Barrett (1999) described emotional reactions they termed *core affects*. These refer to primitive emotional reactions that are consistently experienced but often not acknowledged; they blend pleasant and unpleasant as well as activated and deactivated dimensions that we carry with us at an almost unconscious level. Because different core affects can push people toward either negative or positive interpretations, identical situations are often evaluated by different people or at different times very differently (Smith & Mackie, 2008). Indeed a variety of studies support the observation that many of our emotional responses operate at an unconscious level (Bargh & Williams, 2007).

Figure 2.1 illustrates how a combination of biological, cognitive, behavioral, and sociocultural factors influence our emotional states and reactions.

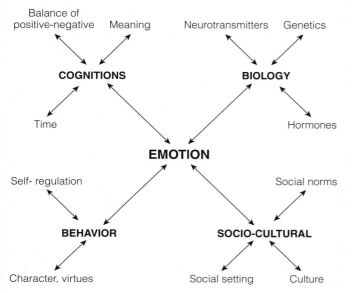

FIGURE 2.1 Components of Emotion

THE COMPONENTS OF EMOTION

The Biology of Emotions

Neurotransmitters and the Chemicals of Pleasure Empirical evidence indicates that at least some of our pleasurable responses are caused by the release of certain chemicals in the brain called neurotransmitters. Neurotransmitters are chemical messengers that relay information between nerve cells. Specifically, increased levels of the neurotransmitter dopamine have been implicated in the experience of happiness (Ashby, Isen, & Turken, 1999). In the mid-1970s, a Scottish team of researchers discovered a variety of neurotransmitters that seem to act like the brain's natural opiate system. These encephalins or endorphins appear to increase pleasure and decrease the experience of pain. Increased levels of endorphins are partially involved in the "runner's high" that can accompany physical exercise (Farrell, Gustafson, Morgan, & Pert, 1987). Endorphin levels also increase as much as 200 percent during sexual intercourse (Pert, 1997).

Recently a considerable amount of attention has been given to the effects of the hormone oxytocin, or the "love hormone". Studies have found that oxytocin is associated with social bonding, trust, and emotional support within couples, and is released during breastfeeding (Dickerson & Zoccola, 2009). In addition to this research on neurotransmitters, recent work has suggested that the brain makes its own version of tetrahydrocannabinols or THC, which is the active ingredient in marijuana (Fackelmann, 1993).

Does this mean that positive emotions such as joy and love are simply patterns of neurotransmitter and hormonal activity? As a recent bumper sticker humorously expressed, "I'm not really happy, it's just a chemical imbalance!" Although our biological processes are certainly part of the equation, science has just begun to explore the various components of our emotional experiences.

The "Happy" Brain John Davidson of the University of Wisconsin has conducted significant research to determine which parts of the brain are involved in positive emotions. Specifically, the left prefrontal cortex is more activated when we are happy (see Lutz, Dunne, & Davidson, 2007). This area of the brain has also been associated with greater ability to recover from negative emotions as well as enhanced ability to suppress negative emotions (see Urry, Nitschke, Dolski et al., 2004). In a unique series of studies involving long-term Buddhist meditators, Davidson found that people can train themselves to increase activation in this area of their brains (also see Kringlebach & Berridge, 2009).

Neuroplasticity Until recently scientists assumed that once our brains are formed in childhood, little change takes place for the remainder of our lives. Several fascinating studies in recent years have challenged this assumption, and in fact it now appears that our brains can change throughout our lives as a result of our experiences. The term for this new idea is **neuroplasticity**. Neurologist Oliver Sacks has said (2010):

> While it is often true that learning is easier in childhood, neuroscientists now know that the brain does not stop growing, even in our later years. Every time we practice an old skill or learn a new one, existing neural connections are strengthened and, over time, neurons create more connections to other neurons. Even new nerve cells can be generated.

In particular, studies have found that structures of the brain increase in size as a result of learning music (see chapter 7) and practicing meditation (see chapter 10).

The Genetics of Emotion Another biologically-based perspective on emotion concerns the question of whether heredity impacts our emotional responses. It is quite obvious that some people are typically cheerful and easygoing whereas others seem more prone to anxiety and worry. Is it possible that being a cheerful person, an anxious person, or someone who always seems to take things in stride is a product of our genes and not necessarily of any coping skills we have learned over the years? Indeed, Micheal Eid and Randy Larsen (2008) argued that reactions such as happiness and satisfaction have been shaped by our evolutionary history.

David Lykken and Auke Tellegen (1996) suggested that up to 80% of a long-term sense of well-being is due to heredity. Specifically, they found in their studies of twins that 40% of the variability among people in positive emotionality, 55% of the variability in negative emotionality, and 48% of the variability in overall well-being

stems from genetics (Tellegen, Lykken, Bouchard, Wilcox, & Rich, 1988). They also found that shared family environment or learning accounts for only 22% of positive emotionality and an extremely small 2% of negative emotionality. Figure 2.2 shows their findings on the heritability of emotionality.

In other words, our families are important to our eventual emotional lives as adults because they provide us with genetic material that largely determines our base emotional responsiveness to the world. Therefore, concluded Lykken and Tellegen,

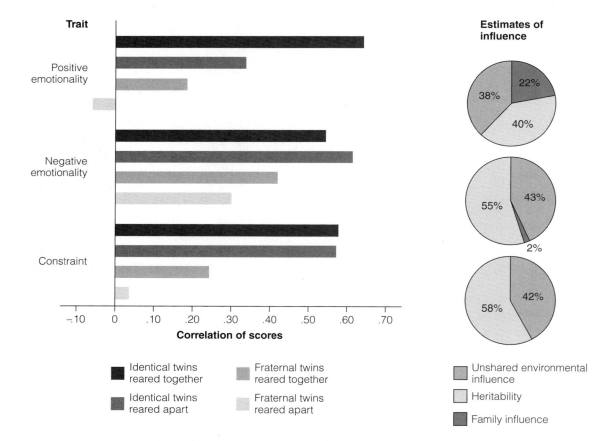

F I G U R E 2.2 Genetic Influences on Well-Being. Left: For three basic personality traits, identical twins were more similar than fraternal twins, even when twins were reared apart (Tellegen et al., 1998). Right: Estimates of heritability derived from the correlational data were relatively high; although investigators also found evidence of environmental influence, the family influence appeared to be neglible for two of the traits (ibid.).

SOURCE: Adapted with permission from Tellegen et al., "Personality Similarity in Twins Reared Apart and Together," *Journal of Personality & Social Psychology*, 54(6), pp. 1031–1039. Copyright © 1988 by the American Psychological Association.

genetic makeup is far more important to the long-term quality of our emotional lives than is learned behavior or the quality of our early childhood environment. Richard Lucas (2008) agreed that genetic factors are vital for average well-being, but insofar as his estimate of genetic influence is somewhat lower at 30%–50%, it is apparent that family environment and learning can also impact well-being.

The Happiness Set Point   Based on results from a variety of empirical studies, Lykken and Tellegen (1996) proposed the measure of a **happiness set point**. That is, heritability studies indicate that most people return to an average level of happiness—or a set point—after temporary highs and lows in emotionality (see also Lucas, 2008). So even though very intense feelings of joy or sadness keep people off their set points for varying periods of time, eventually everyone returns to an average or baseline level of well-being—a level set by genetics. People whose set points lean toward positive emotionality tend to be cheerful most of the time. By contrast, those whose set points direct them toward more negative emotionality tend to gravitate toward pessimism and anxiety.

Do Our Genes Rule Our Emotional Lives? Scientific evidence for a genetic contribution to long-term well-being is very compelling However, the research can be misinterpreted. Note that it does not state that long-term well-being is completely determined by genetic inheritance. Second, research conclusions are often based on group averages compiled over several years. Contained within these group averages can be significant individual variations that occur over time. Third, the studies are based on well-being scores from relatively global assessment measures that do not specify how people uniquely define their own happiness or life satisfaction. Even David Lykken, one of the major proponents of the heritability and set-point theory, pointed out that we can influence our level of well-being by creating environments more conducive to feelings of happiness and by

working with our genetic makeup. He contended (2000):

> The basic point one must remember is that genes affect the mind largely indirectly, by influencing the kinds of experiences people have and the kinds of environments they seek out.... If your happiness set point is below average, that means that your genetic steersman is guiding you into situations that detract from your well-being and is tempting you to behave in ways that are counterproductive. If you let your genetic steersman have his way, then you will end up where he wants to go. But it is *your* life and, within wide limits, you can choose your own destinations instead of having them all chosen for you (p. 60, original italics).

In fact, more recent research has not supported an extreme or "strong" interpretation of set-point theory—that is, one in which genes are considered the determinant factor in overall well-being.

Ed Diener (2008), one of the major researchers of subjective well-being, has criticized extreme set-point theory as being overly deterministic. For example, Frank Fujita and Diener (2005) examined longitudinal data on life satisfaction collected over 17 years in Germany. They found that 24% of people changed significantly between the first five years of the study and the last five years. That is, although their genetic makeup obviously did not alter over time, almost one in four people showed changes in their well-being over the years; indeed, sometimes those changes were quite dramatic.

Bruce Headey (2008) used the same data set and also found clear evidence that life satisfaction can change considerably over time. In particular, from 5%–6% of people dramatically increased their life satisfaction over a 15- to 20-year period. Headey also found that the goals people pursued had a major impact on their life satisfaction. How so? Goals associated with greater life satisfaction consisted of commitments to family and friends, social or political involvement, and altruism. He called these *nonzero-sum goals* because the person involved as well as others can benefit. In contrast, *zero-sum goals*, or those in which one person gains advantage at the expense of others, did not promote life satisfaction.

Felicia Huppert (2007) argued that because interventions to increase well-being can be successful, genes do not completely determine happiness. After analyzing data from a 26-year longitudinal study, Headey, Muffels, and Wagner (2010) concluded that, contrary to the implications of set-point theory, human beings can increase their happiness over time.

So although genetic makeup is not destiny, the genetic influence on long-term positive and negative emotionality or disposition is fairly well-established. At the same time, interventions to increase well-being can be successful in light of large survey findings that nontrivial percentages of individuals change their well-being fairly dramatically over time.

Cognition: How We Think Impacts How We Feel

One of the more significant contributions of psychology in the twentieth century was the revival of the ancient Greek notion that our thoughts in large part determine our emotional states. In cognitive therapy, the goal is to help people change negative styles of thinking as a way to change how they feel. This cognitive approach to our emotional lives has been remarkably successful, and changing how we think about other people, our future, and ourselves is partially responsible for this success (Caprara & Steca, 2010). Over 2,500 years ago, Gautama Buddha said, "We are what we think. All that we are arises with our thoughts. With our thoughts we make the world" (Byrom, 1993).

The thinking processes that impact our emotional states vary considerably. Under the right circumstances (Wood, Perunovic, & Lee, 2009), changing one simple thought from "I'm lonely" to "I am loved by someone" can make all the difference in our emotional lives. Similarly, if we are faced with a challenging event and can find a way to interpret it in positive terms, we can change a potential crisis into an opportunity. Having some dexterity at cognitive control of emotions can be a very useful skill (Kryla-Lighthall, 2009). Martin Seligman has done considerable work in this area by working with what he called *learned optimism* (Seligman, 2006). He has found that people can unlearn negative styles of thinking and instead learn how to interpret events with more realistic optimism (Carver, Scheier, & Segerstrom, 2010). Taking this idea a bit further, we can say that a more complex yet positive interpretation of events can help create a sense of meaning and purpose in life (McKnight & Kashdan, 2009; Steger, Oishi, & Kasdan, 2009; Wong, 2009a).

Our thinking can also impact our well-being through an unusual avenue, namely, our perspective on time. Philip Zimbardo (2009) and Ilona Boniwell (2009) studied how our ideas about time influence our happiness or satisfaction with life. They found that future-oriented people can better delay gratification and work toward long-term goals than more present-oriented ones. The former can be satisfied in a stressful situation if they see how it will lead to a better future. In contrast, present-oriented people tend to live for the moment. They find satisfaction in enjoying current pleasures but are less inclined to work hard toward future goals. However, an important caveat to this conclusion: An ability to pull attention away from the chronic inner chatter of our thoughts can be quite advantageous to well-being (see chapter 4). For a variety of reasons, a change in our orientation to time can dramatically impact how we think about the nature of happiness.

Behavior: How We Act Influences How We Feel

It might seem that our behavior has little to do with our sense of well-being. However, consider a situation in which you are reluctant to confront a friend about her insensitive behavior. Because of your hesitation, you keep your feelings to yourself. Soon your emotions may fester and change into resentment, eventually explode in anger, and make the situation even worse. However, if you draw on your assertiveness and speak to your friend, then you may significantly change your emotions. Your behavior can, in fact, strongly influence your emotions. One of the more significant contributions of positive psychology is its focus on positive behaviors. Often these are viewed in terms of strengths, virtues, and character.

Virtues, Strengths, Character, and Our Emotions
In chapter 1 we saw that Aristotle proposed a theory of well-being based on the cultivation of certain virtues. Most of the virtues involve how we behave in social relationships. For instance, the degree of our truthfulness, magnificence, and sense of justice are all determined by how we relate to other people. How we conduct ourselves as members of a society is referred to as our **character**. Blaine Fowers (2005, 2006) argued that the development of character is essential because how we treat each other is the foundation of ethics, morality, civil society, and well-being. Robert Emmons and Cheryl Crumpler (2000) defined virtues as follows: "Virtues are acquired excellences in character traits, the possession of which contributes to a person's completeness or wholeness. Virtues represent ideal states that facilitate adaptation to life" (p. 57). Therefore, strengths and virtues are more than just useful tools for adaptation to stress or difficult circumstances. They may serve those functions, of course, but they are important because they help a person to grow psychologically toward optimal character development. They are also operative in many situations throughout life.

Another perspective on virtues comes from Sandage and Hill (2001) who argued that virtues: "(a) integrate ethics and health; (b) are embodied traits of character; (c) are sources of human strengths and resilience; (d) are embedded within a cultural context and community; (e) contribute to a sense of meaningful life purpose; and (f) are grounded in the cognitive capacity for wisdom" (Emmons & Paloutzian, 2003, p. 387). The reference to wisdom implies that virtues also contribute to a larger perspective on life that takes into consideration how current actions might impact the welfare of self, others, and the community.

The study of character in positive psychology evolved out of work by the Gallup Institute examining what makes top achievers in business different from their peers. What they found was that top achievers tended to use their **strengths**. These are the unique positive qualities we each have, which we bring to our encounters both with other people and with ourselves. Gallup found that organizations work better when people are allowed to develop their strengths rather than constantly focusing on fixing their weaknesses (Buckingham & Coffman, 1999). This significant line of research is captured by the phrase: *Focus on your strengths*. A corollary is: *Manage your weaknesses*. That is, manage those areas in which a lack of knowledge, skills, or talent has a negative impact on yourself or others. However, the majority of effort should be placed on your strengths.

Donald Clifton and colleagues developed the *Clifton StrengthsFinder* as a way to measure strengths (see Buckingham & Clifton, 2001; Clifton, Anderson, & Clifton et al., 2006). The *StrengthsFinder* evaluated thirty-four themes, such as adaptability; connectedness; and responsibility. Positive psychology emphasizes personal strengths as a way to make changes in our lives by focusing on what we already know how to do well.

Various psychologists have brought an emphasis on personal strengths into schools and universities as the *StrengthsQuest* program. The notion is to "enable students to identify the talents they bring into the learning environment that they can capitalize upon in order to achieve academic success and personal growth" (Schreiner, 2006). They ask students to take the *StrengthsFinder* test and focus their attention on their signature (most salient) strengths. Although all strengths are important and work together, these psychologists believe that a focus on a small number of strengths—even one at a time—is the best strategy to work toward excellence. They advise students to follow a few basic principles as they work on using their strengths: (1) value their talents and assume responsibility for developing them; (2) place their talents in the context of a personal mission; (3) healthy relationships facilitate strengths; (4) reflect on their success with strengths; (5) practice over and over again; and (6) teach others what they are learning. The *StrengthsFinder* has been given to over 100,000 college students. Studies have found that students who participated in the *StrengthsQuest* program felt more hopeful and confident, reported higher well-being, acted more altruistically, and had higher grade-point averages (Hodges & Clifton, 2004; Hodges & Harter, 2005).

Christopher Peterson and Martin E. P. Seligman also developed a classification system for strengths and virtues. They referred to their work on strengths, virtues, and character as the *Values in Action (VIA) Project* (Peterson & Seligman, 2004). Using the *VIA Survey of Character*, Peterson and Seligman assessed 24 different strengths that define six different core virtues. Their list appears in Table 2.1.

As can be seen in the table, this list includes aspects of how people relate to their own inner psychological world; how they relate to others in their world; how they relate to the future; and how they view their responsibilities to community. The most important strengths for each individual are his or her **signature strengths**, or those "positive traits that a person owns, celebrates, and frequently exercises" (Peterson & Park, 2009, p. 29). In a factor analysis of strengths, researchers found two correlated continuous dimensions: one from *Focus on Self* to *Focus on Others*, and the other from *Heart* (emotion) to *Mind* (thinking) (Peterson & Park, 2009). Most of the strengths related to happiness tended to be in the realm of heart, with either a *Focus on Self* or *Focus on Others*. Peterson and Seligman noted that their list is certainly neither comprehensive nor exhaustive for other virtues may be useful in specific social contexts. For instance, in certain religious or spiritual contexts the virtue of selflessness may be prized and fostered.

Nansook Park, Peterson, and Seligman (2004) investigated the relationships between life satisfaction and VIA scores and found that strengths of love, hope, curiosity, zest, and gratitude were the ones most significantly related to life satisfaction.

T A B L E 2.1   Values In Action (VIA) Classification of Character Strengths and Virtues

Wisdom & Knowledge	**Justice**
Curiosity, interest in world.	Teamwork: working well as Member of a group or team.
Love of learning, knowledge.	Fairness.
Open-mindedness.	Leadership.
Creativity, novel solutions.	**Temperance**
Perspective: provide wise counsel.	Forgiveness.
Courage	Prudence, caution, discretion.
Authenticity, honesty, integrity.	Modesty.
Bravery.	Self-regulation.
Perserverance: finishing what one starts.	**Transcendence**
Zest: excitement, energy.	Appreciation of beauty & excellence.
Humanity	Gratitude.
Kindness, generosity.	Hope.
Love: capacity to love, be loved.	Humor.
Social intelligence: aware of motives & feelings of others.	Religiousness.

SOURCE: Adapted from Peterson, C. & Park, N., "Classifying and Measuring Strengths of Character," in C. Snyder & S. Lopez (Eds.). *Oxford Handbook of Positive Psychology, 2nd edition* (page 28). Copyright © 2009 Oxford University Press.

Later in a survey of almost 13,000 people from the U.S. and Switzerland, the most significant predictors of life satisfaction were, again, love; hope; curiosity; and zest (Peterson, Ruch, Beermann, Park, & Seligman, 2007). Gratitude was also a strong predictor in the U.S. sample, while perseverance was an additional predictor in the Swiss sample. A recent study by Brdar and Kashdan (2010) found hope; zest; curiosity; and sense of humor to be the strongest predictors of well-being. Interestingly, the most frequently reported virtues among nearly all nations are: kindness; fairness; authenticity; gratitude; and open-mindedness (Peterson & Park, 2009). This implies that the strengths most associated with well-being are not often the most frequently found strengths in a population.

Seligman, Steen, Park, & Peterson (2005) tested the impact of strength interventions on happiness using an Internet sample. Among the five interventions tested were two devoted to signature strengths. After completing the VIA character scale, participants were asked to note their top five strengths and either "use one of these top strengths in a new and different way everyday for a week" or use the top five strengths "more often during the week." The researchers found that using a single strength in a new and different way increased happiness one week after the post-test and continued to show increases for six months. In contrast, using strengths more often increased happiness at post-test but not in follow-up tests. It appears that how we use our signature strengths is very important in the subsequent impact on well-being.

Courtesy of Christopher Peterson

Christopher Peterson

Of course, our troublesome qualities should not be ignored. In fact, making an effort to remedy our weaknesses can also be beneficial to well-being (Rust, Diessner, & Reade, 2009). It may be that strengths and vulnerabilities are not opposite ends of a continuum but are analogous to the independence of positive and negative emotions discussed earlier. Veronika Huta and Lance Hawley (2010) found that VIA strengths are only moderately correlated with dysfunctional attitudes, suggesting that working on increasing strengths and on decreasing vulnerabilities are both advantageous to well-being. Somewhat tongue-in-cheek, Jonathan Haidt (2002) has remarked, "It's more fun to work on strengths than weaknesses (but it may not be better for you)." Fortunately, it seems that any efforts made in a positive direction can be helpful. But too often in the past focus has been on fixing weaknesses—an emphasis that can lead to a preoccupation with, or even a reinforcement of, personal difficulties.

In addition, other systems exist that classify strengths and virtues. Schwartz's (1994) model of 10 basic values also appears to have universal applicability. The Temperament and Character Inventory by C. Robert Cloninger measures three core character traits (that is, cooperativeness, self-directedness, and self-transcendence), rather than the six used in the VIA (Cloninger, 2004). The Search Institute's Developmental Assets Scale measures forty areas of potential strength and support in the lives of children and youth (see Benson & Scales, 2009). Undoubtedly, the most influential system of personality classification in psychology has been the Big Five (McCrae & John, 1992). Noftle, Schnitker, and Robins (2011) found significant overlap between the VIA and the Big Five and suggested that the VIA measures normal dimensions of personality. However, the most influential system in positive psychology has been the VIA.

Social and Cultural Influences on Emotions

How we experience our emotional lives is also influenced by the social situation we are in at the time. Research on emotions supports a *social constraints model* of mood regulation, which asserts that people regulate their moods based on their understanding of a social situation (Erber & Erber,

© Randy Glasbergen.
www.glasbergen.com

"I was in a good mood once, but I couldn't find any practical purpose for it."

2000; Tamir & Gross, 2011). In addition, researchers studying the sociology of emotion (Stets & Turner, 2008) look at how social status and class structures, as well as culture, can influence our sense of self, our identity, and our understanding of both emotions and emotional expression.

How we experience emotions is also partially determined by the broader culture we live in (see Matsumoto, 1994). Although it is true that some aspects of positive emotionality are innate, at the same time there is considerable variation in how people express, label, and promulgate positive emotions around the world (see chapter 11). For instance, most people in the United States think of happiness as an exuberant, energetic feeling that produces outwardly expressed enthusiasm and joy (Bok, 2010). However, Chinese typically view happiness in terms of quiet contentment that is a somewhat private emotion (Tsai, Knutson & Fung, 2006; Tsai, 2007). Similarly, Algoe, Fredrickson and Chow (2011) noted that emotions in collectivist cultures do not exist so much *within* people as *between* people—that is, as part of social relationships. Because of such differences, Kennon

Sheldon's (2004, 2009) multilevel model of well-being includes an assessment of cultural factors along with personality variables and biological factors.

Even within a specific culture, changes over time can affect how we experience emotion. In the Western world during the Victorian era, it was considered highly erotic for women to expose their legs in public. For men, a minor insult might require a deadly duel in order to protect one's "honor." Today these emotional reactions seem quaint and somewhat silly. Nevertheless, society at the time dictated these emotional reactions to particular events, and most people complied with social expectations for emotionality.

MOODS AND WELL-BEING

Any discussion of emotion must eventually turn to the topic of moods. Although moods are different from emotions, not all psychologists agree on exactly how they are different. What everyone does seem to agree on is that moods are more diffuse, more global, and more pervasive than emotions (Morris, 1999). That is, emotions are focused feelings that can appear or disappear rapidly in response to events in the environment. Moods, however, are generally pervasive and maintain their general tone despite undergoing minor changes over time. Morris (1999) suggested that a basic function of moods is to provide us with information about the adequacy of our current resources to meet current or future demands. In his view, moods provide us with a continuous monitoring system that gives ongoing information about how well we cope with life events.

Recent studies have found that emotions and moods can have a significant impact on almost any psychological process, such as memory, attention, perception, and our experience of self. In particular, being in a happy or positive mood seems to foster greater adaptation to the world in significant ways. In fact, an extensive review of research by Sonja Lybomirsky, Laura King, and Ed Diener (2005) found that the impact of positive emotionality can be substantial, ranging from higher well-being to better romantic relationships, more displays of altruism and generosity, more successful careers, the promotion of creativity, and better health. The advantages of positive mood can impact almost every area of life.

However, the goal of studying positive psychology is not simply to create a high level of positive emotion throughout an entire day, every day over the course of an entire lifetime. That goal is not possible and, further, it leaves out valuable information gained from negative emotions. Actually, the challenge of creating greater well-being is far more interesting than can be expressed by that overly simplistic formula. Nonetheless, the message for a positive psychology is that positive moods help us to adapt better and provide us with opportunities to learn and grow. Obviously, good moods are not all that is required for greater flourishing and thriving, but they are an important piece of the puzzle.

POSITIVE PSYCHOLOGY AND MOTIVATION

Early Theories of Motivation

If positive psychology in part involves the promotion of human flourishing, then somehow people must be motivated to pursue that goal. In fact, motivation and emotion are so intertwined that it is often difficult to separate their individual effects. This section examines how psychology has explained the forces that propel people toward their goals.

As might be expected, there is no simple answer to what causes us to pursue certain goals. Over 50 years ago, Robert W. White (1959) argued that people can be motivated by more than simple drives to fulfill physiological needs, or "tissue needs." White urged psychologists to consider the relevance of motivations that propel people toward a sense of competence—or *effectance motivations*. He said that people are also compelled to engage their immediate environment in ways that produce effective outcomes. In his view, people are driven to engage the world in ways that give them a sense of competence and accomplishment that go beyond the basic meeting of physiological needs.

Intrinsic and Extrinsic Motivation

One of the more interesting lines of research into motivation concerns the difference between intrinsic and extrinsic motivation. *Intrinsic motivation* is operating when we are compelled to engage in some activity for its own sake, regardless of any external reward. *Extrinsic motivation* comes into play when we act to obtain some external reward, be it status, praise, money, or another incentive that comes from outside ourselves. Recently Richard Ryan and Edward Deci (2008) have favored the terms **autonomous motivation** over intrinsic motivation and **controlled motivation** over extrinsic motivation. Autonomous motivation is self-chosen and is congruent with one's true self, while controlled motivation is driven by external rewards or guilt and is not congruent with a person's core values. They view the difference between autonomous and controlled motivation as extremely important for an understanding of mental health, achievement, and well-being as well as for an understanding of basic motivation.

Indeed, Ryan and Deci (2000) earlier went even further, writing, "Perhaps no single phenomena reflects the positive potential of human nature as much as intrinsic motivation, [or] the inherent tendency to seek out novelty and challenges, to extend and exercise one's capacities, to explore, and to learn (p. 70)." Though at first glance Ryan and Deci's statement seems a bit overly enthusiastic, when the research literature is examined there is justification for their energetic endorsement of autonomous motivation. A positive relationship has been found between being autonomously motivated and achieving positive outcomes in numerous areas, such as health; work; intimate relationships; parenting; education; religious participation; and even political activism (Ryan & Deci, 2000; Deci & Ryan, 2008). Studies also indicate that people who are autonomously motivated tend to show enhancements in performance; persistence; creativity; self-esteem; vitality; and general well-being when compared to people who are motivated by external rewards. It seems that the more a person's behavior is autonomously motivated, the greater the impact on well-being (Ryan, Huta, & Deci, 2008).

It should be mentioned that activities that are controlled or extrinsically motivated can also be of value (Brdar, Majda, & Dubravka, 2009). Doing something in order to get an external reward can eventually lead to acquiring desirable skills and competencies. Studies have found that the relative weights given by a person to her or his autonomous and controlled activities are crucial for well-being (see Ryan, Huta, & Deci, 2008). In the context of multiple goals, the more importance given to autonomous goals, the more likely well-being is fostered and nurtured.

Motivation and the Pursuit of Goals

Although some researchers have investigated motivation by looking at innate drives, others have focused on our expectations or hopes for the future. For instance, when we discuss our hopes and dreams for the coming years, then we are talking about our goals. The unique goals we have for our life determine where we place our efforts and commitments. In addition, the specific character of our goals and our relationship to them at any moment in time may also determine our emotional state. This is especially true the more important those goals are to us. In fact, goals may be extremely important to our positive emotional state at any point in time—and to our general emotional well-being.

Researchers who have studied goals and their relationship to well-being have found that certain types of goals are more effective in producing happiness and satisfaction than are other types (see Emmons, 1992; Lyubomirsky, 2001). In general, goals that are the result of *intrinsic* or *autonomous motivation*, are *personally valued*, are *realistic*, and are *freely chosen* seem better at raising subjective well-being. The pursuit of goals that are *meaningful* to us is more fulfilling than chasing after goals that are imposed by others or that we don't value. For example, Niemiec, Ryan, and Deci (2009) found that attainment of intrinsic goals lead to greater well-being while attaining extrinsic goals actually resulted in less well-being. Similarly, Oishi, Diener, Suh, and Lucas (1999) obtained ratings on how much satisfaction college students gained from engaging in a variety of activities. They found differences among activities such that higher subjective well-being was related to ones involving both interpersonal relationships and community contributions. Further, even higher subjective well-being was found when the activity reflected a person's individual values.

For instance, students who valued benevolence experienced higher subjective well-being when they were involved in helpful social activities or when showing other people they cared for them. High congruence between one's personality and goals is referred to as **self-concordance** by Kennon Sheldon (2008) and as "regulatory fit" by E. Tory Higgins (2000). Studies have found that when there is a better fit between a person's values and her or his goal, then a more positive evaluation of the goal, greater motivation, greater commitment to the goal, and higher well-being ensue (Wehmeyer, Little, & Sergeant, 2009).

In general, it also appears that well-being is enhanced by seeking goals associated with *positive relationships* and *helping others*, while relatively self-centered goals decrease well-being. One example is a study by Kasser and Ryan (1993), who found that subjective well-being was enhanced when people pursued goals that facilitated affiliation, intimacy, self-acceptance, and community involvement. Conversely, Cantor and Sanderson (1999) reported that well-being was lowered when people sought relatively self-centered goals related to physical attractiveness, fame, and wealth. Goals that are *valued by one's society or culture* may also be more effective in raising well-being (Cantor & Sanderson, 1999). Obviously, pursuing goals admired in one's culture can lead to more social rewards.

The next issue concerns approach versus avoidance goals. *Approach goals* motivate us to move toward something (for example, "I want to get a Ph.D. in psychology"). *Avoidance goals* motivate us to avoid difficulties, dangers, or fears (for example, "I try to avoid speaking in public because it makes me nervous"). Studies have found that approach goals are more likely to be associated with subjective well-being than are avoidance goals. Well-being is higher when people move toward something they value rather than avoid something difficult or painful. However, motivations are complex, and both approach and avoidance goals can feel good depending on the situation.

What is also important is the rate at which people approach their valued goals. Making *adequate or better-than-expected progress* toward important goals translates into higher well-being (Lent, Singley, Sheu, Gainor, Brenner et al., 2005). That is, the rate of progress a person has made, or expects

to make, toward goals may even be more important than actual achievement. Acceptable rates of progress are associated with more positive emotions. For instance, a goal such as "to learn to play the piano well" is one that is never quite reached because you can always play better than you do now. For most people satisfaction comes, in part, from learning to play better with an acceptable rate of progress.

The impact that our goals have on our sense of happiness or life satisfaction also depend upon how specific such goals are. In terms of specificity, Emmons (1992) has found that highly *abstract goals* may decrease immediate well-being because their abstractness makes it hard to know when they have been achieved. For instance, if your goal is to be a caring and compassionate person, it is hard to know when you have treated people with enough compassion. In contrast, with *concrete goals,* you know almost immediately if you have achieved them. An example of a concrete goal is to treat at least one person every day with caring, compassion, and understanding. At the end of the day, you know immediately if you have met your goal. However, not having any abstract or high-level long-term goals that serve to orient one's life direction is associated with lower well-being. Little (1989) poetically termed this dilemma the conflict between "magnificent obsessions and trivial pursuits." Emmons (1992) suggested that it is best to find a *balance between concrete and abstract goals* by setting concrete, short-term goals that are directly linked to more abstract and meaningful longer-term goals. For example, we might work toward the goal of ending world hunger as long as we do it step-by-step.

Another important aspect of our goals concerns the relationship among them. The first issue here concerns their levels of congruence versus conflict. In particular, greater well-being is associated with *more congruence* among different goals and *less internal conflict* between competing goals. For instance, people who have eight or ten major goals in life that are all "very important" may end up creating conflicts among those goals due to lack of time to fully accomplish them all. Note that the contemporary wish to "have it all" in terms of career, family, self-development, community involvement, and leisure can actually aggravate internal conflicts among goals and thus lower happiness. Social adaptation and adjustment can be defined as the process that reduces conflicts among our important life goals.

Sheldon, Kasser, Smith and Share (2002) developed a program to foster goal attainment. They taught students four strategies: (1) *own your goal* (for example, reinforce personal reasons for pursuing the goal); (2) *make it fun* (for example, enhance intrinsic motivation); (3) *remember the big picture* (for example, remember how small goals fit into long-term goals); and (4) *keep a balance* (for example, balance goals and other aspects of life). They found that participants who were already high in personality integration (they were "prepared to benefit") showed the greatest satisfaction with the program and an increased well-being and vitality.

Strivings and Well-Being Robert Emmons (Emmons, 1986, 1992; Emmons & King, 1988) suggested that it is possible to group several smaller goals around common themes. Personal **strivings** are groupings of smaller goals that can help to facilitate larger, more abstract goals. As an example of a personal striving, Emmons listed *find that special someone*. Note that many smaller goals, such as *be open with other people*, *take an interest in other people*, and *get out and socialize more,* can be part of this personal striving—that is, related to the higher-level goal of *find a lasting and satisfying intimate relationship*. Emmons found that personal strivings were related to subjective well-being in ways similar to goals. For instance, people with high life satisfaction believed their personal strivings were "important, valued, not likely to produce conflict, and [they] expect[ed] to be successful at them" (Emmons, 1986, p. 1064).

Emmons (1999) related four styles of striving to types of motivation. *Extrinsic strivings* are done for the sake of someone else or only for extrinsic rewards. *Introjected strivings* are pursued not necessarily for personally relevant reasons but because if you

didn't, then you'd feel guilty or that you have let someone down. Similarly, *identified strivings* relate to pursuing a goal that someone else says is important. However, in this case a person has adopted the goal as her or his own. *Intrinsic strivings* are engaged in because they are personally meaningful and have been freely chosen by a person. Once again, strivings that are freely chosen and meaningful seem better at increasing well-being than do extrinsic strivings, at least in Western cultures.

Hope Theory A crucial element in whether people are motivated to pursue their goals is their expectation or hope that they will eventually attain them. In most cases, it is hard to bring much enthusiasm to the pursuit of an important goal that you know you will never reach. Thus, many older theories of hope and motivation are based on an expectation of success in attaining goals. However, is that all there is to our hopes for the future? Are they based simply on an expectation that we will reach our goals?

Hope theory says that hope is actually the result of two processes: (1) *pathways,* or believing that one can find ways to reach desired goals; and (2) *agency,* or believing that one can become motivated enough to pursue those goals (Snyder, Rand, & Sigmon, 2002). Therefore, this theory holds that hope for the future is the result of believing we can create both realistic plans and enough drive to reach important goals. People who are hopeful also tend to feel more positive emotions. Besides several other positive benefits, people who are high in hope tend to anticipate greater well-being in the future; are more confident; may be able to deal with stress more successfully; are flexible enough to find alternative pathways to their goals; and tend to have higher social support (Rand & Cheavens, 2009).

Affective Forecasting Daniel Gilbert (2006) developed an intriguing twist to the literature on goal pursuit. In his studies he found that people were not very good at **affective forecasting**— that is, at predicting how they would feel when they reached their goals. For example, when we finally attain the job we have wished for or marry our dream lover, do we actually feel the way we imagined we would feel? Gilbert's research found that we are often disappointed when we achieve our major goals. He suggested this is because we do not imagine those future events accurately.

How so? Our predictions are poor simply because we skip over the specific details in our broad imagining. Gilbert advised us to obtain more accurate assessments of how we would feel by finding other people who had satisfied what we wanted and asking how *they* felt as a result (Gilbert, Killingsworth, Eyre, & Wilson, 2009). He observed that most people do not use this "surrogation strategy" because they falsely believe their own experiences will be too unique and that therefore reports from others will not be useful. Gilbert's research argues for putting more effort into realistic appraisals of how we might feel when we reach important goals rather than holding on to unrealistic expectations about goal attainment and emotional transformation. Equally important, we should also try to enjoy the journey toward our goals because their ultimate satisfaction may not be quite what we expected.

WELL-BEING AND POSITIVE EMOTION

For many years in psychology, positive emotions have been studied far less than negative emotions. As mentioned in chapter 1, one of the barriers to the development of positive psychology was the assumption that positive and negative emotions were simply opposite and balanced ends of an emotional continuum. Therefore, if one studied the predictors of negative emotions, then one automatically knew something about the predictors of positive emotions. We have learned that this assumption proved to be false.

Another barrier to the study of positive emotions is that there seem to be fewer basic positive ones than negative ones by a ratio of one positive to every three or four negative emotions (Fredrickson,

1998). It may be that because negative emotions are used to alert us to possible dangers and threats, we need a variety of them to warn us against numerous potential threats. Also, positive emotions seem fairly diffuse and tend to have nonspecific markers in terms of autonomic activation. By contrast, there are relatively specific biological and neurological processes associated with certain negative emotional responses triggered by the *fight-or-flight* response to unexpected danger. Indeed, many negative emotions are associated with urges to act in certain ways that are called *specific action tendencies*. For example, the response to unexpected fear can be immediate behavioral responses designed to protect us by either fighting off an attack or fleeing from the danger. Unexpectedly, however, this direct linkage between emotion and action does not appear to be found among the positive emotions.

So by an interesting twist in our biology, negative emotions are simply easier to study in scientific laboratories. Roy Baumeister and his colleagues also postulated that negative emotions are stronger than positive emotions because the former are more likely to influence our behavior than the latter. In their words, "bad is stronger than good" (Baumeister, Bratslavsky, Finkenauer, & Vohs, 2001). Anyone who has tried to resist a strong unwanted impulse can recognize this point.

But what about positive emotions? Is their function simply to make us feel good after all of the dangers have been taken care of and the "important" negative emotions have done their job? In fact, many scientists believed this to be the only function of positive emotions. Yet, a recent theory has begun to change that assumption decisively.

The Broaden-and-Build Model

Barbara Fredrickson (1998, 2001; Cohen & Fredrickson, 2009) formulated what she called the **broaden–and–build model** of positive emotions. In her model, the purpose of positive emotions is quite different from the purpose of the negative emotions. For Fredrickson, positive emotions help preserve the organism by providing *nonspecific action tendencies* that can lead to new adaptive behavior.

Courtesy of Barbara Fredrickson

Barbara Fredrickson

How would these processes work? One of the examples she (1998) provided concerns the emotion of joy. She cited Frijda's (1986) point that joy "is in part aimless, unasked-for readiness to engage in whatever interaction presents itself and [it is also] in part readiness to engage in enjoyments" (p. 304). In children, for example, the feeling of joy is associated with urges to play, to explore, to investigate, and to create. When adults feel positive emotions they are more likely to interact with others; to seek out new experiences; to take up creative challenges; and to help others in need. In your own life, think of how much more open and curious you are about the world when you feel good.

Second, positive emotions also provide the spark for changes in cognitive activity that can lead to newer and more adaptive *thought-action tendencies*. This means that people behave in specific ways because they have learned to associate certain cognitive activities or ways of thinking with certain actions. Returning to our example of children's play, when children allow themselves to be motivated by joy and happily engage in playful activities, they are simultaneously learning about their environment and about themselves. Therefore Fredrickson's broaden-and-build model posits that positive emotions *broaden* our awareness and then *build* upon resultant learning to create future emotional and intellectual resources (Garland, Fredrickson, Kring, Johnson, Meyer et al., 2010). In Fredrickson's (1998) words:

> Not only do the positive emotions ... share the feature of broadening an individual's momentary thought-action repertoire, but they also appear to share the feature of building the individual's personal resources.... Importantly these resources

are more durable than the transient emotional states that led to their acquisition. By consequence, then, the often incidental effect of experiencing a positive emotion is an increment in durable personal resources that can be drawn on later in other contexts and in other emotional states (p. 307).

The reference to broadening thought-action responses has another meaning in addition to increasing awareness of potential options; it also changes how people process information. Fredrickson found that increased positive emotionality resulted in greater cognitive flexibility and openness to experience and helped create a sense of meaning (Fredrickson, 2008; Cohn & Fredrickson, 2009). Positive emotion can also enhance an attention bias for positive information, so it helps us notice more positive emotion in the future (Strauss & Allen, 2006). Once again, a contrast with negative emotions is helpful. One characteristic of thought-action tendencies in negative emotions is that they generally lead to a narrowing of options for thought and behavior.

For instance, when we are under immediate threat or danger it is more adaptable to make a quick decision and then act to avoid the danger. It is not very helpful to leisurely mull over your available options if you notice that your kitchen is on fire. Rather, the situation demands quick decision-making and decisive action.

With positive emotions, a narrowing of attention is not what is required. Positive emotions help us to broaden our available options so as to maximize our future resources. For instance, the emotion of love leads not just to thoughts about how to immediately express that love; it also leads to thoughts about how to express love in the future, how to share love with others, how to maximize the potential for love, and how to help other people feel love. Positive emotions such as love and joy often lead to a desire to share those feelings with others, such as to convey loving kindness. Think, for example, how many people spend considerable time sharing their positive experiences with others. So not only can positive emotions broaden our awareness and build up

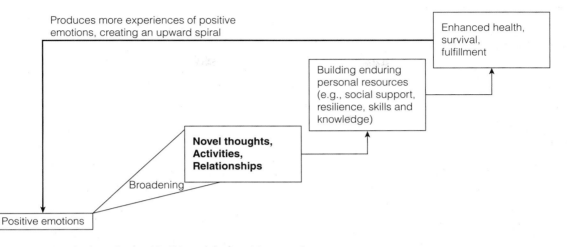

F I G U R E 2.3 The broaden-and-build model of positive emotion

SOURCE: Adapted from Cohn, M. & Fredrickson, B., "Positive Emotions," in C. Snyder & S. Lopez (Eds.). *Oxford Handbook of Positive Psychology, 2nd Edition* (page 16). Copyright © 2009 Oxford University Press.

resources, but also those resources are more enduring than the positive emotions that initiated them.

In another example, think about social support and the numerous advantages it provides for people throughout their lives. Those bonds of closeness, caring, compassion, and love are forged by allowing ourselves to act on positive emotions that compel us to interact with others. Those bonds in a reciprocal fashion increase the likelihood that we will experience more positive emotions in the form of supportive feedback from others. And that, in turn, leads to more positive interactions that, once again, foster the deepening of those relationships and other social attachments. See Figure 2.3 for a representation of the broaden–and–build model of positive emotions.

Positive Emotions as Antidotes to Stress
Another advantage of positive emotions, according to Fredrickson (1998, 2001), is that they may act as antidotes to the unfortunate effects of negative emotions. Her **undoing hypothesis** states that positive emotions help both the body and the mind regain a sense of balance, flexibility, and equilibrium after the impact of negative emotions. Several empirical studies by Fredrickson and colleagues found that positive emotions help shorten the aftereffects of stress

reactions. For example, when you are able to laugh at yourself following a particularly stressful mistake, then you relieve psychological tension and help cleanse your body of stress hormones. In Frederickson's view, the same response can help to restore flexibility and openness of thought after we experience the narrowing of attention associated with the negative emotion of panic. A variety of studies support the restore-and-cleanse functions of positive emotions (Cohn & Fredrickson, 2009; Suzuki, 2005).

A Critical Positivity Ratio In Fredrickson's later research, she examined how much positive emotion might be optimal for well-being. Since it is unreasonable to expect a person will experience only positive emotions, she speculated whether there might be an optimal balance between positive and negative emotions. In an interesting analysis based on nonlinear dynamic systems, Fredrickson and Marcial Losada (2005) found that when the mean ratio of positive to negative emotions was at or above 2.9, then people tended to flourish in life. To get a sense of what this means, imagine that you ask people to list their positive and negative emotions throughout the day. You might give people a beeper that would alert them to times they should stop and record their feelings, behavior, or situation. (This research strategy is called the *experience sampling method*.) After a few weeks you record all the emotions and review how many positive and negative emotions the person felt on average during the day. Fredrickson and Losada found that, on average, those who had high well-being and were flourishing experienced at least 2.9 times more positive emotions than negative emotions (also see Larsen, 2009).

At this juncture, one might well ask whether positive emotion is always beneficial. In fact, Fredrickson and Losada found that a positivity ratio of about 11.6 seems to be an upper limit beyond which flourishing begins to disintegrate. Although that ratio is quite high, they did find that too much positivity is not advantageous to well-being. Other studies have suggested that happiness makes novelty seem attractive (as Fredrickson suggested), but a negative mood helps the familiar feel more comfortable (de Vries, Holland, Chenier, Starr, & Winkeilman, 2010). Feeling happy may also make people feel overly secure, a situation that can result in carelessness, selfishness, and a lesser valuation of trust (Forgas, 2010; Lount, 2010). Therefore, although a positive mood seems a very powerful predictor of well-being and numerous positive outcomes in life, positivity should be used wisely. We investigate this topic in the next section.

Emotional Intelligence

At this point, it should be clear that emotions can serve a very useful function if used properly. One might even consider an ability to use emotions wisely as a type of intelligence. Indeed, some researchers believe there is such a thing as emotional intelligence. Mayer, Caruso, and Salovey (2000) defined **emotional intelligence (EI)** as follows:

> Emotional intelligence refers to an ability to recognize the meanings of emotions and their relationships, and to reason and problem-solve on the basis of them. Emotional intelligence is involved in the capacity to perceive emotions, assimilate

emotion-related feelings, understand the information of those emotions, and manage them (p. 267).

People who are high in EI have an ability to use their emotions wisely, and they appear to have a deeper understanding of their emotional lives. In addition, EI is associated with an ability to accurately read the emotions of other people, a practical knowledge of how to manage one's own feelings and impulses, as well as a deeper sensitivity to the emotional undercurrents that lie behind many social interactions. An allied notion to emotional intelligence is found in the research on *social intelligence*, which consists of an ability to handle social interactions well.

The Dimensions of Emotional Intelligence

Peter Salovey and John Mayer (1990) presented the original model for emotional intelligence. They proposed five characteristics that aptly define the idea:

1. The first is KNOWING ONE'S EMOTIONS, or the ability to recognize an emotion as it happens. People high in EI are able to accurately recognize what they are feeling when they are feeling it. This can include an ability to accurately express the emotion.

2. Second, it includes an ability to HANDLE INTERPERSONAL RELATIONSHIPS well. People high in emotional intelligence are socially competent and good at creating and maintaining effective interpersonal relationships.

3. Third, EI includes an ability to use emotions to MOTIVATE ONESELF. This means that people high in EI are able to control and marshal their emotions in order to reach goals and remain focused.

4. Fourth, EI is related to the ability to RECOGNIZE EMOTIONS IN OTHERS. This refers to the skills of reading what other people are feeling and being empathetic.

5. Fifth, EI involves an ability to MANAGE ONE'S EMOTIONS. This can include abilities to regulate one's moods, handle stress, and rebound after an emotional setback. Interestingly, high EI may be found most often with moderate ability to regulate one's own emotions rather than with high emotional control (Salovey, Meyer, & Caruso, 2002). Too little control of emotions leads to passivity; however, too much control leads to repression and an inability to use information from our emotions to learn about our world and ourselves.

Mayer, Caruso, and Salovey (2000) presented the necessary skills for the development of EI as a hierarchy of increasingly complex abilities. In someone with high EI, an (1) ability to perceive and express emotions leads to (2) skills at assimilating emotions into cognitive representations of emotion and cognitive processing of feelings, which leads to (3) deeper understanding of the complexities of emotion as they relate to the social world, which leads to (4) being able to regulate emotions more effectively.

Does having high emotional intelligence enhance well-being? The answer from research is a definite *yes*. Salovey, Mayer, Caruso, and Hee Yoo (2009) found that people higher in EI had better relationships with friends and family and more satisfying romantic relationships, as measured by lower levels of conflict, more emotional support, more intimacy, and more affection. Those higher in EI also reported higher life satisfaction and psychological well-being. People who showed higher EI at work tended to contribute to a positive workplace environment and had both higher merit pay and higher rank within the company. A recent study found that both men and women physicians who had higher empathy had more satisfied patients and even better clinical outcomes (Hojat, Lousi, Markham, Wender, Rabinowitz et al., 2011). One interesting study found a greater frequency of orgasm in women who were higher in EI (Burri, Cherkas, & Spector, 2009). Mayer, Caruso and Salovey (2000) also found that EI scores increased with age, especially when people had

more experience dealing with emotions. Their results also suggested that a large component of EI is the degree of empathy developed over the years. Therefore, women tend to score higher on this measure of EI than men.

Note that Salovey, Meyer, and Caruso defined EI in terms of various abilities or skills. However, some researchers view EI as a trait (Petrides & Furnham, 2001). A newer perspective sees EI in terms of three qualities: knowledge; abilities; and traits (Milolajczak, Petrides, Coumans, and Luminet, 2009). However, all perspectives assume that EI can be cultivated and developed. In summary, EI comprises insight into the richness of one's emotional life, a moderate degree of self-control, high empathy, and good social skills.

Other aspects of our emotional lives can help us find more meaning and fulfillment in life. For instance, current ideas about EI present it as an aid to problem-solving and social interaction. James Averill (2009) also proposed a theory of **emotional creativity**. His idea is that people can use their emotions in creative ways that foster a greater sense of meaning, vitality, and connectedness in life. That is, it may be possible to teach people how to use their emotions more wisely and more creatively. Although research in this area is fairly new, there seems little doubt that an ability to understand and use our emotions wisely and creatively is related to personal well-being.

Attempts to increase emotional intelligence began with the ancient Greeks as they pursued wisdom and virtue. Certainly one could argue that most forms of psychotherapy focus on increasing EI. Another promising area involves EI training in the workplace. Some interesting programs have found that training managers in EI is associated with higher business growth rates (see Salovey, Mayer, Caruso, & Hee Yoo, 2009). Efforts using contemporary models of EI have been implemented in many school systems. In general, these interventions teach skills such as awareness of one's feelings; accurately labeling one's emotions; enhancing communication; appropriately disclosing one's feelings; managing one's emotions and conflict; and enhancing empathy and validation of others (Salovey, Caruso, & Mayer, 2004). Unfortunately, few of these efforts at teaching EI in the schools have used traditional research designs that could measure their effectiveness.

One well-designed study found that EI could be increased with a four-week training program (Nelis, Quoidbach, Mikolajczak, & Hansenne, 2009). In the study, they taught the four-branch ability model of EI: (1) emotional perception and expression; (2) emotional facilitation of thinking; (3) understanding and analysis of emotions; and (4) reflective regulation of emotion. The program involved lectures, group discussions, practicing skills, and development of coping skills. Results indicated significant increases in emotional identification and emotional management at posttest and at the six-month follow-up.

Research on **emotional regulation** has investigated several topics relevant to EI (Gross, 2008). A study of emotional regulation by Berking, Wupperman, Reichardt, Pejic, Dippel, & Znoj (2008) taught people greater acceptance, tolerance, and active modification of negative emotions over six weeks using techniques of cognitive-behavioral therapy. These comprised education; relaxation training; emotional labeling; imagery training; and goal setting as major interventions. After six weeks, researchers found significant increases in skills at emotional regulation.

DEFINITIONS OF HAPPINESS AND WELL-BEING

As we have indicated, definitions of what should constitute happiness, well-being, and the good life are quite numerous and focus on an amazing variety of emotional outcomes. In an attempt to bring some order to this variety, researchers have created models of the ways in which people define and pursue well-being. These models help determine how well-being is studied, measured, and ultimately pursued. Since there is an enormous variety of behavior that people engage in to enhance their well-being, usual practice is to distill this into the smallest manageable dimension necessary to adequately capture the nature of well-being. Therefore, we begin with perspectives that distill the variety into a single fundamental idea.

One-Dimensional Theories

Hedonic Perspectives One of the oldest approaches to the good life is hedonism. The perspective of **hedonism** focuses on pleasure as the basic component of the good life. Hedonism in its most basic form is the belief that the pursuit of well-being is fundamentally a pursuit of individual sensual pleasures. Although a single-minded pursuit of pleasure is one of the oldest ideas of the good life, this form of hedonism has been seen as self-defeating and unworkable by most societies throughout history. Nearly everyone realizes that sensual pleasures are short-lived, that they require a constant struggle to sustain them, and that when focused on exclusively produce no lasting changes in personality and no personal growth (see Ricard, 2010). The hedonic approach, however, does not have to mean simple self-indulgence or a "me first" attitude toward life.

A socially responsible form of hedonism, although considering pleasure as the basic motivating force behind most human behavior, yet affirms that certain pleasures require positive social relationships with those close to us and with society at large. For instance, some variations of a hedonic approach view family life or civic involvement as ways to maximize pleasure and contentment for all persons involved. According to this more socially responsible hedonic approach to the good life, the goal is to create a high level of happiness for oneself and others. This form of hedonism has been a basic assumption behind many conceptualizations of the good life throughout history and is very much alive today (see Kahneman, Diener, & Schwartz, 1999). Given this caveat, the main goal of a hedonic perspective is to increase happiness in a variety of ways. The good life is defined in terms of positive emotions such as happiness, contentment, satisfaction, and joy. The focus of this approach is on fostering positive emotionality (see chapter 3).

Eudaimonic Perspectives A eudaimonic approach to well-being generally focuses on fulfilling one's potential or developing to the fullest extent one's skills, talents, or personality. It is also associated with fulfilling one's "true nature" and finding one's "true self" (Ryan & Deci, 2001; Schlegel, Hicks, Arndt, & King, 2009; Waterman, 1998). In this latter case, well-being may or may not be associated with a maximization of positive emotions at all times. For the ancient Greeks and Aristotle in particular, **eudaimonia** (also spelled *eudaemonia*) was associated with living one's life in accord with those values and virtues that are most desirable and most indicative of the *highest good*. Richard Ryan, Veronica Huta, and Edward Deci (2008) viewed eudaimonia as involving those processes that result in a person "living well." They defined *living well* as actively pursuing virtues and strengths, using both reflection and reason, and voluntarily pursuing goals that enhance our real self. Outcomes of living well include a sense of inner peace; a deep appreciation of life; a sense of connection to both other people and a greater perspective; and a sense that life "feels right." In contrast, these psychologists viewed the outcome of hedonic approaches as a life that "feels good."

Since the time of the ancient Greeks, hedonic and eudaimonic approaches to well-being have exerted a major impact on how people think about the nature of the good life. In addition, empirical research supports these two conceptualizations as important to how psychology thinks about and measures well-being today (Compton, Smith, Cornish, & Qualls, 1996; McGregor & Little, 1998; Ryan & Deci, 2001).

There are physiological correlates of eudaimonic and hedonic approaches. A study that compared hedonic and eudaimonic measures of well-being found that both were associated with left prefrontal activity and positive emotionality. Further, eudaimonic well-being was also associated with a unique pattern of brain activation not found with hedonic well-being (Urry, Nitschke, Dolski et al., 2004).

Conclusions drawn from research are also impacted by these differences. For instance, most studies on genetics and well-being use hedonic measures, but the impact of hedonic activity fades with time. Eudaimonic activity, which is associated with greater meaningfulness and personal expressiveness, though not often measured in genetic studies may lead to a more stable type of well-being (Huta, 2007).

One of the difficulties with the *eudaimonic perspective* is that it encompasses a fairly broad collection of approaches to well-being. For the ancient Greeks it referred to *wisdom;* for twentieth century existentialists to *authenticity;* for humanistic psychologists it tends to mean *self-actualization;* and for many positive psychologists, it connotes *flourishing.* Although all these approaches share some qualities, they are certainly not identical conceptualizations of well-being. In addition, hedonic and eudaimonic motivations are often closely linked so that clear distinctions between them may be tricky to make in real life (Tamir & Gross, 2011). Nevertheless, eudaimonia has been a very useful perspective in positive psychology.

Engagement Perspectives A third unidimensional perspective on well-being and happiness tends to focus less on emotion and more on how we use our attention and our level of involvement in activities. Engagement theory views well-being as a function of how absorbed we are in the activities of life. Because of its emphasis on activities, this perspective has occasionally been referred to as *activity theory*. From its vantage point, a sense of happiness comes from being captivated by, wrapped up in, or absorbed in what we are doing in the moment.

Nancy Cantor and Catherine Sanderson (1999) associated well-being with goal pursuit insofar as this latter implies an *active participation in life*. The pursuit of goals is simply an indication that people are taking part in life; they are involved, interested, and active participants in living a full life. Cantor and Sanderson contended that greater well-being is found through participation in activities that are intrinsically motivating, freely chosen and desired, and that involve realistic, feasible goals. Of course, the type of activities people choose to be involved with certainly changes over their lifespans. Therefore, it is not necessarily *which* activities people choose; it is the *process* of being fully involved in an active life that really matters.

Multidimensional Theories

As you read about the hedonic, eudaimonic, and engagement perspectives on well-being, it has perhaps occurred to you that a more complete perspective might include all three, and possibly others as well. Indeed, several researchers have suggested that a thorough understanding of well-being requires more than one dimension. Often the differences among such multidimensional perspectives revolve around how many dimensions are necessary to capture the complexity of well-being without becoming overly complicated and unwieldy.

Self-Determination Theory Deci and Ryan (1985) analyzed research on intrinsic and extrinsic motivation and thereby developed **self-determination theory**. It postulates that certain inherent tendencies toward psychological growth, along with a core group of innate emotional needs, are the basis for self-motivation and personality integration. In self-determination theory the three basic needs are: (1) COMPETENCE: the need for mastery of experiences that allows a person to deal effectively with her or his environment; (2) RELATEDNESS: the need for mutually supportive interpersonal relationships; and (3) AUTONOMY: the need to make independent decisions about areas in life important to the person. Ryan and Deci (2000) observed that these three needs "appear to be essential for facilitating optimal functioning of the natural propensities for growth and integration, as well as for constructive social development and personal well-being" (p. 68).

That is, if these three needs are met, then people show better adaptive functioning and higher well-being. As mentioned earlier in this chapter, these researchers tended to speak less about intrinsic

motivation, preferring to see motivation as either *controlled* or *autonomous*. Studies have found that a combination of high autonomy and a perception of a low level of coercive control by others is associated with better ego development; higher self-esteem; higher self-actualization scores; greater consistency of self; more persistence in working toward goals; more satisfaction at work; and fewer experiences of boredom (Deci & Ryan, 2008; Knee & Zuckerman, 1998).

One recent study looked at autonomy, relatedness, and competence as predictors of well-being both in the moment and on a daily basis (Howel, Chenot, Hill, & Howell, 2009). Feeling autonomous and connected were both associated with well-being at all times, but the findings for competence were slightly more complicated. That is, efforts to increase competence by learning a new skill were not enjoyable in the moment, but well-being increased later on a daily basis. In other words, initial difficulties of learning translated into more happiness and life satisfaction—later on. Therefore, if positive psychology is partially defined as the investigation of factors that support human flourishing, then one way to measure the success of these factors is to examine the extent to which they foster a sense of competence, contribute toward the development of positive relationships, and enhance a sense of healthy autonomy.

Deci and Ryan (1985) presented cognitive evaluation theory as a subset within self-determination theory in order to better explain social and environmental factors that lead to greater autonomous motivation. Conditions or activities that help to meet needs for autonomy, relatedness, and competence involve: personal challenge as well as positive supportive feedback; freedom from demeaning and belittling evaluation; and novelty or a sense of aesthetic value. Also necessary are situations that foster an internal locus of control by giving a person choices and opportunities for self-direction and that acknowledge feelings. Further, social contexts in which a person feels somewhat secure and knows that social support is available are conducive to meeting these three needs.

Authentic Happiness and Well-Being Theory
The next two perspectives on well-being both come from Martin Seligman, whose initial ideas led to the founding of positive psychology. We begin with his early theory and continue by discussing his latest approach to well-being. Seligman's original ideas focused on *authentic happiness*, which involves the cultivation of three broad life domains: *the pleasant life*; *the good life of engagement*; and *the meaningful life* (Seligman, 2002). The pleasant life is focused on POSITIVE EMOTIONS. These can be physical pleasures such as having a good meal or more sophisticated pleasures such as enjoying a complex work of art. The latter are *higher pleasures,* which are complex combinations of emotions that produce feelings such as joy or rapture.

The good life is found primarily through ENGAGEMENT in activities that are absorbing and promote full participation in life. Consistent with the earlier discussion of strengths and virtues, Seligman has focused his description of the good life and the meaningful life on *signature strengths*. These are positive personality characteristics that are representative of each person's identity and that add to his or her uniqueness. When people exercise their signature strengths, they tend to feel invigorated and enthusiastic as well as have a sense that their "real me" is being expressed. For Seligman (2002), authentic happiness is "identifying and cultivating your most fundamental strengths and using them every day in work, love, play, and parenting" (p. xiii). Taking the notion of signature strengths further, Seligman defined "gratification" as our emotional response to activities that allow us to enact our signature strengths and virtues. Therefore, the search for authentic happiness means "using your signature strengths every day to produce authentic happiness and abundant gratifications" (p. 13).

Lastly, the MEANINGFUL LIFE uses signature strengths in the service of something larger and more significant than one's individual self. It involves going beyond individual concerns to take a wider perspective on life. People want to understand their world and have life make some type of sense. In particular, people seem to live with a sense of fulfillment when they believe they matter as individuals and that their lives have some significance.

When developing his ideas for *Authentic Happiness*, Seligman believed that authentic happiness theory was based on positive mood. Therefore, the primary goal of positive psychology should be to cultivate positive mood as measured by life satisfaction. Recently, Seligman (2011) argued that his original theory left out too many elements important to well-being and was disproportionately tied to mood. He now advocates what he calls **well-being theory**, writing: "I now think that the topic of positive psychology is well-being, that the gold standard for measuring well-being is flourishing, and that the goal of positive psychology is to increase flourishing" (Seligman, 2011, p. 13). Well-being theory argues that positive emotion, engagement, and meaning are not sufficient to cover the dimensions of a life well-lived. Seligman has added two more dimensions: positive relationships; and positive accomplishments. The acronym for the elements of well-being theory is PERMA (that is, Positive emotion; Engagement; Relationships; Meaning; Accomplishment).

In terms of POSITIVE RELATIONSHIPS, Seligman observes that wherever people are located around the world and in whatever period of history they live, fundamental is a need for positive, supportive relationships with others. He has added POSITIVE ACCOMPLISHMENTS because people also seem to need goals in life and challenges for which they can strive; they also want to feel a sense of competence and mastery both of themselves and their environment.

One of the advantages that Seligman sees in well-being theory is that no single measure can be used to define well-being. Of course, the five elements comprise the core features of well-being and flourishing that can be measured. However, none of the five by themselves can serve as an adequate measure of well-being. Therefore, well-being is a multifaceted construct that cannot be reduced to overly simplistic ideas, such as those found in "happiology." Note that Seligman's theory tends to combine both the hedonic and the eudaimonic perspectives on well-being.

Psychological Well-Being   Carol Ryff has summarized many years of research on positive mental health and created a six-dimensional structure to measure well-being. She (1985, 1995) reviewed classical theories of positive mental health and added more recent research from developmental, clinical, and personality psychology. In this way, she developed six major criteria, along with associated subcategories, for what she called *the Psychological Well-Being Scale* (1989a, 1989b, 1995). Ryff's six-dimensional model of psychological well-being consists of the following factors:

1. SELF-ACCEPTANCE: (a) positive self-evaluation; (b) an ability to acknowledge multiple aspects of self; and (c) an ability to accept both positive and negative qualities in a balanced picture of one's abilities.

2. PERSONAL GROWTH: (a) a capacity to grow and to develop potentials; (b) growing self-knowledge and effectiveness in personal changes over time; and (c) openness to new experiences.

3. POSITIVE RELATIONS WITH OTHER PEOPLE: (a) close, warm, and intimate relationships with others; (b) a concern for the welfare of others; and (c) empathy and affection for other people.

4. AUTONOMY: (a) independence and self-determination; (b) an ability to resist social pressures; and (c) an ability to regulate behavior from within.

5. PURPOSE IN LIFE: (a) a sense of purpose and meaning to life; and (b) a sense of direction and goals in life.

6. ENVIRONMENTAL MASTERY: (a) a sense of mastery and competence; and (b) an ability to choose situations and environments conducive to meeting goals.

Ryff's Psychological Well-Being Scale has often been used as a measure of eudaimonic well-being. Research with this scale has supported the six psychological dimensions as a valid measure of well-being in a variety of samples over the course of the lifespan (Ryff, 1995; Ryff & Keyes, 1995).

The Modes of Fulfillment   Another way to think about well-being is to consider how people choose to cultivate happiness by focusing on a particular emotion or specific goal. Richard Coan's research on well-being uncovered what Coan called the five basic **modes of fulfillment** (Coan, 1974, 1977), derived from an analysis of a six-hour battery of psychological tests (Coan, 1974). These modes

T A B L E 2.2   Comparing Dimensional Theories of Well-Being

Ryff	Seligman	Deci & Ryan	Coan[a]
Positive relationships	Positive relationships	Relatedness	Relatedness
Environmental mastery	Accomplishment	Competence	Efficiency
Purpose in life	Meaning		Self-transcendence
Autonomy		Autonomy	
Personal growth			Inner harmony
Self-acceptance			
	Positive emotion		
	Engagement		
			Creativity

[a]Note: Coan's theory is not additive. Not all dimensions are necessary for high well-being.

comprise a person's core focus in his or her search for well-being. These consist of goals sometimes passionately pursued, but often never fully achieved, in a search for fulfillment.

In contrast to many theories of psychological well-being reviewed so far, Coan's is not necessarily an additive model that assumes a rewarding sense of well-being must be built by adding or combining fulfillment through several life domains. That is, it does not assume that the more fulfillment in each area of life, the greater overall one's sense of well-being (Coan, 1991). In contrast to additive theories, Coan's perspective allows for a passionate pursuit of a single emotional goal, sometimes to the neglect of others (see also Vallerand, 2008). Interestingly, unlike most other perspectives on well-being, Coan included literature from Eastern psychology (that is, Hinduism; Buddhism; Taoism) in his literature review and his conceptual model.

Coan's five basic modes of fulfillment are:

1. EFFICIENCY. This refers to a focus on an exceptional use of one's talents or skills. People who pursue excellence in specific endeavors, such as sports or a profession, are focused on this mode of fulfillment (see chapter 7).

2. CREATIVITY. This mode is the one chosen by artists or people who have an artistic temperament (see chapter 7).

3. INNER HARMONY. As might be guessed, this mode refers to a focus on psychological criteria such as personality integration and the search for one's true self. Most theories of optimal personality development focus on this mode (see chapter 9).

4. RELATEDNESS. This mode has as its focus the development of interpersonal relationships and the presence of love. Anyone whose search for happiness revolves around love, family, or emotional intimacy is committed to this mode (see chapter 5).

5. SELF-TRANSCENDENCE. This mode takes as its focus a person's relationship to God, spirit, or the ultimate ground of being, however conceptualized. Note, however, that this mode is associated not only with organized religion but also with contemplative spirituality, self-transcendence, and mysticism (see chapter 10).

Coan asserted that fulfillment can be found through any of these modes. He implied that if we are diligent, committed, persistent, and passionate in pursuit of our chosen goal, then we can find personal fulfillment in life. Coan's model has attracted much less research attention than other models. However, we offer it as an interesting alternative that addresses issues that other models overlook.

Quality of Life Michael Frisch (2006) has created another multidimensional approach to well-being that he called **quality of life therapy** (QOLT). Built on ideas from cognitive-behavioral therapy, Frisch's theory asks people to rate their satisfaction with 16 areas of everyday life. These include such life domains as health; self-esteem; work; learning; love; friendship; home; and community. Because people can be satisfied with different life domains while feeling various levels of positive emotion, they are asked to rate their satisfaction with these 16 life areas rather than how they feel about them. Frisch's model is also not an additive one. That is, QOLT does not assume that optimal well-being necessarily requires full satisfaction in all sixteen life areas. In fact, it is easy to see that full satisfaction in all sixteen areas is a rather Herculean task that few persons could possibly accomplish.

QOLT is built upon what Frisch called the CASIO model of assessment. In this model, when we attempt to increase our sense of well-being we can evaluate and change: our objective life circumstances (C); our attitude or interpretation of life domains (A); our standards of fulfillment or goals (S); how important we believe an area is to our life (I); or we can focus attention on other areas that already give us a sense of satisfaction (O). QOLT uses the results of CASIO assessment to create interventions that can be used to increase life satisfaction. Indeed, studies of QOLT have found that it can be a very useful strategy for fostering greater well-being (Frisch, Clark, Rouse, Rudd, Paweleck et al., 2005).

SUMMARY

This chapter has reviewed topics that are relevant to positive psychology. Quite appropriately, the first examined has been positive emotionality. Current psychological perspectives on emotion see positive emotional experience as multidimensionally determined by biology; cognition; behavior; our current social situation; and by the society and culture in which we live. The uniqueness of positive emotions has been explored through broaden-and-build theory. That is, positive emotions can help us adapt by broadening our response options and building psychological and social resources for the future. Newer theories of motivation view people as actively involved in seeking intrinsically satisfying experiences and engaged in a process of continuous development centering on needs for competence, relatedness, autonomy, and hopeful expectations for the future. Finally, theories of well-being have been discussed that provide the foundation for ideas and research in positive psychology.

LEARNING TOOLS

Key Terms and Ideas

neuroplasticity

happiness set point

signature
   strengths

broaden-and-build
   model

self-determination
   theory

strivings

affective forecasting

emotional
   intelligence

well-being theory

Psychological well-
   being theory

Books

Clifton, D., & Anderson, E. (2002). *StrengthsQuest: Discover and develop your strengths in academics, career, and beyond.* Washington, D.C.: Gallup Press.

Fredrickson, B. (2009). *Positivity: Groundbreaking research reveals how to embrace the hidden strength of positive emotions, overcome negativity, and thrive.* N.Y.: Crown Archetype.

Gilbert, D. (2007). *Stumbling on happiness.* N.Y.: Vintage.

Linley, A., Willars, J., & Biswas-Diener, R. (2010). *The strengths book: Be confident, be successful, and enjoy better relationships by realising the best of you.* N.Y.: CAPP Press.

Seligman, M. E. P. (2011). *Flourishing: A visionary new understanding of happiness and well-being.* N.Y.: Free Press.

On the Web

http://www.posneuroscience.org   Positive neuroscience.

http://www.strengthsquest.com/home.aspx   Home page for StrengthsQuest.

http://www.viacharacter.org   Web site for the VIA Institute on Character.

http://www.unh.edu/emotional_intelligence/index.html   Devoted to research and measurement of emotional intelligence.

Personal Explorations

1. Psychologists have found that we each have a happiness "set point" that seems relatively resistant to major change. Yet our moods certainly change from day-to-day and sometimes fluctuate within the same day, too. Over the next week, record your mood on a 10-point-scale (1 = extremely unhappy to 10 = extremely happy) each day at these eight times:

   a. when you wake up in the morning;
   b. when you are leaving your home in the morning for school or work;
   c. when you are having lunch;
   d. when you are talking to a family member;
   e. when you visiting the Internet, such as a social networking Web site;
   f. when you are having dinner;
   g. when you are watching television or listening to music in the evening;
   h. when you are getting ready for sleep.

   After one week, you will have recorded a total of 56 entries. (a) What was your average number in total? Does it surprise you? Why or why not? (b) What was your average number for each of these eight activities? Do any of these numbers surprise you? Why or why not? (c) What was the range of your numbers, from lowest to highest? (d) From this activity, what insights have you gained about your moods and their relative stability or changeability in terms of the various times and activities of your day?

2. What things intrinsically interest you? What would you do even if you were not paid for it? Are you studying that interest area now in school? If not, why not? Remember, there are no "right" answers to this question. That is, some people work at jobs that truly interest them, while others explore their interests in their time outside of work.

   List the things that have intrinsic interest for you—things you just love to do. Next, list how frequently you have done these things in the past month. For the exercise, double the frequency of two or three of these activities for the next two weeks. Record how you feel after the two weeks.

3. Use your signature strengths (see Seligman, 2011). Begin by taking the VIA Survey of Character (www.viacharacter.org). Take a look at your top five strengths and ask whether they are your signature strengths. If yes, then make time during the next week to use your signature strengths in new and different ways. It helps to create a clearly defined opportunity in your schedule to do this. It is also important that you use them in new and different (and positive) ways.

Chapter 3

Subjective Well-Being

Happy individuals are more likely than their less happy peers to have fulfilling
marriages and relationships, high incomes, superior work performance,
community involvement, robust health, and a long life.
LYUBOMIRSKY, KING, & DIENER (2005)

What does it mean to be happy? Is it possible to increase one's level of happiness? Is it even important to be happy? These are questions taken up by researchers, in the area of subjective well-being, who have tended to link subjective well-being with scores on three variables: happiness; satisfaction with life; and neuroticism. When researchers ask people about their **happiness**, the focus is on their *emotional* state: how they *feel* about their world and themselves. Questions about persons' **satisfaction with life** address a more global *judgment* about the "rightness" of their lives; they need to weigh their outcome in life against alternatives and assess whether they're satisfied with the result. A third factor—low **neuroticism**—completes the basic triad of measures of subjective well-being.[1] Although a sharp distinction between emotional and cognitive measures has been called into question (Crooker & Near, 1998), most studies nevertheless have shown that these three areas should be considered as separate facets of subjective well-being and must be measured as such (Diener & Lucas, 1999). Therefore, high subjective well-being is found when people report they are feeling very happy; are very satisfied with life; and are experiencing a low level of neuroticism. Research on subjective well-being became the first systematic study of happiness to focus on large groups of people and to utilize the statistical procedures and methodology of contemporary science.

THE MEASUREMENT OF SUBJECTIVE WELL-BEING

Among the main obstacles that held back research on happiness was how to measure it. The solution in subjective well-being research was to use a straightforward approach, with investigators allowing participants themselves to define terms of happiness. In this way, the true judge of how happy someone was would be "whoever lives inside a person's skin" (Myers & Diener, 1995, p. 11).

Therefore, researchers would simply ask participants "Are you happy?" or "How happy are you?" Investigators reasoned that insofar as evaluations of happiness are subjective phenomena, they should be measured with subjective reports. Somewhat unexpectedly, this solution seemed to work quite well (Diener, 1994; Diener, Oishi, & Lucas, 2009). That is, early investigations of subjective well-being found that people who reported higher levels of happiness and life satisfaction also tended to behave as if they were indeed happier and more satisfied; in addition, others perceived these people as being happier and more satisfied. Therefore, researchers found it empirically acceptable simply to ask people about their perceived happiness and life satisfaction.

Self-Report Measures of Subjective Well-Being

Several different measurement instruments were devised for this research endeavor. The actual measurement scale might assess self-perceptions of happiness (for example, Fordyce, 1988): It might

ask people to compare themselves with others (Lyubomirsky & Lepper, 1999), respond to a question such as, "In most ways my life is ideal" (Diener, Emmons, Larsen, & Griffin, 1985), or provide a series of cartoon faces that varied from big smiles to deep frowns and ask people to choose which one fit how they feel (Andrews & Withey, 1976). Figure 3.1 gives examples of these measurement strategies.

Although the specific questions posed varied slightly, they were all based on two assumptions. First, all assumed that the amount of happiness or satisfaction a person experienced could be meaningfully translated into a numerical scale. In this way, if one scored a "6" on a test of happiness before getting married and an "8" on the same test subsequent to getting married, then it was scientifically justifiable to say that his or her happiness had increased after marriage. The second assumption was that if two people both scored an "8" on the same test, then they both had approximately the same level of happiness. For example, if one person was super rich and lived on the French Riviera and

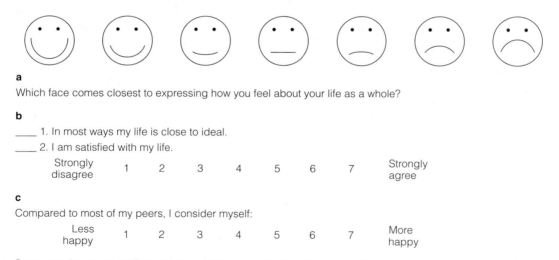

a

Which face comes closest to expressing how you feel about your life as a whole?

b

____ 1. In most ways my life is close to ideal.

____ 2. I am satisfied with my life.

| Strongly disagree | 1 | 2 | 3 | 4 | 5 | 6 | 7 | Strongly agree |

c

Compared to most of my peers, I consider myself:

| Less happy | 1 | 2 | 3 | 4 | 5 | 6 | 7 | More happy |

Some people are generally very happy. They enjoy life regardless of what is going on, getting the most out of everything. To what extent does this characterization describe you?

F I G U R E   3.1   Measurement Scales: (a) Subjective well-being faces; (b) Satisfaction with life scale (partial); (c) Subjective happiness scale (partial)

SOURCE: (a) Andrews & Withey (1976); (b) Diener, Emmons. Larsen, & Griffin (1985); (c) Lyubormnsky & Lepper (1999).

the other was a New York taxi driver—but both scored an "8" on the same test of happiness—then they were about equally happy. Surprisingly to some investigators, empirical results tended to affirm the validity of these two assumptions (Diener, 1984).

The Stability of Subjective Well-Being

The other question was whether scores on measures of subjective well-being represented stable aspects or were temporary reactions to ongoing events—that is, were mere fluctuations in mood. Fortunately for researchers, the scientific evidence has supported the notion that one's average level of happiness and life satisfaction are both relatively stable (Costa, McCrae, 1984, 1986, 1988; Diener, 1994; McCrae, 2011). Indeed, studies have found that self-ratings of subjective well-being are relatively stable over many years (Diener & Lucas, 1999). Positive personality traits have been found to be stable for up to 30 years (Costa, McCrea & Zonderman, 1987). In a clever study related to the stability of happiness, Harker and Keltner (2001) found that positive emotion in high school was significantly related to well-being 30 years later. That is, investigators asked women to bring in their high-school yearbooks in order to measure the intensity of their smiles in the yearbook photos. A genuinely felt smile, called a "Duchenne" smile, involves one's entire face including the muscles around the eyes. Harker and Keltner found that the intensity of women's smiles in high-school yearbook photos was significantly related to well-being and quality of marital relationships 30 years later.

Although self-reports of subjective well-being appear quite stable over time, it is nevertheless possible that this finding exists only because the social environments were stable—that nothing traumatic or intensely stressful happened to the "happy" people. Yet this hypothesis does not seem to be accurate. Why? Because most people are relatively consistent in reporting their subjective well-being despite highly negative events that may have occurred in their lives (Diener & Larsen, 1984; Lucas, 2008).

Ed Diener

These measurement strategies did not completely solve all the issues. Self-reports of happiness do not show a perfect match with other indicators of well-being. Life events, moods, and other daily fluctuations do impact how people evaluate their subjective well-being on a daily basis (Diener, Oishi, & Lucas, 2009). Ed Diener (2008), a leading researcher in this field, proposed that studies of well-being should include multiple indicators in order to help solve some of these problems. Nevertheless, self-report measures of well-being are still the most widely used assessment tool in most studies of happiness and life satisfaction.

Why Is Happiness Important?

When researchers began measuring subjective well-being, what did they find? A quick glance at various social indices might lead one to conclude that happiness is a rare commodity. After all, the mass media depict a society with high rates of divorce and drug problems, and sales of pop psychology books designed to fix a plethora of human miseries are on the rise. However, instead of affirming this apparently bleak situation, studies in many Western industrialized nations found that most people reported "above average" levels of happiness and satisfaction with their lives.

David Myers (2000) reported on surveys done by the National Opinion Research Center, which found about 60% of Americans described themselves as "pretty happy" and 30% said they were "very happy." The Gallup Organization reported that in 2010, 48.4% of Americans said they felt "a lot of happiness [and] enjoyment without a lot of stress [and] worry" (Witters, 2011). The Gallup Healthways Daily Index of Well-Being tracks daily reports of subjective well-being. As of June 2011, the well-being index in the U.S. is 66.5 out of a possible 100. This is slightly up from the 66.2 rating of one month earlier. Diener analyzed subjective well-being reports from over one million people in 45 nations and found that the average global self-report of subjective well-being was 6.75 on a 10-point scale, or 67.5 on a 100-point scale (see Myers & Diener, 1995). Therefore, when studying the causes and correlates of happiness, it does not seem necessary to laboriously discover individuals who actually feel happy. In some countries at least, they seem to be everywhere! Or at least that's what they tell researchers.

Though there seem to be many people who feel fairly happy, almost all investigators believe there is room for improvement. Indeed, research has supported the notion that a little more happiness might be a good thing in most people's lives. In an impressive review of over 225 research papers on subjective well-being, Sonja Lyubomirsky, Laura King, and Ed Diener (2005) found that people who reported feeling happier and more satisfied with life tended to be successful in a wide range of life domains. Compared to people who said they were only moderately happy or not so happy, people who said they were happy and experienced more positive emotions had better marriages, more fulfilling friendships and social relationships, were healthier, were more involved in their communities, had better coping skills, were more satisfied with their jobs, and tended to have higher incomes. In addition, feeling positive emotion may help students learn better (Parish & Parish, 2005); may reduce racial bias (Johnson & Fredrickson, 2005); and may help people process visual information more accurately (Anderson, 2009).

In other words, higher subjective well-being is related to a large array of elements that most people associate with having a better life. Of course, the issue of causality is important: are people's lives functioning well because they're happy or are they happy because their lives are functioning well? Lyubomirsky, King, and Diener found interesting evidence that suggested *being happier* came first and was partially responsible for other positive outcomes in life.

The scientific consensus seems to be that being happier can help people lead more satisfying lives

for themselves, the people around them, and their communities. The next question might be: Is it possible to be too happy? Apparently, the answer is yes. Diener and Seligman (2002) studied "very happy" undergraduates—those measuring in the upper 10% of happiness scores. These students did seem to be functioning very well in many social areas. Although experiencing many positive emotions, they did not report many ecstatic emotions, and they said they felt negative emotions as well. In other words, they were happy but not deliriously so, and they were not happy all the time. Later, Ed Diener and colleagues reported that people who scored a "10" on a 10-point scale of happiness were actually worse off than those who scored an "8" or "9" (Oishi, Dienr, & Lucas, 2007). Those who scored less than "10" were more successful than the super happy in several areas, including income, educational achievement, and political participation. The researchers concluded that if someone scores a "7" or "8" on happiness, that may be enough for daily well-being, and therefore the pursuit of total happiness may be counterproductive (University of Illinois at Urbana-Champaign, 2008). You will recall that Barbara Fredrickson found that a positivity ratio above 11.6 was detrimental to well-being (chapter 2).

Top-Down and Bottom-Up Theories

In general there are two ways to approach the question of how to calculate our well-being. The first approach advocates that we create an overall assessment of our current well-being by examining how satisfied we are with domains of life and then combine the various satisfactions into a totality of current well-being. That is, we might assess the quality of our marriage or friendships, how satisfying our job is, our yearly income as well as several other areas of life, and thereby create a summary statement of our overall "satisfaction." This perspective is known as the **bottom-up theory** (see Michalos, 1985; Schimmack, 2008).

According to the other approach, subjective well-being evaluations reflect how we evaluate and interpret our experiences. From this perspective, we bring our tendencies toward positive interpretations to situations we encounter in life. This approach is known as the **top-down theory**. Often this approach has been measured by looking at personality traits, attitudes, and cognitions—that is, what goes on "inside" a person.

Note that if a bottom-up perspective is correct, interventions should focus on changing the environment and situations that one experiences—such as obtaining a better job, safer neighborhood, and higher after-tax income, to enumerate a few options. But if a top-down model is correct, then interventions to increase happiness should focus on changing people's attitudes; beliefs; perceptions; or personality traits.

In support of the bottom-up theory, research shows that poverty is associated with lower levels of subjective well-being and that certain negative life events can have a lasting impact on happiness (Diener, Oishi, & Lucas, 2009). That is, external circumstances *do* matter. The top-down theory is supported by studies that find certain attitudes, self-perceptions, and personality traits, are highly correlated with subjective well-being (Diener & Lucas, 1999).

At this point, you may be wondering which approach do investigators actually use to calculate subjective well-being. Earlier studies favored the top-down approach by a wide margin; some researchers estimated that 52% of well-being was due to top-down processes and only 23% was due to bottom-up factors (Diener & Larson, 1984). More recently, investigators have tended to argue that that bottom-up predictors may be more important (for example, Lucas, 2008). Schimmack (2008) presented evidence that both top-down and bottom-up evaluations are important, but utilized in different situations and times in life.

We next turn to the important predictors of subjective well-being. We classify these as top-down and bottom-up as a way to organize the discussion. However, note that the division between these two types of predictors is fluid at times and often depends on how constructs are defined and/ or measured.

TOP-DOWN PREDICTORS OF SUBJECTIVE WELL-BEING

Investigations have found several variables that are reliably associated with happiness and satisfaction with life. Chapter 2 provided an introduction to the research on genetic contributions, basic needs, and the pursuit of goals. In this section, we turn to research on personality traits that predict who is happier or more satisfied with life (see Diener et al., 1999; Diener, Oishi, & Lucas, 2009; Myers, 1992).

Cognition: Is the Glass Half Full or Half Empty?

Cognitive theories of subjective well-being argue that the causes of high subjective well-being are not necessarily due to external events in our lives but rather to how we *interpret* those events. This notion is actually an old one that has been given new life in contemporary psychology. For example, Shakespeare's Hamlet alluded to it when he declared, "There is nothing either good or bad, but thinking makes it so."

Theorists who support the cognitive model would also contend that people who are happier and more satisfied with life choose to view the world and their own future in positive ways. That is, happiness is a belief system founded upon assumptions, expectations, or interpretations of reality (Robinson & Kirkeby, 2005). One's freely chosen interpretations of reality are termed *construals* (Funder, 1997). Consistent patterns of positive interpretation create relatively stable ways of relating to the world. These, in turn, create personality descriptions such as "cheerful" or "optimistic." Years of research support the conception that how we *feel* is often determined by how we *think* about and interpret the events of our lives., In support of this idea, research indicates that happier people initially encode events in more positive ways (Seidlitz & Diener, 1993). That is, having a positive mood seems to lead us to interpret events in positive ways, which then become encoded as positive memories. Thus, when asked to recall various events, happier people recount positive memories. In this regard, many people's recollections appear to be positively biased, a situation that, in part, produces an "above average" score on happiness (Walker, Skowronski, & Thompson, 2003).

Sonja Lyubomirsky (2001) proposed a "Construal Theory of Happiness" that regards happiness as a function of how people construe and interpret their experiences of the world. Similarly, Diener and Lucas (2000) formulated what they called "Evaluation Theory," positing that well-being is determined by how we evaluate the constant flow of incoming information. How we do so, depends on our mood and temperament; the comparison standard we use to measure progress; our life situation; and our culture. Central to the process is an assessment of how well our major goals are fulfilled and how likely they are to be met in the future. Those who are good constructive thinkers, or who are more flexible in their thinking, report higher well-being and less neuroticism (Harris & Lightsey, 2005). In addition, being in a positive mood can prompt biases in attention and information processing such that we favor positive information, and therefore we "see" positive events all around us (Robinson & Compton, 2008). In contrast, unhappy people focus on the negativities they perceive.

Sonja Lyubomirsky

Dana Patrick/Courtesy of Sonja Lyubomirsky

For example, think of a crowded airport waiting area. According to the view just presented, happier people will pleasantly see smiling couples and doting parents, whereas unhappy people will observe mainly the tense and impatient. Concerning the issue of information processing, a recent study found that people were less happy when their minds were wandering and they were thinking randomly about matters unrelated to what they were doing (Killingsworth & Gilbert, 2010).

Self-esteem   As might be expected, the first trait identified as important for both happiness and life satisfaction is positive self-esteem. Campbell (1981) found that self-esteem was the most important predictor of subjective well-being. A more recent review affirmed that high self-esteem does lead to increased happiness (Baumeister et al., 2003). Indeed, it is difficult to imagine anyone with chronically low self-esteem who feels happy or satisfied with life. High self-esteem is composed of at least four components: (1) feeling that one is accepted by others; (2) being the recipient of positive evaluations from others; (3) believing that one compares favorably to other people or to one's ideal self; and (4) believing that one can initiate effective action in the world (Hewitt, 2009). In addition, happier people might construct their self-concepts in more abstract terms (for example, "I am a cheerful person") rather than use concrete terms that define the self by specific behaviors , such as "I feel happy when I watch my favorite TV show." (Updegraff & Suh, 2007).

Although happiness and positive self-esteem are highly correlated, self-esteem is a rather tricky predictor of well-being. That is, self-esteem is related more to optimism and achievement while happiness appears related more to positive social relationships and extraversion (Furr, 2005; Lyubomirsky, Tkach, & DiMatteo, 2006). Also, positive self-esteem may be more useful for defending against negative emotions than for promoting happiness (Robinson & Compton, 2008). Finally, it is important to note that emphasis on self-esteem is strongly related to cultural context. That is, high self-esteem is valued far more in the United States than in many other countries around the world (Hewitt, 2009). In collectivist nations such as China, where autonomy and self-assertion are secondary to family unity and social cohesion, self-esteem is a less important predictor of well-being (Diener & Suh, 2000). The precise relationship between cultural conceptualizations of the self and subjective well-being is explored later in chapter 11.

Optimism and Hope   Generally, people who are more optimistic about the future and more hopeful are happier and enjoy greater life satisfaction than others (Carver et al., 2009; Rand & Cheavens,

2009; Seligman, 2011). As compared with pessimists, optimists engage in more effective coping behavior, have better physical health, and experience better relationships with other people (Carver, Scheier, & Sagerstrom, 2010). Optimists also possess greater self-confidence and perseverance when faced with challenges (Carver et al., 2009). Researchers suggest that a key element in optimism is the presence of positive expectancies; therefore, the impact of optimism on well-being is especially apparent when optimists encounter difficulties or challenges in life. Expectations of positive outcomes in the future not only enhance mood but also foster better coping strategies concerning stress. That is, when faced with stress and challenges, optimists tend to use problem-focused coping, realistic acceptance of their situation, humor, and positive reframing (Carver et al., 2009). For example, an optimist who loses her job might say, "This will spur me to get a better, more satisfying position" instead of sinking into depressive self-pity.

Optimism has been conceptualized in two major ways (Peterson, 2000). First, it can be viewed as *dispositional optimism*, or a global expectation that events will turn out well in the future (Scheier & Carver, 1985, 1987). Second, optimism has been defined as an explanatory style, or a way in which people interpret the causes of past events in their lives (Peterson & Steen, 2009). That is, if they believe their past failures are due to transient causes, then the future might seem bright because the causes of failure are no longer operant. However, if they believe their past failures are due to permanent causes, then the future may seem gloomy. Seligman (1998) proposed that people could learn to be more optimistic by paying attention to how they explain life events to themselves. He has referred to this process as **learned optimism**. But are optimists just looking at the world through rose-colored glasses because they can't stand the harsh light of reality?

Lisa Aspinwall (Aspinwall & Brunhart, 2000) argued that this hypothesis is incorrect and that optimists may be the true realists. She found that optimists were more willing than pessimists to receive negative feedback about their performance,

to absorb bad news about their health, and to raise difficult issues in their personal relationships. Sandra Schneider (2001) advanced a similar case for *realistic optimism*, which is optimistic thinking that does not distort reality. Realistic optimism is an honest recognition that there may be opportunities for positive growth or learning experiences in even the most difficult situations. However, research has also firmly established that some people hold optimistic beliefs that are unrealistic and even dangerous (Weinstein, 1980, 1984).

Hope is closely related to optimism. The most widely used definition of hope comes from C. R. Snyder (Snyder, 1994). As we saw in chapter 2, Snyder's definition has two components: (1) "pathways," or an ability to find ways to reach one's goals; and (2) "agency," or motivation to reach these goals. For Snyder, hope is "the belief that one can find pathways to desired goals and the belief that one can muster the motivation to use those pathways" (Rand & Cheavens, 2009, p. 324). From this perspective, hope is an optimistic belief that desired goals can be attained. The agency element of hope may be a better predictor of life satisfaction than the pathways portion (Bailey et al., 2007).

Sense of Control and Self-efficacy   A sense of having personal control refers to a belief that "one has the means to obtain desired outcomes and to avoid undesirable ones (Thompson, 2009, p. 271). Some researchers speculate that a need for control is the central motive that drives every other motive in life (Thompson, 2009) and that it is an innate need (Ryan & Deci, 2000). However, a high sense of control may be more important to well-being in Western cultures (Suh & Koo, 2008).

In the past, this particular predictor has usually been measured as locus of control (Rotter, 1966). A person with a strong *internal locus of control* tends to attribute outcomes to self-directed efforts. An *external locus of control* is a belief that outcomes in one's life are due to factors outside of one's immediate control. Last, a belief in *chance* is essentially a belief that no one is in charge of outcomes. During the past 40 years, there has been a huge amount of psychological research on locus of control, in general linking high internal locus of control to a variety of positive outcomes throughout the lifespan (Lefcourt, 1981).

Many researchers now understand this factor as a sense of personal control (Thompson, 2009; Peterson, 1999). A sense of **personal control** "encourages emotional, motivational, behavioral, and physiological vigor in the face of demands" (Peterson & Stunkard, 1989, p. 290). This newer, expanded vision of personal control encompasses locus of control theory as well as other concepts such as intrinsic motivation and empowerment (Peterson, 1999).

It is disconcerting to note that external locus of control scores for American college students have risen significantly since the 1960s. Today's college students "increasingly believe their lives are controlled by outside forces rather than their own efforts" (Twenge, Zhang, & Im, 2004, p. 308). The authors of the large meta-analysis on locus of control stated that the implications were almost uniformly negative. We hope that positive psychology can play a useful role in reversing this trend.

Self-efficacy is a concept with strong associations to control and hope. According to Bandura (1997), it involves a belief in one's capacity "to produce desired effects [and outcomes] by [one's] own actions" (as cited in Maddux, 2009, p. 335). Obviously, self-efficacy is very similar to a sense of control, hope, and optimism. Like these other constructs, it is related to higher well-being throughout the lifespan (Maddux, 2009; Vecchio et al., 2007). Self-efficacy is usually measured in relationship to specific outcomes. For example, separate measures exist for academic, social, and health self-efficacy as well as for many other forms. Specific measures of self-efficacy generally do better at predicting positive outcomes than do global measures.

A Sense of Meaning in Life   Having a sense of meaning and purpose in life is also an important predictor of higher subjective well-being (Park, 2011; Steger, 2009). Moreover, a sense of meaning is an important component of well-being at all stages of life (Steger, Oishi, & Kashdan, 2009).

Evidence suggests that the relationship is reciprocal, insofar as having a greater sense of meaning in life increases well-being, and feeling more positive emotions induces people to feel that their lives are meaningful (King et al., 2006). In subjective well-being studies, a sense of meaning in life has often been assessed by measures of religiosity (see Myers, 2000, 2008). However, a sense of meaning and purpose in life need not be tied to religious beliefs (Compton, 2000; Steger, Kashdan, & Oishi, 2008). For instance, research found that when people were actively engaged in pursuing a variety of personally meaningful goals, their well-being increased (Oishi, Diener, Suh, & Lucas, 1999).

It is important to note that the impact of meaning on well-being depends on whether one has reached a comfortable sense of meaning or is still searching. That is, feeling secure about one's current sense of meaning in life is associated with higher subjective well-being. However, searching for meaning is not related to higher levels of well-being and may even be related to lower well-being (Steger et al., 2008). Nevertheless, searching for well-being is associated with greater openness to and absorption in experiences as well as more curiosity about the world. Having the curiosity and drive to search for a significant sense of meaning may be the key element. A study of curiosity found that its exploration component (Kashdan, Rose, & Fincham, 2004) was more related to well-being than was the absorption component (Gallagher & Lopez, 2007). Chapter 10 continues the discussion of a sense of meaning in life.

Comments on the Cognitive Predictors   Epictetus, a Greek-born sage of the first century CE, declared, "Men are disturbed not by things, but by the view which they take of them." It is clear that all cognitive predictors of happiness and life satisfaction involve beliefs, interpretation of events, or future expectations. It is also clear that these judgments and expectations need not be entirely accurate to increase happiness or life satisfaction. Indeed, some provocative research has suggested that happiness is often related to inaccurate perceptions of reality—a phenomenon known as having *positive illusions* (Taylor & Brown, 1988).

Studies show that positive illusions about self and control are related to higher self-reported well-being and optimism. As you might expect, some thinkers strongly object to the prescription that we should all wear rose-colored glasses and deliberately avoid seeing the world accurately (for example, Colvin & Block, 1994; Colvin, Block, & Funder, 1995). Nevertheless, a bias for positivity is clearly associated with feeling happier and more satisfied with life. Baumeister (1989) suggested that there may be an "optimal margin for illusions." That is, we can afford to lose some objectivity if it means gaining a bit more optimism about a future that we cannot totally predict anyway. However, it is also true that better mental health is associated with accurate perceptions of self and others (Compton, 1992; Shedler, Mayman, & Manis, 1993). In short, the advantages of positive illusions depend on context and on one's goals of well-being.

If our sense of subjective well-being is intimately tied to the judgments we make about ourselves, then what criteria do we use? Greenberg, Pyszczynski, and Solomon (1986) suggested that social and cultural standards of behavior provide us with both a context for comparison and the actual standards we use to make such judgments; the results determine our feelings of value and self-worth. Their concept is described as involving **social comparison processes**. Of course, these comparisons can be made in many ways, one of which is to set an absolute internal standard for what we *should* be like and then gauge how close we are to it. Research on the difference between our *actual self* (that is, the attributes we currently possess) and our *ideal self* (that is, the attributes we think we should possess) has used this approach. Studies have found that less discrepancy between our actual self and our ideal self is related to more positive self-esteem and a higher sense of well-being (Morretti & Higgins, 1990). However, a perfect agreement between actual and ideal self indicates defensiveness; therefore, a moderately strong relationship indicates greater well-being (Katz & Ziglar, 1967).

A second way to evaluate our well-being is to compare ourselves with other people. In such a comparison, we ask ourselves whether other people seem happier, more satisfied, more talented, or more successful than we are. But exactly which people? That is, we can reference those whom we regard as similar to ourselves (that is, *lateral social comparisons*); those we regard as better on some dimension (that is, *upward social comparisons*); or those we view as less fortunate (that is, *downward social comparisons*).

Studies have found that happier people often use downward social comparisons (see Fujita, 2008; Lyubomirsky & Ross, 1997). For instance, if someone asks you to evaluate how satisfied you are with your life, research indicates that you will probably look around and compare yourself with other people. If you choose persons whom you believe are getting more out of life than you are, then you will feel less satisfied with your own life. But if you recognize that others have more difficult lives than you—if you feel grateful for what you have even if it isn't all that you had hoped for—then you'll tend to feel more satisfied with your life.

However, happy people don't always use downward comparisons. Rather, they are able to select the type of comparisons that maintain their happiness and also help maintain positive social relationships. In a way, they utilize social comparison processes to their advantage. Happier people are also less impacted by social comparisons with others that turn out negative (Lyubomirsky, Tucker, & Kasri, 2001). One of the ways happy people do this is by not expecting the best possible life at all times. Rather, they expect a "good enough" life, and therefore social comparisons that result in feeling their lives as good enough are quite acceptable. Finally, though happier people utilize social comparisons wisely, they tend to do so infrequently. That is, a tendency to make frequent comparisons to others is associated with negative emotions such as anger or sadness (Fujita, 2008).

Additionally, high subjective well-being created by way of social comparison can be built by egocentrism (Goetz et al., 2006). Under these circumstances, comparison processes will eventually lead to problems. In the fourth century BCE the Greek philosopher Demosthenes declared,

"Nothing is so easy as to deceive one's self; for what we wish, we readily believe."

Positive Relationships with Other People

A strong and important predictor of subjective well-being is the presence of positive social relationships (see Diener et al., 1999; Myers, 2000). A need for social interaction may be innate to our species. It may also be that a significant relationship between high subjective well-being and satisfaction with family and friends is found universally in cross-cultural studies of well-being (Diener, Oishi, & Lucas, 2003). The perception that one is embedded in supportive social relationships has been related to higher self-esteem; successful coping; better physical health; and fewer psychological problems. It is interesting to note that the impact of other predictors of subjective well-being is increased if people have good social support (Aspinwall & Taylor, 1992). That is, when individuals feel they have social support, there are enhanced effects on subjective well-being, such as positive self-esteem, optimism, and perceived control. Positive social support helps to create a "rising tide" that increases the effects of all other predictors.

Intimate social relationships provide even greater enhancements of subjective well-being. For example, several studies have found that intimacy—defined as relationships with spouse and family and "high quality" friendships—was the strongest predictor of life satisfaction (for example, Cummins, 1996). As you might guess, companionship and self-validation are two of the strongest components of quality relationships (Demir & Weitekamp, 2007). Having people around us who validate and support us can have a very powerful effect on how we feel. Diener and Seligman (2002) studied the happiest 10% of college students and observed that one factor stood out: such students enjoyed a highly fulfilling social life. Parlee (1979) found that engaging in intimate talk was the most frequently reported friendship experience for women (listed by 90% of women).

Despite popular assumptions about American men's supposed avoidance of emotional intimacy, having an intimate talk was the second-most frequently reported friendship experience for men (listed by 80% of men). A recent MTV and Associated Press poll of 13- to 24-year-old Americans asked, "What makes you happy?"[2] The most frequently reported answer was spending time with family, followed by spending time with friends; almost 75% stated that spending time with their parents made them happy.

One might wonder whether people seek companionship when they're happy or when they're sad. One study found that people most wanted companionship when they were very happy (see Middlebrook, 1980). That is, feeling happy increases social contact. Because positive social contact also seems to increase well-being, the relation between subjective well-being and positive social relationships appears reciprocal: Associating with people we care about who also care for us increases our well-being, and when we increase our sense of well-being others in turn wish to be closer to us. If emotional intimacy is important to subjective well-being, then you would expect that marriage is important as well; indeed, this appears to be the case. Further discussion of the relationship between well-being and marriage is addressed in chapter 5.

Personality Traits

Extraversion   Extraverted persons are interested in things outside themselves, such as physical and social environments (English & English, 1958). In contrast, introverts are more interested in their own thoughts and feelings and less interested in social situations. Many studies have found extraversion to be a leading predictor of subjective well-being (Diener et al., 1999); some have found correlations as high as .80 between extraversion and self-reported happiness (Fujita, 1991). In addition, extraversion has been shown to predict levels of happiness up to 30 years in the future (Costa & McCrae, 1984).

Recent studies have examined exactly how extraversion impacts well-being. Investigators initially thought it was the sociability component of extraversion that was most decisive (Bradburn,

1969). For example, studies found that number of friends was related to well-being such that the more friends one had, the higher one's well-being (Okun, Stock, Haring, & Witter, 1984). Therefore, psychologists believed that extraverts had greater opportunities for positive relations with other people and for obtaining positive feedback about themselves. However, more recent studies found that, although extraverts do engage in some types of activities more than introverts, there was not much difference between the two in the overall domain of social activity, and the greater sociability of extraverts did not account for their greater happiness (Lucas, Le & Dyrenforth, 2008). In addition, extraverts were happier than introverts whether living alone or with others, or engaged in social or nonsocial occupations (Diener, Larsen, and Emmons, 1984).

Extraversion may be associated with higher self-reported happiness because being extraverted is often a better "fit" with contemporary life, which is often highly social. This seems especially true for American culture, which tends to reward behaviors displayed by extraverts (Helgoe, 2010). In contrast, imagine a person who chooses to live as a contemplative monk in a remote mountain monastery; he or she would be a better personality "fit" in that introverted setting.

Some researchers have suggested that the tendency of extraverts to report higher levels of happiness stems from their greater sensitivity to positive rewards, or stronger reactions to pleasant events (Larsen & Ketelaar, 1991; Rusting & Larsen, 1998). Indeed, a positive relationship between extraversion and sensitivity to rewards was even found in cross-cultural studies (Lucas, Diener, Grob, Suh, & Shao, 2000). However, more recent reviews of research studies have not supported this hypothesis (see Lucas, 2008).

Today, most researchers believe that the tendency of extraverts to report greater happiness is due to one particular facet of extraversion: Extraverts tend to have a "cheerful" disposition (Schimmack et al., 2004). That is, they have a general tendency to experience more positive emotions; to laugh more than others; and to joke more frequently, and to experience more positive emotions. A cautionary note, however: Although extraversion correlates with long-term positive affectivity, it does not correlate with long-term negative affectivity (Schimmack, 2008). That is, since positive and negative emotions are not significantly correlated, extraverts may be disposed to cheerfulness, but they may be no better or worse than introverts in avoiding negative emotions.

Are introverts necessarily doomed to depression and ennui? Not at all. For example, Larsen and Kasimatis (1990) found that though extraverts rated themselves as feeling happier than did introverts during the week, both types reported levels of happiness that were above the neutral point and both types reported they were "happy". In their study, Hills and Argyle (2001) found happy introverts as well as unhappy extraverts. They also found that happy introverts and happy extraverts tended to create their well-being in similar ways, implying that activity may be more important than personality type. Other studies have found that introverts are less social because they desire solitude. For introverts, the pursuit of happiness may be less their top priority in life than a search for meaning. Also, introverts may prefer more neutral emotional states such as contentment over more arousing emotions such as happiness. It is fascinating to note there may be differences in brain structures such that introverts do not need as much stimulation as extraverts in order to maintain an optimal level of physiological arousal (Helgoe, 2010).

Agreeableness and Conscientiousness Agreeableness and conscientiousness have also been reliably associated with higher subjective well-being. Along with extraversion, openness to experience and neuroticism, these two comprise the five basic dimensions of personality (see Costa & McCrae, 1986). Agreeableness refers to being honest; trustworthy; modest; compliant (as opposed to oppositional); tender-minded; and altruistic. People who are high in conscientiousness tend to be orderly; self-disciplined; achievement-oriented; deliberate; dutiful; and competent. Persons scoring high on both agreeableness and conscientiousness are able to navigate social and vocational situations far more successfully than those measuring low on both traits.

Neuroticism   At the beginning of the chapter we mentioned that the third pillar of high subjective well-being is low neuroticism. Indeed, some researchers have argued that an effective way to increase happiness and life satisfaction is to focus on eliminating neuroticism (Larsen & Prizmic, 2008). One facet of neuroticism is the most important for subjective well-being: depression (Schimmack et al., 2004). While low levels of anxiety, anger, and self-consciousness are important for mental health, the greatest impact comes from the absence of depression.

BOTTOM-UP PREDICTORS OF SUBJECTIVE WELL-BEING

Bottom-up factors stem from evaluations of various life domains such as income and marital status. We examine demographic factors such as gender, race, and age as well. Let's begin with one of the dominant notions about what makes people happy.

Money, Income, and Wealth

Are people with more money happier than those with less? The assumption that money brings happiness and satisfaction is one of the most persistent messages of many societies (see Myers, 2000). Cross-cultural studies are quite consistent in finding a significant relationship between income and subjective well-being in various countries (Biswas-Diener, 2008). Studies have found that the Gross Domestic Product (GDP) of countries is positively correlated with average life satisfaction at about .50 (Diener, Diener, & Diener, 1995). Studies within countries have also found that higher income is associated with greater self-reported happiness (Diener & Lucas, 2000). A recent longitudinal analysis spanning 33 years in the United States found that being in the lower quarter of income distribution reduced the odds of being happy by about

26%, while being in the upper quarter increased the odds by about 13% (Yang, 2008). Note, however, that being poor decreased the odds more than being wealthier increased the odds. Similarly, a study that examined happiness reported by people included on *Forbes'* annual list of wealthiest Americans found them somewhat happier than others (Diener, Horowitz, & Emmons, 1985). Such research suggests that (1) living in a wealthier country and (2) having more money within it tend to increase happiness.

Money does matter to happiness, in both expected and unexpected ways. As you might expect, possessing disposable income can provide a buffer against stress, offer access to better health care, and lessen chronic worry about daily necessities. Indeed, the *livability theory* suggests that access to the social and economic benefits found in wealthier countries might account for differences in well-being among countries (Veenhoven, 1999). Indeed, differences in life satisfaction among countries have been associated with the ability of societies to meet the basic needs of citizens (Tay & Diener, 2011). Interestingly, Diener and Biswas-Diener (2002) suggested that money may not cause happiness; rather, it may be the other way around (see also Lyubomirsky, King, & Diener, 2005). They suggested that being happier can facilitate obtaining higher income partially because the personality factors associated with high subjective well-being are certainly assets in the workplace. In general, the results of large-scale studies are rather clear: Having more money is associated with higher subjective well-being. When the finer details are examined, however, this general conclusion becomes more complicated.

First, all studies agree that the relationship between income and subjective well-being is curvilinear (Biswas-Diener, 2008). This means that the importance of income to happiness is greatest at lower income levels but becomes less important at higher income levels. In essence, money matters more if you have very little of it, but money matters less when you have more of it. A recent study actually attempted to calculate the precise tipping point below which money is important to well-being and above which point money is less important. In examining individual income, Daniel Kahneman and Angus Deaton (2010) asserted that such a tipping point was around $75,000 (in 2010 U.S. dollars). Beyond that point, additional income did little to improve happiness but continued to raise life satisfaction.

It is also clear that the cross-cultural data on GDP and subjective well-being do not apply to every country. For instance, in 2010 the World Database on Happiness listed Guatemala among the 10 happiest countries on earth, and in 2008 the World Values Survey listed Puerto Rico and Columbia among the top 10 happiest countries, with impoverished El Salvador the 11th (see *Business Week*, 2008). Of course, none of these countries had a GDP even approaching the U.S. or major European nations. Another cross-cultural example comes from a study conducted in the slums of Calcutta, India, which found positive levels of life satisfaction among those who lived in extreme poverty, although satisfaction levels were still lower than those of more prosperous groups in India (Biswas-Diener & Diener, 2001). In addition,

homeless street people in Calcutta reported higher satisfaction than their counterparts in the United States.

Several other investigations cast further doubt on the existence of a simple relationship between income and well-being. Studies conducted in the United States indicate that levels of happiness have not risen dramatically from 1946 to the present—a lengthy period during which personal income has risen substantially (Stevenson & Wolfers, 2008) (see Figure 3.2).

Some reports indicate that happiness ratings in the U.S. have actually decreased during this time period (see Lane, 2000). Cross-cultural studies have found that happiness levels in Switzerland and Norway have also shown no change since 1946.[3] Another study found that increased salary levels over a ten-year period did not lead to increased self-reported happiness (Diener et al., 1993). Studies conducted of lottery winners have shown that most people return to their prior level of happiness relatively quickly (Brickman, Coates, & Janoff-Bulman, 1978). In addition, people who choose a "voluntary simplicity" or "environmentally friendly" lifestyle

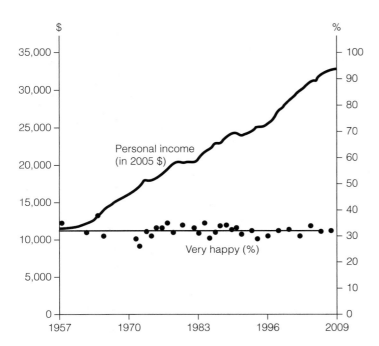

FIGURE 3.2 Income and Percent Very Happy by Years

SOURCE: Income data from U.S. Commerce Department, Bureau of the Census, and Economic Indicatorc; happiness data from General Social Surveys, National Opinion Research Center, University of Chicago; data complied by David G. Myers. Used with permission.

often achieve a high level of subjective well-being despite their low income (Brown & Kasser, 2005; Jabob & Brinkerhoff, 1999). Last, some studies suggest that the higher subjective well-being of people in the highest income brackets may be the result of snob appeal: Researchers in Britain and Wales found that having more income enhanced happiness only if the extra income increased people's social standing (Boyce, Brown, & Moore, 2010).

Some studies even suggest that money may be hazardous to well-being, for among consistent findings about money is that rising income usually spurs materialistic aspirations (Diner & Biswas-Diener, 2002). How so? Because a rise in personal income usually translates into greater expectations about what one needs to be happy. This situation has been dubbed by researchers as the **hedonic treadmill**. When applied to satisfaction with income, it means that a person keeps setting ever-higher materialist goals in hopes of finally becoming happy with their income (Brickman and Campbell, 1971). For example, Schor (1999) reported a survey in 1995 of people who earned more than $100,000 per year ($148,270 in 2011 U.S. dollars). Incredibly, 27% of those surveyed stated they could not afford everything they "really need[ed]" and 19% said they spent *all* their income on "basic necessities" (as cited in Diener & Biswas-Diener, 1999)! Similarly, people who hold "financial success" as their core value tend to report lower global adjustment ratings and more behavior disorders (Kasser & Ryan, 1993). The evidence is clear that people who place a high value on money for personal happiness are less satisfied with their lives than those who don't (Kasser & Ryan, 1993; Sirgy, 1998). Investigators have also found that materialistic behavior is partially stimulated by feelings of insecurity and anxieties about one's mortality (Kasser & Sheldon, 2000; Arndt, Solomon, Kasser, & Sheldon, 2004).

Researchers have found that the act of gazing at relatively small amounts of money while engaged in unrelated tasks resulted in people's enjoying these tasks less. That is, their capacity to enjoy life's little pleasures was undermined (Quoidbach et al., 2010). Viewing money may also cause people to be more solitary and less willing to help others or donate funds to social causes (Vohs, Mead, & Goode, 2008). Consistent with such findings, surveys have consistently shown that wealthier people contribute a smaller percentage of their income to charity than do others (see Flores, 2010; Lyubomirsky, 2010). In a similar way, the act of gazing at luxury goods, such as expensive watches or shoes, can lead to increased self-interest as compared with interest in others (Chua & Zou, 2009). Finally, researchers have found that when people worked toward goals involving wealth, fame, or beauty, their well-being actually decreased (Niemiec et al., 2009).

How Money can Increase Subjective Well-being
We hope you are not too confused at this point. So far, we have seen that money or income is both important to subjective well-being and potentially harmful as well. Therefore, we now turn to studies that focus on how money can enhance well-being. First, evidence indicates that happiness comes from what people do with the money they have; that is, some researchers have distinguished between spending money on "material purchases" (that is, material goods) versus spending money on "experiential purchases" (that is, experiences shared with family and friends, such as a family vacation, or to help fulfill personal goals). As you might suspect, spending money on experiential purchases was more associated with personal happiness than was spending on material purchases (Van Boven & Gilovich, 2003). That is, money can be associated with happiness if we use it to foster relationships with family and friends; enhance our competence in a skill or hobby; gain autonomy (Niemiec et al., 2009); or practice "inconspicuous consumption" rather than "conspicuous consumption" (Frank, 2007).

Using money to fulfill psychological needs, such as learning new skills and gaining respect or autonomy, can increase positive emotions (Diener et al., 2010). This means that money increases happiness if it is spent on activities that enhance personal growth or provide new learning experiences—or even if we spend it on small pleasures such as a massage or a long phone call to a friend abroad. Elizabeth Dunn and colleagues (Dunn, Akin, & Norton, 2008) found that when people spend money on others or donate to charities, this type of spending does increase happiness. A recent study found that priming people to think about having more time for social connections tended to increase happiness, but priming them to think about money did not (Mogilner, 2010).

In an intriguing article, researchers in Britain asserted that "friends are worth more than a new Ferrari" (see Powdthavee & Wilkinson, 2010). They attempted to calculate how much certain factors are worth to happiness (figures are in 2010 US dollars): excellent health (about $2,000,000); marriage (about $323,000); and regularly talking to neighbors (about $184,000). Continuing with this same theme, other researchers noted that successfully completing psychotherapy is at least 32 times more cost-effective in raising happiness than merely gaining more income (Boyce & Wood, 2011). Blanchflower and Oswald (2004) used similar calculations to discover that increasing the frequency of sexual intercourse from once a month to once a week increased happiness as much as a $50,000 raise in salary (Blanchflower & Oswald, 2004; Oliviero, 2005). It may be that the problem of the hedonic treadmill can be overcome by using wealth in ways that reflect our core values or that stimulate factors known to be related to greater well-being. As Rabbi Hyman Schachtel famously said, "Happiness is not having what you want, but wanting what you have." Indeed, a study partially confirmed the rabbi's statement by finding that wanting what you have was a predictor of happiness, although having what you want was also important (Larsen & McKibban, 2008).

Gender: Are Men or Women Happier?

Once again, the answer to this question is a little complicated, for studies have found all possible answers to this fascinating question (see Nolen-Hoeksema & Rusting, 1999). In an earlier analysis designed to resolve the inconsistency of findings, Wood, Rhodes and Welan (1989) concluded that women generally report slightly higher levels of happiness than men—and most analyses published prior to 1990 would have agreed. However, several more recent analyses present a very different picture.

A recent compilation of studies covering 33 years in the U.S., Europe, and other parts of the world found that women's average happiness has fallen steadily since 1972. Women were happier than men before about 1985 and were equal to men in happiness around 1989, but they now report lower happiness than men (Stevenson & Wolfers, 2009). This association was found regardless of such factors as marital status; number of children; chronological age; or income level. This decrease in women's self-reported happiness was found in the U.S. and in all 12 European countries examined with the exception of Germany. Additional data taken from around the world indicated similar trends in 125 of 147 countries. Although this same study found that life satisfaction scores have decreased in recent years for both men and women, the declining well-being ratings for women nevertheless were dramatic and significant. However, other research found that women are happier than men before about age 48, but then the relationship switches; that is, men are happier than women after midlife (Plagnol & Easterlin, 2008; Yang, 2008).

The issue of happiness and gender becomes even more complicated. For example, women report they experience and express *all emotions*—pleasant and unpleasant—more frequently and more intensely than men. Also, women report a greater capacity for joy (Fujita, Diener, & Sandvik, 1991). Some studies suggest that because women talk more than men about emotional issues, then both genders are happier if they have a sister (see Devlin, 2009). However, Deborah Tannen (2010), well-known for her research on men's and women's communication styles, suggested that this increased well-being derives little from mere talking but rather from sharing information in a friendly, comfortable, and important relationship. In her view, the particular topic or even the emotional depth of the conversation is secondary.

Women and men also appear to calculate their well-being differently. Women generally enhance their well-being through positive self-esteem, greater harmony and closeness in their relationships, passive leisure, and religion, whereas men primarily use positive self-esteem, active leisure, and greater mental control (Reid, 2004; Tkach & Lyubomirsky, 2006). In summary, although the decreasing happiness of women around the world is certainly cause for concern, neither gender is inevitably doomed to be less happy than the other.

Several studies should be mentioned that relate to gender, the first of which focuses on physical attractiveness and well-being. A substantial body of research has found that most people tend to automatically attribute a variety of positive qualities to good-looking people (Feingold, 1992). Of course, the attributions may not always be correct. But what about good looks and subjective well-being: Is there an important relationship? A study of married couples found no significant relationship between these two variables (Diener, Wolsic, & Fujita, 1995). A more recent study found that physical attractiveness was related to well-being for women, but only for those living in urban settings (Plaut, Adams, & Anderson, 2009). If people believe that being physically attractive is important, then will cosmetic surgery improve their well-being? The evidence suggests that cosmetic surgery can enhance well-being in specific circumstances, but the psychological elements responsible for a positive outcome are difficult to determine (see Askegaard, Gertsen, & Langer, 2002). However, appearing better-looking may be simpler than undergoing costly and potentially dangerous cosmetic surgery. That is, most people appear more attractive merely by smiling (Reis, 1990). We have more to say about physical attractiveness in chapter 5.

Finally, it is worth noting that a recent study suggested that being taller may have an impact on one's well-being. Deaton and Arora (2009) found that people taller than average reported more enjoyment of life and less pain and sadness than others. However, taller individuals also reported more stress, and for women, more worry. Interestingly, Deaton and Arora calculated that each additional inch in height above the average boosted happiness as much as a 4.4% rise in family income for men and a 3.8% increase in income for women.

Age: Is One Age Group Happier than Another?

What about the social message that young people are happier than older people—is it true? Once again, the research does not support the cultural myth. Indeed, many studies have found that older persons tend to be *more* satisfied with life than their younger counterparts (Diener & Suh, 2000; Yang, 2008). These results, which remain significant even when factors such as income, education, and race are included (Yang, 2008), are also found in many countries around the world (Diener & Suh, 2000; Lucas & Gohm, 2000). One study even found high levels of happiness among centenarians, defined as people over 90 years old (Jopp & Rott, 2006). However, some studies have found that satisfaction with life is higher among older persons but happiness declines in old age (Diener, Oishi, & Lucas, 2009; Lucas & Gohm, 2000). The other caveat is that older people remain relatively happy and satisfied only if they retain good health. One longitudinal study found that subjective well-being was higher among older persons but began to decline approximately four years before their death (Gerstorf et al., 2008).

Researchers have speculated about these consistent findings regarding happiness and age. First, they have noted that older persons often have a smaller discrepancy between their life goals or aspirations and their actual accomplishments (Cheng, 2004). Second, satisfaction with social relationships is both higher and more important for older persons (Herzog, Rogers, & Woodworth, 1982) than for their younger counterparts. Other factors that contribute to higher subjective well-being among older persons include greater self-efficacy and optimism (Jopp & Rott, 2006), a higher felt sense of autonomy (Sheldon et al., 2005), a more realistic view of the future (Lachman et al., 2008), a more successful resolution of developmental life stages (Sheldon & Kasser, 2001), and a greater sense of meaning (Dzuka & Dalbert, 2006).

It does appear that young people experience more frequent negative emotions than do older people (Csikszentmihalyi & Larson, 1984) and that the frequency of negative emotions declines as people age (Carstensen et al., 2000). Because of this change, "periods of highly positive emotional experience [are] more likely to endure among older people" (Carstensen et al., 2000, p. 644). In addition, the emotions of young people are more intense because they have less practice and skill at self-regulation. This means, of course, that *all* emotions tend to be experienced more intensely by younger persons, so they experience more frequent anger, sadness, jealousy, disappointment, and other negative feelings. In this light, research indicates that the intensities of positive and negative emotionality are significantly correlated (Diener, Larsen, Levine, & Emmons, 1985).

There also appear to be effects that impact people who have gone through a similar experience at a specific point in time (that is, "cohort effects"). For instance, most people who grew up during the Great Depression and World War II undoubtedly were strongly affected by those events. A recent study found that people in the United States who were born between 1945 and 1960—the Baby Boomers—tended to experience lower self-rated happiness than people born either before or after that time period (Yang, 2008). Several other reasons for the greater subjective well-being of older persons are explored in chapter 8.

Race, Education, Climate, and Politics

When examining the relationships between subjective well-being and race, it is possible to investigate differences between racial groups within a specific culture and differences among ethnically diverse cultures. This section focuses on differences in subjective well-being within specific cultures in the United States. Differences found among countries and diverse ethnic groups are explored in chapter 11.

Studies in the United States have found that white Americans tended to report higher subjective well-being than did African-Americans, Latinos, or Native Americans (Argyle, 1999; Yang, 2008).

Asian-Americans tended to report high self-esteem as well as levels of happiness comparable to that of Caucasian-Americans (Chang, 2001). However, rates of depression may be higher among Asian-Americans, especially among young women, than among Americans of European background (Oishi, 2001). A Gallup poll found that 39% of African-Americans stated they were "very satisfied" with their personal lives, in contrast to 58% of whites (Carroll, 2007). Similarly, 44% of African-Americans said they "very happy," compared to 52% of whites. However, African-American men aged 70 or older also reported being happier than older white men did (Yang, 2008), and African-American children reported higher self-esteem than white children (Argyle, 1999). In a study of African-Americans, the significant predictors of happiness and life satisfaction included being older; being married; having more income; attending religious services; having good health; and having friends with whom to discuss important issues (Taylor et al., 2001). Not surprisingly, these predictors were almost identical to significant predictors for other racial groups. It also appears that social changes in attitudes and levels of discrimination do have an impact. In the past 30 years, and especially after 1995, disparities in well-being between African-Americans and whites in the United States has been diminishing (Yang, 2008).

Young Native Americans report fairly high levels of self-esteem. Unfortunately, the self-esteem of Native Americans decreases when they encounter white urban culture and face unemployment, discrimination, and cultural clashes (Fuchs & Havinghurst, 1973). In fact, racial or ethnic discrimination within a specific society can negatively impact subjective well-being for all minority groups (see Lewis, 2002). In general, however, when factors such as income, education level, and occupational level within a society are taken into account, then the effects of ethnicity on subjective well-being are smaller (Yang, 2008). Nevertheless, these do not disappear entirely.

Although education is a means to a better job for most people, does it affect happiness? A recent analysis found that a college degree could increase the odds of being "happy" by about 37% (Yang, 2008). However, another study found that once an individual attained a middle-class income level, further education did not impact happiness in any significant way (Diener, Suh, Lucas, & Smith, 1999).

A note for anyone who has fantasized about escaping to a lush tropical island: People may believe that relaxing in such a place will bring the joy they crave, but they are often wrong about what will make them happy. Nevertheless, climate does have an impact on moods. For example, Hawaii is consistently rated among the three "happiest" states (see chapter 11). Studies have found that pleasant warm weather does improve mood but only in the spring (Keller et al., 2005). A two-week vacation on a Caribbean island can certainly relive the tension of a high-stress job—but only temporarily. So, a trip to that lush tropical island might be a good source of relaxation and well-being, but it probably won't produce lasting happiness.

A study of Koreans and Americans examined how good they were at predicting their well-being in retirement (Oishi et al., 2009). Many participants believed that a happy retirement derived from living in a pleasant climate and having a variety of recreational options. However, actual retirees reported that practical factors—such as access to health care and shopping convenience—were more important to their well-being. Although long-term well-being is only mildly influenced by where a person lives, most Americans reported a preference for natural environments over urban settings (see Martens, Gutscher, & Bauer, 2011).

Finally, several studies have examined political affiliation of Americans and subjective well-being. For many years now, research has indicated that Republicans are both more satisfied with their lives and happier than either Democrats or Independents, who score similarly to one another on these two dimensions. No one has been able to explain precisely why this difference exists. However, Republicans are more likely than Democrats to have higher income; be married; attend church; and be healthier. In addition, Republicans more than Democrats have positive expectations of their

future and tend to believe their career success is due to their own efforts. As we have just seen, all these variables are related to higher subjective well-being. It seems clear that several variables specifically related to economic aspects, such as fewer sources of financial worry and stress, are partially responsible for these differences (Taylor, 2008). Nonetheless, a small Republican advantage still exists after controlling for these factors.

Other investigations have suggested psychological differences. Republicans, or more accurately conservative Republicans, tend to worry more about changes to the status quo indicating the collapse of social institutions such as marriage, and tend to believe that without adequate social controls our sexual and aggressive emotions will run wild. In contrast, liberal Democrats tend to worry about a society so rigid and over-controlled that intense emotional experiences are restricted and repressed (McAdams & Albaugh, 2008). Whatever the final answer, no researcher has suggested that a change of party affiliation is a reliable way to increase or decrease your subjective well-being.

Bottom-Up Predictors and the "Happiest Man in America"

In summary, the economic, social, and demographic factors of our lives do matter to our happiness. Bottom-up predictors such as gender, income, race, and marital status interact in relatively complex ways throughout the lifespan to influence levels of subjective well-being. However, none of these factors need dictate our happiness and well-being. To affirm this view, imagine a "very happy" person based on bottom-up predictors. In fact, the Gallup organization recently used several significant demographic characteristics to find the "happiest man in America" (Rampell, 2011). He was Mr. Alvin Wong of Honolulu, Hawaii, a 69-year-old Chinese-American who is 5'10" tall, has been married for over 35 years, has two children, owns his own business, and is a kosher-observing Jew. According to most of the bottom-up predictors, Mr. Wong fits the profile of the happiest man. It turns out that Mr. Wong says he is quite happy.

However, there is obviously more to greater well-being than the statistical predictors used in this somewhat tongue-in-cheek analysis.

CAUTIONARY TALES: THE DOWN SIDE OF FEELING UP

Beyond a doubt, research supports the notion that feeling more positive emotions is advantageous in many life domains. However, several cautions are in order when thinking about how to be happier. We have already seen that feeling too happy (that is, a "10" on a 10-point scale) may actually interfere with well-being and may decrease physical health.[4] It also appears that when happy people make decisions they are prone to more stereotypical thinking; rely on shortcuts too often; and are less likely to check for errors (see Lyubomirsky, King, & Diener, 2005). People who are happier may also be more susceptible to the primacy effect in impression formation; that is, they may too hastily form opinions about others on the basis of first impressions (Forgas, 2010). In essence, being extremely happy can mean that we don't pay much attention to what's occurring around us. Similarly, being in a positive mood tends to make us more selfish (Tan & Forgas, 2010). Perhaps a bit of sadness increases our empathy, interpersonal sensitivity, and sense of fairness.

Turning now to self-esteem, we suggest that most people realize it is possible for self-esteem to be too high. Holding overly favorable views of one's abilities is actually a common judgment error (see *positive illusions*), which often decreases ability to distinguish accuracy from error in many decision-making tasks (Kruger & Dunning, 2009). Baumeister and his colleagues showed that when people with very high self-esteem feel threatened, they can set unrealistic goals that have a greater potential for failure (Baumeister, Heatherton, & Tice, 1993; Baumeister, Smart, & Boden, 1996). Further, there are two types of high self-esteem: secure and fragile (Kernis, 2003). High self-esteem that is fragile is quite unstable and has been associated with elevated hostility (Zeigler-Hill, Clark, & Beckman, in press).

As we have seen, because optimism is a belief, it can be a false belief. For example, most people believe their own risk for developing cancer or heart disease is much lower than their statistical risk for those events (Weinstein, 1980). This type of *unrealistic optimism* creates a false sense of security and a bias in risk perception that, in some cases, can literally be fatal. People who are highly optimistic may also give up on difficult tasks more quickly than other people (Aspinwall & Brunhart, 2000). That is, unless optimists are highly motivated to complete a task, they may not wish to damage their outlook by risking failure.

James Collins (2001) wrote about the "Stockdale paradox," which he named after Admiral James Stockdale's experience as a prisoner of war during the Vietnam War. Stockdale said he never lost hope he would survive imprisonment; however, he also added that those who didn't survive were "the optimists." In this case, the optimists believed their ordeal would soon be over, so they were constantly disappointed. Stockdale observed that people must not confuse faith in an eventual happy outcome with denial of the reality of their current predicament.

Finally, the "power of positive thinking" can have a downside for some people. Those who possessed low self-esteem actually felt worse after repeating affirmations ("I'm a lovable person") or when asked to think about how an affirmation was true for them (Wood, Perunovic, & Lee, 2009). Similarly, those who scored high on neuroticism did not feel less negative emotion when asked to reappraise a past negative event (Ng & Diener, 2009).

INCREASING HAPPINESS AND LIFE SATISFACTION

As we begin this section on strategies to increase subjective well-being, it might be wise to consider whether well-being can be changed significantly. You will recall from chapter 2 that set-point theory suggests genetics largely determines our level of long-term well-being. We hope you will also recall that newer research affirms that people can change over time and that our genetic inheritance does not completely determine our long-term happiness (for example, Headey, Muffels, & Wagner, 2010). However, another issue impacts how successful we can be at changing our level of well-being.

When exposed to a certain level of stimulus, we become habituated and adapt to that level relatively quickly. When we adapt to a positive stimulus and no longer feel its effects, this is called *hedonic adaptation*. Earlier we saw that one outcome of such adaptation can be the hedonic treadmill, in which we need an ever-increasing income level to obtain a positive boost from a rise in income. When we initially feel something pleasant from a positive experience, our happiness has much to do with the fact that a baseline level of happiness has just changed. We notice the change. It grabs our attention. At that instant, the difference between our earlier state and the present one is more pronounced than it will ever be again. For almost immediately, adaptation takes place so that the new level of happiness is inevitably transformed into our new baseline. When this new level of happiness becomes the new baseline, we don't notice it as much; as we feel more positive emotion, we *adapt* to it—and that level becomes "the new normal." So then we need more positive emotion in order to feel "happy" again.

Despite hedonic treadmill theory, several large studies now confirm that adaptation to positive emotions is not inevitable (for example, Lucas, 2007). Diener, Lucas, and Scallon (2006) argued there are at least five important reasons to believe the theory of a hedonic treadmill is wrong, which means that people *can* make positive changes in their lives. These researchers noted that people in Western countries generally report levels of happiness "above average," so they can't be simply adapting to positive emotion (adaptation would imply a return to a neutral point). Also, people may have multiple set-points (for example, one for work satisfaction, another for marital satisfaction, and so on),

and some set-points may be more fluid than others. In addition, research is clear that people can increase their happiness and life satisfaction. For example, the use of better styles of coping can definitely result in higher well-being.

In order to avoid the hedonic treadmill, one must adopt one of two strategies (Larsen & Prizmic, 2008). The first is to find ways to speed up adaptation to negative events. If this is successful, then we could adjust more quickly to negative emotions so as to experience them more briefly in our lives. The second strategy is to slow down adaptation to positive events. If this is successful, then it would take longer for us to adapt to positive events with the result that we would feel positive emotions for greater amounts of time. Therefore, interventions to increase life satisfaction, and especially to increase happiness, must either serve to discharge negative emotions (like anger, resentment, or worry) more rapidly—or help maintain positive emotions like gratitude, admiration, or joy for longer. Either strategy can be successful in amplifying well-being, and people who report being happier are perhaps more skilled at both strategies (Larsen & Prizmic, 2008).

Intensity and Frequency of Positive Emotion

Now that we know a neutral happiness and life satisfaction can be changed for the better, how should we go about changing? Do some general guidelines exist? First to consider is whether more intense or more frequent positive emotions should be the goal. That is, are people happier if they feel mild positive feelings everyday—or if they feel extremely happy once a week? The *peak-and-end rule* in emotion research states that we select a few moments from our memories in determining how we will feel about an entire past event (Fredrickson, 2000). Specifically, we select the most intense emotion from our memories as well as the last emotion. For instance, if your romantic evening was mostly routine and mildly enjoyable, but you experienced one spectacular moment of fun, and the date ended with the most passionate kiss of your life, then you'll remember that entire evening as being fabulous. Therefore, intensity of emotion seems more crucial for happiness.

However, frequency is actually more important than intensity (Diener, Sadvik, & Pavot, 1991). Consistently feeling moderate subjective well-being has a more beneficial effect than an occasional experience of bliss. Partially this is because super joyful experiences are rare and therefore unlikely to affect everyday well-being. So though movies and novels about a brief but passionate romance or a sad-and-struggling athlete who wins the gold medal often fuel popular imagination, in reality a daily dose of mild positive feeling is more likely to induce long-term benefits than a single, tremendous dose of positive emotion.

Strategies for Creating a Good Mood

A straightforward way to change one's subjective well-being is to do something that increases the ratio of positive to negative emotions in one's life. Most people develop various strategies to increase the frequency of positive emotions. Indeed, people are fairly clever at finding ways to bring themselves out of bad moods (Thayer, Newman, and McClain, 1994). For example, many persons report they improve their moods by listening to music. However, music that positively impacts well-being may depend upon the particular type as well as one's own characteristics. For example, one study found that males reacted more aggressively after hearing heavy-metal music (Mast & McAndrews, 2011), and another study found increased rates of suicide in metropolitan areas of the U.S. with a larger audience for country music (Stack & Gundlach, 1992).

Fordyce's Happiness Training Program

An early intervention to increase happiness was the Happiness Training Program developed by Michael Fordyce (1977, 1981, 1983, 1988). He devised a package designed to teach the "fourteen fundamentals of happiness" (1981), grouped in the following way: (1) change your activities (that is, be more active; be productive at meaningful work; get organized); (2) change your thinking (that is, think

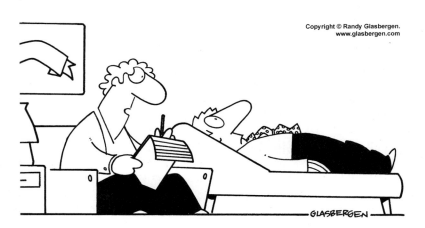

Copyright © Randy Glasbergen.
www.glasbergen.com

"Look at it this way. If your problem belonged to someone else, it wouldn't seem like any big deal at all!"

optimistically; orient yourself to the present; lower your expectations and aspirations; value happiness—put it first in your life); (3) nurture relationships (that is, develop and nurture close relationships since they are the number one source of happiness; develop an outgoing and sociable personality; spend more time socializing); (4) value personal growth (that is, work on a health personality; be yourself); and (5) decrease negative emotions (that is, eliminate negative feelings; stop worrying).

The correspondence between this list and the subjective well-being literature is obvious. Fordyce's (1977, 1983) studies found that scores on standard measures of happiness were increased following implementation of his program. Of course, other factors are also helpful. For instance, Smith, Compton, and West (1995) found that happiness scores increased further when people practiced a simple meditation technique in addition to implementing Fordyce's program for happiness.

Comments on Fordyce's Program   While there are certainly many correspondences between Fordyce's fourteen Fundamentals and the subjective well-being literature, two of Fordyce's fundamentals deserve special attention. Fordyce asserted that we should "lower expectations and aspirations." The research basis for this fundamental comes from studies that show greater satisfaction among those whose actual self and ideal self (or whose actual achievements and goals) are close together. Often the farther apart these are, the less one feels well-being. Thus, people should be less perfectionistic both about themselves and others, and they should not set their goals unrealistically high. However, it can be difficult to distinguish how realistic a goal actually is for any particular person. It is better to allow people to set their goals high and then teach them how to use struggle, challenge, and even failure for personal growth.

Fordyce also proposed that people place the pursuit of happiness *first* in their lives. However, many other theorists dating back to Maslow

(1971) have argued that happiness is a byproduct of other activities and is in fact more elusive when relentlessly pursued (see Oishi, Diener, & Lucas, 2007).

Sustainable Happiness

The **sustainable happiness model** (SHM) suggests that changes in subjective well-being can be made and sustained if the focus of change is in the proper domain (Lybomirsky, Sheldon, & Schkade, 2005; Sheldon & Lybomirsky, 2006). According to the SHM, long-term happiness is a function of (a) one's genetically determined *set-point*; (b) *circumstantial factors*, such as where a person lives, age, gender, and past life events (for example, previous traumas); and (c) *intentional activity*, or how people choose to spend their time, interact with others, and think about situations. People can do very little to modify their set-point, and often circumstances are difficult to change.

However, there are considerable options to change intentional activity. Indeed, consistent with SHM, Sheldon and Lybomirsky (2006a) found that college students who changed their activities (for example, who began pursuing a new goal or life passion) experienced a larger increase in well-being than those who changed their circumstances (for example, who improved their living arrangements or financial situation). One study found that even reading stories written in the active voice increases happiness more than reading stories written in the passive voice (Lucas, Lloyd, & Magaloni, 2005). It is also advantageous to mix several daily activities that each fulfill different needs (Tay & Diener, 2011).

To achieve lasting changes in well-being, making these changes in the correct way is key. For instance, the pursuit of goals can increase well-being, but only if the goals fit a person's interests and values (Sheldon et al., 2002). In another study, Lyubomirsky, Tkach, and Sheldon (2004) asked participants to perform five acts of kindness per week for six weeks. They found the exercise increased well-being. Similarly, they asked participants to "count their blessings" or recognize things for which they were grateful. The researchers again found increases in well-being but only if all five acts were performed in one day.

Barbara Fredrickson's Positivity

Barbara Fredrickson (2010; Cohn & Fredrickson, 2009), who developed the broaden-and-build model of positive emotions (see chapter 2), recommended several ways in which positive emotions might be fostered. She (2008, 2009) listed helpful strategies for increasing positive emotionality in life, many of these are covered in more detail in later chapters. These strategies include: be more open and increase awareness in order to appreciate the sensory experiences of life, be sociable, cultivate kindness, cultivate healthy distractions to take your mind off your troubles, dispute negative thinking, find nearby nature or natural settings (see also Burns, 2009), apply your strengths and virtues, use mindfulness meditation, do good or help others, practice gratitude, savor or relish positive feelings, visualize your future, and imagine you have reached your own best potential. She also advised relaxation strategies such as meditation; positive imagery; massage; and muscle relaxation (Fredrickson, 2000). A unique style of meditation called *loving kindness* is especially helpful (Fredrickson, Cohn et al., 2008; see chapter 10). Fredrickson (2009) also suggested people keep a daily diary of positive events—that is, to record the good things they experienced daily. Many of Fredrickson's suggestions advised people to stop ruminating about issues and instead to focus attention on sensory sensations, activities, or helping other people. Other suggestions asked people to notice the things in life that are positive, including little events that bring joy.

Hope Training

Hope training is based on the premise that hope drives the emotions that define well-being (Lopez, Floyd, Ulven, & Synder, 2000). It is derived from *hope theory*, which posits that well-being is enhanced when people have well-developed goals and believe they have the capacities and resources to reach them. (Rand & Cheavens, 2009; see chapter 2). Therefore, hope therapy helps people conceptualize clearer goals, conceive numerous paths to them, and summon the energy and commitment to reach them. In addition, one's goals should be personally meaningful.

Hope training alerts people to a few common pitfalls in behavior-change strategies. First, people need to set goals that are specific, measurable, and achievable. Note that you have *not* met these criteria if your stated goal is "to be happy." Rather, you should consider what happiness means to you. Do you wish to be more content; feel more pleasant emotions; be more fully engaged in life; or give more love to those you care about? You should also have some notion of how much happier you wish to be and consider what your "good-enough" level of happiness will be. Hope training helps us to focus on more concrete and immediate goals that lead to greater happiness (for example, to express gratitude to someone you love).

Hope training can also prevent people from falling victim to the *false hope syndrome* (Polivy, 2000). This occurs when people believe that behavior change is easy and that results will be obvious in a short period of time. Such overconfidence can breed false hope, which when unrealistic expectations are not quickly fulfilled will eventually undermine one's efforts to change.

Comparing Interventions: Which Ones Work Better?

Seligman, Steen, Park, and Peterson (2005) completed an interesting study that tracked people's behavior for six months and compared the effectiveness of five different positive psychology interventions designed to increase subjective well-being. Two of the five exercises had a lasting impact on well-being. The first asked people to "write down three good things that went well each day and their causes every night for a week" (p. 416). The second exercise asked people to complete the VIA Survey of Character (see chapter 2) and to use one of their signature strengths "in a new and different way every day for a week" (p. 416). Both exercises increased happiness and deceased symptoms of depression for six months. Another in this group was a gratitude exercise that asked people to write and deliver a letter of gratitude to "someone who had been especially kind to [you] but had never been properly thanked" (p. 416). This exercise substantially increased happiness for about one month, but the impact tapered off over the six months. However, the study showed that changes in activities for only one week could have a significant effect on subjective well-being.

Richard Wiseman created the "Science of Happiness Project" in Britain to evaluate the effectiveness of four happiness interventions (see Scott, 2009). Around 2,000 people participated by practicing one of four happiness interventions: (1) express gratitude; (2) smile more; (3) recall a pleasant event that happened the previous day; or (4) perform an act of kindness. Wiseman found that all four interventions increased happiness, but the greatest increase occurred among those who recalled a pleasant event from the previous day. He concluded that the greatest increase in happiness comes from simply reliving happy memories.

Sheldon and Lyubomirsky (2006) compared two interventions. The first was the gratitude exercise mentioned earlier. The second asked people to write about their "best possible selves" or to imagine what life would be like in the future when "everything has gone as well as it possibly could" and you have "succeeded at accomplishing all your life goals [and] the realization of your life dreams." They found that both activities decreased negative mood. Even the control condition that asked people to "pay greater attention to the daily details of your life" decreased mood. The best possible selves' intervention produced the largest immediate increase in well-being, followed by the gratitude exercise. In addition, the best possible selves exercise produced the greatest motivation to continue. Finally, the fit between a particular exercise and a participant's personality was important for motivation and hence for the exercise's success.

Maintaining Happiness

The interventions mentioned above are a small subset of effective ways to increase subjective well-being. The trick is, of course, to maintain a greater sense of well-being over time through the ups-and-downs of life. In her book *The How of Happiness*, Lyubomirsky (2007) recommended 12 intentional happiness activities that have proven effective in fostering greater happiness. Many of the interventions mentioned above are on her list, along with cultivating optimism; nurturing relationships; pursuing goals that fit one's personality; and taking care of one's physical and spiritual life. She also described five strategies, or how-to's of sustainable happiness, to foster a greater feeling of well-being.

The first was to cultivate positive emotion on a consistent basis. She noted that it is the small, pleasant experiences that happen everyday that can have the largest impact on happiness. Her second how-to was to vary the timing and variety of activities. By so doing, one avoids falling into a rut and ensures that favorite activities provide an ongoing stream of fresh positive experiences (see also Sheldon & Lyubomirsky, 2007). Her third how-to was to cultivate and nurture social support for one's efforts at change. Fourth, Lyubomirsky advised people to resolutely commit to activities and practice the exercises diligently. Her last how-to was to turn one's new approach to happiness into a habit through repetition and practice.

General Comments on Increasing Happiness

Research has shown that it is possible to increase scores on measures of happiness and life satisfaction through psychological and physiological interventions. One caveat is that evidence on the heritability of positive affect suggests that it is not possible for everyone to be cheerful, jovial, and optimistic most of the time. Interesting findings from a study indicated that college students had difficulty distinguishing among pleasure, happiness, and contentment (Evans et al., 2008). That is, some people who diligently pursue happiness might really like more contentment.

In a similar way, another study found that feeling relaxed, energized and activated, and safe/content all impacted well-being, but feeling safe/content resulted in the greatest reduction in depression, anxiety, stress, and self-criticism (Gilbert et al., 2008). This study also suggested that feeling energized, relaxed, and safe/content represent three basic dimensions of positive emotionality. Last, it could be that all the constructs we use to assess our well-being are simply aspects of a more general orientation to life. The construct of *love of life* refers to generally positive feelings toward one's own life. It combines positive attitudes toward life, perception of positive outcomes, and possession of a sense of meaningfulness (Abdel-Khalek, 2007).

Nostalgia Our emotions are also difficult to categorize as simply *positive* or *negative*. A good example of how a blend of positive and negative emotions can be psychologically beneficial comes from *nostalgia*. The word derives from ancient Greek, combining *nostos* (to return home or to one's native land) and *algos* (referring to pain, suffering, or grief). The term was first formulated in 1688 by a Swiss physician named Johanes Hofer, who discussed the phenomenon in his medical dissertation. He used *nostalgia* to describe the extreme emotional condition of Swiss soldiers stationed far from home, whose symptoms included sadness; diminished senses; and physical weakness. For several centuries thereafter, nostalgia carried a medical and essentially pathological connotation associated with homesickness. But in the 1950s, popular American usage demedicalized and depathologized it as well. In a seminal study involving American college students, sociologist Fred Davis (1979, p. 18) redefined nostalgia as a "positively toned evocation of a lived past" and asserted (1979, p. 4) that it "allows human beings to maintain their identity in the face of major transitions … in the life cycle [such as] from childhood to pubescence, from adolescence to adulthood, from single to married life, from spouse to parent."

Subsequent psychological research (Batcho, 1995; Holak & Havlena, 1992, 1998) characterized nostalgia as both intense and complex, comprising mainly positive emotions like warmth, joy, gratitude, and affection yet also including negative emotions such as sadness, longing, and wishfulness. For this reason, investigators (see especially Havlena & Holak, 1991) have described nostalgia as "bittersweet," typically combining a pleasant memory of the past with a sense of loss from recognizing that the past is gone. Research also indicates that men and women experience nostalgia differently due to their different socialization experiences (Csikzentmilhalyi & Rochberg-Halton, 1981) and that some people have a greater disposition for nostalgia than others (Holbrook, 1993; Zimmer, Little, & Griffiths, 1999).

In a series of studies, Zhou, Sedikides, Wilschut, and Ding-Guo (2008) found that nostalgia relieved individuals' feelings of loneliness and increased their perceived social support. The restorative function of nostalgia was particularly salient among those with high resilience. The investigators concluded that nostalgia is a psychological resource that fosters mental health by strengthening one's sense of social connectedness and belongingness. In other words, nostalgic memories from our childhood or adolescence—such as involving family trips and birthday parties—amplify our sense that we are loved by others, even though we cannot physically relive those bygone joyful moments.

Depression as an Opportunity? It is also true that sadness and depression can at times be helpful emotions. In a recent paper titled "The Bright Side of Being Blue," Andrews and Thomson (2009) presented their analytical rumination hypothesis, which proposes that feeling depressed and sad can have positive consequences. The idea is that when we are depressed, we can take time to reflect and analyze the complex problems that might have prompted the depression (Andrews & Thomson, 2009). Of course, this valuation might not apply to cases of severe depression. Negative emotions can also prompt creative ways to deal with difficult feeling. A clever insight led to the creation of the "complaints choirs," which allow people to sing about what irritates them.[5] People in the choirs can sing about something as personal as a noisy neighbor, which they get to sing about in large groups! One person explained, "When everyone is singing your complaint, it's very cathartic. It's as if you have a lot of support for your complaint" (see Tarm, 2007).

Finally, it should be remembered that other perspectives on well-being and the good life do not focus exclusively on conventional ideas about happiness. The happiness of a new mother or father is very different from that of a gold medal-winning athlete—and different from that of a Buddhist monk. The relationships among emotions and sense of well-being are complex—like life itself—and the psychological models used to explain them have just begun to explore the intricacy involved in an apparently simple judgment that "life is good."

SUMMARY

This chapter presented research on subjective well-being, which studies happiness and life satisfaction. Investigations in Western countries show that people generally report above-average levels of happiness, and yet the desire to be happier seems universal. Researchers have found several variables that are predictors of subjective well-being, including high self-esteem; positive relationships; optimism; a sense of control; extraversion; and a sense of meaning and purpose in life. Although earning more income is related to higher well-being, the relationship between these two factors is complex and nonlinear. In general, gender, age, race, and geographic climate account for small portions of subjective well-being. We discussed several other factors that impact subjective well-being, such as adaptation, cognition, and social comparison. Finally, a few interventions to increase happiness were highlighted.

NOTES

1. Neuroticism is a fairly general term that refers to chronic problems of anxiety; worry; mild depression; and low self-esteem. It is an older term that is still used for research purposes in psychology but is no longer applied as a diagnostic label. David Watson and Lee Anna Clark (1984) have proposed a more general trait, *negative affectivity*, that combines trait anxiety; neuroticism; general maladjustment; and other tendencies to experience distress and discomfort across many situations.

2. http://www.mtv.com/thinkmtv/research/.
3. "Happiness trends in 24 countries, 1946–2006, Ingehart, Welzel, & Foa (www.worldvaluesurvey.org).
4. http://www.egodevelopment.com/extreme-happiness-can-damage-your-health/.
5. The web site for complaints choirs worldwide is http://www.complaintschoir.org/.

LEARNING TOOLS

Key Terms

bottom-up theory	learned optimism	hedonic treadmill
top-down theory	social comparison processes	sustainable happiness model

Books

Diener, E., & Baswas-Diener, R. (2008). *Happiness: Unlocking the mysteries of psychological wealth.* Wiley-Blackwell.

Frisch, M. (2006). *Quality of life therapy: Applying a life satisfaction approach to positive psychology and cognitive therapy.* Hoboken, NJ: John Wiley & Sons. A workbook on how to increase life satisfaction based on the CASIO method discussed in chapter 2.

Harris, R. (2008). *The happiness trap: How to stop struggling and start living.* Trumpeter. A different approach to well-being based on acceptance, mindful awareness, and being engaged in life.

Lyubomirsky, S. (2008). *The how of happiness: A scientific approach to getting the life you want.* New York: Penguin Press. Practical steps on how to increase your happiness by a leading researcher in the field.

Tal Ben-Shahar (2007). *Happier: Learn the secrets to daily joy and lasting fulfillment.* NY: McGraw-Hill. A how-to book by the man who teaches the most popular course at Harvard University—a course on happiness.

On the Web

http://www.well-beingindex.com/ Gallup-Healthways Well-Being Index. Multiple survey results on well-being in the U.S. and U.K.

http://internal.psychology.illinois.edu/~ediener/ The home page of Dr. Ed Diener (affectionately known as "the Jedi master of happiness"), one of the most respected and prolific researchers on subjective well-being.

http://www.ocf.berkeley.edu/~wrader/pleasures.html A big list of simple pleasures.

http://zenhabits.net/75-simple-pleasures-to-brighten-your-day/ More simple pleasures and other suggestions for well-being.

http://www.eur.nl/fsw/research/happiness The World Data Base of Happiness. Numerous resources on happiness around the world.

Personal Explorations

1. Think of the happiest person you know in your own life, such as a family member or relative, friend or neighbor, teacher or member of the clergy. Interview this person in depth and see if you can identify the various factors that contribute to his or her happiness. It might be useful to ask such questions as: (a) Were you always such a happy person? If not, what helped you to become happier? (b) Does anything affect your happiness on a day-to-day basis? If so, what? (c) Do you ever find yourself in a bad mood? If so, are there ways you've learned to put yourself back in a pleasant mood? (d) Do you have any advice for others who would like to become as happy as you are? If so, what tips or suggestions can you offer?

2. Imagine that you have found the famous "Aladdin's Lamp" whose genie has granted you three wishes. What would you wish for? (Sorry, you can't wish for more wishes.) (a) What do your answers tell you about your idea of happiness or the good life? (b) Are your answers based on any specific assumptions about human nature or of relationships between people and the societies they live in? What are those assumptions?

Chapter 4

Leisure, Flow, Mindfulness and Peak Performance

> Miracles … seem to me to rest … upon our perceptions being made finer, so that
> for a moment our eyes can see and our ears can hear what is there
> about us always.
> WILLA CATHER, AMERICAN AUTHOR

LEISURE

Certainly any exploration of personal well-being must focus on leisure, which refers to how we spend our spare time, what we do to relax, the activities in which we engage to have fun, and how we express our passions and interests. A comprehensive list of activities that fall under the category of leisure would be endless. People are remarkably creative in finding ways to amuse themselves. The emotions associated with leisure activities also span the entire range of human experience. Some people prefer active adventure sports that contain an element of danger or risk, such as mountain biking or kayaking. Others are happier with more traditional sports, such as basketball or soccer that are partially driven by a sense of competition with others. Still others are drawn to quieter activities that foster contemplation and relaxation, such as sailing, walking in the woods, or needlework.

Although it may seem obvious to associate leisure with well-being, is there any evidence for a relationship between the two variables? Indeed, there is considerable research now on how leisure relates to life satisfaction and well-being.

Leisure and Well-Being

In a Time Warner/CNN poll (1991), about 70% of people said they would like to slow down and live a more relaxed life. They especially wished for more time with their families. Another survey found that 88% of Americans said that working too many hours results in not having enough time with family and friends (www.newdream.org). The term **time affluence** refers to a perception that one has enough time for leisure and activities that are personally meaningful. In contrast, *time poverty* refers to a feeling of being constantly busy and pressed for time. As you might expect, Tim Kasser and

Kennon Sheldon (2009) found that subjective well-being is associated with time affluence across all income levels. That is, having more time is more important than having more money.

An earlier empirical study of subjective well-being, conducted by Campbell, Converse, and Rogers (1976), found that satisfaction with leisure—defined as "life outside work"—was one of the variables that showed up as a strong predictor of global well-being. Ruut Veenhoven and his colleagues reviewed a substantial number of studies on well-being and found that happiness was significantly correlated with satisfaction with leisure (see Argyle, 1999). In one study, satisfaction with leisure was also found to be the most important predictor of satisfaction with community life (Allen & Brattie, 1984).

It might be assumed that vacations would give a big boost to happiness because they provide a constant opportunity for leisure. One study indeed found that when people are about to go on vacation, they tend to feel happier. However, only people who experienced a very relaxing vacation continued to feel happier after they returned from vacation (Nawijn, Marchand, Veenhoven, & Vingerhoets, 2010). Other studies have found a memory bias for vacations such that many people recall their vacations as being happier than they actually felt at the time (Wirtz, Kruger, Scollon, & Diener, 2003). This evidence raises the fascinating question: Do we really know what makes us happy, or is happiness more of a retrospective phenomenon, as Maslow (1996) hypothesized?

The impact of leisure on satisfaction begins during adolescence. It has been found that, contrary to expectations, high school students who receive higher grades and tend to excel scholastically are also involved in more activities outside of class (Erickson & Compton, 1982). In a longitudinal study, Glancy, Willits, and Farrell (1986) followed 1,521 high school children for 24 years and found that participation in leisure activities in high school predicted higher life satisfaction during adulthood. At the other end of the life cycle,

studies have shown that successful aging is correlated with regular participation in activities. In fact, participation in leisure activities may be the most important contributor to life satisfaction among older adults (Heo, Lee, McCormick, & Pedersen, 2010; Kelly & Ross, 1989). Finally, at least one form of leisure has been reliably associated with changes in mood. Studies on exercise have found that increases in aerobic exercise can decrease the symptoms of depression and anxiety as well as increase levels of happiness (Alfermann & Stoll, 2000; Stubbe, de Moor, Boomsma, de Geus, 2007). In summary, over the years researchers have consistently found a positive relationship between our satisfaction with leisure and our well-being.

Although it is fairly clear that leisure helps people feel better about their lives, it is also true that simply having leisure time does not automatically increase our well-being. For instance, higher scores on life satisfaction are associated with participation in a greater variety of leisure activities and participation in more active types of leisure than are lower scores (Pressman, Matthews, Cohen, Martire, Scheier et al., 2009). Examining this link from the opposite vantage point, one study found that happier people participate in more active forms of leisure than less happy people (Robinson & Martin, 2008). This same study also found that happy people watch up to 30% less TV than unhappy people. However, an interesting paradox attaches to this finding because people generally report that they enjoy watching TV. The researchers suggest that watching TV might provide people with short-run pleasure but at a cost of long-term dissatisfaction. Another study found that life satisfaction among older persons was strongly related to having personally meaningful activities (Ogilivie, 1987). Therefore, it appears that we must be involved in endeavors that we personally enjoy or that are meaningful to us in some way.

Another study found, as expected, that non-work activities on the weekend were associated with greater indices of well-being (Ryan, Bernstein, Warren Brown, 2010). However, leisure activities in which people gain new life experiences may also be more rewarding than investing time in material purchases (Van Boven & Gilovich, 2003). For instance, it feels better to spend money on learning to play guitar than buying another TV. In addition, as predicted by self-determination theory, increases in well-being are often due to meeting needs for autonomy, relationships, and competence. So what is the key? To be actively involved, it seems, in an activity that we connect with on an emotional level or that fulfills basic needs. Somewhat poetically, Pieper expressed this perspective by saying, "Leisure, it must be understood, is a mental and spiritual attitude—it is not simply the result of external factors, it is not the inevitable result of spare time, a holiday, a week-end or a vacation … [it is] a condition of the soul" (Pieper, 1963, p. 40; quoted in Neulinger, 1974).

What Turns an Activity into "Leisure"?

Since it seems well-established that leisure is important to the life satisfaction of many people, it may be obvious to ask, "Why do people engage in leisure at all?" Although the easy answer might be, "To have fun," the real answer is more complex than a simple pursuit of pleasure. Some types of leisure provide merely relief from stress (which is necessary), while others provide revitalization and renewal. In a study with British people, the highest-ranking reasons for engaging in leisure were that leisure (1) fulfilled needs for autonomy; (2) allowed enjoyment of family life; (3) provided for relaxation; and (4) offered an escape from routine (Kabanoff, 1982; cited in Argyle, 1987). The study reminds us that for many people leisure activities are those that allow autonomously-motivated behaviors. Related to this is an ability to simply make a choice about how to spend time. Boredom, after all, is not necessarily a state of having nothing to do, but rather a state of not being able to choose what to do.

The association of leisure with autonomy suggests that leisure is related not only to quietude and relaxation but also to challenge and skill. Indeed, people like to challenge themselves to develop and acquire skills, talents, and abilities, and to gain knowledge as a way to grow and expand potential.

One recent study found evidence for a "leisure personality style" associated with higher satisfaction with leisure. The personality style consisted of high scores on extraversion, conscientiousness, and openness to experiences along with low neuroticism (Kovacs, 2007).

Another association with leisure is that of play. Although an association between children's play and healthy development has been established (see McMahon, Lytle, & Sutton-Smith, 2005), imaginative play in which children engage in "make believe" may provide even more benefits (Spiegel, 2008). There is also some recent interest in adult play, or the value of **adult playfulness**. Stuart Brown, founder of the National Institute of Play, argued that adults need to play in order to develop emotionally, socially, and creatively (Brown & Vaughn, 2009). One study found that adult playfulness was positively correlated with being more extraverted, more open to experience, and more agreeable, while negative correlations were found with neurosis, aging, and maleness (Mixter, 2009). (Pay attention, men!) The similarity of playfulness to the "leisure personality style" mentioned above is quite striking.

Among the most powerful reasons for leisure activities is a chance to be with other people. Although many activities are performed because they involve solitude (for example, a walk in the woods), countless others are fun precisely because we do them with other people. In fact, Crandall, Nolan, and Morgan (1980) found that satisfaction with the social component of leisure is the best predictor of overall leisure satisfaction. For example, in the Hollywood musicals of the 1930s and 1940s, many people enjoyed watching Fred Astaire dance his solo numbers. But when he danced with Ginger Rogers, the interactions between the two created magic on the screen that allowed the audiences to feel what it is like to be in love.

The relationship between activities that are personally meaningful and leisure satisfaction is also found in the creation of what Argyle (1987) called *leisure worlds*. One often hears phrases like the "world of ballroom dancing" or the "world of tennis." These phrases refer to the somewhat esoteric knowledge one must acquire to understand the intricacies of the activity. These include the nuances of vocabulary, the types of specialized knowledge, and the hidden meanings that all combine to make certain activities uniquely special to those who understand their intricacies. An example familiar to many people is the unique "world of *Star Trek*" with its specialized conventions and costumes taken from the TV shows and movies. Some people in this "world" even choose to learn the Klingon language. For those not familiar with the phenomenon, the Klingon language was created entirely for an imaginary race of aliens who are characters on *Star Trek*. One adventuresome student at the University of California at Berkeley even tried to meet his foreign language requirement by learning Klingon! It didn't work, but it was an interesting idea.

In summary, leisure activities appear to be important to a sense of well-being and life satisfaction. Activities that provide this sense of well-being should be meaningful to the person involved; provide a sense of autonomy; build competence; serve as a break from routine; and frequently involve positive relationships with other people. However, so far our discussion has not addressed what a *fun* activity feels like to one engaged in it. Our next perspective on well-being begins by exploring what fun feels like.

FLOW AND OPTIMAL EXPERIENCE

Mihalyi Csikszentmihalyi (pronounced ME-hi Chick-SENT-me-hi) began his studies of psychological well-being by asking people to describe in their own words what it felt like when they were doing something really enjoyable and the activity was going extraordinarily well for them (Csikszentmihalyi, 1975). He was interested in finding out what it felt like to experience intense enjoyment, fun, play, and also creativity. In his initial study,

Courtesy of Mihalyi Csikszentmihalyi

Mihalyi Csikszentmihalyi

Csikszentmihalyi interviewed over 200 people who were deeply involved in activities that required considerable amounts of time and for which they received little or no money or recognition. What he got from his interviewees were wonderfully rich and compelling descriptions of moments of wonder and magic, when everything was working just right and everything just happened effortlessly.

During the interviews, chess masters and basketball players related what it felt like to be totally engaged in a game; dancers spoke about those moments when they were dancing at their best; composers spoke of what it was like when the muse was working and music just seemed to happen by itself; rock climbers went into vivid detail about the moment-to-moment experience of climbing as one's skill was pitted against the possibility of failure. Csikszentmihalyi performed a *phenomenological analysis* of the described experiences. That is, he examined the verbalizations of experience for common themes. These common themes appeared to describe a fairly recognizable state of consciousness. His initial name for the experience was the *autotelic experience*, but he later settled on the simpler term *flow*.

Definition of Flow

After the interviews and his content analysis of the responses, Csikszentmihalyi defined the **flow** experience (1975, p. 43):

> Flow denotes the holistic sensation present when we act with total involvement ... It is the state in which action follows upon action according to an internal logic which seems to need no conscious intervention on our part. We experience it as a unified flowing from one moment to the next, in which we feel in control of our actions, and in which there is little distinction between self and environment; between stimulus and response; or between past, present, and future.

Readers who are sports fans may recognize the experience that Csikszentmihalyi is describing. In the past few years it has become commonplace to refer to these experiences in sports as being *in the zone* (Cooper, 1998; Kimiecik & Stein, 1992).

Csikszentmihalyi's theory of flow has been very popular, both in psychology as well as reported in the mainstream media. This is probably because the experience of being in flow is fairly common, so that many people instantly recognize just what Csikszentmihalyi is talking about. For example, he (1997) wrote of surveys that ask people, "Do you ever get involved in something so deeply that nothing else seems to matter, and you lose track of time?" (p. 33). American and European samples have found that about 20 percent of people report having these flowlike experiences often, sometimes several times a day. Only about 15 percent of people say that they never have that experience. Of course, the percentage of people who have had very intense flow experiences is much smaller. For those who have had the flow experience, either intensely or mildly, they immediately appreciate the link between flow and psychological well-being.

Characteristics of Flow

What exactly is the flow experience like? Csikszentmihalyi has said that the state of flow can be described with eight parameters (see also Nakamura & Csikszentmihalyi, 2009):

1. A Merging of Action and Awareness   People who experience flow are involved in an activity to the point that they feel "inside" the activity. They do not have to think about what they are doing before they do it. There is no sense of being an observer who is watching and evaluating the activity. In fact, this type of divided consciousness or "outside" perspective destroys the flow experience. For instance, an expert rock climber told Csikszentmihalyi (1975) what it was like when he was on a climb: "You are so involved in what you are doing, you aren't thinking of

yourself as separate from the immediate activity … you don't see yourself as separate from what you are doing."[1]

2. Complete Concentration on the Task at Hand
The merging of action and awareness is made possible by complete concentration and a centering of attention on the activity of the moment. This concentration appears effortless, however, and is not associated with mental strain or aggressive efforts to control or repress thinking. A composer described it as, "I am really quite oblivious to my surroundings after I really get going [that is, composing]. I think the phone could ring … or the house could burn down … when I start working I really do shut out the world."

3. Lack of Worry about Losing Control, which Paradoxically Results in a Sense of Control
The loss of worry apparently allows people to maintain concentration and focus on the task. This focus allows them to feel as if they are in complete control of their actions. Often they feel more in control than they have ever been. A dancer expressed it as follows:

> If I have enough space, I am in control.
> I feel I can radiate an energy into the
> atmosphere…. It's not always necessary
> that another human being be there to
> catch that energy. I can dance for the walls,
> I can dance for the floors … I become one
> with the atmosphere.

4. A Loss of Self-consciousness   Once again, this criterion appears to reinforce the merging of awareness and action as well as the focused concentration. During flow, that part of consciousness that evaluates and plans before acting—the ego—is quieted. We don't have to think before we act; we are not trapped in an internal conflict between various options. A music composer described what it felt like when he was writing at his best:

> You yourself are in an ecstatic state to such
> a point that you feel as though you almost

don't exist … My hand seems devoid of myself, and I have nothing to do with what is happening. I just sit there watching it in a state of awe and wonderment. And it just flows out by itself.

As Csikszentmihalyi & Csikszentmihalyi (1988) have stated, "In flow the self is fully functioning, but not aware of itself doing it … At the most challenging levels, people actually report experiencing a *transcendence* of self" (original italics, p. 33).

5. Time No Longer Seems to Pass in Ordinary Ways   Time may seem to pass more quickly than usual, or it may appear to be vastly slowed down. This element of flow can be very dramatic and may be one of the more distinctive reasons for describing flow as an alternate state of consciousness. For instance, people have described this feeling while playing sports. Often they say that all of a sudden it seems as if they have all the time in the world to shoot a basket, throw a pass, or position the racket for their next shot. For many, time seems to slow down as they feel a sense of relaxation, a lack of worry, and extreme confidence that their next move will be perfect. A chess master said, "Time passes a hundred times faster. In a sense, it resembles the dream state. A whole story can unfold in seconds, it seems."

6. Autotelic Nature of the Experience   This term refers to the fact that the experience is done for its own sake rather than as a means to another goal. A rock climber said:

> The mystique of rock climbing is climbing; you get to the top of the rock glad it's over but really wish it would go forever. The justification of climbing is climbing … you don't conquer anything except things in yourself … The purpose of the flow is to keep on flowing, not looking for a peak or utopia but staying in the flow … There is no possible reason for climbing except the climbing itself; it is a self-communication.

Csikszentmihalyi (1990) noted that there may even be an autotelic personality style. This personality style is associated with a person who consistently does things for their own sake, with involvement and enthusiasm, rather than in response to external threats or rewards. Such individuals are characterized by autonomy and independence. According to Csikszentmihalyi (1997), the major characteristic that defines autotelic individuals is that "their psychic energy seems inexhaustible" (p. 123). In addition, he suggested that autotelic persons are less self-centered and generally less concerned with themselves, tending to be "free of personal goals and ambitions" (p. 125).

7. Flow Accompanies a Challenging Activity that Requires Skill   Csikszentmihalyi believes that when the personal challenge of an activity pushes one's skill level so that intense focused concentration is required, then conditions are right for flow. If the demands are high and skills are low, then a person will feel anxiety. If the demands are low and skills are high, a person will feel bored. It is only when the demands of a situation present a challenge to a person's skills that a feeling of flow is possible.

8. An Activity has Clear Goals and Immediate Feedback   Once again, this describes the parameters of flow. The following quote from professional tennis player Billie Jean King illustrates this quality:

> On one of those days everything is just right … my concentration is so perfect that it almost seems as though I'm able to transport myself beyond the turmoil on the court to some place of total peace and calm. I've got perfect control of the match, my rhythm and movements are excellent, and everything's in total balance … It's a perfect combination of aggressive action taking place in an atmosphere of total tranquility … just totally peaceful.

An activity during flow must have clear goals and immediate feedback so that a person doesn't have to wonder about how well he or she is performing.

Csikszentmihalyi contended that these eight qualities capture the essence of the flow experience. Not all are necessarily present in every such experience, but in very intense flow experiences most of them should be present. Note that the first six characteristics describe what flow *feels like* as one experiences it. They were abstracted from the phenomenological descriptions given to Csikszentmihalyi. The last two characteristics, however, describe the *conditions under which* flow experiences tend to occur. These two are not necessarily descriptions of internal experience. Instead they relate to the fit between a person's level of learned competencies or skills and the demands or challenges of the current situation. The distinction between level of challenge and level of skill is often used to describe the optimal environment for inducing flow. In the model seen in Figure 4.1, an optimal activity for flow balances a high challenge with a person's high skill level.

This balance has been referred to as *just manageable challenges* (Nakamura & Csikszentmihalyi, 2002). In order to continually experience flow in an activity, it is assumed that a person must continue to engage in progressively more complex challenges and keep pushing his or her own skill levels (Nakamura & Csikszentmihalyi, 2009).

Contexts and Situations of Flow

The range of contexts in which people report flow is quite fascinating (Nakamura & Csikszentmihalyi, 2009). Csikszentmihalyi's original study included people who were actively involved in creative artistic pursuits, hobbies, and sports. In addition to the contexts listed thus far, people report flow when participating in activities such as religious rituals (Han, 1988); using computers (Ghani & Deshpande, 1994); teaching in the classroom (Beard, Stansbury, & Wayne, 2010); driving a car (Csikszentmihalyi, 1997); interacting with one's family (Rathunde, 1988); undergoing solitary retreats (Logan, 1985); participating in psychotherapy sessions (Grafanaki, Brennan, Holmes, Tang, & Alvarez, 2007); experiencing online learning (Shin, 2006); cramming for exams (Brinthaupt & Shin, 2001); and even engaging in military combat (Harari, 2008). Of course, almost any sports activity can create a context for flow, or being in the zone (Stavrou, Jackson, Zervas, & Karterolitis, 2007).

Today, because many people report they experience flow during work (Fullagar & Kelloway, 2009), a new construct called *work engagement* has been developed to capture this blend of vigor, dedication, and absorption. Csikszentmihalyi (1990) speculated that flow experiences may be the key to job satisfaction. One of the most frequently mentioned contexts for flow is when reading for pleasure (McQuillan & Conde, 1996). Social activities may also be more enjoyable if all members of the group experience flow. One study found that *social flow* was more enjoyable than solitary flow (Walker, 2010). Indeed, in team sports it is possible for an entire team to experience flow during a game (Cosma, 1999), a phenomenon called *cohesion* (Sugarman, 1998). Similarly, musicians, dancers, and actors often report group flow experiences during performances. Csikszentmihalyi also refers to the experience of **microflow**. This refers to moments

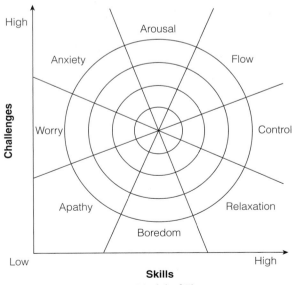

F I G U R E 4.1 Current Model of Flow

SOURCE: From M. Csikszentmihalyi, *Finding Flow: The Psychology of Engagement with Everyday Life.* Copyright © 1997 Mihaly Csikszentmihalyi. Reprinted by permission of Basic Books, a member of Perseus Books, L.L.C.

when we are leisurely involved in a relatively simple, almost automatic activity, such as doodling.

Since children seem able to enter flow states spontaneously and frequently, the ability to experience flow might be innate. It may be that we don't need to learn how to flow, but we can be taught how to repress flow. Csikszentmihalyi and his wife Isabella asserted that the flow experience is a universally human one found in all cultures of the world (Csikszentmihalyi & Csikszentmihalyi, 1988). In fact, studies have found that descriptions of flow are remarkably similar in various countries around the globe (Asakawa, 2004; Fave & Massimini, 2004).

However, interesting variations have emerged. For instance, Japanese tend to report flow during activities of high challenge and high skill, while Chinese report it during activities of low challenge and high skill (Moneta, 2004). In general, Csikszentmihalyi (1990) has argued that flow is the experience that allows people to enjoy life, feel happier, and function better in several different contexts.

Unique Qualities of Flow

The uniqueness of this theory comes from its association of happiness and well-being with a remarkable experience that involves altered perceptions of self, time, and ability. It should be obvious by now that when Csikszentmihalyi describes very intense experiences of flow, he is describing a state of consciousness that is qualitatively different from normal consciousness. As such, his theory of flow—at least of flow in its more intense forms—is one of the few psychological perspectives that associates higher well-being with an alternate state of consciousness.

There is also evidence that the experience of flow has a physiological counterpart. Daniel Landers and colleagues (Landers et al., 1994) measured the brain wave activity of athletes (namely, of archers, marksmen, and golfers) just seconds before they performed. The researchers found that being in the zone coincided with less activity in the left hemisphere, which is associated with analytical and intellectual thought, and greater activity in the right hemisphere, which is associated with verbal

and spatial ability. (At least this was true for right-handed people.) The experience of intrinsic enjoyment and flow is also associated with specific patterns of evoked potential in brain waves (Vaiti et al., 2005; Hamilton, Haier, & Buchsbaum, 1983). The ability to selectively attend to stimuli that is found in flow is associated with different states of awareness or consciousness. The ability to voluntarily switch attention among various stimuli is called *attentional switching*. Greater skill at attentional switching has been associated with higher psychological well-being (Peters, Wissing, & Steyn, 2006).

Galway (1975) proposed four stages a person might go through as he or she moves from micro-flow to a very intense flow experience. The first stage is *paying attention* or simply focusing attention on physiological processes. The second stage is *interested attention*. This state of mild flow is a result of persistently maintaining focus on an activity while continually bringing attention back to the present. In this stage, one doesn't have to concentrate hard on focusing attention and eliminating distractions but rather is able to stay with an activity and enjoy it. The third stage is *absorbed attention*. At this point, a person is so absorbed in activity that it is almost impossible for attention to wander or to be distracted by extraneous stimuli. This stage is often accompanied by altered perceptions of time and space. The fourth stage is *merging*, in which a person is no longer aware of a separation between self and activity. A transcendent experience, such as being in the zone, defines this stage (see Edlin & Golanty, pp. 114–115).

Flow and Subjective Well-Being

Any discussion of the relationship between flow and well-being must acknowledge the potential for circular reasoning that comes with this territory. That is, since Csikszentmihalyi originally asked people to describe moments when activities were going extremely well, the theory of flow was constructed by asking people about moments of well-being. So one answer to the question of whether flow is associated with well-being must be yes, insofar as feelings of well-being were the starting point of the initial interviews. The real question, therefore, is whether experiencing more frequent flow in the present really increases our sense of happiness or life satisfaction later when the feeling of flow is over.

One answer to this question comes from research on leisure. Since flow is a significant component of many pleasurable leisure activities, flowlike experiences seem to be related to leisure and satisfaction. As noted earlier in this chapter, research has supported the positive relationship between leisure activities and subjective well-being. It is also obvious that flow is a significant aspect of intrinsically motivated activities, in that people return again and again to activities that allow them to experience flow even when they receive no recognition or money to do so.

After almost 40 years of research, many studies have found relationships between being in flow and aspects of well-being (Nakamura & Csikszent-mihalyi, 2009). For example, Lefevre (1988) found that the more time people spent in flow, the greater was their quality of experience during the day. Higher quality of experience included greater concentration, creativity, and more positive emotionality. Interestingly, life satisfaction was not higher; people simply reported a higher quality of experience. Wells (1988) studied the relationship between self-esteem and flow in working mothers and found that flow was significantly correlated with feeling better about oneself as a parent. That is, if their interactions with their children were easy, comfortable, and tension free—if they flowed—then the women studied felt they were better mothers. However, their overall sense of self-esteem was not associated with flow experiences. Mothers could feel good about themselves with or without flow.

Another study found that adolescents felt more happy, cheerful, excited, and involved, as well as had a high self-concept when they perceived their family environment at home as autotelic (Rathunde, 1988). An autotelic family context is one that finds an optimum balance among choice, clarity, centering, commitment, and challenge.

Why does Flow Increase Well-being? In his analysis of why flow increases well-being, Csikszentmihalyi (1990) began with what he regarded as a "simple truth." That is, he suggested that the quality of our lives is determined by how well we are able to control our consciousness. The ability to exert a measure of control of consciousness leads to order and greater well-being compared to a lack of this ability, which leads to various states of dissatisfaction and disorder, or what he called "psychic entropy." Nevertheless, control is not some kind of mental muscle that rigidly squashes all unwelcome thoughts and emotions. Rather, control is a learned skill that involves balanced regulation of thoughts, emotions, behavior, and attention. One of the primary reasons that flow leads to well-being, therefore, is that it helps create order in consciousness. This order allows for the smooth functioning of consciousness.

Csikszentmihalyi (1990) stated, "When the information that keeps coming into awareness is congruent with goals, psychic energy flows effortlessly" (p. 39). That is, part of the flow experience is a lack of internal conflict between competing goals. The ability to control consciousness and increase the probability of optimal experiencing can also create an increase in a sense of mastery and participation in life, and an ability to determine the content of life on a moment-by-moment basis. In addition, an ability to control the contents of consciousness can give us an independence of the social environment, so that external circumstance need not determine our emotional or intellectual states.

After a flow experience a further ordering of consciousness occurs. Csikszentmihalyi (1990) theorized that because of a flow experience the organization of the self is more complex. In addition, the sense of self is more integrated after the flow experience as the various elements that make up the complex self work together more harmoniously. He (1997) also suggested that an ability to stay absorbed and interested in our daily experience is one of the key ingredients of a happy and fulfilling life. In his view, the "first step" to enjoying life more is to learn how to engineer daily activities in order to foster rewarding experiences. For example, musicians often have a favorite instrument that increases the likelihood of flow when they play it. Couples often use this strategy as a way to increase the flow that comes with special romantic evenings: They enjoy dinner by candlelight and listen to "their song." Women wear that special dress, men bring flowers—and if it works, the rest of the world fades away as the two people get lost in the flow of their romantic evening together.

This principle of engineering daily experiences was adopted in the Key School, an experimental elementary school that believed school could be enjoyable as well as rigorous (Whalen & Csikszentmihalyi, 1991). Part of the project was to create the *Flow Activities Room* where students could engage in intrinsically motivated free play that challenged their skills and focused concentration. The school was able to increase student well-being as well as attention to coursework by providing focused activities that were challenging, freely chosen, and allowed for skill development.

Flow is also experienced in what Mark Leary and Jennifer Guadagno (2011) described as a **hypoegoic** state, in which self-awareness is low and attention is focused on concrete rather than abstract stimuli. They argued that many positive emotional experiences occur during this state because self-talk is decreased along with its accompanying anxiety and distress. Along these same lines, flow is also a very task-focused activity rather than self-focused. Task-focused attention often leads to greater well-being (Robinson & Tamir, 2011).

Absorption and Curiosity

Research indicates there may be more to the flow experience than merely balancing skills and challenge. The descriptions above of the flow experience suggest several aspects that may be necessary for it to occur. What are these? The first is **absorption**, or the ability to become deeply involved in an experience. Auke Tellegen suggested that an ability to be wrapped up in an experience is a trait in which people vary in their ability

to accomplish at will (Tellegen & Atkinson, 1974). This trait impacts people's ability to enter flow. Recall that Csikzentmihalyi stated that "the autotelic personality" is a significant element of flow.

A study that examined fantasy found that higher well-being was associated with the ability to control fantasies, more "vividness" of fantasies, and greater absorption (Matsui & Kodama, 2004). An investigation of adolescents found that higher well-being, more prosocial behavior, and higher grade-point averages were associated with more **engaged living**, which comprises social integration and absorption (Froh, Kashdan, Yurkewicz, Fan, Allen et al., 2010). Engaged living involves a passion to help others and complete immersion in one's day-to-day activities. In contrast, one study found that people who were prone to adoring celebrities had lower well-being scores and their tendencies for absorption took on qualities of an addiction (Maltby, McCutcheon, Ashe, & Houran, 2001).

Another factor related to flow is curiosity. Todd Kashdan has conducted considerable work on **curiosity** and found that its increase is associated with greater well-being, more frequent personal growth-oriented behaviors, more search for meaning, and greater persistence of meaning from day-to-day (Kashdan, 2009; Kashdan & Steger, 2007; Silvia & Kashdan, 2009; see also Gallagher & Lopez, 2007). He described trait curiosity in two dimensions: *exploration,* or the disposition to seek out novel situations; and *absorption,* or the disposition to be fully engaged in situations.

McQuillan and Conde (1996) found that the probability of flow when reading depended on whether a person had an interest in a book's subject matter. In their study, fiction passages were more likely to enhance flow than were nonfiction passages, and therefore they suggest that fiction is more personally engaging. Webster, Trevino, and Ryan (1993) studied flow and playfulness when people used computers. The researchers found that flow was fostered by intrinsic interest in and curiosity about a task. Such investigations suggest that it is more difficult to experience flow when involved in a task in which one lacks interest.

Comments on the Theory of Flow

The concept of flow is one of those psychological constructs that is immediately recognizable to many people. Further, the association between flow and well-being is also quite obvious to many. However, not all studies have supported the predictions of the flow theory. Csikszentmihalyi reported that flow is produced by balancing one's skills with the challenge of a situation that requires those skills (Nakamura & Csikszentmihalyi, 2002). Certainly types of flow activities such as being in the zone during sports activities occur more often when a person is fully exercising learned skills and competencies in a context that provides high challenges and immediate feedback. However, it may be that the balance of challenge and skill required for flow is problematic for an understanding of flow, leisure, play, and relaxation. A few examples can help illustrate the problems.

One of the more frequently observed aspects of the flow experience is that it is not always present in a specific activity, or if it is present, then it may not be present throughout the duration of the activity. Just playing a thrilling game of tennis does not guarantee a flow experience. The challenge of the game may force moment-to-moment attention and bring a person to the very edge of his or her skill level, and yet the magic doesn't happen and flow is not experienced.

Conversely, even trained musicians may experience flow from pieces that are relatively easy to play but are nonetheless deeply moving. A few years ago, Bill Moyers produced an entire documentary on the song "Amazing Grace" (Mannes, 1990). He found that this nineteenth century song has a special place in the hearts of many people all over the world. The emotions that this song produces in people seem to transcend barriers of race, religion, social class, and educational attainment. And yet the song itself is really quite simple, and even very inexperienced musicians can experience flow when playing that song or other simple songs as well.

Taking a different approach, Clarke and Haworth (1994) examined differences between flow (that is, when skills are balanced by challenges) and what they call *optimal experiencing* (that is, when skills slightly exceed challenges). Note that Clarke and Haworth's definition of optimal experiencing is somewhat unique and a bit confusing because Csikszentmihalyi often uses the term *optimal experiencing* to describe flow. Nonetheless, Clarke and Haworth found that British college students perceived moments of optimal experiencing to be more enjoyable than moments of flow. Further, students who spent a greater percentage of their time in optimal experiencing had higher well-being scores than students who spent more time in flow. In their study, well-being is related to flow but more strongly linked to optimal experiencing. American adolescents also reported more happiness when engaged in low-challenge, high-skills situations (Csikszentmihalyi & Rathunde, 1993).

A study that examined flow and subjective well-being in older persons (70–86 years) found that higher-quality flow experiences were associated with well-being, but too-frequent flow experiences were associated with lower well-being. In addition, in this study the balance between challenge and skills did not predict subjective well-being (Collins, Sarkisian, & Winner, 2009). A small-scale study of flow at work found that individual descriptions of absorption in work did not always fit the definition of flow. In this study, a sense of meaning was more important to entering flow than a balance between challenge and skills (Wright, Sadlo, & Stew, 2007). Finally, Csikszentmihalyi (1997) reported that happiness and flow often go together, but not always. For instance, people report positive experiences of flow at work but at the same time may feel less happy at work than in other contexts (however, see Nakamura & Csikszentmihalyi, 2009 for comments on the "paradox of work").

Some of the problems with the construct may be due to the notorious difficulty of measuring it. Stopping a flow activity to fill out a psychological questionnaire will generally end the flow experience. Indeed, Martin and Jackson (2008) found that different ways of measuring flow produced different research results. Some difficulties may be inherent in the construct itself. To begin with, flow is not simply an emotion. Antonella Delle Fave (2009) has described flow as "a multifaceted experiential state, in which cognitive, motivational and emotional components coexist in a coherent and complex reciprocal integration" (p. 285). Although that description may not clarify too much for the average reader, the basic point is that flow is the result of several factors, all of which must be precisely balanced in order for it to occur and continue over time (also see Ceja & Navarro, 2009; Nakamura & Csikszentmihalyi, 2009).

Delle Fave also suggested that a sense of meaning must be connected to an activity in order for the magic of flow to occur. For instance, other frequently reported contexts for flow are watching movies; participation in religious rituals; and listening to music (Csikszentmihalyi, 1990). As with reading, an experience of absorption in the movie, the music, or the ritual also requires an emotional connection with the activity (also note that the "skills" required in these activities are minimal). In particular, a religious ritual is only meaningful if a person has a personal connection with the underlying belief system or is open to spirituality. Therefore, the induction of flow experiences appears to be more than a simple matching of one's skills with the challenges presented by an activity.

MINDFULNESS

The next perspective on well-being also asks us to pay attention to what is actually happening to us in the moment. **Mindfulness** is paying attention to one's own ongoing experience in a way that allows openness and flexibility. It is being fully present and aware during our daily activities. When people are mindful they are open to new experiences and points of view, able to create new categories for information processing, and they pay attention to life process or their own lived experience as well as to outcomes or goal attainment.

In order to get a better feel for what mindfulness is, it is helpful to describe its opposite—mindlessness. When we are in a state of mindlessness, our thoughts wander, we are not paying attention to what's going on around us, we "space out." Often this is helpful. Granted, it would be difficult to actively process all of the information that comes to us every moment of the day. On the other hand, when we live in a chronic state of mindlessness, we are on automatic pilot and we respond habitually to our world without thinking what we are actually doing or saying; we rely on rigid cognitive processing that may restrict our ability to respond reasonably or compassionately.

It is very important to note, however, that the concept of mindfulness can be confusing insofar as there are two somewhat different definitions and research traditions on mindfulness. We begin with Ellen Langer's research and follow up with the Buddhist tradition of mindfulness.

Ellen Langer's Approach to Mindfulness

The first perspective on mindfulness comes from Ellen Langer (1989) and represents a cognitive style that centers on awareness and the quality of attention that we bring to everyday experiences. Langer found that a particular type of attention is related to increased well-being and better adaptation.

Langer's investigations of mindfulness began with one of the more interesting, and simple, little experiments in the psychological literature. She and her colleague Judith Rodin (1976) went to a nursing home and performed a small intervention in order to investigate the sense of control. Some residents received a small houseplant to care for and were given minor increases in decisional control over their daily lives, whereas others were not given these opportunities. A year-and-a-half later, those who had been given the responsibility for the plants were more cheerful, alert, and active than the other group. In addition, "less than half as many of the decision-making, plant-minding residents had died as had those in the other group" (Langer, 1989, p. 1). Langer and Rodin suggest that the difference between the two groups was the added incentive for the plant group to pay attention to their environment, to notice what was happening around them, and to be more mindful of their own experience.

In another experiment, Langer and her colleagues sent out memos to several offices at their university (this era was before e-mail and texting; see Langer, 1989). The memos simply said, "Please return memo immediately to room 247." The memos were designed either to look exactly like usual memos or were different from usual ones. When memos were designed to look like usual ones, 90% of them were returned! Even 60% of those that looked different from usual memos were returned. Incredibly, most people looked at the memo and blindly followed the instructions, despite the fact that the instructions were nonsensical. For Langer, the roots of mindlessness are found in habits, premature cognitive commitments to categories, and on a focus on future goals rather than on immediate processes.

In Langer's view, well-being is not associated with moving through life on automatic pilot but with actively participating in the ongoing experiences of life with attention and openness. Many of us go through life waiting for something important, significant, or meaningful to happen, and all the time we forget to notice our real lives as we live them. Rock singer John Lennon remarked that our life is happening now, at this moment, while we are obliviously waiting for our "real life" to begin.

However, mindfulness allows us the opportunity to experience our world with fresh eyes and ears. Langer proposed that mindfulness comprises three core qualities: it can help us to *create new categories of experience*; *be open to new information*; and enable us to *see more than one point of view*. In this way, mindfulness can aid in breaking down the rigid categories we use to make information processing easier, at the expense of understanding and complexity. Langer (2009) stated that mindfulness is a flexible state of mind—an openness to novelty, a process of actively drawing novel distinctions. When we are mindful, we are sensitive to context and perspective; we are situated in the present ...

When mindful, we are actively varying the stimulus field (p. 214).

Therefore, her understanding of mindfulness involves an active search for distinctions, novelty, and the unexpected, reducing our tendencies to prematurely evaluate, categorize, and judge our experiences. Finally, mindfulness can help us focus on the process of living our lives and use that focus to create new ways of thinking, acting, and feeling that are responsive to the ever-changing tapestry of our experiences. The old maxim to "stop and smell the roses" is a reminder that we must pay attention to our journey as well as to our goals. Langer (2006) also applied her perspective on mindfulness to creativity. In her view, the creative process can be enhanced by the deliberate use of more mindfulness and the paying of attention.

Studies have found that Langer's form of mindfulness is a useful facilitator of well-being in many contexts. It can be used to enhance classroom learning (Ritchart & Perkins, 2002); to help lawyers give better attention to their clients (www.linkedin.com/in/daveshearon); as a factor in greater marital satisfaction (Burpee & Langer, 2005); and also to help young girls overcome gender differences in learning mathematics (Anglin, Pirson, & Langer, 2008). Mindfulness has also helped reduce the use of stereotypes about aging (Djikic, Langer, & Stapleton, 2008) as well as reduce the negative effects on creativity of social comparison (Langer, Pirson, & Delizonna, 2010). A state of increased mindfulness also helped people regulate their heart rates (Delizonna, Williams, & Langer, 2009). Finally, the mindful practice of actively creating novel distinctions helped musicians perform pieces that were more enjoyable for their audience (Langer, Russell, & Eisenkraft, 2009).

The Buddhist Approach to Mindfulness

The second perspective on mindfulness comes from Eastern psychology, specifically Buddhism. For over 2,500 years, Buddhist meditative practices have included a type called *mindfulness*. Within this venerable tradition, mindfulness is defined as an open or receptive awareness in which attention is focused on one's ongoing immediate experience (Brown & Ryan, 2003). Mindfulness meditation, however, adds another interesting element to a focused awareness: *attention to experience without attachment to one's experiences.* Such meditation involves a calm observation of one's own ongoing experiences without automatic reaction or impulse to associate thoughts and memories. Using the term *bare attention,* Buddhist monk Nyanaponika Thera (www.buddhanet.net) stated:

> By bare attention we understand the clear and single-minded awareness of what actually happens to us and *in* us, at the successive moments of perception. It is called "bare" because it attends to the bare facts of a perception without reacting to them by deeds, speech or mental content" (p. vii).

In mindfulness meditation, individuals are taught to allow their thoughts, images, and sensations to occur, to observe these nonjudgmentally, and then to let them dissipate as they are naturally replaced by other thoughts and sensations.

A group of researchers have proposed that mindfulness be defined by two components (Bishop, Lau, Shapiro, Carlson, Anderson et al., 2004). The first involves a *self-regulation of attention,* in which a person sustains attention to immediate experience, inhibits secondary elaborative processing (that is, inhibits getting lost in thought), and also switches attention to a desired stimulus. Most of these skills are encapsulated by the concept of *attentional switching* (see a similar notion in the section on flow earlier). The second component is a specific type of *openness to experience* encompassing curiosity, acceptance, and a reduction in strategies normally used to avoid its unwelcome aspects.

Application of Buddhist-style mindfulness to Western psychology came primarily from the research of Jon Kabat-Zinn (1990, 1993) at the University of Massachusetts Medical Center. He initially took on the difficult task of treating chronic-pain patients, many of whom had not responded well to traditional pain-management therapy. In many ways, such treatment seems completely paradoxical—you teach people to deal with pain by helping them to become more aware of it! However, the key is to help people let go of the constant tension that accompanies their fighting of pain, a struggle that actually prolongs their awareness of pain. Mindfulness meditation allowed many of these people to increase their sense of well-being and to experience a better quality of life. How so? Because such meditation is based on the principle that if we try to ignore or repress unpleasant thoughts or sensations, then we only end up increasing their intensity.

Buddhist-style mindfulness meditation consists of three core elements: intention; attention; and attitude (Shapiro & Carlson, 2009). *Intention* is a commitment and dedication to meditation practice. *Attention* refers to an observing of the contents of one's experience. *Attitude* refers to *how* a person pays attention to experience. Jon Kabat-Zinn pointed out that mindfulness should be understood "not just as bare attention, but as an *affectionate* attention" (see Shapiro & Carlson, 2009, p. 11; original italics). Shauna Shapiro and Linda Carlson (2009) listed 12 attitudes toward one's experience that are conducive to a Buddhist-style mindfulness meditation (see Table 4.1).

The beneficial impacts of mindfulness meditation have been used for psychological well-being as well as for pain management (Shapiro & Carlson, 2009). Studies have found that people who were more mindful throughout the day tended to also show enhanced self-awareness and reported more positive emotional states (Brown & Ryan, 2003). Improved mindfulness also helps increase self-regulation skills (Evan, Baer, & Segerstrom, 2009). Numerous studies have found stress-reduction benefits, increased focusing abilities, better physical health, and greater subjective well-being (Shapiro & Carlson, 2009). New adaptations of mindfulness to psychotherapy appear on a regular basis, particularly in newer forms of psychotherapy (Hayes, Strosahl, & Wilson, 1999; Linehan, 1993; Segal, Williams, & Teasdale, 2002). In this light, Jeffery Martin (1997, 2002) asserted that the use of mindfulness is a common factor in all successful styles of psychotherapy.

T A B L E 4.1   Elements of Attitude in Mindfulness Meditation

Nonjudging: Impartial witnessing, observing the present moment without evaluation and categorization.

Nonstriving: Non-goal-oriented, remaining unattached to outcome or achievement.

Nonattachment: Letting go of grasping and clinging to outcome, and allowing the process to simply unfold.

Acceptance: Seeing and acknowledging things as they are in the present moment.

Patience: Allowing things to unfold in their time.

Trust: Developing a basic trust in your experience.

Openness (Beginner's Mind*): Seeing things freshly, as if for the first time.

Curiosity: A spirit of interest, investigation, and exploration.

Letting go: Nonattachment, non holding on to thoughts, feelings, experience.

Gentleness: A soft, considerate and tender quality; however, not passive, undisciplined or indulgent.

Nonreactivity: Ability to respond with consciousness and clarity instead of automatically reacting in a habitual, and conditioned way.

Loving-kindness: A quality embodying friendliness, benevolence and love.

NOTE: These categories are offered heuristically, reflecting the general rule that there are specific attitudes that modulate attention during the practice of mindfulness.
* see: *Zen Mind, Beginner's Mind* by S. Suzuki, Shambala Press.
SOURCE: From Shapiro, S. & Carlson, L., *The Art and Science of Mindfullness: Integrating Mindfullness into Psychology and the Helping Professions* (page 11). Copyright © 2009 American Psychological Association. Used with permission.

Intense Mindfulness Experiences   As with the experience of flow, levels of intensity exist in the mindfulness experience. Buddhist psychology teaches that very intense forms of mindfulness may precede profound enlightenment experiences. Of course, there are other moments, outside of deep meditation practices, when a person may experience a relatively intense form of mindfulness or absorbed attention to immediate experience. In a study that looked at mindfulness and subjective well-being, Jacob and Brinkerhoff (1999) interviewed people who moved from the city to the country in search of a less complicated lifestyle that was closer to nature and allowed them to live more completely within their ecological and environmentally-based values. One respondent described a very special moment in the following way:

> Time … seems to stand still … The world for the moment appears whole and the mind moves toward a stillness … One's being … appears to be drawn into the ongoing stream of perceived universal reality, with the potential for finding tranquility, union and wholeness (p. 349).

For many respondents in this study, these brief moments of intense mindfulness contributed to a deeper sense of subjective well-being. Greater mindfulness throughout the day permitted them to focus on the wonder they felt in the everyday events of their world.

Comparison Between Ellen Langer's and Buddhist Styles of Mindfulness

It is worth noting the contrast between a Buddhist approach to mindfulness and Ellen Langer's perspective. In Langer's style of mindfulness, a greater awareness of experience is a first step, and one follows up new information with active attempts to create new categories of knowledge, actively build new perspectives, and foster creativity. The new knowledge gained from being more mindful is used to actively create new ways of thinking about one's life.

© Bradford Veley.

However, in the Buddhist style of mindfulness, no suggestion exists that information gained should necessarily be used in any specific way. The process is simply to be aware of ongoing experience while creating an attitude of calm detachment from it. In fact, efforts to actively use the knowledge gained tend to create greater mental activity, which hinders an ongoing experience of mindfulness meditation. A further difference with Langer's approach is that the formal practice of Buddhist mindfulness meditation often involves attempts to deepen attention to one's ongoing experience with extremely subtle levels of awareness, increasing clarity and vividness.

SAVORING

Most people have at times paused in the middle of an activity to fully experience something that is pleasurable. It could be taking time to really taste an ice cream cone on a hot summer day or absorbing all one's bodily sensations while sitting quietly on an isolated beach at sunset.

Fred Bryant and Joseph Veroff (2007; Bryant, 1989) referred to such moments as **savoring**. It involves an awareness of pleasure along with quite deliberate attempts to focus attention on the sensation at hand and delight in it. In a sense, savoring seeks to extract every nuance and association contained in the complexity of a pleasurable experience.

Bryant and Veroff identified four basic types of savoring: (1) *basking*, or receiving praise and congratulations; (2) *marveling*, or getting lost in the wonder of a moment; (3) *luxuriating*, or indulging in a sensation; and (4) *thanksgiving*, or expressing gratitude. They also suggested five basic ways to enhance savoring. The first is *absorption*, or allowing oneself to be immersed in an experience. Since a person must focus on sensations, the second is *sharpening the senses*, or fixating on one sensation while blocking out others. The third way to promote savoring is through *memory-building*. Here the idea is to do something that will help you remember the experience later on. Indeed, this is why many people buy souvenirs: to help them recall moments of joy or savoring.

Fourth, one can foster savoring by *sharing with others*, for most people automatically seek out others with whom to share their positive experiences. The fifth way to promote savoring is through *self-congratulation*. This suggestion may initially seem a bit odd; however, the idea is to allow yourself to feel good about having had an experience of savoring, to relish the experience, and even to permit yourself a bit of healthy pride. Bryant and Veroff implied we can do more than simply stop and smell the roses. We can stop and really savor the scent of roses.

PEAK PERFORMANCE

Although deep flow is often associated with a feeling of being in the zone, does that mean that people actually perform better while in flow? Jackson and Csikszentmihalyi (1999) noted that athletes often experience flow during moments when they feel they are performing at their best—when they feel

© 1997 Randy Glasbergen. www.glasbergen.com

"hot." The following quote illustrates one such moment:

> During one particular swim meet … I was delegated to swim "third leg" on a free-style relay team … Well, I hit the water, and I remember nothing else about the race, except my coach's ecstatic face when I lifted my head. Somehow I had come in ahead of everyone and put our team out front … To this day I can never remember doing that well in another swim meet. It definitely was not my usual level of functioning (Privette, 1981, p. 60).

It seems fairly obvious that this athlete had a very profound flow experience during the meet. But is it true that being in flow *causes* athletes to perform at their best?

The evidence is that simply being in flow and feeling as if you are performing better does not always translate into objectively better performance. One study found that flow related positively to actual performance in athletes; however, the challenge component was primarily responsible, not the athletes' skills (Stavrou, Jackson, Zervas, & Karteroliotis, 2007). Another study, this one of marathon runners, found that flow or being in the zone was related to future motivation to run, but it was not related to performance (Schuler, & Brunner, 2009).

Peak performance is the term that Gayle Privette (1981, 1983) utilized to describe those moments when we perform at a level beyond our normal level of functioning—and conceptualized as behavior that is "more efficient, more creative, more productive, or in some ways better than [a person's] ordinary behavior … and may occur in any facet of human activity: intellectual, emotional, or physical" (Privette & Landsman, 1983, p. 195). Almost each of us can recall at least one incident in which we somehow, miraculously, performed far better than we normally do. Some people recall a superior performance on an exam, others remember an incident of unusual courage or perseverance, or an episode like the one quoted above of peak athletic performance. As a dramatic example of peak performance, Privette (1983) cited the experience of someone who saved farm animals trapped by a dangerous fire (p. 196):

> The barn caught fire from a brush fire! The children were safe, but animals in an adjacent shed were not … I had no tools, and the oak boards were thick—nailed with 20-penny nails! [I ran to the shed and] pulled at a board and it came off with ease, as if a wrecking bar was being used. The animals were free. After the fire died away it took five minutes to straighten the nails and remove them from the oak plank … On inspection we verified that the oak board was well attached to the locust posts, and removing it by hand was virtually impossible. But it happened to me.

For most people, such an experience is superbly memorable despite having no idea how it happened or how to make it happen again.

Note that Privette defined peak performance as "behavior that transcends or goes beyond predictable functioning to use a person's potential more fully than could be reasonably expected" (1981, p. 58). That is, peak performance entails superior *behavior* at a task, and unlike flow is not simply a subjective experience while engaged in a task. Privette says that peak performance is not a specific type of activity; rather, it is an especially high level of functioning. That is, peak performance is not specific to any particular context, activity, or situation. It can occur in any activity—it is the "full use of any human power" (Privette, 1983, p. 1362). In earlier writing, Privette (1965) referred to the same phenomena as **transcendent functioning**. In her view, this is a universal potential in human beings, so that anyone can show peak performance under the right conditions (Privette & Landsman, 1983).

Privette's investigations found that peak performance can be described by four parameters: (1) clear focus on self, object, and relationship; (2) intense involvement in an experience; (3) a strong intention to complete a task; and (4) a spontaneous expression of power. Although Privette's investigations revealed that many people in varied situations have experienced moments of peak performance, it is still difficult to understand the precise triggers for such experience.

Also, peak performance can happen in two very different ways. The first type consists of incidents of unusual courage during a crisis. The fire quote above speaks to a spontaneous moment of peak performance that happened during a crisis situation. Incidents like this require no previous training and are not deliberately induced.

The other type of peak performance is associated with superior performance at a learned skill. People will train for years to master a specific skill and then a peak performance happens without planning or expectation. The swimmer's comment that opened this section is an example of this second type of peak performance. Often it is associated with sports performance, athletic competition, or creativity.

Peak Performance in Sports

Sport psychologists have eagerly adopted Privette's concept of peak for sports and athletics (Williams, 1993). Despite the difficulty in determining just what it takes to make an athlete "hot," a tremendous amount of research has been conducted on how to increase peak performance in athletics. Since the flow experience has often been compared to being in the zone during an athletic event, one might reasonably ask whether flow is involved. The relationship between peak performance and flow was addressed by Williams and Krane (1993) in this way: "One may be in flow and not necessarily have a peak performance; however, when an athlete experiences peak performance, he/she appears to be in a flow state" (p. 140).

Privette (1981) contended that the key to peak performance is to maintain a clear focus on both self and object, and particularly a strong sense of self in relationship with the object. The object might be almost anything, but it must be something that evokes in a person deep commitment and intense fascination or involvement. She stated that "the task that elicits peak performance represents an intrinsic value to the person and culminates in a direct, active engagement with the valued subject" (Privette, 1981, p. 64). From this broad perspective, peak performance most often arises from activities or situations in which a person is deeply involved, committed, absorbed in, and emotionally connected with.

Peak Performance in Elite Athletes   In a study that involved interviews with hundreds of elite athletes, Garfield and Bennet (1984) found eight conditions that accompanied those moments when actual performance was at its best:

1. Mental relaxation and a sense of calm, of high concentration, and often of time slowing down.

2. Physical relaxation with loose and fluid movements.

3. Self-confidence and optimism even in the face of challenges.

4. Focus on the present and a sense of one's body performing automatically.

5. High energy level along with positive emotions such as joy, as well as a sense of being "hot" or "charged."

6. Extraordinary awareness of one's own body. Often this is accompanied by an uncanny ability to know what the other athletes are going to do and an ability to respond instantly to them.

7. A sense of total control without undue effort to create or maintain that control.

8. "In the cocoon." This refers to a sense of being in an envelope that protects one from distractions. Additionally, it allows easy access to one's powers and skills.

Almost all characteristics of flow are represented in these descriptions. Research with top-performing athletes has found that in addition to flow experiences, those who actually perform better have a psychological advantage. According to Williams and Krane (1993), most coaches acknowledge that once a certain skill level is achieved, as much as 90% of athletic success is due to psychological factors.

Training for Peak Performance   Sport psychologists have developed a wide range of training programs to help athletes develop their full potential. Greenspan and Feltz (1989) reviewed studies that investigated the effectiveness of various psychological interventions to increase levels of performance. The investigations looked at athletes from diverse sports, including figure skating, baseball, karate, and gymnastics, and concluded that psychological interventions can be helpful in improving the performance of adult athletes in competitive situations.

How do such interventions actually improve performance? A key aspect seems to involve enhancing flow or "being in the zone." Sports psychologist Susan Jackson joined with Csikszentmihalyi (1999) to offer several practical hints for induction of the zone in athletic performance. Their suggestions were to: (1) move beyond your comfort zone and challenge yourself; (2) focus on process or moment-by-moment activity; (3) be self-aware, *not* self-conscious; (4) believe in your skills and stop nagging self-doubt; (5) "set the stage," or do all necessary preparations before a competition; and (6) practice a simple meditation exercise to help focus on the present and help control unnecessary and distracting thoughts. They suggested that athletes set up environments so that flow may occur, practice cognitive control over distractions, and prepare for competitions.

COMMENTS ON FLOW, MINDFULNESS, SAVORING, AND PEAK PERFORMANCE

In this chapter, we have examined several major concepts concerned with leisure, flow, mindfulness, and savoring. The range of experience covered by these perspectives includes simple efforts to pay attention to the details of one's life; relaxed and focused contemplation; intense involvement in enjoyable activities in which we forget about time; and even altered states of consciousness. Is there anything that can be condensed from these differing perspectives? What, if anything, can be said about the nature of contemplation and enjoyment?

In order to answer these questions, it is necessary to note the unique perspective on well-being that has been presented in this chapter. The literature on leisure, flow, peak performance, and mindfulness share a common assumption about happiness and satisfaction. In one way or another, all these perspectives find significant well-being through active participation in the immediate, ongoing experiences of our lives. Likewise, they all suggest that a deep appreciation of our moment-by-moment experiences can be satisfying and even fulfilling.

It is worth contrasting other perspectives on well-being. For instance, models based on the *goal-achievement gap* postulate that people are oriented toward goals and that our well-being depends in large measure on where we currently stand in relation to completion of those goals. *Cognitive* models of well-being focus on the content of consciousness. They examine whether our thoughts are positive and whether our interpretations of life help sustain optimism and meaning. Cognitive models focus on altering thoughts and interpretations, on changing the contents of our self-talk or inner chatter. In contrast, the perspectives featured in this chapter all focus on an *appreciation* of our current experience rather than an *evaluation* and *alteration of* our experience. A person might, therefore, reasonably ask what factors facilitate an appreciation of the moment.

Among these factors is a decrease in self-focused attention and internal dialogue. Experiences similar to flow, such as relaxation, hypnosis, and meditation, are also associated with a decrease in internal chatter. Descriptions of how to induce flow in activities, such as tennis (Galway, 1974)

and Zen archery (Herrigel, 1971), often explicitly include instruction on how to get a sense of self-consciousness "out of the way" and to let the body perform without interference from self-evaluation and self-monitoring. Interestingly, neurosis and depression are associated with increased rumination, which is partially an obsessive preoccupation with our thoughts, emotions, or memories. In addition, time is often distorted during flow or peak performance, and the experience of time appears to be related to how we experience the self. That is, some people experience themselves entirely in the present, others in the past, and still others in an imagined future (Fenchel, 1985; 1998).

Additional research must be conducted to identify more precisely the differences between various states of optimal experiencing. In Csikszentmihalyi's model of flow, a balancing of skill with challenge partially defines flow. However, as mentioned, many activities that induce flow—such as reading for pleasure, participating in a religious ritual, or being with close family members—are enjoyable precisely because they demand few skills and present few challenges.

In fact, it seems that an ability to switch self-focused attention to activities or experiences of the moment is the core element found in leisure; flow; mindfulness; savoring; and peak performance. The key factor is *absorption*. Although this factor shares qualities of a personality trait, research on mindfulness has demonstrated that absorption can be taught so that people increase their ability to become wrapped up in their environments. The material in this chapter argues that temporarily forgetting awareness of self and appreciating the moment can lead to greater well-being.

SUMMARY

In this chapter, we have examined topics associated with leisure and optimal experiencing. Satisfaction with life appears to be involved with having adequate leisure time to explore intrinsically satisfying pastimes. The huge variety of leisure activities

speaks to a human need to find activities that are personally meaningful and freely chosen. At times, activities become opportunities for optimal experiences. Many of these states have been described as *flow*. The intensity of flow experiences ranges from a mild and pleasurable involvement to an intense focus in which our sense of time, control, and self are all significantly altered. In sports, these intense experiences of flow are called being *in the zone*.

We have also discussed the concepts of *mindfulness* and *savoring*. These refer to moments when people are concentrated on an experience of the moment. The state of mindfulness can enable us to break old habitual patterns and be more in touch with the ongoing reality of our lives. A related concept is that of *peak performance*. This refers to moments when people perform activities at levels far above what is normally possible for them. From the intriguing perspective of sports psychology, we discussed the parameters of peak performance and suggested how to facilitate it.

NOTE

1. Unless noted, all quotes describing the flow experience in this section of the chapter are taken from Csikszentmihalyi's original paper on flow (1975).

LEARNING TOOLS

Key Terms and Ideas

time affluence	microflow	engaged living	savoring
adult playfulness	hypoegoic	curiosity	peak performance
flow	absorption	mindfulness	transcendent functioning

Books

Bryant, F., & Verhoff, J. (2007). *Savoring: A new model of positive experiences*. Mahwah, N.J.: Lawrence Erlbaum. *(popular)*

Csikszentmihalyi, M. (1990). *Flow: The psychology of optimal experience*. New York: Harper & Row. Csikszentmihalyi has several interesting books on flow written for the general public.

Hayes, K., & Brown, C. (2004). *You're on! Consulting for peak performance*. Washington DC: American Psychological Association. *(professional/popular)*

Kashdan, T. (2009). *Curious? Discover the missing ingredient to a fulfilling life*. N.Y.: William Morrow. *(popular)*

Langer, E. J. (1989). *Mindfulness*. Reading, MA: Perseus. See Langer's other books on mindfulness as well. *(popular)*

Shapiro, S., & Carlson, L. (2009) *The art and science of mindfulness: Integrating mindfulness into psychology and the helping professions*. Washington DC: American Psychological Association. *(professional/popular)*

On the Web

http://www.ted.com/talks/mihaly_csikszentmihalyi_on_flow.html   Csikszentmihalyi talks about his concept of flow.

http://psychcentral.com/blog/archives/2010/02/27/the-mother-of-mindfulness-ellen-langer   Ellen Langer's concept of mindfulness.

http://www.youtube.com/watch?v=3nwwKbM_vJc   Jon Kabat-Zin discusses mindfulness meditation and leads the audience in a meditation exercise.

http://psywww.com/sports/index.htm   Information on sports psychology topics such as training, flow, and peak performance.

Personal Explorations

1. Think back to your childhood and describe a hobby or special interest that you once had. This might have involved participating in or following a sport; learning about a particular topic involving nature or technology, fashion or design; or collecting something that intrigued you. (a) How did this hobby or special interest first develop? Did someone such as a family member or friend stimulate it for you, or did it just seem to suddenly appear in your life? (b) Why did you lose this hobby or interest? Did something specific happen or was it gradual? (c) On a daily basis over the next week on a daily basis, see whether you can reawaken your early interest, such as by reading about the subject on the Internet. (d) Describe how you have felt in revisiting your early interest. What were have been your reactions, and did have they motivated you to reconnect with your special interest in any way?

2. Have you experienced flow? If so, in what contexts or situations? Do you return to flow activities as often as you'd like? The next time you engage in such activity, practice flow by trying to balance your skills with the challenges of the situation. Describe what has happened.

3. In what contexts or situations do you experience mindfulness? How often do you seek out those contexts or situations? Try to bring more mindfulness into your life by focusing on the details of your moment-to-moment activities. Each time you find yourself "spacing out," return to the experience of the moment. Practice this for a week and describe what has happened.

Chapter 5

Love and Well-Being

> At no time in history has so large a proportion of humanity rated love so highly,
> thought about it so much, or displayed such an insatiable appetite
> for word about it.
> MORTON HUNT (1959)

It should be obvious to even a casual observer of human behavior that the search for loving and supportive relationships is a significant factor in the lives of many people. References to finding one's "soul mate" and to "living happily ever after" are everywhere in Western culture. One might wonder why so much attention has been placed on this single emotion. Is it truly that important to well-being and happiness? Indeed, the presence of positive relationships is one of the most significant predictors of happiness and life satisfaction. As we will see in the next chapter on health, love is a significant buffer against stress and increases resistance to illness. Romantic love does seem an important factor in psychological and physical well-being. This chapter explores what we know about this somewhat elusive emotion that is nevertheless so vigorously sought.

GENES, HORMONES, AND MARRIAGE

Evolution and Love

From an evolutionary perspective, love has adaptive properties (Shakelford & Buss, 1997). As social animals, we need involvement with fellow humans in order to create a life for ourselves, our families, and our social groups. From a strictly biological point of view, these bonds compel us to protect those close to us and particularly our children, despite the fact they may cause us difficulty and strain. This overtly biological perspective, however, does not describe the emotional experience that inspires romance novels, love songs, sonnets to one's beloved, and that famous commitment vow: "Till death do us part." The compelling experience of romantic love, holding as it does the utmost fascination for most people, cannot be totally understood by knowing only about genes, hormones, and neurotransmitters.

The Biochemistry of Love

Whenever we experience any emotion, there are always some changes to our biochemistry. Among the hormones that can increase in response to affection and love is **oxytocin**, known affectionately as the "molecule of love" or the "cuddle hormone." In fact, studies have found that oxytocin is associated with social bonding; trust; feelings of closeness and intimacy; and other prosocial emotions (Dickerson & Zoccola, 2009). Studies of new mothers have found that oxytocin is released during breastfeeding and leads to calm feelings of contentment (Nissen et al., 1998). If these effects were not enough, oxytocin is also related to reduction in both stress and anxiety as well as to increase in motivation to seek out social contact and support. However, oxytocin is not the only hormone involved with social bonding and stress: Endogenous opioids are also associated with social affiliation and can help decrease the impact of stress.

Shelly Taylor and her colleagues (Taylor et al., 2000) began some of this research when they studied the impact of stress on female mice and their pups. They found that mother mice moved to protect their pups when under stress or threat. Insofar as such nurturing behavior appeared to contradict the usual "fight-or-flight" response to stress, it was named the "**tend-and-befriend**" response and associated with oxytocin.

However, several cautions are in order before we leave the topic of the "cuddle hormone." First, an emotional response of love is very complex; no single hormone can account for all the feelings associated with romantic love. Second, studies have shown that oxytocin can also promote envy, gloating, and jealousy (see Panksepp, 2009). Therefore, although oxytocin and the opioids appear to be significantly involved in social-bonding behavior, there is still a lot that scientists do not know about the biochemistry of love.

Researchers have also found that experiences of "love" versus "lust" activate different areas of the brain (see Brown, 2011). In one study, people looked at photos while scientists recorded fMRI scans of brain activity. Photos of loved ones activated areas on the right side, while photos of attractive people activated areas on the left side of the brain. Of course, most people recognize a difference between love and lust, but it's interesting that our cortical responses are different as well.

Marriage and Well-Being[1]

You will recall from chapter 3 on subjective well-being that positive social relationships are a central factor in whether we feel satisfied and happy with our lives. But what about more intimate relationships: Do these offer an even greater sense of contentment, joy, and life satisfaction? Indeed, one of the most frequent findings in the literature on subjective well-being is that of an association between marriage and self-reported happiness and life satisfaction (Argyle, 1987; Diener et al., 1999; Myers, 2000). Studies have shown that married people are consistently happier and more satisfied with life than single people, at least when comparisons are made between groups of individuals (Figure 5.1). This fact is true across all ages, income levels, education levels, and racial groups. In addition, this relationship is found almost universally around the world (Diener, & Suh, 2000). Several studies have found that marriage is the *only* really significant bottom-up predictor of life satisfaction for both men and women. And although marriage does tend to increase happiness and satisfaction, people who are more satisfied with their lives before marriage may reap greater benefits (see Diener & Diener McGavran, 2008).

Quality of marriage is also a significant predictor of subjective well-being (Demir, 2008). Marriages with more positive interactions, more emotional expressiveness, and greater role sharing are associated with greater life satisfaction (see Diener et al., 1999). Why so? Among the variables important in these relationships is that of self-disclosure. Supportive relationships that furnish

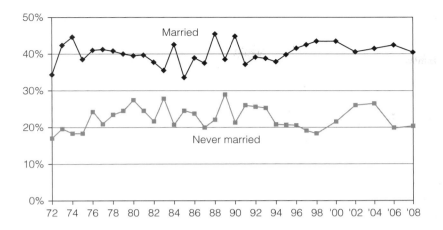

FIGURE 5.1 Percent "very happy" among married and never married Americans (NORC suryeys, 1972–2010)

SOURCE: Courtesy of David G. Myers, Ph.D.

opportunities for emotional intimacy, trust, and openness provide positive effects in a variety of life areas. Research has also found that the salutary effects of romantic relationships are greatest in couples that are married (Kamp Dush & Amato, 2005; Powdthavee, 2005). Since the percentage of cohabiting couples is steadily rising in Western countries, this has implications for relationship well-being in the West today.

Interestingly, the effect of marriage on well-being is stronger for men than for women. Generally, single men are less happy than single women, but married men are as happy or happier than married women (Lee, Seccombe & Shehan, 1991). So although both men and women's average level of happiness increases after marriage, the amount of increase is greater for men. This difference is also seen in ratings that men and women give on how much they love their partner. In a survey conducted by NBC News Today and *Prevention* magazine, 53% of men and women rated their love for their partner a "perfect 10" or as simply perfect. However, when examined closer, 59% of men rated their love as a "perfect 10" while only 47% of women did so (Gorman, 1998). In other words, men were more enthusiastic about their marriages than were women.

Some studies have also found that an increase in men's well-being is due to increased happiness after marriage, whereas women's increase is due mainly to increases in life satisfaction (see Diener et al., 1999). That is, men's increase in well-being after marriage may reflect a resulting increase in positive emotions, whereas women's increase in well-being after marriage may be more attributable to cognitive judgment.

We find dismaying a steady decline in the positive relationship between marriage and well-being in the United States since the 1970s (Diener et al., 1999). This is because married women report less happiness than they used to and single men report more happiness than previously (Glenn & Weaver, 1988). In addition, the number of American households consisting of a husband-and-wife couple has been declining steadily for years as single-parent household's increase among all U.S. households. Apparently, more people believe that living unattached is preferable to marriage, even when there are children involved.

Marriage and Physical Health Being married also has positive benefits for physiological health (see Maisel & Gable, 2009). For example, married people have greater cardiac adaptability to stress (Randall, Bhattacharyya, & Steptoe, 2009) and less risk for strokes (American Friends of Tel Aviv University, 2010). Marital quality is also associated with better health status (Holt-Lunstad, Jones, & Jones, 2008). In one interesting study, couples who interacted in positive ways showed lower blood pressure and lower physiological reactivity to negative interactions (see Gottman & Notarius, 2000).

As expected, a later study found that more positive emotionality in couples was associated with less blood pressure reactivity (Holt-Lunstad et al., 2008). Interestingly, in this same study, the poorest health indicators were found when couples reported high ambivalence in emotionality (that is, both high positive and high negative emotionality).

Positive marital relationships may actually be associated with greater longevity. A study of 67,000 Americans found that people who had never married were 58% more likely to die earlier than those who were married (Kaplan & Kronick, 2006). Of course, the quality of the marriage also matters. A longitudinal study of couples found a lower mortality rate for people in high-quality marriages (Coyne et al., 2001). Indeed, being in a poor-quality marriage increased risk just as much as smoking, obesity, or high blood pressure. The physiological benefits of marriage are also greater for men than for women: When compared with unmarried men, their married counterparts have fewer infectious diseases and live longer. Married women also benefit physiologically from marriage, but the quality of the marriage is a more significant factor for women. In sum, men seem to benefit simply from being married, whereas women need a good marriage in order to show increased health benefits.

THE VARIETIES OF LOVE

Considering that love is so important to emotional well-being, it is surprising that comparatively little research has been devoted exclusively to it. However, considerable research has been conducted on what makes people satisfied with their relationships and which factors predict their stability. Regarding the topic of love, a few theoretical perspectives on its varieties are helpful in understanding this all-too-puzzling emotion.

Michael Barnes and Robert Sternberg (1997) grouped perspectives on love into explicit and implicit theories. Explicit theories analyze love in terms of its core elements or dimensions. Not surprisingly, several

of these perspectives regard love unidimensionally. Sigmund Freud is among the first modern thinkers to consider love as a single phenomenon that encompasses many feelings, behaviors, attitudes, and motivations (Freud, 1921/1952). From this perspective, love is essentially one experience that can take a variety of forms, and therefore any attempt to unpack love into its constituent parts will destroy the essential experience. Although empirical support exists for a unidimensional theory of love (see Barnes & Sternberg, 1997), most perspectives view it as a multidimensional experience.

A Two-Factor Theory of Love

The two-factor theory of love proposed by several researchers (see Barnes & Sternberg, 1997) comprises passionate love and companionate love. From these two fundamental elements derive all varieties of love that people experience, both good and bad. *Passionate love* is an intense longing for a beloved, which can be experienced in a joyous emotional union and sexual fulfillment or in the terrible despair of rejection. *Companionate love* is a quieter form of love associated with affection, companionship, friendship, and long-term commitment to relationship. Interestingly, Hatfield (1988) argued that although both ecstasy and misery can intensify the feeling of passionate love, only pleasurable experiences can deepen companionate love.

The Love Styles

Another multidimensional theory of love is that of *love styles*. Susan and Clyde Hendrick expanded on work done by John Alan Lee to create six styles of love (Hendrick & Hendrick, 1992). In their formulation, the first love style is *eros*. This is passionate love, or an experience of love that draws you irresistibly to someone with a desire to be the exclusive focus of that person's attention. Under the influence of eros, you become obsessed with thoughts of your lover, and you may even physically ache when you can't be with him or her. Eros is the stuff of countless works of art and is what most people mean when they say they want to be in love. Curiously, John Gottman, who ranks among the world's leading relationship scientists, has stated that eros or *limerence* (the scientific term for this feeling) is *not* a major driving force for many newly married couples (see Fefer, 2002). That is, many happy newlyweds have not experienced that "madly in love, swept off one's feet" type of love in their relationships. In addition, erotic love has not been found to predict either later marital satisfaction or long-term relationship stability.

The second style of love is *storge*, a type that is primarily affectionate, close, and emotionally intimate. This is almost identical to Hatfield's idea of companionate love discussed above. It is akin to the feelings we have for close friends. *Storge* is also related to long-term commitment and those qualities that allow relationships to endure.

The third love style is *ludus*. This style has been described as "game-playing" love. Here relationships are seen as a way to play with feelings of affection and attraction. Those who are fascinated with this style of love often enjoy having more than one lover at the same time or enjoy toying with their lovers, such as by deliberately making them jealous. For such persons, love is a game of emotional manipulation.

The fourth love style is *pragma*, which describes a pragmatic approach. People who prefer this love style seek a person who fulfills certain conditions or who possesses such qualities deemed necessary for a suitable partner. For instance, someone focused on the *pragma* love style looks only for a partner who is gorgeous or wealthy.

Mania is the fifth of the six love styles. It is similar to eros in that both involve passionate emotionality and an almost obsessive focus on one's lover. In mania, however, the experience of love always seems to be painful. As one song puts it, "Love is sharp, it cuts like a knife/love is cold, it chills your soul in the middle of the night."[2] You probably know people whose relationships seem always in turmoil and are marked by frequent periods of wonderful highs and awful lows. Indeed, people who prefer the *mania* style often believe that this wild emotionality indicates true love.

The last love style is *agape,* involving selfless love. It asks nothing from the lover and is oriented toward giving, not getting. Although this quality is present in most relationships, a lover who prefers this style is not so much engaged in a relationship as in a one-sided expression of compassion for another.

All of these styles of love would be merely an interesting exercise in scholarship if they didn't have some practical value. Susan and Clyde Hendrick conducted a study involving 57 dating couples, examining their love styles, relationship satisfaction, and relationship stability (Hendrick, Hendrick, & Adler, 1988). First, they found that happy partners showed similar love styles; for instance, those who scored high on the *eros* style tended to be paired with partners who also scored high on it. So, similarity of love style was related to whether people were attracted enough to each other even to begin forming a relationship. Second, the researchers found that higher relationship satisfaction was linked to higher scores on the *eros* style for both men and women: Passion related to satisfaction. However, the *ludus* style in women significantly decreased satisfaction for their male partners, and the *mania* style in men decreased satisfaction for their female partners. The Hendricks also found evidence that the particular love style expressed by the woman in a relationship was more important for her partner's satisfaction than the man's style was for her satisfaction. They found that when women were more passionate (*eros*) and altruistic (*agape*), then their male partners were more satisfied with the relationship.

Sternberg's Love Triangle

The most frequently mentioned multidimensional perspective on love is Robert Sternberg's (1986a, 1988) triangular theory. According to Sternberg, all experiences of love are built on three emotional components: passion; intimacy or liking; and commitment. *Passion* is an intense emotional response to another person (the eros/passionate love mentioned above). *Intimacy* is warmth, closeness, and sharing of self in a relationship.

Commitment is a decision to maintain the relationship. By combining two of the love types in various ways, Sternberg derives four other types of love: romantic love (intimacy + passion); companionate love (intimacy + commitment); and fatuous love (passion + commitment). Finally, **consummate love** is a combination of all three: passion plus commitment plus intimacy. Certainly, most people wish for consummate love in their lives. Figure 5.2 schematically illustrates Sternberg's types of love in a love triangle.

Sternberg argued that these three components of love often progress differently across the lifespan. At the beginning of a relationship, passion is very high, but over time it often decreases. He suggested that, in contrast, intimacy increases steadily throughout a relationship. Commitment may start out very low but increases over time until it reaches its highest point and then remains steady (Sternberg, 1986a). However, studies of elderly persons have found that sexual activity and interest in sexuality remain strong into the seventies and even the eighties (see Belsky, 1997). Sternberg now contends that consummate love is more frequent in long-lived relationships, even among older couples. His cogent perspective indicates how many different types of emotion are lumped together under the heading of "love." It is no wonder that the simple exclamation "I love you" can be interpreted so very differently.

Love as a Prototype or an Ideal

There are also implicit theories of love, which view it as an extremely personal experience in which people define their own ideas of love in relation to a culturally ideal standard. From this theoretical viewpoint, we compare our current feelings with a cultural standard or ideal and see how closely the real matches the ideal. Of course, if our ideal is beyond the reach of any flesh-and-blood person, then we will be continually disappointed in our relationships.

Empirical studies offer evidence that the core aspects of our prototypes of love are intimacy, passion, and commitment (Fehr, 1988). Although this finding appears to make the same assertion as Sternberg's model, note that a difference exists. In implicit models, what people mean when they say they're in love can be similar and yet somewhat different from one another. For example, your best friend and you may both view love as involving a combination of intimacy, passion, and commitment, but the way that intimacy, passion, and commitment must be combined and expressed in order to match your "ideal love" might be very different for you than for your friend. In implicit theories of love the match between one's real lover and one's "ideal" lover is primary (see Zenter, 2005).

The Love Hierarchy

All of these intriguing possibilities that people invoke to express and experience love may seem a bit confusing and overwhelming. Barnes and Sternberg (1997) noticed this variety of perspectives on love and decided to bring some order to its

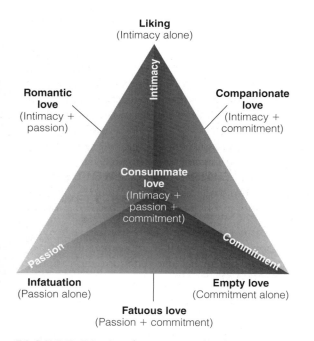

FIGURE 5.2 Sternberg's Love Triangle

SOURCE: Adapted with permission from R. J. Sternberg, "A Triangular Theory of Love," *Psychological Review*, 93, pp. 119–135. Copyright © 1986 by the American Psychological Association.

categories. Thus, their research prompted a hierarchical classification of the types of love. They asked people to report on satisfaction and what was important to them in their romantic relationships (both the good and the bad). They found three levels of hierarchically arranged meanings that people used to describe love.

At the lowest level in their hierarchy, they identified eight clusters that describe the qualities people value in their relationships: trust; sincerity; mutual understanding; compatibility; fulfillment; sexuality; intimacy; and mutual needs. The next higher level consists of *compatibility* (the first five traits on the above list) and *passion* (the last three traits). They described the compatibility factor as the "warm" factor that allows for commitment over time and feelings of companionship; friendship; and respect (that is, companionate love). The passion factor is the "hot" factor that defines feelings of desire; romance; and sexual need (that is, passionate love). The highest level is the single factor called *love*. Their analysis suggests that what we call love can be described at several levels by a variety of components. Of course, if two people use the word *love* in different ways, this can cause considerable confusion.

FINDING ROMANCE AND LOVE

What Attracts Us to Someone?

In order for love to develop in the first place, people must be attracted to each other. Research has found that important variables that impact attraction are proximity; physical attractiveness; attitude similarity; and reciprocity or a mutual exchange of positive evaluations. Proximity simply means that the two people involved spend some time near each other. It takes time for two people to get to know each other and to learn whether they feel comfortable and attracted to one another. Some people might read this last statement and reply that they know someone whose relationship began with a single glance across a room and a "spark" that told the beholder, "This is love at first sight." Despite the Hollywood emphasis on such chance encounters, they are far from the norm and do not necessarily guarantee either relationship satisfaction or stability.

Physical allure is another factor in love attraction but is not as important as many people think. Nevertheless, it certainly influences our behavior. After all, you can't learn whether someone is kindly, intelligent, or ambitious unless you are motivated to meet him or her. An interesting sidelight to this notion is a study by Diener, Wolsic, and Fujita (1995) that found no significant relationship between a partner's physical attractiveness and self-reported relationship happiness. That is, physical allure may be a factor in initial attraction, but it seems to have little to do with enduring happiness and satisfaction. One study found that fashion models reported slightly lower well-being and greater maladjustment than other women (Meyer et al., 2007). Concerning the matter of clothes, one study found that both men and women were more sexually attracted to people who wear the color red (Elliot & Niesta, 2008), but of course, many women know this already.

Ideals of attractiveness also differ among cultures. For instance, Americans tend to rate smiling faces as "more attractive," whereas Japanese tend to rate smiling faces only as "more social" (see Matsumoto, 1994). The basic message is that physical allure is not a major predictor of long-term relationship satisfaction. The old adage may actually be true that "beauty is only skin deep."

Another factor in romantic attraction involves similarity of attitudes and values. In the research literature, this quality has been termed *homogamy,* or the pairing of like with like. Over 70 years ago, in one of the earliest psychological studies of married couples, Lewis Terman found that, at least in terms of romantic relationships, opposites do not attract (Terman & Buttenweiser, 1935). Happy spouses tended to be very similar to each other in terms of a variety of attitudes. These were as specific as whether to have a pet canary and what each thought of insurance salesmen! A high similarity of attitudes and values between happily married spouses over the years is among the most frequent findings in the research. One study found that the similarity of interests and values initially shared by married couples often lasts throughout years of marriage (Caspi, Herbener, & Ozer, 1992). Hojjat (1997) hypothesized that similarity in life philosophy is an overriding factor that determines much of relationship satisfaction. It may also be that promoting and building similarity in a couple's emotional experiences heightens their tendency to feel identically about issues (Gonzaga, Campos, & Bradbury, 2007).

So studies tend to disprove the old adage that "opposites attract." However, one study found that attitude similarity is important to satisfaction only in the early stages of a relationship. Once a couple is committed, then similarity of personalities is more important (Luo & Klohnen, 2005). The "rule" for relationship success seems to be: similarity of either attitudes or personality, or both.

Finally, we tend to be attracted to people who show that they like us. The obvious advantage of this reciprocity or mutual exchange of positive emotions is that it allows us to feel good about ourselves. It may also help us to self-disclose more to the other person and he or she to us. As positive emotions increase along with a sense of trust in our partner's positive regard, the probability of deeper communication increases (Murray, Holmes, & Collins, 2006; Waugh & Fredrickson, 2006). This pattern can create an interpersonal cycle of risking self-disclosure; being validated by the other person, building trust, and then risking more self-disclosure. This is among the more familiar patterns seen in building close relationships of any kind.

RELATIONSHIP SATISFACTION: WHY DO CARING RELATIONSHIPS MAKE US FEEL GOOD?

One of the first issues to clarify when discussing satisfaction in intimate relationships is that "satisfaction" is not a state that couples achieve at one time and then no longer worry about. Satisfaction in any intimate relationship is a dynamic process that changes over time in response to situations, stresses,

and the personal growth of each partner. Although there seem to be several predictors of relationship satisfaction, we begin with a few more commonly discussed ones.

Personality Traits

Among the major factors that influence the quality and satisfaction of intimate relationships are personality traits. Indeed, in surveys that ask which qualities men and women look for in a partner, one of the highest-ranked characteristics for both men and women can be summarized as a healthy personality. For instance, a survey that asked for "the most desirable personality traits" found the following: confidence, integrity, gentleness, warmth, and an ability to love (Tavris & Wade, 1984). Another survey asked men and women what they "look for in a partner" and found: kindness, intelligence, and dependability (Buss, 2000). College students when asked which traits were "the most sought after in a romantic partner" listed: emotional stability, easy going nature, friendliness, and a good sense of humor (Kenrick, Groth, Troust, & Sadalla, 1993). In fact, one study found that women preferred men who were humorous to men who had other positive qualities (MacCrae, 2009). Other traits important to both friendship and relationship success include trustworthiness, honesty, loyalty, warmth, affection, and emotional support (Sternberg & Hojjat, 1997).

At the opposite end, among the most frequently found predictors of poor relationship quality is neurosis (Sternberg & Hojjat, 1997). This is not to say that people must be completely free of worries, nervous habits, or little quirks of personality in order to have happy relationships. Everyone has little anxieties and insecurities. However, big problems enter relationships when either or both partners are persistently anxious; worried; fearful; or suffer from very low self-esteem. Part of the damage comes from the fact that chronic neurosis often leads to chronic focus on the self—allowing little time for attention to one's partner. Without that sense of mutual support and validation, most relationships will inevitably suffer. What people want in their long-term relationships are personality traits that keep the other person interesting and allow trust, stability, and nurturance to develop.

One of the difficulties with predicting relationship satisfaction or stability from personality traits is that traits are broad summaries of behaviors over time. Although such descriptions are helpful, they do not illuminate the psychological processes that underlie relationship satisfaction. At an individual level, a great deal of what makes a relationship good is determined by small behaviors that define the unique relationship between two people. For instance, countless men and women in the world are warm, tolerant, affectionate, considerate, funny, and capable of forming secure attachments to others. Now imagine yourself in a room with 100 of these people. Could you fall in love with every one of them simply because they possess these personality traits? Of course not. At an individual level, love must involve more than general personality traits, though these are certainly important. Therefore, in order to further understand satisfaction and stability in relationships, researchers have looked at other variables that describe how we think about our partners and how we create impressions. The behavior discussed next is at the top of almost everyone's list of important qualities.

Communication

Interpersonal factors in relationships have often been accorded the greatest attention both by

psychologists and by the general public. By far, the most studied aspect of interpersonal relationships is the style of communication expressed. In numerous studies of married couples, communication has been reported as the primary determinant of marital satisfaction (Hooley & Hahlweg, 1989; Gottman, 1998). In the NBC News Today/ *Prevention* poll mentioned earlier, couples listed the following aspects they wanted to improve about their relationships: spending more time together (31%), better communication (30%), fewer worries about money (21%), more romance (6%), and more sex (3%). In other words, the majority of couples wanted more time and better talks together, not more sex.

Studies have found that compared to dissatisfied couples, those who report being more satisfied are more mutually supportive, laugh together more; withhold comments that might be received negatively, and agree more about a variety of topics. Communication between dissatisfied couples is characterized by greater disagreement; less humor and laughter, more expression of negative emotion, fewer helpful or supportive comments, and more criticism (Gottman, 1998).

John and Julie Gottman are considered by many to be the premier researchers in the world on what makes relationships work (www.gottman. com). They have found that a simple index helps distinguish satisfied from unsatisfied couples. In these studies, couples that are more satisfied turn towards each other more often and seek from the other little gestures that indicate attention; support; humor; or affection. These small gestures that help each partner stay connected to the other are what the Gottmans call **bids for attention**. They are usually not grand expressions of love but rather small interactions in which one person invites the other to respond with support or affection. For example, imagine a couple on their way to dinner when the wife says, "I just don't know whether I should spend money on that new dress for the office party next week." Her husband turns to her, looks her in the eye, and says, "It's up to you, but I think you would look nice in that dress." The wife's bid for attention has succeeded.

John and Julie Gottman

Courtesy of John and Julie Gottman

In an unsuccessful bid for attention the husband might respond with a noncommittal "uh-huh". These seemingly trivial moments can really add up, both positively and negatively.

Research has also demonstrated that the type of things people talk about is important to relationship well-being. One study asked participants to record snippets of their conversation for four days (Mehl et al., 2010). Coding of the data revealed that those who talked more with their partners were happier. In addition, those who engaged in more substantive conversation—rather than small talk—were the happiest. The investigators concluded that engaging in substantive and meaningful conversation helped foster increased relationship satisfaction and happiness.

Capitalization   Among the obvious reasons for engaging in conversation is to gain social support. Recent studies have looked at a specific example of social support called **capitalization**, or the sharing of positive events with others (Maisel & Gable, 2009). Capitalization can be helpful to the person sharing, the person listening, or both. Note that self-disclosure is usually described as revealing hidden aspects of oneself to another, but capitalization means revealing positive things about oneself or one's experiences. Shelly Gable found that this intriguing aspect of communication can be very important for couple satisfaction (Gable & Gosnell, 2011).

Imagine a situation in which a woman comes home from work with a big smile on her face and announces she has been offered a promotion at work. Her husband has four options for a response. A *passive-destructive* response ignores the message. For example, "Did you stop at the dry-cleaning store before you left for work?" An *active-destructive* response provides a negative interpretation, such as "Have you even thought about how much extra work and stress this will mean!" A *passive-constructive* response reflects a positive tone but is subdued and short. For example, "That's nice. Congratulations. So where do you want to go for dinner?" In contrast, an **active-constructive** response provides excitement and enthusiasm for the other's good news. For example, the husband might say, "That's great! I'm so proud of you. You've really worked hard, you're absolutely the best person for the job, and you deserve it!" You have probably guessed already that the active-constructive response style is the one most associated with high couple satisfaction. It is interesting to note that these styles of positive communication in couples closely mirror recommendations for good communication in psychotherapy and counseling (Hill, 2009; Rogers, 1961).

Self-Disclosure   Another major factor in healthy relationships is self-disclosure. As a theoretical construct, it dates back more than 50 years to the groundbreaking work of Sidney Jourard, a leading figure in humanistic psychology. During a prolific fifteen-year period ending only with his sudden death in 1974, Jourard's work on self-disclosure not only influenced psychology but the broad American public as well (Jourard, 1967, 1968, 1971a, 1971b). Although some of Jourard's specific ideas have required nuanced reformulation, his overall notion regarding self-disclosure's importance for healthy communication has stood the test of time remarkably well.

The starting point for understanding this viewpoint can be found in Jourard's (1959) influential article, in which he argued:

> Activities such as loving, psychotherapy, counseling, teaching, and nursing all are impossible without the disclosure of the client. It is through self-disclosure that an individual reveals to himself and [others] just exactly who, what, and where he is. Just as thermometers, sphygmomanometers, etc. disclose information about the real state of the body, self-disclosure reveals the real nature of the ... self. You cannot love your spouse, your child or your friend unless he has permitted you to know him and to know what he needs to move toward greater health and well-being (p. 505).

Over the ensuing years, Jourard advanced his conception of self-disclosure as both a vital feature of healthy personality and as a means of achieving successful personal relationships, such as in romantic love, parenthood, and friendship. He contended that transparency allows others to see our *whole* self—that is, to hide nothing. Transparent people are therefore able to live more zestfully, for they needn't waste time and energy disguising or covering up their true feelings and thoughts. If we're not transparent to others, Jourard insisted, we ultimately become closed to ourselves. And if we're unaware of *all* parts of our self, then we cannot grow and actualize our full potential.

Jourard's position was radical for its time, but a large body of research has supported its validity. Investigators have affirmed that self-disclosure is an important contributor to positive personal relationships, such as in marriage (Hendrick, 1981; Mount, 2005); premarital dating (Greene, Delega & Matthews 2006); and adolescent friendship (Bauminger et al., 2008), and also in validating self-worth and self-identity (Beals, 2003; Greene et al., 2006). Does this mean that we should reveal everything about ourselves to everyone we meet as quickly as possible? Of course not. Jourard himself never advocated such indiscriminate soul-baring. Today, psychological practitioners generally value transparency as an ideal in everyday intimate relationships, but necessarily tempered by sensible judgment and situational appropriateness. They also suggest caution (Madaus, 2002; Myers, 2007) in extending Jourard's notion of self-disclosure to nonintimate relations, especially the workplace.

RELATIONSHIP STABILITY: WHAT MAKES IT LAST?

Although satisfaction with one's relationships is an important variable, their stability is at the heart (pun intended!) of what makes them so central to well-being. Right at the start of this discussion, however, it must be clarified that high satisfaction with a relationship does not necessarily translate into long-term stability. After all, it is certainly possible to be satisfied with each relationship in a series of relatively brief involvements. It is also possible to be satisfied in a long-term relationship marked by frequent arguments. In spite of these caveats, we believe that for most people a substantial benefit of intimate relationships comes from their endurance over time. Nevertheless, for several reasons, such as increased longevity and financial autonomy, many people today meaningfully choose to end an unsatisfying long-term marriage to find greater happiness, even in their elder years. In this regard, we certainly do not view all terminated marriages as "failures" or all families marked by divorce as constituting "broken homes." For example, investigations of low-quality marriages have found they provide no benefits to spouses as compared with divorce, and adversely affect children involved (Cunningham & Thornton, 2006; Hawkins & Booth, 2005).

Most researchers begin with the assumption that people remain committed to relationships because they are satisfied with them and that they end relationships when satisfaction wanes. As Bersheid and Lopes (1997) noted, however, "it is surprisingly difficult to find hard empirical evidence to support this seemingly obvious assumption, at least with respect to marital relationships" (p. 130). In view of this reality, what do we know about relationship stability?

One way to determine what may sustain relationships is to ask couples that have been together for many years what they regard as important. Lauer, Lauer & Kerr (1990) studied over 300 married couples that had been together for at least 15 years. (The average length of first marriages in the United States is about eight years; the median length is about eleven years.) Interestingly, both husbands and wives listed the same seven qualities as most important to a successful marriage:

1. My Spouse is My Best Friend.
2. I Like My Spouse as a Person.
3. I Believe that Marriage is a Long-Term Commitment.

4. We Agree on Aims and Goals.

5. My Spouse has Grown More Interesting Over the Years.

6. I Want the Relationship to Succeed.

7. Marriage is a Sacred Institution.

People in such long-term marriages also recognized that marriages inevitably have hard times and that therefore spouses need to tolerate differences between them—as well as relish their shared similarities.

What Does the Research Say about Stability?

John and Julie Gottman have concluded from their research studies that friendship is absolutely essential to a satisfying and stable relationship (Gottman, 1998; Gottman & Gottman, 1999). By *friendship* they are referring to specific ways that happy couples interact with each other. For instance, such couples frequently communicate affection; fondness; admiration; and interest in one another. Happy couples have a genuine interest in their partners' lives; they often turn toward each other during conversation and offer one another potential ways to express positivity (see *bids for attention* earlier). The Gottmans insisted so strongly on nurturing a **culture of appreciation** that couples who attend their marital enrichment seminars are asked to spend at least five minutes daily simply expressing sincere appreciation to their spouses (Gottman & Silver, 1999). The Gottmans also asked husband and wife to take time every morning to find out one specific thing that their spouse will be doing during the day. They reminded couples that it is important to express real interest in each other and to never take the other person's affection for granted.

Studies also find that romantic love need not fade as years pass by. Indeed, romantic love remains strongly associated with marital satisfaction for both short- and long-term relationships (Acevedo & Aron, 2009). Similarly, research has also found that marital boredom is a significant predictor of lower marital satisfaction nine years later (Tsapelas, Aron, & Orbuch, 2009).

Studies have also found that a few specific correlates of satisfaction do change over the course of long-term relationships. What predicts satisfaction may be different for newer, older, or long-lasting couples (Carstensen, Gottman, & Levenson, 1995). In newer couples, the effect of passion may still be strong, and resilient illusions may be operating to conceal differences. Older and longer-lasting couples have often found a way to acknowledge, accept, and work with a partner's shortcomings and foibles. Gottman remarked, "They give each other the message that they love and accept each other, 'warts and all'" (Gottman & Silver, 1999, p. 154).

Skolnick (1981) reported on a 27-year longitudinal study of marriage. In her data set, the most stable marriages were attributed to couples who married when they were older; had higher incomes; higher education; and higher religious participation. She also found that similarity of attitudes and values was important for stability. Finally, the personality traits of self-confidence and nurturance were significantly correlated with stability. In general, she found that stability and satisfaction were related to "a strong affective commitment to the spouse, that is, an affectionate and enjoyable personal relationship between husband and wife" (1981, pp. 288–289).

Skolnick also observed tremendous variation in the behavior exhibited by satisfied and unsatisfied married couples. She concluded that it is relational processes rather than specific behaviors that are the important elements of satisfied marriages. As long as behaviors enhance affection, support, and other necessary processes, then the specifics of how to act in relationships is less important.

MINDING RELATIONSHIPS

John Harvey and Julia Omarzu (1999) developed their theory of close relationships around the idea that paying more attention to relationships helps create closeness. The term *minding* is related to the idea of mindfulness (see chapter 4). That is, **minding** is a way of paying close attention to relationships, of not acting out of habit, and of allowing creative new ways to experience a relationship and one's partner. The concept of minding is used here to discuss several research factors in satisfying and stable relationships.

Minding comprises five components that help enhance closeness, intimacy, caring, and commitment: (1) knowing and being known; (2) attributions; (3) acceptance and respect; (4) reciprocity; and (5) continuity (Harvey & Pauwels, 2009). Because much of the research on relationships can be found within these five categories, the discussion that follows is numbered accordingly.

Knowing and Being Known

The first component of minding describes a real desire to know and understand your partner. John and Julie Gottman call these **love maps** for storing information about your relationship and details about your partner. These can include the preferences, habits, and quirks of your partner as well as memories of important events and significant moments of your relationship.

Minding also encompasses self-disclosure and willingness for your true self to be known by your partner. An ability to be open; truthful; honest with yourself; and to operate in congruence with your deepest beliefs is called **dispositional authenticity**. Amy Brunell and her colleagues found that people who possessed more dispositional authenticity tended to feel more positive about their relationships; reported more intimacy; acted in less destructive ways with their partner; and described feeling enhanced well-being (Brunell et al., 2010). Couples who consistently show greater mindfulness tend to report increased relationship satisfaction (Barnes et al., 2007; Burpee & Langer, 2009). *Trait mindfulness* produces greater awareness of one's partner (that is, more complex love maps) and also helps increase emotional regulation.

Attributions

Attributions are judgments we make about the causes of behavior. In the context of intimate relationships, these refer to how we determine the causes of our partner's behavior. Several investigators have found strong correlations between the attributions people make about their partners and their relationship satisfaction (see Hojjat, 1997). You may wonder: If we need to guess about why our partner behaves in a certain way, why don't we just ask him or her? This is, of course, a reasonable solution that can improve relationship satisfaction and stability. However, often we don't have time to continually ask why others behaved as they have. Or perhaps we have decided by prior attributions that they do not know their own motivations, or even worse, are deliberately lying about them. Note that studies have found a wide variety of cultural variation in how people use attributions (Matsumoto, 1994). Therefore, the following discussion applies mainly to the use of attributions by people from Western cultural backgrounds.

One of the most studied attribution processes in psychology is the *fundamental attribution error* (Ross, 1977). This error in judgment attributes the causes of other people's behavior to enduring personality dispositions or traits while at the same time seeing the causes of our own behavior as due to temporary aspects. If, for instance, you ask your partner to send in the car payment and he forgets, then you might engage in an attribution process to determine why he forgot. If you decide that he is "under too much stress" (that is, an unstable, situational attribution), you might respond with increased support. However, if you decide that he forgot because he is "too self-centered" (that is, attributing a stable, internal trait), then your response may be to blame him for his negative personality trait. The first attribution can enhance the quality of the relationship while the second will hurt it. In fact, this pattern is exactly what research has found.

Couples who are satisfied with their relationships tend to make dispositional and stable attributions for their partner's positive behavior along with situational and unstable attributions for each other's negative behavior (see Hojjat, 1997; Bradbury & Fincham, 1990). So, your partner's stopping to help a stranger on the street is evidence that she is always a "compassionate person" (a stable disposition), while her abruptness with a waiter is because of "too much stress at work"—that is, is a transient reaction to an atypical situation. In this example, note how attributions of both politeness and rudeness are explained in a way that helps to enhance the relationship. As might be guessed, this pattern is reversed for couples who are distressed and less satisfied.

Another personality factor related to attributions is the use of optimistic or pessimistic explanatory styles. We saw in chapter 3 that optimism is an important predictor of subjective well-being. In a similar fashion, couples who are more optimistic have a better chance of making their relationship work (Assad, Donnellan, & Conger, 2007). This notion makes perfect sense. If a wife consistently explains her spouse's behavior in optimistic terms, she is more likely to support and validate her husband and less likely to bring overly negative attacks into their disagreements. Studies of optimism in marriage have found that the more positive the explanations are for a spouse's behavior, the more satisfied and stable are the relationships.

Positive Romantic Illusions: Is Love Really Blind?   The importance of how we view our partners cannot be overestimated in relationship satisfaction. You may have already surmised that such cognitive processes have one curious feature: They need not be accurate. The old adage that "love is blind" is sometimes true. Of course, everyone is familiar with a young couple so enamored of each other that each is oblivious to faults in the other that are obvious to everybody else. Who hasn't observed a friend madly in love and thought, "What does she see in him?" Most people believe such illusions fade with time, and that they are not important in long-term relationships.

However, such a consensus is mistaken. Sandra Murray and John Holmes (1996, 1997) investigated relationships and found that positive romantic illusions are central in successful relationships. You will recall from chapter 3 that a slight positivity bias toward oneself can at times enhance one's own sense of happiness. Similarly, happier couples idealized their partner's attributes, held exaggerated beliefs about their control over the relationship, and were overly optimistic about the future of the relationship. It is interesting to note that their illusions were also more stable insofar as those relationships indeed lasted longer! For many couples, the strength of their illusions about their partners increased as the relationship progressed. Indeed, the more idealizations believed by one partner, the more satisfied was he or she. As Murray and Holmes (1997) declared, "Such findings suggest that the willingness to make a leap of faith—to possess hopes for a relationship that reality does not seem to warrant—is critical for satisfying dating and marital relationships" (p. 598).

Happy couples also seem willing to deliberately distort information about their partner in order to enhance or maintain the relationship. For example, Simpson, Ickles, and Blackstone (1995) discovered a phenomenon they termed "motivated inaccuracy." That is, when couples tried to infer information about their partners their accuracy was lower when that information threatened the relationship (for example, "Does your partner ever think about leaving you?"). In essence, each partner deliberately (and unconsciously) guessed wrong about the other's thoughts, attitudes, or motives—but *only* when knowing the truth would be harmful to the relationship. Unfortunately, for many people the first indication that they have been engaging in positive illusions comes when their relationship breaks up. It is at that stressful moment that many people "see" those qualities in their former partner they had never noticed before. As one song puts it, "You won't really know her 'till you've seen her walking away."[3]

Holding positive illusions, then, can be helpful to both self-esteem and to relationship satisfaction. However, the very nature of love is such that you see qualities and potentials in your partner that she doesn't perceive in herself. One must wonder whether these positive perceptions are illusory or in fact represent favorable qualities that those who know the person less intimately simply can't glimpse. Ironically, couples who hold positive romantic illusions may be more successful at relationship, so their optimism is self-fulfilling.

The Michelangelo Phenomenon Discussion of romantic positive illusions is closely related to another popular theory of positive relationships. Anyone who has ever experienced a supportive, emotionally intimate coupling knows that when relationships are going well, then each person feels like a better person. **The Michelangelo phenomenon** describes how "close relationship partners are often active participants in each other's personal development and goal pursuit" (Gable & Gosnel, 2011, p. 271). When a relationship is working well, then each partner helps the other move closer to his or her ideal self; each brings out the best in the other.

The downside is that when a relationship is not going well, then each partner may hinder the personal development of the other. The reference to Michelangelo comes from his famous description of the sculptor's purpose, which is to release the figure trapped inside a block of marble. That is, a final statue is present from the beginning, and a sculptor must chip away unnecessary material to reveal the form hidden inside. Research has found that partners do influence each other's movement toward one's ideal self, primarily via *partner affirmations* (Drigotas, Rusbult, Wieselquist, & Whitton, 1999) that subtly reinforce the other's best qualities.

Acceptance and Respect

The third component of minding relationships is acceptance and respect, which focuses on what you do with the increased knowledge about your partner. Acceptance requires acknowledgement of one's partner really with some degree of honesty (bearing in mind the romantic illusions just discussed). It also requires that partners respect differences between each other and recognize that a healthy relationship is a balance between independence and dependence—that is, one of interdependence. This often entails a good deal of empathic accuracy of one's partner as well as forgiveness at times. Studies suggest that an ability to forgive is extremely important to relationship satisfaction and stability (Fincham, Hall, & Beach, 2006). In fact, the degree of commitment to a relationship may be related to the presence of forgiveness (Finkel et al., 2002).

Another factor that enters into relationship satisfaction is a sense of gratitude (see Gable & Gosnel, 2011). Studies have found that feelings of gratitude are very important to relationship stability and depth of affection. Building a relationship based on gratitude has been termed "find, remind, and bind" (Algoe, Haidt, & Gable, 2008). That is, partners need to find reasons to be grateful for each other, to remember these qualities, and use them to bind themselves together.

The sense of acceptance and respect that comes with any satisfactory relationship can also bring about openness to one's partner and a dropping of defenses, allowing another entry behind our usual emotional barriers. Along these lines, Arthur Aron and colleagues have studied the **self-expansion model** of relationships (Aron et al., 2004) in which a person is motivated to expand his concept of self by incorporating qualities of those he feels close to. Most of us are aware of how new relationships make us feel more expansive, more open, more willing to include other people. Indeed, studies have found that romantic partners incorporate qualities of one another into their own self-concepts. Romantic feelings do lead to more self-other integration over time; each of us may become "more" than we are through intimate relationships.

Reciprocity

Reciprocity is the degree to which each person in a relationship feels a fair balance of benefits from being together. Even though some people view relationships as a vehicle for sacrifice and selfless giving, most researchers agree that a healthy relationship should involve clear benefits for each partner. In social psychology, two theories have dominated this aspect of marital satisfaction and stability: balance theory and social exchange theory.

Balance Theory   The balance theory of relationship stability assumes that it is not the presence of negative emotions or behaviors that is important for stability but how they are regulated. Couples for whom patterns of emotionality are balanced and predictable are termed *regulated couples*. Regulated couples who are stable and free from undue conflict are called *validating couples*. However, note that a stable but argumentative relationship can also describe a regulated couple. An example is a couple who has been together for decades, yet is routinely quarrelsome and curt to one another. Although they quarrel often, such a pattern is predictable and stable, even if at the price of personal happiness.

According to balance theory, those partners given to unbalanced and unpredictable patterns of emotionality are called *nonregulated couples*. Their relationships by comparison are characterized by more negative emotionality, more severe problems, less positive affect, lower satisfaction, and a greater likelihood of ending.

Social Exchange Theory   Probably the most cited perspectives in research on relationship stability are social exchange theories, which assume that relationships are an exchange of rewards and costs. These *bank account* theories consider satisfaction the result of a cost-benefit analysis that evaluates the ratio of positive interactions to negative interactions. If these are more positive than negative, the result is satisfaction. From this perspective, determining the probability of any relationship staying together is a relatively simple calculation. If rewards outnumber costs, then it is more likely the relationship will continue. If the costs outnumber the rewards for too long, the relationship will probably end. Although this principle holds general validity, how people judge what is positive and what is negative is requires further determination.

Kelly and Thibaut's (1978) social interdependency theory postulates that people make separate decisions about (1) whether they are satisfied in a relationship and (2) whether they should maintain or end that relationship. A decision about satisfaction is one's *comparison level,* or how attractive a relationship is. To arrive at this judgment, people evaluate other relationships they have experienced or observed and consider what they deserve. The stability judgments involve a *comparison level for alternatives,* or an evaluation of the best alternatives to a current relationship. In truth, often people engage in both types of analyses. Notably, some studies have found that people who are highly committed to a relationship will often devalue alternative partners as a way to keep satisfaction high (Johnson & Rusbult, 1989).

Rusbult (1991) examined the role of commitment in maintaining relationships, defining commitment as a combination of three elements: relationship satisfaction; relationship alternatives; and relationship investment. That is, commitment increases if we have invested a considerable amount of time and emotional effort in a relationship. Johnson (1991) argued that commitment can also entail the degree to which people believe they ought to maintain a relationship—that is, its moral dimension. Levinger (1976) used the term *barrier forces* to describe the costs of relationship dissolution, such as financial concerns, worries over the emotional health of the children, or family pressures.

Continuity

This component of minding has to do with paying attention to a relationship over time. All relationships change as each partner grows as an individual and learns more about the other. Continuity requires flexibility; adaptability; and an ongoing desire to recommit to minding, despite external stresses or an over-familiarity that can lead to boredom.

Relationships as a Vehicle for Personal Growth
Much of the discussion so far has focused on how to create stable relationships that can withstand the vicissitudes of life and maintain mutual respect, friendship, and love. Some psychologists suggest

that this dynamic quality of relationships can actually become a vehicle for personal growth. That is, couples can use their relationships as an impetus for self-exploration; as a way to challenge their own assumptions; as a way to take emotional risks; and as a means of deepening their understanding of their partner and of themselves. We must point out that although virtually no empirical research exists on this aspect of long-term relationships, couples often mention personal growth as a unique benefit of such commitment. How might this work?

All relationships eventually experience some difficulties. Their source can be external, such as job stresses or the birth of children, or internal, such as the fading of certain positive illusions—the familiar "honeymoon is over" phenomenon. Whatever the cause of inevitable difficulties, each partner is forced to look at how his or her own expectations, personal desires, needs, or unconscious issues are impacting the relationship. When partners successfully cope with these psychological challenges, they develop greater psychological maturity in themselves and in their relationship (Tashiro, Frazier, Humbert, & Smith, 2001; Welwood, 1997). This element of relationship satisfaction and stability is a ripe area for research.

Virtues and Marital Well-being   Insofar as positive psychology is partially defined as the search for strengths and virtues, one might wonder whether the development of these is also important in relationship satisfaction and stability. Blaine Fowers (2000, 2001) emphasized this in his theory of marital happiness, specifically advising couples to build virtues of loyalty, courage, generosity, and justice. He argued that relationships need a strong commitment to these virtues in order to manage and overcome difficulties. His point is illustrated by imagining a couple trying to increase satisfaction by deliberately using more *bids for attention* every day. Such a strategy is backed up by quality research on relationships. However, if this couple doesn't express such virtues, it is unlikely that any satisfaction they gain will be maintained over time. The

exercise of these virtues in a positive relationship helps to build another important quality. This is a sense of **felt security** (see Maisel & Gable, 2009), that one is protected against a threat of rejection and other forms of psychological harm.

POSITIVE FAMILIES

Our discussion of romantic relationship leads to a focus on family. Generally families are the crucible in which children learn about the world and develop into adults. The topic of family dysfunction leaped out of mental health treatment and into popular American culture nearly a generation ago. For a while it seemed from countless depictions in movies, television dramas, and pseudohistorical documentaries that all families are mired in heart-wrenching conflict, abuse, and pathology. Although psychologists never really endorsed this dismal picture, the mass media has promoted it in the absence of strong research on positive family life. Fortunately, this situation is rapidly changing due to growing professional interest in how families in diverse cultures nurture, support, and aid their members throughout the lifespan.

When discussing families, the question arises as to the impact of children on romantic relationships. It may come as a shock to some, but research has generally found that children have little impact on couple satisfaction, and possibly even a negative impact (see Powdthavee, 2009). A variety of reasons for this result have been proposed, ranging from the stress of parenthood; our poor ability to predict how we will feel in a future that includes children (that is, affective forecasting); an illusory focus only on the good times of parenthood and ignorance of the difficulties (Powdthavee, 2009); and the "family life cycle," which will be discussed shortly. The good news is that couples who decide not to have children may not adversely affect their well-being. Despite this research, of course, most people desire to have a child, and many feel more positive about parenthood than certain research results have indicated.

For example, Luis Angeles (2009) analyzed data from 10,000 British households and found that parenthood increases the life satisfaction of couples under the right circumstances. He found that satisfaction even goes up as the number of children increase (the "optimum" number of children was found to be three). However, these results did not apply to all parents. In general, couples who experienced an increase in life satisfaction with children were married, over 30 years old, middle class, and college-educated. Women also seemed to derive a bigger boost from childrearing than did men. People outside these demographics did not show an increase in life satisfaction with children. Angeles therefore concluded that couples with children increase satisfaction "under the right circumstances."

What Makes a Flourishing Family?

Among the earliest psychologists to qualify healthy family life was Alfred Adler. In the 1920s and 1930s, Adler laid the conceptual and therapeutic groundwork for family intervention and parental training. Originating in his native Vienna, Adler's approach gradually became influential throughout Western Europe and the United States. Known as Individual Psychology, it emphasizes Adler (1930, 1938) the universal struggle of children to achieve a sense of competency in the world and, within their family-of-origin, to seek validation for their talents and abilities. That is, from infancy onward every child seeks parental attention and recognition; if parents fail to reward positive behavior and psychological growth when they occur, their children will inevitably engage in misconduct to assert themselves. Aiming his message at parents as well as at mental health professionals, Adler declared that a psychologically healthy family exhibits four vital characteristics: (1) warmth and respect among family members; (2) democratic rather than authoritarian decision making; (3) emotional maturation and autonomy; and (4) friendly and constructive relations with other families and the wider community (Hoffman, 1996).

Some years later, Diana Baumrind (1973) conducted now-classic research studies on what makes a healthy family. In her influential view, a psychologically healthy family is able to foster *instrumental competence* in its children—that is, an ability to function with confidence and a sense of mastery. She noted four types of parental behavior: (1) restrictiveness; (2) appropriateness; (3) communicability; and (4) warmth and support). Of the three parenting styles she classified, the two that she considered least effective are the permissive (that is, few rules; low demands; low communication; low warmth) and the authoritarian (that is, strict rules; moderate demands; low communication; low warmth). The most effective parenting style is the **authoritative parenting style** (that is, reasonable rules; high demands; high communication; high warmth and support). Baumrind argued that healthy families set firm and reasonable rules; expect appropriately mature behavior; instill good communication among all members; and provide considerable warmth and support. One study found that college students with higher self-actualization scores tended to report authoritative parenting styles in their homes (Dominguez & Carton, 1997).

Marissa Diener and Mary Beth Diener McGavran (2008) reviewed research on subjective well-being in families and have added another element to Baumrind's analysis. They pointed out that relationships between parents and children must change as children grow up. When children are infants, a secure attachment to a caregiver is extremely important. As adolescents, children flourish more if they feel close to both their mother and father. Throughout childhood, several parental behaviors are predictors of higher well-being in children: maintaining continuity in positive caregiving, modeling emotional regulation skills, and high but reasonable emotional involvement with the children. Diener and Diener McGavran also noted that positive relationships with siblings are important and that positive relationships between parents and young children often evolve into positive relationships between parents and their adult children. Another major factor is maintaining a positive continuity of care throughout the lifespan, which is central to creating consistently higher subjective well-being in both children and their parents.

The Resilient Family Of course, families at times experience difficulties and challenges. Healthy families, which adjust well and flourish during and after such challenges, are referred to as *resilient families*. Researchers studying children who functioned unexpectedly well despite exposure to adversity originally developed the concept of *resilience* (Garmezy, 1991; Masten, 1994; see chapter 8 for more details). Resilience initially referred to an ability to cope effectively with severe stress or emotional loss. However, the research scope of resilience in both children and adults has considerably broadened to encompass such aspects as self-regulation; optimism; problem-solving ability in everyday life; as well as successful adaptation to adverse events.

Can such features be meaningfully applied to families, too? Family theorists such as Ganong and Coleman (2002) argued in the affirmative, though they contended that the parameters of family resilience may not be identical to those involving individuals. In extending the notion of resilience to families, Patterson (2002) identified three relevant aspects of research: (1) a *family-level* outcome must be conceptualized, so that it is possible to assess the degree to which a family is competent in accomplishing a desirable outcome; (2) there must be some *risk* associated with the possibility that a family will not be successful; (3) there is a need to understand the *protective mechanisms* that prevent poor expected outcomes, such as child psychopathology. In a similar vein, Conger and Conger (2002) conjectured that family resilience encompasses marital happiness as well as the maintenance of close, supportive relations between parents and children. In addition, they suggested that resilient families are able to cope well with adversity, whether unusual or ordinary lifespan transitions.

Due to the relative methodological infancy of this field, investigators are still seeking to identify specific traits most conducive to happy and productive family life. In this respect, several different taxonomies have been presented, although as Ganong and Coleman (2002, p. 348) noted, "Clinicians and practitioners have been ahead of researchers in conceptualizing family resilience." The most frequently mentioned traits found in psychologically healthy families include:

1. a secure and loving marital relationship;
2. a commitment of family members to one another;
3. respectful patterns of communication among all members;
4. clear household rules and boundaries between children and parents;
5. a preference for discussion and negotiation in the decision-making process;
6. an authoritative rather than authoritarian or permissive parenting style;
7. encouragement of individual autonomy and responsibility;
8. a religious orientation;
9. shared leisure and recreational activities;
10. effective strategies for dealing with stress;
11. emotional intimacy among members; and
12. the presence of humor and laughter (Peterson & Chang, 2003).

Research has suggested a few additional elements of happy families (see Lopez, 2009). The living space in the home is important, especially the availability of a private space for each family member and a specified gathering place for family members to meet and interact. Happy families also have traditions, ceremonies, and a shared family narrative that allows positive storytelling. One element that does not seem to be important is economic or social class. Nonetheless, extreme poverty certainly can cause additional stress in any family.

Family-centered positive psychology (Sheridan & Burt, 2009) provides a "framework for working with children and families that promotes strengths and capacity building within individuals and systems, rather than focusing on the resolution of problems or remediation of deficiencies" (quoted in Sheridan & Burt, 2009, p. 554).

Most of the material on positive families listed above has been adopted and central concepts from positive psychology have been added. Specifically, there is a focus on *strengths* in the family and in individuals, as well as on *assets* that help promote better families regardless of the level of risk (that is, factors that promote resilient families). This approach is quite family-focused and promotes partnerships with community resources. (Chapter 7 discusses resilience in more detail.)

The Family Life Cycle

One stressor most families face is the arrival of children. Numerous studies have found that marital satisfaction decreases after the arrival of children. Figure 5.3 shows that, as might be expected, marital satisfaction is high during the initial years of marriage. Average satisfaction levels begin to drop as children arrive in the household. This drop continues until reaching bottom when the children are in early adolescence. It should be mentioned that even though a

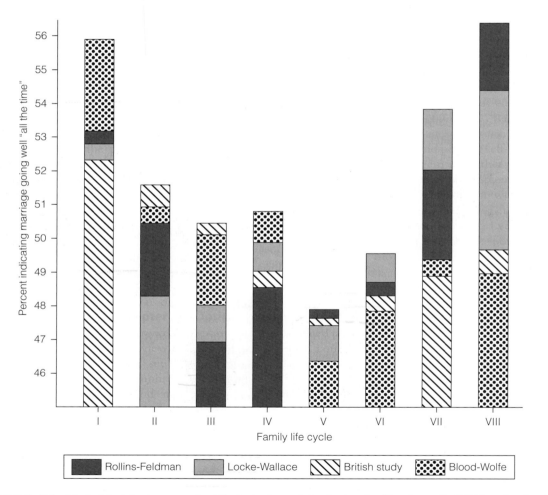

FIGURE 5.3 Marital Satisfaction over the Life Cycle. Stage I, Beginning families; Stage II, Child-bearing families; Stage III, Families with preschool children; Stage IV, Families with school-aged children; Stage V, Families with teenagers; Stage VI, Families as launching centers; Stage VII, Families in the middle years; Stage VIII, Aging families.

SOURCE: © Cengage Learning, 2013; Based on Table 18.4, "Marital Satisfaction by Stage of Family Life Cycle," in well-Being: Foundations of Hedonic Psychology, D. Rahneman, E. Diener, and N. Schwarz (eds.) © 1999 Russell Sage Foundation, 112 East 64th Street, New York, NY 10021.

NOTE: The lines on the graph indicate four different studies that have looked at marital salisfaction and lhe life cycle.

couple's satisfaction with marriage goes down during this period, satisfaction with parental roles and other elements of family life rise. This pattern can be described as a "parental paradox." When later the children leave the home, the often-discussed *empty nest syndrome* turns out to be a myth. An 18-year longitudinal study found that marital satisfaction for women increased during the empty-nest stage (Gorchoff, John, & Helson, 2008). Evidence shows that when couples are once again alone and freed of parental responsibilities, marital satisfaction returns about to the same levels as in early marriage.

It is comforting to know there may be a solution to the drop in marital satisfaction after children are born, which has been attributed mostly to decline in the wife's satisfaction (Shapiro, Gottman, & Carrere, 2000). This may be due to an increased anxiety in being a new mother and increased demands placed on the wife for child care. Shapiro et al., also found that if a couple felt their life was more chaotic after the baby arrived, marital satisfaction decreased.

The good news is that about one-third of couples did not experience a decline in satisfaction after arrival of the first child. Among these couples, new mothers were more satisfied if their husbands continued to express fondness and if attention was paid to the relationship despite the demands of the new baby. These couples found ways to build affection into the relationship; to keep in touch with each other's lives; and to approach parenting demands as something they could resolve together. In other words, they stayed attuned to each other's lives in spite of added stress and saw parenthood as a team effort.

Social and Cultural Influences

The impact of society and culture on long-term commitment can be significant, especially when changes in social expectations over time create unforeseen stress. For example, when issues such as social mores and economic need are no longer significant barriers to divorce or to single parenthood, then relationships can suffer. Social exchange theory evaluates relationships by looking at costs and benefits. If the social costs of separating are reduced (such as the stigma of single parenting), then people must look to other reasons for maintaining a relationship, particularly to the strength of emotional bonds. This is particularly true in societies such as the United States that prize individualism and place a high priority on the experience of love. People then become

© 1999 Randy Glasbergen. www.glasbergen.com

"I'm forming a support group for women who feel overwhelmed by cooking, children, and housework. We meet every weeknight from 5:00 to 10:00 PM."

preoccupied with the quality of their relationship and with emotional interactivity.

As Sternberg and Hojjat (1997) observed, when there are few barriers that prevent relationship dissolution then, "both partners must spend much time and energy 'taking the pulse' of the relationship and attending to even the slightest symptom of malaise, for fear that it ultimately will prove fatal to the relationship" (p. 135). This contemporary perspective suggests that if we are not careful, we may pay a price for economic and social freedom: Namely, we base all decision about relationship commitment on changeable emotional qualities. At worst this can lead to an obsessive preoccupation with the emotional tone of a relationship. Hunt (1959) noted a cultural and historical factor as well:

> The physical isolation and rootlessness of modern life, however, is only half the reason love has assumed such great significance. The other half lies in the fact that our society, more so than most others, conditions us from earliest childhood to measure and rate ourselves by the amount of love we receive (p. 373).

Within highly pluralistic societies, differences between ethnic and cultural backgrounds of two people can also create stress for a relationship. In the United States, for example, a relationship between "mixed couples"—such as one spouse from European and the other from Latino background—can create marked tensions (see Menard, 2003). Different cultures have quite different ideas of love. For instance, one study found that Americans and Europeans place a much higher value on experiencing feelings of love than do Japanese (see Simmons, vom Kolke, and Shimizu, 1986, in Matsumoto, 1994). The researchers cogently suggest that romantic love is more highly valued in Westernized cultures, which have meager extended-family ties and are less influenced by strong traditional kinship networks.

A positive psychology focus on family life is also emerging from the domain of cross-cultural psychology. For example, researchers interested in strength-based counseling among Latinos have noted the importance of family relations in life satisfaction and peak experiences of children and adolescents (Diaz-Loving & Draguns, 1999; Hoffman & Ortiz, 2010; Van Horn & Marques, 2000). In such countries as Brazil and Mexico, *familism* as described by researchers (Carlo et al., 2007; Koller & Lisboa, 2007) has also been identified as a vital factor mitigating the stresses of economic deprivation.

Likewise, investigators examining Chinese culture from a positive psychology framework have found that family closeness is a major source of individual life satisfaction. Under the influence of Confucianism, Chinese culture highly emphasizes family values, family relationship, and filial piety. The psychologically healthy family is regarded as one that encompasses harmony; affection; mutual trust; support; compatibility; equity in marriage; and an ability to adapt to change (Xu, Xie, Liu, Xia, & Dalin, 2007). In addition, attributes related to family, positive conduct, harmonious social relations, and personal maturity are perceived as "ideal child" characteristics by parents in Hong Kong (Shek & Chan, 1999). Researchers have also identified indigenous personality traits of social harmony and family-oriented behavior as salient predictors of life satisfaction among Hong Kong adolescents (Ho, Cheung, & Cheung, 2008; Koch & Koch, 2009).

As the United States becomes an increasingly multiethnic country in coming years, it is likely that the study of family life from a positive psychology perspective will acquire a corresponding prominence. This trend will certainly not negate professional gains in understanding and treating dysfunctional families, but it will provide a much-needed and long-overdue balance.

WHAT HURTS RELATIONSHIPS?

Conflict

Stated quite boldly, conflict is the number one cause of marital dissolution and communication problems are the number one reason given for divorce (Gottman, 1998). However, studies have found that the number of conflicts people have and the matters they argue over are less important than how they handle conflicts. Gottman has identified a type of communication often found between distressed couples that is particularly destructive to relationships: a **harsh setup** that leads to **negative reciprocity**. This style refers to a sequence wherein an initial negative comment, often designed to hurt, only serves to stimulate a negative response from the partner and an increasing cycle of disagreeable comments (Gottman & Silver, 1999). Indeed, some researchers have commented on the negative power of the harsh setup by observing, "One zinger can erase 20 acts of kindness" (Notarius & Markham, 1993, p. 28). That is, one cruel and thoughtless act or comment can wipe out an entire month of affection and tenderness.

The Demand-Withdraw Pattern and Stonewalling

Another sequence manifested by couples in trouble is a **demand-withdraw pattern** (Gottman & Gottman, 1999). This is a four-step pattern particularly destructive to relationships. It begins with (1) criticism and complaint from one partner that often takes the form of a harsh setup and negative reciprocity, followed by (2) a sense of contempt from the other that (3) leads to defensiveness and (4) ends with withdrawal. When step (4) becomes so extreme that one person withdraws attention in a passive-aggressive attempt to punish the other, this becomes what the Gottmans call **stonewalling**. They considered this four-step pattern culminating in stonewalling so destructive that they term it the "Four Horseman of the Apocalypse," in reference to the four horsemen in the Bible who signal the end of the world.

The negative ferocity of personal attack in arguments can overwhelm one or both partners and result in *negative sentiment override*, in which a person becomes shellshocked and retreats into a responsive mode that seeks protection. This response pattern the Gottmans called *flooding*, which their studies have found causes several physical reactions, such as increased heart rate and blood pressure as well as stimulation of a "fight-or-flight" stress response. The result is an inability to engage in positive problem solving.

Related to flooding is the concept of *repair attempts*. This refers to efforts to calm down a tense situation or to de-escalate tension so that flooding does not occur. When repair attempts fail or are not even attempted, a couple is in trouble. Another negative indicator is when distressed couples choose to remember mostly negative moments in their shared history. Although they used to remember their positive moments together, now they can't help recall difficulties, hurts, and disappointments. In effect, their shared history is rewritten.

In a longitudinal study that followed couples for 14 years, Gottman and Levinson (2000) could predict later divorce at over 90% accuracy by direct observation of couple interaction along with information from questionnaires and physiological measures. Accuracy of prediction that high is nearly unheard of in psychology. A major indicator of later problems was a demand-withdraw pattern of communication. Sadly, for some couples this destructive pattern of interaction was present very early in their relationships, manifesting just a few months after the wedding day.

HOW TO NURTURE POSITIVE RELATIONSHIPS THAT LAST

In *The Seven Principles for Making Marriage Work* (Gottman & Silver, 1999), John Gottman summarized the suggestions offered in the Gottman's marriage enrichment seminars:

1. ENHANCE YOUR LOVE MAPS. This principle suggests that partners should pay attention to, and take an interest in, each other.

2. NURTURE YOUR FONDNESS AND ADMIRATION. Couples should use positive attributions and optimism to focus on the positive qualities of their partner, remember the positive events of the relationship, and view their shared past in positive terms.

3. TURN TOWARD EACH OTHER INSTEAD OF AWAY. This principle refers to the *bids for attention* mentioned earlier. In essence, couples need to seize little moments

throughout the day to "stop, look, and listen" to each other.

4. LET YOUR PARTNER INFLUENCE YOU. This principle asserts that couples need to share power and influence. Stubbornness never helps.

5. SOLVE YOUR SOLVABLE PROBLEMS. Based on their research, the Gottmans suggested the following five steps for conflict resolution:

a. Soften your setup.

b. Learn to make and receive repair attempts.

c. Soothe yourself and each other.

d. Compromise.

e. Be tolerant of each other's faults.

6. OVERCOME GRIDLOCK AND MOVE TOWARD DIALOGUE. Movement toward dialogue is partially accomplished by acknowledging and nurturing what the Gottmans call each person's "dreams." These consist of the hopes, goals, aspiration, and wishes that each person has for his or her life. Dreams define our identity on a deep level. Often, conflicts are based on differences between dreams, differences that must be acknowledged and respected before a compromise can be found.

7. CREATE SHARED MEANING. This principle holds that couples should create a "culture of appreciation" in which their shared life together, is appreciated and valued over and over again.

The Gottmans also urged couples to work on building their relationship daily. They said that "**the magic 5 hours per week**" is enough to change a relationship in a more positive direction. Referring to research on marriage and physical health, they stated, "Working on your marriage every day will do more for your health and longevity than working out at the health club" (Gottman & Silver, 1999, p. 261). Although no one should neglect his or her physical health, the well-documented benefits of intimate relationships confirm their importance for well-being and happiness.

John and Julie Gottman now insist that mainstream marriage counseling—in which spouses express their resentments and disappointments about the marriage—almost never benefits the husband. They say that men find such discussions to be inherently threatening and painful, and report feeling more distant from their wives after such sessions. Rather, the Gottmans now almost exclusively have spouses focus on what each partner is doing right and how to amplify that on a daily basis. They have decided that spousal dwelling on negatives almost never is productive, and that if there are a lot of positives in a marriage, then the negatives take care of themselves; these exist but diminish in importance. The Gottmans therefore look at a couple's friendship, meaning, and conflict profiles while trying to maximize the fun and happiness in their marriage, keeping these the focus of therapy (http://www.psychotherapy.net/interview/john-gottman).

Another list of suggestions came from W. Kim Halford and Brett Behrens (1997), who focused rather on five overt behaviors (cited in Harvey & Pauwels, 2009): affection, respect, support and assistance, shared quality time, and appreciation. They insisted that couples need to build a relationship in which demonstrating and sharing appreciation of one's partner is so routine and normal that this expression becomes integral to their everyday life together.

SUMMARY

This chapter has covered the topic of love. The search for love is one of the most significant ways that people pursue well-being. Needs for love and intimacy may be biologically innate. Most theoretical perspectives on love consider it a multifaceted experience that combines at least two elements: passion and compatibility. Relationship satisfaction is associated with a couple's similarity in attitudes and values; positive personality traits; the type of attributions made to explain a partner's behavior; and healthy styles of communication. Relationship stability is associated with factors such as friendship; commitment; conflict management; and the effects of external stressors.

Indeed, the major cause of relationship instability and dissolution is conflict. Suggestions for enhanced relationships focus on deepening involvement in couple interactivity and emotional life as well as simply paying more attention to each other.

NOTES

1. Throughout this chapter the term *marriage* is used to denote an emotionally intimate and committed relationship between two people. Since most of the research has looked at heterosexual relationships, the latter provide the context for most of the discussion. Unfortunately, we do not know how many of these findings apply to same-sex couples. However, researchers do know that same-sex relationships tend to be shorter—on average, by about six years. This may be due to the social factors that tend to keep heterosexual couples together (for example, legal complications in breakups; presence of children). Conversely, John Gottman, among the leading researchers of relationship satisfaction and stability, believed that same-sex couples have an advantage: They tended to discuss issues more positively and with greater affection and humor than do heterosexual couples (*Time, 1/19/04*).

2. Michie, Chris. "*Love is sharp.*" Kulberg/Michie Music.

3. Collins, Will D. "*You won't really know her.*" Power Diamond Music.

LEARNING TOOLS

Key Terms

bids for attention

capitalization

active-constructive responding

minding relationships

love maps

dispositional authenticity

the michelangelo phenomenon

self-expansion model

authoritative parenting

demand-withdraw pattern

culture of appreciation

Books

John Gottman has written several books on making marriage work (for example, Gottman & Declaire, 2001; Gottman & Silver, 1999). Just pick one that looks interesting!

Isay, D. (2007). Listening as an act of love: A celebration of American life from the StoryCorp project. NY: Penguin. NPR's StoryCorp is an oral history of people telling about the most important moments in their own lives. *(popular)*

Kirshenbaum, M. (1997). *Too good to leave, too bad to stay.* NY: Plume. Practical advice on how to decide whether a relationship is working. *(popular)*

Rosenberg, M. (2005). *Speak peace in a world of conflict: What you say next will change your world.* NY: PuddleDancer Press. Rosenberg created his system called Non-Violent Communication years ago and has applied it to many situations. *(popular)*

Tennov, D. (1998). *Love and limerence: The experience of being in love*. NY: Scarborough House. A classic work on differences between love and eros/limerence. *(popular)*

Cultural issues within pluralistic societies can create unique problems for relationships: Menard, V.

(2003). *Latinas in love: A modern guide to love and relationships*. NY: Marlowe & Company.

Whitfield, K., Markham, H., Stanley, S., & Blumberg, S. (2001). *Fighting for your African American marriage*. San Francisco: Jossey-Bass.

On the Web

http://www.gottman.com   John Gottman's Web site with information on what makes relationships work.

http://www.clemson.edu/fyd/bfs.htm   Clemson University's site for building family strengths.

Personal Explorations

1. People in the United States, and increasingly around the world, are influenced by Hollywood films. Think of two romantic love movies that you like very much. For each one, answer the following questions: (a) How do the two lovers meet? What are the circumstances? (b) When they meet, is there "love at first sight" or does it develop gradually? (c) How does the audience know that the two have "fallen in love?"? That is, through what sort of scenes is a state of romantic love depicted? (d) Does something cause the two lovers to separate from each other? If so, what is it (such as a misunderstanding or an external event like a disaster)? (e) What brings the two lovers back together? (f) What makes this movie so appealing to you? Do you often cry at romantic movies? If so, why do you think you do?

2. Interview someone who has been married or romantically involved for at least 15 years. What does this person believe is important for a successful long-term relationship? How does she or he handle conflict or differences of opinion in the relationship? How have passionate love, companionate love, and consummate love changed over the course of his or her relationship?

Chapter 6

Positive Health

> Health is a state of complete physical, mental, and social well-being,
> and not merely the absence of disease and infirmity.
>
> WORLD HEALTH ORGANIZATION (1946)

The idea that physical health and vitality are important to the good life is one of the oldest assumptions about psychological well-being. The ancient Greeks believed that certain mental illnesses such as depression are caused by an imbalance of physical elements in the body, which they called the four humors.[1] In contrast, early Christian perspectives tended to view the body as a source of temptation and sin, denigrating the "flesh" in a quest for the "spirit." Nineteenth century Romantics also emphasized the importance of emotional and physical health to well-being. Henry David Thoreau suggested that in order to achieve emotional well-being, one has to "first become a good animal." In other words, a healthy and vital physical body is necessary for mental health. For many scientists, however, mind and body remain separate aspects of a person, physical health is defined as an absence of illness or disease, and psychological states have no connection to physical health.

Wellness

More recently, researchers have begun to expand specifications of physical health and well-being. Years ahead of most scientists on this point, the World Health Organization's official position in 1946 was that "health is a state of complete physical, mental, and social well-being, and not merely the absence of disease and infirmity." For over 65 years, the World Health Organization has recognized that, although being disease free is a worthy goal, a state of enhanced vitality defines a more encompassing sense of well-being.

Although initially researchers studied physical health as a pathway to increased energy and longevity, this began to change in 1961 when Dunn coined the term "high-level wellness" to describe a state of enhanced physical and emotional well-being. Thereafter, the term **wellness** has been used to refer to states of optimal physical, mental, and emotional health. For Dunn, wellness is a state in which a person has:

1. A ZEST FOR LIFE;
2. A WAY OF LIVING THAT MAXIMIZES POTENTIAL;
3. A SENSE OF MEANING AND PURPOSE;

4. A SENSE OF SOCIAL RESPONSIBILITY; AND

5. SKILLS FOR ADAPTING TO THE CHALLENGES OF A CHANGING ENVIRONMENT.

The wellness perspective has had a distinctly practical and applied emphasis, producing a whole new research agenda, educational focus, and occupational category to satisfy interest in this area. It encompasses the benefits of exercise, nutrition, stress management, emotional self-regulation, social support, and personal growth (Corbin, 2003). Research on *embodied cognition* also suggests that the state of our body is crucial to how our minds work (see Jostmann, Lakens, & Schubert, 2009). The United States Department of Health and Human Services sees health promotion as one of its central objectives (Healthy People, 2000).

POSITIVE HEALTH

Ideas from earlier theories of wellness have been transformed by positive psychology into a concept of positive health as not merely absence of disease but as excellence in three measures: biological markers, subjective experiences, and functional abilities (Seligman, 2008, 2011). Biological markers include any measures of physiological functioning that can impact health or well-being, such as cardiac or pulmonary health. Subjective experiences include any measure of subjective well-being, such as optimism, positive emotionality, energization, and sense of vitality. Functional measures include assessments of how well daily activities are accomplished and behavioral signs such as adjustment to normal aging or occasional disability. Positive health brings a new emphasis on empirical studies investigating health outcomes such as longevity, quality of life, health costs, and other measures of health status.

The goal of positive health is to describe adaptation to challenges that do not simply return a person to homeostasis but toward a better quality of life. This process is not just coping and adaptation but positive growth. O'Leary and Ickovics (1995) termed such a process psychological **thriving**. Epel, McEwen and Ickovics (1998)

expanded this concept to include both enhanced psychological and physical functioning after successful adaptation. That is, we are thriving when we adapt to challenges creatively with better adaptations and acquire even more potent coping skills in the future. Just as in the broaden-and-build model of positive emotions, certain ways of dealing with challenges and stress actually help to build more effective psychological resources for the future.

Vitality and Positive Health

Richard Ryan and Edward Deci conceptualized **vitality** as the energy available to the self (Ryan & Deci, 2008), defining it as a "positive feeling of aliveness and energy" (Ryan & Frederick, 1997, p. 529). In their studies, they found that vitality is enhanced by activities that satisfy self-determination needs for competence; autonomy; and relatedness (Ryan & Deci, 2008). This finding was particularly strong when activities are intrinsically motivated (Nix, Ryan, Manley, & Deci, 1999). Vitality is also related to better health outcomes (Ryan & Frederick, 1997) and may be a factor in longevity because of its association with autonomy (Kasser & Ryan, 1999). Although many studies have found that effort expended on discipline and self-control can deplete energy available to the self for other tasks (Baumeister & Vohs, 2007), Ryan and Deci (2008) found that when discipline is self-motivated, efforts lead to greater energy and vitality.

Exercise and Positive Health

Earlier models of wellness tended to focus on physiological interventions and measures of health. There is still good reason for examining these measures, particularly of physical exercise. Numerous studies have supported the idea of regular exercise as beneficial to both physical and psychological well-being (Penedo & Dahn, 2005). A recent study found that physically fit adults had a greater sense of personal accomplishment and more self-efficacy (McAuley et al., 2010). For older persons, moderate walking for 40 minutes three times a week can help improve cognitive processes and keep aging brains healthier (Voss et al., 2010). Other possible benefits of exercise include a greater ability to fight off colds (see Montagne, 2010), better sleep, (Reid et al., 2010), and greater self-acceptance and mindfulness (Ulmer, Stetson, & Salmon, 2010). Teenage boys who have better cardiovascular health tend to score higher on intelligence tests (Åberg et al., 2009). A recent study found that even better posture—in this case sitting up straight in one's chair—resulted in increased self-confidence (Briñol, Petty, & Wagner, 2009). Physical exercise is an effective treatment for depression and anxiety and can prevent illness (Otto et al., 2009). However, too much activity, or overtraining, can have a negative impact on well-being (Paluska & Schwenk, 2000).

Studies now affirm that several different factors play a role in the type of benefits reaped from physical exercise. A positive attitude toward exercise increases motivation, and even preconscious positive attitudes can increase the amount of physical activity people engage in (Conroy, Hyde, Doerksen, Ribeiro, 2010). In one study, hotel maids were advised that their daily work furnished an effective means to reduce weight. One month later, the maids lost an average of two pounds, lowered blood pressure, and trimmed body fat (Crum & Lang, 2007). Apparently, this was due to their thinking about their daily routine in a different way. Another factor is level of activity. Most experts agree that healthy aerobic activity need not be strenuous. For example, the regular practice of *tai chi chuan*, a Chinese form of slow, gentle movement, can be beneficial to health (Gorman, 2002) and is gaining in popularity among older persons because of its less strenuous demands. Finally, studies in recent years have also found that the well-known "runner's high" results from a combination of hormonal factors and is not simply due to the release of endorphins (Dietrich & McDaniel, 2004).

Vagal Tone and Heart Rate Variability (HRV)

For thousands of years, poets have written about the heart as a metaphor for love, connection, and compassion. Strikingly, the physiology of the heart is among the most intriguing research areas in well-being studies. Stephen Porges at the University of Illinois-Chicago has introduced polyvagal theory, which hypothesizes that activity of the vagus nerve to the heart is involved in social behavior (Porges, 2001, 2007). When the vagus nerve to the heart is functioning well, our heart rates show more variability in response to several different social and interpersonal situations. Polyvagal theory and the neurovisceral integration model (Hagemann, Waldstein, & Thayer, 2003) both postulate connections between parasympathetic processes and an ability to self-regulate. High heart rate variability (HRV) can serve as an index of self-regulatory strength. Indeed, several studies have found that better HRV is associated with greater ability to regulate one's thoughts, emotions, and behaviors (Segerstrom, Smith, & Eisenlohr-Moul, 2011). People with high HRV experience more positive emotions and feel more socially connected (Kok & Fredrickson, 2010). McCraty and Rees (2009) suggested that sustained positive emotions can help generate congruence among the emotional, cognitive and physiological systems, creating a state of "psychophysiological coherence." HRV can be increased by physical exercise; yoga; meditation; and positive self-relevant feedback (Sunkaria, Kumar, & Saxena, 2010; Segerstrom, Smith, & Eisenlohr-Moul, 2011).

Health Psychology and PNI

During the 1970s, the American Psychological Association created a new specialty area focusing on the contributions of psychology to an understanding of illness and disease. The goal of the health psychology division was to examine all behavioral factors that might affect a person's health (Brannon & Feist, 2000). Interestingly, the early focus of health psychology is compatible with positive psychology—namely, how to use psychological knowledge to enhance health status beyond the curing of disease and toward greater wellness.

The issues discussed so far have focused on how psychological processes are associated with physical health. The more difficult question is: Can mental processes actually *cause* changes to the chemical processes of the body? As late as 1985, an editorial in the *New England Journal of Medicine* stated that belief in a connection between disease and mental state was "largely folklore." However, scientists today in a new research domain have begun publishing findings that are turning such thinking on its head.

Research in the new area of **psychoneuroimmunology** (PNI) examines the relationships between psychological processes (especially emotion); the functioning of the nervous system; and the body's immune system. The major pioneer in PNI research was Robert Ader. In the mid-1970s, Ader and immunologist Nicholas Cohen performed an experiment in which they conditioned the immune system of rats to respond to saccharin as if it were an immunosuppressant drug (Ader & Cohen, 1975; see also Ader & Cohen, 1993). Their experiment provided evidence that the immune system could "learn," which suggests a direct influence between the brain and immune responses. Their results were initially met with considerable skepticism and resistance.

However, once it became scientifically respectable to conduct research on the links between psychological functioning and the immune system, several studies began to support their hypothesis. One of the first studies to provide strong evidence for a direct causal connection between health status and psychological factors was published in 1991. It suggested a direct connection between psychological stress and vulnerability to the common cold (Cohen, Tyrrell, & Smith, 1991). Later Cohen, Doyle, Skoner, Rabin, and Gwaltney (1998) advanced a more rigorous test of the stress-cold connection hypothesis, discovering that the larger a person's social network, the less likely he or she would be to develop a cold. In fact, those with lower social support were four times more likely to become ill than those with higher social support.

PSYCHOLOGICAL FACTORS IMPORTANT TO HEALTH

Research in PNI has shown that psychological factors can have a measurable impact on our immune system. Certainly, among the most fascinating research areas in PNI is the idea of consciously influencing the immune system through psychological interventions. Studies have demonstrated that under certain circumstances, people can learn how to either increase or decrease the number of cells in their own bodies associated with immune functioning (for example, T-cells or S-IgA antibodies). A substantial amount of research has found scientifically measurable relationships between cognition, emotions, and the immune response (Ironson & Powell, 2005; Kendall-Tackett, 2009). Therefore, we now turn to psychological factors that improve health status, often through improvements in functioning of the immune system.

Positive Emotionality

Our discussion of Fredrickson's broaden-and-build model of positive emotion in chapter 2 mentioned that positive emotions are advantageous to both psychological and physical well-being. People who feel more positive emotions tend to be healthier (Chesney, Darbes, Hoerster, Taylor, Chambers, et al., 2005; Richman, Kubansky, Maselko, Kawachi, Choo, et al., 2005). How so? Positive emotions may have a facilitative influence on the autonomic nervous system, especially the parasympathetic system, as well as on the immune system (Jencke, 2010). Lyubomirsky, King, and Diener (2005) reviewed over 225 research papers on well-being and found that more frequent positive emotionality was associated with several factors related to higher ratings on self-perceived health and better health status: Happier people perceived themselves as healthier, and objective measures confirmed this. Happier people also showed more energy, were more involved in enjoyable activities, engaged in healthier behaviors (for example, consumed less alcohol), and had better coping skills. Finally, the evidence suggested that happier people had healthier functioning immune systems. Representing a somewhat different research perspective, Leitschuh & Rawlins (1991) found that higher self-actualization is related to better self-reported health. Later researchers found that possessing a sense of meaning and purpose in life is linked to lower risk for Alzheimer's disease (Boyle, Buchman, Barnes, & Bennett, 2010).

Examining health from yet another perspective, Isen (1987) found that physicians who felt more positive emotions tended to integrate patient information better when making diagnoses. Presumably, they made better diagnoses. Please note, however, current research suggests the presence of negative emotions such as depression and anxiety is a better overall predictor of poor health status than are positive emotions of positive health (Dua, 1994).

Social Support

The positive impact of social support on health has been documented in numerous studies over many years (Cohen & Syme, 1985; Stroebe, & Stroebe, 1996). Social support can include either (1) emotional support or (2) a willingness of others to offer their time or other tangible forms of assistance. The perception that we are loved or embedded in a supportive social network is important to our health status. Social support has been associated with positive health outcomes such as greater resistance to disease, lower rates of coronary heart disease, faster recovery from heart disease and heart surgery, and lower mortality (see Salovey et al., 2000). Support from family and friends has also been associated with fewer arterial blockages in patients with Type A personalities (Burg, Blumenthal, Barefoot, Williams, & Haney, 1986). Social support can help increase compliance with medical treatments, reduce the levels of medication, speed up recovery, and help with adoption of health-promoting behaviors (Pilisuk & Parks, 1986; Wynd & Ryan-Wenger, 2004). A classic epidemiological study in Alameda County, California, found that a lack of social support was as strongly related to mortality as was smoking (Berkman & Syme, 1979). For ethnic minorities, a perceived closeness to one's ethnic or racial group and a positive racial identity can serve to reduce health risks (Williams, Spencer, Jackson, & Ashmore, 1999). Conversely, perceived racial or ethnic discrimination can have a negative impact on health (see Lewis, 2002).

For women, social support has been correlated with lower complications during pregnancy and delivery (Nuckolls, Cassel, & Kaplan, 1972). One study found that women in labor with a supportive person present showed a decrease in mean delivery time of more than 50% compared to women who did not have such a support (Sosa, Kennell, Robertson, Klaus, & Urrutia, 1980). This effect, however, was greater for women under high stress. The benefits of social support and relaxation training may even extend to problems of infertility. Alice Domar (Kolt, Slawsby, & Domar, 1999) has given workshops for infertile women and found that a program based on support groups and relaxation training shows a significant increase in pregnancy rates and diminished depression.

One of the better-known studies in health psychology involved social support and cancer. David Spiegel and his colleagues ran support groups for women who were diagnosed with breast cancer (Spiegel, Kraemer, Bloom, & Gottheil, 1989). They found that women in support groups lived an average of 18 months longer than women who were given only conventional treatment. A study with female mice found that social isolation resulted in larger mammary gland tumor growth (Hermes et al., 2009); researchers suggested that social isolation altered the expression of genes responsible for the tumor growth. A review of studies, however, concluded that the causal relationships between psychotherapy and cancer survival is unclear (Coyne, Stefanek, & Palmer, 2007). Nonetheless, the quality of life for some cancer patients can be greatly improved through social support. In addition, since Spiegel's seminal work involving group therapy, a growing body of research has found positive health benefits for social groups and the quality of our social networks (Jetten & Haslam, 2011).

How does social support impact our health? Specifically, how does having a confidant influence our health? Medical researchers are far from answering this question precisely, but most believe that it involves both direct and indirect effects. In a direct way, the presence of a close friend enables us to receive guidance from someone familiar with our personality quirks who cares about our happiness.

Having a close relationship thereby enables us to make better, more careful decisions in such domains as work and family—and thus reduces our vulnerability to the pressures of everyday living. Social support may help to increase positive emotions such as hope, confidence, and a feeling of security. In a reciprocal fashion, an increase in positive mood from better social support increases the probability of gaining more social support (Salovey et al., 2000). Another critical factor in positive relationships and social support is empathy. People who can be empathic with others are liked better by others and feel closer to them as well (Feshbach, 1984). High levels of empathy are also associated with lower levels of anger and aggression (Novaco, 1975). This can be critical for some, as chronic hostility along with trait negative affect have been linked to heart disease (Bleil, Gianaros, Jennings, Flory, & Manuck, 2008). In a series of studies focusing on nurses in the U.S., Sandra Thomas (1997) found that those who had someone to talk to about emotional issues were less likely to be intensely and chronically angry at work than counterparts who lacked such a relationship. She thus argued that, especially for women, the importance of having a "sympathetic ear" is vital to one's well-being.

Friendship and Confidant Relationships   How are you when it comes to friendship? Is there someone with whom you share the major ups and downs of life? Can you always count on this person to stay loyally by your side or rather is he or she only a fair-weather friend? Is your relationship one of unconditional trust or do you frequently withhold facts and feelings from each other? Such questions are not only intriguing for most of us to ponder, but according to mounting evidence from psychology and medicine, their answer holds a key for individual wellness, vitality, and longevity. As American novelist Kathleen Norris (1931) remarked, "Anything, everything, little or big becomes an adventure when the right person shares it. Nothing, nothing, nothing is worthwhile when we have to do it alone."

Although behavioral scientists for the past 20 years have been affirming a measurable link between friendship and well-being, the concept is

hardly new. The Greek philosopher Aristotle addressed the topic nearly 2,500 years ago in his major work on ethical conduct and character virtues, *The Nicomachean Ethics*. He described three types of friendship based on *utility; pleasure;* and *virtue*. Those founded on *utility* are essentially business relations based on mutual tangible benefits, such as money or power. Friendships based on *pleasure* are predicated on fun interests, such as attending sporting events or concerts together. For Aristotle, *virtuous* friendship is the highest of the three, involving emotional concern and compassionate care. In his view, friendship based on virtue has the greatest impact on well-being in everyday life.

In the Middle Ages, Aristotle's outlook was extended by the influential rabbinic scholar and physician Moses Maimonides. Living in Spain and Egypt more than 800 years ago, he contended that friendship is vital for individual wellness. In a treatise of health advice written for a young prince in Saladin's royal court, Maimonides advises, "It is well known that one requires friends all his lifetime. When one is in good health and prosperous, he enjoys the company of his friends. In time of trouble, he is in need of them. In old age, when his body is weak, he is assisted by them." Although Maimonides was esteemed a healer, no medical specialties existed in his day. It was not until the late nineteenth century that scientific personality study and psychotherapy began, with the work of Sigmund Freud. Curiously, although Freud was a prolific writer, he has virtually nothing to say about the role of friendship as a positive force for men and women in adult life.

Although Freud essentially ignores the topic of friendship in personality development and health, his longtime associate and eventual rival Alfred Adler has much to say. After witnessing the horrors of human aggression while serving as an Austrian Army physician during World War I, Adler developed his influential concept of social feeling (Hoffman, 1996). He argued that humans have an inborn capacity for affection, caring, and love, but unless it is strengthened during childhood by family members and teachers, this capacity will be weak. Adler emphasizes the presence of friends as an important indicator of a child's emotional well-being. Arguing mainly from clinical experience rather than research data, he warned that friendless children and teens are a high-risk population for mental health problems and that professional intervention is necessary to teach them social skills.

Since the advent of behavioral medicine in the mid-1970s, investigators have closely studied social support. Increasingly, researchers have come to focus on one specific aspect of social support—friendship and the confidant relationship. As Julianne Holt-Lunstad, Brandon Jones, and Wendy Birmingham (2008) recently observed in their review of cardiovascular disease and psychosocial factors, "There is reason to believe that certain relationships may be more important than others [and that] perceptions of closeness within a specific relationship may be a particularly important ... factor contributing to our understanding" (p. 210).

Over the past three decades, research conducted mainly by psychologists and physicians has verified a measurable link between the presence of a confidant and individual wellness. The range of studies has been wide, from drug abuse and depression among American and Canadian teenagers to condom use among young Mexican men. Repeatedly, research indicated that having a trusted friend lowered virtually all forms of risky and self-destructive behavior (MacLean, 2005; Sattah, 2002). It also demonstrated that people who reported a confidant had better overall health and were less likely to suffer from a variety of chronic medical problems, such as cardiovascular impairment; high blood pressure; or asthma (Loerbroks, 2010; Surtees et al., 2004; Wainwright, 2007). They also showed greater psychological resiliency and less vulnerability to depression. A recent study of morbidity patterns in hospitalized patients with obesity found that those who lacked a confidant were significantly more likely to die within a specified time period than those experiencing this vital social bond (Dickens, 2004). In an investigation of heart disease conducted in Britain, Dickens (2004) estimated that the presence of a confidant added *four years* to women's life expectancy and *five years* to men's.

Indirectly, an ability to share personal feelings with a trusted individual makes us less likely to engage in unhealthy behaviors generated by worry, such as smoking; overeating; substance abuse; and leading a sedentary lifestyle. In this regard, the presence of a confidant buffers us from our own tendencies to seek out unhealthy avenues for relief from inner turmoil. In our 24/7 society of today, stress is unlikely to disappear soon, so having a trusted friend becomes ever more important for our daily well-being.

Internet Use and Positive Relationships   Though behavioral science is shedding increasing light on friendship and confidant relationships, some questions remain unanswered. One concerns the role of the Internet and how it affects social support. Can the positive impact of close relationships be maintained solely by electronic means or is face-to-face contact necessary? Does emotional intimacy require frequent off-line encounters involving the essentials of body language and vocal tone or can "virtual" interaction be just as effective?

Studies of Internet usage on well-being have found that too much time spent online may be slightly related to decreases in well-being (Huang, 2010). Of course, overuse of the Web can lead to an obsessive reliance (see Wang et al., 2010). The impact of the Internet on well-being, however, seems to depend upon the type of use, the amount of time spent online, and when people are online (Cotton, et al., 2011). A recent survey of college students found that increased Internet use was associated with decreases in well-being. The students also believed that face-to-face interactions were more beneficial to their own well-being (Schiffrin et al., 2010).

Undoubtedly coming years will see a deepening scientific understanding of friendship and its powerful effect on mental and physical health. Though technology changes around us, the human need for a trusting bond strengthened by shared feelings is timeless. In this regard, though Aristotle would be amazed by the intricacies of iphone messaging, he would hardly be surprised by the enduring nature of true friendship.

Social Support and the Immune System Many of the most fascinating breakthroughs in PNI research have come from studies that link social support to measurable changes in the immune system. In the 1980s, Janice Kiecolt-Glaser and her husband Ronald Glaser began collecting immunological and psychological data on medical students as they progressed through the academic year. They found that the stress of medical school and final exams was related to a decrease in certain cells associated with immune functioning (Kielcolt-Glaser, Speicher, Holliday, & Glaser, 1984). The effect was greater for medical students who reported greater feelings of loneliness. Similarly, Kielcolt-Glaser and Glaser studied couples and found that those who were in a happy relationship were more likely to have healthier immune systems than their unhappy counterparts (Kiecolt-Glaser, Fisher, Ogrocki, Stout, Speicher, & Glaser, 1987; Kiecolt-Glaser, Newton, Capioppo, MacCallum, Glaser, & Malarkey, 1997). Later researchers also found that loneliness can have negative effects on immune functioning, health, and psychological well-being (see Miller, 2011).

Social Support from Pets? The health benefits of relationships even extend to pets. Several studies have found that pets can enhance people's health in many ways including lowering blood pressure; reducing rates of angina; and increasing longevity (Siegal, 1990). Swedish physician Kerstin Uvnäs-Moberg found that levels of oxytocin increased when people petted their dogs (see Child, 2010). Levels of oxytocin also increased in dogs when petted by their owners. People can gain health benefits by caring for a variety of pets, not just dogs. Even watching a natural environment such as a fish swimming in a tank can help lower some people's blood pressure. Support from diverse animals can be a positive source of health and well-being.

Love and Positive Health

Positive health benefits have also been found for feeling loved (see Seligman, 2005). These effects are particularly evident in men. When compared with unmarried men, married men have fewer infectious diseases; less risk of stroke; and may even live longer (Goldbourt & Lackalnd, 2010). Positive marital relationships and love have been shown to have specific effects on heart disease. A study in Israel of 10,000 married men over 40 years old found that those who believed their wives loved them had a smaller chance of developing symptoms of angina pectoris (chest pain caused by poor blood supply to the heart). Incredibly, belief in their wives' love and support was a *better* predictor of future angina for the men than physical factors such as cholesterol levels, age, and blood pressure (Medalie & Goldbourt, 1976). The perception of being loved by one's wife has also been associated with decreased risk for ulcers (Medalie, Strange, Zyzanski, & Goldbourt, 1992).

Married women also benefit physiologically from marriage, but for them it is the quality of the marriage that is a more significant factor. Men seem to benefit simply from being married, whereas women require a good marriage in order to show increased health benefits. For instance, a study found that being married decreased days in the hospital for men, but decreased hospital stay was found only among women who reported high-quality marriages (Kulik & Mahler, 2006). Finally, the perception that one is loved—or that one was loved as a child—has been associated with several health benefits. These include less risk for heart disease, ulcers, hypertension, and alcoholism (Russek & Schwartz, 1997).

Touch The simple act of touching another person is related to love and is similarly associated with positive health (Field, 2001). Tiffany Field of the Touch Research Institute at the University of Miami notes that our skin is our largest organ, covering about 20 square feet. Physiologically, a caring touch releases oxytocin (the "cuddle hormone"; see chapter 2), which increases feelings of caring and compassion. Touch therapies, such as massage, can help reduce the experience of pain and may help in the treatment of psychological disorders (Field, 1998, 2002; Rich, 2002; the Mayo Clinic, 2010).

In one study, blood pressure and hormonal activity were measured in married couples after they discussed a happy moment together, watched five minutes of a romantic film, and shared a twenty-second hug (Light, Grewen, & Amico, 2005). After the romantic intervention the couples showed lower blood pressure, lowered stress hormones, and higher levels of oxytocin.

Other research has found that supportive touch from a teacher results in more class participation, and sympathetic touch from a physician can give patients the impression a visit lasted longer and was more helpful (see Carey, 2010). Caring and supportive touch may also help people make better decisions (Ackerman, Nocera, & Bargh, 2010). One interesting study (Kraus, Huang, & Keltner, 2010) found that the frequency of touch among basketball players helped predict actual performance during games! The maxim "Give hugs, not drugs" now has real scientific support.

Compassion and Health   The association between empathy and health mentioned earlier recalls a study by David McClelland suggesting that simply watching someone be kind and sympathetic to others can influence changes in our immune system. McClelland (1985) showed people two films and measured immune system functioning prior to and after viewing the films. He showed *Triumph of the Will*, the famous World War II Nazi propaganda film, and *Mother Teresa*, a film about the life of Nobel Peace Prize winner Mother Teresa as she worked among the sick and dying in India. Immediately after seeing the film on Mother Teresa, participants showed increased immune system functioning (see Figure 6.1). Some participants were also asked

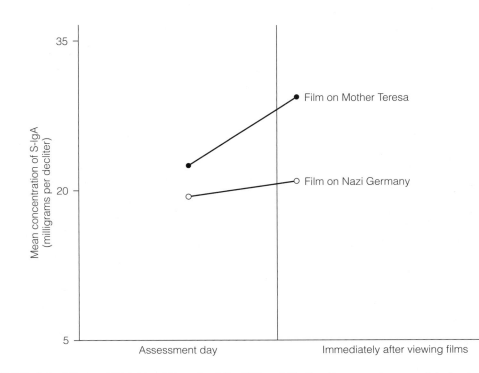

FIGURE 6.1   Effects of Watching *Triumph of the Will* and *Mother Teresa* on Immunoglobulin A

SOURCE: From D. McClelland, *Human Motivation, 1st edition* (Figure 6.1, p. 368). Copyright © 1985. Reprinted by permission of Pearson Education, Inc., Upper Saddle River, NJ.

Copyright 2006 by Randy Glasbergen.
www.glasbergen.com

"**According to my research, laughter is the best medicine,
giggling is good for mild infections, chuckling works for minor
cuts and bruises, and snickering only makes things worse.**"

to recall times in theirlives when they had felt loved. For respondents with positive personal associations, their immune responses remained high for up to an hour after watching the film.

Altruism   If feeling compassion for other people is related to better health, could acting on those feelings also have health benefits? Indeed, research has found better health status in people who engage in altruistic behaviors such as volunteering. Higher volunteering was associated with increased longevity at rates higher than those for engaging in physical exercise or attending religious services— and was rated even slightly better than not smoking (Post, 2005). Giving help may actually be more related to well-being than receiving help. Altruism seems to take people away from preoccupations with their own concerns, increase social bonds, and promote positive emotions. As baseball great Jackie Robinson said, "A life is not important except in the impact it has on other lives." Practicing random acts of kindness is good for your health.

Humor and Positive Health

Research findings even suggest that physicians should prescribe jokes. Hippocrates, the father of Greek medicine, prescribed laughter to his patients as early as the fourth century BCE (Viney & King, 1998). Vaillant (1977; see chapter 8) found that the defense mechanism of humor, or being able to laugh either at oneself or at a situation, is associated with greater personal adjustment and well-being.

Research correlating humor with health gained considerable recognition after writer Norman Cousins helped cure himself of a degenerative and possibly fatal illness, ankylosing spondylitis. He refused to accept the fatalistic diagnosis of his physicians and instead added an unusual component to his treatment. In addition to ingesting high-dose vitamins, he watched funny movies and TV shows (Cousins, 1981). His unorthodox treatment apparently contributed to the cure of his disease. Later experimental studies found that laughter can increase S-IgA antibodies that help fight off infections (Dillon, Minchoff, & Baker,

1985–86), increase natural disease-fighting killer cells, and lower blood pressure (du Pre, 1998). Thorson, Powell, Sarmany-Schuller, and Hampes (1997) found that people who scored high on a sense of humor scale also tended to score high on measures of optimism, extraversion, and capacity for intimacy, and scored low on measures of neurosis. They also showed higher self-esteem and tended to use better coping strategies to deal with stress. In general, having a good sense of humor can help people recover from illness, cope with life stresses and anxiety about death, enhance immune system functioning, reduce the psychological experience of pain, and increase the chances of successful infertility treatments (Friedler et al., 2010; Lefcourt, 2002). Even anticipation of laughter can lower stress hormones (Berk, Berk, & Tan, 2008). We have only to think about laughing to benefit!

Laugh Clubs! As scientists today debate the value of a good belly laugh, some people around the world are insisting that a hearty, deep, full-body laugh is good for us. They have formed laugh clubs that meet once a day, where they laugh together as hard as they can for 15–20 minutes. Citing research that the physical act of laughing is healing in itself (Neuhoff & Schafer, 2002), advocates of laugh clubs say you don't need to even feel like laughing; just do it. (www.laughteryoga.org). Is a good belly laugh actually exercise? One researcher calculated how fast laughter burns calories. Dr. Maciej Buchowski of Vanderbilt University calculated that 15 minutes of laughter a day can produce a weight loss of 4.5 lbs. over the course of a year (Buchowski et al., 2007).

Music and Health

In a similar fashion, some researchers and physicians are now proposing that music can aid the healing process. Relaxing sounds have been shown to lower stress hormones and blood pressure, raise endorphin levels, and increase positive moods (Gaynor, 2002; Halpern & Savary, 1985). Cancer specialist Dr. Mitchell Gaynor has had success using varied music as an adjunctive therapy with his patients (Gaynor, 2002), playing sounds of Tibetan singing bowls; Gregorian chants; the chanting of Jewish prayers; and drumming.

A fascinating series of studies has even suggested that the normal human heartbeat sounds musical. When cardiologists Peng, Goldberger, Stanley, and colleagues recorded human heartbeats, they discovered it was possible to graph the intervals between beats and convert these into a series of musical notes (Peng et al., 1993; Peng, Havlin, Stanley, & Goldberger, 1995). They found that healthy heartbeats sounded musically pleasing while unhealthy hearts sounded somewhat off-key or arrhythmic (see polymer.bu.edu/music). The Boston Museum of Science used this research to create an exhibition that allowed museumgoers to record their own heartbeats and turn them into music. Similarly, a recent study looked at the dynamic patterns and sequences of brain activity over time. It seems that these patterns are more similar to music than to language and speech (Lloyd, 2011). Perhaps a better metaphor than saying that we talk to ourselves is that we are singing.

Emotional Expression and Health

Writing About Our Lives James Pennebaker conducted several studies on the use of writing as a method of dealing with trauma and difficulties. In particular, he focused on the effect of emotional expression on health and well-being. His central research question asked whether psychologists are right to assume that "keeping it all inside" is bad for one's mental and physical health. Pennebaker concluded that confiding in others or sharing one's experiences can be therapeutic and that the nonverbal expression of emotions through art or music can also be helpful (Berry & Pennebaker, 1993; Pennebaker, 1990, 1993). His most surprising finding was that the simple act of writing down one's thoughts about a traumatic event could be therapeutic.

In one study, Pennebaker, Kiecolt-Glaser, and Glaser (1988) asked a group of college students to write about a personal traumatic experience. Another group was asked to write about superficial topics. The group writing about its traumatic experiences showed a significant decline in visits to the university health center, exhibited better immune system responses, lower blood pressure, and less distress. Those who wrote about traumatic events they had not previously shared with others indicated the greatest improvement. Further benefits were found for those who were more self-reflective and open to their emotions (Pennebaker & Seagel, 1999). One interesting finding was that sharing negative emotions was more helpful to the resolution of trauma than trying to focus only on positive emotions. However, Laura King (King, 2001; King & Miner, 2000) found gains when people wrote about how they had grown from a traumatic event.

Does this mean that we sometimes have to feel worse in order to feel better? Apparently people who keep diaries and daily journals know something the rest of us should learn. It seems that efforts to control or suppress negative emotions related to trauma are counterproductive. However, those seeking to use writing as a tool for emotional healing should realize that people in the study often reported feeling worse immediately after writing about difficult experiences. The positive effects from the exercise came only a few days later.

Pennebaker's studies offer a method for acknowledging and grappling with difficult emotions in a healthy way. He provided the following suggestions for using writing as a way to deal with stress, difficult emotions, and painful memories (adapted from Smyth & Pennebaker, 1999, and Sattler & Shabatay, 1997):

1. Write about any issue that currently concerns you.
2. Find a location in which to write where you will not be disturbed. It is helpful if the place is special and unique, acting as a situational cue for the type of writing you will do.
3. Don't worry about spelling, grammar, or your prose. Just put words down on paper. If you run into a mental block, repeat what you just wrote. This can help to unblock the thinking process. It is not be necessary to write everyday. In order to get the ball rolling, however, you might find it useful to set aside 20 minutes each day and write for three or four days consecutively. Be sure to leave a few minutes at the end to compose yourself.
4. Write about what happened as well as your feelings surrounding an event. Explore your deepest emotional reactions to that episode. Really let go. Include both positive and negative emotions, but make a special effort to find the positive emotions associated with the event. Try to explore the complexity of the issue. How has this event and its related emotions affected your life, your relationships, and how you see yourself? How do these relate to your future self? Try to construct a narrative that can explain the events and put them into a meaningful context.
5. Generally, it is helpful if you plan to keep your writing private. You may even wish to destroy what you've written after you have finished.
6. Remember that after you're finished, you'll probably feel somewhat sad. No one can express difficult issues without generating some negative emotions. However, most people find that negative feelings fade away within an hour or so. Be aware, though, that for some people negative emotions may persist for several days. If the negative emotions generated by this exercise are very strong or continue for weeks, it is advisable to seek professional counseling.

A study by Sonja Lyubomirsky, Lorie Sousa, and Rene Dickerhoof (2006) suggested that how we process emotional material is very important. Like Pennebaker, these researchers found that the act of writing about difficult events produced better emotional and physical health, and that relating negative experiences could also be beneficial. However, merely thinking about traumatic experiences did little to help people work through their emotions. In addition, Lyubomirsky and her colleagues found an effect with significant implications for positive psychology interventions: Namely, people who systematically analyzed and processed positive experiences (for example, analyzing the *how* and *why* of positive experiences) showed *reduced* levels of well-being and physical health. They felt worse! Those who simply replayed positive events or recalled positive memories experienced an increase in well-being. It seems that analyzing negative experiences can help to process them, but analyzing positive experiences takes the "fun" from them; it may be better just to enjoy them and replay them through reminiscences.

Those interested in using writing as a method for personal growth may wish to read the work of Ira Progoff (1983, 1992). He named his technique the intensive journal method, in which one begins by writing down an answer to a single question, "Where am I now in my life?" Answers to this question are then addressed in various sections of the journal workbook, such as career, family, and spirituality. The intent is to create an ongoing dialogue between aspects of a person's inner and outer lives. Progoff's journaling method has been used in many settings including university classes; alcohol treatment centers; prisons; divinity schools; and businesses (see Gestwicki, 2001).

Regrets Regret is a common psychological phenomenon experienced by nearly all adults during the lifespan (Landsman, 1987). Much is known about which life domains elicit the biggest regrets: education; career; and romance (Jokaisaari, 2003; Roese & Summerville, 2005; Stewart & Vandewater, 1999). Yet surprisingly, there is little empirical data on what makes our life regrets big or small.

Since the mid-1990s, investigators (Gilovich & Medvec, 1995; Kahneman, 1995) have distinguished between regrets over one's *actions* versus regrets over one's *inactions*. Although systematic research has yet to be undertaken, available evidence (Gilovich, Kahneman, & Medvec, 1998) suggests that regrets over actions tend to elicit primarily "hot" emotions such as anger ("How could I have been so stupid to have done that!") while regrets over inaction generally elicit feelings of wistfulness ("What if I had moved to New York with Kathy that summer instead of remaining in Cleveland?") or despair ("Why didn't I go to law school when I had the opportunity? I've wasted my life selling life insurance."). In research reviewed by Bonnefon and Zhang (2008), people experienced more regret in the short-term over their actions compared to inactions leading to the same bad outcomes. In contrast, long-term regrets usually involved failures to act.

One explanation for this is that consequences of actions are clear in both the short-term and long-term, but the impact of our failures to act often becomes apparent only later on. Thus, the perceived consequences of inactions become clearer and increase as time passes, whereas the perceived impact of actions are immediately clear and stable over time.

Several researchers (Bauer, Wrosch, & Jobin, 2008; Wrosch et al., 2005; Wrosch et al., 2007) have explored the impact of regret upon emotional and physical wellness. The findings clearly indicate that severe regret is associated with lower subjective well-being and more health problems, especially among older adults (Wrosch et al., 2005, 2007). For example, intense regrets are associated with cortisol dysregulation in the elderly (Wrosch et al., 2007). This stronger association between regret and indicators of quality of life among older adults is attributed to age-related reduction of opportunities for overcoming the effects of regret. Thus, regrets have far-reaching implications for emotional and physical well-being, especially in late adulthood.

Can we learn to minimize our regrets and thereby improve our emotional well-being? It would seem so. In an experimental study, Wrosch et al., (2007) found that older adults who engaged in a writing program similar to Pennebaker's lessened both their feelings of regret and chronic sleeping problems.

A recent line of research on life longings (or *sehnsucht*) is highly related to studies of regret. A **life longing** is a "strong feeling that life is incomplete or imperfect, coupled with a desire for ideal (utopian), alternative states and experiences of life" (Scheibe, Kunzmann, & Baltes, 2009, p. 176). Therefore, life longings tell us both that something is missing from our lives and that we may not be able to correct the situation. The emotions associated with these longings are often ambivalent and bittersweet, alerting us to both gains and losses in life. An example is that of a middle-aged single woman who finds herself with a growing desire for children. A key element in the relationship between life longings and well-being is a sense of control. When people are unable to control the onset, duration, or intensity of longings, they experience decreased well-being. On the other hand, if put in a larger perspective and viewed as inevitable consequences of necessary life choices, longings can enrich an understanding of life's complexities.

Crying: Tears of Hurt Pennebaker's research suggests that sometimes it is helpful to briefly feel bad in order to feel good. Then can having a good cry be an effective stress reducer? The research on crying does not support the view that this is always true (DeFruyt, 1997; Vingerhoets, Cornelius, Van Heck, & Becht, 2000). Not everyone benefits from crying, in part because there is a variety of styles of crying and there are many reasons to cry. For instance, crying can be a coping mechanism, or it can be a response to joyful events like weddings. Studies have found that only people who are extraverted and emotionally stable find relief and "feel better" after crying (DeFruyt, 1997). In contrast, those who score high on neurosis tend to cry more often and to use weeping as a coping style but may not experience significant relief from crying. Apparently, having a good cry is not universally helpful.

Crying: Tears of Joy Though nearly everyone has experienced crying due to happiness, this phenomenon is relatively unexplored. Anderson (1996) identified nine characteristics of "transformative weeping" associated with such feelings as gratitude, joy, and wonder. These include a sense of reconnecting with lost parts of one's self as well as a sense of inner freedom or vastness. This type of crying often occurs in response to profound spiritual experiences. In this instance, it is weeping for joy. Placing such experiences in a broad philosophical or religious context, Braud (2001) in a qualitative study related joyful crying to such positive emotions as awe, compassion, gratitude, love, and yearning. Suggesting that this somatic response might be physiologically rooted in the human organism, he observed, "For me, wonder-joy tears are responses to encountering and appreciating what is truly important—an 'empathy indicator' or 'compassion indicator' or 'gratitude indicator'" (p. 106).

Consistent with this view, Rottenberg et al. (2008) in research with Dutch women found that crying in response to positive events was associated with greater empathy. Those with higher scores measuring anhedonia (an inability to feel pleasure) or alexithymia (an inability to express emotions) were less likely to report this type of experience. Finally, crying may also be a generalized response to powerful emotions, whether negative or positive. Being open to aesthetic experiences and deeply moved by works of art is also related to frequency of crying (DeFruyt, 1997). A great deal of empirical investigation concerning gender, age, and cultural factors remains to be done before psychologists understand the intriguing phenomenon of "tears of happiness."

Cognition and Thinking: Optimism, Hope and Control

Several researchers have proposed that our emotional reactions to life events are shaped by our cognitive interpretations. Overly negative or unrealistic interpretations can lead to unnecessary increases in stress, worry, or unwise and impulsive behaviors. Higgins and Leibowitz (1999) presented an interesting variation on this idea, suggesting that the perceived challenge of an event is related to how much personal redefinition it involves. In their view, if an event challenges our basic definition of self, it is more stressful than if our self-concept were left intact.

Richard Lazarus (2007) argued that what is crucial to a cognitive mediation approach is the meaning we bring to a situation. Stressfulness is viewed neither as a quality of a person nor a situation but rather as a quality that emerges from the *relationship* between a person and a situation. Individual judgments of stressfulness are also influenced by current mood; state of health; past experience; and other factors sensitive to a situation. Today, almost all stress management programs incorporate the notion that we can change our emotional reactions to events by changing how we think about or interpret those events. Studies have also shown that cognitive styles are very important for positive coping.

Optimism   Several years ago, Schier and Carver (1985; 1987) produced compelling evidence that optimism is related to both physical and psychological well-being. They also examined the potential health consequences of optimism and found that a generalized expectancy that good things will happen is related to better health outcomes, including less distress in women with breast cancer and faster recovery from surgery (Scheier & Carver, 1992). A recent meta-analysis of 83 studies supports these conclusions by finding that optimism is a significant factor in better health status (Rasmussen, Schier, & Greenhouse, 2009).

Scheier and Carver also examined the factors that might account for these relationships. They found that optimists had a tendency to use problem-focused coping strategies to deal with challenges and stress (also see Lopes & Cunha, 2008). This was especially the case under circumstances that were actually controllable. At the same time, optimism was positively correlated with the seeking of social support, which also aids health. A related finding was that women who were more hopeful were more informed about risk factors for breast cancer; more willing to visit health

professionals; and more likely to perform self-examinations for early signs of cancer (Irving, Snyder, & Crowson, 1998). Similarly, a greater sense of hope has been associated with stronger immune system responses (Scioli, 2010). A recent study found that when patients expected to get better more quickly, they had better outcomes (Barefoot et al., 2011). In general, optimists tended to have better health outcomes than pessimists (Peterson, Seligman, & Vaillant, 1988). In Seligman's (1998) theory of **learned optimism**, he stated that we can learn to be more optimistic if we focus on the positive and what is possible; then we can learn to respond to stressors with an attitude of optimism and hope.

Although being optimistic or feeling hopeful can have advantages, several qualifications must be made. For example, optimism has been associated with less adherence to weight loss programs (Saito, 2009) and decreased well-being among some colostomy patients (Smith et al., 2007). Suzanne Segerstrom (2010) found that dispositional optimism did not predict overall health status in first-year law students, but it did predict better responses to situational stress. It may be that optimism helps people confront easy stressors but is not as helpful for handling persistent and uncontrollable stressors (Segerstrom, 2005). Too much optimism may lead people to work too hard at solving unsolvable problems—a situation, of course, that tends to increase stress. Finally, one study found that pessimism was a better predictor of poor health outcomes than optimism was of better health when a full range of incomes was taken into account (Robb, Simon, & Wardle, 2009).

Perceived Control   Research strongly supports a relationship between a perceived sense of control and health. Indeed, a longitudinal study of over 3,000 community residents found that belief in self-control, social support, and exercise predicted better health status 10 years later (Lachman & Agrigoroaei, 2010). Most discussions of perceived control begin with Rotter's (1966) seminal work on internal and external locus of control. A review of the research on locus of control and health behaviors by Strickland (1978) concluded that people who described themselves as more internal (that is, who viewed themselves as "masters of their destiny" rather than as passive observers of events) engaged in more adaptive coping styles and also in more positive health-related behaviors. However, the review also noted that this conclusion is tentative and must immediately be qualified in some ways. Among the most important caveats is that internally oriented people have an advantage over externally oriented ones in terms of positive coping and greater adaptation only under circumstances in which some control is possible.

Similarly, better health status was found for people with higher health locus of control and optimism (Ustundag-Budak, Meltem, & Sense-West, 2005). However, an internal health locus of control was beneficial for men, and a chance locus of control—usually considered a negative perspective—was beneficial for women. Like the research implications for optimism, it may be that too much internal control is problematic. A study of Chinese women who survived cancer found that those who worked too hard at emotional control had lower well-being (Ho, Chan, & Ho, 2004). Higher well-being was found in women who expressed all their emotions, both positive and negative. Last, a perceived lack of control is associated with negative affectivity or neurosis, but that finding relates only to complaints about one's health and not to actual health status (Watson & Pennebaker, 1989). It may be that moderated control is more effective. Kashdan and Rottenberg (2010) proposed **psychological flexibility** as also an important factor in health status. Greater flexibility allows us to adapt to changing circumstances and can maximize the probability of better adjustment.

Related to optimism and control is the phenomenon known as the placebo response. This is activated when a patient believes that a medicine or treatment is effective even if there is no scientific reason to support that view. For many years, the placebo response was considered a nuisance in medicine insofar as many thought it complicated the search for "real" medical treatments. What was neglected was an acknowledgment that people actually got better—apparently by simply believing

they would. Herbert Benson (1996) argued that to view the placebo response as merely false belief misses the point because that belief can lead to measurable changes in physiology. He renamed the placebo response "remembered wellness," indicating that it just might be an untapped power for healing that all people possess. It may be that a person's belief in the efficacy of a placebo releases natural painkillers in the body.

Self-Efficacy   Among the best-known cognitive perspectives is Albert Bandura's (1977) theory of self-efficacy. He postulated that people are able to make changes in their behavior if they believe they have the ability to perform or the capacity to learn the behaviors necessary to reach desired goals. People with high self-efficacy tend to believe they have more control over their own health and are able to manage pain better (see Brannon & Feist, 2000). They also show better adherence to programs that improve health, such as smoking-cessation programs. Note that the concept of self-efficacy shares many qualities with optimism; perceived control; and the agency pathway of hope.

Recently, researchers have expanded the ideas of Bandura and others with the construct of *problem-solving appraisals*, which refers to beliefs about one's problem-solving abilities. Studies have found that positive problem-solving appraisals are associated with psychological adjustment; better health status; and use of more effective coping skills (Heppner & Lee, 2009).

HARDINESS AND MINDFULNESS MEDITATION

As the above discussion indicates, several personality factors have been identified as related to health. A few researchers have therefore proposed general personality styles that combine coping resources. One such healthy personality styles is explored next, followed by a discussion of a practical technique that combines physiological and cognitive interventions for better health.

Hardiness

Suzanne Kobasa[2] (Kobasa, 1979; Kobasa, Maddi, & Kahn, 1982) examined coping resources by looking at physical illness as an indicator of poor coping. Kobasa found three factors that differentiated a group with high stress and low illness from a group with high stress and high illness. The term she used to describe those in the first group is **hardiness**. She found that people with a hardy personality style showed both better mental and physical health (Kobasa et al., 1994).

Hardiness is defined as a combination of three cognitive factors involved in the interpretation of life events. Kobasa's point is that the events of our life may not matter as much as our interpretation of them. Those found hardier tended to have:

1. A sense of CONTROL over their lives. They may not have known how they would cope with a crisis, but they felt confident they would be able to cope. This factor included: (a) decisional control, or autonomy; (b) cognitive control, or "the ability to interpret, appraise, and incorporate various sorts of stressful events into an ongoing life plan and, thereby, deactivate their jarring effects" (Kobasa, 1979, p. 3); and (c) a greater variety of available coping methods.

2. A sense that the stress they were facing presented them with a CHALLENGE, rather than a crisis. They tended to see that each problem could be used for some potential good and be a catalyst for growth. This quality provided greater cognitive flexibility.

3. A sense of COMMITMENT to the various areas of their life. This third characteristic involved: (a) a meaning system that minimized the perceived threat; (b) a sense of purpose that prevented surrender; and (c) an involvement with others in positive social relationships.

What do hardy people do that differs from others? People who are high in hardiness engage in *transformational coping*. They are not victims of threatening change but instead actively determine the direction that change will take (Gentry & Ouellette-Kobasa, 1984). Interestingly, the same cognitive processes that help produce subjective well-being may also help create a sense of hardiness. Compton, Seeman, and Norris (1991) found that high hardiness was related to strong self-enhancement processes that helped produce a positive self-concept and fewer beliefs that success was due to luck. When examining the three qualities of the hardy personality, it is obvious that a hardy person is someone who can use certain cognitive skills to reinterpret the events of his or her life in adaptive ways.

Mindfulness Meditation

The use of mindfulness meditation was mentioned in chapter 4 as a way to enhance well-being. Jon Kabat-Zinn (1982, 1990) introduced mindfulness techniques into Western psychology by working with medical patients who suffered from chronic pain. Since then, studies have found that mindfulness can also help reduce anxiety, stress, and worry, probably by promoting cognitive, emotional, and physiological regulatory mechanisms (Kuyken et al., 2010; Miller, Fletcher, Kabat-Zinn, 1995; Mohan, Sharma, Bijlani, 2011). Mindfulness has been shown to help increase immune system functioning (Davidson et al., 2003). In medical settings, the use of mindfulness has also been an effective adjunctive therapy for several problems including cancer, insomnia, multiple sclerosis, and has been used to foster greater attention of health professionals to patient's needs and concerns (Epstein, 2003; Grossman, 2010; Shapiro & Carlson, 2009). However, the impact of mindfulness meditation may be greater for people who already have higher trait mindfulness (Shapiro, et al., 2011).

Each year now more than 100 new studies are published, and mindfulness research and training

Jon Kabat-Zinn

© Naushon Kabat-Zinn

programs are offered at more than 250 medical institutions around the United States. Today hundreds of health care professionals are applying the mindfulness-based stress reduction (MBSR) program to problems ranging from anxiety and drug addiction, to cardiovascular disease, chronic pain, cancer, insomnia, and many others (Chang et al., 2010; Chen et al., 2010; Dautovch et al., 2010; Howell et al., 2008; Kingston et al., 2007: Lovas & Barsky, 2010; Matousek & Dobkin, 2010).

Typically, the MBSR program comprises an 8-to-10 week course for groups of up to 30 participants who meet weekly for 2 to 2.5 hours for instruction and practice in mindfulness skills, together with discussion of stress, coping, and homework assignments. An all-day (7-8 hour) intensive mindfulness session is usually held around the sixth week. A variety of mindfulness skills are taught, including a 45-minute body scan exercise in which participants lie down with eyes closed, a sitting meditation in which participants focus on their breathing, and mindfulness cultivation during every-day activities like standing, walking, and eating. Participants in MBSR are instructed to practice these skills outside group meetings for at least 45 minutes per day, six days per week. In all mindfulness exercises, participants learn to focus attention on the target of observation in the present moment, and to experience non-judgmentally their feelings, thoughts, or sensations when they arise. An important consequence of mindfulness practice is the realization that most of these experiences fluctuate or are transient, passing by "like waves in the sea." (Linehan, 1993, p. 87)

Psychologists are interested too in offering mindfulness as a preventative method for ensuring emotional well-being and stability. That is, mindfulness may be useful as a psychological "prophylaxis" for asymptomatic individuals (Ma & Teasdale, 2004) or for those at risk for depression relapse (Teasdale et al., 2000). It is also interesting to note that even the U.S. military is exploring the benefits of mindfulness training. In a study designed to assess its effects on working memory and emotion, investigators (Jha et al., 2010) found that an 8-week course improved working memory and decreased negative affect. While in this study mindfulness training did not significantly bolster positive emotionality, the results were encouraging enough for the investigators to say that mindfulness might reduce the likelihood of long-term psychological disorders, posttraumatic stress, anxiety, and it could help soldiers act more effectively and ethically. Although some empirical literature on mindfulness contains methodological weaknesses (Baer, 2003; Wisner, Jones & Gwin, 2010), the evidence is robust that it is the mindfulness component of these interventions that is largely responsible for a reduction of impairments involving mind and body.

The topic of brain plasticity is also relevant to mindfulness meditation. Studies have found that long-term mindfulness may actually increase the grey matter of the brain in areas associated with meditation (Hölzel et al., 2008). In general, mindfulness meditation has a positive impact on a plethora of factors related to both well-being and health (Brown, Ryan, & Creswell, 2007; Shapiro & Carlson, 2009). Indeed, the research to date suggests that mindfulness meditation may be among the most useful ways to help improve emotional and physical well-being, wellness, and positive health. Fortunately, the benefits of mindfulness can be found in a relatively short period of time and increased benefits are found with more consistent and frequent practice of meditation (Carmody & Baer, 2009; Shapiro et al., 2008). In fact, more recent studies have found that even three days of mindfulness meditation for 20 minutes a day can impact the perception of, and sensitivity to, pain (Zeidan, Gordon, Merchant, & Goolkasian, 2009).

For people who think that meditation sounds like too much work, there may be an easier way to gain at least some of the benefits. Studies have shown that a simple 15-minute focused- breathing exercise can lower negative mood and decrease reactivity to distressing stimuli (Arche & Craske, 2006). Focused-breathing may even help generate joy (Hendricks, 1995). An intriguing study by Herbert Benson and colleagues found that the relaxation response style of meditation can help activate the expression of genes partially responsible for counteracting stress (Dusek et al., 2008).

POSITIVE AGING

Zestful Old Age

The topic of optimal functioning in old age is finally beginning to receive attention in psychology. This reflects the fact that people are increasingly surviving into late adulthood with considerable physical and mental well-being. In the United States, Japan, Germany, Italy, and other industrialized countries, millions of men and women are active in their 70s, 80s, and even 90s. This development, unprecedented in human history, is likely to surge dramatically in coming years. Until recently, the notion of thriving during the elder years seemed almost nonsensical, and so psychology had almost nothing to say about it. This situation is rapidly changing.

Erikson (Hoare, 2002) was among the first thinkers to address this issue from a positive perspective. In his view, "peak aging" encompasses three broad dimensions, insight, wisdom, and playfulness. Erikson viewed insight as "discernment" and perception of "heightened reality," a quality he often links to intuition and that he considers nurtured through sensory experience and empathy. In later years, Erikson came to see wisdom as a blend of emotional maturity; sound judgment; and able reasoning. However, he did not regard wisdom as something that suddenly or magically appears in old age but rather that accumulates over one's lifetime. From this standpoint, some college students may certainly be wiser than others.

Erikson views playfulness as an extremely important quality of elder living, stating that "the opposite of play is death" (cited in Hoare, 2002, p. 113). He viewed children's playfulness as an important model for adult zestfulness, mixing wonder and trust. He regarded early childhood play as marked by glee and exuberance, contending that the widespread absence of playfulness during adulthood stems from feelings of shame and guilt. In Erikson's view, adults today do not so much suppress their sexuality—as rampant today as in Freud's era—as their joyfulness.

How to nurture playfulness? Erikson recommends creative activities such as painting as well as heightened involvement with children. His many specific tips include:

> "See children as a gift … both one's own and those of others. Avoid seeing each child as that which the adult is better than (weak, mischievous, immature, careless); instead see the child as one who has what so many adults have managed to lose— energy, a willing laugh, the bounce of glee, and motives devoid of greed and self-promotion" (p. 137).

Longevity

The previous discussions of positive health and zestful aging point to another positive health outcome—namely, longevity. Generally, people have assumed that longevity is due to genetic factors. However, Thomas Perls, who leads the New England Centenarian Study, argues that up to 70% of the factors contributing to longevity are nongenetic (Yong, 2009). Many of the variables mentioned earlier in association with positive health are also correlated with longevity.

Positive Emotions Several researchers have concluded that positive emotionality can have a significant impact on longevity. Ed Diener and Micaela Chan (2011) report compelling evidence that more positive feelings and fewer negative feelings can lead to longer life. Other studies have found similar results (Chida & Stepoe, 2008; Xu, 2006; Shirai et al., 2009). For instance, *the nun study* is a rather famous one that examined how the presence of positive emotions relative to negative emotions appeared to impact longevity. Danner, Snowdon, and Friesen (2001) analyzed the two to three page autobiographies written by a group of 180 Catholic nuns as part of their application to the Order. Written as early as 1930, the autobiographical statements were analyzed for the number of positive emotions expressed. Of those who expressed more positive emotions in their youth, fully 90% were still alive at their 85th birthday. Of the nuns who expressed the lowest number of positive emotions, only 34% were still alive at age 85. By age 94, there were 54% still alive from the happiest group and only 11% still alive from the least happy group.

One clever study (especially for baseball fans) followed the protocol of the study of smiling high school yearbook photos discussed in chapter 3 (Harker & Keltner, 2001). This time the smiles of major league baseball players were measured (Abel & Kruger, 2010). They found that players with larger Duchenne smiles were only half as likely to die in any year compared with nonsmiling players. Though happiness may not be a major protective factor in people who suffer from major illness, it can increase immunity and longevity in healthy people (Veenhoven et al., 2008).

Some caveats to the general conclusion that positive emotions predict longevity: Diener and Chan (2011) suggest that too much happiness can negatively impact longevity insofar as extremely happy people take more risks due to an overabundance of optimism and are less likely to seek medical attention. Results from Friedman and Martin's (2011) Longevity Project found that none of the following factors is associated with longevity: less work, presence of pets, feeling loved, being happier, and, for women, being married. Rather, longevity is associated with commitment to work, having friends, possessing a sense of meaning, and altruism. However, the Longevity Project analyzed longitudinal data from the Lewis Terman study of gifted children begun in 1925, and its results may not be applicable to the general population.

Positive Relationships Positive social relationships are perhaps the greatest psychological influence on longevity. In fact, a strong sense of social integration and supportive relationships may be more vital to longevity than avoidance of smoking or obesity or engagement in physical exercise (Holt-Lunstad, Smith, & Layto, 2010). A study of Danish twins over 75 years old found that positive social ties (that is, spouse; friends; and living twin) were a major factor in longevity (Rasulo, Christensen, & Tomassini, 2005). The impact of relationships was strongest for women. Positive relationships of any kind are extremely important to female well-being, positive health, and longevity. Finally, altruism may

increase longevity. Stephanie Brown and colleagues (University of Michigan News Service, 2008) found that older persons who spent time caring for another lived longer. Other studies have likewise found longevity benefits for caregiving and other altruistic behavior (University of Michigan, 2008).

Competence, Optimism, and Other Positive Beliefs Positive emotionality may further longevity by promoting a wide array of protective factors associated with better health, such as a sense of mastery. In addition, a positive outlook on life helps with handling stress and is correlated with a proactive approach to aging, physical activity, and avoidance of unhealthy behaviors (Ong, 2010, Stessman, Hammerman-Rozenberg, Cohen, Ein-Mor, & Jacobs, 2009). Autonomy and sense of purpose may also affect longevity (Kasser & Ryan, 1999; Langer, 1989). The influence of optimism has been the subject of several studies. In following over 2,000 Mexican-Americans for two years, researchers found that those who were more optimistic tended to live longer (Ostir, Markides, Black, & Goodwin, 2000). Similar results were found in a study conducted at the Mayo Clinic that related optimism scores obtained at admission to survival rates 40 years later. When researchers compared expected lifespans, they found that optimists exhibited a 19% greater longevity than pessimists (see also Tindle et al., 2009). Finally, one's attitude toward aging plays an important role. People with more positive beliefs about aging seem better able to bounce back from illness (Levy & Myers, 2005). A set of personality characteristics that gerontologists call **adaptive competence** refers to an ability to bounce back from setbacks and stress and to adapt to aging with optimism and humor (Lachs, 2011).

The "Blue Zones" In 2004 Dan Buettner in conjunction with *National Geographic* began a study of longevity by identifying those places on earth where people live longest. They located five areas of the world in which people reached the age of 100 at rates 10 times higher than in the United States, gaining an average of 10 more years of life. They called these areas "blue zones" (www.bluezones.com).

In 2008 a team funded by the American Association of Retired Persons (AARP) and *National Geographic* traveled to one such zone, the Greek island of Ikaria. On Ikaria, one in three people was over 90 years old. Compared to people in the U.S., the Ikarians suffered 50% fewer cases of heart disease; 20% fewer cases of cancer; one-ninth the rate of diabetes; and virtually no cases of Alzheimer's disease or other dementias (Buettner, 2010). Many of these people were physically active and vital. One 102-year-old man, a stone mason who built walls using heavy field stones, had only decided to stop working at age 100! The team found that people in blue zones shared nine characteristics:

1. They remained physically active in their environments.
2. They had a strong sense of purpose, or a reason to get up in the morning.
3. They "downshifted," or found ways to decrease stress every day. As the Ikarians say, "Work gets done when it gets done."
4. They did not overeat and ate their smallest meals in the afternoon and evening.
5. They ate small portions of meat and in comparison more fruits and vegetables.
6. They drank alcohol in moderate amounts.
7. They belonged to a faith-based community.
8. They put their families first and experienced rich social connections.
9. They shared in supportive social circles and groups of friends.

The team condensed these nine characteristics into four maxims: (1) move naturally; (2) keep the right outlook and attitude; (3) eat wisely; and (4) connect with others.

POSITIVE COPING

We have seen how a variety of emotions and behaviors can impact health and wellness. These include better social support, the use of humor, increased compassion, and, for some people at least, taking time out for a good cry. It is by means of such positive coping that wellness is enhanced, for one of life's certainties is that it is sometimes challenging.

A Definition of Positive Coping

Positive coping has been defined as "a response aimed at diminishing the physical, emotional, and psychological burden that is linked to stressful life events and daily hassles" (Snyder & Dinoff, 1999, p. 5). Effective coping reduces the burden of challenges from short-term stress and contributes to the relief of longer-term stress by building resources that inhibit or buffer future challenges. These resources can be physiological, such as better health status; psychological, such as greater subjective well-being; and social, such as more intimate social support networks. More effective coping programs generally take a multidimensional approach and impact many core areas that can be used for resource building (see Synder, 1999).

The Importance of Daily Hassles

The above definition of coping includes responses to major life events as well as to daily hassles and minor irritations that hinder life from going smoothly. An important question asks: Which is more detrimental to our well-being—the big and significant life events that we must confront from time-to-time or the smaller hassles that we cope with on a daily or weekly basis? Surprisingly, studies have shown that it is the smaller, daily hassles that are more problematic for us (Lazarus, 1984). Why so? Many significant life events, such as marriage; the death of a family member; and the birth of one's child, not only occur infrequently but are associated with socially prescribed or religious rituals, such as weddings and funerals, that help people handle the changes involved. Daily frustrations are likely to upset a person's current mood, and persistent negative mood is likely to affect well-being. Therefore, the cumulative effects of many small stressors in a relatively short period of time can be more important than the impact of relatively infrequent major life events. This conclusion suggests that stress management and positive coping need to be built into one's daily routine.

Dimensions of Positive Coping

In general, positive coping strategies follow two approaches. The first focuses on the external environment, physical health, and health behavior, suggesting, for instance, an increased exercise regime to enhance physical well-being. The second approach focuses on psychological factors, usually cognitive factors such as expectations, attitudes, and beliefs through which people give meaning to life events. These interpretive habits are habitually stimulated by potential stressors and if a resultant interpretation is negative, actually produce or exacerbate a stress. That is, an interpretive meaning system intervenes between an actual objective event and its psychological effect on a person. In practice, any good stress management program combines these two approaches (for example, Davis, Eshelman, & McKay, 1988).

Coping Styles

Lazarus and Folkman (1984) contended that specific coping styles can be grouped into three subtypes: (1) attempts to change emotions (*emotion-focused coping*); (2) attempts to change the situation that caused a stress (*problem-focused coping*); and (3) simple avoidance of the challenge presented by a stressor (*emotional avoidance*). Newer perspectives recognize that these three styles do not capture all the important ways that people adapt to challenges. Annette Stanton argues that emotion-focused coping should itself be divided into two types: emotional processing and emotional expression (Stanton, Parsa, & Austenfeld, 2002). Similarly, problem-focused coping has also been divided into two types: behavioral and cognitive. A summary of these coping styles appears as follows:

1. *Emotion-Focused:* Focus primarily on emotional reactions to a stressor.
   a. *Emotional processing:* Understand reaction to a stressor.
   b. *Emotional expression:* Express emotions related to a stressor.

2. *Problem-Focused:* Focus primarily on the situation or cognitions related to a stressor.
   a. *Behavioral:* Take action to fix a real-world situation.
   b. *Cognitive:* Change thinking to fix a problem.

3. *Emotional-avoidance:* Avoid, ignore, or deny the reality of either the stressor or the emotional consequences, or both.

According to Lazarus and Folkman (1984), **emotion-focused coping** is "directed at regulating emotional responses to problems" (p. 150). The goal is to grapple with emotional reactions to a stressor. In Stanton's conception, an approach-oriented, emotion-focused coping is a movement towards the emotions involved with a stressor rather than one away from them (Stanton, Parsa, & Austenfeld, 2002). One way of embracing the emotional components of stress is through *emotional processing*, which consists of acknowledging feelings; taking time to discover one's true feelings about an event; and simply allowing feelings to be present.

Another way to take on the challenge of our emotions is through *emotional expression*, which conveys the affects associated with a stressor by articulating them; engaging in the arts; and even having a good cry. Studies have found that emotion-focused coping is an adaptive and therefore helpful way of handling stressors. In terms of positive health, it can be an effective and wise way to cope with the challenges of diseases or conditions such as cancer, chronic pain, and infertility (Austenfeld & Stanton, 2004).

The other major approach, **problem-focused coping**, involves the use of (1) behavioral strategies that change a situation or context in which stress occurs; or (2) cognitive strategies that alter our perceptions of the stressor Behavioral problem-focused coping is exemplified by a person in a stressful and unfulfilling job who switches careers. Cognitive problem-focused coping requires changing one's thinking about a situation through cognitive reappraisal, which entails doing so in a realistic and honest manner. We can change our attitudes, beliefs, or expectations about an event and thereby decrease our stressful reaction to it.

Finally, the goal can also be to forget an anxiety, eliminate a worry, or just not deal with a stressor via *emotional avoidance*. This is accomplished through defensive reappraisals, which consist of attempts to draw attention away from the more painful elements of a situation by reinterpreting it, using positive thinking to block out negative emotions, or by the use of selective attention.

People often combine these types of coping. For instance, if you consistently take your work problems home to your spouse and the discussions help you decide on a course of action that might change a situation, then you employ both emotion-focused coping and problem-focused coping to help solve a problem.

These three major styles of coping are not equally effective for each individual or in each situation. Some people prefer an emotional approach while others prefer to tackle head-on the external context in which stress occurs (Stanton, Kirk, Cameron, & Danoff-Burg, 2000). Of course, some situations simply demand one style of coping.

For instance, if one has been laid off, emotion-focused coping helps with the emotional reaction, but behavioral problem-focused coping is the only way to find a new job. Even denial or avoidance can be helpful under certain restricted circumstances. Denial can protect a person against overwhelming anxiety during the early stages of a serious illness (Froese, Hackett, Cassem, & Silverberg, 1974), though it is usually a poor long-term solution to the anxiety associated with illness (Breznitz, 1983).

Comments on Positive Coping and Health

Coping styles, resources, and strategies interact in rather complex ways. Our appraisal of events is impacted by a sense of optimism, which is enhanced by good physical conditioning and in turn is affected by a sense of control or self-discipline to maintain a consistent exercise regime. Positive emotions are central to the development of positive health and even longevity. Research is just beginning to investigate how psychological factors interact to enhance health. Results so far indeed confirm that emotions are important to our health. Further, the old Cartesian distinction between mind and body is finally giving way to a more interactive model—a dynamic system that considers psychological, physical, and spiritual factors affecting our health.

SUMMARY

This chapter opened with a discussion of wellness—that is, the notion that total well-being is an interaction of physical, emotional, and spiritual well-being. The fields of health psychology and psychoneuroimmunology were introduced. These areas have begun to change how scientists believe mind and body interact. It appears that psychological factors have a direct influence on certain physical processes such as our immune system responses.

We next reviewed psychological factors that impact health, such as positive emotionality, social support, optimistic orientation, and confidence in one's ultimate ability to bounce back from temporary difficulty. Positive coping strategies often involve interpretation of the events of our lives and the meaning we give to them. We have noted that coping is quite personal: What strategy works for each person is determined by a unique combination of personality and situational variables.

NOTES

1. Note that this idea is almost exactly the same as the contemporary idea that psychological problems are caused by a "chemical imbalance." Today the chemicals are neurotransmitters rather than the four humors, but the concept is the same.

2. Kobasa has also published under her married names of Ouellette and Ouellette-Kobasa.

LEARNING TOOLS

Key Terms

wellness

positive health

psychoneuroimmunology

thriving

hardiness

adaptive competence

emotion-focused coping

problem-focused coping

Books

Anderson, N. (2004). *Emotional longevity: What really determines how long you live.* NY: Penguin. Explains how biology, psychology, emotions, and spirituality all contribute to longevity. *(popular)*

Lazarus, R. (2006). *Stress and emotion: A new synthesis.* NY: Springer. A leader in the field talks about psychological influences on our emotions and stress. *(popular)*

Lewis, M. (2002). *Multicultural health psychology: Special topics acknowledging diversity.* NY: Allyn & Bacon. *(undergraduate textbook)*

Ornish, D. (1999). *Love and survival: 8 pathways to intimacy and health.* NY: Harper. How love and caring are central to health. *(popular)*

Sapolsky, R. (2004). *Why zebras don't get ulcers* (3rd ed.). NY: Holt. A best-selling book on stress-related illness and stress management. *(popular)*

On the Web

http://www.laughology.info/Laughology/Laughology.html   A documentary on the new laughter movement and the benefits of laughter.

http://www.uwsp.edu/hphd/empWell/wellnessDimensions/wellquiz/ A wellness Web site from the University of Wisconson-Stevens Point providing a quick evaluation of seven dimensions of wellness and other resources.

http://reylab.bidmc.harvard.edu/heartsongs and http://polymer.bu.edu/music   Two sites that introduce the Heartsongs project by the cardiologist's son who turned heartbeats into music.

http://healthpsych.com/links.html   A health psychology library that provides general information; listing of books; research; and other resources.

Video

Moyers, B. (Host). (1993). *Healing and the mind.* This five-part video series explores issues such as mind-body interaction; the relations between emotions and health; and the impact of psychological interventions on health and well-being. Important figures in health psychology and psychoneuroimmunology (PNI) are interviewed for the series.

Pochmursky, C. (Director). [2009]. *The musical brain.* A documentary about how music affects the brain. Appearances by Sting, Wyclef Jean, and others.

Personal Explorations

Studies have shown that daily hassles affect our mood and consequently have an impact on our long-term wellness. Over the next week, keep a log and record each event that you experience as a hassle—such as a traffic jam or waiting in line at the post office. Describe: (a) the nature of the hassle; (b) how long it lasted; (c) how it affected your mood; and (d) how long your mood was affected. That is, did your mood return to normal as soon as the hassle ended? If not, how long before your normal mood was restored? At the end of the week, describe what you have learned from this activity. Has it provided any insights about how you react to daily hassles and how you might respond more effectively?

The topic of optimism is an important one in positive psychology, having been linked to both mental and physical health. Over the next week, record in your log-keep a log and record every event that has turned out *better* than you expected. These events can be major or minor—what matters is that they contradicted your negative expectation. Examples includeForare example, such events can include getting a higher exam grade or completing an errand more quickly than you anticipated. After you have completed the week's activity, describe what you have learned about your degree of optimism or pessimism in daily life. As a result, have you become more optimistic?

Chapter 7

Excellence, Aesthetics, Creativity, and Genius

> Genius is 1% inspiration and 99% perspiration.
> THOMAS A. EDISON

People who exhibit excellence are able to perform some behavior, talent, or skill much more fluently and expertly than are other people. **Excellence** has been defined as the acquisition of extraordinary skill in a specific area of expertise (Ericsson & Charness, 1994; Ericsson, 1996). The skill or talent can be in anything—from basket weaving to theoretical physics. The ability to perform something extraordinarily well comprises the first section of this chapter. Our next section discusses an ability to deeply appreciate beauty in the world. The last section of the chapter addresses creativity and that often overused term, "genius."

THE PURSUIT OF EXCELLENCE

The Foundations of Excellence

The first question for consideration is whether excellence is the result of innate ability. That is, is it genetically determined, and therefore experts basically are born but not made? After all, the achievements of certain highly creative artists seem to transcend what "normal" people could ever learn to accomplish. The fact that Mozart composed his first symphony at age nine and his first opera at age twelve is so far out of reach of other children's abilities that the innate genius hypothesis appears the only reasonable explanation.

Despite the intuitive appeal of innateness, considerable research suggests that learning is more important than biology for acquisition of extraordinary skills (Ericsson & Charness, 1994). Such research has generally demonstrated that amateurs given opportunity for intensive practice can indeed mimic the superior abilities of experts. In addition, studies have shown that even child prodigies typically learn their skills in the same way as ordinary people do. Thus, the difference is not so much in innate capability but insofar as prodigies start to learn their craft earlier than others, and work harder at perfecting their skills.

Finally, the learning of excellence is supported by the fact that for many skills and talents, the accomplishments of absolute top performers are constantly bested by the next generation. The most obvious example is seen in sports. For example, the winning time for the first Olympic marathon almost a century ago was "comparable to the current qualifying time for the Boston Marathon attained by thousands of amateur runners every year" (Ericsson & Charness, 1994, p. 737). Similarly, in classical music today there are pieces in the standard performance repertoire that were considered unplayable when composed in the nineteenth century. Or consider mathematics, when in 2007 Alexis Lemaire set a new world record for calculating the 13th root of a 200-digit number. This calculation took just a little over one minute to perform. Lemaire remarked that he simply taught himself to think like a computer (Montagne, 2007).

What many researchers believe is that if any portion of excellence is inherited, it is likely to be physical or emotional characteristics that match with requirements for particular sports, and personality dispositions that match with particular interest areas. In this regard Ericsson and Charness (1994) boldly stated: "Our analysis has shown that the central mechanism[s] mediating the superior performance of experts are acquired; therefore acquisition of relevant knowledge and skills may be the major limiting factor in attaining expert performance" (p. 737).

Much of the research today supports the view that excellence can be learned. However, before readers buy a book on how to compose like Mozart or paint like Picasso, two important caveats. First, though there have been a few Renaissance figures like Leonardo DaVinci—who shines as a painter, sculptor, architect, and inventor—almost always a person's expertise is specific to a single domain. As Ericsson and Charness (1994) note, elite athletes are able to react faster and make better decisions in their realm of expertise, but they are no better than others on standard

Leonardo DaVinci

reaction time and decision-making tasks unrelated to their sport. Second, excellence takes considerable effort.

The Development of Excellence

If superior performance is learned, then the obvious question is: *How* do those who exhibit excellence do it? In 1946 Adriaan de Groot, who was an expert chess player, published his studies of chess masters. In his initial work he demonstrated that chess masters could remember the positions of chess pieces on a board with incredible accuracy after only a brief exposure to the chessboard. He attributed their expertise to superior memory abilities. Later studies, however, showed that chess masters were no better than others at remembering positions of pieces placed randomly on a chessboard. What appeared an obvious advantage of memory was only possible if the pieces on the board *meaningfully* represented arrangements found in a real chess game. Therefore, chess masters were not better at overall memory skills but, more limitedly, at recognizing familiar chess patterns—patterns learned over years of experience with chess (see Ericsson & Charness, 1994).

Real excellence involves cognitive skills, the first element of which is a *large knowledge base* in one's specific domain. For example, expertise in tennis requires a thorough knowledge of the game that includes a familiarity with different strategies, the different styles of potential opponents, with different types of equipment such as rackets and shoes, and even with the game's colorful history. Expert performers often have an almost endless curiosity about their specific domain and can become quite enthusiastic about its minutiae. This bottomless interest and discovery can foster a sense of well-being surrounding one's chosen area of expertise (see Kashdan, 2009).

In addition to memory skills for *relevant* areas of interest and possession of a large knowledge base, research shows that expert performers also tap into well-organized cognitive schemas (Bedard & Chi, 1992). That is, the knowledge base of an expert is not just a random collection of facts but rather an

© Georgios Kollidas/Shutterstock

organized cluster of information that involves numerous conceptual linkages. These allow quicker and easier access to memory and to problem-solving strategies. The ability to utilize these cognitive shortcuts has led many people to associate expertise with intuition. However, the literature on excellence generally views intuition as simply rapid access to information facilitated by shortcuts and schemas.

A second element in expert performance is the motivational factor of *commitment*. How so? People who excel are committed to their particular domain. They are determined to succeed and can persevere despite difficulties. This commitment to learn all they can about their area frequently leads to formation of mentor relationships. The detailed knowledge and specific expertise they require to develop superior skills are usually found only in those who have likewise committed themselves to the same area. In certain realms, the necessity of a mentor is often formalized. For example, in classical music circles, a person who reaches high proficiency instrumentally or vocally can access a fairly well-known list of potential teachers at varied levels of expertise who can guide the next phase of the student's training.

Finally, the most important factor in acquiring performance expertise is that of *practice*. This is confirmed in at least three ways. First, those who truly excel at a specific discipline often begin to practice early in life. Studies have found that people who reach high levels of expertise tend to begin regular practice schedules two to five years earlier than less masterful, though still quite talented, performers. Second, those who are most accomplished tend to practice more hours each day or week than others. Ericsson, Krampe, and Tesch-Romer (1993) found that by age 20, top-level violinists had practiced on average at least 10,000 hours over the years. This figure was about 2,500 more than for violinists ranked at the second-highest level of accomplishment. Again, it should be appreciated that even this secondary level of expertise is filled with highly accomplished musicians.

Consistency of practice also is crucial for the development of expertise. The most accomplished musicians practice approximately four hours per day, seven days per week. The great classical pianist Arthur Rubinstein was purported to have said that if he missed practice for one day, then he knew it; if he missed practice for two days, then his colleagues knew it; if he missed practice for three days, then the public knew it. Studies have found that individuals who have achieved eminence in their field are usually more productive than their less eminent peers. That is, leading composers have written more music, major artists have completed more artwork, and top scientists have published more scientific papers than others in their respective field (see Runco, 2004). This dedication to constant practice is a key factor in determining who reaches a high level of excellence.

Third, in addition to practice time, studies have found that a particular style of practice called **deliberate practice** is important. It is defined as practice that is focused, planned, concentrated, and effortful (Ericsson & Charness, 1994). Deliberate practice is focused on the immediate task with attention to what one is doing correctly or incorrectly at every moment. Anyone who has taken music lessons and ended up half-heartedly performing musical scales while mentally wandering to more enticing topics can understand how far that performance departs from deliberate practice. However, such dedication is not always fun. In contrast to the intrinsic motivation found in leisure activities of flow (see chapter 4), attaining advanced levels of expertise or excellence requires periods of intense effort and discipline.

Having noted that excellence requires extensive practice, we must also point out that too much practice may be harmful. Especially in sports, there is a recognized danger to what is known as overtraining. People who achieve a high level of excellence seem to keep practice to a specific amount of time—about four hours per day—which allows them to perfect their skills while obtaining needed rest and sleep. Excellence, therefore, would appear to require a sensible balance of hard work and rest.

So now that we have identified top performers as those who are knowledgeable in their field, motivated, and dedicated to intense practice

T A B L E 7.1   **The Ten-Year Rule at Work**

	Origin	10 Years	20 Years	30 Years and Beyond
Freud	Charcot's hysteria research	"Project"* The *Interpretation of Dreams***	*Three Contributions to the Theory of Sex*	Social works
Einstein	Light-beam thought experiment	Special theory of relativity*	General theory of relativity**	Philosophical works
Picasso	Barcelona circle	*Les demoiselles d'Avignon** Cubism	Neoclassical style	*Guernica***
Stravinsky	Rimsky-Korsakov influenced works	*Le sacre du printemps**	*Les Noces***	Later styles
Eliot	"Prufrock" Juvenilia	*The Waste Land**	*Four Quartets***	Playwright /critic
Graham	St. Denis troupe	First recital	*Frontier**	*Appalachian Spring*** Neoclassical style
Gandhi	Anti-Indian laws in Natal	South Africa Satyagraha	Ahmedabad*	Salt march**

*Radical breakthrough

**Comprehensive work

SOURCE: From Howard Gardner, *Creating Minds.* Copyright © 1993 Howard Gardner. Reprinted by permission of Basic Books, a member of Perseus Books, L.L.C.

schedules, how long do they have to deliberately work before they reach elite status in their field? Interestingly, the answer is fairly consistent across various disciplines. The **ten-year rule** states that it takes at least a decade of dedicated, consistent practice before one can attain a high level of excellence (Ericsson & Charness, 1994).

Table 7.1 illustrates how the ten-year rule fits the careers of a few well-known people who have achieved not merely excellence in their particular field but eminence or even genius.

While a minimum of ten years is typically necessary for superb performance, the age at which people generally attain recognition and make big breakthroughs does vary across disciplines. For instance, the peak age for creative achievement in mathematics, physics, and lyric poetry occurs in the late twenties and early thirties, while the peak age in philosophy and for writing fiction is the late forties and early fifties (Simonton, 1988). Of course, it should be remembered that these ages are group statistics or averages. Individual variation is certainly possible.

That excellence need not be tied to age is exemplified by the American architect Frank Lloyd Wright. By the time Wright was in his fifties, he had already established himself as one of the most creative architects of the twentieth century. At that point in his life, however, he was revered more as an historic figure than as a still-relevant force in architecture (Norwich, 1975). Despite this presumed irrelevance by his colleagues, Wright surprised everyone by renewing his career at the age of 69 with the completion of one of his masterpieces: the private home known as Fallingwater. From that point on, Wright designed some of his most memorable buildings. Indeed, after the age of 80, Wright was busier than he had ever been in his professional life. This period of creativity culminated in another of his masterpieces, the Guggenheim Museum in New York City, which was completed only a few months after Wright's death at the age of 92.

Resonance

Another perspective on excellence comes from the work of Doug Newberg and colleagues (Newberg, Kimiecik, Durand-Bush, & Doell, 2002). They created the concept of *resonance*, deeming this a cyclical process that guides the development of excellence in many different areas of expertise. They found that "performance excellence was the byproduct of living … life in such a way that [people are] fully engaged in what they do" (p. 251). However, in an interesting twist to other perspectives on excellence, their model grounds excellence in a desire to experience specific emotions—namely, those associated with full engagement in a preferred activity. Therefore, in the resonance model, people who achieve excellence "consciously identify unique feeling[s] they want to experience in their daily pursuits and place themselves in situations and environments that elicit these feelings" (p. 257).

The Resonance Performance Model (RPM) constitutes four stages. The first stage is *the dream*, or the feelings a person experiences when engaged in an activity. Stage two involves intense *preparation* along with consistent engaged practice. Inevitably, people encounter *obstacles* and enter the third stage. In the RPM when obstacles are encountered, however, people do not simply try harder. That is, they do not necessarily believe that "when the going gets tough, the tough get going." Instead, they *revisit their dream*, or reconnect with the feelings that gave spark to their dream. This reconnection with original feelings allows them to embrace the obstacles, to avoid the trap of "trying harder and enjoying it less," and thereby to move forward.

Passion

Among the more obvious factors necessarily involved in attainment of excellence is dedication to—and even a passion for—one's chosen area (Robinson & Aronica, 2009). Canadian psychologist Robert Vallerand and colleagues have conducted considerable work relating to passion (Vallerand, Carbonneau, & Lafrenière, 2010). They defined **passion** as

> a strong inclination toward a self-defining activity that one likes (or even loves), finds important, and in which one invests time and energy. These activities are so self-defining that they represent central features of one's identity (Vallerand, 2008, pp. 1–2).

Therefore, passion is an intense interest in and personal commitment to an activity one regards as central to one's true self. Vallerand found that 84% of college students in his studies described an activity about which they were at least moderately passionate, devoting an average of 8.5 hours per week to it.

Vallerand clarified his concept of passion by postulating a dualistic model comprising harmonious and obsessive types. *Harmonious passion* is a result of autonomous motivation, is freely chosen, seems to "fit" with one's identity, and is engaged in joyously and effortlessly. Often activities based on harmonious passion are accompanied by flow (see chapter 4). *Obsessive passion*, however, results in feelings of being controlled, often involves rigid persistence, and may create conflicts within one's identity and life as well as feelings of anxiety and even shame. As examples of obsessive passions Vallerand identified gambling and Internet preoccupation. Many psychological addictions exemplify obsessive passion. For this reason, only harmonious passion of these two passions is reliably associated with greater well-being.

In a series of studies with swimmers, water polo team members, basketball players, and classical musicians, Vallerand and colleagues examined how passion evolves over time to produce performance outcomes. They found that harmonious passion increased goals of mastery and resulted in high-quality deliberate practice, which in turn predicted high-level performance or excellence. In addition, harmonious passion, in contradistinction to obsessive passion, led to greater subjective well-being even before performance outcomes were achieved (see Figure 7.1). In the figure, note that only harmonious passion was significantly related to subjective well-being (.39).

Grit

Angela Lee Duckworth combined concepts of persistence and passion into a new construct she calls **grit** (Duckworth, Peterson, Matthews, & Kelly, 2007). People who are very self-disciplined and score high on measures of persistence and passion toward their goals are high in grit. Studies have found that high grit scores predicted better

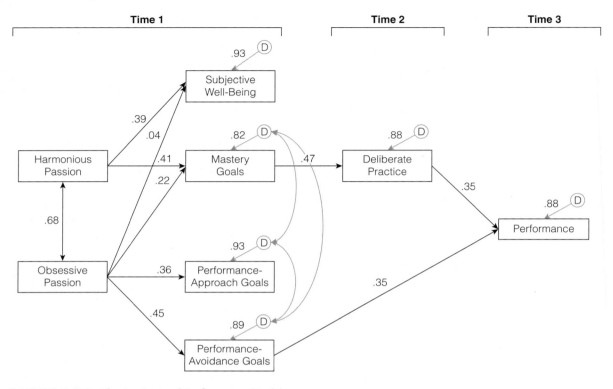

F I G U R E 7.1   The Passion and Performance Model
SOURCE: From Vallerand, Robert J., "On the psychology of passion: In search of what makes people's lives most worth living" *Canadian Psychologist,*
49(1), p. 7. Copyright © 2008. Reprinted with permission.

grade-point averages, retention of first-year cadets at West Point Academy, and performance at the Scripps National Spelling Bee (Duckworth, & Quinn, 2009). Grit was a better predictor of academic performance than IQ and SAT scores. Duckworth also found that grit increases with age, with people over 65 scoring higher than other age groups (Seligman, 2011).

AESTHETICS AND THE GOOD LIFE

Why is the topic of aesthetics important in a book on positive psychology? Perhaps the relevance is easy to understand if you try a little thought-experiment. Imagine that you live in a world in

which all buildings are concrete block structures painted gray, all clothes are identically gray with no ornamentation, and nowhere is any attempt made to beautify the environment or the people in it. Would you enjoy living in such a world? Most people would find it lacked an important quality—beauty—that enhances our experience of being human. Yet, some people *do* live in this world—for it is that of the prison environment. Indeed, in prison the lack of aesthetics is part of the punishment. So although a discussion of aesthetics initially seems a bit out of place in a book on well-being, a moment's reflection reveals its pertinence.

Further, why does the topic of beauty appears in a chapter on excellence and creativity? First, there is an obvious relationship between beauty and creativity. Second, a way to conceptualize the aesthetic sense is in terms of an appreciation of excellence. **Aesthetics** has been defined as "an appreciation of the beautiful and the sublime" (Averill, Stanat, & More, 1998, p. 153).

Why Is the Aesthetic Sense Important?

Even a casual museum visit indicates that people have applied their artistic sense since before recorded times. We know that virtually all societies have had some forms of artistic expression. The compellingly beautiful cave paintings at Lascaux and Vallon-Pont-d'Arc in France, which are 12,000 to 20,000 years old, are an example of universal artistic expression that includes music, dance, art, and story. Even nomadic peoples use beadwork on leather and cloth, paintings on pottery, as well as feathers, bones, and beautiful stones to enhance the aesthetic value of their living accommodations. It appears then that a desire to stimulate the aesthetic sense has existed since the beginnings of humanity. But what purpose does it serve?

Four Attributes of the Aesthetic Experience

Averill, Stanat, and More (1998) propose four basic attributes of aesthetics, pleasure, absorption, intrinsic interest, and challenge. Although these four are not the only constituents of aesthetic experience, this model serves as a framework for understanding aesthetics.

Pleasure   Looking at an attractive object increases our sense of well-being—even if only momentarily. Witness in today's world wherein a large percentage of disposable income is spent on jewelry, the latest fashions, new furniture, new cars, and new "dream" homes. All are intended to bring their owners a greater sense of beauty. Though some objects are acquired simply for social status, many more are obtained for the aesthetic pleasure they offer. Artwork, photographs, drawings, and other objets d'art that people place in their homes can also serve as pleasant reminders of places visited or things and people loved. Often

such objects furnish stimuli for positive emotions by elevating us—even momentarily—from day-to-day concerns that can consume our emotional lives if we are not careful.

Absorption   The renowned American philosopher and psychologist John Dewey (1934) proposed a similar function of art in his book *Art as Experience*. He believes an appreciation of art builds on experience, "which intensifies the sense of immediate living" (Sarason, 1990, p. 86). In Dewey's view, an aesthetic sense is necessary for well-being insofar as it creates a heightened vitality that is restorative. The aesthetic sense helps us to transcend the overly mundane by intensifying our relationship with immediate experience. It heightens our awareness, energizes our appreciation of the moment, and allows a more complete "interpenetrating of self and the world of objects and events" (Sarason, 1990, p. 86).

Intrinsic Interest   Among the frequently mentioned places that people like visiting for leisure are beaches or other natural areas such as national parks. When asked what is appealing about these areas, people often reply, "The scenery." They go on vacations to appreciate the beauty of the natural world. Indeed, research studies have found that landscapes that seem both mysterious and also somewhat easy to understand can reliably arouse people's interest (see Kaplan, 1992).

A sense of aesthetics can also help us learn about the world around us. Interesting objects, intriguing patterns, and unexpected color combinations stimulate our sense of curiosity. Such objects in our surroundings keep us interested in life and provide varied stimulation. Even infants only a few weeks old already show preferences for objects that are aesthetically interesting and stand out from the rest of their environment. Sarason (1990) argues that artistic expression is often suppressed in childhood when children hear a message that "art" is something to be judged and that only "creative" people can do it correctly. He contends that in adults this suppressed need for artistic expression creates a "festering source of dissatisfaction in quotidian living" (p. 5). In other words, the fallout from suppression of our aesthetic needs is an attitude that life is boring and uninteresting.

A frequent justification for arts education has often been that art fosters intellectual development. Indeed, scientific evidence exists that it does just that (Evans, 2010). In the popular media, the "Mozart effect" is supposed a facilitator of intelligence. Listening to Mozart's music, it has been said, helps children learn, even those still in the womb. Never claiming that listening to Mozart's music enhances intelligence, the researchers who conducted the original studies therefore felt obliged to write a rejoinder to all the misinformation about their work (Evans, 2010). Nevertheless, arts in the schools can help children by providing emotional expression, teaching communication and persistence, engaging interests that fall outside traditional curricula, teaching the use of metaphor and imagination, and enhancing understanding of themselves and others.

Challenge   Another use of aesthetics, albeit one less common, is as a pathway to greater personal growth. Art can be used to express emotions, intuitions, and meanings that people find hard to express in words. Poetry, of course, is the art of using words to express something that lies beyond the words themselves. From this perspective, art can challenge us to look deeper within ourselves; to search for new ways to express emotion; and to help us step outside our personal comfort zones to experience life in fresh ways. This may be to what Sigmund Freud was alluding when he said, "Everywhere I go, I find a poet has been there before me."

From a challenge perspective, art by stimulating people to think and feel differently leads them to view the world, others, and themselves in new ways. The view that art should point the way toward a new vision of the future was the rallying cry of the *avant-garde movement* that began in the nineteenth century. Avant-garde artists of the period deliberately set out to shake up the bourgeoisie, whom they criticized as overcontrolled, emotionally timid, and stifled by a rigid social

system that demanded conformity rather than creativity (Hughes, 1980). Although an extreme position, art can certainly be used to shake up a complacent sense of who we are. Actor and film director Orson Welles aptly stated that "an artist is always out of step with the times. He has to be."

An example of this use of the aesthetics comes across in a story whose author described his young niece and her first experience of Beethoven's Ninth Symphony. The young woman was simply overwhelmed by the music and speechless as she left the concert hall. She stammered to her uncle, "What do I do now? Now that I know such music exists?" She had no idea that she could experience so many new and intense emotions as a result of the music. Rather dramatically for her, the old boundaries of her experiential world were shattered. She knew she had to adjust to the shock and discover how to adapt to a newly expanded vision of what is possible in life. Her confusion called for a creative readaptation to her life.

A powerful example of how art may impact us occurs when our personal boundaries of what is "acceptable" art are pushed. A famous case of how changes in aesthetics are not always welcome comes from the first performance of Stravinsky's *Le Sacre du Printemps (The Rite of Spring)* in Paris in 1913. Stravinsky had composed a piece of music so counter to the audience's aesthetic sense of what was considered acceptable that the normally conservative Parisian society unanimously exploded! The following passage describes, with the help of Jean Cocteau, the most famous premier in the history of Western music (adapted from Brockway & Weinstock, 1958):

> The first performance of *Le Sacre du Printemps*, at the Theatre Des Champs-Elysées, on May 29, 1913, was a scandal unmatched in the annals of music.... The *Great Sacred Dance* [movement] ... is the high-water mark beyond which the brutal modern [musical] technique has not gone, possibly cannot go. Its constantly changing rhythms thudded out in screaming, searing discords engender a physical agitation in

the listener that is closely akin to sexual excitation, acting chiefly on atavistic, deeply veneered strata of being…. Jean Cocteau, the star reporter of *Smart Paris*, so describes it: "The audience behaved as it ought to; it revolted straight away. People laughed, booed, hissed, imitated animal noises … and a handful of musicians, carried away by their excessive zeal, insulted and even roughly handled the public in the loges. The uproar degenerated into a free fight." The cause of all this disturbance was the most beautiful, the most profoundly conceived, and most exhilarating piece of music thus far composed in the twentieth century (pp. 599–601.)

Although this account might seem somewhat comical from a safe distance of 100 years, it reminds us that artistic expression can have a profound impact on our sense of identity and emotional security—and push us to examine the boundaries by which our lives might be constrained.

Finally, a desire for aesthetic experience may be growing in the wider population. Attendance at museums, the theater, and music and dance events has grown significantly in recent decades. People seem to want more of the pleasure, absorption, interest, and challenge that art has to offer.

Music and the Brain

The Stravinsky example brings us to the topic of new research on music. Several years ago, the New York Academy of Sciences published a collection of papers on music entitled *Biological Foundations of Music* (Zatorre & Peretz, 2001). This as well as other research indicates that music can help patients heal faster after surgery, cancer patients with the healing process, Alzheimer's patients to remember events from their past, people cope better with severe pain, boost our immune systems, and even raise children's test scores (Dalla Bella et al., 2009). There is some evidence that music can actually lead to increased brain size. Gottfried Schlaug and his colleagues

(Schlaug, 2001; Schlaug et al., 1995) compared brain scans of 30 nonmusicians and 30 musicians and found that the corpus collosums in the musicians were measurably larger. For musicians who began playing a musical instrument at an early age, the difference was even greater. (Note that the corpus collosum is the thick bundle of neurons that connects the right and left hemispheres of the brain.)

Recent findings indicate that listening to music, even anticipating a favorite musical passage, can stimulate dopamine release and activate regions of the brain involved in the experience of pleasure, euphoria, and craving (Salimpoor, Benovoy, Larcher, Dagher, & Zatorre, 2011). Many other benefits come from playing music. Studies have found that three- and four-year-old children who learned how to play the piano scored 34% higher on tests of abstract reasoning skills than children taught computer skills. Other studies have found that children with attention deficit hyperactivity disorder learned to concentrate and control their aggression better after playing games based on musical rhythms (see Zatorre & Peretz, 2001).

Charles Limb and his collaborator Allen Braun conducted some clever studies on brain activity of musicians. Using an fMRI machine they measured blood flow in the brains of jazz musicians and rappers while they were improvising. They found decreased activity in areas of the brain associated with self-monitoring and increased activity in self-expression and all sensory areas (Limb & Braun, 2008). Since this pattern is often seen in REM sleep, Limb speculates that improvising musicians may be in a state similar to that of a waking dream (see Zagorski, 2008).

Art, Music, and Dance Therapy

Recent research on neuroplasticity and the brain has given new life to various therapies that make use of the arts. Music therapy has risen rapidly in popularity as studies have found that using the right kind of music can help enhance pain-blocking nerve pathways, calm the central nervous system, and help regain healthy functioning in heart rate variability (Sauter, 2010; Sethi, 2009). Although it seems obvious, studies have now confirmed that "happy" music can boost mood by impacting areas of the brain responsible for emotions. One study found that patients who felt positive emotion while listening to music they enjoyed showed better ability to heal from visual neglect after a stroke (Soto et al., 2009). However, the style of music might be important. Mood, mental clarity, tension, and cardiovascular health may be improved by listening to classical music and music designed for relaxation or meditation, but heavy metal, grunge rock, and techno music can actually be physiologically harmful (McCraty, Barrios-Choplin, Atkinson, & Tomasino, 1998; Trappe, 2010).

Another study found that when people listened to music that made them feel "joyful," their blood-vessel functioning improved (Miller, Beach, Mangano, & Vogel, 2008). Music therapy has helped improve the well-being of hospitalized children (Longhi & Pikett, 2008), and singing has helped improve well-being along with increased levels of oxytocin (Grape, Sanderson, Hansson, Ericson, & Theorell, 2003). Finally, music making may help increase well-being, neuroplasticity, and quality of life in older persons (Solé, Mercadal-Brotons, Gallego, & Riera, 2010; Wan & Schlaug, 2010). Results like these led Eckhart Altenmüller and colleagues at the Institute of Music Physiology and Musician's Medicine to develop music-supported training exercises (MUT) to use along with traditional medicine (Sautter, 2010).

Art therapy has also been useful in a variety of contexts. In particular, research has found that artistic expression can increase feelings of well-being and help people process the emotions associated with cancer (Reynolds & Lim, 2007; Puig, Lee, Goodwin, & Sherrard, 2006; Zammit, 2001), adjust to dementia (Hannemann, 2006), handle chronic disability (Reynolds & Prior, 2003), and reduce stress (Adams-Price & Steinman, 2007). Art activities also offer a valuable tool for older persons to adjust to aging, increasing their satisfaction with life and their sense of meaning (Flood, 2007; Hickson & Housley, 1997).

Recently a program was launched in Sweden that helps people suffering from mental health problems by taking them to cultural events like visiting museums and attending concerts (Visscher, 2010). One study asked college students to keep a "beauty log—that is, a diary recounting beautiful events in nature, beautifully constructed objects, or experiences found morally beautiful (ones uplifting or inspiring human behavior) (Diessner, Rust, Solom, Frost, & Parsons, 2006). These researchers found that engagement with moral beauty was especially associated with increase in hope and sense of well-being.

Finding Beauty Outside the Arts

An appreciation of beauty need not be confined to traditionally recognized forms of art, for we can awaken to beauty in many guises. For example, the beauty of a scientific theory, of a mathematical equation, and of the sheer immensity of the universe emotionally moves many scientists. Some scientists have even suggested that a scientific theory should be judged partially on its "elegance." Susan Fitzpatrick (2001) recalls how she entered the field of science because of the beauty she discerned in the Kreb's cycle of cellular respiration. She advises her colleagues to tell their students about "the moment you recognized beauty in the work of another scientist and fell in love" (p. 4).

Fitzpatrick (2001) tells a story about beauty, this time in the context of the world's most demanding bicycle race, the Tour de France:

> One image I see over and over is the moment in the race when [Lance] Armstrong decided the time had come for him to put his definitive mark on the grueling 21-day event, ending all speculation about the eventual outcome. A French rider, Laurent Roux, out in front, all alone, was leading the day's stage for more than 60 miles when, during a mountain climb, Armstrong blew by him. Literally. There is no other way to describe it. In the post race interview Roux was quoted as saying, "When he passed me,

I had the impression it was a motorcycle at my side. It was beautiful to see." It was beautiful to see? Can you imagine that you are a Frenchman within sight of claiming victory of one of the most demanding stages of your country's most famous athletic event when some kid from Texas passes you like you are standing still? "It was beautiful to see"; that's how Laurent Roux described it.... These athletes ride for glory, and for fame, and … for the sheer beauty of the sport (p. 4).

SOURCE: From Susan M. Fitzpatrick, "Commentary," *The Scientist* (October 1, 2001), p. 4. Reprinted by permission of *The Scientist*.

Origins of the Aesthetic Sense

Where does our sense of aesthetics come from? Kaplan (1992) argues for the "savannah hypothesis" that finds evolutionary significance in our elemental interest in and curiosity about landscapes, insofar as such typically human traits encouraged early humans to explore their environment. Swiss psychologist Carl Jung considers our emotional responses to primordial forms and universal images to be innately patterned by a deep collective unconscious. Ellen Dissanayake (2009) has proposed that our aesthetic sense develops from the attunement between mother and infant. She believes that early imitation of the mother sets the stage for later artistic expression.

It is obviously true that many judgments of what is beautiful are learned from the culture and historical period in which we live. For example, many people in Western societies find the music of India strangely discomforting and not particularly pleasing. Primarily this is because Indian music uses a quarter-tone scale while Western music uses a halftone scale. Similarly, the highly stylized form of Japanese drama called Noh is completely incomprehensible for most Westerners even though the aesthetic of Japanese gardens is very accessible. At the same time, we can learn to appreciate odd aesthetic experiences that we initially find quite unappealing.

Can Tragedy and Sadness Be Beautiful?

The discussion of aesthetics for a positive psychology raises an interesting question about the role of tragedy in art. Why is it that people are drawn to plays, books, poetry, movies and other art forms that portray tragic stories? For instance, the tragic play *Romeo and Juliet* is one of Shakespeare's most popular despite the fact that both lovers die unnecessarily at the end. In the latest film version of the *Titanic* tragedy, Leonardo DeCaprio and Kate Winslet portray two people who fall madly in love only to be separated by the death of DeCaprio's character as the ship sinks into the frigid Atlantic Ocean. In spite of this tragic ending, the film grossed hundreds of millions of dollars and some fans returned to see the movie over 20 times. After each viewing they left the movie theater having cried sympathetic tears as the lovers are separated forever by fate. Why would people voluntarily immerse themselves in an artistic tragedy that they know will make them feel negative emotions?

People know, of course, that tragic events are part of life; they realize that in order to face human mortality, they must inevitably experience sadness in some way. Through the medium of art, people can experience tragedy and gain at least three benefits. First, empathy for characters reminds us of our shared humanity and may even serve to increase compassion and charity. Second, out of compassion we might resolve not to allow such tragedies to occur if we can prevent them. Third, allowing life's sad and tragic moments through a substitute work of art enables us to feel certain emotions without having to live through the actual experiences that gave rise to them. After all, people *do not want to really* lose their lovers in tragic deaths. Rather, the power of artistic tragedy is a paradoxical one: when we are genuinely engaged by negative emotions that can lead us to positive feelings of compassion, hope, relief, empathy, and courageous resolve. As the musician said, "There's nothing like the blues to make you feel good."

CREATIVITY

Among the more interesting ways that people pursue well-being is through creativity. Creating as a vehicle through which one derives pleasure, satisfaction, and a sense of well-being is actually quite common. Everyday people around the world are engaged in hobbies, crafts, and amateur performances in the arts. More broadly, creativity is responsible for virtually all the advances that humans have made over time immemorial. We literally would not have emerged from caves or savannas without it. What is perhaps historically modern is an engagement with our creative powers as part of a journey toward an enhanced well-being. Indeed, for some people an actualization of creative potential is the primary goal in life. However, it is only within the last 200 years that the social role of *artist* has been created in contemporary society.

What is Creativity?

Although we all use the word *creativity*, just what do we mean by this elusive term? The lack of consensus for a simple definition has truly baffled psychologists. Creativity is a quality that is enormously difficult to pin down. Dean Simonton (2009) defined it as "adaptive originality." To be creative, an idea or product must be original, novel, surprising, or unexpected as well as be adaptive—that is, it must provide a useful solution to a real-life problem. These dual criteria mean that if you are the only person to see your latest painting as inventive, inspiring, and original, then it isn't really creative. John Nicholls (1972) suggests that a creative solution must be original and "make a meaningful contribution to culture." From this perspective, if we invent a novel solution to the problem of how to dust our apartment, it might be considered clever but it is not true creativity.

However, considering that many creative breakthroughs have not been recognized as such at their point in history, any judgment that a creation makes "a meaningful contribution to culture" is unavoidably tied to particular observers of a particular period. Part of the problem here is that an assessment of creativity can apply to a very wide range of behavior, from an unusual usage of mulch in one's vegetable garden to a literary style of writing that transforms the way a society looks at life.

"Little c" and "Big C" Creativity

One way to address types of creativity is to distinguish "little c" creativity from "big C" creativity. "Little c" creativity enhances life by finding unique solutions to problems, but the solutions are not necessarily groundbreaking innovations (Simonton, 2009). "Little c" creativity is referred to as "everyday creativity," in which the focus is more on originality concerning routine or common problems (Caralynn, 2009). In contrast, "big C" creativity transforms culture and history. It is the creativity we associate with genius. "Little c" and "big C" creativity may represent differences of degree that fall along the same continuum (Simonton, 2002).

Research Perspectives on Creativity

Creativity has also been a difficult subject for researchers to study due to the difficulty of measuring it quantifiably. Psychological measurement scales usually rely on interval measurement, in which one indicator is higher or lower than another indicator. For example, if we score "8" on a happiness test and our friend scores "6," then we are "happier" than he is. But how does one measure creativity on a 10-point scale? In actuality, most psychologists don't try to be that precise. Rather, they measure relative degrees of creativity.

For instance, Lubart and Sternberg (1995) asked 48 adults to tap into their creativity via tasks such as depicting "hope" in a drawing or designing a TV ad for the Internal Revenue Service. The participants' work was rated by such qualities as novelty; overall creativity; and perceived effort. The researchers were not very interested in whether one person's drawing of hope represented a "6" or an "8" on a 10-point Likert-type scale. Instead, they conducted a global assessment of whether the drawing was "creative" or not. In this study as in several others, the finding was of considerable agreement among raters as to which solutions were creative and which were not. It turns out that many people can recognize creativity when they see it, at least creativity in general.

Another finding of the Lubart and Sternberg study is that creativity in one domain, such as painting, is only moderately associated with creativity in a different domain, such as writing. This is not surprising in light of earlier discussion that manifestations of excellence and expertise for most people are confined to a single domain. The same appears to be true for creativity. For instance, Andy Warhol transformed twentieth century art with the invention of pop art. But though the films he created are viewed today as interesting experiments, these have not had the transformative effect his paintings have had. Evidence indicates that artistic excellence in one area does not usually translate into excellence in another.

One caveat is that crossovers appear easier within related artistic disciplines. For instance, it is fairly common for artists to be creative at both painting and sculpture because the media are closely related. Note that research does *not* indicate a *difference in kind* of creativity across domains. No matter what the medium or field, creative work evinces a few common elements (Tardif & Sternberg, 1988).

Mark Runco (2004) observes that four traditions dominate research concerning creativity focusing on: person, process, press, and product. Studies of creative *persons* investigate personality traits and other attributes associated with individuals. *Process* studies look at how creativity happens. *Press* refers to the environmental influences that help or hinder creativity. Finally, a *product* approach focuses on actual outcomes of creativity.

The Creative Person A common hypothesis about creative people assumes exceptional intelligence at work. The reasoning is that if highly creative people are better at problem solving than those who are not creative, then they must be more intelligent. Although this hypothesis seems logical, the data do not support it. Studies have found that correlations between tests of creativity and scores on standard IQ tests are usually between .10 and .30, that is, in the modest range (Barron &

Harrington, 1981). Research studies have generally concluded that having an average to moderately high IQ is often associated with creativity and may even be beneficial to it, but it is not necessary in order to be creative. Again, this conclusion should sound familiar given the earlier discussion of excellence.

Personality characteristics of creative people do seem to overlap with those who achieve excellence. However, this relationship is a one-way street because not all people who achieve excellence are highly creative. Creative people are intensely interested in their field and willing to work hard and long (recall the ten-year rule). Creativity generally takes time, particularly to acquire a firm and thorough expertise in one's medium or field. Further, people who work on finding solutions must often wait for insights. For a product to be novel, original, and to break new ground, its creator must thoroughly understand the existing ground. Occasionally possession of a firm knowledge base is not a requirement for creativity, although this exception that may be more common in the visual arts than in other disciplines. An example comes from the art world, where there is considerable interest in folk art these days. Creators of folk art have no training in, or even knowledge of, formal elements of art such as design, color, and composition. Nashville artist William Edmonson, who created stone sculptures in the folk tradition with no such formal training, nevertheless managed to capture the essence of his subjects in powerful and moving ways. He carved his works in relative obscurity, often as tombstone ornaments for friends, until a Nashville artist with friends in New York saw his work. In 1937 Edmonson became the first African-American to have a one-person show at New York's Museum of Modern Art. In 2000–2001, a major retrospective of his works traveled around the United States to rave reviews from critics.

Although highly creative people share many qualities with those who excel in a particular area, the former do exhibit distinct differences that enhance their ability to produce the novel, the unique, and the unexpected. A discussion of these differences observed in creative people follows. Yet note, as Tardif and Sternberg (1988) stress, that no studies have found any single personality trait to hold *the* key to creativity.

One consistent trait that creative people do tend to share is an *openness to experience* (Sternberg, 1999; Tardif & Sternberg, 1988). Greater openness implies a person more willing to consider the unusual, the unexpected, the out-of-the-ordinary, and the unconventional. Therefore, creative people tend to be *highly flexible in their thinking* and quite *tolerant of ambiguity* or even outright disorder. In fact, they may even have a preference for complexity. They often delight in seeking the simplicity that lies beneath apparently complex, difficult, and even chaotic problems. Insofar as complex problems lead to more dead-ends and exasperating failures than those simpler in structure, creative people are marked by a *higher tolerance for frustration*.

Studies have also found that highly creative people tend to be very *independent*. This quality can manifest as an ability to resist social pressures to behave and think in conventional ways. Of course, many aspiring young artists seem only to mimic this unconventionality and in so doing are paradoxically quite conforming to the conventional stereotype of "rebellious artist." Rather than simply resisting social pressures to appear different, truly creative people resist conventions that are stifling to the freedom they need for their work. They also may prefer to work alone so they can take their own path toward their own solutions. Because of this, many creative people have seen themselves as loners. Highly creative people also display a *willingness to restructure problems* or cognitive templates that have served people in the past, and to play with ideas, traditions, existing forms, and solutions. This often sets them apart.

Many researchers agree that creativity involves tension and conflict. It may be that creativity consists of a struggle to resolve seemingly incompatible questions. Tardif and Sternberg (1988) observe in creative people "what seems almost to be an aesthetic ability that allows such individuals to *recognize 'good' problems in their field* and apply themselves to these problems while ignoring others" (p. 435). Creative people often sense where the "fit" lies between their talents and the problems just waiting for a creative solution.

Creativity also is associated with being *intrinsically motivated*. Creative persons love to stimulate their creative impulses in activity. Often they exhibit a passion for their area of focus. Working intensely on a creative endeavor may actually give them more personal energy rather than deplete it. Gardner (1993) has found that creative people are often productive in some way every day.

Other personality characteristics associated with creativity include: *receptivity*; *sensitivity to problems*; *fluency in thinking*; and *willingness to take risks* (Arieti, 1976; Sternberg, 1999). Therisa Amabile (1983) summarizes three major characteristics of creative persons. First, they are experts in their chosen field or artistic medium. Second, they possess and make use of the cognitive skills and personality characteristics mentioned earlier. Third, they are intrinsically motivated. Table 7.2 compares personality factors related both to excellence and creativity.

The Creative Process   Styles of thinking have been associated with creativity, specifically convergent and divergent thinking (Guilford, 1967). *Convergent thinking* is a process in which various

T A B L E 7.2   Comparisons Between Excellence and Creativity

Excellence	Creativity
Large Knowledge Base	Large Knowledge Base
Commitment	Commitment
Practice: Consistent	Practice: Consistent
Deliberate	Deliberate
10-year Rule	10-year Rule
	Openness to experience
	Flexible in their thinking
	Tolerance for ambiguity
	Tolerance for frustration
	Independent
	Intrinsically motivated
	Willing to restructure problems

SOURCE: K. Ericsson & N. Charness (1994), Simonton (2000), & R. Sternberg (1988).

problem-solving strategies converge on a single correct answer to a problem. Tests of convergent thinking often are scored in terms of whether a person has answered correctly or not. In contrast, *divergent thinking* is an ability to think in many different ways, using a number of strategies that, at least initially, may or may not show any direct relevance to a solution. It is an ability to produce many different solutions to the same problem. Tests of divergent thinking are usually scored by counting the number of different but plausible solutions generated. For instance, a divergent thinking test might ask someone to generate as many uses as possible for a burned-out light bulb.

At first glance, divergent thinking should be more related to creativity than convergent thinking. Unfortunately, neither style is highly correlated with creativity (Barron & Harrington, 1981). Actually, both may be necessary: divergent to generate ideas and convergent to hone in on a solution based on those ideas (Rathunde, 2001). Research has shown associations of a single style of thinking with creativity to be overly simplistic (Sternberg, 1999).

The Role of the Unconscious in Creativity

Freud (1901/1960) associates creativity with the unconscious id, or primary process thinking, which he considered illogical, emotional, and symbolic. His ideas have led to the notion, taken up by Jung, that creativity is related to an ability to tap into unconscious processes. However, for Jung the level of the unconscious viewed as central to creativity, invention, and spontaneity is a deeper one. Psychodynamic theorists have since proposed that creativity is based not on unconscious processing but on preconscious thinking (Kris, 1952; Kubie, 1958). The more influential of these perspectives comes from Ernst Kris (1952), who contends that creativity results from a specific cognitive process he terms *regression in service of the ego*. This is an ability to temporarily submerge the rational and control functions of the ego and tap into cognitive processes that are more allegorical, symbolic, and holistic.

Natalie Rogers, daughter of Carl Rogers (see chapter 9), has created Expressive Arts Therapy as a way for people to give creative expression by submerging the rational control function of the ego. She sees artistic expression is a means of accessing deep and often remote emotions as well as unconscious processes. Therapists trained in this approach offer people an opportunity to explore their deepest emotions in a safe, supportive environment that values expression, spontaneity, and intuition over control and conformity.

Rollo May (1975) presents an influential perspective on the creative process. Drawing upon existentialist philosophy, he argues that genuine creativity involves an intense relationship or encounter in which the artist is fully absorbed in and engaged with the artistic subject. He contrasts this condition with "escapist" creativity, which lacks a genuine encounter. Like Friedrich Nietzsche, it is May's contention that genuine creativity gives access to both the Dionysian (that is, irrational) and the *daimonic* (that is, negative) forces of the psyche. May sees creativity as evolving out of the tension between our positive and negative tendencies, the Jekyll and Hyde aspects of who we are.

The Four Stages of the Creative Process

A connection with unconscious or preconscious processes is also found in the renowned four-stage theory of creativity proposed by Joseph Wallas (1926). The first stage is one of *preparation*—that is, a time when information is gathered, initial efforts to solve a problem are attempted, a variety of ideas are tossed around, and in general the stage is set for a creative solution. If a solution is not found, then the second stage of *incubation* begins. Here attempts to find a creative solution are handled at an "unconscious" level of processing. This stage can last hours or years. Numerous stories of how creative breakthroughs are reached involve such a stage of latency and apparent—though not actual—abandonment of the problem. Recent research suggests that though a period of incubation is often associated with a new solution, this stage consists of normal cognitive processes operating beneath the surface rather than the primary process thinking of the id (Trotter, 1986). Consistent with this view is recent evidence that getting adequate amounts of sleep can enhance a person's ability to problem solve (Wagner et al., 2004).

The third stage, termed *illumination*, is initiated when a creative solution often emerges rapidly and unexpectedly as an insight. People frequently recall answers emerging from dreams and other less rational avenues of cognitive processing, but an insight may be stimulated by more everyday occurrences. The following excerpt from an interview with Paul McCartney, who with the late John Lennon formed part of the most successful songwriting team in history, illustrates the mysterious quality of illumination at play in artistic creativity:

> RD: You've said that [the song] "Yesterday" emerged fully formed from a dream. What is your personal understanding of inspiration?
>
> McCartney: I don't understand it at all. I think life is quite mysterious and quite miraculous.… Every time I come to write a song, there's this magic … and I just sit down at the piano and … suddenly there's a song there … it's a faith thing … with creativity, I just have faith.… It's a great spiritual belief that there's something really magical there. And that was what helped me write "Yesterday." Something to do with me, something to do with my love of music, and my faith in the process. But I don't quite know what it is and I don't want to know (*Readers Digest*, November 2001, pp. 85–87).

The American photographer Ansel Adams references these three stages of the creative process in his description of creativity as "chance favoring the prepared mind."

Many researchers recognize that what is commonly known as *insight* plays a relatively small, if important, part in the creative process—which may be surprising. In this view, insight is not a special unconscious process but rather involves the use of rather ordinary cognitive skills at a preconscious level. This process leads to the last stage in this theory of the creative process, that of *verification*. Here the creative breakthrough must be worked with to give it final form. Often this entails work on turning an insight into a real-world solution with practical application.

Left Brain/Right Brain and Creativity   Finally, research on right- and left-brain cognition deserves mention. For a number of years it was popular to assume that logical and rational thinking was produced in the left hemisphere of the brain, while creative, holistic, and generally artistic processes were associated with the right hemisphere. Back in the 1970s and 1980s, many popular books and workshops offered to teach people how to "think with your right brain." Although researchers initially dismissed this notion, some support exists for a distinction between cognitive processes performed by the left and right hemispheres. Indeed, research has found the left hemisphere holds a small advantage for logical thought and the right hemisphere for symbolic thinking (at least in right-handed people). The overall conclusion, however, is that both hemispheres are involved in both styles of thinking, and the differences between the two are a matter of emphasis (Trope, Rozin, Nelson, & Gur, 1992).

Creative Environments, or Press   Creativity also correlates with supportive environments, which can range from family environments to social, even historical environments. Families of creative people seem to share several characteristics. Often the childhoods of creative people haven't been the happiest or most stable. Many highly creative people come from somewhat turbulent childhoods in which they received comparatively little emotional comfort. Interestingly, these families also score high in encouragement of their children to achieve, providing many opportunities and resources for learning and new experiences.

Speaking of families, we must point out that one factor that does *not* seem important for creativity is heredity. In studies of characteristics of identical twins raised apart, correlations between twins' creativity scores are lower than correlations between their IQ scores (Nichols, 1972). Since we

© 2006 by Randy Glasbergen.
www.glasbergen.com

"You see clutter. I see an environment that encourages the random juxtaposition of disparate elements for the potential generation of creativity born of chaos!"

know that IQ is influenced both by hereditary factors and environmental factors, this suggests that genetic influences on creativity are small.

Sometimes a special group of people together create a unique synergy that allows for greater creativity. Again, the *Beatles* band is instructive. It is universally included among the most creative innovators in the history of popular music. However, after the band's breakup, its four individual members never quite cast the magic that the *Beatles* en masse were able to create. Their producer George Martin remarked: "It is absolutely true that the sum of the four of them was much, much greater that the sum of the individual parts." John Lennon commented on the group of which he was a part, "Beatlemania is when we all get together. The Beatles go into the studio and IT [creativity] happens" (both quotes from Herstgaard, 1995, p. 135). Work environments that encourage exploration and diversity of thinking also foster creativity.

Certain environments have fostered such creative magic more than others, such as Paris in the 1920s and 1930s, New York City in the 1950s and 1960s and California's high-tech "Silicon Valley" in recent years. Creative people who regard themselves as loners tend to congregate in stimulating settings of similar minds. Richard Florida (2004)

postulates a "creative class" of people in the U.S. today who partially drive its economic engine and who congregate in areas amenable to their iconoclastic tastes and sensibilities. On a more limited scale, certain environments are more conducive to creativity than others. Many creative people decorate their homes in ways that fuel creativity. In this respect, Alain de Botton (2006) argues for a "happy architecture" that promotes well-being and higher values through such qualities as balance, elegance, and harmony in building. Indeed, most people notice buildings that feel more pleasurable than their ordinary counterparts.

Also some historical periods have notably nourished creativity, such as the Italian Renaissance, particularly in Florence, and the end of the nineteenth century in America. The decades around the turn of the nineteenth century in the United States saw an astounding number of inventions. Someone who lived during the fifty years between 1875 and 1925 saw the introduction of new inventions such as the automobile, airplane, telephone, and phonograph. Filings at the United States patent office hit an all-time high during this period. Today we may well be living in a similarly fertile period of creativity as communication and entertainment media merge with computer and Internet technologies.

The Product Approach to Creativity   As mentioned earlier, a product approach focuses on the outcomes of creativity. Runco (2004) suggests this approach can be quite objective insofar as products are quantifiable. This is because the products readily available for study are usually those creators who have already achieved a place in cultural history. A problem with such an approach, discussed in an upcoming section, is that those identified as geniuses do not necessarily fit the patterns found in other creative people.

The Confluence Approach   Another difficulty is that each discipline in psychology has studied creativity from its own perspective. That is, social and personality psychologists have studied personality traits associated with creativity, cognitive psychologists have looked at cognitive processes, still others have focused on motivational theories. Situations like this are often compared to the parable of five blind persons each trying to describe an elephant only by the sensation of touch. In this story, the first one who is holding the trunk says that elephants are long and round and therefore like a snake; the second one holding a leg says that elephants are round but wide, with toes like a horse; the third one holding the ears says that elephants are wide and flat and have wings like a huge bird; and so on. Each person explains the entirety of an elephant from only a limited perspective.

Avoiding this trap, Guilford (1950) explains creativity as a cognitive function composed of multiple factors. Influenced by his perspective, later researchers have tried to group various approaches to creativity as representative of only one piece of a pie. A **confluence approach** to creativity requires multiple factors in place for real creativity to occur. The confluence model proposed by Lubart (1994) states six resources need to work together for creativity: intellectual ability, knowledge, personality traits, motivational style, thinking style, and an environment supportive of both the creative process and creative output. Barron (1988) argues that the relationship between persons and products (or problems) is what ignites creativity, analogous to an "open

system of mutual interdependence." This implies that creativity is not simply the product of a unique individual. In fact, Csikszentmihalyi (1997) proposes that in order for creativity to really flower, a special synergy of person, environment, culture, and historical period needs to take place.

How to Enhance the Potential for Creativity

Since creativity is valuable both to individuals and society, many people are interested in how to nurture creativity. (Note: It may be impossible to develop interventions that consistently and reliably increase creativity.) German artist Joseph Beuys once famously declared, "Everyone is an artist" (Spivey, 2005). If he is correct, how can each of us find the artist within? Csikszentmihalyi's work with flow was originally designed as a partial study of creativity. Indeed, highly creative people are often referring to flow experiences when during periods of total engagement they describe creative juices as flowing (Csikszentmihalyi, 1997)! Some studies have found that positive mood can increase cognitive flexibility and thereby the potential for creativity (for example, Nadler, Rabi, & Minda, 2010).

However, research is mixed: Other studies do not support a link between positive mood and creativity (Kaufman, 2009). For instance, one recent study found that positive mood only helped extraverts be more creative (Stafford, Ng, Moore, & Bard, 2010). An interesting study used EEG biofeedback to induce alpha/theta hypnagogic states of relaxation in order to increase creativity (Boynton, 2001). Ellen Langer's (2005) work with mindfulness has also been used to increase potential for creativity. How? By helping people focus on the moment, break out of old habits, and avoid distractions. Other suggestions to improve creativity are to follow your passions, take breaks when solutions don't come easily, remember to do aerobic exercise, and expand your horizons by exploring other cultures (Bronson & Merryman, 2010).

The Knight Foundation has created one of the more charming ways to stimulate creativity by supporting "Random Acts of Culture" throughout

© 2002 by Randy Glasbergen.
www.glasbergen.com

**"I drank 40 cups of coffee to help me feel more creative!
Does hallucinating count as 'thinking outside of the box'?"**

the United States (Kino, 2011). One of the more famous involved members of the Opera Company of Philadelphia mingling anonymously among Christmas shoppers in a department store. When a secret cue was given, members of the opera began singing the "Hallelujah Chorus" from Handel's *Messiah*, accompanied by the store's famous pipe organ. Shoppers were enthralled and many enthusiastically joined in singing at the top of their lungs (http://www.youtube.com/watch?v=wp_RHnQ-jgU).

We now know that an old standby recommendation for creativity, brainstorming, is not effective. In the 1970s and 1980s, organizational psychologists often recommended getting together with others and collectively generating as many solutions as possible, even ridiculous ones, to enhance creativity. Recent research has found this tactic does not help improve creativity (Rusco, 2004).

Undoubtedly, among the more unusual examples of finding creativity is the true story of Dr. Tony Cicoria. In 1994 when Dr. Cicoria was 42 years old and a prominent orthopedic surgeon, he was struck by lightning and underwent an out-of-body experience (see Sacks, 2007). After he recovered, he began to develop an insatiable need to listen to and play piano music. Within three months of the accident, Cicoria was spending most of his time playing piano

and composing. His first composition for piano debuted in 2007 and since then he has made numerous appearances as pianist and composer. (We hope that no readers who wish to paint like Picasso or compose like Mozart are now looking around the room for an electrical outlet!)

Creativity and Personal Growth   Outside formal research in psychology there has also been quite a bit of interest in creativity and its role in personal growth. Maslow (1971) refers to *primary creativity* as an ability to be inspired, to be taken up by the moment, and to perceive the world in new and unique ways. Similarly, Averill (2009) has done work with what he calls **emotional creativity**, or the ability to use emotion in creative ways to enhance life and expand potential. He draws inspiration from German philosopher Nietzsche's advice to "spiritualize the passions." In this formulation, Nietzsche means to embrace the full range of emotional expression, both highs and lows, in order to transcend more mundane approaches. These latter seek only to control emotion in order to grasp a small, yet unstable, security and predictability (see also Hergenhahn, 2009).

GENIUS

Before leaving the topic of creativity, we turn to the concept of genius. It is an oft-stated myth that the word *genius* was invented during the Renaissance to describe Leonardo DaVinci. Although DaVinci certainly deserves to be called a genius, the term actually comes to us from the ancient Romans who used the word to describe a guardian spirit. During the Renaissance (probably, in part, due to persons like DaVinci) *genius* began to take on a meaning of special talent or ability beyond the normal range. Since that time, it denotes a person of extraordinary creativity and inventiveness.

Howard Gardner's (1993) study of genius investigated such luminaries as Freud, Picasso, and Einstein. He found that these well-known geniuses were both similar to yet also different from other highly creative individuals. Those labeled as geniuses exhibited the same qualities associated with people who achieve excellence in their fields, insofar as they were intensely dedicated to their area of expertise,

© Bettmann/Corbis

Albert Einstein

extremely motivated, willing to work long and hard, and absorbed in a search for deeper knowledge about their craft. Yet not only were they often loners, they were so intensely involved in their work that they appeared self-absorbed. Also in contrast to those found "merely" creative, the geniuses tended to exhibit an extremely high level of self-confidence that might well be called arrogance. Freud's unyielding confidence in the absolute correctness of his theories, for instance, was the primary reason for his difficult splits with his former allies Adler and Jung.

Additionally, Gardner found that many geniuses would probably not be a very good friend. Often they made friends only when they needed support and could abandon those friendships easily,

quickly, and sometimes heartlessly if they felt it necessary. For instance, Picasso's relationships with other people—especially women—were once described as "ruthless". Similarly, Frank Lloyd Wright was famous for his egotism and could occasionally be cruel in his most intimate relationships. Despite this personality characteristic, creative geniuses tended to find an older person—often prior to a big breakthrough—to serve as mentor. Yet this vital person in their lives could also be abandoned quickly.

Finally, Gardner suggests that many creative geniuses made what he calls a "Faustian bargain" in order to be creative. This is a reference to the medieval legend of Faust, a character who sold his soul to the devil in order to gain knowledge and power. Gardner contends that creative geniuses "strike a deal" with themselves: that they will sacrifice something important in order to become creative and famous. Often what is sacrificed is the quality of their personal relationships in romance and marriage, parenthood, and friendship. Apparently, genius has its costs as well as its rewards.

Genius and "Madness"

Those costs for some highly creative people have entailed mental illness. The association between creativity and mental problems is part of the popular conception of the creative artist. Even Aristotle said, "There was never a genius without a tincture of madness." However, this time-honored notion seems to be a myth. Rothenberg (1990) argues quite logically that the type of cognitive skills associated with creativity have absolutely no inherent relationship to mental illness. Judith Schlesinger (2009) reviewed the classic papers that argue for a creativity-mental illness link (that is, Andreasen, 1987; Jamison, 1989; Ludwig, 1995) and found numerous problems with their research methods and conclusions, particularly with the subsequent reporting of results both in the popular media and in the psychological literature.

For example, James Kaufman (2001) coined the term "the Sylvia Plath effect" after his study found female poets more likely to suffer from mental illness than either female or male writers, or eminent women from diverse occupations. Kaufman (2009) later noted the unfortunate misinterpretation of his results to support a general link between creativity and mental illness, emphasizing that his results applied only to female poets and that the other creative women in his study did not show significantly more mental illness. Several authors have commented on the curious tendency of the public, and some psychologists, to either pathologize creativity or to romanticize the "suffering, mad artist" (Kaufman, 2009).

Dean Simonton (2010) interestingly adds to this puzzle with the observation that if there is any relationship between creativity and mental illness, it must depend on how creativity is measured. For "little c" creativity, there is actually a positive relationship between creativity and mental health! This is the opposite of the prevailing cultural assumption. With "big C" creativity, the picture becomes more complex. Genius-caliber creative people do tend to exhibit some personality traits associated with poor mental health, such as primary process thinking and nonconformity. However, they also possess compensatory characteristics that balance the impact of negative traits. That is, "big C" creative people often have more effective coping skills than other people, and this capacity allows them to function effectively.

There is a genetic factor in the type of mental illness associated with creativity in some earlier studies. Richards, Kinney, Lunde, and Benet (1988) conducted an interesting study that looked more directly at genetic contribution to creativity in genetic-linked mental illness. This study illustrates the complexities of the research, for they examined rates of both bipolar disorder and cyclothymia (a milder form of bipolar disorder). They reasoned that since bipolar disorder has a very strong genetic component, then close relatives of creative artists who have bipolar disorder should show higher rates of both bipolar disorder and higher rates of creativity. When they looked at creativity, they indeed found that first-degree relatives of artists with bipolar disorder or cyclothymia were more creative than a comparison group. However, when they investigated further, higher creativity scores were found for either relatives with cyclothymia or for those who did not have a mood disorder, but not for relatives diagnosed with bipolar disorder. In other words, creativity was more easily expressed by those who did *not* exhibit the symptoms associated with bipolar disorder. Therefore, this study suggests that if there is a shared genetic contribution to both creativity and bipolar disorder, then serious mental illness such as bipolar disorder may actually *inhibit* the expression of creativity.

SUMMARY

This chapter has covered excellence, passion, the sense of beauty or aesthetics, creativity, and genius. Much of the research concludes that excellence is learned rather than the result of innate genetic factors. Key factors in excellence include: dedicated and frequent practice; a strong intrinsic interest in one's area of expertise; and a persistence to develop one's expertise over many years. A major factor in excellence is having a passion for one's interest area.

The relevance of aesthetics for well-being has also been discussed. An appreciation of beauty enhances our sense of wonder at and appreciation of the world. The development of creativity shares most of the characteristics of excellence but adds certain cognitive styles. These include, but are not restricted to: openness to experience; cognitive flexibility; tolerance for ambiguity; and willingness to consider unconventional solutions. Characteristics of the creative person; creative process; creative environment, or press; and creative product were highlighted. Finally, we discussed characteristics of genius. The condition of genius builds on qualities of both excellence and creativity, yet adds an intense drive to succeed that can involve a willingness to sacrifice even important psychological needs in order to achieve one's high goals.

LEARNING TOOLS

Key Terms and Ideas

excellence

deliberate practice

ten-year rule

passion

aesthetics

little c and big c creativity

divergent thinking

confluence approach

emotional creativity

Books

Kaufman, J. (2009). *Creativity 101 (Psych 101)*. NY: Springer. Summary of creativity research for students.

Robinson, K. & Aronica, L. (2009). *The Element: How finding your passion changes everything*. NY: Penguin. *(popular)*

Simonton, D. (2009). *Genius 101 (Psych 101)*. NY: Springer. Summary of the research on genius for students.

Spivey, N. (2005). *How art made the world: A journey to the origins of human creativity*. NY: Perseus. Argues that art and imagination are key factors in the development of civilization. *(popular)*

Tharp. T. (2003). *The creative habit*. NY: Simon & Schuster. Renowned choreographer Twyla Tharp presents her ideas on learning how to be creative. *(popular)*

On the Web

http://www.youtube.com/watch?v=86x-u-tz0MA Elizabeth Gilbert (author of *Eat, Pray, Love*) discusses creativity.

http://www.youtube.com/watch?v=iG9CE55wbtY Sir Ken Robinson (see **References** above) discusses the need for creativity in schools.

http://www.psychologytoday.com/basics/creativity Links to articles on creativity from *Psychology Today* magazine.

Personal Explorations

1. Identify within a space of five minutes as many different uses of a pencil as possible. The goal is to "think outside of the box," so allow yourself to describe highly unconventional, even absurd, uses. As long as the pencil usage is possible, it counts. Second, perform the same activity with regard to a wooden ruler. And, finally, do so for a CD.

2. Write an imaginative one-page story about the below photo accompanying this activity. Feel free to invent a main character; subordinate

characters; a plot that involves tension or conflict; and—since this is a course on positive psychology—a happy ending.

3. As imaginatively as possible, write a one-page story that begins with this opening paragraph:

"So this is what feels like to be rich and famous!" thought Jason as he stepped onto his yacht for the first time. It had all happened so fast. Only one year ago," …

Feel free to invent any additional characters or plot that you like based on this opening paragraph.

Harbor in Japan

Chapter 8

Well-Being Across the Lifespan

> The marvelous richness of human experience would lose something of rewarding joy if there were no limitations to overcome. The hilltop hour would not be half so wonderful if there were no dark valleys to traverse.
> HELLEN KELLER

Psychologists have long been concerned with how people grow and develop over the course of a lifetime. However, early behaviorist perspectives were based on an image of human beings as passively reacting to events; people were viewed as merely responding to stimuli. Further, responses were regarded as a result of past conditioning that allowed little room for independent action. In contrast, newer theories of development begin by assuming that we are active participants in shaping our own development. That is, besides merely reacting to events, people can also anticipate upcoming changes and prepare for them before life challenges turn into crises. Positive psychology declares that adult development is a continuous process of anticipating the future, appraising and reappraising goals, adjusting to current realities, and regulating expectations so as to maintain a sense of well-being in the face of changing circumstances.

It may seem obvious that how we think about well-being, happiness, and satisfaction with life will change in some ways as we mature. However, many assumptions about the ways in which well-being can change turn out to be cultural myths. In addition, research into the relationship between well-being and age turns out to be fairly complicated. This section begins with a discussion of studies that investigate subjective well-being at different ages. The next section covers studies that look at how well-being is impacted by both anticipated and unexpected life events. Many studies have specifically investigated how our sense of well-being changes as we age and as we are inevitably challenged by the vicissitudes of life. Of course, many events in life are expected and welcome, but they nevertheless require adjustments and effort. The Peruvian-born writer Carlos Casteneda once said, "We either make ourselves miserable, or we make ourselves strong. The amount of work is the same."

In any culture as people grow throughout adulthood, a variety of significant life events require change and adjustment. Indeed, many such events have rituals associated with them to give social support for the challenges of undergoing them. These challenges are referred to as *normative* life events, depending on a particular culture, these include launching a career, marriage, becoming a parent or grandparent, and retirement. Unexpected life challenges, such as unanticipated illness or financial crisis, are referred to as *non-normative* life events (see Ryff, Singer, & Seltzer, 2002). Some events, such as relocating for one's career or caring for aging parents, even if not universal comprise normative events. Regardless of whether challenging life events are expected or not, people generally adopt two basic methods of adjustment: assimilation and accommodation.

Adjustments that use *assimilation* allow us to keep striving without major alterations in goals, assumptions, or in sense of identity. For instance, a goal of becoming a world-famous chef does not have to be abandoned when one's first child is born, but how that goal is pursued will certainly need to be altered to fit the new role of parent. Adjustments that use *accommodation* require us to change goals, assumptions, or identities because the old ones are no longer workable. For example, after paralysis of his left hand, Robert Schumann was forced to abandon his desire to be a concert pianist. Luckily for the world, he created a new life for himself as a composer (Brandtstäder, 2002). Earlier research on adaptability to change defined *ego resiliency* as an ability to adapt flexibly to challenges and to restore a sense of positive well-being (Block & Block, 1980). Studies have found that high ego resiliency at age 21 predicted positive adaptation to challenges many years later in life (see Pals, 2006b).

WELL-BEING OVER THE LIFESPAN

In the study of personality development over time, researchers have used three basic models to understand life changes: stage or growth models, lifespan models, and life-course models (Pulkkinen & Caspi, 2002). Stage or growth models postulate recognizable stages that need to be addressed, roughly at different ages. In contrast to stage theories, lifespan models do not postulate age-specific challenges but rather see personality development as a continuous process of adjustment to challenges. Often these adjustments are viewed in terms of various phases of life, such as adolescence, early adulthood, and middle adulthood. Life-course models also tend to look at phases of life but emphasize the social-role demands at each phase. Such models are particularly sensitive to cultural and historical differences in social-role expectations. The next sections focus on understanding well-being through stage, lifespan, and life-course models of personality development.

Stage Models and Well-Being

The most influential model of life stages in Western psychology has been Erik Erikson's (1950) eight stages of psychosocial development (see Table 8.1).

Erikson's theory presents a very captivating idea in that each life stage is defined by a specific "crisis" or challenging situation that compels us to move out of our comfort zone and readjust to changing life circumstances. The successful resolution of each crisis helps to build a specific virtue. From an Eriksonian perspective, at least some of the virtues and strengths applauded by positive psychology are developed through

Erik and Joan Erikson

© Jon Erikson

TABLE 8.1   Erikson's Stages of Psychosocial Development

Ego Conflict		Ages: (approx.)	Virtue
Adaptive	**Maladaptive**		
Trust	Mistrust	0–1	Hope
Autonomy	Shame/Doubt	1–3	Will
Initiative	Guilt	3–5	Purpose
Industry	Inferiority	6–11	Competence
Ego Identity	Role Confusion	11–18	Fidelity
Intimacy	Isolation	18–25	Love
Generativity	Self-absorption	25–50	Care
Ego Integrity	Despair	50+	Wisdom

SOURCE: Adapted from Benjafield, J. (2010) A History of Psychology, 3rd Edition (pp. 246–348). Copyright © Oxford University Press.

successfully resolving tensions between opposing goals and emotions. You may recall from chapter 1 that Aristotle, and later Maimonides, declared that virtues are found by searching for a "golden mean" between opposing emotional and behavioral tendencies. Studies have found that greater maturity in adulthood is associated with movement through Erikson's stages and resolution of stage crises as he hypothesized (Sheldon & Kasser, 2001; Tucak & Nekic, 2007; Vandewater, Ostrove, & Stewart, 1997). For instance, a 45-year longitudinal study of women examined Erikson's last stage of *ego integrity versus despair* and found, as expected, that one's ego integrity was predictive of better intimate relationships and higher psychological well-being (James & Zarrett, 2006). The researchers also found that identity status in 1951 predicted one's level of generativity in 1996. Stage seven of Erikson's stage theory, *generativity versus stagnation*, has recently been the focus of considerable research interest.

Generativity: Nurturing and Guiding Others Erikson, Erikson, and Kivnick (1986) defined **generativity** as "the responsibility for each generation of adults to bear, nurture, and guide those people who will succeed them as adults, as well as to develop and maintain those societal institutions and natural resources without which successive generations will not be able to survive" (pp. 73–74). Dan McAdams and his colleagues have analyzed life narratives in order to assess generativity (McAdams & Diamond, 1997; McAdams & de St. Aubin, 1998). In general, studies have shown that a higher level of generativity is associated with greater well-being (for example, Ackerman, Zuroff, & Moskowitz, 2000; McAdams, de St. Aubin, & Logan, 1993). As Erikson predicted, generativity is also associated with other factors related to increasing maturity or greater personal growth. For instance, studies have found an association between generativity and use of more principled moral reasoning; balance between individualistic and communal concerns; and increasing importance of other-directed behaviors in midlife (An & Cooney, 2006; Pratt, Norris, Arnold & Filyer, 1999; Mansfield & McAdams, 1996).

In other words, generativity is related to many traits central to the concept of the good life in positive psychology. In fact, Ackerman, Zuroff, and Moskowitz (2000) found that increased generativity is the best predictor of well-being in midlife adults. Greater generativity is also associated with having more education and being at least middle-aged (McAdams & de St. Aubin, 1998). This suggests that learning and maturity are conducive to generativity, as well as access to resources and opportunities that enable generative activities (Keyes & Ryff, 1998). However, women tend to be more generative than men, probably due to women's higher scores on empathy. A recent study by

Monika Ardelt, Scott Landes, and George Vaillant (2010) examined resilience in World War II veterans. They found that although simple exposure to combat during the war was unrelated to later psychosocial adjustment and maturity, men who had endured high combat exposure and were more generative showed higher subsequent psychological growth, maturity, and wisdom. Higher generativity helped the men adjust better and even to thrive.

McAdams, Diamond, de St. Aubin, & Mansfield (1997) suggested how generativity might be related to well-being (also see Keyes & Ryff, 1998). They found that the identities of highly generative people, as revealed through their life stories, were often partially constructed with a **commitment script**. A common theme in this type of life narrative is that initial difficulties in life were faced, which then led to a greater sensitivity to other's suffering and, finally, to a positive outcome that benefited society. This indicates that self-identity for highly generative people is based in part on a personal life story that emphasizes overcoming difficulties and, as a result, growing into greater understanding, empathy, and compassion for others.

Another intriguing finding was that highly generative people did *not* experience either more positive events or fewer stresses compared with less generative people; rather, the difference between highly generative people and others was in *how* those life events were interpreted. For generative people, both positive and negative life events are seen as events that foster empathy, compassion, and a deeper understanding of others. Once again, the important factor is not the number or types of events encountered in life, but how one perceives them or makes events meaningful.

George Vaillant (2002) proposed a theory of successful aging based on both Erikson's theory and on Vaillant's analysis of longitudinal data covering over 50 years of people's lives. He presented a series of six developmental life tasks: identity, intimacy, career consolidation, generativity, keeper of meaning (or wisdom), and integrity. Viewing the tasks as requiring continuous refinement throughout life, he postulated that mastery of all life tasks is a hallmark of successful aging.

For his research, Vaillant conducted in-depth interviews with people to elicit their personal stories and unique perspectives on life. He wrote of his research participants, "Their lives were too human for science, too beautiful for numbers, too sad for diagnosis, and too immortal for bound journals" (Vaillant, 1977, p. 11).

Lifespan and Life-Course Models and Well-Being

A substantial body of research has found that the processes we use to create a sense of well-being differ at different phases of life. For instance, imagine a man who has never seemed to take steps into adulthood—the stereotypical 45-year-old guy who still lives in a basement room in his parent's house; or a 50-year-old woman who continues to relate to the world as if she were still sweet-16 years old. Although these people might claim they were happy, most observers would feel somewhat saddened by a sense that a fuller and richer adult life has passed them by. By examining life stages in this way, we can add to our understanding of life's complexities and of how its challenges demand adaptability and flexibility. We begin with adolescence, since healthy childhood development has been the subject of many other books.

Positive Youth Development   In psychology's early years, leading thinkers believed that preteen years and adolescence are a time of "storm and stress," that is, a period with many emotional upheavals when myriad potentially wrong turns and bad decisions could impact a young person far into adulthood. Adolescence was considered a time when the inevitable problems of growing up had to be carefully managed and controlled. However, current developmental studies have found many pathways through adolescence, most of which involve little upheaval or storm and stress (Lerner, 2009). This newer vision has been conceptualized as **positive youth development**, which assumes that youth possess resources that can be developed, nurtured, and cultivated. Strength-based assessments of children have identified a variety of strengths, virtues, and positive character traits that help children and adolescents not simply to adapt but to flourish as they enter adulthood. These include hope, optimism, and benefit-finding—that is, the ability to reinterpret seemingly negative events in a positive light (Kirschman, Johnson, Bender, & Roberts, 2009). Of course, curiosity and openness to experiences must also be added to this list.

Richard Lerner (2009) presented positive youth development as a process that fosters the "five C's": *competence*; *confidence*; *connection*; *character*; and *caring*. He described young people who actively seek to nurture and develop these qualities as "thriving youth" (see King, Dowling, Mueller, White, Schultz et al., 2005). In addition, Lerner suggested that a "6th C" should be added to the list: *contribution*, or the effort to help or serve others. A major resource for positive youth development is an alignment of young people with the social contexts in which they live, such as families, schools, and community organizations.

These supportive contexts are referred to as **developmental assets**. That is, positive youth development is not only focused on developing individual strengths in youth but devotes significant effort to developing a good relationship between young people and social-community resources. Instances of developmental assets outside the home include churches, YMCA or activity centers, Big Brothers/Big Sisters, 4-H Clubs, and colleges and universities. Among the more striking changes in how researchers think about positive development and resilience is an increased emphasis on the social environment. How so? It is becoming clear that emotional bonds and social connections are far more important than previously realized. It really does "take a village" to raise healthy children (see Clinton, 2006).

The Penn Resiliency Program, which evolved from research on optimistic and pessimistic explanatory styles, is devoted to positive youth development. It teaches children *learned optimism*, or how to reinterpret life events in a more positive and realistic fashion (Gillham, Reivich, Jaycox, & Seligman, 1995). Children who go through the program are able to avoid symptoms of depression, increase

optimism, and even become healthier (Gillham & Reivich 2004).

Early and Middle Adulthood   Discussion of subjective well-being in chapter 3 covered basic relationships among happiness, life satisfaction, and age. This section focuses on how well-being is affected by chronological age and passage through the lifespan.

Jochen Brandtstäder (2002) investigated how people pursue goals as they encounter the vicissitudes of life. In particular, he postulated a dual-process model of adaptation and adjustment: First, as people pursue goals they may run into difficulties that require them to intensify efforts or alter paths. This entails a process of assimilation as they keep the original goal intact. Second, important goals may become impossible to attain or be substantially blocked. At such times, a person must use accommodative processes to adjust by downgrading the importance of the goal; switching to a new goal; or using other strategies to adapt to the loss of an important goal. Brandtstäder found that both assimilative and accommodative processes after unexpected life events force us to adjust our original goals can lead to a sense of well-being and life satisfaction. Over 100 years ago, William James (1892) declared that we increase our sense of self-esteem by either succeeding more or by giving up our "pretensions"—our overly ambitious goals and self-evaluation.

Although the successful completion of normative life events is associated with greater well-being, the specific type of event varies by age. Ryff and Heidrich (1997) found that young people associated participation in positive social and leisure activities with greater well-being, whereas middle-aged people found positive relationships most important, and an older group associated well-being more with previous educational and work experience.

As noted throughout this book, a major tenet of positive psychology is that people need to focus on their strengths and virtues. Derek Isaacowitz, George Vaillant, and Martin Seligman (2003) examined the relative importance of personal strengths at different ages. They found that for younger groups strengths centered on exploration of their world, and that the strength of hope was a predictor of life satisfaction. For the middle-aged group, life satisfaction was predicted mainly by a higher capacity for loving relationships. The older group reported greater use of interpersonal and self-regulatory strengths.

Intriguingly, differences appear among age groups in terms of how people calculate their subjective well-being. Older persons often experience a smaller discrepancy between their life goals or aspirations and their actual achievements in life; this accomplishment tends to increase a sense of happiness and life satisfaction. Rates of discrepancy between ideal self and actual self vary with age. Heidrich (1996) found that for younger and middle-aged groups, significant differences existed between ratings of ideal self and actual self. However, for an older group, both ratings were quite similar.

When compared to young people, older persons are more satisfied with their past accomplishments and their present lives but less satisfied with their anticipated futures (see Argyle, 1999). Satisfaction with social relationships has been found to be more important for older persons (Herzog, Rogers, & Woodworth, 1982). Ryff and Singer (2006) highlighted several studies using Ryff's Psychological Well-Being Scale. Their results showed that some scale scores increase as people age (in autonomy, environmental mastery, and self-acceptance—but only for men), some decrease (in purpose in life and personal growth), while still others remain relatively stable throughout life (in positive relationships with others and self-acceptance—but only for women). The researchers attributed the decrease in personal growth and purpose in life to retirement and change in social roles. As we have noted, however, subjective well-being research indicates no decline in happiness or life satisfaction in old age, though increasing health problems associated with advancing age do exert a negative impact on subjective well-being.

Conclusions on relationship between life phases and well-being depend on how well-being is measured. Corey Keyes, Dov Shmotkin, and Carol Ryff (2002) examined different age groups in terms of both subjective well-being (SWB) and psychological well-being (PWB—that is, Ryff's Psychological Well-Being Scales). Since they measured both, they looked at a four-fold classification at different life stages (that is, high/low SWB with times high/low PWB). They found that those who had both high SWB and high PWB

Courtesy of Carol Ryff

Carol Ryff

were more likely to be midife or older, with a higher level of education; they were also more conscientious and extraverted, and had lower neurosis scores. Younger people with less education tended to be found in the groups low on either measure of well-being. Adults with higher PWB than SWB tended to be younger, better educated, and more open to experiences than adults who had higher SWB than PWB. Thus, conclusions about well-being at different age groups were somewhat different depending upon how well-being was measured (i.e. PWB or SWB).

Is there a Midlife crisis?   Recent studies suggest that the often-clichéd midlife crisis is not only indeed real but a universal phenomenon as well. David Blanchflower and Andrew Oswald (2008) examined the relationship between age and well-being in a huge sample of over 2 million people from nearly 80 countries. When they viewed a subset of a half-million people from American and Europe, they found that well-being tended to be relatively high at younger ages, decrease in midlife, then rise again after about age 60. Therefore, they argue that well-being shows a U-shaped curve over the course of the lifespan. Specifically, women reach a minimum level of well-being around their mid-forties and men in their late forties or early fifties. Statistically, the researchers controlled for the impact of education, income, marital status, race, and other demographic variables, so they interpret these findings as a picture of well-being over the lifespan when all other factors are equal except age. An intriguing finding from their statistical analysis is the presence of a similar U-shaped curve in most countries of the world.

Brockmann (2010) analyzed data on German adults and found some evidence for cohort effects (that is, baby boomers versus prewar cohorts) but concluded that major factors influencing the dip at midlife were gender-specific and related to mid-career re-evaluation. He argued that midlife creates many "frustrated achievers" because it is a time when people reevaluate where they are in life, what they have or have not accomplished, and the inevitability of aging. Then as people come to terms with these realities and adjust their aspirations, they regain a greater sense of well-being. However, Brandtstäder cautioned that "attempts to define personal well-being exclusively in terms of efficient goal pursuit are seriously incomplete" (p. 381), insofar as accommodation encompasses more than merely changing one's goals.

Other analyses have also found differences between the subjective well-being of men and women as they pass through the lifespan, but not always a midlife dip. In older studies that examined both gender and age at the same time, older women tended to be less happy than older men (Argyle, 1999). In terms of change over time, men's happiness ratings showed a relatively steady increase as they aged, while women's happiness ratings increased up to age 25, then showed a slight dip in happiness from age 25 to 35, which was followed by steadily increasing happiness ratings (Mroczek & Kolarz, 1998).

The Middle-aged Brain Many people have complained about decreasing mental capacities as they enter middle-age. Popular jokes about "senior moments" when memory suddenly fails reinforce this phenomenon. Nonetheless, current research has found this notion not quite accurate. Some mental functions, such as reaction time and abilities to multitask and remember names do manifest a decline. However, other functions actually show improvement with age. These include complex reasoning skills, empathy, inductive reasoning, verbal memory, making financial decisions, and ability to see connections or to grasp the big picture (Strauch, 2010). Studies today suggest that the middle-aged brain may be "less quick, but more shrewd" (Trudeau, 2010).

Successful Aging and Aging Well Developmental psychologists who currently study aging have abandoned previous assumptions that getting older inevitably leads to rapid cognitive, emotional, and physical decline. Today, terms such as *successful aging*, *aging well*, and *positive aging* capture a view that being older is one of the most exciting and invigorating times of life (Depp, Vahia, & Jeste, 2010; Williamson & Christie, 2009). We have already seen that older persons tend to be the happiest and most satisfied of any age group. One caveat: This conclusion holds only as long as a person remains in good health and active.

Some intriguing lines of research suggest why studies often find increased subjective well-being with age. One interpretation is that the increase in well-being is due primarily to a decrease in negative emotionality rather than to an increase in positive emotion (Gomez, Krings, Bangerter & Grob, 2009; Larsen & Prizmic, 2008). That is, the positivity ratio for older persons increases because negative emotionality goes down, a phenomenon known as the *positivity effect* (Scheibe & Carstensen, 2010). For example, a study by Kisley, Wood, and Burrows (2007) measured brain activity in people aged 18–81 as they gazed at images that were positive (for example, a chocolate ice cream cone); negative (for example, a decomposing calf); or neutral (for example, an electrical outlet). They found that younger adults were slightly more reactive to both positive and negative images than older persons. On the other hand, older persons reported less negative emotion toward negative images, while responsiveness to positive events remained relatively constant over age groups. Other studies have found no changes in response to positive images with age (Scheibe & Carstensen, 2010). Magai (2008) suggested that the positivity effect is due partially to a reduction in the frequency of anger as people age.

Other researchers investigating how emotions are processed have discovered that older persons lead somewhat more interesting emotional lives than younger people (see Magai, 2008). It seems that older people are better able to regulate their emotions (Kryla-Lighthall, 2009), score higher on measures of emotional intelligence (see Scheibe & Carstensen, 2010), have a greater appreciation for the emotional aspects of life, and better thrive with emotional complexity than younger people.

Readers may be wondering how these findings fit with research reported earlier that young people feel emotions more strongly than older persons. Although older persons may emotionally react with less intensity, recent studies have found that when their emotions are aroused, these are felt with just as much intensity as for their younger counterparts. A greater ability of older persons to control their emotional responses is due to better skills in antecedent-focused emotional regulation. That is, older people are better at selecting less stressful environments and using anticipatory coping strategies to regulate emotion (Scheibe & Carstensen, 2010).

Older persons may also be less prone to one type of positive illusion (see chapter 3). In this case, a study looked at *temporal realism*, or the ability of people to accurately recall their past well-being and to predict their future well-being. They found that older persons showed more temporal realism—that is, were more accurate—than younger persons (Lachman, Röcke, Rosnick, & Ryff, 2008). In contrast to many studies on positive illusion, it also found that greater temporal realism is associated with more adaptive functioning at all ages.

Fascinating findings on the greater complexity of emotions reported in older people indicate both increased range and type of emotions and more overlap among these, especially of positive and negative emotions. Older people may experience more highly nuanced and poignant blend of positive and negative emotion, as Maslow (1996) suggested. The higher well-being of many older persons may also be due to increased feelings of connectedness to others and greater focus on the present moment

(Kamvar, Mogilner, & Aaker, 2009). As we have observed, greater autonomy tends to predict higher subjective well-being. One study discovered that older persons have a greater sense of autonomy even when performing social or civic duties (Sheldon, Kasser, Houser-Marko, Jones, & Turban, 2005).

Jochen Brandtstäder (2002) found that people in older age groups report a greater sense of well-being when they downgrade the importance of earlier goals, give up some need for instrumental control, and use other accommodative strategies. This can result in satisfaction with how life has turned out. A study of centenarians (mean age 99.8 years) looked at *congruence*, or a perception that life has been satisfying and that one has received what he or she expected out of life (Bishop, Martin, MacDonald, & Poon, 2010). Researchers found that higher congruence was related to better subjective reports of health and economic security, which was ultimately tied to higher self-reported happiness.

Paul Baltes (1993) proposed a model of aging based on how people adapt to difficult circumstances. Baltes termed his model **selective optimization with compensation**. He argued that optimal adjustment to aging is accomplished by accepting that certain capacities decline with age and finding ways to compensate for those inevitable losses. By such self-acceptance, one can retain optimum enjoyment with activities that give a sense of satisfaction. Classical pianist Arthur Rubinstein, who continued to perform into his eighties (Baltes, 1993), is a case in point. As he aged, Rubinstein certainly couldn't play at the same technical level that he could when younger. But he adapted by selecting fewer pieces to perform, practicing more often, and deliberately slowing down his playing just prior to faster passages to give the impression of playing faster. These strategies allowed Rubenstein to continue performing music, an activity that gave him deep satisfaction.

Laura Carstensen (1992, 1995) proposed a theory also relevant to how people actively regulate aspects of their emotional lives throughout the lifespan. She noted that older people often regularly bypass opportunities for social contact, yet report levels of subjective well-being as high or higher than younger people. If, as we saw in chapter 3 on subjective well-being, positive social relationships are correlated with well-being, then how can this be true? Carstensen's answer is a theory of **socioemotional selectivity**. This states that basic psychological goals, such as the development of a positive self-concept or the regulation of emotion, remain throughout the lifespan, but their salience changes depending on one's place in the life cycle. Specifically, drives to seek out information and to develop a positive self-concept are most important during adolescence and become less important with age. In contrast, the drive for emotional regulation is less important during adolescence and then rises in significance with advancing age, until in old age it becomes dominant.

Carstensen (1995) further observed that as people enter old age, fewer others can provide novel and interesting information that seems relevant and, therefore, people are "less motivated to engage in emotionally meaningless (but perhaps otherwise functional) social contacts, and will make social choices based on the potential for emotional rewards" (p. 153). Note that a reduction in social contact can be adaptive for older persons. This process, however, is more akin to social selection than to social withdrawal. Indeed, studies find that in comparison to younger people, older persons tend to prefer familiar social partners and have smaller social networks, albeit ones comprised of people they feel closer to emotionally (Scheibe & Carstensen, 2010). This means that intimate relationships may become more important but less numerous with age. Similarly, the *value-as-moderator model* of subjective well-being by Oishi, Diener, Suh, and Lucas (1999) proposed that shifting values across the lifespan predict shifts in how well-being is calculated based on those values.

In a study designed to test some of these ideas, Carstensen and her colleagues (Carstensen, Mayr, Nesselrode, & Pasupathi, 2000) found that though age was unrelated to the frequency of positive experiences, extended periods of positive emotionality were more likely experienced in older persons. They also found that older persons felt more complex and more poignant emotional experiences than younger people. In their view, therefore, older people have learned how to recognize more nuances of emotional experience and how to regulate their emotions in more adaptive ways. Carstensen's theory suggests that the type of activities and goals people seek in life is intimately related to issues that are salient at their particular place in the life cycle. Interestingly, in this case, age does seem to have its advantages. With advances in medicine and more emphasis on fitness, physically active older persons may eventually prove to be the happiest, most satisfied of all age groups.

DIFFERENT PATHS TO MATURITY: INDIVIDUAL DIFFERENCES IN LIFESPAN DEVELOPMENT

Several studies of well-being across the lifespan have looked at how individuals take different paths to managing the challenges of life. Ravenna Helson and Sanjay Srivastava (2001) used an individual differences approach to examine data from a well-known longitudinal study of women. For over 50 years, the Mills Study has been following women who graduated from Mills College in 1958 and 1960. The 2001 study used information gathered when the women were nearly 60 years old. Helson and Srivastava examined four criteria of maturity: competence, wisdom, ego development, and generativity. They discovered three relatively distinct paths to positive adult development that the women had followed throughout life: *achievers, conservers,* and *seekers.* A fourth group, *the depleted,* had a pattern of unresolved emotional difficulties in their lives.

The women who fit the profile of *achievers* tended to be highly achievement-motivated, competent, career-oriented, and ambitious, and they scored highest on the measure of generativity. *Conservers* tended to also be quite competent but somewhat conventional, emotionally reserved, and less open to change. The women who were *seekers* were quite open to new experiences, continued to question and challenge themselves throughout life, valued personal growth over career success, and scored highest on measures of wisdom and ego development. In terms of self-identity, the *achievers* had the most integrated sense of self-identity; the *conservers* were comfortable with their identity, but they had accepted the self-identity others and society had expected of them; and the *seekers* had definitely not accepted conventional definitions of who they should be. In fact, some *seekers* had been searching for a stable self-identity as late as their early forties.

The emotional lives of the three groups were also distinct. Over the course of their lives, the *achievers* had tried to maximize their positive emotions while minimizing their negative feelings; the *conservers* had adopted a strategy of dampening all their emotions so that both positive and negative feelings were kept in check; and the *seekers* had amplified all their emotions so that both positive and negative feelings were experienced more deeply. What is fascinating about this study is that women in each of the three groups had created a positive sense of subjective well-being by handling their emotional lives in quite different ways.

A study by Gisela Labouvie-Vief and Marshall Medler (2002) also used an individual differences approach in a study of adult emotional development. Their study encompassed a sample of 156 community residents stratified by age and sex, with age ranges from 15 to 86. Labouvie-Vief and Medler assumed that people regulate their emotions by using primarily two strategies. The first is **affect optimization**, or attempt to maximize positive emotions and dampen negative emotions. The second is **affect complexity**, or attempt to coordinate positive and negative emotions into cognitive-emotional schemas (that is, organizational structures) that are both flexible and integrated. They found four groups that

each used a different emotional regulation style. The first was the *integrated group*, which emphasized positive emotions as well as emotional complexity. However, people in this group had only moderately high levels of self-complexity, and their use of certain defense mechanisms indicated some distortion of reality in order to maintain their positive emotions. The second group was the *defended group* that also emphasized positive emotions but scored low on affect complexity and had a somewhat underdeveloped sense of self. This group used stronger defense mechanisms to maintain positive emotions. A third group was labeled the *complex group* because members tended to have only moderate levels of positive emotions but high levels of emotional complexity (that is, blended patterns of both positive and negative emotions) and a highly complex sense of self. The lower scores for defensiveness in this group indicated greater openness to experiences, even if experiences involved negative emotions. The last group, the *dysregulated group*, scored low on both positive emotions and emotional complexity, and they were clearly having emotional difficulties. In terms of age differences, the younger group (15–29 years old) had the smallest percentage of *integrated* members and the older group (60–80 years old) tended to use defense mechanisms more than the other age groups to maintain their positive emotionality and subjective well-being.

The studies by Helson and Srivastava (2001) and by Labouvie-Vief and Medler (2002) used different methods and studied different populations but came to several similar conclusions. That is, both teams of researchers found that different styles of emotional regulation across the lifespan create different types of positive adaptation. These styles of positive adaptation can be understood by looking at the relative emphasis of positive over negative emotions, the complexity of emotional experience, and the type of defense mechanisms used to maintain a subjective sense of well-being. The importance of defense mechanisms for well-being is covered later in the chapter.

© Dan Rosandich.
www.danscartoons.com

"Oh, I have my good years and my bad years."

Narrative Approaches to the Lifespan: Telling Stories to Make Sense of Our Lives

A narrative approach to lifespan development examines how we build stories or self-narratives that help us define and understand our lives (Gergen & Gergen, 2006; McAdams, 1993). To get a feel for the narrative tradition in psychology, simply reflect on how you and your friends tell stories about your lives. Note that some are happy stories and others sad; some provide a message or lesson for you; and some illustrate a personal strength and some a potential weakness. Finally, note that the stories are not simply objective accounts of absolutely everything that happened at the time, as if a documentary of the event. Rather, most stories are creative constructions from actual events that we take bits and pieces of and from which we build a coherent narrative. This last quality of creative construction is why life stories are important to our sense of well-being. We literally write our own autobiographies and, in turn, the story we create helps to define our life for us.

Major functions of our personal stories or life narratives are, first, to aid in the creation of a self-identity or sense of self; and second, to help create a sense of meaning (McLean, Pasupathi, & Palls, 2007). By telling stories about ourselves, we create our identity as well as create meaning in our lives. In fact, a search for meaning is often a search for a narrative that makes sense, that gives us hope, and that enlivens us. Among adolescents and young adults, more sophisticated life meanings have been associated with more mature identity status (McLean & Pratt, 2006). Our earlier discussion on generativity focused on how commitment scripts often lead to more altruism. Studies on reminiscing found that taking time to review our life narratives can lead to improved well-being (Bryant, Smart, & King, 2005; Staudinger, 2001).

Also, telling our stories to other people is quite helpful in the creation of new meaning in life (Thorne, McLean, & Lawrence, 2004). As an example in your own life, think of a time when you weren't sure how you felt about an issue until you began to talk about it with someone else. If telling our life narratives to other people is a necessary part of identity creation and meaning-making, then this might explain why having quality interpersonal relationships is so universally associated with well-being.

Themes in Life Stories Of course, there are many different types of stories that people tell about their lives. Jennifer Pals, Kate McLean, and their colleagues have conducted considerable research on the relationship between life stories and personal well-being. Their analyses reveal two types of narrative processing (McLean, Pasupathi, & Pals, 2007; Pals, 2006a, 2006b). One path they term **coherent positive resolution**, which involves the creation of a narrative about a difficult event that has a positive ending and conveys a sense of emotional resolution and closure. For instance, someone might say, "Yes, it was difficult growing up with an alcoholic father, but I learned to be independent and to build my own sense of self-worth." The other path they term **exploratory narrative processing**, which involves a willingness to fully understand a difficult situation and to analyze it with openness and full recognition of the negative emotional impact the event had on one's life. This process leads to greater depth and more complexity in a person's understanding of life events. For instance, high exploratory processing is indicated by someone who says, "Not a day goes by that I don't feel the pain of the loss. But I know that people get sick and die. It's no one's fault; it's just the cycle of life and we need to accept it."

Research has found that high coherent positive narratives are often associated with building positive relationships and with high scores on subjective well-being. High exploratory narratives, in contrast, are associated with personal growth and with high scores on maturity, wisdom, and ego development. That is, people tell positive or happy stories in order to support and nurture interpersonal relationships, but they tell stories about difficult or negative events to help understand life in a more complex and compelling way (McLean, Pasupathi, & Pals, 2007).

By looking at both high and low styles of coherent positive and exploratory processing, it is possible to create a 2x2 matrix of life narrative styles (Pals, 2006a) that displays **transformation processing**, or both high coherent positive and high exploratory processing. This term refers to narratives that contain both high positive resolution and high processing of negative emotions, which are more consistently associated with indices of greater well-being. In this light, Pals suggested that positive adaptation to difficult life events is a two-step process: first, to explore the meaning and emotional impact of the event; and second, to construct a coherent and positive resolution. She wrote:

> Subjective well-being is associated with the capacity to construct a coherently structured story about a difficult experience, the ending of which emphasizes the restoration of the positive in the person's life and also a sense that the person has moved on emotionally (Pals, 2006a, p. 1083).

Laura King has also explored the ways in which narratives impact well-being. In studies of how people adjust to important life transitions, she and colleagues found two important processes (see King & Hicks, 2006). When life transitions are required, people must be able to relinquish old goals that are no longer possible and embrace potential *second chances* in life. In addition, people must be willing to acknowledge the emotional consequences of lost goals and to recognize that they have been changed by the necessary transition. That is, people must be able to let go of both old goals and old selves, then work to create new goals, or second chances and *newfound selves.*

A final comment about narratives concerns the cultural aspect of life stories. Studies have found that the stories we create reflect the values and perspectives of our particular culture (McLean, Pasupathi & Pals, 2007). For instance, stories by native Chinese tend to be less focused on the self and more focused on both morality and connectedness to family than are stories by Americans. In contrast, American stories frequently portray a theme of **redemptive sequence**. That is, a difficult or challenging experience is transformed by a person's own active intervention, creating a change in the self that becomes the focal point of the story. The old "Horatio Alger" stories of individual success in America are examples of a redemptive sequence. One study found that narratives Americans wrote after the 9/11 terrorist attack contained redemptive themes along with coherent positive resolution (Adler & Poulin, 2009).

It is also possible that some narrative themes are universal and cross-cultural. For example, comparative mythologist Joseph Campbell (1949) described what he calls the "myth of the hero." The theme of this universal story is similar to one of redemptive sequence except for the ending: In the hero myth the protagonist returns to the community to teach others what he or she has learned from the struggle with a difficult life event.

The impact of cultural narrative on subjective well-being can also be seen in goal pursuit. In chapter 2, we noted that people tend to feel happier when they make adequate progress toward goals that are valued by their culture. Similarly, people feel better when they reach culturally valued milestones in life at ages considered socially appropriate. For instance, people tend to feel better about themselves when they get married, have children, or reach career milestones at the "right" time or at the "correct" age. Such an accomplishment impacts in part because it helps create a positive identity in a life narrative that says, "I've been a success in life."

A similar notion is advanced in the concept of **age identity**. This term describes how old we feel, rather than our actual chronological age. Some people feel younger than their actual age while others feel older. One study that examined adults in the United States and Germany found that feeling younger than one's actual age was associated with greater subjective well-being (Westerhof & Barrett, 2005). Another study found that feeling younger than one's actual age was associated with better cognitive abilities 10 years later (Schafer & Shippee, 2010).

In summary, ample evidence exists that individuals do create unique methods of adapting to life events over the course of their lives. Of course, often life does not go the way we expect or hope. Sometimes significant adjustments must be made, and it is to these adjustments that we turn next.

ADJUSTING TO DIFFICULT LIFE EVENTS

When thinking about the course of one's life, the familiar aphorism that "the only thing constant is change" reminds us that change can bring the unexpected or the unwelcome. This certainly applies to the human journey through life. Indeed, studies have found that up to 60% of adults have faced a major crisis or a trauma at some point in their lives (Greve & Staudinger, 2006). Statistics like this suggest that dealing with a crisis is a normal part of adulthood. Despite the frequency of difficult events, most adults find ways to recover from temporary setbacks. Researchers investigating adjustment to life difficulty have recognized many ways people can adapt. If you recall our earlier discussion, it is easy to surmise that some adaptations involve assimilation to an established sense of self and world, while others require life-altering accommodation.

Differing nomenclature in the research on positive adaptation to crisis or trauma is a difficulty. Here we adopt the terminology suggested by Christopher Davis and Susan Nolen-Hoeksema (2009). In their view, the term **benefit finding** describes common but potentially transient adjustment to adversity. This often takes the form of positive cognitive interpretation of setbacks that thereby place the troublesome event in a different light—that is, proverbially seeing the glass as half full rather than as half empty. In contrast, the term **posttraumatic growth** refers to significant changes in life goals and life commitments that require major alteration in one's sense of identity or life narrative. This approach views adaptation as eventually leading to improved mental health (Davydov, Stewart, Ritchie, & Chaudieu, 2010).

Resilience is the familiar descriptor for "a broad array of abilities for constructively and positively adapting to risk, adversity, or some monumental negative event" (Dunn, Uswatte & Elliot, 2009, p. 656). Masten and Reed (2002) defined resilience as a "pattern of positive adaptation in the face of significant adversity or risk" (p. 75). Resilience is found when a person responds favorably to a significant event that would otherwise produce a major decrease in well-being. Resilient people "bounce back" from difficult situations. Various degrees of resiliency can be found on a continuum extending from benefit finding on one end to posttraumatic growth on the other. Note, however, that some studies conceptualize resilience rather as a protective mechanism, similar to *psychological immunity*—that is, a mechanism that provides a buffer against future challenge (Davydov, Stewart, Ritchie, & Chaudieu, 2010).

Resilience: In Children

Historically, research on resilience began with observations of children. One assumption of early child development theories was that a poor family environment inevitably caused less-than-healthy adult personality development. Later studies found that poor childhood environment did not necessarily result in psychological problems for children when they reached adulthood. In fact, what is surprising is that some children who grow up in highly dysfunctional families emerge quite well-adjusted as adults (Anthony & Cohler, 1987). These studies consistently indicate that some children thrive despite a variety of difficult backgrounds that include chronic poverty, parental neglect, parental psychopathology, abuse, and living in the midst of war. Such findings should not be accepted as evidence that early family environment is unimportant, rather, that some children learn how to adjust to difficult environments and are less negatively affected than others.

Garmezy and colleagues (1984) described one such child: an 11-year-old boy who came from a poor home with an alcoholic father, a troubled mother, two brothers involved in crime, and two disabled siblings. In this home, both parents were depressed and approached life with a sense of hopelessness and helplessness. Nevertheless, the school

principle described this boy as someone who got along well with others and was liked by everyone. He was a fine athlete who had won several trophies, was well-mannered, bright, and "a good kid." Similarly, Anthony (1987) followed 300 children of schizophrenic parents for 12 years and found that about 10% of the children were very well-adjusted despite some very bizarre family environments.

Emily Werner (1989, 1995) followed the progress of children in Hawaii for over 30 years and also found exceptional children who emerged from difficult childhoods. Approximately one-third of the children from difficult backgrounds emerged as competent and caring adults. Werner (1995) described a core group of characteristics she believed are typical of resilient children across various studies. First, they are able to find a nurturing surrogate parent. It appears that an ability to emotionally detach from a disturbed parent is only a first step. Besides distancing themselves from unhealthy relationships, resilient children must be able to find someone else who can fill the role of caring and supportive parent. Also, such children often manage to form a close relationship with at least one teacher who serves as a role model. In contrast to classic attachment theory, these children thrive because they can detach themselves emotionally from their disturbed parents. Second, such children have good social and communication skills and at least one close friend. They also seem to have a desire to help others, provide some nurturance to other people, and have a capacity for empathy and altruism. Third, resilient children have creative outlets, activities, or hobbies they can focus on when life becomes even more difficult than normal. Competence with this activity also gives them a sense of pride and mastery. Fourth, these children are fairly optimistic, seem to have an internal locus of control, and have a positive self-concept. Resilient children also develop a style of coping that combines autonomy with an ability to ask for help when necessary. Last, families that hold religious beliefs providing meaning in difficult times are also common for resilient children.

Werner (1995) suggested that family factors that promote resiliency appear to be different for boys and girls. For resilient boys, important factors are a household with good structure and rules, a male role model, and encouragement of emotional expressiveness. Resilient girls seem to need homes that emphasize risk-taking and independence as well as provide reliable support from an older female. Werner found that a particularly positive influence on girls is a mother who is steadily employed. She also noted that these "protective buffers" can be found in resilient children regardless of differences in ethnicity, social class, and geographic location.

Among the more intriguing conclusions of these studies is that resilient children are actively involved in creating or finding environments and people who are supportive and reinforce their competencies. That is, when their own families fail to provide these qualities, resilient children do not react passively to the loss and neglect; they are not pawns of their environments. Rather, they seek what they need and avoid unhealthy relationships as much as possible.

New Perspectives on Resilient Children Early research on resilience tended to focus on the personality traits of highly resilient children. More recent studies affirm the obvious fact that the personalities of young children change and develop rapidly as they mature (Luthar, 2006). In addition, family and school environments of children can have an extraordinary impact on how well they adjust to difficulties, stress, and trauma. Indeed, researchers today view family factors, such as having a good relationship with at least one parent or supportive relationships with competent siblings, as the most important influence on children's adjustment.

Besides family factors, the role of supportive communities may be next in importance for children. Community factors that help foster adjustment include positive relationships with peers, friends, or a trusted teacher; participation in positive social or religious organizations; and a sense of social cohesion or community involvement in the child's neighborhood. In a somewhat intriguing reversal of earlier conclusions, the personality of children now takes a secondary role to family and community factors; nevertheless, it is still an important aspects of how well a child copes. In addition to the personality factors listed earlier, research has suggested the following as also important: an ability to inhibit unwanted behavior and regulate emotions, high emotional intelligence, high self-efficacy and persistence, as well as insight into the complexities of situations and behavior. Table 8.2 presents an overview of some protective factors.

T A B L E 8.2   Protective Factors for Resilience in Children and Youth

In the Family and Close Relationships:

Positive attachment relationships

Authoritative parenting

Organized home environment

Positive family climate with low discord between parents

Connections to pro-social and rule-abiding peers

Socioeconomic advantage

In the Community:

Effective schools

Ties to pro-social organizations

Neighborhoods with high "collective efficacy"

High levels of public safety

Good public health

In the Child:

Good problem solving skills

Self-regulation skills for self-control of attention, arousal, and impulses

Positive self-perceptions or self-efficacy

Positive outlook on life

Faith and a sense of meaning in life

Easy temperament as child; adaptable personality when older

SOURCE: Adapted from Masten, A., Cutuli, J., Herbers, J., & Reed, M-G. (2009). Resilience in development. In C. Snyder, & S. Lopez (Eds.). *Oxford handbook of positive psychology* (2nd edition). Oxford: Oxford University Press, p. 126.

Another intriguing line of research relevant to resilience comes from Carol Dweck's studies on motivation in children (Dweck & Master, 2008, 2009). In essence, she found a somewhat paradoxical relationship between giving children praise for their work and their ability to adjust to difficult challenges. Unexpectedly, she found that when children were praised for their intelligence (for example, "That's great. You are so smart!"), then it was more difficult for children to adapt to later difficulties. Why would this be? Dweck assumed that praise for a child's "intelligence" is praise for a skill or ability that is fixed and might be lost at some point in the future. That is, the child becomes afraid that if she or he gives a wrong answer later on, then the "intelligence" is gone and the praise will go away with it. For Dweck, this worry creates a **fixed mindset** in children and makes it more difficult for them to handle challenges in the future.

An alternative is to praise children *for their efforts* and *for being engaged in* the process of learning and discovery. Effort and engagement can't be taken away and are always resources for a child. Therefore, parents should teach their children to love both effort and challenge and to welcome difficult tasks. This process helps children believe that their talents and abilities can be developed through dedication, persistence, and passionate commitment. This attitude toward learning and challenge Dweck has called a **growth mindset** (Dweck, 2006). Research by Dweck and her colleagues has found that children with growth mindsets are more likely to persist in difficult tasks and to overcome challenges. She also found that children can be taught to use a growth mindset by recognizing and valuing the process of transformation that occurs when such an attitude is operating.

Finally, Dweck and her colleagues found that the concepts of fixed and growth mindsets applies equally well to adults. In one study, they measured participants' brainwaves while they were solving difficult problems (Dweck, 2006). Those with a fixed mindset lost interest in the problems after they were told their answers were incorrect. However, those with a growth mindset stayed involved by seeking out the correct answers; they also scored better when tested again at a later date. Creating such an attitude

improved performance; sparked a zest for learning; increased receptivity to feedback; and built an ability to confront and surmount obstacles. Practical application has included teaching a growth mindset to business managers, teachers, and university students. Such workshops teach that effort put into learning helps create new brain connections (see the discussion of neuroplasticity in chapter 2), encouraging individuals to notice how such effort improves their lives and those of others.

Resilience in Adulthood

The concept of resilience has recently been applied across the lifespan. Indeed, compelling arguments have been made for the necessity of challenge in life. Theorists have recently suggested that lifespan development is, in fact, *guided by* how we deal with a series of crises or challenges in life—in other words, some difficulty and challenge in life are necessary for healthy development. In this light, a recent study found some support for Nietzsche's adage, "Whatever does not kill us makes us stronger." The researchers found higher levels of resilience only among those with a history of handling moderate adversity (Seery, Holman, & Silver, 2010). In contrast, lower levels of resilience were found for people who either had no history of major adversity or who had experienced major traumas and losses.

Cultivating Resilience in Adults Review of research on resilience in adulthood has found similar results to those found with children (Greve & Staudinger, 2006)—that is, a greater emphasis on family and community factors and a somewhat lesser one on individual personality factors. Community and family factors tend to emphasize strong social supports both on the instrumental or practical level and on the emotional level. Important factors in how adults deal successfully with difficulties are the supportiveness of one's social network of family and friends, having a sense of community involvement, and social participation in religious activities. These indicate that positive social relationships and a sense of meaning in life can do much to buffer the impact of stress and unwelcome life events.

One factor quite relevant to positive psychology that can increase resilience is positive emotionality. Several studies have found that feeling positive emotions daily helps moderate reactions to stress (Ong, Bergman, Bisconti, & Wallace, 2006; Tugade, & Fredrickson, 2007). An ability to represent positive emotions with precision and specificity, as with higher emotional intelligence, is even more helpful (Tugade, Fredrickson, & Barrett, 2005). Other factors that enhance resilience include task- or problem-focused coping (Campbell-Sills, Choan, & Stein, 2006), commitment to goals, humor, patience, optimism, faith, altruism (Connor & Zhang, 2006), and the use of mature defense mechanisms (Simeon, Yehuda, Cunill, Knutelska, Putman et al., 2007; Vaillant, 1977).

However, it may be that trying too hard to regulate emotion is less likely to facilitate resilience (Kashdan, Breen, & Julian, 2010). Resilience requires finding that delicate balance between too much and too little emotional control. Although lists of individual resilience factors are quite extensive and vary from study to study, they often also include high self-complexity along with self-integration, both emotional and practical intelligence, capacity for empathy, and greater openness to experience. Resilience is also understood by looking at how we create narratives or stories that help us understand what has happened to us and what we can learn from it (Hildon, Smith, Netuveli, & Blane, 2008). Indeed, the studies discussed earlier on life narratives are relevant to resilience. The American Psychological Association cautions that resilience is not a trait (see "On the Web" below). Rather, it is a way of dealing with adversity that can be developed, and each person goes about this process in her or his unique way. The APA suggests the following factors are generally important for the cultivation of resilience:

1. Make connections with family, friends, or community.
2. Avoid seeing crises as insurmountable problems.
3. Accept that change is part of living.
4. Move toward your goals.
5. Take decisive action, use problem- and task-focused coping.
6. Look for opportunities for self-discovery.
7. Nurture a positive view of yourself.
8. Keep events in perspective.
9. Maintain a hopeful outlook.
10. Take care of yourself; attend to your needs and feelings.

Posttraumatic Growth Occasionally, a traumatic event is such that it requires both assimilation and accommodation. The end result is an adaptation that enhances flourishing and moves a person to a higher level of psychosocial functioning and well-being. These types of changes are termed *posttraumatic growth*. Ronnie Janoff-Bulman (2004) suggested that posttraumatic growth involves changes in self-understanding and in one's worldview, or meaning-making. Some attempts to accomplish these changes, however, require less intense processing than others. Davis and Nolen-Hoeksema (2009) contended that benefit finding and self-protective functions such as adoption of positive illusions provide emotional relief but may not produce robust and lasting accommodation to trauma. In fact, benefit finding has not been consistently related to increased psychological well-being (Helgeson, Reynolds, & Tomich, 2006). Such protective processes may produce "pseudo growth" that, ironically, makes a person more vulnerable to future crises. The possibility that a self-reported increase in resilience might instead indicate pseudo growth is a challenge researchers face in attempting to unravel complexities in this domain (Lechner, Tennen & Affleck, 2009). As Davis and Nolen-Hoeksema commented, posttraumatic growth requires "more than revisionist autobiography."

Authentic posttraumatic growth can be seen when a person renegotiates personal goals and life priorities in important ways (Davis, & Nolen-Hoeksema, 2009). This renegotiation requires significant disengagement from old activities, strivings, and core projects. The next step is to create new goals and priorities that are intrinsically motivating and personally meaningful. Posttraumatic growth comes through actions and activities that move a person toward important new goals that provide a renewed sense of meaning and purpose. Central to this understanding of posttraumatic growth is the notion that cognitive reappraisal, by itself, is insufficient to indicate authentic posttraumatic growth. It may help in re-evaluating a situation, but true personal growth comes only from taking action in the world—an effort that moves a person's life in a significantly different direction.

Sense of Coherence   We saw in chapter 6 that Suzanne Kobasa's theory of *hardiness* is a way to incorporate the major psychological factors that improve health status. Similarly, there are perspectives on resilience and posttraumatic growth that try to capture the major personality factors that foster personal growth after crisis or trauma. Indeed, hardiness is often mentioned in the resilience literature as an important resource for positive adaptation to difficulty. However, the theory advanced by Israeli psychologist Aaron Antonovsky (1979, 1987) seems to capture the complexities of posttraumatic growth more decisively. Partially, this is due to his choice of research participants in developing his theory.

Antonovsky explored people's ability to cope well with trauma and stress. Most researchers assume that homeostasis, or a state of balanced equilibrium, is the desired or baseline state of the human organism. In such a view, stressors are then abnormal pathogens that disturb equilibrium. In contrast, Antonovsky assumes that humans are inherently active; curious; exploratory, and variety-seeking. If this is true, then people don't really want equilibrium but rather seek active growth, development, and positive change. Therefore, researchers interested in resilience and stress should adopt a **salutogenic orientation** that examines how to enhance an active, exploratory, and variety-seeking perspective on life. This approach, you will recall, is similar to that taken by positive psychology.

Taking this perspective as his starting point, Antonovsky developed a **sense of coherence** model, which he saw as a unique set of personality traits that creates an orientation to life allowing people to interpret life stressors in a positive and adaptive way—that is, as coherent and understandable despite adversity. He began his empirical research by examining the lives of people who met two criteria. First, they had undergone a severe trauma that bore inescapable consequences for their lives: namely, the death of a loved one, a severe personal disability, or economic deprivation. For Antonovsky, this requirement entailed an investigation of one of the most horrific experiences a person can endure: He interviewed people who had lived through Nazi concentration camp internment. The second requirement was that such a person must function remarkably well in her or his current life. In other words, Antonovsky's subjects showed evidence of highly adaptive coping skills and competence in spite of experiencing severe stress and trauma in their past.

Here is an excerpt from one interview with a 90-year-old concentration camp survivor with a strong sense of coherence:

> How we overcame all difficulties in our lives? You need patience. You have to believe in the Promise, a word I learned in Bulgaria.... It doesn't have to be God. It can be another force, but you have to have faith. Otherwise you can't suffer so much and go on" (Antonovsky, 1987, p. 68).

Contrast that interview with the following excerpt from a 50-year-old woman with a weak sense of coherence:

> "I'm a sick woman, I always suffered from something, and even before the tragedy three years ago when my husband died.... I believe in fate. True, I don't know who runs it, because I don't believe in God anymore.... My life has been full of losses even from before.... Things are rough, I don't have any faith left in anyone.... All of life is full of problems, only in dying there are no problems.... I don't even think of going out with a man or of getting married again" (1987, p. 72).

The difference is quite obvious between the hope and determination of the first interviewee and the despair and hopelessness of the second.

For Antonovsky, a sense of coherence comprises three major factors:

1. The first, and most important, factor he calls Meaningfulness, which he defines as the extent to which life makes sense on an emotional level. Meaning gives a person a willingness to take up the challenges of life. It gives a person a sense that he or she is "a participant in the process shaping one's destiny as well as one's daily experience" and "that at least some of the problems and demands posed by living are worth investing energy in, are worthy of commitment and engagement" (Antonovsky, 1979, p. 128). Notably, this factor doesn't imply that when life makes sense, then we are always happy. Instead, a life that is meaningful allows a person to accept the disappointment and suffering that are inevitable in life.

2. The second most important factor in sense of coherence is COMPREHENSIBILITY. This is the extent to which life events appear ordered, consistent, structured and clear; life does not appear to be chaotic and random. Someone who scores high on comprehensibility "expects that the stimuli he or she will encounter in the future will be predictable or, at the very least, when they do come as surprises, that they will be ordered and explainable" (1987, p. 17). Again, this factor does not imply that life events are always desirable.

3. The third factor is MANAGEABILITY. This is the belief that our personal resources and coping skills are adequate to meet the demands of the tasks that confront us. It is "the extent to which one perceives that resources are at one's disposal which are adequate to meet the demands posed by the stimuli that bombard one" (1987, p. 17). In essence, this factor means a sense of control derived from confidence in one's coping skills.

Research studies have shown that a higher sense of coherence is often associated with higher psychological well-being (Frenz, Carey, Jorgensen, 1993; Feldt, Metsäpelto, Kinnunen, & Pulkkinen, 2007; Jeges & Varga, 2006; Togari, Yamazaki, Takayama, Sasaki et al., 2008). Studies have also found that a high sense of coherence is related to other variables associated with well-being, such as job satisfaction (Strümpfer & Mlonzi, 2001), social support (Bíró, Balajti, Ádány, & Kósa, 2010), and better health status (Jeges & Varga, 2006; Julkunen & Ahlström, 2006). One study found that sense of coherence and neurosis were almost perfect opposites of each other (that is, having a correlation of −.85), suggesting a strong link between sense of coherence and mental health (Feldt, Metsäpelto, Kinnunen, & Pulkkinen, 2007). Finally, a high sense of coherence has been found to be a quite stable trait over the middle years of adulthood (Hakanen, Feldt & Leskinen, 2007).

Master Resilience Training   The Master Resilience Training program is the largest attempt to teach resilience that has ever been undertaken. At the moment, thousands of soldiers in the United States Army have been given the training. If evaluation of the training continues to be positive, then when fully implemented it should provide training to the entire United States Army and their families (Seligman, 2011). The aim of the program is to teach skills that inoculate against posttraumatic stress disorder (PTSD) and set the seeds for future posttraumatic growth. The program teaches resilience skills through three modules: building mental toughness, building character strengths, and building strong relationships.

Mental toughness skills are taught by using techniques from learned optimism training as well as rational emotive and cognitive therapies. These focus primarily on changing pessimistic and catastrophic thoughts into more rational and adaptable ones. Keeping a "gratitude journal" is also part of this module. Character strengths are taught by using the VIA Survey of Character to pinpoint individual signature strengths, especially those that help overcome challenges (see chapter 2). The strong relationships module teaches Carol Dweck's ideas on growth mindset (see above),

Shelly Gable's research on active constructive communication (see chapter 5), and assertiveness training to enhance both professional and personal relationships.

In summary, studies on resilience have found that people can be remarkably adaptable to a variety of difficulties in life. Tragically, sometimes adaptability is only a partial achievement and chronic difficulties remain long after an unwelcome event (Seery, Holman, & Silver, 2010). However, many people find creative, and sometimes heroic, ways to grow from setbacks, disappointments, and tragedies in life. Be aware: It is helpful to know that unexpected difficulties are an expected part of a full life. At times, life really isn't fair, so it's best to just accept a challenge and get on with life.

Healthy and Adaptive Defense Mechanisms

Although Sigmund Freud's personality theory has generated considerable controversy, almost all perspectives that followed his have agreed with one of Freud's points: People can sometimes hide their true feelings or true motives from conscious awareness (Bargh & Chartrand, 1999). It is now accepted in psychology that at times people can keep unpleasant emotions or thoughts out of awareness (Cramer, 2000). That is, under certain circumstances, people use what are called *defense mechanisms*. George Vaillant has focused on how the use of various defense mechanisms can help or hinder our progress toward positive mental health. Defense mechanisms describe one way we choose to we deal with stress, which has consequences for well-being.

The story of Vaillant's research study began in 1937 when philanthropist William T. Grant and Dr. Arlie V. Bock decided to begin a systematic inquiry into the kinds of people who are healthy and function well (Vaillant, 2000). They believed that too much medical research was weighted toward the disease end of the spectrum and studies of healthy functioning were needed. The Grant study began by selecting a group of 268 Harvard sophomore men who were chosen because they appeared to be healthier than their peers—they were the "best and

the brightest." The study followed those men through their lives for the next 40 years and beyond. George Vaillant joined the staff of the Grant Study in 1967 and began to summarize the research on what differentiated people who continued to adapt well throughout life from those whose earlier promise was not sustained as they aged. Later, he also examined data gathered from two other longitudinal studies: a study begun in the late 1950s that examined adolescent boys from disadvantaged neighborhoods in Boston; and another that examined women who were part of the Terman study of gifted women initiated at Stanford University in 1920 (see Vaillant, 2000, for more details).

Vaillant (1977) began by recognizing that an adequate definition of mental health or adaptation is a very slippery concept. He felt that mental health could *not* be defined by an average or by reference to what was "normal" behavior. He felt that such a criterion represented only the "average amount of disease and incapacity present in the population" (1977, p. 5). Vaillant also rejected a criterion of absence of psychological conflict because all the men in the Grant Study had at times been despondent, anxious, overly temperamental, or reacted childishly to stressors. He followed the advice of Frank Barron (1963) and assumed that good mental health was "a way of reacting to problems and not an absence of them" (p. 64). In addition, he decided to define positive adaptation in terms of a person's actual behavior and the number of areas in life in which people functioned well, rather than use definitions based on emotional state.

Mature Defense Mechanisms   Vaillant found that what differentiated healthy adaptation from unhealthy is the type of defense mechanisms used when people face conflicts and difficulties. Surprisingly, he found that the type of defense mechanisms used by a young person could predict well-being over 20 years later (Vaillant, 2000). He classified defense mechanisms on a continuum from extreme to mild, based on the degree of unconsciousness and involuntariness involved: *psychotic, immature, neurotic,* and *mature* or *adaptive* styles. The psychotic defense mechanisms were clearly unhealthy, involving severe distortions of reality in an attempt to avoid anxiety (for example, delusional projection; psychotic denial). Immature defense mechanisms are often used by adolescents and persons with severe depression (for example, projection; hypochondriasis; passive-aggressive behavior; and acting out).

By contrast, Vaillant saw neurotic defense mechanisms as average or "normal" styles that most people use to cope with anxiety, threat, and conflict (for example, repression; intellectualization; reaction formation; displacement/conversion; and neurotic denial/dissociation). Finally, the **mature** or **adaptive defense mechanisms** that Vaillant identified are: sublimation, altruism, suppression, anticipation, and humor. These defense mechanisms deal with anxiety by attempting to maximize gratification but at the same time allow awareness of underlying feelings, impulses, ideas, and consequences of behavior. The mature defenses "synthesize and attenuate rather than deny and distort conflicting sources of human behavior" (Vaillant, 2000, p. 97).

Vaillant found that in the Harvard and Boston samples those men who used more mature defenses more often, as well as the other defenses less often, had higher incomes, better psychosocial adjustment, more social supports, more joy in living, better marital satisfaction, and higher self-rated health (but not actual health status). He also found they had jobs that fit their ambitions, were more active in public service, had rich friendship patterns, happier marriages, and still engaged in competitive sports in midlife. In the Boston sample from the disadvantaged neighborhood, those who used mature defenses were more likely as adults to have escaped poverty.

Interestingly, Vaillant also found that self-perception of happiness was not always associated with better adjustment. In fact, those in the *mature* category did not always score higher than others on self-reported measures of happiness. Specifically, only 68% of the men in the mature category were in the top third of self-reported happiness, while 16% of the men in the immature category rated themselves in the top third of happiness. Vaillant's results would suggest that if self-assessments are based on immature defenses, then the resulting happiness may be fragile and transitory.

SUMMARY

This chapter has covered a variety of topics related to positive lifespan development and successful aging. Studies have found that well-being can be experienced differently across the lifespan due to changing life circumstances. For instance, recent evidence suggests a midlife drop in subjective well-being. The higher well-being frequently found in older persons compared with those younger may be due to recognizable ways in which happiness and satisfaction are calculated as we age. Recent studies of resiliency in childhood have shown that despite difficult early environments, some children grow into healthy adults and may even thrive. Similarly, studies have found that many adults adapt with remarkable ingenuity to changes as they age.

LEARNING TOOLS

Key Terms and Ideas

generativity	socioemotional selectivity	growth mindset	salutogenic orientation
selective optimization with compensation	resilience	posttraumatic growth	mature defense mechanisms

References

Bornstein, M., Davidson, L., Keyes, C., & Moore, K. (Eds.). (2003). *Well-Being: Positive development across the life course. Crosscurrents in Contemporary Psychology Series*: Psychology Press. (*professional*, but the interested student will find it helpful)

Strauch, B. (2010). *The secret life of the grown-up brain: The surprising talents of the middle-aged mind.* NY: Viking.

Vaillant, G. (2003). *Aging well: Surprising guideposts to a happier life from the landmark Harvard study of adult development.* NY: Little, Brown & Co.

On the Web

http://www.taosinstitute.net/positive-aging-newsletter *The Positive Aging Newsletter.* Gergen, K., & Gergen, M. (Eds.).

http://adultdevelopment.org Society for Research on Adult Development.

http://www.soc.duke.edu/~cwi *The child and youth well-being index.*

http://www.apa.org/helpcenter/road-resilience.aspx *The road to resilience.* The American Psychological Association.

Personal Explorations: Flourishing through the Lifespan

A. Erikson's theory of human development encompasses eight stages. Each stage presents a particular task whose mastery builds personality strength and resilience. When a stage isn't well-mastered, we're likely to struggle with its issues throughout our life. Though we can't undo the past, awareness and insight can help us complete what remains unfinished in our personality growth. Here are some guiding questions to answer:

1. *Basic trust vs. mistrust.* Is it relatively easy for you to trust others—or difficult? When treated with unexpected kindness, are you generally accepting or suspicious? Are you usually idealistic or cynical about people's motives?

2. *Autonomy vs. shame and doubt.* Do you like your body? Do you enjoy using it to the best of your ability? Or do you typically envy how others look and neglect your body as a source of self-esteem and pleasure?

3. *Initiative vs. guilt.* Do you take an active approach to life, or do you tend to be passive and cautious? Do you initiate new relationships and activities with ease—or do you prefer familiar situations as much as possible?

4. *Industry vs. inferiority.* How conscientious and persevering are you? When working on something, are you energetic—or more of a slacker? Do you typically stick to projects until they're successfully done or give up along the way?

B. Some theories of well-being say that our perspective on life changes as we age. For this exercise, interview someone who is at least 25 years older than you and ask what they believe is important for a fulfilling and happy life. (If you are past middle age, then interview someone 25 years older or 25 years younger.) How do their answers differ from yours?

Chapter 9

Optimal Well-Being

> If you deliberately plan on being less than you are capable of being, then I warn
> you that you'll be unhappy for the rest of your life.
> ABRAHAM MASLOW

A core assumption of positive psychology is that human beings have the potential to conduct themselves with extraordinary competence, compassion, and dignity. Positive psychology research has focused on how people are able to achieve these admirable behaviors despite the numerous temptations that entice them toward selfishness, indulgence, or greed. Throughout history many cultures have generated ideas on what human beings are like when they operate at their best. Today, various researchers working from a positive psychology perspective have investigated topics such as how to nurture "your best self" (Sheldon, & Lyubomirsky, 2006) and how to foster your "true self" (Schlegel et al., 2009). This chapter seeks to identify what people are like when operating at the higher levels of their potential, or at optimal levels of personality development.

It might be asked, however: Hasn't this topic already been addressed? Isn't it the basic concept of flourishing? Indeed, the theories in this chapter might well be considered more focused perspectives on high-level flourishing; they provide greater detail about how flourishing could be defined and recognized. For example, all perspectives on flourishing indicate that positive relationships, romantic love and friendship are central to any list of necessary criteria. But which is more vital for flourishing— close interpersonal relationships or relationships based on community engagement and a deep commitment to world betterment? How wide should one's zone of concern extend? Are only close family members included or should a person be concerned with humanity's general welfare? Further, how should people create positive relationships? What if one's close friendships are driven by deep, unacknowledged fears of isolation and loneliness? Do such relationships still qualify as examples of flourishing? Most importantly, how does one make choices among the myriad ways that personal relationships can be created and maintained?

The theories in this chapter flesh out the details of how flourishing can be understood, and what choices we should make in order to actualize specific types of flourishing. As the previous paragraph suggests, not all of these theories agree on precisely how optimal flourishing should be defined; however, they concur that if we wish to establish goals for well-being in terms of developing our highest potential, then we must make specific choices. These theories provide guidelines on the choices available and how we might decide among various options.

Attempts to describe optimal psychological well-being date back to the earliest days of psychology. William James was strongly interested in mental health issues, especially in exceptional states of well-being (see Rathunde, 2001). For example, in his nearly final book *Energies of Men* (1907), James declared:

> We ought somehow to get a topographic
> survey made by the limits of human power
> in every conceivable direction, something
> like an ophthalmologist's chart of the limits
> of human field of vision; and we ought
> then to construct a methodical inventory
> of the paths of access, or keys, differing
> with the diverse types of individual, to the
> different kinds of power (p. 145).

James (1902/1958) asserted that the psychologically healthy personality was "harmonious and well balanced." He also felt that fulfillment of one's creative and aesthetic potentials were the hallmarks of mental health. In this regard, he considered a career as a painter before deciding upon an academic career. Soon other psychologists would create their own ideas on the optimal personality. However, we begin with one of the oldest perspectives on well-being.

WHAT WISDOM DID KING SOLOMON HAVE?

Wisdom has been one of the most frequent terms used to describe optimal maturity throughout Western history (Robinson, 1990). The Bible tells us that King Solomon was "wise," and the Greek philosophers speculated for centuries about wisdom and how it should be the *ultimate* goal of life. In the Jewish tradition, wisdom is a venerated quality

associated with leading a righteous—that is, highly ethical—life. The ancient Judaic text *Pirkey Avoth (Ethics of the Fathers)* taught that wisdom involves sacred study derived from the Bible and a life that contributes to the well-being of others. In the past, research psychologists have tended to avoid the topic of wisdom due to its seemingly abstract nature. Nevertheless, several investigators have attempted to describe what people mean by the term *wisdom* (for example, Sternberg, 1990).

Preliminary Wisdom About Wisdom

In general, wisdom is a unique, positive result of long developmental processes, not merely an accumulation of information or opinions. Also, wisdom implies knowledge that is social, interpersonal, and psychological—and that may be difficult for the average person to grasp. Hence, the wise person is the one to approach when you're wrestling with life's most perplexing questions. You don't seek out the counsel of the wise to learn where is the best place in town to buy pizza. Kramer (2000) stated that wisdom entails "exceptional breadth and depth of knowledge about the conditions of life and human affairs" (p. 85). According to Clayton (1982), "Wisdom is ... the ability that enables the individual to grasp human nature, which operates on the principles of contradiction, paradox, and change. Human nature is being used here to refer to understanding of self and understanding of others" (p. 316).

Labouvie-Vief (1990) proposed that wisdom involves a dialectical integration of two forms of knowledge: *logos* and *mythos*. Logos is knowledge gained through the use of analytical, propositional, and other formal structures of logic. Mythos is knowledge gained through speech, narrative, plot, and dialogue. It is exemplified in oral traditions, social relationships, and many forms of art. It is knowledge that is embedded in the context of social relationships and social experiences, and includes intuition and openness to unconscious processes.

Pascual-Leone (1990) sounded similar themes in his perspective on wisdom. What he added is a theoretical statement on what he calls the "ultra-self" or "transcendent self" as a hallmark of wisdom. This ultraself operates as a higher, more encompassing center of information processing able to integrate cognitive and emotional elements, particularly love and care. Deirdre Kramer (2000) referred to this ability as a form of self-transcendence that consists of a "detached, but encompassing, concern with life itself" (p. 86).

Kramer (2000) also reviewed much of the existing research on wisdom. In her view, the two major elements of wisdom are greater openness to experience and a "capacity to reflect on and grapple with difficult existential life issues" (p. 99). Among the other qualities is an ability of wise people to find meaning in both positive and negative life experiences. She noted that persons who are wise seem able to transform negative experiences into life-affirming ones; through this process, they may even possess a sense of serenity that others lack. This outlook can be manifested in a self-effacing sense of humor that recognizes life ironies (Webster, 2003). Kramer also regarded individual wisdom as a potential resource for communities; that is, she urged communities to recognize that wise people do exist and that they could be utilized more fully than at present.

A study by Wink and Helson (1997) suggested that two forms of wisdom exist. The first is *practical wisdom*, encompassing good interpersonal skills; clarity of thinking; greater tolerance; and generativity. The second is *transcendental wisdom,* which deals with the limits of knowledge, the rich complexity of the human experience, and a sense of transcending the personal and individual aspects of human experience.

Despite their difficulties with a precise definition, psychologists are fairly sure about what wisdom is *not*. The first point made by most researchers is that wisdom is not an inevitable outcome of advanced age (Clayton, 1982). Having made that comment, however, it is also true that profound wisdom is seen more often—though not exclusively—in persons who are at least middle-aged. Baltes & Staudinger (2000) suggested that the optimal age to attain wisdom may be about 60 years old. The second point upon which most psychologists agree is that wisdom is not merely intelligence as measured by IQ tests. In this regard,

Clayton (1982) observed that IQ tests measure domains of knowledge that are essentially nonsocial and impersonal (for example, facts, vocabulary, and the ability to manipulate objects in space). Most psychologists assume that wisdom cannot be totally understood by examining only these nonsocial domains of intelligence.

Wisdom and Well-Being

Although the attainment of wisdom seems a universal goal across cultures, is there any evidence that it enhances personal well-being? The answer appears to be *yes*. A study by Ardelt (1997) revealed that wisdom was significantly correlated with life satisfaction for both men and women. She found that wisdom was a better predictor of life satisfaction than objective circumstances such as physical health. Wisdom also is related to well-being through association with increased striving for the good life and greater preferences for personal growth and self-actualization (Scheibe, Kunzmann, & Baltes, 2009). Studies have also found that wise people show emotional and motivational preferences that impact well-being. They report fewer self-centered pleasant feelings but more process-oriented and environment-centered emotions, such as interest and inspiration (Kunzmann, 2004). Wise people also prefer values focused on personal growth; insight; social engagement; and the well-being of friends, as opposed to values focused mainly on pleasure and a comfortable life (Scheibe, Kunzmann, & Baltes, 2009). Finally, wise persons prefer cooperative conflict-management styles that reflect a joint concern for both their own and other persons' interests; that is, they reject approaches to conflict management in which one person wins at the expense of another (Kunzmann, 2004).

Wisdom as a Stage of Life

The most familiar perspective on wisdom in general psychology was advanced by Erik Erikson (1950). He regarded wisdom as the virtue that results from a successful resolution of the last psychosocial stage of development: integrity versus despair (see Table 8.1). This last life-stage challenge involves the necessity to review one's life and see what has been accomplished. Some people do so with regret or bitterness, while others reflect and find some value and meaning in what they have done in life. For Erikson, wisdom involves both an acceptance of life as it has been lived and the reality of approaching death. He also viewed wisdom as "involved disinvolvement," or a commitment to the processes of life with a calm detachment from any insistence that life turn out a specific way. For Erikson, those who can approach their death without fear have found wisdom. From this view, wisdom is a personal experience involving acceptance and a sense of spiritual meaning that resolves the last existential crisis anyone on earth will ever face.

Wisdom as Post-Formal Cognitive Development

A second perspective describes wisdom in terms of post-formal cognitive thought and dialectical modes of thinking. The last stage in Piaget's theory of cognitive development, is formal–operational thinking, involves the ability to use abstract concepts in solving problems, and most people begin utilizing it during adolescence. Some theories view wisdom as a stage of cognitive thought that goes beyond formal-operational thinking—that is, as a highly complex style of problem solving. Indeed, most contemporary theories of wisdom encompass some of this perspective. Many researchers describe wisdom by referencing qualities such as a greater capability to handle paradox, to grapple with difficult issues, to transcend self-oriented concerns, and to adopt a larger perspective.

For example, though both Pascual-Leone (1990) and Labouvie-Vief (1990) posited the ability to deal with contradiction and paradox as central to any definition of wisdom, others view post-formal development in terms of maturity and ego development (see Cook-Greuter, 2000). The theory of *emergent wisdom* proposes that wisdom involves a unique kind of thinking that moves from simple to complex considerations, from valuation of independence and individualism to interdependence, and from self-focus to a concern for the common

good (Basset, 2006). In this theory, wisdom involves four major components: (1) *discerning,* or a deep understanding of fundamental patterns and relationships; (2) *respecting,* or considerate and thoughtful dealing with others; (3) *engaging,* or acting in ethical ways for the common good; and (4) *transforming,* or looking inward and tolerating paradox, ambiguity, and uncertainty (www.wisdo minst.org).

Wisdom as a Form of Excellence

A third psychological approach regards wisdom as a specific type of excellence (see chapter 7). In this instance, wisdom is defined as excellence in the performance of one's life. In their research studies on wisdom, Baltes and Staudinger (2000) found it useful to conceptualize wisdom as a multifaceted phenomenon that can be understood only by examining many different predictors. This orientation seems similar to the confluence approach utilized in the study of creativity. In addition, they contended that any search for the causes of wisdom must acknowledge that many paths can lead to it. In another interesting parallel with creativity, Baltes and Staudinger (2000) argued that wisdom is a joint product between the individual and his or her environment. Wisdom is therefore partially carried in the knowledge and expertise of a culture at a specific historical point; that is, what many wise people do is recognize and utilize the knowledge that exists in their surrounding culture.

Baltes and Staudinger (2000) took their understanding of wisdom even further and implied a relationship with ethics. They stated that wisdom is "knowledge with extraordinary scope, depth, measure, and balance ... a synergy of mind and character; that is an orchestration of knowledge *and virtue*" (p. 123, italics added). Ute Kunzmann (2004) added that wisdom is an integration of knowledge and particular emotional experiences, such as a greater ability to regulate one's emotions and higher capacity for other-centered emotions. These researchers also regarded the concept of wisdom as complex, highly differentiated, and associated with diverse cultural meanings. They even suggested that the concept may be so complicated that it "may be beyond what psychological methods and concepts can achieve" (p. 123). In other words, the idea of wisdom may be too complex for the necessary restrictions of the scientific method. Nevertheless, as enterprising psychologists they have taken this particular bull by the horns and undertaken a series of empirical studies into the construct of wisdom.

The Predictors of Wisdom   The research studies of Baltes and Staudinger (2000) found that wisdom can be predicted by looking at four general factors: (1) intelligence; (2) personality dispositions; (3) cognitive styles; and (4) life experiences (see Figure 9.1). In terms of intelligence, they found that high scores on measures of fluid and crystallized intelligence were significant predictors of wisdom. However, these factors accounted for only about 2% of the variation in wisdom scores. Similarly, personality dispositions such as openness to experience and psychological mindedness were significant predictors but accounted for an equally small percentage. The type of life experiences people underwent did a somewhat better job of predicting wisdom, accounting for about 15% of wisdom. In this regard, the researchers examined the traits

of clinical psychologists as part of their study, assuming that those who work as psychotherapists and who deal with life's difficulties, complexities, and meanings have learned something about wisdom along the way.

The factor of cognitive styles also accounted for about 15% of wisdom. Among the better predictors were creativity and thinking styles termed *judicial* and *progressive,* which describe the ability to evaluate and compare issues as well as tolerate ambiguity. For Baltes and Staudinger, all of this evidence implied that wisdom is "meta-heuristic"—that is, it entails a highly organized strategy of searching relevant information from multiple sources and integrating it into solutions that optimize knowledge and virtue. Note that the reference to virtue implies an ethical component to wisdom.

A Balance Theory of Wisdom

Robert Sternberg has been a leading researcher of intelligence and wisdom for many years. His Balance Theory of Wisdom begins with the concept of *tacit knowledge,* or knowledge embedded in individual experience and acquired through personal experiences, insight, or absorption in activities.

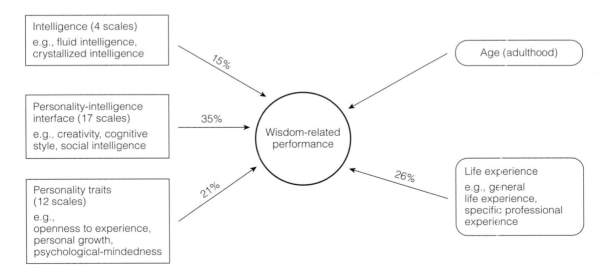

FIGURE 9.1 The Pattern of Predictive Correlates of Wisdom-Related Performance in Adults

SOURCE: From P. Baltes and U. Staudinger, "Wisdom: A metaheuristic ... excellence," *American Psychologist,* 55(1), Fig. 3, p. 130. Copyright © 2000 by the American Psychological Association. Reprinted with permission.

NOTE: Percentages indicate shared influence. Age is not significant.

Tacit knowledge is difficult to translate into words and hard to teach to others but can be extraordinarily useful in various situations. A woman who is an excellent psychotherapist, for instance, has a storehouse of tacit knowledge about people, relationships, and growth that may be difficult to articulate but nevertheless contributes to the expertise, she uses everyday with every patient in therapy. In this light, Sternberg (1998) defined wisdom as the application of tacit knowledge and personal values "toward the goal of achieving a common good" (p. 353; see Figure 9.2). That is, wisdom is using tacit knowledge and personal values to contribute to the common good, "not just to one's own or someone else's self-interest" (p. 354). He further stated that the common good is achieved by balancing personal, interpersonal, and social interests and concerns in order to find solutions that are appropriate to a situation. Of course, Sternberg acknowledged that the "common good" may turn out to be better for some people than others. However, a wise person seeks solutions based on higher values that support broader humanitarian concerns.

By basing his theory on tacit knowledge, Sternberg affirmed that wisdom is specific to certain domains of experience. For example, the psychotherapist mentioned above may be wise about human relationships and love but naïve about economic matters and financial investments. Sternberg has strongly advocated that wisdom be taught in

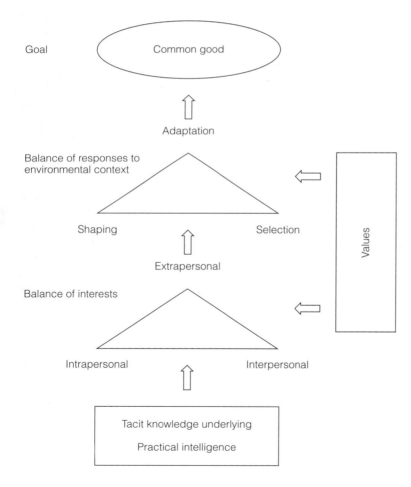

Goal

Common good

Adaptation

Balance of responses to environmental context

Shaping   Selection

Values

Extrapersonal

Balance of interests

Intrapersonal   Interpersonal

Tacit knowledge underlying

Practical intelligence

FIGURE 9.2 A Balance Theory of Wisdom

SOURCE: From Sternberg, R. J., "A balance theory of wisdom," *Review of General Psychology*, 2(4) pp. 347–365. Copyright © 1998 American Psychological Association. Reprinted with permission.

our public schools. In his view, intelligence, creativity, and wisdom are all necessary skills in today's world and should therefore be central to a standard curriculum (Sternberg, 1990, 1998).

Wisdom as the "Master" Virtue

The early Greek philosophers such as Socrates, Plato, and Aristotle considered their philosophies as pathways to wisdom. For them, optimal personality development meant the development of wisdom. In positive psychology, we have seen that Aristotle's virtue theory has been vital to the current notion of strengths and virtues (Seligman, 2002). For Aristotle, wisdom was the "master virtue" that allowed a person to discern which virtues were most important and how the various virtues should be balanced in life. The appropriate development of strengths in one's virtues allowed the cultivation of **practical wisdom** (Fowers, 2008; Schwartz & Sharpe, 2010), enabling a person to navigate inevitable conflicts and to translate character strengths and virtues into concrete action in real-life situations. For instance, when is honesty the best policy, and under which circumstances is it better to keep what you know to yourself? When is courage a virtue, and when is it simply being foolhardy? In a practical wisdom perspective, strengths and virtues should not be treated in isolation from each other. They must act in accord and also be balanced in the right proportions. Furthermore, the use of virtues must be sensitive to specific contexts; the timing of how they are used is important (Schwartz & Sharpe, 2010).

Blaine Fowers (2005) described five character types, each defined by how well the virtues are acknowledged and balanced. These move from those in which people ignore the basic human virtues (that is, the "beastly" and "vicious" types) to those in which people know what they should do but struggle to act in ways that are consistent with those values (that is, "incontinent" and "continent" types). The most mature character type is the *virtuous*. The *virtuous character* type is "able to act consistently in a way that is fitting, given the circumstances. Virtuous character is guided by a clear vision of what is good and admirable, and the individual acts consistently and gladly in the service of those goods" (Fowers, 2008, p. 645). In addition, the virtuous character is motivated by a love of what is good. There is no struggle to act well because one's desires are harmonious with the higher virtues.

How to Cultivate Wisdom

All theories of wisdom assert the difficulty of teaching people how to be wise. After all, tacit knowledge is built from personal experience, and wisdom takes time to develop—often until 50 or 60 years of age. Most theories, however, agree on a minimum set of parameters for wisdom. First, wisdom requires an ability to use post-formal thinking to work with contradictory, conflicting, or paradoxical ideas. Second, it requires openness to experience along with "the ability to transcend one's narrow perspective and self-interest" (Leary & Guadagno, 2011, p. 142). Third, truly wise people act according to high ethical standards and seek a common good.

How can one cultivate wisdom, given these criteria? Alina Reznitskaya and Robert Sternberg (2004) suggested that practicing dialectical and reflective thinking skills about difficult problems can promote wisdom. That is, one can practice thinking about all sides of issues and become more aware of how thinking is swayed by personal values, opinions, and assumptions. Note this process requires that people be challenged by problems and not retreat to facile solutions. People may also read the writings of important thinkers throughout history. Another recommendation is to acquire a greater understanding of human nature through the great works of literature and art that deal with the human situation. One can read books, watch plays, see movies, and listen to songs that convey the complexities of human life. Note that facile solutions, which are initially satisfying but ultimately simplistic, are not helpful for wisdom development. Finally, one can also read biographies of wise and admirable people to get a sense of how they thought about life.

Since wisdom is also associated with emotion, empathy and compassion seem necessary aspects of being wise. Therefore, it is important to strive to understand the complexities of human motivation and to recognize people's tendencies to make dumb mistakes. Greater emotional regulation also is required of those who are wise. All of the above are more likely to promote wisdom if one discusses these strategies and processes with other people. Why? Because, dialogue and interaction develop wisdom. Engaging in volunteer work and helping others in need can also help develop empathy. Lastly, one must want to develop wisdom; it must be a priority in one's life. Interestingly, some psychologists suggest that if people want to develop wisdom, they should find role models and mentors who are wise and then consciously emulate them (Scheibe, Kunzmann, & Baltes, 2009). Though wisdom is most easily recognized in older persons, it can be found at any point over the entirety of the lifespan (Ardelt, & Jacobs, 2009). The development, cultivation, and use of wisdom can begin at any time. With practice, we just get better at it.

EARLY PSYCHODYNAMIC IDEAS OF OPTIMAL PERSONALITY

For many people, modern ideas of mental health originated with Sigmund Freud, although his vision of humanity was somewhat pessimistic. Because he saw people as inevitably trapped in a conflict between the id's needs for aggression and sex versus the ego's concern with social adaptation, happiness and satisfaction were always compromises and therefore less-than-perfect solutions. Freud (1930) stated: "The goal toward which the pleasure principle impels us—of becoming happy—is not attainable; yet we may not, nay cannot, give up the effort to come nearer to realization of it by some means or other" (p. 39). When Freud was asked his definition of mental health, he replied "*lieben und arbiten*"— that is, when a person is able "to love and to work." Freud also suggested that maturity is marked by a humanitarian concern for other people and a desire

to do something good for society (Maddi, 1972). Although Freud's simple goals for humanity do require substantial effort, they do not speak eloquently for ultimate possibilities of psychological growth and optimal well-being. Many theorists who followed Freud created more optimistic models than did his psychology.

Alfred Adler

Alfred Adler (1870–1937) was an early colleague of Freud. In contrast to Freud, Adler declared that an innate striving for prosocial interaction and altruistic concern for others drives self-realization. The term most closely associated with Adler's theory of optimal mental health is *gemeinschaftsgefühl*, a German word created by Adler that has no exact equivalent in English. It was translated initially as *social sense* and then later as *social feeling* or **social interest** (Adler, 1938). It is a feeling of intimate relationship with humanity, empathy with the human condition, and a sense of altruism. Adler taught that social feeling could propel a person toward a type of self-realization that would inevitably include greater empathy and compassion for others.

For Adler, the concept of social feeling described an ideal or a goal that offered possibilities for behavior rather than a condition that could realistically be achieved. Adler stated, "We conceive the idea of social interest, social feeling, as the ultimate form of mankind.... It is a normative ideal, a direction-giving goal.... Everything we find valuable in life ... is forever a product of this social feeling" (in Ansbacher, 1992, p. 35). Adler insisted that people are inherently social beings who need satisfying social relations to develop their personalities most fully. Indeed, Adler taught that one could discern whether psychotherapy was effective or not by observing how much a client was motivated by social feeling: to the extent that it was present, the better therapy was working.

Carl G. Jung

Carl G. Jung (1875–1961) was also a member of the early inner circle of Freud. Jung, like Adler, taught that individuals possess an innate potential for

Copyright by The Erich Fromm Estate, c/o Rainer Funk

Erich Fromm and D. T. Suzuki

optimal mental health that needs to be actualized. In addition, for many decades, Jung's was the only major theory of personality that respected concepts of traditional Eastern psychology.

Jung's personality system continues to offer a unique perspective in Western psychology. Jung taught that there exists a *collective unconscious* deeper than the personal unconscious that Freud described, contending that it contains tendencies toward emotional responses shared by everyone across cultures and even historical time periods. The contents of the collective unconscious he called *archetypes*.

The process of **individuation**, or self-realization, leads to the development and refinement of what Jung termed the Self archetype, which is the archetype of inherent wholeness of the personality. He taught that optimal mental health could only be obtained by balancing opposites of the personality, listening with openness to messages from the collective unconscious, and allowing archetypes some control and direction

over one's personality. Jung's de-emphasis on the controlling functions of the ego has a distinctly spiritual or religious element (see chapter 10 for more on Jung and religion).

Erich Fromm

Erich Fromm (1900–1980) agreed with Adler that we are inherently social beings and that the structure of the society in which we live is extremely important to our well-being. Fromm was a founding member of the Frankfurt School, which critiqued social and economic systems that stifle personal growth and well-being. For Fromm (1941/1994), our sense of being a fundamentally separate and distinct self constitutes a double-edged sword for humanity—creating a mindset of both freedom and isolation. This situation creates conflicts and anxiety because we desire intimate connections with others, but fear rejection; we desire freedom, but fear isolation; we desire pleasure, but fear pain. The tension between our fear of isolation and our desire for freedom generates the basic dynamic force that drives personality development.

The healthy way to deal with these fundamental conflicts and fears is to accept them as part of life and wrestle with the difficulties that real freedom brings. The mentally healthy person takes a courageous stance toward the inherent conflicts and paradoxes of life, working with these to find meaning and a true sense of psychological freedom. The unhealthy methods of dealing with this fundamental anxiety result in what Fromm termed *escape mechanisms*. As the term implies, these are attempts to avoid real issues—or hide from the necessary struggle of facing one's fears openly and honestly. Fromm (1941/1994) declared:

> What then is the meaning of freedom for modern man? He has become free from the external bonds that would prevent him from doing and thinking as he sees fit. He would be free to act according to his own will, if he knew what he wanted, thought, and felt. But he does not know. He conforms to anonymous authorities and adopts a self which is not his (pp. 254–255).

The Productive Orientation Fromm (1955/1990) called his ideal of optimal mental health the *productive personality* or the **productive orientation**. The term that Fromm used is unfortunate because "productive" has associations with profits and marketing, which were anathema to Fromm. Rather, it is helpful to think in terms of the production of a real self. For Fromm, this process entails dealing honestly with life's basic dichotomies and paradoxes. It is accomplished by courageously and creatively forging a unique identity, resisting escape mechanisms, opening oneself to mature love, and following ethics derived from a deep understanding of autonomy, community, and the human condition. Such a stance results in an approach to life that encourages a complete

expression of one's true self and allows people to fully meet their potential.

Creating the Productive Personality It was not until his later writings that Fromm (1996) provided specific suggestions for how people could begin to change their own lives toward a more productive orientation; indeed, some of these suggestions were published posthumously. In these later writings, Fromm asserted that optimal mental health involves an orientation toward *being,* which is the spontaneous expression of one's total self when it is created from a position of complete openness to, and awareness of, experience. Its opposite is a *having* orientation, which hides isolation and anxiety behind possessions, rigid beliefs, and diversions designed to protect people from the truth rather than to reveal it. Fromm (1976) explained the difference between being and having when he wrote, "People look for pleasure and excitement, instead of joy; for power and property, instead of growth. They want to *have* much, and *use* much, instead of *being* much" (p. 40).

Fromm asserted that the path toward a being orientation comprised self-analysis and the development of particular values including honesty, tolerance, patience, self-respect, humility, self-control, and generosity. In order to perform self-analysis effectively, one needs to practice five specific ways of confronting both inner and outer experience.

First, one must *will one thing*. This is a commitment to one definite goal. He or she must focus on that goal and devote all one's energies on a path that is freely chosen. This gives meaning and purpose to life. Second, one must be *fully awake*. By this phrase, Fromm referred to a dynamic attention and alertness to experience—that is, a direct and immediate participation in a moment-to-moment experiencing of the world. This is the quality of being appreciative of each life moment. In many ways, this quality seems to be similar to the attention aspect of the flow experience (Csikszentmihalyi, 1990). An illustration that is actually quite relevant to Fromm's theory involves the famous Zen Buddhist scholar D. T. Suzuki who, when asked about the ultimate meaning of Zen, replied with a single word: *Attention!* The questioner was not satisfied and continued: "Is that all? Isn't there more?" Suzuki paused and added, *Attention, attention, attention!*

Third, one must be *aware*. This quality refers to an awareness of our psychological experiences. Fromm described this quality as receptivity to how our perceptions of self, our well-being, and our psychological reality are affected by our transactions with both the external and internal worlds. A progressive dropping of unhealthy escape mechanisms is definitely one aspect of such awareness. We must be attentive to the ongoing experience of the world and be aware of how our own psychological processes both create and shape our interpretation of that experience.

Fourth, one must have the ability to really *concentrate* and to focus one's attention despite distractions. It is not enough to pay attention and be aware; one who aspires to optimal well-being must also be able to voluntarily concentrate on a single aspect of experience when necessary. Concentration is also central to the last skill.

Fifth, Fromm stated that a being orientation involves the ability to *meditate*. In his description of this quality, Fromm specifically mentioned the practice of Buddhist mindfulness meditation (see Chapters 4 and 6). In an earlier classic work, Fromm made direct comparisons between his model of optimal well-being and the goals of Zen Buddhist meditation (Suzuki, Fromm, & DeMartino, 1960).

EXISTENTIALISM
AND AUTHENTICITY

Existentialism initially encompassed a diverse movement in European philosophy that many people find difficult to summarize (see Barrett, 1962). Nevertheless, all seminal existentialist thinkers objected to a society that they criticized as superficial in its suppression and denial of certain aspects of human experience. In their view, modern society has fostered a restricted awareness in order to maintain a rigid social order. Social pressures that either reward the presentation of a false self or punish expression of the true self can lead to a false self-presentation. Existentialists argue that the consequences of this bargain mean that people no longer lead lives that confront the world openly and honestly. The existentialists' major goals, therefore, have to point individuals in the direction of choosing to live with full honesty, self-awareness, and openness.

The focus on honest awareness implies that we are aware of fears and limitations in our lives; such knowledge inevitably creates anxiety or dread (that is, *angst*). At this juncture, most approaches to well-being would say that if we feel anxiety, then the solution is to find a way to avoid it. However, existentialist philosophers contend that if we retreat or hide from anxiety, we have chosen to live an inauthentic life. Therefore, the truly authentic life is one in which we live with full awareness of choice, responsibility, freedom, anxiety, guilt, fate, and the impossibility of escape from the full range of our human experience—both the joyful and the tragic. The following famous passage from Henry David Thoreau's book *Walden* (1854/1960) illustrates the existentialists' drive to extract deeper levels of honesty, understanding, and meaning from life experiences:

> I went to the woods because I wished to live deliberately, to front only the essential facts of life, and see if I could not learn what it had to teach, and if not, when I came to die, discover that I had not lived.
>
> I wanted to live deep and suck out all the marrow of life, to live so sturdily and Spartan-like as to put to rout all that was not life, to cut a broad swath and shave close, to drive life into a corner, and to reduce it to its lowest terms, and, if it proved to be mean, why then to get the whole and genuine meanness of it, and publish its meanness to the world; or if it were sublime, to know it by experience and be able to give a true account of it in my next excursion....

Let us settle ourselves, and work and wedge our feet downward through the mud and slush of opinion, and prejudice and tradition, and delusion, and appearance, that allusion which covers the globe ... till we come to a hard bottom of rocks in place, which we can call reality (p. 66).

Rollo May

Rollo May (1909–1994) was the foremost interpreter of European existentialism in American psychology (May, 1950/1977; May, Angel, & Ellenberger, 1958). May insisted that the psychological problems that people in modern society must confront are significantly different than in the past. Due to the nature of the world we find ourselves in, we face unique forms of anxiety and are prone to a sense of powerlessness. In addition, we also face an erosion of core values that once helped to sustain men and women throughout life. May declared that today, more than ever, we are cognizant of potential threats to ourselves and to our loved ones, and we increasingly feel we have little power to change many of the political, economic, or social conditions that impact us. Further, our values are increasingly subject to attack because we know they are relative to situations and time periods and, therefore, at a deeper level we can't adequately explain why they are better than other values. This situation results in a pervasive sense of anxiety and unease.

For May, one of the primary consequences of such a life is the loss of real emotional responses to our experiences. Partly, we avoid real emotions because some of these require us to fully examine existential issues like death, loneliness, and meaninglessness. In order to regain a sense of our lives as authentic and meaningful, we must recognize fundamental paradoxes in life and find a way to integrate them that does justice to both sides of those dualities (Engler, 1991). In much the same way as Erich Fromm, May insisted that we must deal with the basic dualities and paradoxes of life:

we want love, and yet we fear rejection; we want to embrace life, and yet we run from an acknowledgment of our own death.

As an example, May (1969) argued that most of us deny the power of the *daimonic* in our lives. For May, the daimonic is any emotional response of ours that has the power to take us over completely. Because we are afraid of that power, we repress those aspects of our lives. For instance, instead of embracing the risks and power of love, we rush toward sensations of physical sex. Similarly, in order to be "better lovers," we follow sexual techniques that focus on sensation rather than on passion and love. In both cases, we deny the full range of our feelings because we are afraid of their power, and we refuse to grapple with the paradox that such feelings can be both creative and destructive at the same time.

In May's view, optimal well-being is an integration of all aspects of the personality, based on a willingness to open oneself to all aspects of life and to courageously and creatively forge an identity—all the while knowing full well that we risk failure and despair. May's vision of optimal psychological well-being demands uncompromising self-awareness, an almost brazen honesty and courage in the face of despair, and a dedication to deeply lived experience. Like most other existentialist thinkers, May did not promise facile happiness or self-esteem as the fruits of authentic living. He did promise a meaningful life, but that meaning may be forged out of despair as readily as out of joy. Interestingly, in line with May's predictions, a contemporary research study found that greater mindfulness was associated with less defensive reactions to thoughts of death (Niemiec et al., 2010). Paradoxically, greater mindful awareness resulted in less death anxiety.

Viktor Frankl

Viktor Frankl (1905–1997) initially created his style of existentialism out of his experiences as a young psychiatrist imprisoned in the Nazi concentration

Victor Frankl

camps of Auschwitz and Dachau during World War II. He was forced, in the most horrendous of circumstances, to search for a new way to ground his existence. The perspective that Frankl gained from these experiences in the death camps led him to postulate that the search for meaning in one's life, or the *will to meaning,* is our primary drive.

Frankl was quite explicit, however, in his rejection of any notion that finding meaning in life merely involves finding a comfortable belief system. He commented: "I think the meaning of our existence is not invented by ourselves, but rather detected" (p. 157). That is, finding meaning in life is not a search for an abstraction or a belief by which one might find solace from the realities of life. Frankl used the analogy of learning chess, explaining that it would be foolish to ask what is the single best move in chess. The best move at any moment is defined by each opponent and changes throughout the game. Similarly, there is no "best" meaning that a person can unilaterally apply to life. Frankl (1963) declared:

> What matters, therefore, is not the meaning of life in general but rather the specific meaning of a person's life at a given moment.... As each situation in life represents a challenge to man and presents a problem for him to solve, the question of the meaning of life may actually be reversed. Ultimately, man should not ask what the meaning of his life is, but rather must recognize that it is *he* who is asked. In a word, each man is questioned by life; and he can only answer to life by *answering for* his own life; to life he can only respond by

being responsible (pp. 171–172; italics in original).

For Frankl, the meaning of life must be continually created in response to the demands of life. Of prime importance in this process is an ability to take full responsibility for one's choices and to repeatedly actualize the potential meaning of life.

Frankl emphasized that finding meaning through life results in a style of life that is self-transcendent rather than self-actualizing. Therefore, his ideal of optimal psychological well-being is the **self-transcendent person**, or someone able to rise above self-focused concerns to seek some higher meaning and purpose. Specifically, meaning is found in three ways: (1) by doing a deed or taking action, (2) by deeply experiencing, or (3) by suffering. For Frankl, mental health is associated with a deep commitment to self-awareness, honesty, courage, responsibility, and active involvement in whatever life presents to us. In addition, he (1963) contended that suffering offers us a way to "actualize the highest value, to fulfill the deepest meaning.... For what matters above all is the attitude we take toward suffering" (p. 178). Therefore, he viewed our attitude toward "our" unavoidable suffering was a primary way in which we could reject resentment, depression, and anger and thereby transcend this self-focused orientation to create a meaning that embraced *both* the joy and the pain of life.

Authenticity: Finding One's True Self

Certainly, the necessity for valid self-knowledge has been emphasized since the ancient Greeks. Probably the most famous mandate for self-knowledge was inscribed in marble at the ancient Greek Oracle at Delphi: *Know Thyself.* Today we understand this maxim to emphasize valid knowledge of our interior lives and psychological realities; the obverse of this proverbial coin involves honest presentation of oneself to other people. In existentialist psychology, the term that is used to describe this combination of behaviors is *authenticity.*

© Dan Rosandich.
www.danscartoons.com

"Afraid to reveal my true self? Why do you say that?"

Note that some existentialist thinkers view authenticity solely in terms of how a person relates to the traditional values of a society. For these existentialists, authenticity requires nonconformity to several basic social norms. The presentation given here is in line with Eric Fromm and others who see authenticity as an inner psychological process that is related to personal growth; in their cogent view, the results of this process may or may not be nonconformity.

Authenticity involves both the ability to recognize and take responsibility for one's own psychological experiences and also the ability to act in ways consistent with those experiences. Charles Guignon (2000) observed that a key element in Martin Heidegger's idea of authenticity is an ability to take responsibility for making one's own choices in life and to accept full responsibility for their consequences.

Richard Ryan commented that an authentic personality comprises elements that are fully self-endorsed, willingly acted upon, and personally meaningful (see Ryan, LeGardia, & Rawsthorne, 2005). In this light, Susan Harter (2002) stated:

> authenticity involves *owning* one's own personal experiences, be they thoughts, emotions, needs, wants, preferences, or beliefs; processes captured by the injunction to 'know thyself'. The exhortation 'To thine own self be true' further implies that one *acts* in accord with the true self, expressing oneself in ways that are consistent with inner thoughts and feelings (p. 382; italics in original).

Terms such as the "true self" or the "real self" have often been used to describe core elements of authenticity.

Several contemporary researchers have created models of authenticity that specify its major dimensions. Alex Wood et al., (2008) measured authenticity with three dimensions taken from the theory of Carl Rogers (discussed below): self-alienation, authentic living, and accepting external influences. In this model, authenticity involves honest awareness of one's inner reality (or true self), ability to act and express oneself in ways consistent with the true self and in accord with one's real values, and courage to reject external influences and opinions inconsistent with one's own perception of reality. Michael Kernis and Brian Goldman (2005) described authenticity in terms of four dimensions: awareness, unbiased processing, behavior, and relational orientation. *Awareness* refers to better and more complex knowledge about one's motives, desires, emotions, and true self. *Unbiased processing* means an ability to see oneself without undue distortion, bias, or illusions. The *behavior* dimension involves an ability to act consistently in line with one's values as well as an increased sensitivity to how one's behavior fits with environmental demands and its potential impact on others. Finally, *relational orientation* entails an ability to strive for honesty, openness, genuineness, and truthfulness in close relationships.

Authenticity and Well-Being Richard Ryan and Edward Deci (Deci & Ryan, 1985; Ryan & Deci, 2000) described their self-determination theory as a newer perspective to explain how the real or true self can be actualized. According to self-determination theory, the true self is actualized through activities that promote and foster the three basic needs for autonomy, relatedness, and competence (see also Ito & Kodama, 2005). Among the many research findings that support their view, they have found that greater well-being is associated with the pursuit of goals that are more meaningful, more integrated with the self, more aligned with the true self, and more autonomous. That is, when greater authenticity is used as a foundation for pursuing our goals, then greater well-being results.

In a study that examined both the true self and authenticity, Sheldon, Ryan, Rawsthorne, and Ilardi (1997) found that greater authenticity was related to higher self-esteem, more identity integration, and feelings of more autonomy (see also Ryan,

LaGuardia, & Rawsthorne, 2005). Greater authenticity was also related to less depression, less perceived stress, and fewer complaints of physical problems. The investigators also found that the more genuine and self-expressive people felt in a given role, the freer they felt to express their core personality traits. Authenticity has also been associated with greater life satisfaction and positive emotionality (Wood et al., 2008). Kernis and Goldman (2005) found that authenticity was correlated with higher self-reported scores on several well-being variables including life satisfaction, secure self-esteem, autonomy, self-efficacy, and mindfulness. Schlegal, Hicks, Arndt, & King (2009) found that priming individuals to think about their "true self-concept" resulted in enhanced perceptions of meaning in life.

Both Susan Harter (2002) and Emily Impett et al., (2008) examined the development of authenticity in adolescent girls. They found that the ability and willingness to find one's true "voice," or to express one's real opinions and feelings, is related to higher authenticity. Harter also found that adolescent girls with higher authenticity had higher self-esteem, more hope, felt more positive emotions, and were more cheerful. Suggesting that greater authenticity can be forged through more positive interpersonal relationships, she therefore encouraged people to create close relationships based on genuine empathy, willingness to be truthful, unconditional positive regard, and both autonomy and connectedness to others.

Defenses and Authenticity If we are to speak of a true self or a real self, then there obviously must be some conceptualization of a false or an unreal self. Therefore, a guiding assumption of authenticity is that people often deceive themselves about their real motives, true emotions, and actual beliefs. Indeed, research on *illusory mental health* has found that a sense of well-being can be based on distorted self-perception (Shedler, Mayman, & Manis, 1993). Others have found that efforts to maintain high self-esteem can be detrimental to well-being when the struggle stifles the creation of an authentic view of self (Goldman, 2006). George Vaillant's research discussed in chapter 8 showed a clear pattern of diminished well-being in people who consistently used unhealthy defense mechanisms.

Some of the factors that influence the use of defenses are consistent with the basic premises of authenticity. For example, people who score high on autonomy and low on need for control tend to use fewer unhealthy defenses (Knee & Zukerman, 1998; Ryan & Deci, 2000). When investigating her idea of fixed and growth mindsets (see chapter 8), Carol Dweck and her colleagues found that people who believed their valued attributes were fixed were more defensive than those with a growth mindset who believed their valued assets could be developed (Dweck & Elliot-Moskwa, 2010; Nussbaum & Dweck, 2008).

HUMANISTIC PERSPECTIVES

Carl Rogers and the Fully Functioning Person

Carl Rogers (1902–1987) developed his theory of mental health from his experiences as a psychotherapist. Among the major thrusts of his approach to psychotherapy, he addressed ways that people can develop their own unique approach to life in the context of a supportive psychotherapeutic relationship.

Rogers posited that we all have an innate need to develop our potential, which he termed the *self-actualizing tendency* (Rogers, 1959). He taught that, given the right circumstances, people will find ways to fulfill their potential that are both socially responsible and personally fulfilling. The problem, according to Rogers, is that many people lose touch with their innate impulses toward self-actualization; this process of loss begins when we deny our own experiences of self and world in order to gain conditional acceptance from other people, such as initially our parents. He argued that when people exist in environments defined by unconditional love, empathic understanding, and genuineness, they can grow psychologically toward their fullest potential.

The Fully Functioning Person   For Rogers, the definition of psychological adjustment rests on the notion that mental health exists when all the relevant experiences of a person can be integrated into a coherent and flexible self-concept. The name that Rogers chose for those who can achieve this ideal is the **fully functioning person** (Rogers, 1961). Three major criteria and two auxiliary ones could characterize the fully functioning person. The fully functioning person exhibits: (1) openness to experiences; (2) existential living; and (3) trust in one's own organismic experiences. These three results in: (4) a sense of freedom; and (5) enhanced creativity.

By *openness to experience,* Rogers was suggesting a personality that is aware of both internal and external stimuli—one whose use of defense mechanisms is minimized. Actually, he hypothesized that it is possible to live without *any* defense mechanisms. One of the consequences of this openness is that both pleasant and unpleasant experiences are allowed equal access to consciousness. This capacity requires that individuals have a sufficiently grounded sense of self that they will not be overwhelmed by emotions. Although Rogers doesn't specifically mention it as a criterion, it seems that the fully functioning person would also exhibit substantial fortitude and courage.

The second criteria—*existential living*—implies that the fully functioning person favors life as it is lived in the moment; this criterion is not too distant from the adage to "stop and smell the roses." It implies a strong process orientation to life, or a life that is lived as a fluid, dynamic sense of being aware of current experiences, deciding what to do with the experience, taking action and moving on to deal with the next experience. (Note the similarity to the theory of flow in chapter 4.)

Persons open to the moment are also open to cues that come from their physiology, trusting in their own organismic experiences. The fully functioning individual is aware of, trusts in, and values his or her instincts and intuitions, or "felt sense" about a situation. Because such a person is nondefensive, open to the experience of the moment, and willing to experience life as a process rather than a product, it seems quite obvious that he or she would also experience a sense of freedom. Finally, since the fully functioning person is continually adapting to new experiences, a degree of creativity in that adaptation seems manifest. In sense, Rogers' theory, describes a life open to unique and unusual ways of problem solving. It also implies a willingness to be challenged by new experiences. In this way, one's innate need for self-actualization can emerge from adversity and motivate growthful behavior.

Living as a Fully Functioning Person   What is the person like in Rogers' theory of the fully functioning person? Rogers (1961) provided clues:

> It seems to mean that the individual moves toward *being*, knowingly and acceptingly, the process which he inwardly and actually *is*.... He is not trying to be more than he is, with the attendant feelings of insecurity or bombastic defensiveness. He is not trying to be less than he is, with the attendant feelings of guilt or self-deprecation. He is increasingly listening to the deepest recesses of his physiological and emotional being, and finds himself increasingly willing to be, with greater accuracy and depth, that self which he most truly is (pp. 175–176).

The movement is toward self-direction, openness to experience, acceptance of others, and trust in self. It is not toward any particular state but rather is a way of approaching and even welcoming life experiences. Again in Rogers, (1961) own words:

> It seems to me that the good life is not any fixed state. It is not, in my estimation, a state of virtue, or contentment, or nirvana,

or happiness. It is not a condition in which the individual is adjusted, or fulfilled, or actualized. To use psychological terms, it is not a state of drive-reduction, or tension-reduction, or homeostasis (pp. 185–186).

Rogers seems to be describing a person who can balance rationality and intuition but who shows a slight preference for the intuitive modes of understanding the world. It seems that his idea of optimal mental health borrows heavily from a conception of the creative artist (see *The Creative Person* in chapter 7).

Substantial research on self-concordance and self-congruence has been based partially on Rogers' theory. **Self-concordance** is found when there is high congruence between one's personality and one's goals (Sheldon, 2008). In order to have higher congruence, it is necessary to become aware of one's true self, what one really wants in life, and how to strive towards those goals. Studies have found that a good fit between a person's values and her or his goals results in greater motivation and higher well-being (Wehmeyer, Little, & Sergeant, 2009). Striving toward goals that are authentic and fit the real self has also been associated with higher well-being (Sheldon & Kasser, 2001; Sheldon, Ryan, Deci, & Kasser, 2004).

Abraham Maslow and Self-Actualization

The theory of self-actualization developed by Abraham Maslow (1908–1970) refers to the process of fulfilling one's full potential. In his original presentation, Maslow (1954) stated that **self-actualization** "may be loosely described as the full use and exploitation of talents, capacities, potentialities" (p. 200). Although Maslow's theory of the self-actualizing person is among the best-known theories of personality development, it remains

Abraham Maslow

widely misunderstood even in psychology. For instance, Maslow's theory has nothing to do with self-absorption or preoccupation with simply enhancing one's own self-esteem.

Early Studies of Self-Actualizing People   For Maslow, self-actualization was not a state but rather described an ongoing process of development. Beginning with a question about why some people adjusted extraordinarily well, he searched for exemplars of optimal well-being: people who showed evidence of fulfilling their potential. Who were these people who exemplified the process of self-actualization? They were not, in any sense, the average person off the street. To get a feel for the elite nature of his candidates, one has only to look at how some historical figures fared in his classification. Maslow's "fairly sure they are self-actualizer" candidates included Abraham Lincoln (only in his last years) and Thomas Jefferson; the "highly probable group" included Eleanor Roosevelt and Albert Einstein. Beethoven and Freud were in his "partial" group while George Washington Carver and Albert Schweitzer he placed in his "potential" group.

In addition to studying public figures, well-known people from history, and his acquaintances, Maslow also screened 3,000 college students. In this last group he found only one person who fit his criteria—and that person was in the "probable" category. He concluded that self-actualization "was not possible in our society for young, developing people" (Maslow, 1954, p. 200). He believed that a person needed some life experience before he or she could be considered self-actualizing. Indeed, one must have faced some difficult situations and coped with them well. A person had to be "tested by life" before his or her degree of self-actualization could be discerned. Later, Maslow estimated that less than 1% of the adult population in the U.S. could be called self-actualizing.

Maslow developed his definition of self-actualization through an iterative process. That is, first he chose participants, next he evaluated those people, then he adjusted the original definition based on the first evaluation. This process was then followed by his choosing the next group to be evaluated based on the revised definition, and so on. Using this process, Maslow (1954) expanded his explanation of self-actualization:

> Such people seem to be fulfilling themselves and to be doing the best that they are capable of doing, reminding us of exhortation, 'Become what thou art!' They are people who have developed or are developing to the full stature of which they are capable. These potentialities may be either idiosyncratic or species-wide, so that the self in self-actualization *must not have too individualistic a flavor* [italics added] (p. 201).

We have taken the liberty of italicizing part of this last quote to emphasize that from the very beginning Maslow did not equate self-actualization with self-absorption or excessive individualism. Later, many interpreters of Maslow would forget this point.

Maslow's Hierarchy of Needs   Once Maslow identified examples of the self-actualizing person, he began to develop a theory of personality to explain how such people came to be the way they were. He proposed a theory of personality development based on a list of basic needs, a relatively common practice in psychology at the time.

Maslow (1954) initially delineated five basic human needs that must be met in order for people to feel fulfilled in life. Graphically, he presented these needs in the shape of a pyramid (Figure 9.3) The pyramidal shape suggest that lower needs were more pervasive and that higher needs were more tenuous, more easily overwhelmed by the influence of lower needs. Maslow posited all five sets of needs as innate to the human species.

1. *Physiological and safety*. People must have their basic needs met for food, shelter, comfort, and freedom from disease.
2. *Safety and security*. People need to believe that they are relatively safe from physical harm and social disruption and that they have some degree of control over their own destinies.

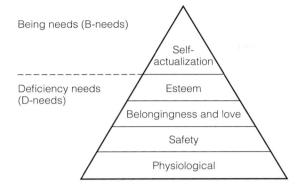

Being needs (B-needs)

Deficiency needs
(D-needs)

F I G U R E 9.3 Maslow's Hierarchy of Basic Needs

3. *Love and belongingness.* People need to feel connected to others and that they are loved and cherished for who they are.

4. *Self-esteem.* People need to feel a sense of competence, achievement, and respect from other people in their lives.

5. *Self-actualization.* People have a need to develop their unique potential.

Maslow (1954) also postulated that certain preconditions were necessary for satisfaction of needs: specific *freedoms* (that is, freedom of speech, expression, inquiry); and necessary *ethical principles* (that is, justice, fairness, honesty, orderliness). He also believed that human needs *to know* and *to understand* formed a second smaller needs hierarchy that was interrelated and synergistic with the basic needs hierarchy. Finally, he stated that for some people there existed a basic need for *aesthetic expression.* For these people (for example, creative artists), a failure to satisfy their needs for creativity and beauty resulted in ennui, boredom, and meaninglessness. Years later, Maslow (1971) added a need for *self-respect* to couple with self-esteem as well as a sixth need above self-actualization: that of *self-transcendence.*

Maslow suggested that the first four needs must be satisfied in a relatively sequential fashion. However, it is not necessary to satisfy each need fully before moving on to concerns of the next higher need. For the sake of illustration, he (1954) stated that a person might have satisfied 85% of his or her physiological needs, 70% of safety needs, 50% of belongingness needs, 40% of self-esteem needs, and 10% of self-actualization needs.

Motivation in Self-Actualizing People   The first four needs are also based on what Maslow termed **Deficiency needs** or **D-needs**. If the D-needs are not satisfied, then we feel we lack qualities necessary for basic psychological adjustment. In this case, we lack a positive sense of self, a sense that we are loved, and a sense of security that allows optimism for the future. Once we feel relatively secure, connected to others and loved, and we hold a healthy respect for our personality, then our need for self-actualization becomes more salient. However, this need creates a new tension that comes from the difference between who we are and who we imagine we can be. Since we acknowledge we are not the person we can be and recognize that our potential is unrealized, this separation between the real self and the potential self produces a desire to fulfill our potential.

Maslow's term for self-actualizing needs was **being needs**, or **B-needs**. Some B-needs are truth, justice, beauty, wholeness, richness, playfulness, meaningfulness, and goodness (Maslow, 1971). One singular characteristic of self-actualizing people is that they are motivated by B-needs more than by D-needs. Maslow (1954) stated, "Our subjects no longer strive in the ordinary sense, they develop" (p. 211). He asserted that when self-actualizing people are motivated by B-needs they are, in a sense, pulled toward a possible future for themselves defined by the need to develop their unique potential as well as by greater being needs. Therefore, part of the tension created by an emerging need for self-actualization comes from a conflict between current security and the risk of change. The American writer Max de Pree said, "The greatest thing is, at any moment, to be willing to give up who we are in order to become all that we can be."

Maslow viewed this type of choice to be a common conflict in life illustrating a general principle: the tension between **security versus growth**. For him, a self-actualizing person is characterized by a willingness to risk the security of the known and comfortable for the potential growth that can come from embracing a new challenge. Similarly, Eleanor Roosevelt advised people to "do one thing every day that scares you." Self-actualizing people also acknowledge, accept, and actually embrace the tensions created by such growth risks. However, they risk potential failure in an attempt to actualize their potential.

Certainly Maslow knew that many people reject personal growth changes due to a variety of fears, such as a fear of moving away from what is known and familiar or a fear that other people in their lives will not accept those changes. He (1971) also identified a fear that he called the **Jonah complex**, which the following quote addresses:[1]

> Our deepest fear is not that we are inadequate. Our deepest fear is that we are powerful beyond measure. It is our light, not our darkness that frightens us. We ask ourselves, 'Who am I to be brilliant, gorgeous, talented and fabulous?' Actually, who are you not to be? You are a child of God. Your playing small doesn't serve the world. There's nothing enlightening about shrinking so that other people won't feel insecure around you.... And as we let our light shine, we unconsciously give other people permission to do the same.

As we mentioned earlier, Maslow asserted that only a tiny percentage of humanity during his era could mange to be truly self-actualizing. He called these the "growing tip" and optimistically predicted that their percentage would steadily increase in coming decades as Western society, and then world society in general, became increasingly democratic and freedom-loving. For those who did manage to self-actualize, what would they be like?

The Personality Traits of Self-Actualizing People   In his study of self-actualizing people, Maslow (1954) extracted 15 personality traits that he believed were characteristic of their behavior. Not every self-actualizing person he studied showed evidence of all 15 traits. Therefore, the list was a useful tool for understanding self-actualizing people, not a rigid checklist. He also recognized that his participants were not perfect. They were not completely free of guilt, anxiety, sadness, or conflict. He felt compelled to remind people that his subjects "are not angels." For the most part, however, they were free of neurotic anxieties and conflicts. With this in mind, Maslow (1954) presented a list of 15 personality traits for self-actualizing people. For the sake of clarity, we have grouped the 15 traits into four categories. (for other classifications, see Sumerlin et al., 1994; Sumerlin & Bundrick, 1996.)

A. OPENNESS TO EXPERIENCE

1. *More efficient perception of reality and more comfortable relations with it.* Maslow believed that self-actualizing people have a keen eye for deception, dishonesty, and superficiality in other people. Since they have settled many questions of self-esteem, they are also more able to perceive the world without the distorting bias of their own wishes, hopes, and anxieties.

2. *Acceptance (self, others, nature).* It follows logically that self-actualizing people should also be better able to detect deception, weakness, and shortcomings within themselves. It was their attitude toward those shortcomings that distinguished Maslow's self-actualizing people. He commented:

> Our healthy individuals find it possible to accept themselves and their own nature without chagrin or complaint or, for that matter, even without thinking about the matter very much. They can accept their own human nature in the stoic style, with all its shortcomings, with all its discrepancies from the ideal image without feeling real concern (Maslow, 1954, pp. 206–7).

Maslow also noted that when self-actualizing persons do feel guilty or dysphoric, it is from recognition of the discrepancy between what is and what could be or ought to be. They can see the possibilities inherent in humanity and are acutely aware of how far short people are from what they could be.

3. *Continued freshness of appreciation*. This characteristic seems to describe an openness to, a joy in, and a gratitude for the moment-to-moment experiences of life. Maslow (1954) stated: "Self-actualizing people have the wonderful capacity to appreciate again and again, freshly and naively, the basic goods of life with awe, pleasure, wonder, and even ecstasy, however stale these experiences may have become to others" (pp. 214–215).

4. *Spontaneity*. Maslow also found his participants to be more spontaneous and showed behavior marked by simplicity, naturalness, and lack of artificiality. This did not mean their behavior was necessarily unconventional, and it certainly was not overly impulsive. By simplicity, Maslow meant that his subjects were not boastful or supercilious. They had an easy-going naturalness about them.

5. *Creativeness*. The creativity he saw was originality, inventiveness, adaptability, and spontaneity in the solution of problems—both large and small.

6. *The mystical experience; the oceanic feeling*. These experiences Maslow (1970) would later describe as *peak experiences*. These are typically brief moments of intense joy and are often accompanied by heightened awareness. Frequently these possess a spiritual or noetic quality (these will be discussed in more detail in chapter 10).

B. AUTONOMY

7. *Autonomy; independence of culture and environment*. The self-esteem of self-actualizing people was not based on how other people thought of them or on culturally defined criteria for success. They could remain fairly stable, even serene and happy, in the midst of

frustrations and stressors. They seemed to find intrinsic satisfactions rather than relying on extrinsic rewards from others.

8. *The quality of detachment; the need for privacy*. Maslow believed that his participants showed a distinct tendency to enjoy solitude and privacy. Not that they were unsociable, but they did not need people around them at all times. In this context, Maslow also characterized a greater ability to concentrate and a quality of detachment that allowed self-actualizing people to "remain above the battle, to remain unruffled, undisturbed by that which produces turmoil in others" (1954, p. 212).

9. *Resistance to enculturation*. Maslow (1954) began his description of this criterion with the very provocative sentence, "Self-actualizing people are not well adjusted" (p. 224). What he meant was that his participants maintained a certain detachment from the culture in which they lived. They lived in their society, usually without overt rebelliousness or unconventionality, but their inner attitudes and beliefs were not shaped and dominated by the messages from that society. They were able to examine their culture more objectively and see the contradictions, inconsistencies, and errors that existed.

C. POSITIVE RELATIONSHIPS WITH OTHERS

10. *Gemeinschaftsgefühl (social interest)*. Maslow deliberately borrowed the name of this criterion directly from his mentor Alfred Adler. Maslow's participants manifested a deep feeling of empathy, compassion, and humanitarian affection for people, despite a piercing awareness of other's imperfections. Self-actualizing people possessed a genuine desire to help humanity that was based on a sense of shared identity with the human family. They felt a need to be of service to others in some way.

11. *Interpersonal relations*. Maslow reported that his participants experienced deeper, more intense, and more profound interpersonal

relationships than the average person. They were able to drop defensiveness and find greater love. In this context, he also stated that self-actualizers tended "to be kind or at least patient to almost everyone. They have an especially tender love for children and are easily touched by them" (1954, p. 218). Maslow also observed that their friendships were extremely close, but not numerous.

12. *Philosophical, unhostile sense of humor.* Maslow's participants did not find humor at other people's expense. They did not laugh *at* other people but rather laughed *with* other people. They found the foibles of the human condition—their own included—to be the greater source of humor. More often the source of their humor was irony, rather than cynicism or malicious satire.

13. *Problem-centering.* Maslow found that his participants tended to be oriented to some problem, task, vocation, or mission in life. The goal of this mission was, in general, not oriented toward personal gain was unselfish. He stated: "Generally the devotion and dedication is so marked that one can fairly use the old words vocation, calling, or mission to describe their passionate, selfless, and profound feeling for their work" (Maslow, 1971, p. 291). In other words, the self-actualizers in Maslow's sample tended to devote a good deal of energy to tasks they believed would benefit others. How they defined service to others often came from a "framework of values that [was] broad and not petty, universal and not local, and in terms of a century rather than the moment" (1954, p. 212).

D. STRONG ETHICAL STANDARDS

14. *The democratic character structure.* Part of this criterion described a lack of pretense and hypocrisy in his participants. Maslow found that they were more willing than most people to listen to and learn from anyone who might have something important to say. Matters of rank, class, status, and educational attainment meant very little to self-actualizers.

15. *Discrimination between means and ends.* This is a somewhat confusing title for this criterion and, in fact, is the least clearly defined of the original fifteen criteria. What Maslow was trying to capture with this unwieldy term was a strong sense of ethics and morality. He stated that his participants were quite clear about the differences between right and wrong and lived according to those values. The reference to means versus ends suggests that self-actualizing people did not use unethical means to obtain a goal they thought was ethical.

Although Maslow didn't use terms from contemporary positive psychology, it seems fairly obvious that his fifteen traits of self-actualization encompass a list of strengths and virtues. His theory posits two primary characteristics of the process of self-actualization. First, self-actualizing people exhibit a specific set of strengths and virtues. Second, they tend to show a unique style of motivation. They are motivated more often by needs for personal growth than by needs for security and safety.

Research on Self-Actualization A chief criticism of Maslow's influential theory is that little empirical evidence supports it. Yet this critique raises a more complicated issue than it might seem. First, it is true that research has generally failed to support Maslow's proposed ascendancy of needs through the needs hierarchy (Wahba & Bridwell, 1976). However, several studies have shown that the predictions of the needs hierarchy are accurate when comparing nations around the world in terms of how well basic needs are met (Drakopoulos, 2008; Hagerty, 1999). For instance, Tay and Diener (2011) recently found that societal factors within a country such as the availability of food, shelter, and a sense of security were important to meeting lower needs for survival and safety. However, meeting the higher needs for respect and belongingness was related to predictors within the person such as cognitive style and personality. They concluded that Maslow's need hierarchy should be evaluated at both the societal level and at the individual level.

Studies that investigate the criteria of self-actualization as a metric for optimal well-being, however, offer a striking contrast with the research on Maslow's needs hierarchy. That is, the research literature on the theory of self-actualization comprises over 1,000 studies, most of which support Maslow's self-actualization criteria as useful indicators of positive well-being (for reviews, see Jones & Crandall, 1991; Knapp, 1990; Welch, Tate, & Medeiros, 1987). For instance, Wahba and Bridwell (1976) did not find support for Maslow's needs hierarchy, but they found support for his distinction between deficiency needs (D-needs) and being needs (B-needs). Apparently, some people are motivated by self-actualization needs more than others.

In general, research has indicated that people who score higher on measures of self-actualization also score higher on other indices of well-being (for example, Hjelle, 1991; Sharma & Rosha, 1992). Among the challenges of measuring relationships between well-being and self-actualization is that the predictors of subjective well-being and self-actualization may not be identical (Compton, 2001, Compton et al., 1996; Vitterso, 2004). Therefore, researchers need to measure well-being with measures that adequately tap into the psychological constructs.

How to be More Self-Actualizing   Initial recommendations of how to be more self-actualizing follow straightforwardly from the 15 personality traits Maslow listed. That is, work for greater autonomy, be more open to experiences, foster deep close personal relationships along with increased tolerance and understanding of others, and operate in the world with the highest ethical principles and in your life with the highest values. In addition, determine what motivates you and experiment with taking more growth-producing risks in your current behavior. Specifically, take those chances in life that you know hold you back from reaching your potential. However, note that Maslow firmly rejected the use of thrill-seeking risks insofar as these are often motivated by D-needs. Finally, recognize how B-needs and B-values are functioning in your life. Nurture the way these motivate you toward self-actualizing goals.

For those interested in applied self-actualization, in *The Farther Reaches of Human Nature* (1971), Maslow provided various recommendations for how people can grow toward greater self-actualization. First, "experience the world fully, vividly, with full concentration and total absorption" (p. 44). Although Maslow was writing before Csikszentmihalyi published his theory of flow, today we would say this recommendation is to increase flow in one's life. Second, Maslow asserted that life is a process of choices and greater self-actualization is found by making growth rather than security choices. Third, we should increase autonomy by listening to our own inner voices and instincts when making decisions. Fourth, "when in doubt, be honest" (p. 45).

Fifth, utilize the first four recommendations to make better choices in life and then advance toward goals that are your own. Sixth, recognize that self-actualization is a process, not a goal, and that we can move toward it every day. Vital to this process is endeavoring to be the best you can at what you really want to be. Maslow declared, "To become a second-rate physician is not a good path to self-actualization. One wants to be first-rate or as good as he [or she] can be" (p. 46). Seven, even though peak experiences cannot be guaranteed, "Set up conditions so that peak experiences are more likely" (p. 46). As C. S. Lewis wrote, "One must be surprised by joy". Last, strive to decrease unhealthy defense mechanisms that inhibit growth, honesty, and intimacy.

Julius Seeman and Personality Integration

Julius Seeman (1959, 1983, 1989, 2008)[2] developed his theory of *personality integration* around systems theory (see *Systems Theory* in chapter 12 for more detail). In a human systems perspective, multiple elements or subsystems work together in complex ways to maintain optimal functioning of the person. In Seeman's *human systems model* of personality integration the subsystems are: the biochemical, physiological, precognitive (for example, dreams, intuitions, preconscious or unconscious motivations), and cognitive. Also, the interpersonal/ecological subsystem has two divisions: person-to-person and person-to-environment (Seeman, 2008). All the subsystems influence each other, both in the present and as developmental processes over time. Interestingly, in Seeman's human system model, emotion is a function of all the subsystems acting together rather than comprising a separate subsystem. That is, emotion emerges from the transactions among the subsystems with the environment.

Seeman (1983) declared, "What is fundamental about the components of a system is not relationship but organization" (p. 215). Central to the organization of the system are two major processes: communication and regulation. Therefore, higher personality integration is found when there is maximal communication among the subsystems, and the greater information available to the system is used to regulate the system in adaptive and healthy ways. Based on these ideas, Seeman (1988) defined self-actualization in the following way: "Persons are maximally actualizing when as total human systems they are functioning at peak efficiency" (p. 309). His research has generally supported his hypotheses about greater communication and regulation. For example, Seeman's studies have found that persons who scored higher on personality integration were better able to voluntarily regulate their hand temperature, showed greater tolerance for ambiguity, and were rated as more empathic and self-congruent than those who scored lower on personality integration (Seeman, 1983).

Seeman was an early colleague and lifelong friend of Carl Rogers, and the similarity between their two theories is evident. Both are based on openness to experience, increased trust regarding one's ongoing experience, and a sense of psychological freedom. However, Seeman argued that receptivity to experience must be augmented by meaningful subsystem integration to achieve optimal well-being.

Personal Growth Initiative

Another approach to personal growth comes from the work of Christine Robitschek (Robitschek, 1998). She created the concept of *personal growth*

initiative to describe how some people are able to foster personal growth changes. She defined personal growth as "active, intentional engagement in the process of personal growth" (Robitschek, 1998, p. 184). People who are high on personal growth tend to be open to experiences, seek improvement in themselves, have a strong sense of life direction, and enduring goals (Whittaker & Robitschek, 2001). Robitschek found that people who have a high level of personal growth initiative know the directions in which they would like to grow, appear able to capitalize on opportunities for personal growth, and seek opportunities for creativity and adaptive solutions (Robitschek & Kashubeck, 1999). For example, college students who scored high on personal growth initiative had stronger career direction and were more open to exploring different experiences in their environments (Robitschek & Cook, 1999).

Personal Growth and Human Potential

Therapists and researchers associated with humanistic psychology have developed many intervention strategies aimed at helping people to move toward optimal well-being (Cain & Seeman, 2002; Schneider, Bugental, & Pierson, 2001). During the 1960s leaders of humanistic psychology created a style of intervention called personal growth therapy or human potential (Mann, 1979). These approaches focused on helping people who were already functioning reasonably well to fulfill more of their potential. The fundamental principle behind the human potential approach is that normal psychological and social adjustments represent a point of departure rather than a goal (Mann, 1979). Another assumption is that most people utilize a tiny part of their potential, yet we all have the capacity to expand and develop our skills, talents, and psychological growth.

There is another way that ideas from human potential have been brought into the public eye. This type of personal growth experience seeks to help people overcome their self-imposed limits, but it tends to be more educational and less focused on inner conflicts and defenses. For instance, people may choose workshops designed to tap into their creative potential or participate in exercises designed to help them build self-confidence, increase their motivation for success, or just relax and communicate better with their colleagues. Personal growth experiences like these, as well as many other types, are offered to individuals in a variety of settings—from one-on-one sessions to religious groups and even corporate boardrooms.

Unfortunately, many personal growth or human potential interventions in the 1960s and 1970s were never adequately assessed for their effectiveness (Mann, 1979). Even today, many remain untested in their usefulness. Recently, however, some well-established styles of humanistic psychotherapy—as well as assumptions that serve as their foundation—have developed solid initial research that supports their usefulness (Bohart & Greenberg, 1997; Cain & Seeman, 2002; Greenberg & Rice, 1997).

THE OPTIMAL PERSONALITY: COMMON THEMES

Marie Jahoda and Positive Mental Health

The first attempt to summarize the relevant literature on optimal well-being was undertaken by Marie Jahoda (1958). (The phrase used by Jahoda was "positive mental health.") Her review and analysis resulted in six criteria and associated subcategories. These comprised:

1. *Attitudes toward the self.* This first criterion addressed ideas such as self-acceptance, self-confidence, and self-reliance. There were four main subcategories: (a) adequate self-awareness; (b) accurate self-concept; (c) self-acceptance; and (d) a positive and "globally benevolent" view of the self.

2. *Growth, development and self-actualization.* Jahoda associated mental health with a striving toward goals in the future including efforts to realize potential. This involved: (a) the ability to accept challenges and tension in the present in the interest of future goals; and (b) full

commitment toward living, or an extension of the self, through involvement in different pursuits, a concern for other people, and a desire to help and benefit others.

3. *An integrated personality.* This criterion refers to a balancing of the important aspects of self such that: (a) desires, impulses, and needs are offset by rationality, responsibility, and social concerns; (b) there is a unifying philosophy of life or a sense of meaning and purpose; and (c) there are anxiety tolerance, frustration tolerance, and an ability to delay gratification.

4. *Autonomy.* There are two aspects of this criterion: (a) regulation of behavior from within; and (b) an ability to act independently of environmental pressures and to resist unnecessary conformity or obedience to authority.

5. *Perception of reality.* This criterion consists of: (a) an ability to see self and others without one's own needs distorting perception of other people or situations; and (b) greater empathy and social sensitivity. Jahoda suggested that if people are free from need distortion, then they are better able to see others clearly and honestly and are able to empathize with them.

6. *Environmental mastery.* This criterion refers to successful adaptation to situational demands and expectations. It includes six different subcategories: (a) the ability to love; (b) the ability to work and play; (c) good interpersonal relations; (d) the ability to meet the demands of situations with a sense of mastery and self-efficacy; (e) the ability to balance one's efforts to change the external world with efforts to change one's inner world; and (f) the ability to utilize adequate problem-solving strategies.

In general, Jahoda's perspective on positive well-being presents the ideal of a person able to balance various personality factors—such as independence with dependence; self-concern with concern for others; and honest self-awareness with healthy self-enhancements. Because of this balance, one can form healthy relationships with others and achieve autonomous change and personal growth.

Personality Traits Important for Optimal Well-Being

Several personality traits not listed above also appear frequently in perspectives on optimal well-being. Among the most frequently named traits is *openness to experience.* You will recall that openness is associated particularly with wisdom, the fully functioning person, and self-actualization. The aspects of openness to experience especially relevant are those related to greater self-awareness, tolerance of other viewpoints, and curiosity about self and others. Relevant to optimal well-being are research studies that associated greater openness with higher life satisfaction (Stephan, 2009), better stress regulation (Williams et al., 2009), better learning strategies (Chamorro-Premuzic & Furnham, 2009), better cognitive performance in older persons (Sharp et al., 2010), and greater ability of adults to be playful (Mixter, 2009).

Another often-identified trait is *curiosity.* Todd Kashdan, Paul Rose, and Frank Fincham (2004) developed the Curiosity and Exploration Inventory to measure two dimensions of curiosity: *exploration,* or seeking out novelty or challenge; and *absorption,* or the ability to be fully engaged in activities. They found both subscales were highly correlated with openness to experience. Both curiosity subscales were also significantly related to well-being, but only the exploration subscale was related to life satisfaction. Gallagher and Lopez (2007) also found the exploration subscale to be very similar to openness to experience and, in their study as well, it was more highly related to well-being than was absorption. Higher trait curiosity has also been associated with more frequent growth-oriented behaviors and greater persistence in forging meaning in life (Kashdan & Steger, 2007). Indeed, Todd Kasdan (2009) refers red to curiosity as "the engine of growth," or the psychological factor that drives personal growth. Kasdan also observed, however, that novelty is not enough to inspire curiosity. In order to be curious about a novel situation—as opposed to being frightened—people must feel they can cope with the novelty.

Courage is another factor that is assumed, but rarely articulated, in most optimal theories of well-being. (See a special issue on courage in *The Journal of Positive Psychology* [2007], volume 2, issue 2.) In this instance, courage is not necessarily an ability to dash into a burning building to save a child or a beloved pet, rather, it is a quality necessary to sustain personal growth. How so? As Maslow commented via his concept of the Jonah complex, the act of taking personal-growth risks—such as being more authentic or self-disclosing—can arouse anxiety. To venture outside one's comfort zone or scrutinize honestly one's personality traits can be difficult. This type of courage has been referred to as "existential courage" (Pury & Lopez, 2009). At times, it can be challenging to act in accord with one's ethical principles due to potential consequences. In addition, psychological growth can also result from acts of "civil courage," such as social action taken to end injustice (Greitmeyer et al., 2007).

Cynthia Pury and Shane Lopez (2009) noted that courage has four dimensions: (1) willfulness and intentionality, (2) mindful deliberation, (3) objective substantial risk, and (4) "a noble or worthy end" (p. 376). Similarly, a study of non-Jews who risked their lives to rescue Jews during the Holocaust found four factors that differentiated rescuers from bystanders who took no risks: a high sense of social responsibility, altruistic moral reasoning; high empathic concern for others, and high risk-taking (Fagin-Jones & Midlarsky, 2007). It is interesting to note Maslow's assertion that all four of these qualities are characteristic of self-actualizing persons. On a less dramatic scale, risk is certainly necessary for any important degree of personal growth.

The topic of fighting for justice leads us to a discussion of *high ethical standards*—another factor appearing in most perspectives on optimal well-being. In some way, most theories associate optimal well-being with living on the basis of high ethical and moral standards, focusing on the common good or the welfare of others. For instance, this notion is found in the tolerant and just reasoning of wisdom; Adler's social interest, Maslow's B-needs, and in the authenticity necessary for resisting dishonorable social values. In all these examples, a high degree of integrity (Pytlik Zillig, Maul, Dienstbier, 2001) and other positive virtues are regarded as operating at optimal levels of well-being.

Consistent with this, Handelsman, Knapp, and Gottlieb (2009) urged greater attention to what they called *positive ethics*—an outlook that encourages us to strive for our highest ideals. An element of positive ethics involves values' clarification and virtue ethics. These ask us to examine closely what we really believe and to ask ourselves: "Who should I be?" They quoted Pipes et al., (2005) who stated, "Virtue ethics ... suggests that the kind of person someone is (in some total sense) drives what the person does and how the person thinks in the professional and personal realm" (Handelsman, Knapp, and Gottlieb, 2009, p. 109). They also suggested techniques such as an "ethics autobiography" and a "morality genogram" to help people clarify through writing and reflection their most important personal values and virtues.

Last, all perspectives concur that *positive interpersonal relationships* are found at the highest levels of personality development. Interestingly, this state is usually attained within a small group of very close friends rather than through a multitude of social contacts. All perspectives also agree that positive relationships are found among people from many walks of life, social classes, and intellectual backgrounds, in keeping with the concept that all people possess intrinsic dignity.

YOUR OWN INNER HERO

This chapter has presented a variety of theories regarding optimal well-being. At the outset, we stated that personal growth requires choices about what particular type of person you would like to become. One of the fallacies that can accompany "developing your full potential" or "finding your true self" is that each of us has a unique optimal personality hidden inside that must be released like a butterfly waiting to emerge fully formed from its chrysalis. Indeed, while the *true self* refers to a more open and honest understanding of our inner life, that understanding must develop and deepen over time—and through this process, we fulfill our potential. However, growth never occurs in a vacuum, so we must choose the kind of person we wish to become. So, how does one choose what direction to take? How does one find what goals fit with one's true self?

One way to make this choice is to become familiar with the various theories on optimal well-being. This chapter has provided a brief introduction to the main perspectives in Western psychology. Another approach is to think about the types of people you admire and respect. That is, who are your heroes? Which people inspire you to be a better person—those who embody the kinds of qualities you would like to develop? Recently, Phillip Zimbardo created *The Hero Project* as a way to help people explore and encourage their inner heroes (see Learning Tools section below). The purpose of Zimbardo's project is to develop and promulgate the image of heroes as basically ordinary, everyday people who are motivated to act on behalf of others or for a higher moral cause. Of course, heroism can be more personal and focus on developing one's own best, most ethical, compassionate, and courageous self.

Lawrence Walker and Karl Henning (2004) refined this idea by noting that our conceptions of "moral excellence" can be divided into three major types of exemplars: the brave, the just, and the caring. When we uphold *brave* people as our heroes we admire their courage, self-sacrifice, and ability to face danger. Exemplars of the *just* hero are those who are fair to all, truthful, principled, and seek the common good. The *caring* exemplar is a person who is compassionate, sympathetic, altruistic, and loving. Making choices about what kind of person you would like to be, or which personality traits express your unique potential, often involves an initial choice among these three types of exemplars. Each expresses a different set of strengths and virtues and each requires a different set of challenges for its development. From an applied perspective, one study found that just thinking about these exemplars helped to foster related behaviors (Osswald et al., 2006).

Therefore, when we think about developing our "best possible self" it helps to consider role models, ideals, or heroes who can serve as examples of where we would like to travel on life's journey. Note that this chapter has covered several major theories of optimal well-being in Western psychology, but not all (see Schultz, 1977). For instance, Karen Horney (1942, 1950) was influential in the psychology of women and created a method of self-realization and personal growth that did not require a psychotherapist. Jane Loevinger's (1966, 1976) theory of ego development described how the ego, or "master personality trait," develops over a lifetime. Her theory also postulated higher levels of ego development similar to self-actualization. Finally, several religious and spiritual perspectives also speak to ideals of optimal personality. We examine some of these in the next chapter.

SUMMARY

This chapter has highlighted several theories of optimal personality development, described as more detailed, specific types of flourishing. The first we addressed was wisdom, which has been viewed as a developmental process, a type of excellence, or the "master virtue." We discussed early psychodynamic theories that posited styles of self-realization. The emphasis on authenticity in existentialism lends focus to the "true self" by integrating both the joys and sorrows of life. The humanistic perspective values openness to experience, authenticity, and self-actualization. The chapter concluded with a short discussion on choosing your own path to optimal personality and finding your personal heroes.

NOTES

1. The quote is from Marianne Williamson (1996). It is often wrongly attributed to Nelson Mandela.
2. The dates 1959–2008 are not a misprint. Julius Seeman began working on his ideas in the early 1950s with Carl Rogers at the University of Chicago. The first formal presentation of his theory was in 1959. He continued to work on his theory of personality integration and publish until his death in 2010. He acted as major professor to one of the authors (W.C.) during the author's doctoral program.

LEARNING TOOLS

Key Terms and Ideas

practical wisdom	productive orientation	authenticity	self-actualization
social interest	self-transcendent person	fully functioning person	being needs or B-needs

Books

Fromm, E. (1994). *The art of being.* NY: Continuum. Presents Fromm's basic thinking about optimal personality development. *(popular)*

Maslow, A. (1999). *Toward a psychology of being* (3rd ed.) (R. Lowry, Ed.). NY: John Wiley. (Original work published 1962, 1968) Maslow's best introduction to what he meant by self-actualization. *(popular)*

Rogers, C. (1961). *On becoming a person.* Boston: Houghton-Mifflin. Rogers' best introduction to his ideas on optimal well-being. *(popular)*

Schwartz, B. & Sharpe, K. (2010). *Practical wisdom: The right way to do the right thing.* NY: Riverhead. A contemporary exploration of wisdom from an Aristotelian perspective. *(popular)*

Zuckerman, A. (2008). *Wisdom: The greatest gift one generation can give to another.* Fifty "wisdom keepers" give their thoughts on what's really important. In addition, there are more focused volumes on love, life, and peace. *(popular)*

On the Web

http://www.youtube.com/watch?v=3BB41MLgoWk Comments from "wisdom keepers" found in Zukerman's book on wisdom.

http://www.selfgrowth.com Links to several resources on self-improvement and personal growth.

http://www.ahpweb.org/index.html The Association for Humanistic Psychology.

http://www.lucifereffect.com/heroism-signup.htm Zimbardo's Hero Project.

Personal Explorations

1. The psychology of wisdom is a growing specialty of positive psychology. Interview three people over the age of 60 in order to gain more information about wisdom. These can include family members, family friends, clergy, and former teachers. Your questions should include the following: (a) In your view, what exactly is wisdom? (b) Do people usually become wiser as they get older? Why or why not? (c) How do people acquire wisdom? (d) Is wisdom the same thing as intelligence? That is, are smart people necessarily wise? (e) Finally, what advice would you give to someone in his or her twenties who wants to gain more wisdom?

2. Think back over the course of your life and identify two people whom you consider to be highly self-actualizing according to Maslow's viewpoint. By definition, these are individuals who: (1) do not exhibit major pathology such as depression or anxiety; and (2) are motivated by higher needs, such as the needs for creativity, aesthetics, knowledge, and for making the world a better place. They also have frequent peak experiences—that is, moments of great happiness and fulfillment. (a) Describe each person in a couple of paragraphs, focusing on the behaviors that you associate with self-actualization. (b) Is either person an inspiring role model for you? If so, how?

Chapter 10

Religion, Spirituality, and Well-Being

> I think that the very purpose of life is to seek happiness. That is clear. Whether
> one believes in religion or not ... we are all seeking something better in life.
> So, I think, the very motion of our life is toward happiness.
>
> HIS HOLINESS THE 14TH DALAI LAMA (1998)

The term *spirituality* refers to a personal or group search for the sacred in life. *Religion* refers to a search for the sacred within a traditional context such as a formal religious institution (George, Larson, Koenig, & McCullough, 2000; Paloutzian & Park, 2005). Therefore, spirituality is the more inclusive term for a search for the sacred, whereas religion refers to a search grounded specifically in institutional forms. Both encompass a need to relate to something greater than oneself and often require a degree of self-transcendence (James & Samuels, 1999). Note that transcendence can take two forms (Hood, 2005). *Vertical transcendence* entails fostering a relationship with a spiritual being who is "higher" or "greater" than oneself, such as the Judeo-Christian conception of God. *Horizontal transcendence* involves forming a relationship with a force that is more immanent in the world and is less often viewed as a spiritual being. For instance, in Taoism the force that underlies and sustains the natural order of the universe is called *the Tao*.

It is interesting to note that although spirituality and religion can be distinguished, most people consider themselves both religious and spiritual. However, about 25%–30% of the U.S. population identifies itself as spiritual but not religious (Hood, 2005). In addition, affiliation with traditional faiths has been declining for young Americans. As reported recently by the Pew Forum (2011), 25% of Americans aged 18–29 say they are not affiliated with any specific religion. By comparison, only about half as many young American adults were unaffiliated in the 1970s and 1980s.

RELIGION AND SUBJECTIVE WELL-BEING

A substantial number of studies have examined how religiousness and spirituality impact well-being (Chamberlain & Hall, 2000; Koenig, 1998; Miller & Kelley, 2005; Paloutzian & Park, 2005; Plante & Sherman, 2001). Research has been relatively consistent in finding that greater religiousness is significantly related to better mental health and higher subjective well-being. That is, people who are more religious in their behavior show better emotional well-being and lower rates of delinquency, alcoholism, drug abuse, and other social problems (Donahue & Benson, 1995). In terms of subjective well-being, David Myers (2008) stated that "in survey after survey, actively religious people have reported markedly greater happiness and somewhat greater life satisfaction than their irreligious counterparts" (p. 324). Indeed, Peacock and Paloma (1999) found that one's perceived closeness to God was the single biggest predictor of life satisfaction across all age ranges. Particularly relevant to positive psychology are studies that have found that religious or spiritual practices can increase positive emotional states such as joy, hope, optimism, and compassion, as well as foster positive virtues such as self-control (for example, Ciarrocchi, Dy-Liaacco, & Deneke, 2008; Francis & Bolger, 1997; Lewis & Maltby, 1995; Mathews–Treadway, 1996). Negative emotional states, such as fear, sadness, or anger, may also be reduced (Oman & Thoresen, 2005). Religious beliefs can also decrease death anxiety (Harding et al., 2005). It is possible that certain positive emotions can enhance religiousness (Saroglou, Buxant, & Tilquin, 2008). For example, Seligman (2002) reported a study finding by Sheena Iyengar that increased well-being brought about by greater religiousness was entirely accounted for by increased hope.

Gender, ethnicity, and age are important variables mediating the relationship between well-being and religion. For instance, women tend to exhibit stronger relationships between well-being and religiousness than men do. In terms of race, African-Americans also manifest stronger relationships between well-being and religiousness than do whites (Argyle, 1999). Older persons tend to show stronger relationships between religiousness and well-being (McFadden, 2005). Indeed, Okun and Stock (1987) found that religiousness and good health were the two best predictors of psychological well-being among older adults. For those in this same age range, belief in life after death has been highly correlated with a belief that their current life was exciting (Steinitz, 1980). Poloma and Pendleton (1990) found that when well-being was defined as having a sense of meaning and purpose in life, the relationship between well-being and religious sense was strengthened.

It is important to know that stronger, more statistically significant correlations are usually based on actual religious behavior rather than on religious attitudes (Witter, Stock, Okun, & Haring, 1985). Indeed, the biggest predictor of the relationship between religiousness and well-being is "public religious participation" or active involvement in religious activities (George et al., 2000). That is, people who actually *do* something related to religious faith (for example, attend church, pray) report greater well-being than those who simply hold pro-religious attitudes.

Although an association between religion and subjective well-being is found frequently, the causal links are unclear. In some cases, strong and fervent religious belief is associated with better well-being, but in other studies moderate religiousness is a better predictor (Miler & Kelly, 2005). Partially this is because religion is a very complex area of life. For instance, studies have also found that committed atheists have just as much resilience to depression as do committed religious believers (for example, Riley, Best, & Charlton, 2005). This finding suggests that allegiance to a belief system is the core psychological process involved.

Religion and Health

A large number of studies and meta-analyses have found strong and consistent evidence of an association between religiousness and better physical health. That is, people who report greater religiousness tend to have fewer illnesses, lower rates for cancer and heart attacks, recover more quickly from illness or surgery, and have a greater tolerance for pain (George et al., 2000). One major study found that people who are more religious live an average of seven years longer than those who are less religious. Even after adjusting for physical risk factors, religious persons show a 25% reduction in mortality (see Oman & Thoresen, 2005). The physiological factors responsible for better health include lower blood pressure, better immune system functioning, and reduced stress and worry. Religious faith also strongly contributes to "learned hardiness," or a sense of hardiness in people who have coped with multiple health challenges (McFadden, 2005). Other factors that contribute to the improved health of strongly religious people are healthier lifestyles; more positive emotions, better social support, greater forgiveness, more volunteer service to others, and greater use of meditation and prayer (Oman & Thoresen, 2005). The ability of religion to provide a sense of meaning, purpose, and coherence is possibly the *most important* predictor of improved health status (George et al., 2000). However, many of these effects are stronger for women than for men. And again, the strongest predictor of health and longevity is active religious participation—that is, whether or not people attend religious services.

In view of these positive findings, one might ask whether religiousness has any negative consequences for physical or mental health. When examining representative samples of people, George et al., (2000) found no evidence that religiousness can be detrimental; however, a proclivity to neglect medical services because of one's religious beliefs can certainly be detrimental. For example, there are higher rates of childhood deaths among families that favor faith healing over standard medical practices (Asser & Swan, 1998), and African-Americans who hold very strong beliefs in the curative power of prayer tend to exercise less frequently and be less interested in taking responsibility for their personal health care (Klonoff & Landrine, 1996). Indeed, African-Americans also hold significantly stronger beliefs in the curative power of prayer than do other ethnic groups (Klonoff & Landrine, 1996). In this last instance, such faith seems to induce people to believe they need not be careful about their health.

Prayer and Well-Being

Among the earliest psychologists to investigate prayer was William James, who called it "the very soul and essence of religion" (1902/1958, p. 505). Prayer was certainly an important feature of American religious life in James' era over a century ago, and it continues to be so. Fully 92% of adult Americans believe in God (U.S. Religious Landscape Survey, 2008), nearly 90% pray (Poloma & Gallup, 1991), and 72% pray on a daily basis (Gallup Report, 1993). For millennia, the world's major religions have emphasized the significance of prayer for the spiritual well-being of adults and even children. Yet the psychology of prayer has been almost completely unexplored until quite recently. Of course, scientific inquiry is concerned with the impact of prayer upon an individual's functioning, not its efficacy in influencing wider events.

The act of praying is not a uniform behavior, for researchers have identified six different types of prayer, each with its own potentially unique and beneficial experiential qualities. These encompass prayers of *adoration*, focused on the worship of God without any reference to one's circumstances, needs, or desires. Prayers of *thanksgiving* are expressions of gratitude toward God, made in reference to specific positive life experiences. *Petitionary* prayers, or those of *supplication,* are requests for divine intervention in specific life events concerning one's self or others, and prayers of *confession* involve one's admission of negative behavior and request for God's forgiveness. Finally, prayers of *reception* convey a passive or contemplative openness to divine wisdom or guidance, and *obligatory prayers,* prevalent in Orthodox Judaism and Islam, are primarily ritualistic and repeated at fixed worship times (Whittingon & Scher, 2010). Within these six categories, the act of praying can be (1) *formalistic,* that is, reading aloud or silently from a prayer book; (2) *colloquial,* that is, speaking to God in one's own heartfelt words; or (3) *meditative,* essentially quieting the mind so as to seek God presence in one's thoughts. Historically in the theologies of Christianity, Islam, and Judaism, each of these categories of prayer has a particular role and value for daily living.

The issue of how prayer affects personal well-being is highly complex, for researchers at the outset must clearly differentiate the type and mode of prayer being studied. For scientific accuracy, they must also differentiate the effects of prayer from personality variables like dispositional optimism and gratitude. For example, it is possible that people who pray regularly are more optimistic than those who do not, so that any differences in mental health or physical wellness between these two groups are attributable to their degree of optimism and not to their frequency of prayer. Finally, it seems plausible that certain types and modes of prayer are psychologically more effective for some persons than for others. For example, *formalistic obligatory prayers* may be most beneficial for individuals with moderate subjective well-being and a strong need for order, whereas *colloquial prayers of thanksgiving* might most benefit those with high subjective well-being and a preference for emotional expressiveness. Aware of such methodological complexities, astute investigators of the psychology of prayer therefore present their findings tentatively and cautiously.

With the rise of positive psychology, researchers today are increasingly interested in the benefits of prayer for mental states. In this light, Whittington & Scher (2010) found the frequency of three types of prayer—*adoration, thanksgiving, and reception*—was positively associated with measures of well-being such as self-esteem, optimism, and meaning in life. In contrast, the other three forms of prayer had negative or null relations with well-being measures. In particular, *confessional* prayer was the most consistent negative predictor of well-being measures. If a causal relationship between prayer type and emotional functioning can be extrapolated, then the types of prayer that appear beneficial are less ego-focused and more focused on God.

Other researchers have examined the impact of prayer upon gratitude (Lambert et al., 2009) and forgiveness (Lambert et al., 2010). In an experimental study involving college students, Lambert and his colleagues (2009) found evidence that daily colloquial prayer (no specific content was presented or suggested to participants) played a causal role in promoting gratitude, an attitudinal state with clear psychological benefits. The researches conjectured that the act of daily prayer helped students to be more aware of the positive features in their own lives. In another experimental study involving prayer, Lambert and his colleagues (2010) found that college students in romantic relationships who were assigned to a prayer condition were more

willing to express forgiveness of their partners than those assigned to a nonprayer verbal activity condition. In a follow-up study relating to friendship, the act of prayer led to greater willingness to forgive and also greater selfless concern, as compared with a control condition.

Several studies have examined the relationship between prayer and health (see Plante & Sherman, 2001), finding that higher frequency of prayer is associated with such indices of health as better postoperative emotional health in cardiac patients, greater vitality and mental health, greater psychological well-being, and decreases in depression after cardiac surgery (Ai, Bolling, & Peterson, 2000; Ai, Dunkle, Peterson, & Bolling, 1998; Maltby, Lewis, & Day, 1999; Meisenhelder & Chandler, 2001). One six-year longitudinal study of older adults found that private religious activities such as prayer predicted longevity. However, prior health status did seem to make a difference in whether prayer had an impact on health. Why might prayer impact health status? Harvard psychiatrist Herbert Benson, who developed the Relaxation Response, also investigated prayer and found that prayer seems to help the immune system function better and can aid in healing (Benson, 1983; Benson & Stack, 1996). Fascinating though scientifically controversial studies have found benefits to people even when they are the recipients of prayers from others (see Oman & Thoresen, 2005).

The plethora of studies on the relationship between prayer and healing prompted one physician to write an article titled "Should Physicians Prescribe Prayer for Health?" (Marwick, 1995). His answer was a qualified "not yet." Similarly, McCullough (1995) reviewed the research on prayer and health and found that most studies had relatively serious flaws and further research was definitely needed. Science is just beginning research efforts in the area of prayer and health, so the exact mechanism responsible for this relationship currently remains quite a mystery. While the scientific evidence is being debated, however, nearly two-thirds of medical schools in the United States currently include course work that focuses on spiritual issues (Sheler, 2001).

Why is Religion Related to Well-Being?

It seems there is a small but significant and consistently reported effect of religiousness on well-being. Why would this be the case? Researchers have hypothesized that religion impacts mental and physical health because of at least six factors (see Emmons, 1999; Myers, 2008; Paloutzian & Park, 2005; Pargament, Smith, Koenig, and Perez, 1998).

(1) Religion Provides Social Support Social support is one of the strongest predictors of subjective well-being, so it seems logical that participation in religious activities within a community of like-minded individuals is a source of satisfaction (Bergan & McConatha, 2000; Myers, 2000). Religious community may be an important factor in physical health given the large impact that social support has on stress and the immune system (see chapter 6). However, unlike other forms of social support, a religiously derived sense of social support extends to what many consider the ultimate source of any supportive relationship—namely, belief in support from God.

(2) Religion Supports Healthy Lifestyles Studies have found that increased religiousness is associated with fewer health-risk behaviors. Adherents of denominations that are more likely to prohibit risky health behaviors (for example, Mormons, Seventh Day Adventists) tend to be healthier than people in other denominations (George et al., 2000). In addition, strongly religious people may be more likely to use preventive health services, such as flu shots and screenings for early detection of disease (Oman & Thoresen, 2005).

(3) Religion Promotes Personality Integration Emmons (1999) argued that religion increases a sense of well-being partially because it facilitates personality integration. He reported research that studied 50 Jesuit novices who undertook a "4-week period of secluded meditation." After the experience, they showed increased personality integration and mental health. In Emmons' view, personality integration was fostered because

an increase in one's religious commitment can help resolve conflicting goals and enable focus on what is significant in life.

(4) Religion Promotes Generativity and Altruism As we saw earlier in this book, generativity, altruism, and volunteering are all associated with greater well-being and better health—especially during middle age and later. Most religious institutions promote the value of helping others.

(5) Religion Provides Unique Coping Strategies Studies of religious-based coping have found a wide range of strategies people use to deal with stress and difficulties in life (Pargament, Ano, & Wachholtz, 2005). Religion can provide hope, offer reasons for unexpected and unwanted stressors (for example, "God gives you trials to help make you strong"), help people place their lives in a larger framework, and create renewed purpose and meaning. Religious forms of coping can also foster forgiveness and suppress negative emotions. Prayer is an obvious form of coping unique to religion.

Religious coping can be divided into positive and negative forms (Pargament, Smith, Koenig, and Perez, 1998). Positive forms of coping are dependent on positive emotions like support, compassion, and hope. Negative forms of coping involve negative emotions such as guilt and fear of retribution from God. As with prayer, it seems only the positive forms of coping have a beneficial impact on mental and physical health (Pargament, Smith, Koenig, and Perez, 1998). In addition, religious forms of coping that view an individual and God as working together to solve problems appear more beneficial than forms that regard all problems as wholly in God's hands (Quick, Nelson, Matuszek, Whittington, & Quick, 1996). However, one intriguing study found that people with terminal cancer who held the strongest religious beliefs were the ones who requested the most intensive end-of-life care (Phelps et al., 2009), suggesting they were less likely to calmly accept their mortality.

(6) Religion Provides a Sense of Meaning and Purpose You will recall from earlier chapters that a sense of meaning and purpose is related to subjective well-being. One obvious reason why people adopt religious perspectives is to gain a sense of meaning and purpose in their lives. However, religion can provide a distinctive type of meaning; it can provide *ultimate meaning* (Paloutzian & Park, 2005). This advantage is so particular to religion that the next section is devoted to meaning.

A SENSE OF MEANING AND PURPOSE IN LIFE

Park and Folkman (1997) defined meaning as simply "perceptions of significance" (p. 116). They argued that what meaning does for people is give life significance; more than almost any other institution, religion offers a larger perspective on human life and gives explanations for why unexpected events happen. Particularly when life is difficult, religion provides solace and hope.

A problem that plagues research on meaning is that the concept itself is extremely broad and has been defined in different ways by different researchers (see Steger, 2009). The type of meaning most relevant to our discussion of religion and spirituality is *cosmic meaning* (Yalom, 1980), or *global meaning* (Park, 2011). This type of meaning addresses questions about whether "life in general, or at least human life, fits into some overall coherent pattern" (Yalom, 1980, p. 423). Cosmic meaning is what people search for when they need to believe that some design or order exists in the universe. Park and Folkman (1997) identified such meaning as a search for enduring beliefs, valued goals, and a sense of order and coherence for existence. In addition, cosmic meaning "centers on what is perceived to be sacred" (Paloutzian & Park, 2005, p. 33). The type of meaning that religion can provide establishes a connection to "concepts of God, higher powers, transcendent beings, or other aspects of life that have been sanctified" (Paloutzian & Park, 2005,

p. 34). This process is so powerful that almost any animate or inanimate object can be seen as sacred. Obvious candidates are religious buildings such as churches and synagogues, but small objects such as crucifixes or Judaic menorahs can also be regarded as having sacred power, as do Native American "power spots" in the southwestern United States and groves of oak trees for Druids. Cosmic meaning can also provide a way to connect with humanity through belief in the interconnectedness of all life.

Ways to Create Meaning

Most researchers who have studied meaning believe that people must create a sense of meaning that is personal and based on their own experience. That is, it is not personally empowering to adopt someone else's criterion of meaning. Park (2011) suggested that making life meaningful entails (1) feeling connected to something outside or larger than one's self; (2) searching for greater depth and significance in one's experience; or (3) adapting to life events that challenge one's current sense of meaning. This last aspect of meaning-making implies a dynamic understanding of life based on current experiences, adjusting and refining one's sense of meaning over a lifetime (see Figure 10.1). Although meaning can be created in many ways, the following six criteria offer more common avenues for greater meaning:

(1) Greater Harmony, Coherence, and Congruence Greater meaning is created when there is greater harmony, coherence, and congruence among the various aspects of our self-identity and our goals in life (Little, 1989; McGregor & Little, 1998). As mentioned before, a religious attitude can pull disparate elements of life into a consistent direction. Park and Folkman (1997) asserted that creating meaning is a process of reducing the discrepancy between our current situation and our global meaning. Often this process is accomplished by renewing a sense of control, predictability, and order as well as by restoring a belief that benevolence, justice, and fairness exist in some way in both humanity and in the cosmos.

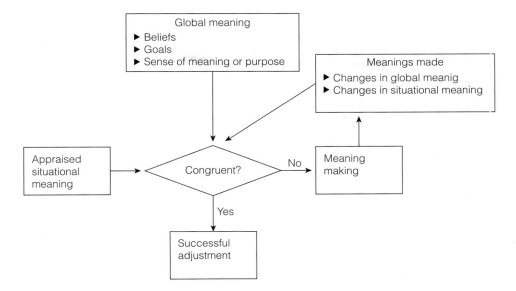

FIGURE 10.1   Model of Meaning Making

(2) Be of Service to Others, or Dedicate Oneself to a Worthy Cause By taking time to help others, we can feel we are contributing to the general welfare and so in some way making a difference in the world, an attitude at the core of a sense of meaning. Feeling that one's life is purposeful often means feeling the world is a different place because one is in it. A similar way to create a sense of meaning and purpose is to dedicate oneself to a worthy cause larger than the individual.

(3) Creativity The creation of something new gives life significance, enabling us to experience life in a different way. Sometimes the creation outlives the creator. Yalom (1980) observed that Beethoven was quite explicit that music and creativity were the only things that kept him from suicide. Scientific creativity is also a source of meaning and purpose, giving new ideas to the world. Further, creativity can be understood in terms of self-discovery, or creating a new self-identity.

(4) Live life as Fully and as Deeply as Possible For some people, finding a sense of meaning involves an effort to live one's life as fully and as deeply as

possible (Yalom, 1980). Note this does not refer to an obsessive seeking of pleasure and avoidance of pain, for that approach usually results in unhappiness and disillusionment. Instead, a desire to experience life fully can provide a sense of active participation and involvement. It is similar to the openness to experience emphasized by Rogers and Maslow (see chapter 9) and to Cantor and Sanderson's (1999) theory on active participation in living a full life.

(5) Suffering As we saw earlier, existential psychotherapist Viktor Frankl (1963) argued that our forbearance of suffering is a primary determinant in experiencing meaning in life. Through undergoing difficulties, people are obliged to re-evaluate their lives and so possibly transform themselves. Emmons (1999) commented that most of the world's major religions regard suffering as a potential stimulus of spiritual growth. Similarly, Tedeschi and Calhoun (1995) noted that suffering brings three potential benefits: (1) a possibility of increased self-confidence; (2) opportunities for enhanced interpersonal relationships; and (3) avenues for changing one's philosophy of life or style of creating meaning.

(6) Religious Experiences Another way to increase a sense of meaning in life is through according profound experiences a religious or spiritual interpretation. Unfortunately, remarked George, Larson, Koenig, and McCullough (2000), science knows "almost nothing about the spiritual experience itself.... Spiritual experience is the most ignored dimension of spirituality" (pp. 112–113). Next, we turn to emotions often associated with religion that have been important to positive psychology. In a later section in this chapter, we focus on religious experiences.

THE SACRED EMOTIONS

Most people know that religion and spirituality entail more than philosophical or intellectual statements of belief. Generally, religious sentiments involve an emotional component as well as behavioral responses consistent with those emotions. Many would argue that the heart of religion and spirituality consists of emotional experiences, which deepen a person's faith through core feelings and expression. For this reason, Emmons (2005) described these emotions as "sacred emotions."

Of course, most of these emotions are also expressed in secular contexts with no specific religious or spiritual connotation. But in all cases, these emotions create positive connections among people and allow us to express our highest values and potential.

Gratitude and Appreciation

What are you most thankful for in your life? How often do you feel grateful, and how easy is it for you to express gratitude? Not surprisingly, such questions have become vital in positive psychology, for expressions of gratitude have enjoyed a long past in human history and in cultures throughout the world, honored as fundamental aspects of both individual personality and social life. For example, gratitude is a cherished human disposition in Buddhist, Christian, Hindu, Jewish, and Muslim religious thought, fostered for centuries through prayer and service to others. As the ancient Greek philosopher Cicero asserted, "Gratitude is not only the greatest of virtues, but the parent of all the others" (cited in Emmons & Shelton, 2001, p. 459).

Yet until recently psychology had remarkably little to say about this trait. Undoubtedly, this reflects the meager attention given to positive

© Randy Glasbergen.
www.glasbergen.com

"I'm trying to develop an 'attitude of gratitude' but the best I can muster is a 'sentiment of resentment'."

human traits in general by traditional psychology. A significant exception was Abraham Maslow, who during the 1960s became convinced, based on his studies of self-actualizing persons, that the abilities to experience and express gratitude are two key signs of emotional health. He also suggested specific experimental techniques for nurturing gratitude (Hoffman, 1996), such as recalling the joys of one's life and imagining that one had only a short time left on earth. Maslow viewed the ancient adage to "count your blessings" as still highly relevant to modern men and women.

The rise of positive psychology has spurred research on gratitude, for as Wood et al., (2008) noted, "Gratitude is perhaps the quintessential positive psychological trait, as it involves a life orientation toward the positive in the world. This positive orientation can be contrasted, for example, with the depressive orientations toward the negative in the self, world, and future" (pp. 854–855). Emmons (2005) has described gratitude as "an emotional response to a gift. It is the appreciation felt after one has been the beneficiary of an altruistic act" (p. 238). In fact, studies have found that grateful people tend to be happy people (Watkins, Van Gelder, & Frias, 2009; Wood, Froh, & Geraghty, 2010). Thus from the outset in launching positive psychology, Seligman and his colleagues (Peterson & Seligman, 2004; Seligman, 2002; Seligman et al., 2005) have highlighted the importance of gratitude in healthy personality functioning and have also developed interventions for nurturing it (see Watkins, Van Gelder, & Frias, 2009). For example, Seligman et al., (2005) recommended a "gratitude visit," in which an individual is given one week to write and then deliver in person a letter of gratitude to someone who had been especially kindly.

Though investigators remain divided as to whether gratitude is primarily an emotion or an attitude, research has clearly indicated its importance in contributing to well-being, such as by increasing perceived social support and lowering stress and depression (Emmons & McCullough, 2003; Wood et al., 2008). There is growing evidence, too, that gratitude functions to maintain and enhance social relationships, including friendships and romantic involvements (Algoe, 2010; Algoe, Haidt, & Gable, 2008). In terms of positive emotions, gratitude has been related to greater life satisfaction, optimism, and both more positive and less negative emotionality (Emmons & Mishra, 2011). Reflecting these findings, marriage and family therapists are increasingly recommending the practice of expressing gratitude to loved ones on a daily basis, as a means to strengthen emotional closeness and intimacy.

Can gratitude be nurtured? Recent experiments have shown that practicing grateful thinking on a regular basis can indeed improve positive emotionality and other measures of well-being (Emmons & McCullough, 2003; Lyubomirsky, Tkach, & Sheldon, 2004). For example, Emmons & McCullough (2003) in three experiments instructed participants to engage in self-guided exercises of "counting your blessings" either on a weekly basis for ten weeks or on a daily basis for two or three weeks. As compared with control participants who focused their attention on routine or negative events during the intervention, those in the gratitude group reported higher positive emotion and physical well-being.

Lyubomirsky et al., (2005) similarly found that students who expressed gratitude once a week (but not three times a week) showed increased well-being after the intervention. Sheldon and Lyubomirsky (2006) found that a four-week gratitude program was effective in lowering negative emotionality. Algoe and Haidt (2009) found that gratitude induced a desire to give back to others, observing that "typically, these grateful sentiments are focused toward the benefactor, but can be redirected under certain circumstances" (p. 122). In other words, our feelings of gratitude can expand outward and truly benefit the world.

Appreciation is a response to the world that is similar to gratitude. Being appreciative allows us to notice people and life experiences and to acknowledge their value and importance. Like gratitude, appreciation allows us to perceive experiences as a gift. Adler and Fagley (2005) viewed appreciation as a combination of many emotions discussed so far, including awe and gratitude. They found that people who were more appreciative also felt more positive emotions, greater life satisfaction, and fewer negative emotions—this was after controlling for the effects of optimism, spirituality, and emotional self-awareness. They believed that greater appreciation is one of the more effective means of increasing positive relationships and creating a sense of meaning.

Forgiveness

Forgiveness has been of interest to psychologists, theologians, and others for some time (see McCullough et al., 2009). Since abuses of various kinds are all-too-commonplace, Archbishop Desmond Tutu has said that "forgiveness is an absolute necessity for continued human existence" (quoted in Enright & North, 1998, p. xiii). Without an ability to forgive, certain emotions such as anger, resentment, and hurt can consume lives and create ever-increasing cycles of hostility and desire for revenge. McCullough (2000) noted that forgiveness allows us to move beyond desire for revenge and to reinstitute social ties. Emmons (2005) viewed forgiveness as one of the more useful ways to regulate negative emotions.

Like other psychological traits, a disposition to forgive varies from person to person. Some people are able to let go of a painful hurt or injustice easily, whereas others keep a grudge for years or actively seek revenge. Undoubtedly you know people in each category. What accounts for such individual differences? At present, research has examined both gender and age as relevant variables, though it should be noted that most studies assess reactions to hypothetical situations rather than to real-life events like personal betrayal or deception.

Investigations have revealed that women are more likely to forgive than men due to greater empathy and less concern with vengeance (Exline

et al., 2008; McCullough, Pargament, & Thoresen, 2000). However, nuances definitely exist in this domain. For example, in a series of seven forgiveness-related studies conducted with college students over several years, Exline and her associates (2008) found to their surprise that men became more forgiving when asked to recall a similar offense of their own, but the effect was minimal for women. This seemingly puzzling result was explained by a suggestion that women begin with a lower disposition to vengeance than men because of early socialization.

As for the impact of age, investigators have consistently found that children and adolescents are less willing to forgive than adults, and that older adults are the most willing to do so of all age groups through the lifespan (Allemand, 2008; Girard & Mullet, 1997; Subkoviak, 1995). For example, Subkoviak and his associates (1995) found that college students were less likely to forgive than their middle-aged parents of the same gender. Why should our tendency to forgive increase with chronological age? Certainly, the stereotype is prevalent of the elderly as stubborn and fixated on the past. According to Allemand (2008), perspective plays a crucial role in this effect of age. That is, older persons, who have a shorter personal time horizon, tend to "let bygones be bygones" out of greater awareness of life's brevity and fragility. Adolescents and young adults, who possess a longer personal time horizon, are less able to see events in broader perspective.

For several years, Robert Enright and his colleagues have studied forgiveness. Following the suggestions of Joanna North, they defined forgiveness as "a willingness to abandon one's right to resentment, negative judgment, and indifferent behavior toward one who unjustly injured us, while fostering the underserved qualities of compassion, generosity, and even love toward him or her" (Enright, Freedman, & Rique, 1998, pp. 46–47). They noted that this definition includes emotional (overcoming resentment), cognitive (changing negative judgments), and behavioral (ending indifference) aspects. In general, their definition suggests that forgiveness means overcoming the hurt, resentment, and aggression, whether minor or severe, that accompany being the target of abuse. Enright and colleagues as well as McCullough (2000) have also been quick to discuss what forgiveness is *not*—that is, it is *not* simply tolerating or forgetting an injustice; it is *not* using denial or suppression; it is *not* forgetting, denying, or minimizing a hurt; and it is *not* condoning what was done. Forgiveness entails recognizing and acknowledging that a transgression occurred against us and finding ways to move beyond it. True forgiveness is about breaking free from both the wrong done to us and from the person who committed the wrong.

Some readers may be asking, "Why should we even bother?" The answer lies in the fact that in the long run anger, resentment, and obsessive rumination about an event only serve to hurt *us*. Forgiveness is a gift we give ourselves. However, Enright cogently remarked that forgiveness should also increase one's sense of shared humanity with a larger community. Forgiveness is an opportunity to use one's painful experiences in order to deepen a connection with others and to increase one's sense of compassion.

McCullough (2000) observed that an ability to forgive promotes well-being, primarily by fostering healthy and supportive interpersonal relationships. In addition, forgiveness helps a person modulate a hostility linked to poor health outcomes. For example, one study found that people able to forgive someone from their past enjoyed better health including lower blood pressure and muscle tension (McCullough, Bono, & Root, 2005).

Four Phases of Forgiveness Enright, Freedman, and Rique (1998) proposed a four-phase model of the steps involved in forgiving. Phase one is the *uncovering phase*. At this point, people explore how their chronic holding onto resentment, anger, or hate has a negative impact on their own lives. The *decision phase* involves making a choice to try and forgive. In the *work phase* one tries to forgive by reframing an incident, accepting its hurt, and trying to gain an empathic understanding of why the

offender acted as he or she did. Phase four is the *deepening phase*, in which one tries to gain a deeper sense of meaning as a result of an injury. This can encompass a recognition of universality with others who have experienced deep hurts, that one is not alone. Research with incest survivors found that those who completed a forgiveness education program gained in an ability to forgive and to hope while decreasing their scores on anxiety and depression (Enright, Freedman, & Rique, 1998).

Self-Forgiveness. Although the necessity to forgive other people for their transgressions is very important, the capacity to forgive ourselves is arguably more crucial for well-being. In chapter 6 we examined how vital it was to deal with regrets in healthy ways. If our recriminations are for harmful actions we committed, then we must forgive ourselves as well as make amends to another person. Self-forgiveness is a process of letting go of resentment toward oneself for a transgression (Wohl, DeShea & Wahkinney, 2009).). We must take responsibility for our behavior, then let go of the self-absorption, self-criticism, and rumination that keep us stuck with guilt and self-reproach. Then we can begin to make amends in some way that helps us and others to move forward with life.

Compassion and Empathy

A common description of great religious figures finds them *compassionate*. Indeed, it is hard to imagine such a person who lacks this crucial quality. Compassion is grounded in an ability to connect deeply with others, especially with their suffering (Cassell, 2009). As such, an ability to empathize with others and to identify with their experiences is central to compassion. In addition,

Mother Teresa

emotional identification with others lends itself to a desire to be of service. Therefore, compassion, empathy, and altruism often go together (Batson, Ahmad, & Lisher, 2009). Note that this complex emotional experience requires a person to in some way feel the suffering of another. However, in order that one's compassion be of help to another, empathy for another's pain must be managed rather than allowed to overwhelm us. Somewhat paradoxically, compassion and empathy toward others can help people feel better about themselves. People with high degrees of empathy have also reported more satisfaction with life and more positive relationships (Grühn et al., 2008).

In the Buddhist tradition, two hallmarks of optimal well-being are compassion and wisdom. To develop compassion, Buddhist monks for many years have practiced *metta*, or lovingkindness meditation. This is designed to generate positive emotions such as compassion, love, generosity, and tolerance. Recently, several studies examining lovingkindness meditation have found it can increase positive emotions, build personal resources (Fredrickson et al., 2008), increase social connectedness (Hutcherson, Seppela, & Gross, 2008), and even improve the negative symptoms of schizophrenia (Johnson et al., 2009). Brain imaging of highly experienced Tibetan Buddhist monks practicing lovingkindness meditation indicates significant alterations in brain functioning (Lutz et al., 2008). Even novice meditators can gain substantial benefits from this practice.

Self-Compassion   The benefits of altruism are obvious in close relationships. But can you be compassionate toward yourself? Ironically, many people find it very difficult to treat themselves with the same understanding, forgiveness, and compassion they give their friends and family. It is as if they believe that compassion is fine for others, but they themselves require tough self-reproach in order to get motivated or to make changes in their lives. Studying self-compassion, Kristin Neff (2003, 2011) found that being kindly toward oneself is a better way to change one's

behavior than through self-criticism. For instance, one study indicated that women who were more self-compassionate were able to eat healthier and stay with healthy dieting (Adams & Leary, 2007). More broadly, Neff's research has suggested that people who are more self-compassionate tend to be happier, more optimistic, more curious, wiser, and less neurotic (Neff, Rude, & Kirkpatrick, 2007). In addition, they feel more positive emotions and fewer negative emotions. Other studies have found that people who are more self-compassionate are less depressed, worried, and anxious (Van Dam et al., 2011). Finally, increased self-compassion might be the primary reason that mindfulness therapies help people improve their lives (Kuyke et al., 2010; Van Dam et al., 2011). Based on Neff's research, the classic maxim that *when the going gets tough, the tough get going* should be changed to *when the going gets tough, the self-compassionate get going.*

An important footnote to this discussion concerns empathy. Recent surveys have found that today's college students score about 40% lower in empathy than students did 20–30 years ago (Konrath, O'Brian, & Hsing, 2011). This startling statistic should be of concern to everyone. The conclusion was based on a meta-analysis of 72 studies involving 14,000 students. The researchers were not sure why empathy dropped so dramatically but suspected decreased face-to-face contacts due to the Internet and increased economic competitiveness today.

Humility

As we found true for the trait of compassion, it is hard to imagine a great religious leader who does not show humility. Being humble involves a relative lack of self-focus and self-preoccupation, an ability to acknowledge mistakes, openness to other opinions and ideas, and an appreciation of the many different ways people contribute to the world (Exline, 2008, Tangney, 2009). True humility does not mean being passive or nonassertive, is based neither in self-deprecation nor low self-esteem, and is not simple modesty. True humility requires strength to forget the self, or to "quiet the ego," in order to learn, to observe, to appreciate, and to connect with others and with a larger meaning in life (see Leary & Guadagno, 2011).

Humility has not been studied as extensively as other sacred emotions. However, research does support the role of humility in positive behavior and positive emotionality. For instance, one study found that greater humility is related to higher self-esteem, gratitude, forgiveness, spirituality, and better health (Rowatt et al., 2006). Another study found that humble people respond better to criticism by taking responsibility for their problems and increasing their efforts to improve their problems (Zell, 2008). Humility seems related to forgiveness and enhances social relationships. Being humble is important for living a life of quiet joy, satisfaction, wisdom, and contentment (this last is another understudied sacred emotion).

RELIGIOUS EXPERIENCES

Religious experiences tend to be brief moments when we feel connected to something larger than ourselves. During these mysterious moments, we feel more whole or complete and believe some hidden truth has been revealed to us, even if we are given merely a glimpse of something profoundly important and meaningful. The word **epiphany** derives from the Greek word for "manifestation" and refers to moments of sudden realization or comprehension of a larger meaning. Religious experiences and the emotions that accompany these can be intensely positive, such as profound spiritual illuminations; deeply calming and contemplative, such as providing comfort and security when entering a religious building; and can serve to regulate other emotions less conducive to spirituality (Emmons, 2005). **Transcendent experiences** are religious or spiritual experiences that are often quite dramatic and leave people feeling they have entered a higher state of consciousness. The depth and intensity of the

experience often provide people with an emotional confirmation that a spiritual reality is alive in this world.

Surveys have found that religious or transcendent experiences occur relatively frequently. Kennedy, Kanthamani, and Palmer (1994) found that 59% of U.S. participants reported either psychic or transcendent experiences. In a famous U.S. survey, Greely and McCready (1975) found that 40% answered yes when asked, "Have you ever had the feeling of being very close to a powerful spiritual force that seemed to lift you out of yourself?"

The emotional consequences of religious or transcendent experiences can be extremely positive (see Hood, 2005; Nobel, 1987). It is common among those who have undergone a profound transcendent experience to say that it was the most meaningful occasion of their life. Leak, DeNeve, and Greteman (2007) found that people who oriented their goals around spiritual and self-transcendent strivings reported more positive emotions; higher subjective well-being, better physical health, more concern for others, as well as additional positive indicators of higher well-being.

Religious experiences that occur fairly often can be of moderate rather than powerful intensity. In such instances, the experience itself may be quite common (such as seeing a dazzling sunset), but interpreted in a religious or spiritual fashion; as with sacred emotions, these experiences may also be given a secular interpretation. Conversely, religious experiences can occur quite infrequently but be so profound that they transform a person's life forever. Such experiences, such as sensing a divine presence guiding one's life, may be quite unique and have few counterparts in a person's normal, everyday routine.

Elation and Awe

A relatively common experience for most people involves witnessing unsolicited acts of kindness, charity, or compassion. For many persons, just viewing these acts can produce a variety of positive emotions. Jonathan Haidt (2000) studied similar experiences of momentary joy that he termed

elation, describing these as our responses to "acts of moral beauty."

To understand what Haidt was referring to, think of a time when you witnessed a spontaneous act of compassion, helping, or truly selfless giving. Most people report a warm feeling in their chest, a sensation of expansion in their heart, an increased desire to help, and a sense of connection with others. Interestingly, our reactions to these acts of charity and kindness may be innate. In his research, Haidt found that simply viewing Mother Teresa's acts of compassion on film was sufficient to produce such feelings of elation. He even observed these effects among seven-year-old to eleven-year-old children—an outcome again suggesting an innate basis for feelings of elation.

Haidt (2000) found that the most common reactions to witnessing compassionate acts were desires to help other people, resolutions to become a better person, increased needs to affiliate with other people, and increased feelings of love, compassion, and overall well-being. He theorized that such experiences have the potential to be life-altering events: For some people, moments of elation are so powerful that they reorient their lives in significant ways.

Similarly, Dasher Keltner (2000) and Jonathan Haidt (Keltner & Haidt, 2003) have written about an experience of **awe**, or "deep appreciative wonder" at the immensity, beauty, and complexity of a phenomenon that takes on universal significance. Keltner found that such experiences are stimulated by nature, art, and observations of human excellence. Paradoxically, one is left diminished contemplating one's smallness in a vast universe while at the same time feeling a heightened sense of connection to all. Keltner and Haidt (2003) suggested two appraisals as necessary for awe: a sense of perceived vastness and an inability to assimilate that experience into current mental structures.

However, some researchers have argued for a distinction between awe and reverence. Reverence is a "response to greatness" in which the reverential is seen in positive terms and is found worthy of praise. Awe may have this quality, but it can also be a response to something that is so vast that it is overwhelming and consequently can produce fear (Emmons, 2005). For example, in Plutchick's (1980) emotion wheel, the feeling of awe combines surprise and fear. That is, one's feeling of awe when contemplating the size of the universe combines surprise at its utter immensity with fear of the seeming insignificance of any single part of the whole.

In his book *The Idea of the Holy* (1958), Rudolph Otto referred to awe in a religious context as the "*mysterium tremendum,*" or "the overpowering feeling of majesty and mystery in the presence of the holy" (Emmons, 2005, p. 240). In this case, a deep and profound experience of awe occurs when we touch on the inexpressible mystery, majesty, and power of the divine. Otto (1958) described this feeling as a "unique emotional moment in religious experience, a moment whose singular *daunting* and awe inspiring character must be gravely disturbing to those persons who will recognize nothing in the divine nature but goodness, gentleness, love, and a sort of confidential intimacy" (p. 19). That is, in an experience of awe, a positive and a negative emotion combine in a unique way to produce an emotion that seems to transcend them both.

Schneider (2009) devoted considerable attention to the importance of awe in optimal psychological functioning. As both a theorist in humanistic-existential psychology and a practicing psychotherapist, he commented that "whereas traditional Eastern or mystical perspectives emphasize the harmony of being; the sense of awe emphasizes the mystery of being. In short, awe is imbued with the sense of adventure or discovery" (Schneider, 2009, p. 20). He identified the following conditions that favor an emergence of awe in one's emotional life: (1) time for reflection; (2) the capacity to slow down; (3) the capacity to savor the moment; (4) a focus on what one loves; (5) a capacity to see the big picture; and (6) an ability to trust in the ultimately unknowable.

Wonder

Closely related to experiences of awe are those involving wonder. Linked especially to qualities of imagination, surprise, and aesthetics, wonder has been celebrated in Western civilization since the Romantic era of the early nineteenth century. At that time, influential poets like Coleridge and Wordsworth deliberately sought to impart a renewed appreciation for the great mystery of life. In particular, Wordsworth cherished nature as a catalyst for such an awareness, noting in his famous poem "Lines Written a Few Miles Above Tintern Abbey" (1798/1994, p. 205): "All which we behold is full of blessings." In his view, expressed also in prose essays, daily existence in bustling society almost inevitably brings boredom and inner weariness. The antidote is a sense of wonder, best induced by nature that "never did betray the heart that loved her" (p. 206). Others have described **wonder** as an opening of the heart to joy, gratitude, and love (Emmons, 2005).

As the founder of American psychology, William James (1902/1985) also had a strong interest in experiences of wonder, which he associated both with exposure to nature's beauty and with religious contemplation. For example, while vacationing in New York State's Adirondack wilderness, James underwent an exalted experience in which, as he later wrote:

> The moon rose and hung above the scene before midnight … and I got into a state of spiritual alertness of the most vital [kind]…. It seemed as if the Gods of all the nature-mythologies were holding an indescribable meeting in my breast with the moral Gods of the inner life…. It was one of the happiest … nights of my life.

James (1902/1985) advocated that psychology vigorously study such experiences of wonder, for he regarded these as key to the heights of human personality. He was convinced that our sense of wonder is rooted in an accurate and higher perception of reality that, amidst our busy, day-to-activities, usually escapes us. Thus late in his career, James wrote (1896/1956): "We are amazed that a Universe which appears to us of so vast and mysterious a complication should ever have seemed to anyone so little and plain a thing" (p. 326). Most of his colleagues, however, had no interest in experiences of wonderment, and his

viewpoint was dismissed as quaintly outdated even before his death in 1910. It was not until Maslow's (1954, 1959, 1968) studies of self-actualizing persons nearly 50 years later that academic psychology once more became interested in these intriguing phenomena, insofar as Maslow had found the sense of wonder a basic feature of peak experiences. As he (1959) noted, "The emotional reaction in the peak-experience has a special flavor of wonder, of awe, of reverence, of humility and surrender before the experience as before something great" (p. 55).

In later writings, Maslow (1970, 1971) urged that educators and educational psychologists promote experiences of wonderment in order to produce more creative individuals in the sciences as well as the arts. Though comparatively little to date has been undertaken to follow this recommendation, Stolberg (2008) investigated events triggering wonder in the life histories of college students planning careers in science education. Such experiences were indeed common and could be categorized into three distinct groupings: (1) *physical*, involving objects, phenomena, or processes found within nature, such as visiting the Grand Canyon or seeing a dazzling sunset; (2) *personal*, involving interactions with people or their work, such as observing one's infant develop; and (3) *metaphysical*, involving intense musing on the meaning of the original stimulus, such as gazing down at the earth from an airplane, or contemplating the Big Bang theory of the universe's creation.

Can we deliberately induce experiences of wonderment? Among those who have studied these phenomena, the answer appears to be a definite yes. For example, Maslow (cited in Hoffman, 1995) elicited such experiences in his life by bird-watching and reading science fiction. It seems no coincidence that the phrase "sense of wonder" was coined by an early science-fiction writer (Hugo Gernsback in the 1920s), for as Panshin and Panshin (1990) noted, "In science fiction, we encounter unknown powers, alien beings, and worlds of wonder where things become possible that are presently impossible to us" (p. 13). Izzo (2004) described the attainment of wonderment during adulthood as essentially a time of "second innocence," building upon the "first innocence" of our early childhood. Among his recommendations for recapturing the experience of wonder is exposure to nature and, more broadly, living fully in the present moment—that is, mindfulness.

Peak Experiences

Another association between religious experiences and well-being comes from Maslow's descriptions of peak-experiences. Maslow viewed these as brief moments when people experience intense joy, wonder, appreciation, or connection to a larger spiritual reality. His (1954) description of **peak experiences** may be instructive:

> There were the same feelings of limitless horizons opening up to the vision, the feeling of being simultaneously more powerful and also more helpless than one ever was before, the feeling of great ecstasy and wonder and awe, the loss of placing in time and space with, finally, the conviction that something extremely important and valuable had happened, so that the subject is to some extent transformed and strengthened even in his daily life by such experiences (p. 216).

Peak experiences are associated with events involving nature, aesthetic delight, special moments when relationships with family or friends are particularly joyful, the birth of a child, religious worship, intense moments of intellectual insight or discovery, moments of achievement, and any number of other "triggers" (Maslow, 1968, 1970).

In recent years, Hoffman and colleagues (Hoffman, 2003; Hoffman & Muramoto, 2007; Hoffman & Ortiz, 2009, 2010; Hoffman, Iversen, & Ortiz, 2010; Hoffman, Resende, & Yee, 2011; Nishimura & Hoffman, 2011) have examined youthful peak experiences—that is, occurring before the age of 14—in the U.S. as well as in southeast Asia, Western Europe, and South America. Their research has indicated that such experiences can be elicited in adults using a retrospective recall methodology and typically leave an enduring impact, such as enhanced self-confidence. The investigators have identified 15 categories of early peak experience, including interpersonal joy, external achievement, skill mastery, developmental landmark, nature, and aesthetics. In every culture studied—including Brazil, Hong Kong, Japan, Mexico, Norway, Portugal, and the U.S.—youthful peak experiences of interpersonal joy were reported most frequently, particularly those involving the subcategories of family togetherness, peer camaraderie, and the birth of a younger sibling.

In terms of well-being, Maslow (1987) asserted that peak experiences could lead to greater psychological health, at least temporarily:

> The main finding relevant to our topic was that an essential aspect of peak experience is integration within the person and therefore between person and the world. In these states of being, the person becomes unified; for the time being, the splits, polarities, and dissociations within him tend to be resolved; the civil war within is neither won nor lost but transcended. In such a state, the person becomes far more open to experience and far more spontaneous and fully functioning (p. 163).

Panzarella (1980) found that self-reported aftereffects of aesthetically produced peak experiences included more positive feelings about self, more positive relationships with other people, vivid and stimulating memories of the experience, enhanced appreciation of aesthetics, and greater optimism. Others report dramatic changes in how they create meaning in life as a consequence of intense peak experiences (Maslow, 1970). The noetic or spiritual quality of certain peak experiences is one of their most prominent features. The poet E.E. Cummings (1958) described how these experiences provide a sense of acceptance, joy, and wonder at the simple events of the world:

> out of the lie of no
> rises a truth of yes
> (only herself and who
> illimitably is)

Making fools understand
(like wintry me) that not
all matterings of mind
equal one violet

SOURCE: "out of the lie of no." Copyright © 1957, 1985, 1991 by the Trustees for the E. E. Cummings Trust, from COMPLETE POEMS: 1904–1962 by E. E. Cummings, edited by George J. Firmage. Used by permission of Liveright Publishing Corporation.

Toward the end of his life, Maslow recognized that certain elements of peak experiences could become almost permanent aspects of daily experience. This phenomenon he termed the **plateau experience** (see Krippner, 1972; Maslow, 1970; Cleary & Shapiro, 1995). In the plateau experience, all aspects of the world take on a sacred quality or are seen as manifestations of a divine presence. Maslow referred to this quality as **resacralization**, or restoring a sense of the sacred to the ordinary world. This process he saw as an antidote to a modern defense mechanism he named *desacralization*, which he found when people repressed a sense of the sacred and instead perceived the world as simply objects with no inherent meaning or value. Elisha Goldstein (2007) conducted a study based on a similar idea by asking participants to deliberately take time each day to cultivate "sacred moments" by meditating on stimuli that had spiritual significance for them. Those who did so experienced an increase in their well-being.

Maslow also described experiences with the same intensity as peak experiences but possessing negative emotionality, which he termed "nadir experiences" (Maslow, 1968, p. 84). These might involve a deep sense of loss, defeat, betrayal, powerlessness, or loneliness. He had earlier found that struggle and difficulties are sometimes necessary for personal growth. Consistent with this view, Ebersole (1970) found that some people reported using moments of deep despair and meaninglessness to forge a renewed sense of meaning and purpose in their lives. Similarly, Spencer and Stephen (1990) asked people to report their "most intense" positive or negative experience. They found that 60%–70% of people reported using *either* positive *or* negative experiences in some way to change their lives. Finally, nadir experiences may immediately precede deeply profound and extremely positive religious experiences. In Christianity, references to the "dark night of the soul" describe nadir experiences that are followed by profound religious illuminations (see Wapnick, 1980).

Numinous Experiences

Highly religious people often report feeling as if they were in the presence of God or a transcendent being. **Numinous experiences** are those in which a person feels he or she has been granted an "awareness of a holy other beyond nature and a sense that one is in communion with this holy other" (Hood, 2005, p. 356). For instance, Greely reported a correlation of .60 between self-reported happiness and a numinous experience in which one felt "bathed in light" (as cited in Argyle, 1999). A numinous experience also imparts an almost unshakable conviction that the transcendent being or presence encountered is wholly real; such experiences may be more common that most people realize. When Glock and Stark (1965) asked individuals, "Have you ever as an adult had the feeling you were somehow in the presence of God?", 72% of respondents answered yes to this question. Interestingly, children may have a greater capacity for numinous experiences, but the frequency declines as they age and as cultural acceptance of such experiences falters (see Hoffman, 1992; Hood, 2005).

Conversion

Occasionally a religious or spiritual experience is so overwhelming that it leads to a radical transformation in one's sense of meaning and purpose in life. Often this change reorients a person's life in a very different direction by altering attitudes, beliefs, values, goals, or overall purpose (Paloutzian, 1981). An intriguing aspect of a conversion experience is that it is usually preceded by doubt, a questioning of one's faith, or a fundamental dissonance between what one thinks religion should be like and what it actually is (for example, the "dark night of the soul" mentioned above). The doubt creates stress, strain, and a sense of disequilibrium as one seeks to reconcile elements of one's faith that seem contradictory. The struggle to resolve this issue can result in a conversion or spiritual transformation—recasting one's sense of meaning in such a way that disparate elements are integrated into a coherent, meaningful system. However, the change usually occurs in a few significant portions of a person's meaning system, and total transformations are rare (Paloutzian, et al., 1999). Because conversion experiences are highly personal and almost impossible to induce, they have been studied after the fact—but rarely experimentally.

CONTEMPLATIVE SPIRITUALITY

It is helpful at this point to examine the model of spirituality presented by contemplative religious or spiritual disciplines. The term *contemplative spirituality* is used to describe religious disciplines that seek a direct and very personal experience of God, or whatever is seen as the ultimate force in the universe (Woods, 1980). Having such a spiritual experience is said to be extremely positive emotionally and can result in a spiritual transformation or spiritual conversion (see Emmons & Paloutzian, 2003). Contemplative spiritual traditions have existed for many centuries in all major religions of the world—Christianity, Judaism, Islam, Buddhism, and Hinduism. Though at any one time there are comparatively few committed practitioners of contemplative religious disciplines, the historical impact of these mystical religious branches has been considerable. Indeed, one area of psychology has tended to specialize in the study of contemplative spirituality and religious experiences, especially as these relate to mysticism—transpersonal psychology.

Transpersonal Psychology

Cofounded by Abraham Maslow and Anthony Sutich in 1969 with its own professional association and journal is the specialty known as transpersonal psychology. It emerged from their combined perspective that spiritual, mystical, and transcendent experiences are basic to human nature and deserve

serious scientific attention. In fact, empirical studies have suggested that spirituality is a distinct dimension of well-being (Compton, 2001a). Maslow arrived at this view mainly through his study of self-actualizing persons and peak experiences (Hoffman, 1996), whereas Sutich's work as a humanistic psychotherapist led him to conclude that people share an identity greater than the sum of their individual egos (Ruzek, 2007).

Of course, the launching of transpersonal psychology in the late 1960s reflected the broader, burgeoning scientist interest in Far Eastern spiritual traditions and their wisdom teachings. For the first time since the work of William James in the early 1900s, American psychologists were turning to such traditions for insights into human personality and human potential, for example as revealed through meditation and exalted states of consciousness. Thus, in the founding issue of the *Journal of Transpersonal Psychology,* Sutich (1969) offered the following definition to inaugurate this specialty:

> Transpersonal psychology is concerned specifically with the *empirical,* scientific study of, and responsible implementation of the findings relevant to becoming, individual and species-wide meta-needs, ultimate values, unitive consciousness, peak experiences … bliss, wonder, ultimate meaning, transcendence of the self … and related concepts, experiences and activities" (p. 5).

Over the ensuing decades, leading figures in transpersonal psychology have addressed theoretical issues related to higher and ecstatic states of human consciousness (Aziz, 2007; Ferrer, 2001; Tart, 1975; Taylor, 2009; Washburn, 2003) as well as the development of assessment tools (Goretzi, Thalbourne, and Storm, 2009; Lazar, 2009) and interventions for enhancing spiritual well-being or growth (Boorstein, 1996; Ingersoll, 2007; Taylor and Mireault, 2008). In the latter category, it is important to note that transpersonal psychotherapy aims at "the daily experience of that state called liberation, enlightenment, individuation, certainty or gnosis according to various [spiritual] traditions" (cited by Boorstein,

1996, p. 3). To this end, practitioners of transpersonal psychotherapy have turned to Kundalini Yoga, Zen Buddhism, Christian monasticism, Kabbalah, Sufism, and Native American shamanism for specific insights and practices.

Partly because transpersonal psychology accepts phenomenological research methods and first-person narrative accounts of spiritual experiences, its influence in academia has remained weak to date. Recently, however, some transpersonal psychologists have asserted the need for their specialty to become more scientifically rigorous (Ruzek, 2007), while others (Anderson and Broad, 2011) have begun to advocate innovations in psychological research methods consistent with its interest in spiritual and transcendental experiences. For example, the latter investigators argue that research itself can be transformative both for researchers and those who read the research reports, and that effective transpersonal research necessarily requires the initial preparedness or experiential adequacy of the researcher. However, transpersonal psychologists are not the only people who study religious and transcendent experiences. Researchers aligned with the psychology of religion and other specialties also study these experiences.

Mysticism

Mysticism has been scientifically difficult to define. Generally, the mystical experience "diverges in fundamental ways from [our] ordinary conscious awareness and leaves a strong impression of having encountered a reality different from—and, in some crucial sense, higher than—the reality of everyday experience" (Wulff, 2004, p. 397). People usually report mystical experiences as among the most profound experiences of their life, and mysticism has been a part of the Western world for millennia (Tarnas, 1991). From the initial interest of William James at the beginning of the twentieth century, a variety of psychological researchers have written extensively on mysticism. Early works by James, Leuba, W.T. Stace, and Evelyn Underhill evolved into more empirical approaches such as those of Ralph Hood (1997, 2005).

Although diverse mystical experiences have been reported throughout history, these have generally shared a few features. First, the experience is typically ineffable or impossible to describe in words; second, it is noetic or involves a sense that profound knowledge has been revealed; third, it is experienced as beyond the conventional understanding of time and space; and finally, it is typically accompanied by a sense of unity, of dropping the usual boundaries of self-identity and merging with a greater reality (Hood, 1975; James, 1902/1958; Wulff, 2004). The results of the experience are often described in tremendously positive terms—as joyous and even ecstatic. For example, a Western psychologist described his experience thus: "Preoccupations, misgivings, worries, and desires all seem to evaporate, leaving everything perfect, just as it is'.... [I felt] awe, wonder, expansiveness, freedom, warmth, love, and a sense of total truth or rightness' ... [a sense] of having been *at one*" (May, 1983, pp. 53–54). Intense mystical experiences have proved difficult to study experimentally. Although some attempts have been made in this regard (see Hood, 1995; Lukoff & Lu, 1988), the experience is difficult to induce and measure.

Janet C'deBaca and William Miller studied what they called instances of "quantum change" (Miller & C'deBaca, 1994, 2001; C'deBaca & Wilbourne, 2004). These were moments of sudden, dramatic personality and behavior change that occurred years earlier and were brought on by spiritual events such as conversion or mystical experiences. Among their sample, 90% reported such positive consequences as release from fear, depression, and anger as well as a deepening of intimate relationships, optimism, trust, and spirituality; only 10% reported negative aftereffects of the experience. A decade later, a follow-up study found participants continued to value spirituality, compassion, humor, personal growth, hope, openness to experiences, and inner peace. They continued to reject self-centered values such as wealth, pleasure, career, and glamour. Interestingly, they continued to place little value on a traditional pursuit of "happiness." This follow-up interview took place, on average, 20 years after the original experience and yet it was still a powerful motivating force in participants' lives.

CONTEMPLATIVE RELIGIOUS TRADITIONS

This next section presents a few examples of contemplative spirituality found in traditional religions. Although the mystical element is more easily observed in Hinduism, Buddhism, and Taoism, all of the world's major religions possess a mystical branch. In each, a major goal is the cultivation of mystical and transcendent experiences.

Monastic Christianity

The contemplative mystical practices of Christianity are most easily recognized in Catholic monastic practices. For thousands of years, monks have prayed, meditated, fasted, chanted, and engaged in a wide variety of activities to seek a personal experience of God. Father William McNamara (1975) remarked, "Mystical experience, the realization of union with God, is simply the highest or deepest form of religious experience…. At the deep root of the mystic's being, at his center, there is a conscious direct contact with Transcendental Reality" (p. 405). Among the "twelve characteristics of the mystic way" listed by Father McNamara are detachment from self, liberation, unification, attainment of peace, and identification with the will of God. (For an Eastern Orthodox perspective, see Chirban, 1986.) Many people are familiar with Catholic monastic practices through the beautiful writings of Father Thomas Merton (for example, Merton, 2000), who lived for many years at Gethsemani Abbey.[1]

Centering Prayer It is interesting to note that centering prayer, developed by such leading practitioners of Catholic monasticism as Thomas Merton and Thomas Keating, has emerged as an alternative to mindfulness-based cognitive therapy (MBCT) for the treatment of emotional disorders. As described by Pennington (1980), centering prayer

involves three simple rules: (1) At the beginning of the prayer, take a minute or two to quiet down; and then (2) move in faith to God's presence dwelling in our depths; (3) At the end of the prayer, take several minutes to come out, mentally praying the "Our Father" or some other prayer. After resting awhile in the center in faithful love, take up a single word, such as *love*, that expresses this response and allow it to repeat itself within your mind. Whenever in the course of prayer you become aware of any intrusion, gently return to God's presence by using the prayer word.

Noting that centering prayer shares features with the well-researched intervention of MBCT, Knabb (2010) recommended the former's potential therapeutic usefulness, especially if emerging research confirms this similarity in efficacy. Knabb (2010) observed that centering prayer appeals particularly to Christian adults seeking therapeutic aid through their own religious heritage.

Moses Maimonides

© Hulton Archive/Getty Images

Kabbalah

In recent years, there has been a worldwide surge of interest in the Kabbalah, the mystical tradition of Judaism. As early as the 1940s, psychiatrist Carl Jung acquired a strong interest in its psychological relevance (Drob, 2009). However, as Jung (1973b, pp. 358–359) later related, he lacked the knowledge of Hebrew and major Judaic sources to explore the Kabbalah in depth. Hoffman (1980) was one of the first psychologists to highlight the Kabbalah for its insights into personality, human potentialities, and methods of personal growth. He (1981/2006) expanded his analysis by connecting the Kabbalah to ongoing trends in both humanistic and transpersonal psychology, such as growing interest in meditation, transcendent and ecstatic experiences, and the mind-body relationship.

Schachter and Hoffman (1983) related counseling techniques in early Hasidism, a mystical branch of Judaism, to current psychotherapeutic interests. By the mid-1990s, various mental health practitioners, especially those with humanistic or transpersonal orientations, sought to apply Kabbalistic teachings in their therapeutic work (Hoffman, 1995). In this light, a challenge has been to separate the Kabbalah's intriguing psychological ideas and techniques from classic Jewish theology and religious practice, a task that traditionalists oppose as invalid (Schachter-Shalomi & Gropman, 2003).

Reflecting more than 1,500 years of Judaic writings, the Kabbalah is a vast body of esoteric speculation and mystical lore. In essence, it teaches that: (1) the cosmos is a unity, with all aspects in interrelation; (2) the forces of creation represent an eternal interplay between an active force and a passive force; (3) the human individual is a microcosm of the universe; (4) in daily life, we are attuned to only one state of consciousness among many; (5) each individual may attain higher states of consciousness, but careful preparation is necessary; and (6) to achieve transcendent mental states, various specific practices and techniques are employed.

Buddhism

Buddhism begins by asserting what it considers the one irrefutable truth of human existence: constant change. Despite our wishes or attempts to prevent it, life always changes; we are born, we age, we die. Pain follows pleasure, or joy follows heartache as surely as night follows day. When we allow ourselves to acknowledge the inescapable reality of change, it creates anxiety, worry, fear, and insecurity (Rahula, 1974).

The second basic truth of Buddhism asserts that the fundamental

© Kasahara Katsumi/ Gamma-Rapho/Getty Images

Dalai Lama

cause of all unhappiness is because, despite the reality of constant change, we crave security, permanence, stability, and a complete end to doubt and worry. In this sense, when we find something that appears to provide pleasure and stability, such as a well-paying career or a comforting belief system, then we latch onto it for dear life. In Buddhism, this craving for something stable that will ensure permanent satisfaction and well-being is referred to as *attachment* or *grasping*. The Buddha declared that all our efforts to control and manipulate life so that we have only positive experiences are doomed to failure. Furthermore, our efforts to completely control life in this way are actually *the primary cause* of human suffering.

Nirvana and Enlightenment   In Buddhism, the cure for these problems—the route to true happiness—can be found in disciplined meditative practice. Meditation allows awareness to develop so that *all* elements of psychological processes are observed without grasping or attachment. When this process develops to a certain point, it is then possible to experience the extinction of *grasping* as the basis of one's life. In Sanskrit this extinction is called **Nirvana**, or "the Extinction of Thirst" (Rahula, 1974). That is, to realize Nirvana is to be released from all needs and desires based on greed, anger, and delusion (Ling, 1972).

The realization of Nirvana is accompanied by profound positive emotions. Buddhist monk and scholar Walpola Rahula (1974) declared that "he who has realized the Truth, Nirvana, is the happiest being in the world.... He is joyful ... free from anxiety, serene and peaceful ... full of universal love, compassion, kindness, sympathy, understanding and tolerance" (p. 43). Someone who experiences Nirvana is said to have an **enlightenment** experience. A person can have numerous enlightenment experiences, each of which may be increasingly deep with insight. Buddhism teaches that the person who experienced the deepest and most profound enlightenment possible was the Buddha; in fact, the term *Buddha* is an honorific one meaning *the enlightened* or *awakened one*.

Buddhists believe that the result of complete and full enlightenment is a *total* elimination of unhealthy mental factors and their replacement by healthy mental states (Goleman, 1975)[2] (see Table 10.1). In general, healthy mental factors represent the two core traits of optimal mental health from the Buddhist perspective—compassion and wisdom.

To Western psychologists probably the most incredible assertion of Buddhism is that all negative emotions, behaviors, and personality traits can be totally eliminated. However, the Buddhist perspective (as well as other Eastern perspectives) is quite serious about this claim. In Buddhism, the **arhat** is an enlightened person who has achieved this state.[3] Goleman (1988) stated:

> The arhat embodies the essence of mental health in [Buddhist psychology]. His personality traits are permanently altered; all his motives, perceptions, and actions that

he formerly engaged in under the influence of unhealthy factors will have vanished....While the arhat may seem virtuous beyond belief from the perspective of Western psychology, he embodies characteristics common to the ideal type in most every Asian psychology. The arhat is the enlightened being, a prototype notable in the main for its absence in Western personality theory (pp. 137–8).

In summary, Buddhism fosters a sense of well-being by encouraging the acceptance of all aspects of life with equanimity through insights into the nature of human consciousness (de Silva, 1979). These are achieved through the practice of meditation, which allows for experiencing the world and the self in fundamentally altered ways, diminishing the need for goal attainment as a source of happiness. Why? Because ultimate happiness is described as potentially present in every moment.

Mindfulness Meditation

A common spiritual practice found in mystical traditions involves the control of attention. Often this encompasses some form of prayer or meditation. Almost all forms of contemplative spirituality practice some form of mindfulness. You will recall that mindfulness meditation is a way of intentionally paying full attention, nonjudgmentally, to the present moment. As Kabat-Zinn (1990) initially reported, mindfulness meditation, originating in ancient Buddhist meditative practices, was a practice long unfamiliar to contemporary Westerners. Typically, Western clinicians who have introduced mindfulness-based therapies into mental health treatment programs teach these skills independently of their religious and cultural origins. In other words, one needn't be a practicing Buddhist or Christian, Hindu, Jew, or Muslim in order to reap the benefits of mindfulness-based therapies. When, however, mindfulness embedded in traditional spiritual practices is applied in a particular religious context, the effects are significantly different from those obtained via Western therapeutic applications.

T A B L E 10.1   Healthy and Unhealthy Mental Factors of Buddhism

Unhealthy Factors	Healthy Factors
Wisdom Factors	
Delusion	Insight
False View	Mindfulness
Shamelessness	Modesty
Recklessness	Discretion
Egoism	Confidence
Compassion Factors	
Agitation	Composure
Greed	Nonattachment
Aversion	Nonaversion
Envy	Impartiality
Avarice	Buoyancy
Worry	Pliancy
Contraction	Adaptability
Torpor	Proficiency
Perplexity	Rectitude

SOURCE: Adapted from Goleman, D. (1975). Mental health in classical Buddhist psychology. *Journal of Transpersonal Psychology, 7*, 176–181.

Several types of mindfulness meditation exercises exist. Many encourage practitioners to focus on inner experiences occurring each moment, such as bodily sensations, thoughts, and feelings. Others focus on outer aspects, such as sights and sounds. All recommend that mindfulness be practiced with an attitude of nonjudgmental acceptance (Lykins & Baer, 2011). That is, phenomena that enter one's awareness, such as fleeting or repetitive thoughts, feelings, perceptions, and sensations, are observed carefully but evaluated as neither good nor bad, true nor false, healthy nor sick, important nor trivial. Thus as Baer (2003) remarked, "Mindfulness is the nonjudgmental observation of the ongoing stream of internal and external stimuli as they arise" (p. 125). What is different about mindfulness in contemplative spiritual disciplines is the depth and intensity of the practice. For instance, adepts say that with practice it is possible to not only observe the ongoing stream of thoughts and sensations but to also become aware of the "space between" individual thoughts and sensations—a space of pure awareness. Further practice allows a person to observe the coalescence of thoughts and sensations into self-identity, and thus to experience a "self-less" awareness (Rahula, 1974).

Indeed, for many centuries Buddhist monks have incorporated this practice in their daily regimen as a way of freeing themselves from confining desires and worries, thereby transcending ego. Further, virtually all the world's major religions have likewise emphasized the value of mindfulness. As we have seen, Moses Maimonides, the influential Jewish philosopher-physician of the thirteenth century, not only discussed the health benefits of mindfulness but also prescribed specific methods for its cultivation (Hoffman, 2009).

MYSTICISM AND THE BRAIN

Although spiritual experiences are difficult to study, there have been recent attempts to provide more scientific evidence. The more fascinating involve brain-imaging studies, whereby scientists are beginning to locate physiological markers of spiritual experience. The new specialty of **neuromysticism** seeks a scientific understanding of extraordinary mental states by examination of their neural activity. Conceptually it dates back more than a century, for William James (1902/1985) urged that transcendental experiences be studied carefully and objectively to provide insights into the heights of human potential. Though many theologians and psychologists quickly embraced this task, it seemed virtually impossible to implement methodologically. After all, wasn't mystical experience by its very nature utterly internal and therefore impervious to objective measurement? How could the alluring self-reports of mystics and sages about elevated states of consciousness in meditation be quantified or even verified? This methodological impasse existed for nearly 70 years, until the advent of biofeedback instrumentation. Arising out of behavioral medicine's attempts at psychophysiological (that is, mind-body) self-regulation, the field came into professional existence in the late 1960s, and in 1969 the Biofeedback Research Society (renamed the Association for Applied Psychophysiology and Feedback) was formed; the term *biofeedback* was coined that same year.

One of the first investigators to use biofeedback with brain waves was psychologist Joe Kamiya at the University of Chicago. Exploring the internal world of perception, he initially found that individuals could learn through EEG (electroencephalograph) feedback to discriminate their brain-wave states—that is, alpha, beta, and theta (the more rapid gamma brain waves were detected later by researchers). Then Kamiya discovered that with biofeedback individuals could learn to generate specific brain-wave states on demand, though the ability to do so varied widely among persons (Green & Green, 1977).

In the early 1970s, researchers Elmer and Alyce Green of the Menninger Foundation in Topeka, Kansas, traveled to India, where they studied the psychophysiology of yogis. In pioneering research that challenged longstanding medical beliefs about the nature of the autonomic nervous system, the

Greens (1977) found that some yogis were able to control seemingly involuntary bodily processes. Subsequent research with practitioners of transcendental meditation (Dillbeck et al., 1981; Dillbeck, 1982; Gallois, 1984) confirmed the conscious human ability to: (1) slow metabolic rate, as confirmed by decreased oxygen consumption and carbon dioxide output; (2) increase beta, alpha, and theta activity during meditation; and (3) increase skin resistance to electrical stimulation, indicating increased tolerance to external stimuli. More recently, research supported by the Dalai Lama involving visual imaging and attention in 78 Tibetan Buddhist monks (Carter et al., 1995) found "new evidence … that different types of meditation and training duration lead to distinguishable short- and long-term changes at the neural level" (p. 413). Such studies provided solid scientific evidence for millennia-old claims by mystics that the human mind has powers over the body—abilities previously doubted by most modern scientists.

If neuroscience could validate such claims by Eastern and Western mystics, how about their accounts of enlightenment and ecstatic oneness? One of the most articulate investigators in this domain is James Austin, an American academic neurologist and Zen Buddhism practitioner. In 1974 he traveled to Kyoto, Japan, to learn Zen meditation under the Zen master Nanrei

© Ed Hoffman

Sand Garden in Japan

Kobori-Roshi, immediately finding the practice puzzling from the standpoint of his training in Western medicine. His questions were: What is Zen? How does the human brain actually function? And, what really occurs during extraordinary mental states like enlightenment? Stimulated by these questions, Austin (1998, 2006, 2009) has written lucidly and comprehensively on Zen mysticism from the vantage of neuroscience theory and research.

In Austin's view, the experience of enlightenment comprises essentially two features: (1) a loss of the sense of "self" central to ordinary consciousness; and (2) a corresponding feeling of unity with the entire world. Neither ancient myth nor religious metaphor, this is a genuine experience that Austin (1998) himself underwent and that he has vividly described:

> It strikes unexpectedly at 9 A.M. on the surface platform of the London subway system. [Due to a mistake] I wind up at a station where I have never been before…. The view includes no more than the dingy interior of the station, some grimy buildings in the middle ground, and a bit of open sky…. Yes, there is the paradox of this extraordinary viewing. *But there is no viewer.* The scene is utterly empty, stripped of every last extension of an *I-Me-Mine.* Vanished in one split second is the familiar sensation that *this* person is viewing an ordinary city scene. The new viewing proceeds impersonally, not pausing to register the paradox that there is no human subject "doing" it…. Three insights … penetrate the experiment, each conveying *Total Understanding* at depths far beyond simple knowledge: This is the eternal state of affairs. There is nothing more to do…. There is nothing whatever to fear (pp. 537–538).

Austin's (1998, 2006, 2009) basic premise was that such extraordinary mental states—whether occurring spontaneously, cultivated by meditation, or drug-induced—all originate in the brain, because the brain is the organ of the mind. Like other researchers, Austin argued that the human brain is "hard-wired" for such experiences and that meditative practices release basic, preexisting neurophysiological functions. He (1998) reported that his mystical experience produced immediate and enduring psychological benefits, such as enhancing calmness and equanimity. However, it is important to note that though some neuroinvestigators of mysticism (Austin, 1998; 2006, 2008; d'Aquili & Newberg, 1999) regarded such states as emotionally and cognitively beneficial, others (Alper, 2001; Persinger, 2001) view them as delusional and potentially harmful. In a cogent literature review of mystical experience and neuroscience, Miller (2007) advocated a "middle way" in which systematic research might reveal precisely how episodes of transcendence contribute to individual well-being.

Neurotheology

Eugene d'Aquili and Andrew Newberg called their approach to the study of religious experiences **neurotheology**, in reference to their use of neurological imaging techniques to study these (d'Aquili & Newberg, 1999; Newberg, d'Aquili, & Rouse, 2001). In one study, they used a neuroimaging technology to record brain activity in very experienced Tibetan Buddhist monks while they were meditating. They found that specific areas of the brain were activated during deep meditative experiences. It is fascinating to note that these are the cortical areas of the brain, involved in creating a sense of self in conscious experience. The researchers argued that activation of those areas led to a sense that the perceptual boundary between *self* and *other* was temporarily breaking down, which could result in a feeling of *oneness* with the world. In other words, they believed they had found preliminary physiological correlates for the experiences reported for centuries by meditators.

A study by Richard Davidson and others (2003) recorded brain activity in a Tibetan Buddhist monk who had extensive experience with meditation. The monk said he could voluntarily induce feelings of universal compassion during meditation.

Indeed, each time during meditation the monk signaled that he was entering the compassionate meditative state, significant and consistent changes in his brain-wave activity resulted. Davidson has also found recognizable patterns of brain activity associated with both positive and negative moods (see Goleman, 2003). He and others have found that for most individuals, meditation changes brain activity toward patterns associated with positive moods. Davidson also found that of all people tested in one study, a Tibetan monk manifested the most intense shift toward the brain pattern associated with positive emotions.

An Unusual Route to Transcendent Experiences

An unusual perspective on spirituality comes from Jill Bolte Taylor, who recounted a very unexpected route to spiritual experiences. In 1996 she suffered a major stroke that interrupted many functions in the left hemisphere of her brain. Unbelievably, this tragedy resulted in her experiencing what seems to have been a mystical state of consciousness (Taylor, 2008). Because Taylor was a Harvard-trained neuroanatomist, she recognized the physiological processes that were affected. As she described her experience, when the left hemisphere functions of rationality, analysis, and language were silenced, then what remained were the right hemisphere functions of awareness, openness, and life in the present moment.

As Taylor recalled in a radio interview, "I felt a sense of euphoria as I lost the boundaries of my body.... I felt I was as big as the universe." She went on to report that the experience "was really wonderful.... It was all about the present moment [in which] there is no judgment, it just is.... It was a total experience of peacefulness and euphoria."

Taylor now believes that insofar as this experience is associated with normal right hemisphere functioning, it is available to all who permit "the left hemisphere verbiage system to shut down enough to allow you to come back to the present moment." Certainly no one would recommend a major stroke as a spiritual intervention, but Taylor's powerful experience does add to a growing body of research that associates spiritual experiences with real, if underutilized, biological and neurological processes.

Entheogens and Religious Experiences

If physiological and biological processes are associated with spiritual experiences, then it is logical to assume that pharmacological interventions might produce experiences that resemble, or are identical with, religious experiences. Drugs used to foster religious experiences are called **entheogens** (Roberts, 2006). In the 1960s, several studies investigated the use of certain drugs to induce spiritual experiences (Pahnke, 1969). However, due to governmental and societal backlash against youthful drug use, serious scientific research on these substances all but stopped. Nevertheless, several researchers in recent years have resumed the study of entheogens (Marsa, 2008). It should be noted that these studies use very experienced professionals to administer the drugs under highly controlled conditions that are quite unlike recreational drug use (see Johnson, Richards, & Griffiths, 2008).

In this light, one study examined the impact of psilocybin on spiritual and religious meaning (Griffiths, Richards, McCann, & Jesse, 2006). The results of a double-blind intervention produced "complete" mystical experiences, indistinguishable from natural mystical experiences, in 58% of participants. In addition, participants rated their experiences as extraordinarily significant and meaningful; 67% said this was among the five most spiritually significant experiences of their lives. After the sessions, people who knew the participants well reported noticeable positive changes in their mood and behavior. A follow-up 14 months after the sessions found these changes persisted at the same intensity and meaningfulness (Griffiths, Richards, Johnson, McCann, & Jesse, 2008).

Currently these experiments have little relevance either to ordinary people seeking spiritual experiences or professionals scrutinizing spiritually-based therapies. However, they do offer an intriguing research opportunity for qualified scientists to experimentally test some of the claims made by mystics throughout history.

PSYCHOLOGICAL THEORIES OF RELIGIOUS MATURITY

Although the relationship between religious experience and subjective well-being is quite robust and appears to be stable, it is also obvious that not all religious involvement is conducive to well-being. It has been painfully true since time immemorial that considerable harm has been done around the world in the name of religion. As a result, several psychologists examining the development of religious beliefs have presented theories that address mature versus immature types of religiousness or religiosity.

Intrinsic and Extrinsic Religiousness

An early attempt to explore types of religiousness came from Gordon Allport. He suggested that what distinguishes healthy from unhealthy religiousness is motivation. To understand this distinction, he developed the concepts of intrinsic and extrinsic religiousness (Allport & Ross, 1967).

For Allport, those whose religious practices were *extrinsic* used their religion essentially as a path to egotistical or secular ends. Extrinsic religiousness "is the religion of comfort and social convention, a self-serving, instrumental approach shaped to suit oneself" (Donahue, 1985, p. 400). Donahue (1985) stated that extrinsic religiosity "is positively correlated with prejudice, dogmatism ... trait anxiety ... fear of death ... and is apparently uncorrelated with altruism" (p. 416).

Intrinsic religiosity, however, is found when religious beliefs and practices are founded upon personal and authentic motivations (Miller & Kelley, 2005). Studies have found that intrinsic religiousness, in contrast with extrinsic religiosity, is associated with various measures of well-being including gratitude (Miller & Kelley, 2009; Watkins et al., 2009).

Several decades after Allport's seminal formulation, other researchers began to add dimensions of religiousness. Frequently articulated has been that of a *quest* orientation (Bateson et al., 1993). Persons with a quest orientation view their religion or spirituality as an evolving system that must develop dynamically as a result of challenging life experiences.

Stages of Religious Cognition

Other psychologists have examined how religious concepts and stories develop over the course of a lifetime and how challenges to our early religious ideas are resolved. As one example, Raymond Fowler (1981) developed an influential stage theory of faith development that changes throughout a person's life. He defined faith as a way we find meaning and coherence in our lives. This entails belief in a "master story" to answer such basic questions as "What is life about?"; "Who's in charge?"; and "How do I live a good and worthy life?" In this sense, faith is how we relate to whatever is of transcendent worth to us; it is a way of trusting, committing, and relating to the world (Fowler, 1981). Fowler's theory suggests that what distinguishes healthy from unhealthy religiousness is how we think about faith and what cognitive processes we bring to bear on religious and moral questions. This view is similar to perspectives on wisdom, for to develop a mature faith over time, we must become wise.

In general, Fowler's six stages of development move from simple and concrete to more complex and abstract notions of faith. During stage transitions, believers become increasingly aware of the contradictions and paradoxes of their faith. As they resolve contradictions, they move to more mature stages of faith, manifested by greater tolerance and openness.

Stage six, the last stage, consists of *universalizing* faith. This stage is rarely achieved, especially in persons younger than 40. Here one operates from universal principals of love and justice, understanding people as part of a universal community to which one responds with compassion. Believers at stage six are usually considered great religious teachers, humanitarians, or even saints.

Psychodynamic Perspectives on Religion

Psychodynamic theorists have explained the processes involved in creating a mature spirituality by exploring our relationship to our unconscious. This view holds that unresolved psychological conflicts can interfere with one's awareness of spiritual needs or religious impulses. In essence, when people become too preoccupied with a resolution of personal psychological issues or with self-focused goals, they are distracted from the spiritual dimensions of life. From this perspective, what distinguishes healthy from unhealthy religiousness is the relationship to one's unconscious—especially the use of defense mechanisms and other self-protective strategies. For instance, early psychodynamic theorists like Alfred Adler (1964) and Erich Fromm (1955) declared that resolution of unconscious conflicts resulted in increased compassion, altruism, social feeling, and deeper spirituality. Other theorists have argued that a deep level of unconscious processing is present within everyone, access to which leads to enhanced spirituality (see Assagioli, 1965; Washburn, 2003). Carl Jung embraced this spiritual dimension more than most other psychodynamic thinkers.

Carl Jung on Religion and Spirituality Jung believed that religion and spirituality are rooted in innate needs that drive us to find meaning in life, to create a sense of wholeness or completeness, and to connect with something larger than our individual selves. He distinguished between the personal and the collective unconscious. The personal unconscious, similar to Freud's idea of the unconscious, contains individual contents, in contrast with the universal **collective unconscious** that contains psychological material shared by all humanity. This latter consists of **archetypes**, or "psychological instincts", which are innate universal tendencies to respond emotionally to environmental stimuli.

Jung asserted that in order to fulfill our innate needs for spirituality, we must increase our awareness of specific archetypes in the collective unconscious—that is, of those universal, psychological, and emotional impulses that drive the religious and spiritual quests of all human beings across all ages and cultures. The Reverend Don Culpitt observed that for Jung, "the real encounter with God was [through] the encounter with your own unconscious" (Segaller, 1989). For Jung, a mature understanding of spirituality and religion was too complex to be captured by mere statements of belief or verbal explanations. Rather, the only way to express such meaning was through images, symbols, and rituals.

Perspectives on Morality and Ethics

The sources of moral and ethical behavior have been of interest to psychologists since the earliest days of the profession. Freud assumed that moral behavior depended on a strong ego to control innate forces that would otherwise drive us toward unchanneled aggressive and sexual impulses. However, Adler, Jung, Rogers, Maslow, and others assumed that people possessed innate tendencies to moral and ethical behavior that needed to be cultivated. In the 1970s Lawrence Kohlberg (1984) proposed that morality developed in a mature stagelike sequence driven by cognitive processes similar to the progression of wisdom. Recently some researchers have again argued that innate physiological and emotional reactions are the sources of moral behavior (Haidt, 2007; Haidt & Kesebir, 2010), although not everyone agrees with this new focus (Narvaez, 2010).

Recent work hints that physiological and cognitive factors combine to influence moral behavior. One of the first brain-imaging studies of positive "inspirational emotions" found them to take more time to process than emotions such as pain or fear (Immordino-Yang et al., 2009). This study discovered that the emotions of compassion and admiration did indeed produce distinct physiological reactions, but they also needed one's persistent attention in order to be fully understood. A disturbing implication is that in today's world of rapid-fire media people haven't enough time to fully understand or process moral and inspirational emotional information. Therefore, the speed of information we consume can confuse our moral compass (DeJong, 2009). Another study implied that the adage "cleanliness is next to godliness" is correct. Researchers found that people acted more fairly and charitably when they inhabited clean-smelling environments (Liljenquist, Zhong, & Galinsky. 2010). Earlier they had found that when people recalled their transgressions, those memories increased their desire to be physically cleansed through actions like washing their hands (Zhong & Liljenquist, 2006). In an interesting twist, however, people who felt more physically clean were more likely to inflict harsher punishments on others for ethical or moral violations (Zhong, Strejcek, & Silanathan, 2010). Apparently feeling physically clean inflated moral self-perceptions, which led to decreased compassion for those who appeared less virtuous.

SUMMARY

This chapter has covered a variety of issues related to religion and spirituality. First, we reviewed studies that found significant relationships between religious participation and both psychological and physical well-being. Second, we considered the topic of meaning, exploring how people create a sense of meaning in life. Next we discussed sacred emotions, including gratitude, forgiveness, compassion, and humility. Following this, we described religious experiences such as elation, awe, wonder; and peak experiences. For some people, such singular dramatic experiences lead to meaningful changes in how they perceive life. In a subsequent section, we highlighted contemplative spirituality, addressing its association with several major religious traditions. Then we discussed studies that use new brain-imaging technologies to scientifically re-create religious and transcendent experiences. Finally, we examined several psychological theories on healthy or mature spirituality.

NOTES

1. Information about the Thomas Merton Institute for Contemplative Living can be found at http://www.mertoninstitute.org/Default.aspx. Information about Gethsemini Abbey can be found at: http://www.monks.org.

2. It is interesting to compare the unhealthy and healthy mental factors of Buddhism with the Seven Deadly Sins and the Seven Virtues of Christianity, as well as with the list of strengths and virtues presented by Peterson & Seligman (see chapter 2).

3. In Mahayana Buddhism, the ideal of the arhat is changed into the ideal of the bodhisattva, a person who vows not to realize final Nirvana until all other beings are saved from suffering first. A bodhisattva is seen as the embodiment of total compassion.

LEARNING TOOLS

Key Terms and Ideas

transcendent experiences	awe	resacralization	transpersonal psychology
elation	wonder	plateau experience	neuromysticism
	peak experience		

Books

Armstrong, K. (2010). *Twelve steps to a compassionate life*. NY: Knopf. A renowned religious scholar teaches the necessity of compassion. *(popular)*

Newberg, A., & Waldman, R. (2010). *How God changes your brain*. NY: Ballantine. Andrew Newberg, who co-created the field of neurotheology, presents recent findings on spirituality and the brain. *(popular)*

Ricard, M. (2007). *Happiness: A guide to developing life's most important skill*. NY: Little Brown. A French scientist turned Tibetan Buddhist monk discusses true happiness. Ricard was one of Richard Davidson's subjects and colleagues in brain scan studies of Buddhist monks. *(popular)*

Vaillant, G. (2008). *Spiritual evolution: A scientific defense of faith*. NY: Broadway. Vaillant is known for his longitudinal studies of well-being (see chapter 8). Here he argued that spiritual emotions are necessary for survival. *(popular)*

On the Web

http://nfb.ca/film/mystical_brain   A documentary from the National Film Board of Canada on neurological studies of meditation and mystics.

http://www.beliefnet.com/Health/2000/07/Opening-The-Heart.aspx?p=1   A lovingkindness meditation from Sharon Salzberg, one of the foremost teachers of Buddhist meditation in the West.

http://www.buddhanet.net/pdf_file/powermindfulness.pdf   A classic text on Buddhist mindfulness meditation by the Venerable Nyanaponika Thera.

http://www.psychologytoday.com/blog/moral-landscapes/   A Psychology Today magazine blog by Darcia Narvaez on "living the life that is good for one to live."

http://www.atpweb.org/   The Association for Transpersonal Psychology.

Personal Explorations

1. Positive psychology has increasingly focused on the link between religiousness and wellness. Interview two persons you know who are actively involved in their religion. If possible, select adherents of different religions. Your interview should include the following questions: (a) When did you first become religious—in childhood, adolescence, or adulthood? (b) Did you have a particular experience that led you to your religion? If so, could you describe it? If not, was your involvement with your religion a gradual process? (c) How often do you pray or meditate? How important is prayer or meditation in your life? (d) How often do you attend religious services? (e) How important is such attendance for you? (f) Do you feel that you have faith? If so, how does that affect your daily life? (g) In your opinion, how does your religion contribute to your well-being? After completing these interviews, describe what you found most interesting. If you could design a study interviewing 200 persons, what would you most like to investigate?

2. Abraham Maslow was the first psychologist to study peak experiences—that is, wonderful moments of joy and fulfillment, often accompanied by a sense of oneness with the world. Subsequently researchers have confirmed that people across the globe have peak experiences, often influenced by their particular culture. Describe a peak experience in your own life with reference to these questions: (a) How old were you when it occurred? (b) Who was with you when it happened, or were you alone? (c) As best you can determine, what "triggered" this moment of tremendous happiness? (d) What impact did this experience have on your subsequent life? For instance, did it affect your view of human existence or your relationships with others? (e) Do you think that people can learn to have more frequent peak experiences? If so, how?

Chapter 11

Positive Institutions and Cultural Well-Being

> No man is an island entire of itself; every man is a piece of the Continent, a part
> of the main ... any man's death diminishes me, because I am involved
> in Mankind; and therefore never send to know for
> whom the bell tolls; it tolls for thee.
> JOHN DONNE (1623)

One of the most significant areas of most people's lives is the world of work. In contemporary global society, work fills the waking hours of hundreds of millions of people. Additionally, work is vital in terms of generating income, enhancing self-esteem and camaraderie, creating opportunities for meaningful activities, and producing the goods and services that society values. Of course, work can include both professional and paid employment as well as managing a household and caring for children. Most research on the impact of work on well-being, however, has almost exclusively studied professional and paid work. It is our hope that the unfortunate neglect among researchers of the work of stay-at-home moms and dads will soon be remedied. In this section of the book, however, the focus is on paid employment.

EMPLOYEE ENGAGEMENT AND JOB SATISFACTION

A Definition of Employee Engagement

To begin, it is helpful to define **employee engagement**. This has been defined as "a positive, fulfilling, work-related state of mind that is characterized by vigor, dedication, and absorption" (Schaufeli et al., 2002, p. 74). According to Maslach and colleagues (2001), engagement is characterized by energy, involvement, and efficacy—the direct opposite of the three burnout dimensions of exhaustion, cynicism, and inefficacy. Research on burnout and engagement has found their core dimensions to be opposites of each other (Gonzales-Roma et al., 2006). Just as past researchers have found that job satisfaction is a complex

© 2005 by Randy Glasbergen.
www.glasbergen.com

**"This job has cost me my health, my family,
and my soul. Can I get a receipt?"**

concept (Pinder, 1998), investigators today view the construct of employee engagement as similarly multidimensional (Saks, 2006). Though this construct is not identical with that of job satisfaction—a worker may be content with his or her job but have little involvement in, absorption with, or dedication to it—the two terms are quite similar in their positive focus.

What Promotes Employee Engagement?

Positive Emotions and Work   Studies have found that disposition to positive emotionality can have a significant impact on an individual at work. People who tend to score higher on measures of positive emotionality are often described as more enthusiastic, more energetic, and more excited about their jobs. They also report greater job satisfaction (Luthans & Youssef, 2009; Warr, 1999). Peterson and his colleagues (2009) suggested that personal zest, which they defined as "approaching life with anticipation, energy, and excitement," is a particularly important form of positive emotionality; they

found it predicted work satisfaction as well as a view of one's work as a calling. Indeed, positive emotions at work can be partially responsible for several processes that enhance both personal fulfillment and worker productivity.

Allison Isen and her colleagues (Isen, 2008, 2009) studied the impact of positive emotions on several basic psychological processes as well as in the workplace. They found that positive emotions generally enhance problem solving and decision making and can lead to more flexible, innovative, and creative solutions. They can also lead to more favorable evaluations of others and increase positive behavior in the workplace, such as helpfulness, generosity, and empathy for others.

Growing evidence also exists that employees who experience more positive emotions at work make greater contributions to organizational effectiveness (Pinder, 1998). When people are in good moods they are more sociable, less aggressive, and better able to recall positive information. More positive moods also contribute to positive *spontaneous behavior* in the workplace (George & Brief, 1992).

This means that without special consciousness, such persons are more likely to be helpful to others, to develop skills that aid the organization, make constructive rather than destructive criticisms, spread goodwill, and take actions that help protect the organization from threats and dangers. Additionally, workers who experience more positive emotions tend to suffer fewer job injuries.

Are happier people more successful than their less happy peers on job-related and performance variables? Researchers affirmed that not only is there a significant link between personal happiness and vocational success, but that positive emotionality precedes and enhances workplace achievement (Boehm & Lyubormisky, 2008; Lyubormisky, King, & Diener, 2005; Staw, Sutton, & Pelled, 1994). In other words, persons who possess higher confidence, optimism, self-efficacy, likability, and sociability have a definite advantage when launching their careers—and are more likely to advance than their less happy peers.

Investigators have suggested several pathways to explain this outcome. First, positive emotions are associated with approach-oriented behavior (Elliot & Thrash, 2002), so that people in a good mood are more apt to enter novel situations, interact with others, and pursue new goals (Carver, 2003). Second, workers who experience positive emotions not only go beyond their required duties at work but tend to be more engaged with their jobs (George, 1995). In other words, happy people show less burnout, less emotional exhaustion, and less absenteeism—and they are less likely to quit their jobs than unhappy people (Herrbach, 2006). Third, those with a positive disposition tend to be more popular and to gain greater social support from both colleagues and supervisors (Feingold, 1983; Iverson et al., 1998). This latter finding certainly confirms most people's experiences, for virtually everyone prefers to be around co-workers who are pleasant and upbeat rather than moody or irritable. Finally, there is experimental evidence that experiencing happiness triggers

helpful behavior toward others, such as volunteering one's time (Baron & Bronfen, 1994) or making a charitable contribution (Cunningham, Steinberg, & Grev, 1980). Thus those with high positivity are more likely to be better team players than their unhappier counterparts and to be valued more highly by coworkers. All of these factors contribute to career success—possibly quite substantially. Fred Luthans and colleagues proposed the notion of **psychological capital (PsyCap)** to explain what catalyzes many of these behaviors (Luthans, Yussef, & Avolio, 2007). PsyCap is defined as a combination of self-efficacy, hope, optimism, and resiliency. New interventions are being created to help people develop their PsyCap (Luthans & Yussef, 2009).

Barry Staw (2000) hypothesized that positive emotionality at work inoculates people against the impact of various stressors. However, he also cautioned that people who exhibit negative traits at work can also serve a useful purpose in organizations. That is, sometimes organizations need someone to be cautious, doubtful, or even worried in order to optimize long-term functioning.

More Frequent Positive Emotions or More Intense Emotions? Although positive emotions provide several positive benefits to people at work, the question remains whether their frequency or their intensity is more important. As in the subjective well-being research, the frequency of positive emotions at work may be more important than their intensity. For example, many employees gain a huge burst of self-confidence, enthusiasm, and camaraderie after attending motivational seminars and workshops and engaging in personal tests of courage, such as outdoor adventures. But the problem is that these bursts of positive emotion don't last. Research therefore suggests that organizations could do more for their employees and for productivity by creating work environments that foster less-intense levels of positive emotions but induce these on a more reliable basis.

It's Not Just a Job, It's a Calling Amy Wrzesniewski and colleagues found that people in jobs ranging from clerical to professional viewed their occupations in three basic ways (Wrzesniewski, McCauly, Rozin, & Scwartz, 1997). Some people saw them as simply a "job," insofar as they focused on the financial gains from work and on the necessity of earning a living. Others conceptualized their work as a "career." For these people, their jobs were a way to motivate achievement, stimulate their need for competition, or enhance prestige and satisfaction. The third way people viewed their work was as a "calling" and a source of personal fulfillment; for many, this sense of meaning came from believing that what they did served a socially useful purpose.

Wrzesniewski found these three ways of conceptualizing work were manifested across many different types of occupations. It appears that matters such as income, status, and job prestige have little to do with what motivates people to work, especially when it is considered a calling. The following comment from a piano tuner suggests that occupations of diverse types can be seen as callings: "Piano tuning is not really business. It's a dedication.... I enjoy every second of it.... There seems something mystic about music, about piano tuning. There's so much beauty [that] comes out of music [and] piano tuning" (Turkel, 1974, p. 322).

Vocational researchers have become increasingly interested in the construct of calling, which has important consequences for individual success, resilience, and job satisfaction. Traditionally, the notion of a calling has been associated with Western religion, specifically with theistic command—for example, Moses in the Bible experienced a divine summons at the burning bush. In the early centuries CE, Catholic monks described feeling called to monastic life; later, during the sixteenth and seventeenth centuries, Protestant reformers led by Martin Luther and John Calvin argued that any occupation could hold spiritual significance.

Today, some vocational psychologists suggest that people may experience a calling without necessarily adhering to a particular faith (Bunderson & Thompson, 2009; Hunter, Dik, & Banning, 2010). A consensus among researchers is emerging that a calling comprises three vital features: (1) *An action orientation,* that is, an emphasis on doing rather than simply being. Specifically, a calling refers to a *course of action,* an activity to be done. (2) A sense of *clarity of purpose, direction, meaning, and personal mission.* (3) *A prosocial intention*—that is, a desire to make the world a better place.

Although empirical research on callings is currently at an early stage, there is increasing evidence that people who experience their work as a calling reap definite benefits. These include more focused career decision making, higher motivation, increased job satisfaction, lower stress and frustration, stronger organizational commitment, and better citizenship behavior (Elangovan et al., 2009). Yet perhaps inevitably, there can be a downside to the sense of a calling in one's life. As Elangovan and colleagues (2009, p. 436) commented, "[It] can be all-consuming and never ending.... Such a state could also result in a permanent state of dissatisfaction, not with one's activities, but with one's performance." In this respect, those who experience a calling may need special guidance in learning how to balance their passion for work with family, social, and leisure activities.

Being in Flow at Work You may recall from the chapter on flow that some people report flow at work. Csikszentmihalyi found that people who enjoy their jobs often report being in a state of flow during work (Csikszentmihalyi, 1990; Csikszentmihalyi & LeFevre, 1989). Indeed, Haworth and Hill (1992) found that for most people, their flow experiences—when high skills were matched with high challenges—came primarily from the work environment. However, Csikszentmihalyi (1997) also found that people report positive experiences of flow at work but at the same time may feel less happy at work than in other contexts (the "paradox of work"). Nonetheless, he suggested that having more flow experiences is a key to job satisfaction, or to what we might term today *engagement*.

What specific features of work contribute to flow? Turner, Barling, and Zacharatos (2002) argued that the job characteristics model (JCM) offers a useful perspective, outlining five core elements that influence workers' attitudes and behavior. These encompass *skill variety* (the degree to which a job requires different activities and skills); *task identity* (the extent to which a job requires completion of a whole and identifiable work product or service); *task significance* (the degree to which a job exerts a meaningful impact on others); *autonomy* (the extent to which a worker has independence in deciding the schedule and process of work); and *feedback* (the degree to which a worker is given information about his or her performance). Although the question of whether flow stems more from personal or work factors has yet received little empirical attention, Fullager and Kelloway (2009) found that situational factors were more important than dispositional factors in a study of flow during design work among advanced architectural students.

Self-Actualizing at Work The construct of employee engagement has attracted considerable interest among practitioners in recent years. Yet it has been hampered by empirical issues, particularly how to measure accurately and meaningfully an employee's degree of job involvement. To help rectify this situation, Hoffman (2004) developed a scale of employee self-actualization based specifically on Maslow's motivational framework, with self-reports focusing on such aspects as creativity, challenge, peak experiences, and contribution to world betterment through one's work. Subsequent research conducted with this scale in Venezuela (Hoffman, Yves-Simon, & Ortiz, 2008) and Italy (Hoffman, Solgian, & Ortiz, 2009) affirmed that Maslow's hierarchy of inborn needs and conception of self-actualization at work indeed possessed cross-cultural validity or, in his unique phrasing, was "species-wide" in both relevance and applicability.

A Strength-Based Approach to Engagement

Myths of Career Satisfaction and Success What can individuals do to enhance their own career satisfaction? An interesting perspective has come from Donald Clifton and colleagues at the Gallup Organization (Buckingham & Clifton, 2001; Buckingham & Coffman, 1999; Clifton & Nelson, 1992; Coffman & Gonzalez-Molina, 2002). They began emphasizing our personal strengths, or those traits, abilities, interests, and skills that show us at our best and make us unique from others. They also described the myths that they say inhibit us from using our strengths.

Donald Clifton

Courtesy of Don Clifton

The first myth is that fixing our weaknesses is a better strategy than fostering and building our strengths. Of course, people must try to improve their weaknesses and must try to change what is less adaptive or even counterproductive. The problem with this strategy is that many people believe fixing what is wrong is the most efficient way to fulfill potential.

The second myth is that people can do anything they put their minds to. In this light, Clifton and his colleagues mentioned two common aphorisms that express this myth: "If at first you don't succeed, try again," and "If you can conceive it, you can achieve it." These adages are touted in motivational seminars, but the reason they are mythical is that for most people they represent impossible goals. If you think about it, the notion that anyone can do anything is ridiculous. There are real limits to what any of us can accomplish in life. It is a better strategy to know what your limits are and to work with them.

Focus on Your Strengths What Clifton and colleagues emphasize is a focus on one's strengths. People should focus on what they do right. That is, we should examine what we do very well and seek to do more of it. So what about our weaknesses? They suggested that weaknesses should be managed, meaning that we should recognize those areas in which we don't function very well (whether it be number-crunching or machinery usage) and find ways to compensate, such as delegating responsibilities to others. The researchers also recommended that we initially focus on only one strength, and as it develops other strengths will rise in salience. Because many people are accustomed to look for self-weaknesses, one might ask: How does a person recognize his or her strengths?

Recognize Your Strengths   Clifton and colleagues observed that all strengths share five characteristics. First, they represent "yearnings"—strong psychological pulls we feel toward certain interests, goals, or directions. They comprise the internal compass that can point out our direction, if we pay attention to it. Second, when we fulfill a strength, we experience intrinsic satisfaction; that is, we feel good about ourselves and about the activity. Third, when we employ a strength in certain contexts, learning comes easier; it is then more facile to absorb information and to integrate it in satisfying ways. Fourth, in moments when we activate a strength, we sometimes perform extraordinarily well. During these moments we glimpse excellence, and sometimes we find ourselves in a flow state. Fifth, when we activate a strength, our performance takes less effort than it does with other activities.

The Development of Strengths   Clifton and his colleagues also asserted that strengths develop best in relation to other persons. They contended that interpersonal support, understanding, empathy, and commitment to relationships help create the crucible in which strengths can grow. Strengths develop when we place positive expectations on others and on ourselves. Note this is *not* the clichéd "You can do anything" type of expectation but rather a realistic trust in potential that can be actualized.

Finally, Clifton and his colleagues posited that strengths develop best within the framework of "a mission"—that is, if we can develop a deep commitment to the future or even a life passion, then it becomes easier to discover our strengths in this context. A mission that expresses in relatively basic terms its central foundation provides a guiding direction or purpose for our life. Clifton and his colleagues cautioned that a mission is not identical to a goal. Goals can be associated with fulfilling a mission, but the two need not be synonymous. This implies that a mission can give us direction in life even if we fail to reach some of its goals. That is, if we possess a mission, then the failure of a single goal does not derail us.

Employee Engagement: A Positive Work Environment

Job Characteristics and Well-Being   Characteristics of a job itself and its work environment are also important to satisfaction. After all, merely having a cheerful personality is not enough to create high satisfaction in any job situation! Once questions about job satisfaction turn to elements of the work environment, the findings become more complicated. Why? Primarily because there are so many factors that create the environments in which people do their jobs. Consider that a work environment is composed of elements such as multiple social relationships, the amount of time one is expected to put into the job, type of organizational structure, opportunities for advancement or recognition, ability to use one's skills and learn new skills, and numerous issues of salary and compensation.

Ten Qualities of Positive Work Environments   Peter Warr (1999) reviewed the research on job engagement and satisfaction and classified the major elements of the work environment that determine well-being.

1. *Opportunity for personal control:* People enjoy a certain degree of freedom, autonomy, participation in decision making, and self-determination on their jobs. The chance to make decisions about how to attain goals and to contribute to various aspects of one's job helps create a sense of competence.

2. *Opportunity for skill use:* Meeting the need for competence is also related to having opportunities for using one's skills and talents on the job.

3. *Reasonable, externally generated goals:* Satisfaction is associated with having moderately strong and clear goals that stimulate challenging work conditions.

4. *Variety:* A 1991 Gallop poll found that "interesting work" and "chances to learn new skills" were ranked second and fourth, respectively, in importance for job satisfaction. People like to learn new skills and to use certain aspects of work to stimulate curiosity and even personal growth.

5. *Environmental clarity:* One element is clarity of feedback, or how well people communicate tasks, assignments, concerns, and goals within an organization.

6. *Availability of money:* Some extent of job satisfaction does relate to one's absolute level of pay. However, studies have also shown that one's satisfaction with income depends substantially on a comparison with what others are earning for doing the same job. Clark and Oswald (1996) found that it is possible to calculate an average salary for different jobs and that the more people believed their pay was lower than the "going rate," the less their overall job satisfaction.

7. *Physical security:* This refers to pleasant working conditions, safety on the job, and ergonomically adequate equipment.

8. *Supportive supervision:* Supportive management and effective leadership.

9. *Opportunity for interpersonal contact:* Items 8 and 9 refer to one of the most important aspects of job satisfaction: gratification from one's social relationships at work. Since coworkers can be a source of support, recognition, validation, and other forms of social rewards, one's work satisfaction tends to be positive when those features are present.

10. *Work is valued by society:* People also need to feel that what they do is important in some way. That is, individuals derive a sense of life purpose from believing their job makes a real difference in the lives of others (London & Strumpf, 1986). In a 1987 Harris poll, researchers found that 48% of respondents listed "My job gives a feeling of real accomplishment" as the most important aspect of their work.

Leadership

In the growing field of positive organizational behavior, leadership has emerged as a key factor for engaged employees and flourishing organizations. This seems hardly accidental, for over 25 years of research affirms its importance for organizational success. Leadership is also a topic with a huge popular and business market, with myriad books on leadership available—including lessons we can learn from Abraham Lincoln and Winston Churchill, Steve Jobs and Bill Gates, King David of the Bible, and Queen Elizabeth I.

The investigation of leadership has undergone many shifts in approach, conceptualization, and attempts at measurement. Initially, the "Great Man" perspective, first advanced in the 1840s by Scottish writer Thomas Carlyle, held sway (Whitman, 2009). In Carlyle's influential view, heroic individuals, by force of their unique personal traits and drive, successfully motivate others to achieve as well. The classic aphorism has been that "Leaders are born, not made." Reflecting the influence of powerful figures like Napoleon Bonaparte and Abraham Lincoln, who rose out of obscurity and poverty to shake the world, this emphasis seemed an indisputable view. Great leaders were like distant gods, whom we could celebrate and revere, but never hope to imitate.

However, by the early 1900s, a dramatic shift propelled by Freudian theory took place. Even renowned historical figures like Leonardo da Vinci came to be viewed as deeply flawed and troubled, seething with inner conflicts. The very notion of heroism or leadership seemed naïve, and some scholars even denied that it existed. For them, history revealed such achievement as totally accidental—a matter of being "in the right place at the right time." Most investigators espoused only a slightly less extreme view: that there is no such thing as overall leadership but only whether a person has the particular traits needed for a specific task. From this vantage point, figures such as Abraham Lincoln, Franklin D. Roosevelt, Queen Victoria, Mahatma Gandhi, and Dr. Martin Luther King Jr. were leaders only because they were thrust into greatness by historical forces that can never be duplicated. That is, the *times* required a Lincoln, a Gandhi, or a Dr. Martin Luther King Jr., and so they led powerfully.

Such an approach produced little tangible results and also contradicted the real-life experience of most organizational practitioners. Thus in their classic work, Warren Bennis and Burt Nanus (1985, p. 1) declared: "Leadership is a word on everyone's lips … but no clear and unequivocal understanding exists as to what distinguishes leaders from non–leaders, and perhaps more important, what distinguishes *effective* leaders from ineffective [ones] and *effective* organizations from ineffective." During the 1980s and 1990s, the research pendulum swung back toward an emphasis on the personality traits or competencies linked to successful leadership. Known as the **transformational leadership** approach, this derives its name from the process hypothesized to account for group or organizational success. This perspective, most notably advanced by Bennis and colleagues (1985, 1994) and Bruce Avolio and Bernard Bass (1990, 1993a, 1993b, 1997), focused on the ability of a transformational leader to increase such qualities as self-confidence, intrinsic motivation, and self-expectation among group members. That is, a transformational leader unleashes the power and harnesses the talent within a group to help it be successful.

But how exactly? Although theorists have disagreed on specific emphases, the following three traits have been regarded as most salient for leadership: (1) *possessing a broad vision*—that is, preferring to think in big-picture terms, rather than on minute details and micromanaging issues; (2) *having optimism and excitement about the future*; and, (3) *valuing individuals for their unique talents* and *seeking to maximize their self-actualization* as the building blocks of organizational success. Three additional leadership traits are often mentioned too: (4) *dedication and hard work*; (5) *integrity*; and, (6) *providing clear directives and specific feedback* to subordinates. Finally, another far-more-nebulous trait is sometimes identified with transformational leadership: (7) *charisma*. Bass (1998) suggested that transformational leaders make followers feel more aware of their own importance and value to the success of the group. Kark, Shamir, & Chen (2003) found that followers socially identified with transformational leaders and felt empowered to take action as a result of their relationship.

More recent studies have moved away from a strong focus on transformational leadership toward a greater emphasis on shared and relational factors, especially on the interaction between leader and follower (Avolio, Walumwa & Weber, 2009). That is, the focus of leadership researchers has changed from concentrating only on the leader to exploring a wider context, including peers, supervisors, work setting, and culture. As Van Dierendonck (2011, p. 1234) observed, "Leadership theories are more and more acknowledging the complex process that leadership actually is."

Conclusions about Employee Engagement

In general, people are more engaged with work in which stress is manageable, when they are provided with challenges and opportunities to learn new skills, and when they are allowed freedom to achieve their own solutions to problems. A good fit between a person's personality style and the demands of an organization is also related to engagement. The conventional assumption that everyone wants a job that pays a huge salary for doing minimal work is a myth: Most people have a psychological need to feel competent and to believe their efforts contribute in a meaningful way to their society.

Ultimately, though, a definitive summary of employee engagement is difficult to compile. For despite voluminous research over decades, there is no consensus yet on precisely what the earlier construct of job satisfaction really comprises, how it is influenced by factors such as work organization, and just what its consequences are for running organizations or managing people (Pinder, 1998). Everyone seem to agree that this broad topic is important, but like many other areas of human behavior, the complexities of the relationships involved have proven quite challenging.

It is also important to note that despite increasing professional interest in promoting positive psychology in the workplace, several organizational analysts have offered critiques. For example, Hackman (2008) argued that the positive organizational behavior (POB) approach has overemphasized individual traits to the exclusion of situational forces and social contexts. He also contended that positive organizational scholarship is generating too many theoretical constructs with weak validity and unproven models and methods. As Hackman (2008, p. 310) commented:

> The field of organizational behavior at its best addresses cross-level interactions among individuals, their work relationships, and the broader organizational or cultural context. It would be a significant step backwards if an emphasis on the well-being and fulfillment of [individuals] eclipsed attention to those cross-level interactions that most powerfully shape organizations.

CAREERS THAT USE POSITIVE PSYCHOLOGY

Our review of positive psychology in the workplace segues well into discussion of how one might build a career around positive psychology. Indeed, there are many ways that positive psychology can become one's major career focus. As we saw above, several consultants in the business world use concepts of positive psychology in their work. In addition, a rather obvious way to employ positive psychology is through research. This entire book has been a survey of the many people in academic settings who have conducted research on positive psychology topics. Another career that for many decades has applied ideas relevant to positive psychology is psychotherapy and counseling.

As we noted earlier, Alfred Adler, Carl Jung, and others in the beginning of the twentieth century all viewed their systems of psychotherapy as ways for people to enhance their well-being and mental health. Similarly, early leading psychotherapists associated with humanistic psychology developed interventions aimed at helping people to achieve states of improved well-being, personal growth, and potential (Mann, 1979). Although research continued on humanistic and other theories of well-being (Cain & Seeman, 2001; Schneider, Bugental, & Pierson, 2001), the dominant thrust of psychology has centered on the treatment of dysfunction and pathology. Fortunately, the development of positive psychology has brought a renewed awareness of the positive side of human behavior.

Positive Psychotherapy

Positive psychotherapy as treatment is built on an enhancement of positive traits and strengths as well as helping clients find untapped resources of positive change. Seligman (2002) declared "treatment is not just fixing what is wrong, it is also building what is right" (p. 4) and as mentioned in chapter 1, a reduction of negative emotions and behaviors does not automatically result in positive emotions or psychological flourishing (Keyes & Lopez, 2002). Therefore, just fixing what is wrong is only part of the psychological challenge. In positive psychotherapy, clients are seen as active seekers of health who are already engaged in trying to solve their problems (Keyes & Lopez, 2002). Such a psychotherapy suggests that therapy focus more on client strengths, capacities for problem solving, and demonstrated competencies (see Linley et al., 2009).

Interestingly, just prior to the development of positive psychology, a small number of new psychotherapy approaches were already choosing to focus on client strengths and competencies. Viewing clients as true experts in their own treatment, they understood the psychotherapist's job as helping clients get unstuck and back on track.

Among the better known of these approaches is *solution-focused therapy* (Berg & Miller, 1992; DeShazer, 1985). Therapists help their clients rediscover what strengths they have employed in the past, remember how they have solved problems similar to their present one, and set realistic goals for newer, healthy behaviors (Durant & Kowalski, 1993). *Well-being therapy* is an eight-session treatment package based on the dimensions of psychological well-being proposed by Carol Ryff (see chapter 2). As developed by Giovanni Fava, well-being therapy helps clients restructure the way they think about aspects of their lives in relation to Ryff's six dimensions of psychological well-being (Fava, 1999; Ruini & Fava, 2004; Ruini et al., 2006). *Positive psychotherapy*, developed by Nossrat Peseschkian (Peseschkian, 1997; Peseschkian & Tritt, 1998), seeks to enhance an individual's competencies instead of reinforcing failed attempts at problem solving. *Narrative therapy* focuses on the stories we all tell ourselves about who we are and our relationships to others (White & Epston, 1990). By helping people change their self-narratives in a more positive direction, narrative therapy helps change emotions. *Acceptance and commitment therapy* (ACT) was one of the first styles of therapy to significantly integrate mindfulness into treatment (Hayes, Strosahl, & Wilson, 1999). In contrast to most forms of therapy, ACT teaches people how to actively accept and embrace all their experiences with mindful awareness and with equanimity, to commit to building their best lives, and to operate from their core values (Hayes & Smith, 2005).

Positive Clinical Psychology Soon after the founding of positive psychology, Seligman and Peterson (2003) proposed a model of positive clinical psychology. They realized that focusing on strengths and competencies could be used as a foundation for work with clients in psychotherapy.

Just what are the strengths that all effective therapy provides? Seligman and Peterson agreed with Jerome Frank (Frank & Frank, 1991), who insisted for many years that all effective psychotherapies instill hope. In addition, they added the traits of courage, insight, optimism, authenticity, perseverance, and an ability to dispute one's own negative thinking. Positive psychotherapy involves more than simply disputing negative thoughts, however; it also employs "deep narration," or telling stories of one's life in ways that build positive resources for the future. A positive orientation to psychotherapy also recognizes that positive traits and adaptive behaviors serve as buffers against future stressors and difficulties. For example, people who know how to dispute their irrationally negative thinking are better able to deal constructively with unexpected setbacks. Later, Duckworth, Steen, and Seligman (2005) presented a model of how positive psychotherapy might work by focusing on interventions that help cultivate pleasure, engagement, and meaning.

Their next step was to test positive psychology interventions. Seligman, Steen, Park, and Peterson (2005) tracked people's behavior for six months and compared the effectiveness of five different positive psychology interventions. They found that relatively brief interventions could increase well-being for up to six months. Within the ensuing few years, several investigators specifically examined positive psychology interventions. Nancy Sin and Sonja Lybomirsky (2009) completed a meta-analysis of 51 studies and found that positive psychology interventions can both increase well-being and decrease symptoms of depression.[1]

Life Coaching As concepts of positive psychology have spread, new types of careers are now emerging. Among these is that of life coaching. Its central premise is that many people who are well-adjusted and functioning satisfactorily can find themselves "stuck" during certain times in their lives; they therefore need a consultant to help them reach a major decision, mark a new direction in work or romance, or find a better way to find personal fulfillment (Biswas-Diener, 2009; Biswas-Diener & Dean, 2007). Because the construct of a life coach is relatively new, few substantive studies have yet been conducted on its effectiveness. However, recent research finds promising support for coaching interventions, especially those that focus on how to attain one's goals (Grant & Cavanaugh, 2011). Unfortunately, there are currently no consistent standards for certification or training in life coaching (Biswas-Diener, 2009). Quite possibly, though, as positive psychologists become interested in life coaching, they will urge organizations to standardize training and certification (Grant & Cavanaugh, 2011).

Positive Psychology in Schools

Among the more obvious areas in which positive psychology can be applied is in the schools. One of America's most famous philosophers was John Dewey, whose writings on education have influenced American educational theorists through the present (Dewey, 1938/1997). Dewey argued that most schools failed to foster exploration, a sense of discovery, or a development of sound judgment skills.[2] He contended that schools should be environments that foster a desire to learn, to expand one's potentials, and to live and work cooperatively with others.

What would positive education look like? First, positive schools would promote the well-being of students as a central goal (Huebner et al., 2009; Miller & Nickerson, 2007). To further that end, positive schools would focus on developing personal strengths and competencies as well as giving students opportunities to be fully engaged in activities (that is, in flow; see Whalen & Csikszentmihalyi, 1991) and in active learning. Positive schools would be caring communities that are built around cooperative relationships between students, faculty, and peers. Such schools would promote "academic buoyancy," or the ability to resiliently bounce back from the challenges that are typical of school life (Martin & Marsh, 2008).

They would also promote peak experiences (Maslow, 1971).

Several programs are already operating that share the ideals of positive schools. The Positive Behavior Support (PBS) initiative provides help for at-risk students and operates according to William Glasser's reality therapy. PBS encourages social competence, responsibility, positive communication, and self-management skills while taking a positive approach, rather than a punitive one, to difficult student behavior (see Scott, Gagnon, & Nelson, 2008). A similar approach came from Michael Wehmeyer (1996). He and his colleagues suggested that students who leave school as self-determined persons will adapt to the world in more positive and healthy ways than those educated to be passive. To this end, they developed instructional methods to enhance self-determination and found that students who learn greater self-determination skills indeed adjust better after graduation.

The notion of utilizing one's signature strengths has been the basis of the *StrengthsQuest* program in college advising for years. Recently this approach has also been brought to elementary schools as advocates have insisted that helping students to learn and use their strengths creates a culture of learning, customizes work to students unique needs, and fosters better bonds among students and teachers.[3] Some innovative teachers have recently begun to incorporate mindfulness meditation into the classroom—a technique that helps students focus, pay attention, and control emotional outbursts (www.mindfuled.org). Kirk Schneider (2005) proposed that students could benefit from an "awe-inspired curriculum." His point is that students need to be inspired and passionate about learning. Such a curriculum would challenge students to make life choices based not simply on empty or mechanized priorities but on what most inspires them and arouses their deepest strivings.

Since one of the stated goals of education is to nurture "intelligence," it is logical that some schools might want to encourage emotional intelligence as well. Indeed, several schools have begun to teach emotional intelligence skills. The Self Science curriculum developed at the Nueva School in California is offered to children in the first through the eighth grades and imparts skills essential to emotional intelligence (see Salovey et al., 2009). Among various skills, the curriculum helps children recognize and label their emotions, be more aware of multiple feelings, take responsibility for their emotions, and improve listening and communication skills (Stone-McCown, Jensen, Freedman, & Rideout, 1998). Several other programs that fall under the general category of Social and Emotional Learning (SEL) programs and Character Education also offer training in skills essential to emotional intelligence.

POSITIVE COMMUNITIES

Social Well-Being

Corey Lee M. Keys and Shane Lopez argued that a complete classification system for mental health should include three general components: emotional well-being, psychological well-being, and **social well-being** (Keys & Lopez, 2001). Emotional well-being refers to subjective well-being. Psychological well-being represents the basic behavioral and emotional dimensions measured by Carol Ryff in her model of psychological well-being. Social well-being was developed by Keys and comprises five dimensions (Keys, 1998).

The first of these is "social acceptance," or the degree to which people generally hold positive attitudes toward others. The second dimension is "social actualization," or the degree to which people believe that society has the capacity to develop and evolve into a better place. "Social contribution" refers to how much people believe their daily activities contribute to society and how much those activities are valued by their community. The fourth dimension is "social coherence," or the degree to which society is understandable, predictable, and logical—how it makes sense. The last dimension is "social integration," or how much a person feels a part of his or her community, as well as how much support and commonality one feels toward others.

Keys (1998) found that the dimensions of social well-being correlated positively with measures of happiness, life satisfaction, generativity, optimism, perceptions of neighborhood trust and safety, subjective perceptions of one's physical health, and degree of community involvement. He also found that this new measure of social well-being was similar to other measures of mental health, but not identical. Thus, social well-being is a distinct way in which people judge their own sense of well-being and is important for overall mental health and well-being.

Flourishing Communities

All perspectives on healthy communities imply that psychologists cannot be concerned exclusively with either the individual or the environment in isolation. Rather, what is most important is the person-environment fit. When the fit between the individual and the environment is poor, then problems can occur; when the fit is good, then the probability of human flourishing increases. But what is the nature of a good fit between a person and his or her community and society? How would we recognize it? One of the difficulties in highly diverse and pluralistic societies is that there are often several competing goals among citizens. Nevertheless, it is possible to identify a few factors that are common to people who wish to create a flourishing society.

Several researchers have investigated the notion of **social capital** as they study societies. This refers to the web of connections among social networks, as well the connections within social networks. When a society has a high level of social capital, then there is a greater sense of trust in other people, more reciprocity and helpfulness, greater participation in social and civic activities, and stronger social ties. Social capital, therefore, has both a behavioral component (for example, civic participation) and an attitudinal component (for example, trust in others) (Yip et al., 2007). Several studies have also found that higher social capital results in better physical health for citizens (Poortinga, 2006; Yip et al., 2007).

During the mid-twentieth century, the anthropologist Ruth Benedict presented her observations of what she called "high synergy cultures" (Maslow, Honigmann & Mead, 1970). These are cultures in which people engage in many activities that are mutually reinforcing and enhancing of their general well-being. In contrast, low-synergy cultures are those in which personal goals often conflict with society's overall well-being. Low-synergy cultures would do a very good job of increasing the well-being of a few members of society—that is, those who achieved their personal goals. As you might guess, however, high-synergy cultures are more likely to increase the well-being of most of its members. Maslow (1971) did much to popularize Benedict's ideas on synergy, especially in emphasizing their relevance for business and organizational success.

Lawrence Kohlberg proposed a similar idea in an extension of his stage theory of moral development. That is, he began to argue in terms of a "just community," in which social bonding and cooperation helped people move to higher levels of moral development (Power & Reimer, 1979). Maslow (1961) advanced his own version of a utopian society—what he called "eupsychia," or the good society. He speculated on what a society would be like if most of its members were self-actualizing people—that is, possessing excellent ability to see the truth in people and situations, functioning creatively and spontaneously, sustaining the greater courage of their convictions, and feeling a strong sense of responsibility to their fellow human beings.

Social Contagion: the Power of Social Networks

Several recent studies have produced very intriguing findings on how powerful social networks can be for our lives. Nicolas Christakis and James Fowler (2011) found that certain behaviors and even emotions can spread through social networks. They call this phenomenon **social contagion**. Their studies and those of others have shown that rates of obesity and behaviors such as quitting smoking can spread throughout social networks (Christakis & Fowler, 2007; Christakis & Fowler, 2008). For instance, they suggested that if one of your friends begins to put on body weight, there is a greater chance that over several years, you will also become heavier. Indeed, the more people in your social network who gain weight, the more likely you will also become heavier.

The same effect occurs when people try to quit smoking. Intriguingly, these effects do not occur only among close friends. That is, your friend may influence you, and then you may influence other people who have no connection with your friend.[4]

Fowler and Christakis also found social contagion effects for happiness (Fowler & Christakis, 2009). They examined what they called a "dynamic spread of happiness" in a single community over a span of 20 years. In their study, they found that happiness spread throughout social networks up to three degrees of separation. That is, if you are happy, this can impact your friend and your friend's friend as well. In addition, the effect does not come from the tendency of people to associate with others who are similar. Physical distance from others moderates the effect. For instance, if you have a friend who is happy and lives within a mile (1.6 km) of you, then the probability that you will be happier increases by 25%. The farther away your friend lives, the smaller the impact on you.[5] Interestingly, the effect did not apply to coworkers: Your happiness will not impact those you work with, and vice versa.

When they looked at faces of Facebook friends[6] in terms of acts of kindness (Fowler & Christakis, 2010), they also found a social contagion effect for smiling. Specifically, they found that each act of kindness spread throughout a social network, and its impact was tripled as it spread. They concluded that "cooperative behavior cascades into human social networks" (p. 5334). Practicing "random acts of kindness" can, in fact, be good for you and those around you. It must be noted that they have also found social contagion effects for loneliness and uncooperative behavior. Therefore, the quality of one's social networks appears to matter a great deal.

Community Psychology

Among the ways that psychology has moved beyond an emphasis on the individual is through the specialty area of **community psychology**, which emphasizes the role of the environment and the social world in both the creation of problems and the solution to those problems. Community psychology studies the person-in-social-context (Rappaport & Seidman, 2000; Smith, 2001). Rappaport (1977) remarked that community psychology should be thought of as a perspective built on three general foundations: cultural relativity, diversity, and ecology.

First, cultural relativity affirms that social rules, mores, and standards differ among cultural groups. Second, in many societies, the reality of cultural diversity presents the necessity of recognizing that differences among community subgroups continue to exist. Finally, the notion of ecology is applied not just to the natural environment but also to the reality of human ecology. The community psychology perspective thus insists that people exist not in isolation but in a constant variety of intricate relationships with their environment. Another implication is that community psychology should focus on competencies. Change happens by identifying the strengths, resources, and efficiencies of people and environments (Smith, 2001).

In addition, community psychology is sometimes involved with social or political activism. Indeed, research found that engaging in political activism can enhance personal well-being (Klar & Kasser, 2009). In their investigation, political activism increased happiness, a sense of vitality, and purpose. Of course, group activism also gives people a sense of social bonding and shared goals. Finally, community psychology tends to be more heavily involved in prevention than are other applied areas of psychology.

Empowerment A key concept in community psychology is that of empowerment (Smith, 2001). This refers to the process of enabling people who are marginalized or underprivileged to increase their personal and political power by taking charge of their lives and thereby enhance their efficacy, competence, and self-determination (Rappaport, 1990). Community psychology interventions are designed to help people take control of their own environments and master their own problems (Orford, 1992).

Former U.S. Vice President Al Gore (2001) suggested that neglected environments characterized by disarray, disorder, and debilitation create a sense of *learned powerlessness*. That is, if peoples' efforts to solve problems in their own neighborhood are consistently unsuccessful, then they're likely to lose hope, optimism, and a sense of self-efficacy in the ability to implement meaningful changes in their own environment. The opposite of learned powerlessness is **learned empowerment**. Through community activity that produces tangible results, people can learn to assert a degree of control over their communities. Indeed, people feel better about themselves and their communities when they believe they have a voice, that they are able to make changes, and that they can participate meaningfully in the democratic process (Huang & Blumenthal, 2009).

Robert Sampson (2001; Sampson et al., 1997, 1999) proposed that one form of learned empowerment is a sense of **collective efficacy**. In general, it is social cohesion in a community that creates local friendship networks and a sense of agency, or a willingness to intervene in making one's neighborhood a better place to live. When collective efficacy in a neighborhood is high, then criminal activity is reduced. Cohesion and informal social ties with one's neighbors buffer community fear and mistrust (Ross & Jang, 2000). Trust can be partially built by a willingness to be involved in one's community. This can take the form of participation in neighborhood organizations such as crime watch, the PTA, and voluntary community cleanups. A sense of agency or willingness to intervene can also come from little things like watching a neighbor's children at the park or paying attention to unusual activity going on at neighbors' homes. Generally research has found that high social organization, high social capital, and a sense of community contribute to better neighborhood quality of life (Shinn & Toohey, 2003).

Community Interventions A unique aspect of community psychology is its emphasis on positive interventions at a community level. If these work successfully they can impact large groups of people by improving both personal lives and the lives of the communities.

For example, many elderly persons face a decline in physical and/or cognitive functioning. Most people in this situation do not wish to leave their homes to receive institutional care.[7] However, they definitely need assistance with various chores at home and also with shopping. To address this problem, the "village movement" was created (Ludden, 2010). Villages are organized networks of volunteers who offer assistance to older persons wishing to continue living in their homes. Volunteers help with transportation needs, household repairs, and even with teaching computer skills. These small gestures can be all that's needed for an elderly person to continue to enjoy a home that holds many comforts and fosters happy memories.

Volunteerism

Earlier in this book we saw that people reported feeling happier when they pursued goals that have personal meaning for them (Oishi et al., 1999; Sheldon, 2002). If one of those goals was to be more involved with their communities, then individuals also tended to feel greater well-being. One way to become more engaged with community is through volunteering.

Every day millions of people around the world donate their time, effort, and emotional support to the welfare of people who are often complete strangers. Mark Snyder (2011) reported that over 100 million people daily donate their time to volunteer organizations and causes. Why would anyone do this? According to some motivational theories, there are no immediate and tangible rewards for volunteering. Yet if one is helping another person in a direct and hands-on fashion, personal benefits can be immediately felt through the other's presence. What about volunteering for a political cause, working on environmental issues, or working for other causes oriented toward future hopes and dreams? Why do people volunteer for these?

Mark Snyder (2011; Snyder, Clary, & Stukas, 2000) and his colleagues found that rather than a single motive existing for volunteerism, several reasons explain why people volunteer. These include altruism, seeking to gain knowledge and understanding, a desire to enhance self-esteem, and social pressure. It is interesting to note that the strength of a person's altruistic motives is not associated with long-term volunteerism. People who volunteer over an extended period tend to be motivated by desire for greater understanding, to enhance their social identity, and for self-esteem. That is, they view their efforts as contributing to their own personal growth. However, the impact of volunteering is greater if a person holds prosocial values and the volunteer activity is compatible with one's self-identity (Hitlin, 2007). As we noted earlier, volunteering has been associated with better health and longevity (Post, 2005).

CROSS-CULTURAL SUBJECTIVE WELL-BEING

One of the least explored influences on subjective well-being is the impact that our culture has on how we think about self, others, and even the nature of reality. Barnouw defines **culture** as "the set of attitudes, values, beliefs, and behaviors shared by a group of people, communicated from one generation to the next via language or some other means of communication" (cited in Matsumoto, 1994, p. 4). If we define happiness as the most unqualified emotional state of feeling good, then studies have found that people in all cultures have some notion of this generic, positive emotional state (Wierzbicka, 1986). Although seemingly all cultures have a conception of the emotion of happiness, there are substantial differences in how this general feeling is understood, expressed, and experienced. Diener, Oishi, and Lucas (2009) reported that there are "profound differences in what makes people happy" in different countries (p. 191).

Studies that have investigated national levels of well-being have found substantial differences among countries (see Diener, 2009c; Diener, Helliwell, & Kahneman, 2010). The Gallup Organization asked people in 124 countries to rate their current lives and expectations of the next five years (Ray, 2011). People who scored at least a 7 out of 10 on current life rating and an 8 on future expectations were considered "thriving." When the data was analyzed, Denmark was at the top of the list with 72% thriving respondents. Chad was at the bottom with only 1% thriving respondents. The U.S. with 59% thriving respondents was 12th from the top of the list. For several years, various research organizations have published rankings of countries on well-being. Table 11.1 gives partial results from a few of these surveys. (Because we are writing from within the U.S., we have taken the liberty of placing U.S. rankings in the table.)

Interestingly, some countries appear at the top of these lists on a fairly regular basis. For many years, Denmark and Scandinavian countries, Switzerland, and the Netherlands have ranked at the top of these lists. These small countries appear to be doing something right for the well-being of their citizens. Differences among various lists are often due to how well-being was measured. For example, in Table 11.1 each survey measured well-being by using a slightly different indicator. Another study took a somewhat different approach and measured well-being by looking at the prevalence of hypertension among countries (Oswald & Blanchflower, 2007). This unique index resulted in a ranking of countries that closely paralleled other rankings of well-being, though it was not identical to any.

For those interested in such rankings, many of the sources listed in Table 11.1 also rank regions within countries (also see Florida & Rentfrow, 2011). For instance, the Gallup-Healthways Well-Being Index ranks individual states within the

T A B L E 11.1 **Top Five Happiest Countries in Surveys of Well-Being (From 1 to 5, Top to Bottom)**

World Database of Happiness (2000–2009)[1]	Gallup Survey (2010)[2]	World Values Survey (2005)[3]	World Map of Happiness (2006)[4]	Legatum Prosperity Index (2011)[5]	United Nations HDI (2010)[6]
Costa Rica	Denmark	Iceland	Denmark	Norway	Norway
Denmark	Sweden	Sweden	Switzerland	Denmark	Australia
Iceland	Canada	Denmark	Austria	Finland	New Zealand
Switzerland	Australia	Netherlands	Iceland	Australia	United States
Norway	Finland	Australia	Bahamas	New Zealand	Ireland
United States ranking from top:					
21	12	12	23	10	4
Least Happy Country in Survey:					
Tongo	Chad	Bulgaria	Burundi	Zimbabwe	Zimbabwe

[1]http://worlddatabaseofhappiness.eur.nl/
[2]see "global wellbeing" at http: www.gallup.com
[3]http://www.worldvaluessurvey.org/
[4]http://www.mapofhappiness.com/world/
[5]http://www.prosperity.com/
[6]http://hdr.undp.org/en/statistics

United States. For 2010, the top five states for overall well-being (in order) were: Hawaii, Wyoming, North Dakota, Alaska, and Minnesota. The lowest ranked state was West Virginia. Looking at Hawaii in first place, you might assume that climate is a major factor in higher well-being. However, the four states right behind Hawaii are hardly known for balmy, warm winters.

Another way to explore differences among countries is to examine how well-being has changed over the years. The World Values Survey found that some countries showed dramatic increases in happiness from 1946–2006 (that is, India, Ireland, Mexico, Puerto Rico, and South Korea); some countries showed decreases (that is, Austria, Belgium, the U.K., West Germany); while others showed relatively no changes in happiness (that is, the U.S., Switzerland, Norway). It is intriguing to note that most countries showed increases in happiness over this period of time. It would seem that many places in the world are becoming happier over the years.

Why Do Cultures Differ in Subjective Well-Being?

Money, Wealth, and Income   The next questions concern why these differences exist among nations. One factor was mentioned earlier in chapter 3: differences involving income and wealth. Those countries with higher life-satisfaction ratings also tend to be countries with higher average incomes and GNPs. In fact, correlations between level of subjective well-being and national wealth vary from .70 to .80 (see Diener et al., 2010). However, similar to individual income and well-being, the impact of national wealth on happiness and life satisfaction may be greatest when nations are less wealthy. That is, once a nation gains a moderate level of prosperity, then further increases have less impact on well-being (Veenhoven, 1999).

The relationship between national wealth and subjective well-being is partly due to the fact that virtually every social indicator measured in these studies is related to the prosperity and wealth of nations (Diener & Diener, 1996). For example, more prosperous nations also tend to have a more adequate food supply, better drinking water, better schools, better medical care, greater longevity, and other indicators of a higher quality of life (Diener & Suh, 2000).

Need Fulfillment   Recent studies have discovered that differences among countries in well-being depend on the extent to which people feel their needs are being met on a daily basis. Louis Tay and Ed Diener (2011) found that differences in life satisfaction were significantly related to how well basic needs for safety, security, shelter, and nutrition were being met. In another study, even at the upper end of the income scale, the more people felt they had adequate disposable income for luxury conveniences, the higher their life satisfaction (Diener, Ng, Harter, & Arora, 2010). This result suggests that income is the most important factor in well-being differences among countries. However, researchers in these studies also found some interesting differences between happiness and life satisfaction. First, they found that the amount of happiness, or positive emotionality, had a small relationship to income. Rather, greater happiness was associated with the fulfillment of psychological needs for learning, autonomy, respect, and opportunities to use one's skills. In countries that had higher incomes, fulfillment of psychological needs was a better predictor of happiness than was income. Therefore, investigators recommended that cross-cultural well-being be measured with two types of prosperity: economic and social-psychological.

Subjective well-being in all cultures appears related to how well people believe they are achieving the things they value (Diener, Oishi, & Lucas, 2003). Because individuals in different cultures differ in what they value, paths to well-being likewise differ among cultures. For example, Latino cultures tend to place a high value on interpersonal reciprocity and building strong emotional family ties (Lewis, 2002), while East Asian cultures tend to value social harmony over individual achievement (Diener & Suh, 2000). Therefore, how people go about pursuing well-being is different in different cultures.

Democracy and Equality Other cultural differences have also been studied, including the amount of political unrest in a country. Studies have found that, as might be expected, political instability in a country is related to lower levels of subjective well-being (Inglehart, 1990). People are also more satisfied if they can engage in the democratic process (Frey & Stutzer, 2000). A more recent study examined surveys from 1981 to 2007 in 45 countries and found that "the extent to which a society allows free choice has a major impact on happiness" (Ingelhart et al., 2008, p. 264). Higher happiness ratings were related to democracy, tolerance for others, a sense of control, and greater ability to make economic choices. Indeed, a higher sense of agency or self-efficacy is associated with well-being across countries (Welzel & Ingelhart, 2010). This aspect of nations seems to be related to collective levels of interpersonal trust. Nations in which people tend to be more distrustful of others or of the government show lower levels of overall subjective well-being in spite of income levels (Inglehart & Rabier, 1986; Tov et al., 2009). For example, the level of justice and sense of fair treatment in a society is strongly correlated with subjective well-being (Wong, 1998).

One characteristic of societies that appears related to democracy is *social equality,* or the extent to which people share in the economic and social advantages. Hagerty (2000) found evidence that the higher the income inequality in a country, the lower its subjective well-being. Richard Wilkinson and Kate Pickett (2009) present compelling evidence that a more equitable distribution of wealth and services leads to a nation that is happier, healthier, has less crime, higher academic achievement, and fewer teenage births. They present compelling evidence that inequality makes societies dysfunctional for all members of a society. They also argued that it is not only the poorer members of a society who benefit from greater social equality; everyone benefits. In this light, a recent brain imaging study found that when people were experimentally made to feel "rich," they reacted in the pleasure centers of their brains—as might be expected. Surprisingly, though, the

"rich" participants reacted even more strongly in their pleasure centers when someone "poor" received money (Tricomi et al., 2010)—they felt happier when someone needy received money than when they received it themselves. The researchers concluded that the human brain is "wired" to respond favorably to social equality.

Finally, Diener and Suh (2000) suggested that satisfaction depends partially on one's values and goals, and these are related to aspects of culture such as social norms, expectations, roles, and attitudes. Indeed, the notion that multiple determinants are necessary to understand the elements of well-being was supported by Sheldon and Hoon (2007). They found that needs, traits, personal goals, social supports, evaluations of self, and cultural contributions all make unique additions to subjective well-being.

Cultural Conceptualization of Emotions Most people in Western cultures assume that emotions are individually experienced internal states or reactions to events. What many Westerners do not realize is that cultures differ in how they define, label, express, and give meaning to emotions (Matsumoto, 1994). As an initial example, consider that Americans tend to think happiness and elation should not be fleeting but should last forever. For many Americans, contentment does not equal real happiness (Bok, 2010). But in many Asian cultures, contentment describes happiness.

In the West, it is common to understand emotions as inner experiences that have personal meaning. Emotions are used to inform people about themselves. In contrast, some cultures view emotions as statements about the relationships among people and their environments. In these cultures, emotions are somewhat shared experiences that are created between people and their social environments and are, therefore, social constructions rather than individual reactions.

People in different cultures also seem to experience emotions in different ways. For instance, Americans and Europeans tend to experience their emotions more intensely and for longer periods of time as well as to associate them more with basic physiological sensations than do the Japanese. However, Japanese report feeling *all* their emotions more often than do Americans and Europeans (see Matsumoto, 1994). Events that trigger emotions also differ; for example, relationship difficulties tend to trigger sadness for Japanese but are more associated with anger for Americans.

People in different cultures also utilize positive and negative emotions differently when they calculate their level of well-being. For example, positive emotional experiences are particularly important for European and European-Americans when they calculate well-being (Wirtz et al., 2009). That is, their satisfaction depends a good deal on the positivity ratio: the more positive emotions, the more satisfaction with life. East Asians and Asian-Americans employ both positive and negative emotions in assessing life satisfaction, but negative emotions are

especially important. Table 11.2 shows several countries with various indices of well-being.

In this table, the "social-psychological prosperity" column is a composite of: relationships with family and friends, opportunities to learn new skills or do "what you do best," sense of respect, and autonomy. The "self-anchoring" column refers to a satisfaction-with-life scale. Positive and negative feelings reflect how often these were "experienced yesterday." When we examine this table, it is clear why Denmark tends to score near the top in most rankings of the happiest country: It has a relatively high social prosperity ranking, the highest life satisfaction, very high positive emotions, and the lowest ranking on negative emotions. However, Japan has a very different pattern, with low social prosperity and moderate satisfaction along with low positive and very low negative emotions. Costa Rica, in

TABLE 11.2   Rankings of Selected Nations on Types of Prosperity (Out of 89)

Nation	GDP/Capita	Social Psychological Prosperity	Self-Anchoring Striving Scale	Positive Feelings	Low Negative Feelings
United States	1	19	16	26	49
Denmark	5	13	1	7	1
The Netherlands	7	36	4	3	26
Japan	14	50	24	44	6
Italy	18	33	20	67	63
Israel	20	56	11	61	64
New Zealand	22	12	9	1	21
South Korea	24	83	38	58	77
South Africa	35	42	53	29	44
Russia	36	72	56	79	42
Mexico	39	22	23	17	28
Costa Rica	41	6	18	4	38
Indonesia	59	63	57	24	43
India	61	85	46	63	22
Ghana	68	51	70	68	20
Nepal	76	88	69	50	10
Sierra Leone	87	80	87	87	86
Tanzania	89	58	86	52	32

NOTE: GDP = gross domestic product.

contrast, has a very high score on social prosperity, moderate satisfaction, and high positive emotions, and high negative emotions. This table illustrates quite well the various ways that cultures influence how people calculate their well-being.

Yong-Lin Moon (2009) suggested that such cultural differences imply different "frames of meaning" among countries. Different frames provide different ways of interpreting experiences and emotions to create judgments of one's level of happiness or satisfaction with life.

Cultural Conceptualizations of Self Recently investigators have shown increased interest in how Western ideas of individualism and self have influenced ideas about happiness, well-being, and social relationships (Diener & Suh, 2000; Kitayama, Markus, Matsumoto, & Norasakkunkit, 1997). Obviously, when we define the self or who we are as individuals, we simultaneously define the other, or who is "outside" of the self. Indeed, cultures differ in how inclusively they define the boundaries of "self." In turn, this determines how we define roles, expectations, and responsibilities for ourselves and others.

In cross-cultural studies, a major difference among cultures is the dimension of individualism-collectivism. Highly **individualistic cultures**, such as the United States and Western European countries, place greater emphasis on individual achievement, autonomy, freedom of expression, and on each person's internal thoughts, emotions, and experiences. These societies place a greater emphasis on self-sufficiency and self-reliance, self-expression, and "actualizing the inner self." Individualistic cultures tend to highlight emotions that encourage the independence of the self.

In contrast, **collectivist cultures** tend to be more socially oriented, placing emphasis on a person's immediate group and on the significant relationships among group members. Autonomy and independence are often de-emphasized in order to focus on the group's welfare. An individual's feelings of self-worth in collectivist societies can depend on how well one can respect authority and fit in through important relationships (Matsumoto, 1994; Price & Crapo, 2002). Collectivist cultures tend

to emphasize socially engaged emotions or those that impact communal relationships, such as humility and indebtedness. This can be particularly true for women in collectivist cultures (Lu, Shih, Lin, & Ju, 1997). In general, East Asian countries such as China and Japan are more collectivist than Western ones.

Studies have found that this broad cultural variable is a significant factor in how people experience subjective well-being. For instance, there is a stronger relationship between high subjective well-being and high self-esteem in individualistic cultures than in their collectivist counterparts (Diener, Diener & Diener, 1995). Similarly, in the United States, it is important to see oneself as acting autonomously by being consistent across various situations and in accord with one's self. However, in South Korea, self-consistency across situations was not a strong predictor of well-being; indeed, high self-consistency regardless of social situation was negatively associated with ratings of likeability by friends and family (Suh, 1999). Rather, well-being was associated with flexibility and adaptability depending on the social context. Suh, Diener, Oishi, and Triandis (1998) examined cultural differences in affect balance—the degree to which pleasant emotions are experienced more than unpleasant emotions (see Table 11.2). They found that a high positivity ratio was more important to subjective well-being in individualistic cultures and associated with feeling frequent positive emotions in many social situations. However, in collectivist cultures, the important information used to make a judgment of subjective well-being involved social norms about how good or acceptable it was to feel satisfied in various social situations. In collectivist cultures, giving oneself a very high rating on "happiness" might even indicate arrogance.

Joan Chiao and colleagues proposed a new area of research called "cultural neuroscience" (Chiao & Ambady, 2007; Chaio, Li, & Harada, 2008). Emerging from this research domain is evidence that neurological differences exist among people in individualistic versus collectivist cultures. In one neuroimaging (fMRI) study, researchers found different neurological markers for representations of the self in people from individualistic versus collectivist cultures (Chiao et al., 2009). Thus, it is quite possible that cultural differences go much deeper than previously believed.

Eunkook Suh and Jayoung Koo (2008) posited an intriguing theory to explain why individualistic countries tend to score higher than collectivist countries on measures of well-being. They began by noting that the goals of collectivist countries are to foster social order and harmony while individualistic countries promote an individual's value. Therefore, they believe, collectivist countries create "potholes in the road to happiness" by trying to maximize social harmony through keeping people "preoccupied with social concerns [that may] create friction in the pursuit of personal happiness" (Suh & Koo, 2008, p. 421). They theorized that a focus on maintaining harmony in collectivist cultures results in preventing potential social disruptions—a situation that produces less time for self-promotion activities. Because the pursuit of happiness is ultimately a quest that requires personal autonomy, focus on individual needs, and self-expression, collectivist countries tend to de-emphasize it.

As true for many aspects of life, there are both advantages and disadvantages with each cultural style. One study found that collectivist cultures were more likely to buffer individual depression (Chiao & Blizinsky, 2010). The researchers speculated that a greater social support in collectivist countries provided crucial aid to those vulnerable to depression. Collectivist cultures also provide its members with a sense of collective control, in which group norms foster a sense of personal control (Thompson, 2009). Another study examined suicide rates and found that the happier countries—which are generally individualistic—tended to have higher suicide rates (Daly et al., 2011). They suggested that the social comparison processes in individualistic countries lead some people to believe they have "failed" as persons, and this self-appraisal can increase the probability of suicide.

Comments on Culture and Well-Being

There seems little doubt that the social context of our lives has a major impact on how we perceive ourselves, our relationships, and our responsibilities. It is also becoming increasingly clear that broad social contexts impact how we view the nature of the self and what goals we pursue in order to achieve greater happiness, satisfaction, or well-being in life. Because cross-cultural research on subjective well-being has rapidly become central to positive psychology research, this development signals a recognition of how social context affects people's experience of well-being and the good life.

Such research indicates that indices of well-being reveal something about how well a country provides for its citizens' needs. Therefore, some researchers have proposed that governments create national well-being indices that can be used to assess how well a country is progressing toward greater well-being (Diener & Seligman, 2004). This would be a companion index to others such as the GDP, which is based solely on economic indicators. It should be clear by now that individual well-being is not simply a matter of economic factors. For example, the king of Bhutan, a small Buddhist nation in the foothills of the Himalayas, proposed the creation of a gross national happiness (GNH) index to measure psychological well-being in his country. He further proposed to launch a gross international happiness project, which would connect efforts in many nations to develop new indices of national well-being. Recently, David Cameron, the prime minister of the United Kingdom, also proposed a national happiness index (Cohen, 2011). Such ideas are special efforts toward measuring the well-being of countries with something more personally meaningful to most people than industry production statistics. French president Nicolas Sarkozy, however, has responded to these ideas by proposing a French index of "ennui" or boredom (Brancaccio, 2011). He declared that "the intention is to 'Keep France French' by insuring that Anglo-American-style happiness does not get out of hand." His comment was not entirely sarcastic, for boredom indeed relates to low work productivity. However, the French response again illustrates that countries calculate well-being in quite different ways.

SUMMARY

This chapter has reviewed the search for well-being in the larger community and across cultures. Our first topic was well-being at work. Job engagement is an important element of overall well-being, and positive emotions at work enhance job performance. Important aspects of higher job satisfaction include dispositional positive emotionality, task variety, job control, and equitable pay. We also mentioned that by focusing on personal strengths and talents, people can increase their job satisfaction. The communities and societies in which we live also impact well-being. We provided some examples from community psychology to illustrate how positive community change can impact people's lives for the better. The final aspect of well-being encompasses cultural values, expectations, and norms. A short review illustrated how factors such as individualism versus collectivism lead to different notions of well-being.

NOTES

1. See a special issue of the *Journal of Clinical Psychology* (2009), 65(5) devoted to positive psychotherapy.

2. http://www.bgsu.edu/departments/acs/1890s/dewey/educ.html.

3. http://www.youtube.com/watch?v=wZYveRLtXXY.

4. For a list of references on social contagion, see Olivia Judson's blog "Social Medicine" for the *New York Times*, November 10, 2009.

5. For an image of the happiness network they found, go to: http://web.med.harvard.edu/sites/RELEASES/html/christakis_happiness.html.

6. http://www.edge.org/3rd_culture/christakis_fowler08/christakis_fowler08_index.html.

7. The Census Bureau reports that only about 5% of people over 65 years of age live in nursing home-style facilities.

LEARNING TOOLS

Key Terms and Ideas

employee engagement	social well-being	learned empowerment	individualistic cultures
psychological capital (PsyCap)	social capital	collective efficacy	collectivist cultures
	social contagion		

Books

Biswas-Diener, R. (2010). Practicing positive psychology coaching: Assessment, activities and strategies for success. NY: Wiley. *(professional)*

Christakis, N., & Fowler, J. (2011). *Connected: The surprising power of our social networks and how they shape our lives.* NY: Back Bay. The book that introduced "social contagion" to the public.

Weiner, E. (2008). *The geography of bliss: One grump's search for the happiest places in the world.* NY: Twelve. Weiner travels to the happiest (and unhappiest) counties in the world to interview people and see what makes them happy. *(popular)*

Wilkinson, R., & Pickett, K. (2009). *The spirit level: Why greater equality makes societies stronger.* NY: Bloomsbury. Presents the idea that more equity in societies results in higher well-being for everyone. *(popular/professional)*

Web Sites

http://www.worldblu.com/ World Blu ranks work places in terms of organizational democracy, or the extent they allow freedom and create opportunities to amplify human potential.

http://www.volunteermatch.org/ Looking for a way to volunteer in your community? Just go to the site, enter information about where you live, and read opportunities in the U.S.

http://www.worldvaluessurvey.org/ World Values Survey has many graphs illustrating different values and indicators of well-being around the world.

http://www.well-beingindex.com/ Gallup-Healthways Well-Being Index. Many graphs illustrate well-being by country, states, and cities in the U.S.

http://www.scra27.org/ The Society for Community Research and Action (APA Division 27—Community Psychology).

Personal Exploration

1. Employee engagement—akin to the earlier construct of job satisfaction—remains an important topic in organizational psychology. Yet little is actually known empirically about people with high intrinsic work motivation, especially over the course of their careers. Interview three people age 40 or older who enjoy their profession a great deal—that is, who display a sense of "calling" whatever their particular field, from education, medicine, or law to computer technology. Of course, these can be individuals whom you know like family members or family friends. Your interview questions should include the following: (a) Did you always want to have a profession in this field? How old were you when you decided upon it? (b) How have you maintained your interest and enthusiasm in your work? To what extent did you rely on yourself and to what extent on colleagues, mentors, and protégés to help in this regard? What gives you the greatest sense of fulfillment and happiness—what Maslow described as peak experiences at work? (d) Finally, if someone right out of school came to you for specific advice or tips about how to stay engaged and excited by your particular profession, what would you say?

   After your interviews with these three people, describe what you found most intriguing in their replies. If you could expand this pilot study to 300 participants, what would you like to investigate?

2. The psychology of altruism is gaining renewed attention in psychology today. Interview three adults who are over 30 years old; they can certainly be friends or family members. (a) Ask them each to recall an experience in detail in which someone acted extremely altruistically to them, perhaps in a way that was quite unexpected or surprising. This might have happened in childhood, adolescence, or adulthood. (b) Then, ask them each whether this experience changed their perspective on human life or social relations in any way? If so, how? Based on your interviews with these three persons, what have you found intriguing in light of this chapter? If you could design a study with 300 interviewees, what would you like to investigate further? (c) Finally, practice random acts of kindness for an entire day: Do helpful or courteous things for people. What was it like for you?

Chapter 12

A Look Toward the Future of Positive Psychology

> We must take care to live not merely a long life, but a full one; for living a
> long life requires only good fortune, but living a full life requires character.
> Long is the life that is fully lived; it is fulfilled only when the mind
> supplies its own good qualities and empowers itself from within.
>
> SENECA THE YOUNGER (ca. 4 BCE–65 CE)

Since positive psychology was created in 1998, it has shown extraordinary growth and has rapidly established a solid footing in the field of psychology. The many books, research articles, scholarly conferences, and related Web sites on positive psychology are increasing at an astounding rate. On a personal note, we have noticed that many undergraduate and graduate students express a very high level of interest in positive psychology. Indeed, their interest is often so strong that students frequently ask us how they can channel it into a career. The subfield is certainly attracting a growing number of eager students and enthusiastic professionals.

The rapid growth of positive psychology has also brought with it several notable accomplishments. Research on well-being has positively exploded in recent years, and there is now a new appreciation for the role that positive emotions play in our lives. As this book has illustrated, positive psychology research on self-development and positive relationships has found application in psychotherapy and counseling, in wellness promotion, self-fulfillment in the workplace, and even in government planning (for example, as a measure of *Gross National Happiness*).

But as any scientific specialty evolves, it must change to meet a growing demand for increased scholarship, research, and practical application. In order for any scientific endeavor to remain relevant, it must provide new knowledge, assimilate new findings, and utilize such knowledge to help better people's lives. Of course, if any specialty in psychology would be expected not only to adjust—but also to thrive—as it meets the challenges of change, that area is positive psychology. Therefore, we highlight several directions in which positive psychology may move in the near future.

HOW DO WE RECOGNIZE A LIFE WELL-LIVED?

At present, many research studies in positive psychology have investigated individual well-being by assuming that happiness and life satisfaction are the only criteria for understanding the good life. Although feeling happy and satisfied with one's life are important individual goals, these are hardly the only criterion relevant for defining a life lived well, one worthy of admiration and respect. Indeed, many of the chapters in this book have explored other psychological dimensions relevant for measuring positive outcomes in life. Of course, one could argue that such dimensions merely lead to different *types* of happiness and satisfaction. But this argument ignores the real complexities of a full and rich life. For instance, although romantic love can be a thrilling and beautiful emotion, it can also be directly tied to other less uplifting experiences like rejection, struggle, painful sacrifice, and conflict. Yet, romantic love becomes more meaningful when it has withstood difficult, uncomfortable challenges and threats that might have destroyed it.

According to Gordon Allport, a founder of modern personality study, happiness should never be a goal but rather a probable consequence of full involvement in life. As Allport (1955) declared, "Nor does the hedonistic conception of the pursuit of 'happiness' help us.... The state of happiness is not itself a motivating force but a by-product of otherwise motivated activity. Happiness is far too incidental and contingent a thing to be considered a goal in itself" (p. 68). Allport suggested that well-being is achieved through a willingness and eagerness to experience all that life has to offer in conjunction with a drive to expand one's sense of self. Similarly, Emmons (1999) quoted Rozick's remarks:

> It is not clear that we want these moments [of happiness] constantly or want our lives to consist wholly and only of them. We want other experiences too ... we want

experiences, fitting ones, of profound connection with others, of deep understanding of natural phenomena, of love, of being profoundly moved by music or tragedy.... What we want, in short, is a life and a self that happiness is a fitting response to—and then give it that response (p. 138).

From a historical perspective, it must also be asked whether an exclusive focus on happiness negates or minimizes the struggles of people who lived in the past. Many who were not happy very often nevertheless possessed dignity, courage, perseverance, faith, and dedication to their families and friends. Shouldn't those experiences also count toward a judgment that life has been lived well? Looking at this issue from a related perspective, Albert Einstein observed, "Only a life lived for others is a life worthwhile" (*New York Times*, 6/20/32).

Today, many researchers in positive psychology agree that happiness ought not to be the sole criterion for the good life (for example, Diener, 2008; Seligman, 2011; also see Gruber, Mauss, & Tamir, 2011). For one thing, the term "happiness" is quite vague and poorly defined from a scientific viewpoint (Algoe, Fredrickson, & Chow, 2011). In addition, when research findings on "happiness" are presented around the world to the general public, an even greater array of folklore on happiness is activated and the potential for misunderstanding is magnified. Thus, for some time now leading researchers of subjective well-being have insisted that happiness may be "necessary" to the good life, but not "sufficient" (Diener, Oishi, & Lucas, 2003).

Focusing on a purely emotional criterion for well-being, as in our contemporary understanding of happiness, brings up another issue. At some point in the near future, the pharmaceutical industry will develop and release a "happiness pill." How people define well-being for themselves therefore becomes very important. For instance, if happiness consists only of positive emotion, then why not just take a happiness pill? However, if well-being means more than positive emotion, then even taking a happiness pill is not sufficient for a life lived well.

Most researchers today agree that positive emotionality needs to be part of a whole life experience that also includes such factors as upholding prosocial values and working toward socially desirable goals. In addition, other approaches to well-being—such as that of contemplative spirituality—define happiness in ways quite different from most empirical investigations of average persons (for example, Ricard, 2007). Nevertheless, Laura King (2011) contended that voluminous research has affirmed the role of positive emotion in a wide variety of positive life outcomes. She argued, therefore, that personal happiness is still a relevant notion, even with its attendant problems concerning definition and measurement.

POSITIVE PSYCHOLOGY NEEDS BOTH POSITIVE AND NEGATIVE EMOTIONS

The previous discussion of happiness lends itself naturally to a consideration of negative emotions. For frequently voiced comments about the future of positive psychology stress the need to integrate positive and negative emotions into a broader conceptualization of well-being and the good life (Brown & Holt, 2011). Several investigators have suggested that in order for people to experience a full life, it is necessary for them to feel both positive and negative emotions rather than to eliminate the latter (Woolfolk, 2002). Years of research in the domains of psychotherapy and counseling, resilience and posttraumatic coping, and creativity have made it abundantly clear that both positive and negative emotions are essential for adaptation and personal growth. Blaine Fowers (2005, 2008) posited that a life well-lived requires a type of wisdom that can balance often-contradictory and competing claims of *the good* with a full range of emotions.

Indeed, an interpretation of emotions as either "positive" or "negative" can change with a specific situation (see Wong, 2011). In this light, Allport insisted it is possible to exhibit optimal mental health and *not* be happy! Similarly, several of Maslow's exemplars of self-actualization experienced troubled and difficult lives (for example, Abraham Lincoln in his last years). In brief, some exposure to unwelcome life events is needed in order for people to cultivate personal strengths (Stokols, 2003).

Studies by Shepela et al., (1999) on courageous resistance illustrated this notion that certain positive outcomes demand a blend of positive and negative emotions. Investigations have examined the characteristics of people who risked their lives in order to help Jews in Nazi Germany resist oppression. Usually, courageous resistors were ordinary people who found themselves faced with a choice: Ignore injustice or do something to help despite the enormous risks. Researchers found that it was difficult to know who would become a courageous resistor until people were faced with a choice.

The Cellist of Sarajevo   What follows illustrates how a combination of various emotions including hope, courage, grief, and anger transformed an unknown musician into a hero, even if only for a few weeks. The report begins in 1992 during the Bosnian war in Sarajevo as the city suffered mass shelling. One afternoon, 22 people were in line waiting for bread outside one of the few open bakeries when a mortar shell struck, killing everyone. The very next day after the tragedy, Mr. Vedran Smajlovic, principal cellist of the National Theater Philharmonic Orchestra, donned his work clothes—a black tuxedo—and began playing his cello in a bombed crater in memory of the victims. He returned for the following 21 days, playing one day for each of the victims.

After this event, a tuxedo-clad Mr. Smajlovic continued playing his cello at bombed sites throughout Sarajevo as mortars exploded around the city. People said it was "unreal" to see him playing in bombed craters; he seemed supernaturally protected from the destruction around him. As Mr. Smajlovic's fame spread he became a hero in Bosnia. A physician in Sarajevo at the time remarked:

> He seemed connected to some sky that was nicer than the one we lived under. We were all trying to find our own spiritual way to survive that hell. It meant a lot to

see that kind of spiritual courage. For some people [his action] was a kind of stupidity, but for me it was a perfect example of how the soul can carry you beyond that kind of horror.

Mr. Smajlovic continued to play until his cello was destroyed and he was forced to leave his homeland (Scott, 1999).

Theories That Integrate Positive and Negative Emotion

Many perspectives on optimal well-being covered in chapter 9 recognize the need for a full range of emotional experience. The two theories discussed next both specifically set out to integrate positive and negative emotions into a positive psychology orientation.

Dov Shmotkin and Well-Being Modules Israeli psychologist Dov Shmotkin's (2005) detailed, comprehensive model of subjective well-being in adulthood addresses our relationship to both positive and negative emotions. Shmotkin stated that our sense of well-being is created out of a dynamic system that fosters "a favorable psychological environment in the face of an actually or potentially hostile world" (p. 295). The assumption is that although we all encounter a potentially threatening world, our sense of subjective well-being is designed partially to protect us from the impacts of anxiety, worry, and fear. Shmotkin borrowed ideas from terror management theory, which postulates that people are often unaware of how death anxiety drives their behavior (Pyszczynski, Greenberg, & Solomon, 1999). That is, our attempt to find protection from inescapable anxiety and various threats to self-esteem can lead either to relatively benign strategies, such as mild positive illusions, or to more serious self-deception employing rigid and inflexible defense mechanisms. Research on terror management theory suggests that our attempts to create a stable sense of well-being are motivated in significant ways by negative emotions.

Shmotkin proposed that subjective well-being is built from four modules, the first of which is concerned with self-awareness, or our subjective awareness of well-being. This is influenced by factors such as need fulfillment, the ratio of positive to negative thoughts, and our movement toward important goals. The second module is concerned with how we report our own well-being to others. This is influenced by how we wish to present ourselves to others and is a factor in how we self-assess our well-being. That is, we may present ourselves to others as "happy" so as to convince ourselves this is true—a tendency particularly prevalent among Americans.

The third module is concerned with the relationships among evaluative dimensions of well-being—that is, positive–negative emotions; life satisfaction–affect balance; and our dispositional optimism (for example, optimism–pessimism). By defining our place in these dimensions and then combining them in various ways, we can create many different definitions of happiness and well-being. The last module is focused on narrative well-being, or the stories we tell ourselves about our own lives (see chapter 8).

Paul Wong and Existential Positive Psychology Paul Wong (2011) also proposed a comprehensive theory of well-being that values both positive and negative emotions. Drawing on his Chinese heritage, Wong interpreted the familiar yin-yang symbol in which positive and negative are intertwined, each interpenetrating and influencing the other. His concept of "tragic optimism" describes a state of optimism that simultaneously allows unavoidable pain into one's life. Wong contended that the search for meaning creates a "meaning mindset," which collects a person's overarching motivations, worldviews, purposes, and assumptions about the good life. He noted that great reformers and visionaries throughout history have functioned by means of a "meaning mindset" rather than a "happiness mindset." Hence heroes from history elevate their search for meaning above a search for personal happiness. Wong argued that his dual-system model, combining existential and positive psychology perspectives, offers a viable alternative for a positive psychology of the future (Wong, 2011).

The models of Shmotkin and Wong join a small group of perspectives that value both positive and negative emotions. Future research in positive psychology should utilize complex models such as these in attempting to understand the complex ways that people create well-being.

ALTERNATIVES TO HAPPINESS

Meaning in Life

If mere happiness is an insufficient criterion for well-being and the good life, then what factors are a better measure of well-being? Several researchers have suggested that considerations of meaning are a better way to conceptualize the good life. As we saw in chapter 9, psychiatrist Viktor Frankl believed that the creation of meaning—not of happiness—must be the major criterion of the good life. As a Holocaust survivor, he was adamant that the creation of meaning cannot be tied to happiness, joy, or any other specific emotional experience. As Frankl (1978) stated:

> The more one's search for meaning is frustrated, the more intensively he devotes himself to … the 'pursuit of happiness.' When this pursuit originates in a frustrated search for meaning … it is self-defeating, for happiness can arise only as a result of living out one's self-transcendence, one's devotion to a cause to be served, or a person to be loved (pp. 82–83).

Michael Steger (2009) suggested that meaning in life entails both purpose and a sense of significance. Indeed, feeling happy without a sense of purpose or significance essentially defines self-indulgent hedonism or, to be more generous, uncomplicated, naïve pleasures. People seem to need a means of making sense of the world (see Antonovsky, 1987). However, Crystal Park (2011) cautioned that the term *meaning* is liable to the same criticisms as *happiness*. That is, if *meaning* is understood simply as a subjectively good feeling, such as that achieved by collecting colorful stamps from

around the world or becoming a chess master, then the experience of it might be quite shallow. In other cases, a sense of meaning may be maintained by defenses or even blatant distortions; it might be highly egocentric or culturally biased.

Therefore, Park argued that meaning must be described in terms of breadth, depth, and dynamic understanding. Breadth connects meaning to goals, beliefs, worldviews, personal experiences, and a wide range of emotional and cognitive factors. Depth requires that meaning help us to confront and understand the fundamental givens of existence. Meaning cannot simply protect us from all worry; it must also push us to deepen our understanding of the human condition. Dynamic understanding refers to a conception of how meaning operates over time in different life situations. From this perspective, meaning is a process rather than simply a product that we create once and forget about.

Park's suggestions for an understanding of meaning applies to a positive psychology of the future, with one exception. Positive psychology does not need more breadth, insofar as its concepts apply to a wide variety of areas. However, positive psychology in the future may need more depth. For instance, studies based on the fundamental givens of life as encountered in existential philosophy and psychology—for example, death, meaninglessness, loneliness, and anxiety—are almost nonexistent in positive psychology (see Park, 2011). You will remember from chapter 10 that among the ways we can find meaning is through our relationship with suffering. Our previous discussion including both positive and negative emotion in positive psychology is relevant to Park's requirement of depth.

Some researchers have recommended a more dynamic positive psychology. Cowen and Kilmer (2002) advised that positive psychology pay more attention to the developmental paths that people take as they move through life. The nature of well-being and of the good life may be quite different at diverse points in life or for different life goals that people pursue. For example, research indicates that people define and create a sense of well-being differently at different ages (for example, Heath, 1991; Ryff & Heidrich, 1997). The nature of well-being changes with different situations, stages of life, life experiences, and many other factors that make up an individual lifespan. Such appreciation of life as lived through time is expressed succinctly in American novelist Willa Cather's dictum, "The end is nothing. The road is all."

Purpose in Life

The celebrated American philosopher Ralph Waldo Emerson implied that purpose in life may be the best criteria for the good life when he noted, "The purpose of life is not to be happy. It is to be useful, to be honorable, to be compassionate, to have it make some difference that you have lived and lived well." The philosopher Søren Kierkegaard (1843/1987) commented along similar lines:

> If I were to wish for anything, I should not wish for wealth or power, but for the passionate sense of the potential, for the eye which, ever young and ardent, sees the possible. Pleasure disappoints, possibility never. And what wine is so sparking, what so fragrant, what so intoxicating, as possibility!"

Although Steger considered meaning to be partially defined by a sense of purpose, others have insisted on separating a sense of purpose in life from a sense of meaning.

For example, Todd Kashdan and Patrick McKnight argued that well-being is best understood in terms of purpose in life (Kashdan & McKnight, 2009; McKnight & Kashdan, 2009), which in turn catalyzes our sense of meaning. By studying purpose in life, researchers gain an understanding of goals, religion, meaning, personal strivings, resilience, and well-being. It is in taking into consideration a strong sense of purpose in life that investigators can better comprehend why people might sometimes deliberately choose negative experiences or emotions over positive ones.

Kashdan and McKnight (2009) suggested three pathways to creating a sense of purpose: (1) through a proactive effort in pursuit of goals; (2) by a transformative life event that gives clarity to a person's life; and (3) in social learning by observation of other people. Wong (2011) added that we must recognize a variety of purposes, particularly higher ones. He cautioned that limiting our purpose in life to superficial pleasures or selfish ambitions robs it of its most important quality: providing a direction for personal growth.

NEW RESEARCH METHODS

When psychologists reflect on the direction in which their discipline is heading, often the call is sounded for newer and better research strategies. In positive psychology as well several researchers have proposed strategies to enhance a scientific determination of well-being and the good life. Namely, well-being needs to be studied with multiple measurement instruments and newer research approaches that offer a better fit with the complexities of human behavior (see Diener, 2008; Magnusson & Mahoney, 2003; Lambert, Fincham, Gwinn, & Ajayi, 2011; Ong & Zautra, 2009). After all, people are inherently complex, and an adequate psychological understanding requires equally complex tools of investigation.

Kevin Rathunde (2001) suggested positive psychology could benefit by focusing on the work of seminal psychologists such as William James, John Dewey, and Abraham Maslow. These early theorists of positive mental health developed their theories on the basis of subjective reports; they considered personal introspection a valuable tool to be used in conjunction with other research strategies. It does seem that experiences of well-being and happiness need to be studied as well from the "inside" and allowed to present themselves in all their human complexity.

Gergen and Gergen (2007) recommended that positive psychologists make research a more collaborative process between scientists and their research participants. For instance, years ago Kurt Lewin (1946) developed what he called "action research" that involved both researchers and participants in collaborative problem solving. In general scientists today agree that the use of multiple new research strategies will be more necessary in the future. Sometimes, however, the complexity of human behavior pushes the limits of the tools that science has to work with (see **Systems Theory** that follows). In some ways, the search for happiness and the good life is the ultimate "individual differences" variable. That is, no two individuals travel the exact same road to greater well-being. Traditional research results can give general guidelines based on average responses, but each individual must tailor a uniquely meaningful search for well-being. As Daniel Molden and Carol Dweck (2006) stated, a research approach "describing only the 'average person' risks describing no one in particular" (p. 192).

Systems Theory

Several researchers assert that positive psychology needs to view people in a more holistic fashion—that is, as integrated systems of mind, body, emotion, and cognition (Magnusson & Mahoney, 2003). Among the more fascinating recent changes in psychological theory is a conceptualization of human beings as integrated organisms described by various subsystems—physical, emotional, intellectual, behavioral, and spiritual. From this perspective, any definition of optimal well-being must include healthy functioning in all the subsystems as well as healthy integration among them. Such a viewpoint has revived the ancient Greek notion of the ideal person, for whom a healthy body, a rational mind, and a sense of social obligation are the hallmarks of the good life. Investigators along these lines have begun to see persons as integrated systems, the different elements of which complement each other rather than constitute isolated parts.

"Billiard ball" Model of Causality   Systems theory describes complex causal relationships among a variety of factors. Early scientific approach to causality assumed a so-called billiard ball model in which one object moved and hit another object, causing this second one to move. Analogous psychological models explained human behavior as a series of stimuli that impacted people and then caused certain responses to occur. Although a stimulus–response model is simple and easily applied to many situations, it rather quickly becomes problematic under certain conditions.

In order to illustrate this idea, let's follow the causal pathways of this model. Start with someone who increases her physical exercise regimen. This behavior results in enhanced mood. That leads to greater willingness to be involved socially, which in turn leads to positive feedback from others, a condition that enhances self-esteem and mood even further. The exercise regimen also decreases stress, a condition that results as well in more positive social relations, less tension, and greater optimism about the future. All of these aspects lead to an increased sense of well-being.

Beyond the Billiard Ball   So far, this explanation follows a billiard ball model of causality. However, a complete understanding of such a process must acknowledge that the enhanced mood, self-esteem, and well-being could also increase the probability that physical exercise would continue as part of the person's life. Indeed, the process need not start with physical exercise. It is also true that a cognitive commitment to better health could enhance the optimism and mood that allow an exercise routine to begin, which would stimulate the process from a different starting point. Once this process is in motion, it is difficult to determine which part of it actually causes another part to occur: Does exercise cause better mood, or does better mood cause more frequent exercise?

The answer is that *both* aspects are true, in which case the billiard ball model of causality—that a specific *A* must cause a specific *B*—doesn't fit the phenomena under observation. Lines of causal influence are distributed throughout the model, and causality is no longer unidirectional (that is, *A* only causes *B*) but is now at least bidirectional (that is, *A* and *B* cause each other) and possibly transactional (that is, causality is a function of ongoing relationship patterns between *A* and *B*).

Moreover, in this more complex model the individual causal connection between *A* and *B* may be less important to behavior than the total organization of the system. That is, how all of the parts work together is more important than any one element of the system. Systems theory was designed to provide a complex model that does not simplistically distort the world. A holistic perspective on psychological well-being, in which the whole is greater than the sum of its parts, is a significant theoretical development.

A Systems Perspective for Positive Psychology
As we saw in chapter 9, Jules Seeman's theory of personality integration is based on a systems perspective by incorporating physiological, perceptual, emotional, motivational, cognitive, and interpersonal systems into a holistic model. Kennon Sheldon (2004, 2011; Sheldon & Hoon, 2006) expanded this model by including biological processes as well as sociocultural influences on behavior, moving from the subatomic level up through the human nervous system to the impacts of personality traits, social interactions, and cultural influences on well-being (see Figure 12.1). He makes two points about the different levels

of his model that are relevant to this discussion. First, each level is irreducible to the level below. For instance, you cannot fully understand cognition by knowing about the nervous system. Second, many behaviors, such as those that enhance well-being, are best explained via cross-level interactions. So, for example, cultural assumptions about the value of individualism can impact social interactions, which may influence how those who tend toward an introverted personality style express autonomy. Interestingly, Sheldon suggested that research in positive psychology should focus from "personality on up" through his model. He argued that topics most relevant to positive psychology, such as joy, integrity, and cooperation, are studied in the most meaningful way at these upper levels. We suspect that others would disagree with Sheldon's exclusions. Nonetheless, his model does provide an illustration of how a systems perspective might be used in positive psychology research.

Although the notion that people are integrated and complex biological, emotional, intellectual, and even spiritual systems is undoubtedly true, what does this mean for how researchers study well-being? The limitations of current research methodologies make it difficult to describe the multiple lines of influence in holistic models. So, even

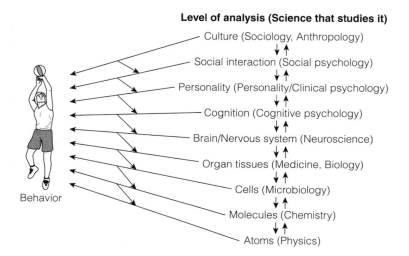

Level of analysis (Science that studies it)

Culture (Sociology, Anthropology)

Social interaction (Social psychology)

Personality (Personality/Clinical psychology)

Cognition (Cognitive psychology)

Brain/Nervous system (Neuroscience)

Organ tissues (Medicine, Biology)

Cells (Microbiology)

Molecules (Chemistry)

Atoms (Physics)

Behavior

FIGURE 12.1 Sytems Model of Processes that Affect Behavior from Kennon Sheldon

SOURCE: Adapted from Sheldon, K., "What's Positive About Positive Psychology? Reducing value-bias and enhancing integration within the field," (page 425) in (eds.) K. Sheldon, T. Kashdan, & M. Steger., *Designing Positive Psychology: Taking Stock and Moving Forward.* Copyright © 2011 Oxford University Press.

though we know that people are integrated systems, it is hard to study them in that way. One possible solution is to explore how environmental scientists study complex biological and ecological systems. A holistic study of well-being remains a future challenge for positive psychology as well as for the science of psychology in general.

INTEGRATE POSITIVE PSYCHOLOGY WITH GENERAL PSYCHOLOGY

Another major research challenge for positive psychology is to integrate findings from other areas of psychology. Several critics have pointed out that some positive psychologists have only minimally utilized research from other areas in either theory or application, with the result that many positive psychology research studies remain relatively isolated. However, there is a strong interest in applying positive psychology interventions that can help people increase their well-being (Biswas-Diener & Dean, 2007; Burns, 2009). Of course, clinical and counseling psychologists (as well as other professionals) have been helping clients change their behavior for over a century. Nevertheless, many positive psychology interventions neglect basic research findings on what makes successful therapy work (for example, building a strong therapeutic relationship), as well as on challenges to successful changes in behavior, emotion, and well-being (for example, client resistance or reluctance; unconscious defense mechanisms; unsupportive social environments).

Observers have also noted that research challenging some fundamental ideas of positive psychology has occasionally been dismissed too easily within the field. Studies on terror management theory, as mentioned earlier, strongly suggest that our attempts to establish a stable sense of well-being are motivated in part by negative emotions such as fear and death anxiety (Pyszczynski, Greenberg, & Solomon, 1999). Further, several positive psychology

interventions are based on reinterpreting thinking patterns from negative to positive (for example, emphasizing optimism, sense of control, self-esteem). However, recent studies of psychotherapy have found that changes in thinking patterns may not be primarily responsible for changes in behavior. Instead, changes in psychological flexibility and mindfulness may be primary determinants of the changes seen in psychotherapy (Flaxman & Bond, 2010; Longman & Worrell, 2007). Also, some researchers have begun to question whether a core idea of positive psychology—namely, that people should focus on their strengths—always leads to better outcomes (Kaiser, 2009). For instance, one study found that working on both strengths and weakness might lead to better outcomes than working on strengths alone (Rust, Diesner and Reade, 2009).

One last point: Some positive psychologists would do better to follow the basic ideals of positive psychology—in particular, the ideal of creating a science-based discipline. At times professional enthusiasm to "bring positive psychology to the people" as quickly as possible has threatened to undercut the rigorous standards of positive psychology as a scientific discipline (Kashdan & Steger, 2011). Delivering positive psychology interventions before adequate research has been conducted can lead to significant problems and erode scientific trust.

THE QUESTION OF VALUES

Another substantive challenge for positive psychology in the future concerns the place of values in science. Every student of psychology has heard that values should be removed as much as possible from science. However, it may be quite difficult to totally remove values from the scientific study of well-being (Kristjánsson, 2010; Sheldon, Schmuck, & Kasser, 2000). Of course, a researcher's belief system and personal values should never interfere with the analysis of data, but values undoubtedly influence research through the choice of research topics, in the forceful advocacy of an invested theory, and in complex methodological procedures (Kurtines, Alvarez, & Azmitia, 1990). In positive psychology, the question of values becomes of central importance insofar as conceptualizations of well-being rest on how best to define the good life (Compton, 2001b; Fowers, 2008).

Maslow was often criticized for choosing exemplars of self-actualization from people he personally liked or admired. Although he was aware of this problem, it is hard to imagine studying individual well-being without making a deliberate choice of whom to study and which traits to investigate. If positive psychology declares it will study "average" men and women, then that scientific choice, too, limits how well-being is defined and measured. For instance, the VIA Survey of Character was developed in part by surveying the major religious traditions of the world (Dahlsgaard, Peterson, & Seligman, 2005). In addition, the choice of particular values and virtues may have been heavily influenced by a contemporary version of nineteenth-century European humanism. That is, despite their seemingly universal significance, values have been emphasized within a specific vision of *the good*. Personally, we find the VIA list of virtues, as well as Maslow's criteria for self-actualizing people, to be quite admirable. However, we recognize that our personal values and belief systems enter into this admiration.

In the future, positive psychology needs to be more explicit about how personal perspectives on well-being influence the choice of research participants, the measurement instruments used, and the theories tested. It also needs to be more explicit about the concept of *the good* driving research (see Fowers, 2008). That is, it must specify more precisely what kinds of ideals of well-being and what types of "happiness" are being pursued through research. None of these psychological factors negate the scientific enterprise but rather bring the underlying assumptions of researchers to the foreground and make the process more open and honest.

The influence of values on the study of well-being can only be managed if the values in question are acknowledged.

CROSS-CULTURAL CONSIDERATIONS

Cross-Cultural Well-Being

Among the frequent criticisms of positive psychology (and Western psychology in general) has been its over reliance on North American and European research participants. It is indeed clear that some research findings are attributed universal significance when they apply only within a specific culture at a specific historical moment (Moon, 2009; Wong, 2009b). In this light, Kyle Smith, Seyda Smith and John Christopher (2007) examined folk conceptions of the "good person" in seven cultures around the world, finding common virtues across cultures but also differences. Most cultures saw the prototypical "good person" as exhibiting benevolence, conformity, and traditionalism. Note that conformity and traditionalism do not appear on any list of positive psychology virtues. In contrast, cultures varied significantly in whether they valued competence, which is one of the hallmarks of well-being in the West. The researchers also found that the virtue of respect was frequently mentioned, though it is not often highlighted in positive psychology.

Such differences have implications for applied work as well. For instance, one study compared responses to therapies that emphasized positive over negative emotions by looking at both Asians and European-Americans. The researchers found that positive emotion-based therapies did not work as well with Asians because they view well-being by contrast more as balance and harmony among both positive and negative emotions (Leu, Wang, & Koo, 2011).

Eastern Psychology Eastern psychological systems such as Hinduism, Buddhism, and Taoism offer alternatives to many topics relevant to positive psychology (for example, Rama, Ballentine, & Ajaya, 1976; Levine, 2000). Although Western psychologists freely borrow techniques such as meditation and yoga from the East, underlying assumptions of Eastern systems are typically ignored or dismissed (see Kabat-Zinn, 2011). For example, mindfulness is extremely popular in positive psychology; yet, this Buddhist meditational style is designed to cultivate an attitude of calm equanimity and acceptance toward all experiences, both negative and positive (Nyanaponika, 1954). Likewise, Western therapies based on Buddhist mindfulness significantly differ from approaches based on increasing the ratio of positive emotions to negative emotions (see Hayes & Smith, 2005; Mikluas, 2002). When Eastern psychological systems are understood properly, they offer clear alternatives to Western ideas on well-being, the nature of emotion, the elements of personality, and on changing behavior in positive ways (Compton, 2012; Davidson & Harrington, 2002).

Post-Modern Considerations

Along with an over reliance on data obtained from Western research participants, positive psychology has been criticized for relying too much on the Western cultural worldview. Ideas from critical theory, social constructivism, and postmodernism address the extent that culture, political systems, and history shape assumptions about well-being in ways that positive psychology and Western psychology in general have ignored. Positive psychologists emphasize positive emotions and say that people matter. Scholars working from a postmodern perspective emphasize culture and say that history matters. For instance, because positive psychology is based on a Western conception of the individual, the good life is defined in terms of

© by Randy Glasbergen.
www.glasbergen.com

GLASBERGEN

"I'm learning how to relax, doctor —
but I want to relax *better* and *faster!*
I want to be on the cutting edge of relaxation!"

personal fulfillment (Christopher & Hickinbottom, 2008; Sampson, 1988 see chapter 11). Becker and Marecek (2008) noted, "Like most of conventional North American psychology, positive psychology typically has taken the individual as the object of study without regard for history, society, or culture" (p. 598). That is, the very notion of what constitutes an "individual" in the Western world is shaped by cultural and historical determinations that are often unexamined. In contrast to Western individualism, the construct of a "person" in Chinese Taoism consists of multiple interdependent relationships, especially relationships with family. Some of these relationships, such as with forces of nature and immaterial natural forces such as *chi*, fall outside traditional Western boundaries of the self.

In addition to individualism, the modernist Western worldview emphasizes instrumentalism, in which "human action is seen as consisting mainly in manipulative or instrumental efforts to gain control over natural and social processes" (Richardson & Guignon, 2008, p. 606). What emerges from the combination is an ideal of a mentally healthy person as one who takes charge of her or his environment and overcomes adversities to successfully reach self-defined goals. The well-being that ensues is an enhanced sense of personal accomplishment and an internalized feeling of happiness and satisfaction. Although this is one legitimate model of well-being among many, almost all of positive psychology today is based solely on this one.

Indeed, an unfortunate consequence is that anyone not flourishing in this heroic sense might be chastised for his or her "failure" to be happier. In fact, a recent study found that priming people to think about their own happiness resulted in lower self-reports of happiness later when experience didn't match expectations (Gruber, Mauss, & Tamir, 2011). Although provoking a happiness backlash is certainly not the intent of any positive psychologist, the modernist Western ideal of individual fulfillment does tend to minimize the day-to-day social, political, and economic realities that define the identities of people throughout the world.

Occasionally critiques question the assumptions of modern scientific instrumentalism as well, in which science is considered the primary method to foster change. Often science is pursued with more regard for the rigor of its research than for its meaning. Specifically, Jeff Sugarman (2007) noted that positive psychology's concern with empirical rigor often results in somewhat meaningless research results. He observed:

> Technically exacting, but nevertheless, vapid and voiceless reports of empirical research fill the literature. Despite the often impressive display of empirical rigor, there is a lamentable absence of profundity, insight, subtlety, imagination, and genuine relevance for anyone seeking guidance for living a happier human life (p. 187).

Making the same point, albeit a bit more humorously, the Scottish poet and novelist Andrew Lang once quipped: "He uses statistics as a drunken man uses lamp posts ... for support rather than illumination."

Although the scientific basis of positive psychology provides a necessary foundation for the study of well-being, the field can better flourish when using additional tools to examine the human condition. Blaine Fowers (2011) asked, "Do we really believe that the good life is a scientific question that, in the end, will produce a technical solution?" The study of well-being is particularly well-suited to collaboration among various scientists and scholars. A thorough understanding of happiness requires input from psychologists, sociologists, philosophers, artists, cultural anthropologists, theologians, and many others. A complete understanding of well-being needs science and wisdom; group statistics and individual lives; objectivity and empathy; understanding and compassion.

Of course, Western psychology in general, not just positive psychology, tends to ignore much of the critique just presented. The impact of unexamined cultural and historical assumptions is a challenge for any psychology in the twenty-first century. In moving psychology toward a new paradigm, positive psychology is well-positioned to take up these challenges (see Mahoney, 2002; Snyder et al., 2002).

TOWARD THE FUTURE WITH OPTIMISM

Positive psychology has touched a vital chord in many professionals and students. With each passing year this specialty draws increasing attention. Many people are enthusiastic about a psychology that emphasizes the positive, adaptive, healthy, and admirable qualities of humanity. Findings are beginning to show that by focusing on human strengths and virtues, it is possible to increase success in central areas of life such as education, job satisfaction, romantic relationships and family life, health, and general well-being. In an era of new challenges and opportunities for humanity, researchers in positive psychology are tasked with exploring personality, lived environments, the

interpretation of life events, various criteria of well-being, and interventions to enhance well-being. Indeed, we are optimistic about the future of positive psychology and of humanity.

We close with a wish kept by the mother of one of the authors (Dr. Bill Compton) for many years on her dressing table. We hope you find it meaningful.

Throughout the coming year, may you have:

Enough happiness to keep you sweet;

Enough trials to keep you strong;

Enough sorrow to keep you human;

Enough hope to keep you happy;

Enough failure to keep you humble;

Enough success to keep you eager;

Enough friends to give you comfort;

Enough wealth to meet your needs;

Enough faith to banish depression;

Enough determination to make each day better than yesterday.

SUMMARY

This chapter has covered issues important for positive psychology in the future. Difficulties with using "happiness" as the sole criterion for well-being have been discussed along with alternative conceptualizations of well-being. We have considered the needs to integrate negative

emotion into positive psychology; to integrate positive psychology into other research areas of psychology; and for new research methods. Critiques of positive psychology from both cross-cultural and postmodern perspectives have also been explored.

LEARNING TOOLS

Books

Jason, L. A., Keyes, C. B., Suarez-Balcazar, Y., Taylor, R. R., & Davis, M. I. (Eds.). (2004). *Participatory community research: Theories and methods of action.* Washington DC: American Psychological Association. Discusses participatory research strategies that involve community residents in the design of research studies. *(professional)*

Sheldon, K., Kashdan, T., & Stegar, M. (Eds.). (2011). *Designing positive psychology: Taking stock and moving forward.* NY: Oxford. A collection of essays to mark the tenth anniversary of positive psychology. *(professional)*

On the Web

http://www.huffingtonpost.com/matthieu-ricard/
pleasure-happiness-difference_b_771048.html
Matthieu Ricard, a Tibetan Buddhist monk born in
France, talks about real happiness.

http://www.meaning.ca Site for the International
Network on Personal Meaning

http://www.tmt.missouri.edu/index.html Site explains
terror management theory and gives references to
scientific articles.

Personal Explorations

1. The Internet offers a vast potential in coming years
for bringing together people of diverse regions and
cultures in both work and social relationships.
Interview two persons residing in foreign countries
who have never visited the United States. Of
course, you can do this by e-mail or through a
social network site. Your questions should include
the following:

   a. Do you have impressions or stereotypes about
   life in the United States, such as provided by
   Hollywood movies and television? If so, what
   exactly are these impressions or stereotypes?

   b. Have you ever met any Americans? If so, how
   did they conform to your impressions or
   stereotypes?

   c. Do you think Americans have any particular
   impressions or stereotypes of life in your own
   country?

   d. If so, what do you think these are exactly?

   e. What do you regard as most admirable about
   values or aspects of life in the United States?

   f. What do you think Americans regard as most
   admirable about values or aspects of life in your
   country?

   g. What do you think makes Americans happy?

   h. What makes people happy in your country?

2. You can be certain that in the near future a drug
company will produce a "happiness pill." This pill
will reliably increase positive mood on a daily basis.
Assume that there are no serious side effects and the
pill is affordable. Would you take it? Why or why
not? What does your answer tell you about your
own definition of happiness and well-being?

References

Abdel-Khalek, A. (2007). Love of life as a new construct in the well-being domain. *Social Behavior and Personality, 35*(1), 125–134.

Acevedo, B. P., & Aron, A. (2009). Does a long-term relationship kill romantic love? *Review of General Psychology, 13*(1), 59–65. doi: 10.1037/a0014226

Ackerman, S., Zuroff, D. C., & Moskowitz, D. S. (2000). Generativity in midlife and young adults: Links to agency, communion, and subjective well-being. *International Journal of Aging and Human Development, 50*(1), 17–41.

Adams, C. E., & Leary, M. R. (2007). Promoting self-compassionate attitudes toward eating among restrictive and guilty eaters. *Journal of Social and Clinical Psychology, 26*(10), 1120–1144.

Ader, R., & Cohen, N. (1975). Behaviorally conditioned immunosuppression. *Psychosomatic Medicine, 37,* 333–340.

Ader, R., & Cohen, N. (1993). Psychoneuroimmunology: Conditioning stress. *Annual Review of Psychology, 44,* 53–85.

Adler, A. (1930). *The pattern of life* (W. B. Wolfe, Ed.). New York: Greenberg.

Adler, A. (1938). *Social interest: A challenge to mankind.* London: Faber & Faber.

Adler, Jonathan M., & Poulin, Michael J. (2009, Aug.). The political is personal: Narrating 9/11 and psychological well-being. *Journal of Personality, 77*(4), 903–932.

Adler, M., & Fagley, N. (2005). Appreciation: Individual differences in finding value and meaning as a unique predictor of subjective well-being. *Journal of Personality, 73,* 79–114.

Ai, A. L., Bolling, S. F., & Peterson, C. (2000). The use of prayer by coronary artery bypass patients. *International Journal for the Psychology of Religion, 10*(4), 205–220.

Ai, A. L., Dunkle, R. E., Peterson, C., & Bolling, S. F. (1998). The role of private prayer in psychological recovery among midlife and aged patients following cardiac surgery. *Gerontologist, 38*(5), 591–601.

Alfermann, D., & Stoll, O. (2000). Effects of physical exercise on self-concept and well-being. *International Journal of Sport Psychology, 31*(1), 47–65.

Algoe, S. B., Gable, S. L., & Maisel, N. (2010). It's the little things: Everyday gratitude as a booster shot for romantic relationships. *Personal Relationships, 17,* 217–233.

Algoe, S. B., Haidt, J., & Gable, S. L. (2008). Beyond reciprocity: Gratitude and relationships in everyday life. *Emotions, 8,* 425–429.

Algoe, S. B., & Haidt, J. (2009). Witnessing excellence in action: The "other-praising" emotions of elevation, gratitude, and admiration. *Journal of Positive Psychology, 4,* 105–127.

Algoe, S., Fredrickson, B., & Chow, S. (2011). The future of emotions research within positive psychology. In K. M. Sheldon, T. B. Kashdan, & M. F. Steger (Eds.), *Designing positive psychology: Taking stock and moving forward* (pp. 115–134). New York: Oxford University Press.

Allemand, M. (2008). Age differences in forgiveness: The role of future time perspective. *Journal of Research in Personality, 42,* 1137–1147.

Allen, L., & Beattie, R. (1984). The role of leisure as an indicator of overall satisfaction with community life. *Journal of Leisure Research, 16*(2), 99–109.

Alper, M. (2001). *The "God" part of the brain: A scientific interpretation of human spirituality and God.* Brooklyn, NY: Rogue Press.

Allport, G. W. (1955). *Becoming.* New Haven: Yale University Press.

Allport, G., & Ross, J. M. (1967). Personal religious orientation and prejudice. *Journal of Personality and Social Psychology, 5,* 432–443.

Amabile, T. M. (1983). *The social psychology of creativity.* New York: Springer-Verlag.

American Friends of Tel Aviv University. (2010). Different strokes for married folks? Retrived from: http://aftau.org/site/News2?page=NewsArticle&id=11993

An, J., & Cooney, T. (2006). Psychological well-being in mid to late life: The role of generativity development and parent-child relationships across the lifespan. *International Journal of Behavioral Development, 30*(5), 410–421.

Anderson, A. (2009, July). Seeing positive: Positive mood enhances visual cortical encoding. *Psychological Science Agenda, 23*(7). Retrieved June 3, 2011 from http://www.apa.org/science/psa/jul09-sci-brief.html

Anderson, R. (1996). Nine psycho-spiritual characteristics of spontaneous and involuntary weeping. *Journal of Transpersonal Psychology, 28*(2), 167–173.

Anderson, R., & Braud, W. (2011). *Transforming self and others through research: Transpersonal research methods and skills for the human sciences and humanities.* Albany: SUNY Press.

Andreasen, N. C. (1987). Creativity and mental illness: Prevalence rates in writers and their first-degree relatives. *American Journal of Psychiatry, 144,* 1288–1292.

Andrews, F. M., & Withey, S. B. (1976). *Social indicators of well-being: Americans' perceptions of life quality.* New York: Plenum.

Andrews, P. W., & Anderson, T. J., Jr. (2009). The bright side of being blue: Depression as an adaptation for analyzing complex problems. *Psychological Review, 116*(3), 620–654. doi: 10.1037/a0016242

Anglin, L. P., Pirson, M., & Langer, E. (2008). Mindful learning: A moderator of gender differences in mathematics performance. *Journal of Adult Development, 15*(3–4), 132–139.

Ansbacher, H. L. (1992). Alfred Adler's concepts of community feeling and of social interest and relevance of community feeling for old age. *Individual Psychology, 48*(4), 402–412.

Anthony, E. J. (1987). Children at risk for psychosis growing up successfully. In E. J. Anthony, & B. J. Cohler (Eds.), *The invulnerable child.* New York: Guildford.

Anthony, E. J., & Cohler, B. J. (Eds.). (1987). *The invulnerable child.* New York: Guilford.

Antonovsky, A. (1979). *Health, stress, and coping: New perspectives on mental and physical well-being.* San Francisco: Jossey-Bass.

Antonovsky, A. (1987). *Unraveling the mystery of health.* San Francisco: Jossey-Bass.

APA Help Center (2011). *How to help a friend or loved one suffering from a chronic illness.* American Psychological Association Help Center. Washington, DC: American Psychological Association. http://www.apa.org.helpcenter.help-chronic.aspx

Arch, J., & Craske, M. (2006). Mechanism of mindfulness: Emotion regulation following a focused breathing induction. *Behaviour Research and Therapy, 44*(12), 1849–1858.

Ardelt, M. (1997). Wisdom and life satisfaction in old age. *Journal of Gerontology: Psychological Sciences, 52B*(1), 15–27. doi: 10.1093/geronb/52B.1.P15

Ardelt, M., & Jacobs, S. (2009). Wisdom, integrity, and life satisfaction in very old age. In M. C. Smith, & N. DeFrates-Densch (Eds.) *Handbook of research on adult learning and development* (pp. 732–760). NY: Routledge/Taylor & Francis.

Ardelt, M., Landes, S., & Vaillant, G. (2010). The long-term effects of World War II combat exposure on later life well-being moderated by generativity. *Research in Human Development, 7*(3), 202–220.

Argyle, M. (1987). *The psychology of happiness.* London: Methuen.

Argyle, M. (1999). Causes and correlates of happiness. In D. Kahneman, E. Diener, & N. Schwartz (Eds.), *Well-being: The foundation of hedonic psychology.* New York: Russell Sage Foundation.

Arieti, S. (1976). *Creativity: The magic synthesis.* New York: Basic Books.

Aristotle (trans. 1908). Nicomachean ethics. In W. D. Ross (Ed.), *The works of Aristotle, Vol. 9.* Oxford: Clarendon Press.

Arndt, J., Solomon, S., Kasser, T., & Sheldon, L. (2004). The urge to splurge: A terror management account of materialism and consumer behavior. *Journal of Consumer Psychology, 14*(3), 198–212.

Aron, A., Aron, E. N., & Norman, C. (2004). Self-expansion Model of Motivation and Cognition in Close Relationships and Beyond. In: M. Brewer & M. Hewstone (Eds.), (Ed.), *Self and social identity.* (pp. 99–123). Malden: Blackwell Publishing.

Asakawa, K. (2005). Flow Experience and Autotelic Personality in Japanese College Students: How do they Experience Challenges in Daily Life? *Journal of Happiness Studies, 5*(2), 123–154.

Asakawa, K. (2010). Flow experience, culture, and well-being: How do autotelic Japanese college students feel, behave, and think in their daily lives? *Journal of Happiness Studies,11*(2), 205–223.

Askegaard, S., Gertsen, M. C., & Langer, R. (2002). The body consumed: Reflexivity and cosmetic surgery. *Psychology and Marketing, 19*(10), 793–812. doi: 10.1002/mar.10038

Ashby, F. G., Isen, A. M., & Turken, A. U. (1999). A neuropsychological theory of positive affect and its influence on cognition. *Psychological Review, 106,* 529–550.

Aspinwall, L. G., & Brunhart, S. M. (2000). What I do know won't hurt me: Optimism, attention to negative information, coping, and health. In J. E. Gillham (Ed.), *Laws of Life Symposia Series. The science of optimism and hope: Research essays in honor of Martin E. P. Seligman* (pp. 163–200). Philadelphia, PA: John Templeton Foundation Press.

Aspinwall, L. G., & Taylor, S. E. (1992). Modeling cognitive adaptation: A longitudinal investigation of the impact of individual differences and coping on college adjustment and performance. *Journal of Personality and Social Psychology, 63*(6), 989–1003.

Assad, K., Donnellan, M., & Conger, R. (2007). Optimism: An enduring resource for romantic relationships. *Journal of Personality and Social Psychology, 93*(2), 285–297.

Assagioli, R. (1965). *Psychosynthesis.* NY: Viking.

Asser, S. M., & Swan, R. (1998). Child fatalities from religion-motivated medical neglect. *Pediatrics, 101,* 625–629.

Austenfeld, J., & Stanton, A. L. (2004). Coping through emotional approach: A new look at emotion, coping, and health-related outcomes. *Journal of Personality, 72*(6), 1335–136.

Austin, J. H. (1998). *Zen and the brain: Toward an understanding of meditation and consciousness.* Cambridge, MA: MIT Press.

Austin, J. H. (2006). *Zen-brain reflections.* Cambridge, MA: MIT Press.

Austin, J. H. (2009). *Selfless insight: Zen and the meditative transformation of consciousness.* Cambridge, MA: MIT Press.

Averill, J. (2009). Emotional creativity: Toward "spiritualizing the passions". In C. R. Snyder & S. Lopez (Eds.), *Oxford handbook of positive psychology* (2nd ed., pp. 249–258). New York: Oxford University Press.

Averill, J. R., Stanat, P., & More, T. A. (1998). Aesthetics and the environment. *Review of General Psychology, 2*(2), 153–174.

Avolio, B., Walumbwa, F., & Weber, T. J. (2009). *Leadership: Current theories, research, and future directions.* Lincoln: University of Nebraska Management Department Faculty Publications.

Aziz, R. (2007). *The syndetic paradigm: The untrodden path beyond Freud and Jung.* Albany: SUNY Press.

Baca, J. C., & Wilbourne, P. (2004). Quantum change: Ten years later. *Journal of Clinical Psychology, 60*(5), 531–541. doi: 10.1002/jclp.20006

Baer, R. A. (2003). Mindfulness training as a clinical intervention: A conceptual and empirical review. *Clinical Psychology: Science and Practice, 10,* 125–143.

Baer, R., & Lykins, E. (2011). Mindfulness and positive psychological functioning. In K. M. Sheldon, T. B. Kashdan, & M. F. Steger (Eds.), *Designing positive psychology: Taking stock and moving forward* (pp. 335–350). New York: Oxford University Press.

Bailey, T. C., Eng, W., Frisch, M. B., & Snyder, C. R. (2007). Hope and optimism as related to life satisfaction. *The Journal of Positive Psychology, 2*(3), 168–175. doi: 10.1080/17439760701409546

Baltes, P. B. (1993). The aging mind: Potential and limits. *Gerontologist, 33*(5), 580–594.

Baltes, P., & Staudinger, U. (2000). Wisdom: A meta-heuristic (pragmatic) to orchestrate mind and virtue toward excellence. *American Psychologist, 55*(1), 122–136.

Bandura, A. (1977). Self-efficacy: Toward a unifying theory of behavioral change. *Psychological Review, 84,* 191–215.

Bandura, A. (1997). Self-efficacy: The exercise of control. New York: W. H. Freeman.

Barefoot, J., Brummett, B., Williams, R., Sieglar, I., Helms, M., et al. (2011). Recovery expectations and long-term prognosis of patients with coronary heart disease. *Archives of General Medicine, 171*(10), 929–935.

Bargh, J. A., & Chartrand, T. L. (1999). The unbearable automaticity of being. *American Psychologist, 54,* 462–479.

Bargh, J. A., & Williams, L. E. (2007). The case for nonconscious emotion regulation. In J. Gross, *Handbook of Emotion Regulation.* (pp. 429–445). New York: Guilford.

Barnes, M. L., & Sternberg, R. J. (1997). A hierarchical model of love and its prediction of satisfaction in close relationships. In R. J. Sternberg & M. Hojjatt (Eds.), *Satisfaction in close relationships* (pp. 79–101). New York: Guilford Press.

Barnes, S., Brown, K., Krusemark, E., Campbell, W., & Rogge, R. (2007). The role of mindfulness in romantic relationship satisfaction and responses to relationship stress. *Journal of Marital and Family Therapy, 33*(4), 482–500.

Barrett, W. (1962). *Irrational man: A study of existential philosophy.* New York: Doubleday Anchor.

Barron, F. (1963). *Creativity and psychological health.* Princeton, NJ: Van Nostrand.

Barron, F. (1988). Putting creativity to work. In R. L. Sternberg (Ed.), *The nature of creativity: Contemporary psychological perspectives* (pp. 76–98). Cambridge: Cambridge University Press.

Barron, F., & Harrington, D. M. (1981). Creativity, intelligence, and personality. *Annual Review of Psychology, 32,* 439–476.

Bass, B. M. (1997). Does the transactional-transformational leadership paradigm transcend organizational and national boundaries? *American Psychologist, 52*(2), 130–139.

Bass, B. M., & Avolio, B. J. (1990). The implications of transactional and transformational leadership for individual, team, and organizational development. *Research in Organizational Change and Development, 4,* 231–272.

Bass, B. M., & Avolio, B. J. (1993a). Transformational leadership: A response to critiques. In M. M. Chemers & R. Ayman (Eds.), *Leadership theory and research: Perspectives and directions* (pp. 49–80). Sydney: Academic Press.

Bass, B. M., & Avolio, B. J. (1993b). *Manual for the multifactor leadership questionnaire.* Palo Alto, CA: Consulting Psychologist Press.

Bassett, C. (2006). Laughing at gilded butterflies: Integrating wisdom, development, and learning. In C. Hoare (Ed.) *Oxford handbook of adult development and learning* (chap. 14). New York: Oxford University Press.

Batcho, K. I. (1995). Nostalgia: a psychological perspective. *Perceptual & Motor Skills, 80,* 131–134.

Batson, C. D., Ahmad, N., & Lishner, D. (2009). Empathy and altruism. In C. R. Snyder & S. Lopez (Eds.), *Oxford handbook of positive psychology* (2nd ed., pp. 417–426). New York: Oxford University Press.

Bauer, I., Wrosch, C., & Jobin, J. (2008). I'm better off than most people: The role of social comparisons for coping with regret in young adulthood and old age. *Psychology and Aging, 23,* 800–811.

Bauer, J. J., McAdams, D. P., & Pals, J. L. (2008). Narrative identity and eudaimonic well-being. *Journal of Happiness Studies, 9,* 81–104. doi: 10.1007/s10902-006-9021-6

Baumeister, R. F. (1989). The optimal margin of illusion. *Journal of Social and Clinical Psychology, 8,* 176–189.

Baumeister, R. F., Bratslavsky, E., Finkenauer, C., & Vohs, K. D. (2001). Bad is stronger than good. *Review of General Psychology, 5*(4), 323–370.

Baumeister, R. F., Campbell, J. D., Krueger, J. I., & Vohs, K. D. (2003). Does high self-esteem cause better performance, interpersonal success, happiness, or healthier lifestyles? *Psychological Science in the Public Interest, 4*(1), 1–44.

Baumeister, R. F., Heatherton, T. F., & Tice, D. M. (1993). When ego threats lead to self-regulation failure: Negative consequences of high self-esteem. *Journal of Personality and Social Psychology, 64,* 141–156.

Baumeister, R. F., Smart, L., & Boden, J. M. (1996). Relation of threatened egotism to violence and aggression: The dark side of high self-esteem. *Psychological Review, 103*(1), 5–33.

Baumeister, R. F., & Vohs, K. D., Self-regulation, ego depletion, and motivation. (2007). *Social and Personality Psychology Compass, 1*(1), 115–128.

Bauminger, N., Finzi-Dottan, R., Chason, S., & Har-Even, D. (2008). Intimacy in adolescent friendship: The roles of attachment, coherence, and self-disclosure. *Journal of Social and Personal Relationships, 25*(3), 409–428.

Baumrind, D. (1973). The development of instrumental competence through socialization. In Pick (Ed.), *Minnesota Symposium on Child Psychology* (pp. 3–46). Minneapolis: University of Minnesota Press.

Beals, K. P. (2003). *Stigma management and well-being: The role of social support, cognitive processing, and suppression* (Unpublished doctoral dissertation). University of California, Los Angeles.

Beard, K., Stansberry, H., & Wayne, K. (2010). The nature, meaning and measure of teacher flow in elementary schools: A test of rival hypotheses. *Educational Administration Quarterly, 46*(3), 426–458.

Becker, D., & Marecek, J. (2008). Positive psychology: History in the making? *Theory and Psychology, 18*(5), 591–604. doi: 10.1177/0959354308093397

Bedard, J., & Chi, M. T. (1992). Expertise. *Current Directions in Psychological Science, 1*(4), 135–139.

Belsky, J. (1997). *The adult experience*. St. Paul, MN: West Publishing.

Bennis, W., & Nanus, B. (1985). *Leaders*. New York: Harper & Row.

Bennis, W. (1994). *On becoming a leader*. New York: HarperCollins.

Benson, H. (1975). *The relaxation response*. New York: Morrow.

Benson, H. (1983). The relaxation response and norepinephrine: A new study illuminates mechanisms. *Integrative-Psychiatry, 1*(1), 15–18.

Benson, H., Malhotra, M. S., Goldman, R. F., Jacobs, G. D., et al. (1990). Three Case Reports on the Metabolic and Electroencephalographic Changes During Advanced Buddhist Meditation Techniques. *Behavioral Medicine, 16*(2), 90–95.

Benson, H., & Stark, M. (1996). *Timeless healing: The power and biology of belief*. London: Simon & Schuster.

Benson, Peter L., & Scales, Peter C. (2009, January). The definition and preliminary measurement of thriving in adolescence. *The Journal of Positive Psychology, 4*(1), 85–104.

Berg, I. K., & Miller, S. (1992). *Working with the problem drinker: A solution-focused therapy approach*. New York: W. W. Norton.

Bergan, A., & McConatha, J. T. (2000). Religiosity and life satisfaction. *Activities, Adaptation, and Aging, 24*(3), 23–34.

Berking, M., Wupperman, P., Richardt, A., Pejic, T., Dippel, A., & Znoj, H. (2008). General emotion-regulation skills as a treatment target in psychotherapy. *Behaviour Research and Therapy, 46*, 1230–1237.

Berkman, L. F., & Syme, S. L. (1979). Social networks, host resistance, and mortality: A nine-year follow-up study of Alameda County residents. *American Journal of Epidemiology, 109*, 186–204.

Berlyne, D. E. (1960). *Conflict, arousal and curiosity*. New York: McGraw-Hill.

Berry, D. S., & Pennebaker, J. W. (1993). Nonverbal and verbal emotional expression and health. *Psychotherapy and Psychosomatics, 59*, 11–19.

Berscheid, E., & Lopes, J. (1997). A temporal model of relationship satisfaction and stability. In R. Sternberg & M. Hojjat (Eds), *Satisfaction in close relationships* (pp. 129–159). New York: Guildford Press.

Bíró, E., Balajti, I., Ádány, R., & Kósa, K. (2010). Determinants of mental well-being in medical students. *Social Psychiatric Epidemiology, 45*(2), 253–258.

Bishop, A. J., Martin, P., MacDonald, M., & Poon, L. (2010). Predicting happiness among centenarians. *Gerontology, 56*, 88–92. doi: 10.1159/000272017

Bishop, S. R., Lau, M., Shapiro, S., Carlson, L., Anderson, N. D., Carmody, J., Segal, Z. V., et al. (2004). Mindfulness: A proposed operational definition. *Clinical Psychology: Science and Practice, 11*(3), 230–241.

Biswas-Diener, R. (2008). Material wealth and subjective well-being. In M. Eid & R. Larsen (Eds.). *The science of subjective well-being.* (pp. 307–322). New York: Guilford Press.

Biswas-Diener, R. (2009). Personal coaching as a positive intervention. *Journal of Clinical Psychology, 65*(5), 544–553.

Biswas-Diener, R. (2010). Practicing Positive Psychology Coaching: Assessment, Activities and Strategies for Success. NY: Wiley.

Biswas-Diener, R., & Dean, B. (2007). *Positive psychology coaching: Putting the science of happiness to work for your clients*. Hoboken, NJ: John Wiley & Sons.

Biswas-Diener, R., & Diener, E. (2001). Making the best of a bad situation: Satisfaction in the slums of Calcutta. *Social Indicators Research, 55*(3), 329–352.

Blanchflower, D., & Oswald, A. (2004). Money, sex, and happiness: An empirical study. *Scandinavian Journal of Economics, 106*(3), 393–415.

Blanchflower, D., & Oswald, A. (2007, February). Is well-being U-shaped over the life cycle? Retrieved June 10, 2011 from http://www.nber.org/papers/w12935

Bleil, M., Gianaros, P., Jennings, J., Flory, J., & Manuck, S. (2008). Trait negative affect: Toward an integrated model of understanding psychological risk for impairment in cardiac autonomic function. *Psychosomatic Medicine, 70*, 328–337.

Block, J. H., & Block, J. (1980). The role of ego-control and ego-resiliency in the organization of behavior. In W. A. Collins (Ed.), *Development of cognition, affect, and social relations: The Minnesota Symposia on Child Psychology* (Vol. *13*). Hillsdale, NJ: Erlbaum.

Boehm, J. K., & Lyubormisky, S. (2008). Does happiness promote career success? *Journal of Career Assessment, 16*(1), 101–116.

Bohart, A. C., & Greenberg, L. S. (Eds.). (1997). *Empathy reconsidered: New directions in psychotherapy.* Washington, DC: American Psychological Association.

Bok, S. (2010). *Exploring happiness: From Aristotle to brain science.* New Haven CT: Yale University Press.

Bolte, J. T. (2008). *My stroke of insight.* NY: Viking.

Boniwell, I. (2009). Perspectives on time. In C. R. Snyder & S. Lopez (Eds.), *Oxford handbook of positive psychology* (2nd ed., pp. 295–302). New York: Oxford University Press.

Bonnefon, J. F., & Zhang, J. (2008). The intensity of recent and distant life regrets: An integrated model and a large scale survey. *Applied Cognitive Psychology, 22*(5), 653–662.

Boorstein, S. (1996). *Transpersonal psychotherapy.* Albany: SUNY Press.

Bowker, J. (2006). *World religions: the great faiths explored and explained.* NY: DK Adult.

Boyce, C., Brown, G., & Moore, S. (2010). Money and happiness: Rank of income, not income, affects life satisfaction. *Psychological Science, 21*(4), 471–475.

Boyce, C., & Wood, A. (2011). Personality and marginal unity of income: Personality interacts with increases in household income to determine life satisfaction. *Journal of Economic Behavior and Organization, 78*, 183–191.

Boyle, P., Buchman, A., Barnes, L., & Bennett, D. (2010). Effects of a purpose in life on risk of incident Alzheimer disease and mild cognitive impairment in community-dwelling older persons. *Archives of General Psychiatry, 67*(3), 304–310.

Bradburn, N. (1969). *The structure of psychological well-being.* Chicago: Adine.

Bradbury, T. N., & Fincham, F. D. (1990). Attributions in marriage: Review and critique. *Psychological Bulletin, 107*, 3–33.

Brancaccio, D. (2011, April 1). France's new measure of well-being; Boredom. Retrieved from: http://www.marketplace.org/topics/life/economy-40/frances-new-measure-well-being-boredom

Brandtstädter, J. (2002) Searching for paths to successful development and aging: Integrating developmental and action-theoretical perspectives. In L. Pulkkinen and A. Caspi (Eds.), *Paths to successful development: Personality in the life course* (pp. 380–408). Cambridge, UK: Cambridge University Press.

Brannon, L., & Feist, J. (2000). *Health psychology: An introduction to behavior and health* (4th ed.). Belmont, CA: Wadsworth.

Braud, W. G. (2001) Experiencing tears of wonder-joy: seeing with the heart's eye. *Journal of Transpersonal Psychology, 33*, 99–111.

Brdar, I., & Kashdan, T. (2010). Character strengths and well-being in Croatia: An empirical investigation of structure and correlates. *Journal of Research in Personality, 44*, 151–154.

Brdar, I., Majda, R., & Dubravka, M. (2009). Life goals and well-being: Are extrinsic aspirations always detrimental to well-being? *Psihologijske Teme, 18*(2), 317–334.

Breznitz, S. (Ed.). (1983). *The denial of stress.* New York: International Universities Press.

Brickman, P., & Campbell, D. T. (1971). Hedonic relativism and planning the good society. In M. H. Appley (Ed.), *Adaptation level theory: A symposium* (pp. 287–304). NY: Academic Press.

Brickman, P., Coates, D., & Janoff-Bulman, R. (1978). Lottery winners and accident victims: Is happiness relative? *Journal of Personality and Social Psychology, 36*, 917–927.

Briñol, P., Petty, R., & Wagner, B. (2009). Body posture effects on self-evaluation: A self-validation approach. *European Journal of Social Psychology, 39*(6), 1053–1064.

Brinthaupt, T. M., & Shin, C. M. (2001). The relationship of academic cramming to the flow experience. *College Student Journal, 35*(3), 457–471.

Brockmann, H. (2010). Why are middle-aged people so depressed? Evidence from West Germany. *Social Indicators Research*, 97(1), 23–42.

Brockway, W., & Weinstock, H. (1958). *Men of music: Their lives, times, and achievements*. New York: Simon & Schuster.

Brown, J. (2011). Is it love or lust? Retrieved from: http://www.life123.com/relationships/dating/dating-intimacy/is-it-lust-or-love.shtml

Brown, K., & Holt, M. (2011). Experiential processing and the integration of bright and dark sides of the human psyche. In K. M. Sheldon, T. B. Kashdan, & M. F. Steger (Eds.), *Designing positive psychology: Taking stock and moving forward* (pp. 147–159). New York: Oxford University Press.

Brown, K. W., & Kasser, T. (2005, November). Are psychological and ecological well-being compatible? The role of values, mindfulness, and lifestyle. *Social Indicators Research*, 74(2), 349–368.

Brown, K. W., & Ryan, R. M. (2003). The benefits of being present: Mindfulness and its role in psychological well-being. *Journal of Personality and Social Psychology*, 84(4), 822–848.

Brown, K. W., Ryan, R. M., & Creswell, J. D. (2007). Mindfulness: Theoretical foundations and evidence for its salutary effects. *Psychological Inquiry*, 18(4), 211–237.

Brown, S., & Vaughn, C. (2009). *Play: How it shapes the brain, opens the imagination, and invigorates the soul*. New York: Avery.

Brummett, B. H., Babyak, M. A., Grønbæk, M., & Barefoot, J. C., (2011). Positive emotion is associated with 6-year change in functional status in individuals aged 60 and older. *The Journal of Positive Psychology*, 6(3), 216–223.

Brunell, A., Kernis, M., Goldman, B., Heppner, W., Davis, P. et al. (2010). Dispositional authenticity and romantic relationship functioning. *Personality and Individual Differences*, 48(8), 900–905.

Bryant, F. B. (1989). A four-factor model of perceived control: Avoiding, coping, obtaining, and savoring. *Journal of Personality*, 57, 773–797.

Bryant, F., Smart, C. M., & King, S. P. (2005). Using the past to enhance the present: Boosting happiness through positive reminiscence. *Journal of Happiness Studies*, 6(3), 227–260.

Bryant, F., & Verhoff, J. (2007). *Savoring: A New Model of Positive Experiences*. Mahwah, N.J.: Lawrence Erlbaum.

Buchowski, M., Majchrzak, K., Blomquist, K., Chen, K., Byrne, D., et al. (2007). Energy expenditure of genuine laughter. *International Journal of Obesity*, 31(1), 131–137.

Buckingham, M., & Clifton, D. (2001). *Now, discover your strengths*. New York: Free Press.

Buckingham, M., & Coffman, C. (1999). *First, break all the rules: What the world's greatest managers do differently*. New York: Simon & Schuster.

Buettner, D. (2010). *The blue zones*. Washington, DC: National Geographic.

Bunderson, J. S., & Thompson, J. A. (2009). The call of the wild: Zookeepers, callings, and the dual edges of deeply meaningful work. *Administrative science quarterly*, 54, 32–57.

Burns, G. (2007). Naturally happy, naturally healthy: The role of the natural environment in well-being. In F. Huppert, N. Baylis, & B. Keverne (Eds.), *The science of well-being* (pp. 405–431). Oxford: Oxford University Press.

Burns, G. W. (2009). *Happiness healing, enhancement: Your casebook collection for applying positive psychology in therapy*. NY: Wiley.

Burpee, L., & Langer, E. (2005). Mindfulness and marital satisfaction. *Journal of Adult Development*, 12(1), 43–51.

Burri, A., Cherkas, L., & Spector, T. (2009). Emotional intelligence and its association with orgasmic frequency in women. *Journal of Sexual Medicine*. doi: 10.1111/j.1743-6109.2009.01297.x

Buss, D. M. (2000). The evolution of happiness. *American Psychologist*, 55(1), 15–23.

Byrom, T. (trans.) (1993). *Dhammapada: The saying of the Buddha*. NY: Rider.

Cain, D. J., & Seeman, J. (Eds.) (2002). *Humanistic psychotherapies: Handbook of research and practice*. Washington, DC: American Psychological Association.

Camfield, L., Guillen-Royo, M., & Velazco, J. (2010). Does needs satisfaction matter for psychological and subjective Well-being in developing countries: A mixed-methods illustration from Bangladesh and Thailand. *Journal of Happiness Studies*, 11(4), 497–516.

Campbell, A. (1981). *The sense of well-being in America.* New York: russel Sage.

Campbell, A., Converse, P. E., & Rodgers, W. L. (1976). *The quality of American life.* New York: Russell Sage Foundation.

Campbell, J. (1949). *The Hero with a thousand faces.* Novato, California: New World Library.

Campbell-Sills, L., Cohan, S., & Stein, M. (2006). Relationship of resiliencey to personality, coping, and psychiatric symptoms in young adults. *Behaviior Research and Therapy, 44*(4), 585–599.

Cantor, N., & Sanderson, C. A. (1999). Life task participation and well-being: The importance of taking part in daily life. In D. Kahneman, E. Diener, & N. Schwarz (Eds.), *Well-being: The foundation of hedonic psychology* (pp. 230–243). New York: Russell Sage Foundation.

Caprara, G. V., Steca, P., Alessandri, G., Abela, J. R., & McWhinnie, C. M. (2010). Positive orientation: Explorations on what is common to life satisfaction, self-esteem, and optimism. *Epidemiology and Psychiatric Sciences, 19*(1), 63–71.

Carlo, G., Koller, S., Raffaeilli, M., & de Guzman, M. R. T. (2007). Culture-related strengths among Latin American families: A case study of Brazil. *Marriage and Family Review,* 3–4, 335–360.

Carmody, J., & Baer, R. (2009). How long does a mindfulness-based stress reduction program need to be? A review of class contact hours and effect sizes for psychological distress. *Journal of Clinical Psychology, 65*(6), 627–638.

Carroll, J. (2007, December 31). Most Americans very satisfied with their lives. Retrieved from: http://www.gallup.com.

Carstensen, L. L. (1992). Social and emotional patterns in adulthood: Support for socioemotional selectivity theory. *Psychology and Aging,* 7, 331–338.

Carstensen, L. L. (1995). Evidence for a life-span theory of socioemotional selectivity. *American Psychological Society, 4*(5), 151–156.

Carstensen, L. L., Mayr, U., Nesselroade, J. R., & Pasupathi, M. (2000). Emotional experience in everyday life across the adult life span. *Journal of Personality and Social Psychology, 79*(4), 644–655.

Carstensen, L. L., Pasupathi, M., Mayr, U., & Nesselroade, J. R. (2000). Emotional experience in everyday life across the adult life span. *Journal of*

Personality and Social Psychology, 79(4), 644–655. doi: 10.1037//0022-3514.79.4.644

Carter, O., Presti, D., Callistemon, C., Ungerer, Y., Liu, G., & Pettigrew, J. (2005). Meditation alters perceptual rivalry in Tibetan Buddhist monks. *Current Biology,* 15, R412–413.

Carver, C., Scheier, M., Miller, C., & Fulford, D. (2009). Optimism. In C. R. Snyder & S. Lopez (Eds.), *Oxford handbook of positive psychology* (2nd ed., pp. 303–312). New York: Oxford University Press.

Carver, C., Scheier, M., & Segerstrom, S. (2010). Optimism. *Clinical Psychology Review, 30*(7), 879–889.

Caspi, A., Herbener, E. S., & Ozer, D. J. (1992). Shared experiences and the similarity of personalities: A longitudinal study of married couples. *Journal of Personality and Social Psychology, 62*(2), 281–291.

Cassell, E. (2009). Compassion. In C. R. Snyder & S. Lopez (Eds.), *Oxford handbook of positive psychology* (2nd ed., pp. 393–404). New York: Oxford University Press.

C'de Baca, J., & Wilbourne, P. (2004). Quantum change: Ten years later. *Journal of Clinical Psychology, 60*(5), 531–541.

Ceja, L., & Navarro, J. (2009). Dynamics of flow: A nonlinear perspective. *Journal of Happiness Studies, 10*(6), 665–684.

Chamberlain, T. J., & Hall, C. A. (2000). *Realized religion: Research on the relationship between religion and health.* Philadelphia, PA: Templeton Foundation.

Chamorro-Premuzic, T., & Furnham, A. (2009, December). Mainly Openness: The relationship between the Big Five personality traits and learning approaches. Learning and Individual Differences, 19(4), 524–529.

Chang, B. H., Casey, A., Dusek, J. A., & Benson, H. (2010). Relaxation response and spirituality: Pathways to improve psychological outcomes in cardiac rehabilitation. *Journal of Psychosomatic Research, 69*(2), 93–100.

Chang, E. C. (2001). A look at the coping strategies and styles of Asian Americans: Similar and different? In C. R. Snyder (Ed.) *Coping with stress: Effective people and processes* (pp. 222–239). London: Oxford University Press.

Change, R., & Page, R. (1991). Characteristics of the self-actualized person: Visions from the east and west. *Counseling and Values, 36*(1), 2–12.

Chen, K. W., Comerford, A., Shinnick, P., & Ziedonis D. M. (2010) Introducing Qigong meditation into residential addiction treatment: A pilot study where gender makes a difference. *Journal of Alternative and Complementary Medicine, 16*(8), 1–8.

Cheng, S-T. (2004, September). Age and Subjective Well-Being Revisited: A Discrepancy Perspective. *Psychology and Aging, 19*(3), 409–415.

Chesney, M., Darbes, L., Hoerster, K., Taylor, J., Chambers, D., et al. (2005). Positive emotions: Exploring the other hemisphere in behavioral medicine. *International Journal of Behavioral Medicine, 12*(2), 50–58.

Chiao, J., & Ambady, N. (2007). Cultural neuroscience: Parsing universality and diversity across levels of analysis. In S. Kitayama & D. Cohen (Eds.). *Handbook of cultural psychology.* (pp. 237–254). NY: Guilford.

Chiao, J., & Blizinsky, K. (2010). Culture-gene coevolution of individualism-collectivism and the serotonin transporter gene. *Proceedings of the Royal Society: Biological Sciences, 277*(1681), 529–537.

Chiao, J., Harada, T., Komeda, H., Li, Z., Mano, Y., et al. (2009). Neural basis of individualistic and collectivistic views of self. *Human Brain Mapping, 30*(9), 2813–2820.

Chiao, J., Li, Z., & Harada, T. (2008). Cultural neuroscience of consciousness. In C. Whitehead (ed.). *The origin of consciousness in the social world.* Charlottesville, VA: Imprint Academic.

Chida, Yoichi, & Steptoe, Andrew, (2008). Positive psychological well-being and mortality: A quantitative review of prospective observational studies. *Psychosomatic Medicine, 70*(7), 741–756.

Child, D. (Producer). (2010). Dogs decoded: How smart are dogs and what makes them such ideal companions? NOVA [television series]. NY: Public Broadcasting Corporation.

Christakis, N., & Fowler, J. (2007). The spread of obesity in a large social network over 32 years. *New England Journal of Medicine, 357*, 370–379.

Christakis, N., & Fowler, J. (2008). The collective dynamics of smoking in a large social network. *New England Journal of Medicine, 358*, 2249–2258.

Christakis, N., & Fowler, J. (2011). *Connected: The Surprising Power of Our Social Networks and How They Shape Our Lives—How Your Friends' Friends' Friends Affect Everything You Feel, Think, and Do.* NY: Back Bay.

Christopher, J. C., & Hickinbottom, S. (2008). Positive psychology, ethnocentrism, and the disguised ideology of individualism. *Theory and Psychology, 18*(5), 563–589. doi: 10.1177/0959354308093396

Chua, R., & Zou, X. (2009, November 2). The devil wears Prada? Effects of exposure to luxury goods on cognition and decision making. Harvard Business School Organizational Behavior Unit Working Paper No. 10–034.

Ciarrocchi, J. W., Dy-Liacco, G. S., & Deneke, E. (2008). Gods or rituals? Relational faith spiritual discontent, and religious practices as predictors of hope and optimism. *The Journal of Positive Psychology, 3*(2), 120–136. doi: 10.1080/17439760701760666

Clark, A. E., & Oswald, A. J. (1996). Satisfaction and comparison income. *Journal of Public Economics, 61*, 359–81.

Clarke, S. G., & Haworth, J. T. (1994). "Flow" experience in the lives of sixth-form college students. *British Journal of Psychology, 85*, 511–523.

Clary, E. G., & Snyder, M. (1999). The motivations to volunteer: Theoretical and practical considerations. *Current Directions in Psychological Science, 8*(5), 156–159.

Clary, E. G., & Snyder, M. (2002). Community involvement: Opportunities and challenges in socializing adults to participate in society. *Journal of Social Issues, 58*(3), 581–591.

Clayton, V. (1982). Wisdom and intelligence: The nature and function of knowledge in the later years. *International Journal of Aging and Human Development, 15*(4), 315–321.

Cleary, T. S., & Shapiro, S. I. (1995). The plateau experience and the post-mortem life: Abraham H. Maslow's unfinished theory. *Journal of Transpersonal Psychology, 27*(1), 1–23.

Clifton, D., Anderson, E., & Schreiner, L. (2006). *StrengthsQuest: Discover and Develop Your Strengths in Academics, Career, and Beyond.* Gallup Press.

Clifton, D., & Nelson, P. (1992). *Soar with your strengths.* New York: Dell.

Clinton, H. R. (1996). *It takes a village: And other lessons children teach us.* NY: Simon & Schuster.

Cloninger, C. R. (2006). The science of well-being: An integrated approach to mental health and its disorders. *World Psychiatry, 5*(2), 71–76.

Coan, R. W. (1974). *The optimal personality.* New York: Columbia University Press.

Coan, R. W. (1977). *Hero, artist, sage, or saint.* New York: Columbia University Press.

Coan, R. W. (1991). Self-actualization and the quest for the ideal human. In A. Jones & R. Crandall (Eds.) *Handbook of self-actualization: Special issue of the Journal of Social and Behavior and Personality, 6*(5), 127–136.

Coffman, C., & Gonzales-Molina, G. (2002). *Follow this path: How the world's greatest organizations drive growth by unleashing human potential.* New York: Warner.

Cohen, M., & Fredrickson, B. (2009). Positive emotions. In C. R. Snyder & S. Lopez (Eds.), *Oxford handbook of positive psychology* (2nd ed., pp. 13–24). New York: Oxford University Press.

Cohen, R. (2011, March 12). The happynomics of life. *The New York Times.* Retrieved July 23, 20100 from www.nytimes.com/2011/03/13/opinion/13cohen.html

Cohen, S., Doyle, W. J., Skoner, D. P., Rabin, B. S., & Gwaltney, J. M., Jr. (1998). Types of stressors that increase susceptibility to the common cold in healthy adults. *Health psychology, 17,* 214–233.

Cohen, S., & Syme, S. L. (1985). *Social support and health.* San Diego, CA: Academic Press.

Cohen, S., Tyrrell, D. A. J., & Smith, A. P. (1991). Psychological stress and susceptibility to the common cold. *New England Journal of Medicine, 325,* 606–612.

Cohen, S., Tyrrell, D. A. J., & Smith, A. P. (1993). Negative life events, perceived stress, negative affect, and susceptibility to the common cold. *Journal of Personality and Social Psychology, 64,* 131–140.

Collins, A. L., Sarkisian, N., & Winner, E. (2009). Flow and happiness in later life: An investigation into the role of daily and weekly flow experiences. *Journal of Happiness Studies, 10*(6), 703–719.

Collins, J. (2001). *Good to great: Why some companies make the leap … and others don't.* NY: Harper Business.

Colvin, C. R., & Block, J. (1994). Do positive illusions foster mental health? An examination of the Taylor and Brown formulation. *Psychological Bulletin, 116,* 3–20.

Colvin, C. R., Block, J. K, & Funder, D. C. (1995). Overly positive self-evaluations and personality: Negative implications for mental health. *Journal of Personality and Social Psychology, 68*(6), 1152–1162.

Compton, W. C. (1992). Are positive illusions necessary for self-esteem: A research note. *Personality and Individual Differences, 13*(12), 1343–1344.

Compton, W. C. (2000). Meaningfulness as a moderator of subjective well-being. *Psychological Reports, 87,* 156–160.

Compton, W. C. (2001a). Toward a tripartite factor structure of mental health: Subjective well-being, personal growth, and religiosity. *Journal of Psychology, 135*(5), 486–500.

Compton, W. C. (2001b). The values problem in subjective well-being. *American Psychologist, 56*(1), 84.

Compton, W. C. (2012). *Eastern psychology: Buddhism, Hinduism, and Taoism.* Seattle, WA: CreateSpace.

Compton, W. C., Seeman, J., & Norris, R. C. (1991). Predicting hardiness: A search for the parameters of deep cognitive structures, *Medical Psychotherapy, 4,* 121–130.

Compton, W., Smith, M., Cornish, K., & Qualls, D. (1996). Factor structure of mental health measures. *Journal of Personality and Social Psychology, 71*(2), 406–413.

Conger, R. D., & Conger, K. J (2002). Resilience in midwestern families: Selected findings from the first decade of a prospective, longitudinal study. *Journal of Marriage and the Family, 64*(2), 361–373.

Connor, K., & Zhang, W. (2006). Resilience: Determinants, measurement, and treatment responsiveness. *CNS Spectrums, 11*(10), 5–12.

Cook-Greuter, S. R. (1994). Rare forms of self-understanding in mature adults. In M. Miler & S. R. Cook-Greuter (Eds.) *Transcendence and mature thought in adulthood: Further reaches of human development.* Lanham, MD.: Rowan & Littlefield.

Cooper, A. (1998). *Playing in the zone: Exploring the spiritual dimensions of sports.* Boston: Shambala.

Corbin, J. M. (2003). The body in health and illness. *Qualitative Health Research, 13*(2), 256–267.

Cosma, J. B. (1999). Flow in teams. *Dissertation Abstracts International 60*(6–A), 1901.

Costa, P., & McCrae, R. (1984). Personality as a lifelong determinant of well-being. In C. Malatesta & C. Izard (Eds.), *Affective processes in adult development and aging* (pp. 141–157). Beverly Hills, CA: Sage Publications.

Costa, P. T., & McCrae, R. R. (1986). Personality stability and its implications for clinical psychology. *Clinical Psychology Review, 6,* 407–423.

Costa, P. T., & McCrae, R. R. (1988). Personality in adulthood: A six-year longitudinal study of self-reports and spouse ratings on the NEO Personality Inventory. *Journal of Personality and Social Psychology, 54*(5), 853–863.

Costa, P. T., McCrae, R. R., & Zonderman, A. B. (1987, August). Environmental and dispositional influences on well-being: Longitudinal follow-up of an American national sample. *British Journal of Psychology, 78*(3), 299–306.

Cotten, Shelia R., Goldner, Melinda, Hale, Timothy M., & Drentea, P. (2011, March). The importance of type, amount, and timing of Internet use for understanding psychological distress. *Social Science Quarterly, 92*(1), 19–139.

Cousins, N. (1981). *Anatomy of an illness.* New York: Norton.

Cowen, E. L., & Kilmer, R. P. (2002). Positive psychology: Some plusses and some open issues. *Journal of Community Psychology, 30*(4), 449–460.

Coyne, J. C., & Benazon, N. R. (2001). Not agent blue: Effects of marital functioning on depression and implications for treatment. In Beach, S. R. H. (Ed.), *Marital and family processes in depression: A scientific foundation for clinical practice.* Washington, DC: American Psychological Association, 25–43.

Coyne, J., Stefanek, M., & Palmer, S. (2007). Psychotherapy and survival in cancer: The conflict between hope and evidence. *Psychological Bulletin, 133*(3), 367–394.

Cramer, P., & Davidson, K. (Eds.). (1998). Defense mechanisms in contemporary personality research. [Special issue]. *Journal of Personality, 66*(6).

Crooker, K. J., & Near, J. P. (1998). Happiness and satisfaction: Measures of affect and cognition? *Social Indicators Research, 44*(2), 195–224.

Csikszentmihalyi, M. (1975). Play and intrinsic rewards. *Journal of Humanistic Psychology, 15*(3), 41–63.

Csikszentmihalyi, M. (1988). *Society, culture, and person: A systems view of creativity* (pp. 323–339). New York: Cambridge University Press.

Csikszentmihalyi, M. (1990). *Flow: The psychology of optimal experience.* New York: Harper & Row.

Csikszentmihalyi, M. (1997). *Finding flow: The psychology of engagement with everyday life.* New York: Basic Books.

Csikszentmihalyi, M., & Csikszentmihalyi, I. S. (1988). *Optimal experience: Psychological studies of flow in consciousness.* New York: Cambridge University Press.

Csikszentmihslyi, M., & Larson, R. (1984). *Being adolescent: Conflict and growth in the teenage years.* New York: Basic Books.

Csikszentmihalyi, M., & LeFevre, J. (1989). Optimal experience in work and leisure. *Journal of Personality and Social Psychology, 56*(5), 815–822.

Csikszentmihalyi, M., & Nakamura, J. (2011). Positive psychology: Where did it comes from, where is it going? In K. M. Sheldon, T. B. Kashdan, & M. F. Steger (Eds.). *Designing positive psychology: Taking stock and moving forward.* (pp. 3–8). New York: Oxford University Press.

Csikszentmihalyi, M., & Rathunde, K. (1993). The measurement of flow in everyday life. *Nebraska Symposium on Motivation, 40,* 57–97.

Csikszentmilhalyi, M., & Rochberg-Halton, E. (1981). *The meaning of things: Domestic symbols and the self.* Cambridge: Cambridge University Press.

Cummings, E. E. (1958). *95 poems by E. E. Cummings.* New York: Harcourt, Brace & World.

Cummins, R. A. (1996). The domains of life satisfaction: An attempt to order chaos. *Social Indicators Research, 38*(3), 303–328.

Cunningham, M. H., & Thornton, A. (2006). The influence of parents' marital quality on adult children's attitudes toward marriage and its alternatives: Main and moderating effects. *Demography, 43*(4), 659–672.

Dalai Lama (with Cutler, H. C.). (1998). *The art of happiness: A handbook for living.* New York: Riverhead.

Dalla Bella, S., Kraus, N., Overy, K., Pantev, C., Snyder, J., et al. (2009). *The neurosciences and music III: Disorders and plasticity (Annals of the New York Academy of Sciences).* New York: Wiley-Blackwell.

Daly, M., Oswald, A., Wilson, D., & Wu, S. (2011). Dark contrasts: The paradox of high rates of suicide in happy places. *Journal of Economic Behavior and Organization,* doi: 10.1016/j.jebo.2011.04.007

d'Aquili, E. G., & Newberg, A. B. (1999). *The mystical mind: Probing the biology of religious experiences.* Minneapolis, MN: Fortress Press.

Danner, D., Snowdon, D., & Friesen, W. (2001). Positive emotions in early life and longevity: Findings from the nun study. *Journal of Personality and Social Psychology, 80*, 804–813.

Dautovich, N. D., McNamara, J., Williams, J. M. (2010). Tackling Sleeplessness: Psychological treatment options for insomnia. *Nature and Science of Sleep, 2*, 23–37.

Davidson, R., & Harrington, A. (Eds.) (2002). *Visions of Compassion: Western Scientists and Tibetan Buddhists Examine Human Nature.* NY: Oxford University Press.

Davidson, R. J., Kabat-Zinn, J., Schumacher, J., Rosenkranz, M., Muller, D., Santorelli, S. F., … Sheridan, J. F. (2003). Alterations in brain and immune function produced by mindfulness meditation. *Psychosomatic Medicine, 65*, 564–570.

Davis, C., & Nolen-Hoeksema, S. (2009). Making sense of loss, perceiving benefits, and posttraumatic growth. In C. R. Snyder & S. Lopez (Eds.), *Oxford handbook of positive psychology* (2nd ed., pp. 641–650). New York: Oxford University Press.

Davis, F. (1979). *Yearning for yesterday: A sociology of nostalgia.* New York: Free Press.

Davis, M., Eshelman, E. R., & McKay, M. (1988). *The relaxation and stress reduction workbook.* Oakland, CA: New Harbinger Publications.

Deaton, A., & Arora, R. (2009). Life at the top: The benefits of height. *Economics and Human Biology, 7*, 133–136.

Deci, E. L., & Ryan, R. M. (1985). *Intrinsic motivation and self-determination in human behavior.* New York: Plenum.

Deci, E. L., & Ryan, R. M. (2008, February). Facilitating optimal motivation and psychological well-being across life's domains. *Canadian Psychology/Psychologie canadienne, 49*(1), 14–23.

De Fruyt, F. (1997). Gender and individual differences in adult crying. *Personality and Individual differences, 22*(6), 937–940.

deGroot, A. D. (1965). *Thought and choice in chess.* The Hague: Mouton. (Original work published 1946)

DeJong, T. (2009, April 13). *Nobler instincts take time.* EurekAlert! Retrieved from: http://www.eureka-lert.org/pub_releases/2009-04/uosc-ttr040909.php

Delizonna, L. L., Williams, R. P., & Langer, E. (2009). The effect of mindfulness on heart rate control. *Journal of Adult Development, 16*(2), 61–65.

Delle Fave, A. (2009). Optimal experience and meaning: Which relationship? *Psychological Topics, 18*(20), 284–302.

DeNeve, K. M., & Cooper, H. (1998). The happy personality: A meta-analysis of 137 personality traits and subjective well-being. *Psychological Bulletin, 124*(2), 197–229.

Depp, C., Vahia, I. V., & Jeste, D. (2010). Successful aging: Focus on cognitive and emotional health. *Annual Review of Clinical Psychology, 6*, 527–550.

de Shazer, S. (1985). *Keys to solution in brief therapy.* New York: Norton.

de Silva, P. (1979). *An introduction to Buddhist psychology.* London: McMillan.

Devlin, K. (2009, April 2). Having a sister makes you happier and more optimistic, say psychologists. *The Telegraph.* Retrieved June 15, 2011 from http://www.telegraph.co.uk/family/5089197/Having-a-sister-makes-you-happier-and-more-optimistic-say-psychologists.html

de Vries, M., Holland, R. W., Chenier, T., Starr, M. J., & Winkielman, P. (2010, March). Happiness cools the warm glow of familiarity: Psychophysiological evidence that mood modulates the familiarity-affect link. *Psychological Science, 21*(3), 321–328.

Dewey, J. (1934). *Art as experience.* Oxford, UK: Minton, Balch.

Dahlsgaard, K., Peterson, C., & Seligman, M. E. P. (2005). Shared virtue: The convergence of valued human strengths across culture and history. *Review of General Psychology, 9*(3), 203–213. doi: 10.1037/1089-2680.9.3.203

Davydov, D. M., Stewart, R., Ritchie, K., & Chaudieu, I. (2010). Resilience and mental health. *Clinical Psychology Review, 30*, 479–495. doi: 10.1016/j.cpr.2010.03.003

Deaton, A., & Arora, R. (2009). Life at the top: The benefits of height. *Economics and Human Biology, 7*, 133–136. doi: 10.1016/j.ehb.2009.06.001

Diaz-Loving, R., & Draguns, J. G. (1999). Culture, meaning, and personality in Mexico and the United States. In Y. T. Lee, C. R. McCauley, & J. G. Draguns (Eds.), *Personality and perception across cultures* (pp. 103–126). Mahwah, NJ: Erlbaum.

Dickens, C. M., McGowan, L., Percival, C., Tomenson, B., Cotter, L., Heagerty, A., & Creed, F. H. (2004). Lack of a close confidant, but not depression, predicts further cardiac events after myocardial infarction. *Heart, 90*, 518–522.

Dickerson, S. S., & Zoccola, P. M. (2009). Toward a biology of social support. In S. J. Lopez & C. R. Snyder (Eds.), *Oxford handbook of positive psychology (2nd ed.)* (pp. 519–526). New York, NY, US: Oxford University Press.

Diener, E. (1984). Subjective well-being. *Psychological Bulletin, 93*(3), 542–575.

Diener, E. (1994). Assessing subjective well-being: Progress and opportunities. *Social Indicators Research, 31*, 103–157.

Diener, E. (2000, October). *Is happiness a virtue?* Paper presented the Positive Psychology Summit 2000, October. Washington, DC.

Diener, E. (2008). Myths in the science of happiness, and directions for future research. In M. Eid & R. Larsen (Eds.). *The science of subjective well-being.* (pp. 492–514). New York: Guilford Press.

Diener, E. (2009a). *The science of well-being: The collected works of Ed Diener (Social Indicators Research Series).* NY: Springer.

Diener, E. (2009b). Assessing well-being: *The collected works of Ed Diener (Social Indicators Research Series).* NY: Springer.

Diener, E. (2009c). *Cultural and well-being: The collected works of Ed Diener (Social Indicators Research Series).* NY: Springer.

Diener, E., & Biswas-Diener, R. (2002). Will money increase subjective well-being? A literature review and guide to needed research. *Social Indicators Research, 57*, 119–169.

Diener, E., & Biswas-Diener, R. (2008). *Happiness: Unlocking the mysteries of psychological wealth.* NY: Wiley-Blackwell.

Diener, E., & Chan, M. (2011). Happy people live longer: Subjective well-being contributes to health and longevity. *Applied Psychology: Health and Well-being, 3*(1), 1–43.

Diener, E., & Diener, C. (1996). The wealth of nations revisited: Income and quality of life. *Social Indicators Research, 36*, 275–86.

Diener, M., & Diener McGavran, M. B. (2008). What makes people happy? A developmental approach to the literature on family relationships and well-being. In M. Eid & R. Larsen (Eds.). *The science of subjective well-being.* (pp. 347–375). New York: Guilford Press.

Diener, E., Diener, M., & Diener, C. (1995). Factors predicting the subjective well-being of nations. *Journal of Personality and Social Psychology, 69*, 653–663.

Diener, E., Emmons, R., Larsen, R., & Griffin, S. (1985). The satisfaction with life scale. *Journal of Personality Assessment, 49*(l), 71–75.

Diener, E., Harter, J., Arora, R., & Ng, W. (2010). Wealth and happiness across the world: Material prosperity predicts life evaluation, whereas psycho-social prosperity predicts positive feeling. *Journal of Personality and Social Psychology, 99*(1), 52–61. doi: 10.1037/a0018066

Diener, E., Helliwell, J., & Kahneman, D. (Eds.). (2010). *International differences in well-Being.* NY: Oxford University Press.

Diener, E., Horwitz, J., & Emmons, R. A. (1985). Happiness of the very wealthy. *Social Indicators, 16*, 263–274.

Diener, E., & Larsen, R. J. (1984). Temporal stability and cross-situational consistency of affective, behavioral, and cognitive responses. *Journal of Personality and Social Psychology, 47*, 871–883.

Diener, E., Larsen, R. J., & Emmons, R. A. (1984). Person X situation interactions: Choice of situations and congruence response models. *Journal of Personality and Social Psychology, 47*, 580–592.

Diener, E., Larsen, R. J., Levine, S., & Emmons, R. (1985). Intensity and frequency: Dimensions underlying positive and negative affect. *Journal of Personality and Social Psychology, 48*(5), 1253–1265.

Diener, E., & Lucas, R. (1999). Personality and subjective well-being. In D. Kahneman, E. Diener, & N. Schwarz (Eds.), *Well-being: The foundation of hedonic psychology* (pp. 213–229). New York: Russell Sage Foundation.

Diener, E., & Lucas, R. E. (2000). Explaining differences in societal levels of happiness: Relative standards, need fulfillment, culture, and evaluation theory. *Journal of Happiness Studies, 1*, 41–78.

Diener, E., Lucas, R. E., & Scollon, C. N. (2006). Beyond the hedonic treadmill: Revising the adaptation theory of well-being. *American Psychologist, 61*(4), 305–314. doi: 10.1037/0003-066X.61.4.305

Diener, E., Oishi, S., & Lucas, R. E. (2003). Personality, culture, and subjective well-being: Emotional and cognitive evaluations of life. *Annual Review of Psychology, 54*, 403–425.

Diener, E., Oishi, S., & Lucas, R. (2009). Subjective well-being: The science of happiness and life satisfaction. In C. R. Snyder & S. Lopez (Eds.), *Oxford handbook of positive psychology* (2nd ed., pp. 187–194). New York: Oxford University Press.

Diener, E., Ng, W., Harter, J., & Arora, R. (2010). Wealth and happiness across the world: Material prosperity predicts life evaluation, whereas psychosocial prosperity predicts positive feeling. *Journal of Personality and Social Psychology, 99*(1), 52–61. doi: 10.1037/a0018066

Diener, E., Sandvik, E., & Pavot, W. (1991). Happiness is the frequency, not the intensity, of positive versus negative affect. In F. Strack, M. Argyle, & N. Schwarz (Eds.), *Subjective well-being: An interdisciplinary perspective*. Elmsford, NY: Pergamon Press, 119–139.

Diener, E., Sandvik, E., Seidlitz, L., & Diener, M. (1993). The relationship between income and subjective well-being: Relative or absolute? *Social Indicators Research, 28*, 195–223.

Diener, E., & Seligman, M. E. P. (2002). Very happy people. *Psychological Science, 13*(1), 81–84.

Diener, E., & Suh, E. M. (2000). *Culture and subjective well-being*. Cambridge, MA: MIT Press.

Diener, E., Suh, E. M., Lucas, R. E., & Smith, H. L. (1999). Subjective well-being: Three decades of progress. *Psychological Bulletin, 125*(2), 276–302.

Diener, E., Wolsic, B., & Fujita F. (1995). Physical attractiveness and subjective well-being. *Journal of Personality and Social Psychology, 69*, 120–129.

Dietrich, A. (2004). Neurocognitive mechanisms underlying the experience of flow. *Consciousness and Cognition, 13*, 746–761.

Dietrich, A., & McDaniel, W. F. (2004). Endocannabinoids and exercise. *British Journal of Sports Medicine, 38*, 536–541. doi: 10.1136/bjsm.2004.011718

Dillbeck, M. C., & Bronson, E. C. (1981). Short-term longitudinal effects of the Transcendental Meditation program on EEG power and coherence. *Perceptual and Motor Skills, 62*, 731–738.

Dillbeck, M. C. (1982). Meditation and flexibility of visual perception and verbal problem solving. *Memory and Cognition, 10*, 207–215.

Dillon, K., Minchoff, B., & Baker, K. (1985–1986). Positive emotional states and enhancement of the immune system. *International Journal of Psychiatry in Medicine, 15*, 13–18.

Dissanayake, E. (2009, winter). The birth of the arts. *Greater Good: Magazine of the Greater Good Science Center at UC Berkeley, V*(3), 20–22.

Djikic, M., Langer, E. J., & Stapleton, S. F. (2008). Reducing stereotyping through mindfulness: Effects on automatic stereotype-activated behaviors. *Journal of Adult Development, 15*(2), 106–111.

Domino, G., Short, J., Evans, A., & Romano, P. (2002). Creativity and ego defense mechanisms: Some exploratory empirical evidence. *Creativity Research Journal, 14*, 17–25.

Dominguez, M. Melina, Carton, John S. (1997). The relationship between self-actualization and parenting style. *Journal of Social Behavior and Personality, 12*(4), 1093–1100.

Donahue, M. J. (1985). Intrinsic and extrinsic religiousness: Review and meta-analysis. *Journal of Personality and Social Psychology, 48*(2), 400–419.

Donahue, M. J., & Benson, P. L. (1995). Religion and the well-being of adolescents. *Journal of Social Issues, 51*(2), 145–160.

Drakopoulos, S. A. (2008). The paradox of happiness: Towards an alternative explanation. *Journal of Happiness Studies, 9*(2), 303–315. doi: 10.1007/s10902-007-9054-5

Drigotas, S. M., Rusbult, C. E., Wieselquist, J., Whitton, S. W. (1999). Close partner as sculptor of the ideal self: Behavioral affirmation and the Michelangelo phenomenon. *Journal of Personality and Social Psychology, 77*(2), 293–323.

Drob, S. L (2009). *Kabbalistic visions: C.G. Jung and Jewish mysticism*. New Orleans: Spring Journal.

du Pré, A. (1998). *Humor and the healing arts: A multimethod analysis of humor use in health care*. Mahwah, NJ, US: Lawrence Erlbaum Associates Publishers.

Dua, J. (1994). Comparative predictive value of attributional style, negative affect, and positive affect in predicting self-reported physical health and psychological health. *Journal of Psychosomatic Medicine, 38*(7), 669–680.

Duckworth, A. L., Peterson, C., Matthews, M., & Kelly, D. (2007). Grit: Perseverance and passion for long-term goals. *Journal of Personality and Social Psychology, 92*(6), 1087–1101.

Duckworth, A. L., & Quinn, P. (2009). Development and validation of the short Grit Scale (GRIT-S). *Personality Assessment, 91*(2), 166–174.

Duckworth, A. L., Steen, T. A., & Seligman, M. E. P. (2005). Positive psychology in clinical practice. *Annual Review of Clinical Psychology, 1*, 629–651. doi: 10.1146/annurev.clinpsy.1.102803.144154

Dunn, D., Uswatte, G., & Elliot, T. (2009). Happiness, resilience, and positive growth following physical disability: Issues for understanding, research, and therapeutic intervention. In C. R. Snyder & S. Lopez (Eds.), *Oxford handbook of positive psychology* (2nd ed., pp. 651–664). New York: Oxford University Press.

Dunn, E., Aknin, L., & Norton, M. (2008, March). Spending money on others promotes happiness. *Science, 319*(5870), 1687–1688.

Dunn, H. (1961). *High-level wellness*. Arlington, VA: Beatty.

Dusek, J. A., Out, H. H., Wohlhueter, A. L., Bhasin, M., Zerbini, L. F., Joseph, M. G., … Libermann, T. A. (2008). Genomic counter-stress changes induced by the relaxation response. *PLoS One, 3*(7), e2576. doi: 10.1371/journal.pone.0002576

Dweck, C. (2006). *The psychology of success*. New York: Random House.

Dweck, C., & Master, A. (2008). Self-theories motivate self-regulated learning. In D. Schunk & B. Zimmerman (Eds.) *Motivation and self-regulated learning: Theory, research and applications* (pp. 31–51). Mahwah, NJ: Lawrence Erlbaum.

Dweck, C., & Master, A. (2009). Student's beliefs about intelligence. In K. Wenzel & A. Wigfield (Eds.) *Handbook of motivation at school* (pp. 123–140). New York: Routledge/Taylor & Francis Group.

Dweck, C. S., & Elliott-Moskwa, E. S. (2010). Self-theories: The roots of defensiveness. In J. E. Maddux & J. P. Tangney (Eds.), *Social psychological foundations of clinical psychology* (pp. 136–153). New York, NY: Guilford Press.

Dzuka, J., & Dalbert, C. (2006, September). The belief in a just world and subjective well-being in old age. *Aging & Mental Health, 10*(5), 439–444.

Ebersole, P. (1970). Effects of nadir experiences. *Psychological Reports, 27*(1), 207–209.

Edelson, E. (2011, February 24). Happy marriage cuts men's risk for stroke. *Tallahassee Memorial Healthcare*. Retrieved April 30, 2011 from http://tmh.org/body.cfm?id=223&action=detail& aeproductid=HealthScoutfeed&aearticleid=32939

Elangovan, A. R., Pinder, C. C., & McLean, M. (2009). Callings and organizational behavior. *Journal of Organizational Behavior, 76*, 428–440.

Elliot, A. J., & Niesta, D. (2008, November). Romantic red: Red enhances men's attraction to women. *Journal of Personality and Social Psychology, 95*(5), 1150–1164.

Elliott, I., & Coker, S. (2008). Independent self-construal, self-reflection, and self-rumination: A path model for predicting happiness. *Australian Journal of Psychology, 60*(3), 127–134. doi: 10.1080/00049530701447368

Emmons, R. A. (1986). Personal strivings: An approach to personality and subjective well-being. *Journal of Personality and Social Psychology, 51*(5), 1058–1068.

Emmons, R. A. (1992). Abstract versus concrete goals: Personal striving level, physical illness, and psychological well-being. *Journal of Personality and Social Psychology, 62*(2), 292–300.

Emmons, R. A. (1999). *The psychology of ultimate concerns: Motivation and spirituality in personality*. New York: Guilford.

Emmons, R. A., (2005). Emotion and Religion. In: Handbook of the psychology of religion and spirituality. Paloutzian, Raymond F. (Ed.), Park, Crystal L. (Ed.), New York, NY, US: Guilford Press, 2005. pp. 235–252.

Emmons, R. A., & Crumpler, C. A. (1999). Religion and spirituality? The roles of sanctification and the concept of God. *The International Journal for the Psychology of Religion, 9*(1), 17–24.

Emmons, R. A., & Crumpler, C. A. (2000). Gratitude as a human strength: Appraising the evidence. *Journal of Social and Clinical Psychology, 19*(1), 56–69 [Special issue: Classical sources of human strength: A psychological analysis].

Emmons, R. A., & King, L. A. (1988). Conflict among personal strivings: Immediate and long-term implications for psychological and physical well-being. *Journal of Personality and Social Psychology, 54*(6), 1040–1048.

Emmons, R., & Mishra, A. (2011). Why gratitude enhances well-being: What we know, what we need to know. In K. M. Sheldon, T. B. Kashdan, & M. F. Steger (Eds.), *Designing positive psychology: Taking stock and moving forward* (pp. 248–264). New York: Oxford University Press.

Emmons, R. A., & McCullough, M. E. (2003). Counting blessings versus burdens: Experimental studies of gratitude and subjective well-being in daily life. *Journal of Personality and Social Psychology, 84,* 377–389.

Emmons, R. A., & Paloutzian, R. F. (2003). The psychology of religion. *Annual Review of Psychology, 54,* 377–402.

Emmons, R. A., & Shelton, C. S. (2002). Gratitude and the science of positive psychology. In R. C. Snyder & S. J. Lopez (Eds.), *Handbook of positive psychology* (pp. 459–471). New York: Oxford University Press.

Engler, B. (1991). *Personality theories: An introduction* (3rd ed., pp. 418–444). Boston: Houghton Mifflin.

English, H., & English, A. (1958). *A comprehensive dictionary of psychological and psychoanalytic terms.* New York: David McKay.

Enright, R. F. (2001). *Forgiveness is a choice: A step-by-step process for resolving anger and restoring hope.* Washington, DC: American Psychological Association.

Enright, R. D., & North, J. (1998). *Exploring forgiveness.* Madison, WI: University of Wisconsin Press.

Enright, R. D., Freedman, S., & Rique, J. (1998). The psychology of interpersonal forgiveness. In R. D. Enright & J. North (Eds.), *Exploring forgiveness* (pp. 46–62). Madison, WI: University of Wisconsin Press.

Epel, E. S., McEwen, B. S., & Ickovics, J. R. (1998). Embodying psychological thriving: Physical thriving in response to stress. *Journal of Social Issues, 53*(2), 301–322.

Epstein, M. (1988). The deconstruction of the self: Ego and "egolessness" in Buddhist insight meditation. *Journal of Transpersonal Psychology, 20*(1), 61–69.

Epstein, R. M. (2003). Mindful practice in action: Technical competence, evidence-based medicine, and relationship-centered care. *Systems & Health, 21*(1), 1–9.

Erber, R., & Erber, M. W. (2000). The self regulation of moods: Second thoughts on the importance of happiness in everyday life. *Psychological Inquiry, 11*(3), 142–148.

Erickson, J., & Compton, W. (1982, April). Who is talking to whom: Some dimensions of noncommunication. Paper presented at the annual meeting of the Western Social Science Association, Denver, CO.

Ericsson, K. A. (Ed.). (1996). *The road to excellence.* Mahwah, NJ: Lawrence Erlbaum.

Ericsson, K. A., & Charness, N. (1994). Expert performance. *American Psychologist, 49*(8), 725–747.

Ericsson, K. A., Krampe, R. T., & Tesch-Roemer, C. (1993). The role of deliberate practice in the acquisition of expert performance. *Psychological Review, 100*(3), 363–406.

Erikson, E. (1950). *Childhood and society.* New York: Norton.

Erikson, E., Erikson, J. M., & Kivnick, H. Q. (1986). *Vital involvement in old age.* New York: Norton.

Evans, A., Guerra, S., Romero, S., & Lucas, D. (2008, April). *Mistaking contentment for happiness.* Poster session presented at the annual meeting of the Southwestern Psychological Association.

Evans, D. R., Baer, R. A., & Segerstrom, S. C. (2009). The effects of mindfulness and self-consciousness on persistence. *Personality and Individual Differences, 47*(4), 379–382.

Evans, K. (2009, winter). Arts and smarts. *Greater Good: Magazine of the Greater Good Science Center at UC Berkeley, V*(3), 16–20.

Exline, J. J., Baumeister, R. F., Zell, A. L., Kraft, A. J., & Witvliet, C. V. O. (2008, March). Not so innocent: Does seeing one's own capability for wrongdoing predict forgiveness? *Journal of Personality and Social Psychology, 94*(3), 495–515.

Fackelman, K. (1993, February 6). Marijuana and the brain: Scientists discover the brain's own THC. *Science News,* Retrieved from: http://findarticles. com/p/articles/mi_m1200/is_n6_v143/ ai_13434805/

Fagan-Jones, S., & Midlarsky, E. (2007). Courageous altruism: Personal and situational correlates of rescue during the holocaust. *The Journal of Positive Psychology, 2*(2), 136–147. doi: 10.1080/17439760701228979

Farrell, P. A., Gustafson, A. B., Morgan, W. P., & Pert, C. B. (1987). Enkephalins, catecholamines, and psychological mood alterations: Effects of prolonged exercise. *Medicine and Science in Sports and Exercise, 19*(4), 347–353.

Fave, A. D., & Massimini, F. (2004). The cross-cultural investigation of optimal experience. *Ricerche di Psicologia: Special Issue: Positive Psychology, 27*(1), 79–102.

Fava, G. A. (1999). Well-being therapy: Conceptual and technical issues. *Psychotherapy and Psychosomatics, 68*, 171–179.

Fava, G., Rafanelli, C., & Cazzaro, M. (1998). Well-being therapy: A novel psychotherapeutic approach for residual symptoms of affective disorders. *Psychological Medicine, 28*(2), 475–480.

Fefer, M. (2002, February 13). A lot of love in the lovemaking: Avoiding chaos relationshipwise [interview with Dr. John Gottman]. *Seattle Weekly News.*

Fehr, B. (1988). Prototype analysis of the concepts of love and commitment. *Journal of Personality and Social Psychology, 55*, 557–579.

Fehr, B., & Russell, J. A. (1991). Concept of love viewed from a prototype perspective. *Journal of Personality and Social Psychology, 60*, 425–438.

Feingold, Alan (1992). Good-looking people are not what we think. *Psychological Bulletin, 111*(2), 304–341.

Feldt, T., Metsäpelto, R.-L., Kinnunen, U., & Pulkkinen, L. (2007). Sense of coherence and five-factor approach to personality: Conceptual relationships. *European Psychologist, 12*(3), 165–172.

Fenchel, G. H. (1985). Time as self and ego experience. *Issues in Psychoanalytic Psychology, 8*(1–2), 73–81.

Ferrer, J. N. (2001). *Revisioning transpersonal theory: A participatory vision of human spirituality.* Albany: SUNY Press.

Feshbach, N. (1984). Empathy, empathy training, and the regulation of aggression in elementary school children. In R. M. Kaplan, V., Konecni, & R. Novaco (Eds.), *Aggression in children and youth* (pp. 192–208). The Hague: Martinus Nijhoff.

Field, T. M. (1998). Touch therapies. In R. R. Hoffman, M. F. Sherrick, & J. S. Warm (Eds.) *Viewing psychology as a whole: The integrative science of William N. Dember* (pp. 603–624). Washington, DC: American Psychological Association.

Field, T. M. (2001). *Touch.* Cambridge, MA: MIT Press.

Field, T. M. (2002). Violence and touch deprivation in adolescents. *Adolescence, 37*(148), 735–749.

Finkel, E. J., Rusbult, C. E., Kumashiro, M., & Hannon, P. A. (2002). Dealing with betrayal in close relationships: Does commitment promote forgiveness? *Journal of Personality and Social Psychology, 82*(6), 956–974.

Fincham, F., & Beach, S. R. (2007). Forgiveness and marital quality: Precursor or consequence in well-established relationship? *The Journal of Positive Psychology, 2*(4), 260–268. doi: 10.1080/17439760701552360

Fincham, F., Hall, J., & Beach, S. (2006). Forgiveness in marriage; Current status and future directions. *Family Relations, 55*(4), 415–427.

Fisher, J. S. (2011). *A tear: the secret message of smells.* The Smart Set from Drexell University. Retrieved from: http://www.thesmartset.com/article/article02171102.aspx

Fitzpatrick, S. M. (2001, October 1). Choose beauty. *The Scientist, 64*, 4.

Flaxman, P., & Bond, F. (2010). A randomized worksite comparison of acceptance and commitment therapy and stress inoculation training. *Behavior Research and Therapy, 48*(8), 816–820.

Flores, T. (2010, August 30). Those with less likely to give more. Retrieved June 10, 2011 from http://www.jconline.com/fdcp/?1283183290627

Florida, R., & Rentfrow, P. (2011). Place and well-being. In K. M. Sheldon, T. B. Kashdan, & M. F. Steger (Eds.), *Designing positive psychology: Taking stock and moving forward* (pp. 385–395). New York: Oxford University Press.

Foley, E., Matheis, R., & Schaefer, C. (2002). Effect of forced laughter on mood. *Psychological Reports, 90*(1), 184.

Fordyce, M. W. (1977). Development of a program to increase personal happiness. *Journal of Counseling Psychology, 24*(6), 511–521.

Fordyce, M. W. (1981). *The psychology of happiness: A brief version of the fourteen fundamentals.* Ft. Myers, FL: Cypress Lake Media.

Fordyce, M. W. (1983). A program to increase happiness: Further studies. *Journal of Counseling Psychology, 30*(4), 483–498.

Fordyce, M. W. (1988). A review of research on the happiness measures: A sixty-second index of happiness and mental health, *Social Indicators Research, 20*, 355–381.

Forgas, J. (2011). Can negative affect eliminate the power of first impression? Affective influences on primacy and recency effects in impression formation. *Journal of Experimental Social Psychology, 47*(2), 425–429.

Forgas, J. P. (2011). Affective influences on self-disclosure: Mood effects on the intimacy and reciprocity of disclosing personal information. *Journal of Personality and Social Psychology, 100*(3), 449–461.

Fowers, B. (2011, March 15). Comments on Pascal Bruckner's article "Condemned to joy". Posted to the Positive Psychology listserve: Friends-of-PP@apa.org

Fowers, B. (2005). *Virtue and Psychology: Pursuing Excellence in Ordinary Practices.*

Fowers, B. J. (2000). *Beyond the myth of marital happiness: How embracing the virtues of loyalty, generosity, justice, and courage can strengthen your relationship.* San Francisco: Jossey-Bass.

Fowers, B. J. (2001). The limits of a technical concept of a good marriage: Exploring the role of virtue in communication skills. *Journal of Marital and Family Therapy, 27*(3), 327–340.

Fowers, B. J. (2008). From continence to virtue: Recovering goodness, character unity, and character types for positive psychology. *Theory & Psychology, 18,* 629–653.

Fowler, J. W. (1981). *Stages of faith: The psychology of human development and the quest for meaning.* San Francisco: Harper & Row.

Fowler, J., & Christakis, N. (2009). Dynamic spread of happiness in a large social network: Longitudinal analyses over 20 years in the Framingham Heart Study. *BMJ, 337,* doi: 10.1136/bmj.a2338

Fowler, J., & Christakis, N. (2010). Cooperative behavior cascades in human social networks. *PNAS Proceedings of the National Academy of Sciences of the United States of America, 107*(12), 5334–5338.

Frank, J. D., & Frank, J. B. (1991). *Persuasion and healing: A comparative study of psychotherapy* (3rd ed.). Baltimore, MD: Johns Hopkins University Press.

Frank, R. H. (2007). Falling behind: How rising inequality harms the middle class. Berkeley, CA, US: University of California Press, 2007.

Frankl, V. E. (1963). *Man's search for meaning.* New York: Pocket Books.

Frankl, V. E. (1978). *The unheard cry for meaning: Psychotherapy and humanism.* New York: Simon & Schuster.

Fredrickson, B. (2007). The broaden-and-build theory of positive emotions. In F. Huppert, N. Baylis, &

B. Keverne, (Eds.). *The science of well-being.* (pp. 217–240). New York: Oxford University Press.

Fredrickson, B. (2008). Positive emotions. In M. Lewis, J. Haviland-Jones, & L. Feldman Barrett (Eds.). *Handbook of emotions (3rd edition).* (pp. 777–796). New York: Guilford Press.

Fredrickson, B. (2009). *Positivity: Groundbreaking Research Reveals How to Embrace the Hidden Strength of Positive Emotions, Overcome Negativity, and Thrive.* Crown Archetype.

Fredrickson, B. L. (1998). What good are positive emotions? *Review of General Psychology, 2*(3), 300–319.

Fredrickson, B. L. (2000a). Cultivating positive emotions to optimize health and well-being. *Prevention & Treatment, 3,* 1–32.

Frederickson, B. L. (2000b). Extracting meaning from past affective experiences: The importance of peaks, ends, and specific emotions. *Cognition and Emotion, 14*(4), 577–606. doi: 10.1080/026999300402808

Fredrickson, B. L. (2001). The role of positive emotions in positive psychology: The broaden-and-build theory of positive emotions. *Journal of American Psychological Association, 54*(3), 218–226.

Fredrickson, B., Cohn, M., Coffey, K., Pek, J., & Finkel, S. (2008). Open hearts build lives: Positive emotions, induced through loving-kindness meditation, build consequential personal resources. *Journal of Personality and Social Psychology, 95*(5), 1045–1062.

Fredrickson, B., & Joiner, T. (2002). Positive emotions trigger upward spirals toward emotional well-being. *Psychological Science, 13,* 172–175.

Fredrickson, B., & Levenson, R. (1998). Positive emotions speed recovery from the cardiovascular sequelae of negative emotions. *Cognition and Emotion, 12,* 191–220.

Fredrickson, B. L., & Losada, M. F. (2005). Positive Affect and the Complex Dynamics of Human Flourishing. *American Psychologist, 60*(7), 678–686.

Frenz, A. W., Carey, M. P., & Jorgensen, R. S. (1993). Psychometric evaluation of Antonovsky's Sense of Coherence Scale. *Psychological Assessment, 5*(2), 145–153.

Freud, S. (1952). Group psychology and the analysis of the ego. In *The major works of Sigmund Freud* (pp. 664–696). Chicago: Encyclopedia Britannica. (Original work published 1921:)

Freud, S. (1960). *The Interpretation of Dreams*. New York: Basic Books. (Original work published 1901)

Frey, B. S., & Stutzer, A. (2000). Happiness prospers in democracy. *Journal of Happiness Studies, 1*, 79–102.

Friedler, S., Glasser, S., Azani, L., Freedman, L., Arie, R., et al. (2011). The effect of medical clowning on pregnancy rates in vitro fertilization and embryo transfer. *Fertility and Sterility, 95*(6), 2127–2130.

Frijda, N. (1986). *The emotions*. Cambridge, UK: Cambridge University Press.

Frijda, N. (2008). The psychologist's pint of view. In M. Lewis, J. Haviland-Jones, & L. Feldman Barrett (Eds.). *Handbook of emotions (3rd edition)*. (pp. 68–87). New York: Guilford Press.

Frisch, M. B., Clark, M. P., Rouse, S. V., Rudd, M. D., Paweleck, J. K., Greenstone, A., & Kopplin, D. A. (2005). Predictive and treatment validity of life satisfaction and the quality of life inventory. *Assessment, 12*(1), 66–78.

Froese, A., Hackett T. P., Cassem, N. H., & Silverberg, E. L. (1974). Trajectories of anxiety and depression in denying and non-denying acute myocardial infarction patients during hospitalization. *Journal Psychosomatic Research, 18*(6), 412–20.

Froh, J., Kashdan, T., Yurkewicz, C., Fan, J., Allen, J., & Glowacki, J. (2010). The benefits of passion and absorption in activities: Engaged living in adolescents and its role in psychological well-being. *The Journal of Positive Psychology, 5*(4), 311–332.

Fromm, E. (1976). To have or to be? NY: Continuum.

Fromm, E. (1990). *The sane society*. New York: Holt, Rinehart, & Winston. (original work published in 1955).

Fromm, E. (1994). *Escape from freedom*. New York: Holt, Rinehart, & Winston. (original work published in 1941).

Fromm, E. (1996). *The Art of Being*. NY: Continuum.

Fuchs, E., & Havinghurst, R. (1973). *To live on this earth: American Indian education*. New York: Anchor Books.

Fujita, F. (1991). *An investigation of the relation between extroversion, neuroticism, positive affect, and negative affect* [Unpublished masters thesis]. University of Illinois at Urbana-Champaign.

Fujita, F. (2008). The frequency of social comparison and its relation to subjective well-being. In M. Eid & R. Larsen (Eds.). *The science of subjective well-being*. (pp. 239–257). New York: Guilford Press.

Fujita, F., & Diener, E. (2005). Life satisfaction set point: Stability and change. *Journal of Personality and Social Psychology, 88*(1), 158–164.

Fujita, F., Diener, E., & Sandvik, E. (1991). Gender differences in negative affect and well-being: The case for emotional intensity. *Journal of Personality and Social Psychology, 61*, 427–434.

Fullagar, C. J., & Kelloway, E. K. (2009). "Flow" at work: An experience sampling approach. *Journal of Occupational and Organizational Psychology, 82*(3), 595–615.

Funder, D. C. (1997). *The personality puzzle*. New York: Norton.

Furr, M. R. (2005). Differentiating happiness and self-esteem. *Individual Differences Research, 3*(2), 105–127.

Gable, S., & Gosnell, C. (2011). The positive side of close relationships. In K. M. Sheldon, T. B. Kashdan, & M. F. Steger (Eds.), *Designing positive psychology: Taking stock and moving forward* (pp. 265–279). New York: Oxford University Press.

Gallagher, M. W., & Lopez, S. (2007). Curiosity and well-being. *The Journal of Positive Psychology, 2*(4), 236–248. doi: 10.1080/17439760701552345

Gallois, P. (1984). Modifications neurophysiologiques et respiratoires lors de la pratique des techniques de relaxation. *L'Enchephale 10*, 139–144.

Galway, W. T. (1975). *The inner game of tennis*. New York: Random House.

Gallup Organization. (1993). *GO LIFE Survey on prayer*. Princeton, NJ.

Ganong, L. H., & Coleman, M. (2002). Family resilience in multiple contexts. *Journal of Marriage and the Family, 64*, 2, 346–348.

Gardner, H. (1993). *Creating minds: An anatomy of creativity seen through the lives of Freud, Einstein, Picasso, Stravinsky, Eliot, Graham, and Gandhi*. New York: Basic Books.

Garfield, C. A., & Bennett, H. Z. (1984). *Peak performance: Mental training techniques of the world's greatest athletes*. Los Angeles: Tarcher.

Garland, E. L., Fredrickson, B., Kring, A. M., Johnson, D. P., Myer, P. S., & Penn, D. L. (2010). Upward spirals of positive emotions counter downward spirals of negativity: Insights from the broaden-and-build theory and affective neuroscience on the treatment of emotion dysfunctions and deficits in psychopathology. *Clinical Psychology Review, 37,* 849–864.

Garmezy, N. (1991). Resilience in children's adaptation to negative life events and stressed environments. *Pediatric Annals, 20*(9), 463–466.

Garmezy, N., Masten, A. S., & Tellegren, A. (1984). The study of stress and competence in children: A building block for developmental psychopathology. *Child Development, 55,* 97–111.

Gay, V. P. (2001). *Joy and the objects of psychoanalysis.* Buffalo, New York: State University of New York Press.

Gaynor, M. P. (2002). *The healing power of sound.* Boulder, CO: Shambhala.

Gentry, W. D., & Ouellette-Kobasa, S. C. (1984). Social and psychological resources mediating stress–illness relationships in humans. In W. D. Gentry (Ed.), *Handbook of behavioral medicine* (pp. 87–116). New York: Guilford.

George, J. M., & Brief, A. P. (1992). Feeling good-doing good: A conceptual analysis of the mood at work organizational spontaneity relationship. *Psychological Bulletin, 112,* 310–329.

George, L. K., Larson, D. B., Koenig, H. G., & McCullough, M. E. (2000). Spirituality and health: What we know, what we need to know. *Journal of Social and Clinical Psychology, 19*(1), 102–116.

Gergen, K., & Gergen, M. (2007). Social construction and psychological inquiry. In J. Gubrium & J. Holstein (Eds.). Handbook of Social Constructionism. (pp. 171–188) Sage.

Gergen, K. J., & Gergen, M. M. (1988) Narrative and the self as relationship. In L. Berkowitz (Ed.), *Advances in experimental social psychology* (Vol. *21,* pp. 17–56). New York: Academic Press.

Gergen, M., & Gergen, K. (2006). Narratives in action. *Narrative Inquiry 16,* 112–128.

Gerstorf, D., Ram, N., Estabrook, R., Schupp, J., Wagner, G., & Lindenberger, U. (2008). Life satisfaction and terminal decline in old age: Longitudinal evidence from the German Socio-Economic Panel Study (SOPS). *Developmental Psychology, 44*(4), 1148–1159.

Gestwicki, R. (2001). Ira Progoff (1921–1998): The creator of the intensive journal method and a new profession. *Journal of Humanistic Psychology, 41*(3), 53–74.

Ghani, J. A., & Deshpande, S. P. (1994). Task characteristics and the experience of optimal flow in human-computer interaction. *The Journal of Psychology, 128*(4), 381–391.

Gilbert, D. (2007). *Stumbling on Happiness.* NY: Vintage.

Gilbert, D. T., Killingsworth, M. A., Eyre, R. N., & Wilson, T. D. (2009). The surprising power of neighborly advice. *Science, 323*(5921), 1617–1619.

Gilbert, P., McEwan, K., Mitra, R., Franks, L., Richter, A., & Rockliff, H. (2008). Feeling safe and content: A specific affect regulation system? Relationships to depression, anxiety, stress, and self-criticism. *The Journal of Positive Psychology, 3*(3), 182–191.

Gillham, J., & Reivich, K. (2004). Cultivating optimism in childhood and adolescence. *Annals of the American Academy of Political and Social Science, 591,* 146–163

Gilovich, T. D., & Medvec, V. (1994) The temporal pattern to the experience of regret. *Journal of Personality and Social Psychology, 67*(3), 357–365.

Gilovich, T. D., & Medvec, V. (1995) The experience of regret: What, where, when and why? *Psychological Review, 102*(2), 379–395.

Gilovich, T. D., Medvec, V., & Kahneman, D. (1998). Varieties of regret: A debate and partial resolution. *Psychological Review, 105*(3), 602–605.

Girard, M., & Mullett, E. (1997). Propensity to forgive in adolescents, young adults, older adults, and elderly people. *Journal of Adult Development, 4,* 209–220.

Glancy, M., Willits, F. W., & Farrell, P. (1986). Adolescent activities and adult success and happiness. *Sociology and Social Research, 70,* 242–270.

Glenn, N. D., & Weaver, C. N. (1988). The changing relationship of marital status to reported happiness. *Journal of Marriage and the Family, 50,* 317–324.

Glock, C., & Stark, R. (1965). *Religion and society in tension.* New York: Rand McNally.

Goetz, T., Ehret, C., Jullien, S., & Hall, N. C. (2006). Is the grass always greener on the other side? Social comparisons of subjective well-being. *The Journal of Positive Psychology, 1*(4), 173–186. doi: 10.1080/17439760600885655

Goldstein, E. D. (2007). Sacred moments: Implications on well-being and stress. *Journal of Clinical Psychology, 63*(10), 1001–1019. doi: 10.1002/jclp.20402

Goldman, B. (2006). Making diamonds out of coal: The role of authenticity in healthy (optimal) self-esteem and psychological functioning. In M. Kernis (Ed.), *Self-esteem issues and answers: A sourcebook of current perspectives* (pp. 132–139). NY: Psychology Press.

Goleman, D. (1972a). The Buddha on meditation and states of consciousness. Part I: The teachings. *Journal of Transpersonal Psychology, 7*(1), 1–44.

Goleman, D. (1972b). The Buddha on meditation and states of consciousness. Part II: A typology of meditation techniques. *Journal of Transpersonal Psychology, 7*(2), 151–210.

Goleman, D. (1975). Mental health in classical Buddhist psychology. *Journal of Transpersonal Psychology, 7,* 176–181.

Goleman, D. J. (1995). *Emotional intelligence.* New York: Bantam Books.

Gomez, V., Krings, F., Bangerter, A., & Grob, A. (2009). The influence of personality and life events on subjective well-being from a life span perspective. *Journal of Research in Personality, 43*(3), 345–354.

Gonzaga, G. C., Campos, B., & Bradbury, T. (2007). Similarity, convergence, and relationship satisfaction in dating and married couples. *Journal of Personality and Social Psychology, 93*(1), 34–48. doi: 10.1037/0022-3514.93.1.34

Gonzales-Roma, V., Schafeli, W. B., Bakker, A. B., & Lloret, S.(2006). Burnout and engagement: Independent factors or opposite poles? *Journal of Vocational Behavior, 68,* 165–174.

Gorchoff, S. M., John, O. P., & Helson, R. (2008). Contextualizing change in marital satisfaction during middle age: A 19-year longitudinal study. *Psychological Sciences, 19*(11), 1194–1200.

Gore, Al, Jr. (2001, November 8). Building healthy communities. Speech at Middle Tennessee State University.

Goretzki, M., Thalbourne, M. A., & Storm, L. (2009). The questionnaire measurement of spiritual emergency. *Journal of Transpersonal Psychology, 41,* 81–97.

Gorman, M. O. (1998, March). Do you love him? *Prevention,* 92.

Gorman, R. M. (2002). *Experiencing psychology.* Albuquerque, NM: Southwest.

Gottman, J. M. (1998). Psychology and the study of the marital processes. *Annual Review of Psychology, 49,* 169–297.

Gottman, J., & Declaire, J. (2001). *The relationship cure: A five-step guide for building better connections with family, friends, and lovers.* New York: Crown.

Gottman, J. M., & Gottman, J. S. (1999). The marriage survival kit: A research-based marital therapy. In R. Berger & M. T. Hannah (Eds.), *Preventive approaches in couples therapy* (pp. 304–330). Philadelphia, PA.: Brunner/Mazel.

Gottman, J. M., & Levenson, R. W. (2000). The timing of divorce: Predicting when a couple will divorce over a 14-year period. *Journal of Marriage and the Family, 63*(3), 737–745.

Gottman, J. M., & Notarius, C. I. (2000). Decade review: Observing marital interaction. *Journal of Marriage and the Family, 62*(4), 927–947.

Gottman, J., & Silver, N. (1999). *The seven principles for making marriage work.* New York: Crown.

Grafanaki, S., Brennan, M., Holmes, S., Tang, K., & Alvarez, S. (2007). In search of flow in counseling and psychotherapy: Identifying the necessary ingredients of peak moments of therapy interaction. *Person-Centered and Experiential Psychotherapies, 6*(4), 240–255.

Grant, A., & Cavanagh, M. (2011). Coaching and positive psychology. In K. M. Sheldon, T. B. Kashdan, & M. F. Steger (Eds.), *Designing positive psychology: Taking stock and moving forward* (pp. 293–312). New York: Oxford University Press.

Grant, A. M., & Sonnentag, S. (2010). Doing good buffers against feeling bad: Prosocial impact compensates for negative task and self-evaluations. *Organizational Behavior and Human Decision Processes, 111*(1), 13–22. doi: 10.1016/j.obhdp.2009.07.003

Grape, C., Sandgren, M., Hansson, L., Ericson, M., Theorell, T. (2003). Does singing promote well-being?: An empirical study of professional and amateur singers during a singing lesson. *Integrative Physiological and Behavioral Science, 38*(1), 65–74.

Greeley, A. M., & McCready, W. C. (1975, January 26). Are we a nation of mystics? *New York Times Magazine,* p. 12ff.

Green, E., & Green, A. (1977). *Beyond biofeedback.* New York: Delacorte.

Green, E., & Green, A. (1989). *Beyond Biofeedback.* NY: Knoll.

Greene, K., Delega, V. J., & Matthews, A. (2006). Self-disclosure in personal relationships.

In A. L. Vangelisti & D. Perlman (Eds), *Cambridge Handbook of Personal Relationships*. Cambridge: Cambridge University Press.

Greenberg, J., Pyszczynski, T., & Soloman, S. (1986). The causes and consequences of the need for self-esteem: A terror management theory. In R. F. Baumeistser (Ed.), *Public self and private self* (pp. 189–207). New York: Springer-Verlag.

Greenberg, L. S., & Rice, L. N. (1997). Humanistic approaches to psychotherapy. In P. L. Wachtel & S. B. Messer (Eds.), *Theories of psychotherapy: Origins and evolution* (pp. 97–129). Washington, DC: American Psychological Association.

Greenspan, M. J., & Feltz, D. E. (1989). Psychological interventions with athletes in competitive situations: A review. *The Sport Psychologist, 3*, 219–236.

Greitmeyer, T., Osswald, F. P., & Frey, D. (2007). Civil courage: Implicit theories, related concepts, and measurement. *The Journal of Positive Psychology, 2*(2), 115–119.

Grepmair, L., Mitterlehner, F., Loew, T., Bachler, E., Rother, W., et al. (2007). Promoting mindfulness in psychotherapists in training influences the treatment results of the patients: A randomized, double-blind, controlled study. *Psychotherapy and Psychosomatics, 76*, 332–338.

Greve, W., & Staudinger, U. (2006). Resilience in later adulthood and old age: Resources and potentials for successful aging. In D. Cicchetti & D. J. Cohen (Eds.), *Developmental psychopathology: Risk, disorder, and adaptation* (Vol. *3*, 2nd ed., pp. 796–840). Hoboken, NJ: John Wiley.

Griffiths, R. R., Richards, W. A., McCann, U., & Jesse, R. (2006). Psilocybin Can Occasion Mystical-Type Experiences Having Substantial and Sustained Personal Meaning and Spiritual Significance. *Psychopharmacology, 187*, 268–283.

Griffiths, R., Richards, W., Johnson, M., McCann, U., & Jesse, R. (2008). Mystical-type experiences occasioned by psilocybin mediate the attribution of personal meaning and spiritual significance 14 months later. *Journal of Psychopharmacology, 22*(6), 621–632.

Grob, C. S., Danforth, A. L., Chopra, G. S., Hagerty, M., McKay, C. R., Halberstadt, A. L., Greer, G. R. (2010, September). Pilot Study of Psilocybin Treatment for Anxiety in Patients With Advanced-Stage Cancer. *Archives of General Psychiatry, 6*.

Gross, J. (2008). Emotion regulation. In M. Lewis, J. Haviland-Jones, & L. Feldman Barrett (Eds.). *Handbook of emotions (3rd edition).* (pp. 497–512). New York: Guilford Press.

Grossman, P., Kappos, L., Gensicke H., D'Souza, M., Mohr, D. C., Penner, I. K., & Steiner, C. (2010). MS quality of life, depression, and fatigue improve after mindfulness training: A randomized trial. *Neurology, 75*, 1141–1149.

Gruber, Mauss, & Tamir (2011). The dark side of happiness: How, when and why happiness is not always good. *Perspectivse on Psychological Science, 6*, 222–233.

Gruhn, D., Rebucal, K., Diehl, M., & Lumley, M. (2008). Empathy across the adult lifespan: Longitudinal and experience-sampling findings. *Emotion, 8*(6), 753–765. doi: 10.2037/a0014123

Guignon, C. (2000). Authenticity and integrity: A Heideggerian perspective. In P. Young-Eisendrath & M. Miller (Eds.), *The psychology of mature spirituality: Integrity, wisdom, transcendence* (pp. 62–74). NY: Brunner-Routledge.

Guilford, J. P. (1950). Creativity. *American Psychologist, 5*, 444–454.

Guilford, J. P. (1967). *The nature of human intelligence.* New York: McGraw-Hill.

Hackman, J. R. (2008). The perils of positivity. *Journal of Organizational Behavior, 30*, 309–319.

Hagemann, D., Waldstein, S., & Thayer, J. (2003). Central and autonomic nervous system integration in emotion. *Brain and Cognition, 52*(1), 79–87.

Hagerty, M. R. (1999). Testing Maslow's hierarchy of needs: National quality-of-life across time. *Social Indicators Research, 46*, 249–271.

Hagerty, M. R. (2000). Social comparisons of income in one's community: Evidence from national surveys of income and happiness. *Journal of Personality and Social Psychology, 78*(4), 764–771. Retrieved from: http://find.galegroup.com

Haidt, J. (2000a, October). *Elevation and the positive moral emotions.* Paper presented at the Positive Psychology Summit.

Haidt, J. (2000b). The positive emotion of elevation. *Prevention and Treatment, 3*(3).

Haidt, J. (2002). *It's more fun to work on strengths than weaknesses (but it might not be better for you)* http://people.virginia.edu/~jdh6n/Positivepsych.html.

Haidt, J. (2006). *The Happiness Hypothesis: Finding Modern Truth in Ancient Wisdom.* NY: Basic Books.

Haidt, J. (2007, May 18). The new synthesis in moral psychology. *Science, 316,* 998–1002.

Haidt, J., & Kesebir, S. (2010). Morality. In S. T. Fiske, D. T. Gilbert, & G. Lindzey (Eds.) *Handbook of social psychology, volume two (5th ed.).* (pp. 797–832). NY: Wiley.

Halpern, S., & Savary, L. (1985). *The music and sounds that make us whole.* San Francisco: Harper & Row.

Hamilton, J., Haier, R., & Buchsbaum, M. (1984). Intrinsic enjoyment and boredom coping scales: Validation with personality, evoked potential and attention measures. *Personality and Individual Differences, 5*(2), 183–193.

Han, S. (1988). The relationship between life satisfaction and flow in elderly Korean immigrants. In M. Csikszentmihalyi & I. S. Csikszentmihalyi (Eds.), *Optimal experience: Psychological studies of flow in consciousness* (pp. 138–149). New York: Cambridge University Press.

Handelsman, M., Knapp, S., & Gottlieb, M. (2009). Positive ethics: Themes and variations. In C. R. Snyder & S. Lopez (Eds.), *Oxford handbook of positive psychology* (2nd ed., pp. 105–114). New York: Oxford University Press.

Harari, Y. N. (2008). Combat flow: Military, political, and ethical dimensions of subjective well-being in war. *Review of General Psychology, 12*(3), 253–264.

Harding, S. R., Flannelly, K. J., Weaver, A. J., & Costa, K. G. (2005). The influence of religion on death anxiety and death acceptance. *Mental Health, Religion, and Culture, 8*(4), 253–261. doi: 10.1080/13674670412331304311

Harker, L., & Keltner, D. (2001). Expressions of positive emotion in women's college yearbook pictures and their relationship to personality and life outcomes across adulthood. *Journal of Personality and Social Psychology, 80*(1), 112–124.

Harris, P. R., & Lightsey, O. R. (2005). Constructive thinking as a mediator of the relationship between extraversion, neuroticism, and subjective well-being. *European Journal of Personality, 19,* 409–426. doi: 10.1002/per.544

Harter, S. (2002). Authenticity. In C. R. Snyder & S. J. Lopez (Eds.), *Handbook of positive psychology* (pp. 382–394). New York: Oxford University Press.

Harvey, J. H., & Omarzu, J. (1999). *Minding in close relationships: A theory of relationship enhancement.* New York: Cambridge University Press.

Harvey, J. H., & Pauwels, B. (2009). Relationships connection: A redux on the role of minding and the quality of feeling special in the enhancement of closeness. In C. R. Snyder & S. Lopez (Eds.). *Oxford handbook of positive psychology (2nd ed.).*(pp. 385–392). New York: Oxford University Press.

Haslam, A., Jetten, J., Postmes, T., & Haslam, C. (2009). Social identity, health and well-being: An emerging agenda for applied psychology. *Applied Psychology: An International Review, 58*(1), 1–23.

Hatfield, E. (1988). Passionate and companionate love. In R. J. Sternberg & M. L. Barnes (Eds.), *The psychology of love* (pp. 191–217). New Haven, CT: Yale University Press.

Havlena, W., & Holak, S. (1991). The good old days: Observations on nostalgia and its role in consumer behavior. *Advances in Consumer Research, 18,* 323–329.

Hawkins, D. N., & Booth, A. (2005). Unhappily ever after: Effects of long-term, low-quality marriages on well-being. *Social Forces, 84*(1), 451–471.

Haworth, J. T., & Hill, S. (1992). Work, leisure, and psychological well-being in a sample of young adults. *Journal of Community and Applied Social Psychology, 2*(2), 147–160.

Hayes, S., Strosahl, K., & Wilson, K. (2003). *Acceptance and Commitment Therapy: An Experiential Approach to Behavior Change.* New York: Guilford.

Hayes, S. C. (2002). Buddhism and Acceptance and Commitment Therapy. *Cognitive and Behavioral Practice, 9*(1), 58–66.

Hayes, S. C., & Smith, S. (2005). *Get out of your mind and into your life: The new acceptance and commitment therapy.* Oakland, CA: New Harbinger.

Headey, B. (2008). Life goals matter to happiness: A revision of set-point theory. *Social Indicators Research, 86*(2), 312–231. doi: 10.1007/s11205-007-9138-y

Headey, B., Veenhoven, R., & Wearing, A. (1991). Top-down versus bottom-up theories of subjective well-being. *Social Indicators Research, 24,* 81–100.

Headey, B., Muffels, R., & Wagner, G. (2010, June). Choices which change life satisfaction: Revising SWB theory to account for change. Retrieved June 23, 2011 from http://hdl.handle.net/10419/36715

Heath, D. H. (1991). *Fulfilling lives: Paths to maturity and success*. San Francisco: Jossey-Bass.

Helgeson, V. S., Reynolds, K. A., & Tomich, P. L. (2006). A meta-analytic review of benefit finding and growth. *Journal of Consulting and Clinical Psychology, 74,* 797–816.

Heidrich, S. M. (1996). Mechanisms related to psychological well-being in older women with chronic illnesses: Age and disease comparisons. *Research in Nursing Health, 19*(3), 225–235.

Helgoe, L. (2010, Sept./Oct.). Revenge of the introvert. *Psychology Today,* 54–61.

Helson, R., & Srivastava, S. (2001). Three paths of adult development: Conservers, seekers, and achievers. *Journal of Personality and Social Psychology, 80,* 995–1010.

Helson, R., & Wink, P. (1987). Two conceptions of maturity examined in the findings of a longitudinal study. *Journal of Personality and Social Psychology, 53,* 531–541. doi: 10.1037//0022-3514.53.3.531

Hendrick, S. S. (1981). Self-disclosure and marital satisfaction. *Journal of Personality and Social Psychology, 40*(6), 1150–1159.

Hendrick, S. S., & Hendrick, C. (1992). *Romantic love.* Newbury Park, CA: Sage Publications.

Hendrick, S. S., Hendrick C., & Adler, N. L. (1988). Romantic relationships: Love, satisfaction, and staying together. *Journal of Personality and Social Psychology, 54,* 980–988.

Hendricks, G. (1995). *Conscious breathing: Breathwork for health, stress release, and personal mastery.* New York: Bantam.

Heo, J., Lee, Y., McCormick, B. P., & Pedersen, P. M. (2010). Daily experience of serious leisure, flow and subjective well-being of older adults. *Leisure Studies, 29*(2), 207–225.

Heppner, P. Paul, & Lee, Dong-Gwi, Problem-solving appraisal and psychological adjustment. (2009). In: S. Lopez & C. R. Snyder (eds.) Oxford handbook of positive psychology (2nd ed.). (pp. 345–355). New York, NY, US: Oxford University Press.

Hergenhahn, B. R. (2009). An introduction to the history of psychology. Belmont, CA: Wadsworth/ Cengage.

Hernstein, R. J., Nickerson, R. S., de Sanchez, M., & Swets, J. A. (1986). Teaching thinking skills. *American Psychologist, 41,* 1279–1289.

Herrbach, O. (2006). A matter of feeling? The affective tone of organizational commitment and identification. *Journal of Organizational Behavior, 27*(5), 629–643.

Herrigel, E. (1971). *Zen in the art of archery.* New York: Vintage.

Hertsgaard, M. (1995). *A day in the life: The music and artistry of the Beatles.* New York: Delacorte Press.

Herzog, A. R., Rodgers, W. L., & Woodworth, J. (1982). Age and satisfaction: Data from several large surveys. *Research on Aging, 3,* 142–165.

Hewitt, J. (2009). The social construction of self-esteem. In C. R. Snyder & S. Lopez (Eds.), *Oxford handbook of positive psychology* (2nd ed., pp. 217–224). New York: Oxford University Press.

Hickson, J., & Housley, W. (1997). Creativity in later life. *Educational Gerontology, 23*(6), 539–547.

Higgins, E. T. (2000). Making a good decision: Value from fit. *American Psychologist, 55*(11), 1217–1230.

Higgins, R. L., & Leibowitz, R. (1999). Reality negotiation and coping: The social construction of adaptive outcomes. In C. R. Snyder (Ed.), *Coping: The psychology of what works* (pp. 20–49). New York: Oxford University Press.

Hildon, Z., Smith, G., Netuveli, G., & Blane, D. (2008). Understanding adversity and resilience at older ages. *Sociology and Health, 30*(5), 726–740.

Hill, C. E. (2009). *Helping skills: Facilitating exploration, insight, and action.* Washington, DC: American Psychological Association.

Hill, S., & Buss, D. M. (2008). Evolution and subjective well-being. In M. Eid & R. Larsen (Eds.). *The science of subjective well-being.* (pp. 62–79). New York: Guilford Press.

Hills, P., & Argyle, M. (2001). Happiness, introversion-extraversion and happy introverts. *Personality and Individual Differences, 30*(4), 595–608.

Hitlin, S. (2007). Doing good, feeling good: Values and the self's moral center. *The Journal of Positive Psychology, 2*(4), 249–259. doi: 10.1080/17439760701552352

Hjelle, L. A. (1991). Relationship of social interest to internal-external control and self-actualization in young women. *Individual Psychology: Journal of Adlerian Theory, Research, and Practice, 47*(1), 101–105. Retrieved from http://www.utexas.edu/utpress/journals/jip.html

Ho, M. Y., Cheung, F. M., & Cheung, S. F. (2008). Personality and life events as predictors of adolescents; life satisfaction: Do life events mediate the link between personality and life satisfaction? *Social Indicators Research, 89,* 457–471.

Hoare, C. H. (2002). *Erikson on development in adulthood: New insights from the unpublished papers.* New York: Oxford University Press.

Hodges, Timothy D., & Clifton, Donald O. (2004). Strengths-Based Development in Practice. In: Positive psychology in practice. Linley, P. Alex (Ed.), Joseph, Stephen (Ed.), Hoboken, NJ, US: John Wiley & Sons Inc, 2004. pp. 256–268.

Hodges, T. D., & Harter, J. K. (2005, Spring). A review of the theory and research underlying the StrengthsQuest program for students. *Educational Horizons,* 190–201.

Hoffman, E. (1980). The Kabbalah: Its implications for humanistic psychology. *Journal of Humanistic Psychology, 20*(1), 33–47.

Hoffman, E. (1994). *The drive for self: Alfred Adler and the founding of individual psychology.* Reading, MA: Addison-Wesley.

Hoffman, E. (Ed.). (1995). *Opening the Inner Gates: New paths in Kabbalah and psychology.* Boston: Shambhala.

Hoffman, E. (Ed.). (1996). *Future visions: The unpublished papers of Abraham Maslow.* Thousand Oaks, CA: Sage.

Hoffman, E. (1999). *The right to be human: A biography of Abraham Maslow.* New York: McGraw-Hill.

Hoffman, E. (2003). Peak-experiences in Japanese youth. *Japanese Journal of Humanistic Psychology, 21*(1), 112–121.

Hoffman, E. (2004). Abraham Maslow's life and unfinished legacy. *Japanese Journal of Administrative Science, 17*(3), 133–138.

Hoffman, E. (2006). *The way of splendor: Jewish mysticism and modern psychology.* Lantham, MD.: Rowman & Littlefield. (Originally published in 1981)

Hoffman, E. (2009). *The wisdom of Maimonides: The life and writings of the Jewish sage.* Boston: Shambhala/Trumpeter.

Hoffman, E., Iversen, V., & Ortiz, F. (2010). Peak-experiences among Norwegian youth. *Nordic psychology, 62*(4), 67–76.

Hoffman, E., & Muramoto, S. (2007). Peak-experiences among Japanese youth. *Journal of Humanistic Psychology, 47,* 524–540.

Hoffman, E., & Ortiz, F. (2009). Youthful peak experiences in cross-cultural perspective: Implications for educators and counselors. In L. Francis, D. Scott, M. de Souza, & J. Norman (Eds.), *The International handbook for education for spirituality, care & well-being* (pp. 469–480). New York: Springer.

Hoffman, E., & Ortiz, F. (2010). Experiencias de cumber en jovenes Mexicanos. *Revista Alternativas en Psicologia, Mexico (Journal of Alternatives in Psychology, Mexico),* 14,(1), 2–10.

Hoffman, E., Resende, A., & Ho, M. Y. (in press). Peak-experiences among Brazilian youth. *Advanced Development Journal.*

Hoffman, E., Solgian, F., & Ortiz, F. (2009). Enhancing employee engagement: A validation study in Italy. *IHRIM Journal, 13*(3), 44–51.

Hoffman, E., Yves-Simon, J. Y., & Ortiz. F. (2008). Enhancing employee engagement: A validation study in Venezuela. *IHRIM Journal, 12*(5), 21–26.

Hojjat, M. (1997). Philosophy of life as a model of relationship satisfaction. In R. J. Sternberg & M. Hojjatt (Eds.), *Satisfaction in close relationships* (pp. 102–128). New York: Guilford Press.

Hojat, M., Louis, D. Z., Markham, F. W., Wender, R., Rabinowitz, C., & Gonnella, J. S. (2011, March). Physicians empathy and clinical outcomes for diabetic patients. *Academic Medicine, 86*(3), 359–364.

Holak, S., & Havlena, W. (1998). Feelings, fantasies and memories: An examination of the emotional components of nostalgia. *Journal of Business Research, 42,* 217–226.

Holbrook, M. B. (1993). Nostalgia and consumption preferences: Some emerging patterns of consumer tastes. *Journal of Consumer Research, 20,* 245–256.

Hooley, J. M., & Hahlweg, K. (1989). Marital satisfaction and marital communication in German and English couples. *Behavioral Assessment [Special issue: Coding Marital Interaction], 11*(1), 119–133.

Holt-Lunstad, J., Birmingham, W., & Jones, B. Q. (2008). Is there something unique about marriage?: The relative impact of marital status, relationship quality, and network social support on ambulatory blood pressure and mental health. *Annals of Behavioral Medicine, 35*(2), 239–244. doi: 10.1007/s12160-008-9018-y

Holt-Lunstad, J., Jones, B., & Birmingham, W. (2008). The influence of close relationships on nocturnal blood pressure dipping. *International Journal of Psychophysiology, 71*(3), 211–217.

Holt-Lundstad, J., Smith, T., & Layton, B. (2010). Social relationships and mortality risk: A meta-analytic review. *PLoS Medicine, 7*(7): e1000316. doi: 10.1371/journal.pmed.1000316

Hölzel, B. K., Ott, U., Gard, T., Hempel, H., Weygandt, M., Morgen, K., & Vaitl, D. (2008). Investigation of mindfulness meditation practitioners with voxel-based morphometry. *Social Cognitive and Affective Neuroscience, 3*(1), 55–61.

Honderich, T. (Ed.) (1995). *The Oxford companion to philosophy.* New York: Oxford University Press.

Hood, R. W., Jr. (1977, June). Eliciting mystical states of consciousness with semistructured nature experiences. *Journal for the Scientific Study of Religion, 16*(2), 155–163.

Hood, R. W., Jr. (1997). The empirical study of mysticism. In B. Spilka & D. McIntosh (Eds.). The psychology of religion: Theoretical approaches (pp. 222–232). Boulder, CO: Westview Press.

Hood, R. W., Jr. (2005). Mystical, spiritual, and religious experiences. In R. Paloutzian & C. Park (Eds.). *Handbook of Psychology of Religion and Spirituality* (pp. 348–364). Guilford Press.

Hood, R.W., Jr., Morris, R. J., Watson, P. J. (1993). Further factor analysis of Hood's mysticism scale. *Psychological Reports, 73*, 1176–1178.

Horney, K. (1942). *Self-analysis.* New York: Norton.

Horney, K. (1950). *Neurosis and human growth.* New York: Norton.

Howell, A. J., Didgeon, N., & Buro, K (2008). Relations among mindfulness, well-being, and sleep. *Personality and Individual Differences, 45*, 773–777.

Howell, R. T., Chenot, D., Hill, G., & Howell, C. J. (2009). Momentary happiness: The role of psychological need satisfaction. *Journal of Happiness Studies, 12*(1), 1–15.

Huang, C. (2010). Internet use and psychological well-being: A meta-analysis. *Cyberpsychology, Behavior, and Social Networking, 13*(3), 241–249.

Huang, P., & Blumenthal, J. (2009). Positive institutions, law, and policy. In C. R. Snyder & S. Lopez (Eds.). *Oxford handbook of positive psychology (2nd ed.).* (pp. 589–598). Oxford: Oxford University Press.

Huebner, E. S., Gilman, R., Reschly, A., & Hall, R. (2009). Positive schools. In C. R. Snyder & S. Lopez (Eds.), *Oxford handbook of positive psychology* (2nd ed., pp. 561–568). New York: Oxford University Press.

Hunt, M. (1959). *The natural history of love.* New York: Alfred Knopf.

Hunter, I., Dik, B. J., & Banning, J. H. (2010). College students' perception of calling in work and life: A qualitative investigation. *Journal of Vocational Behavior, 76*, 178–186.

Huta, V., & Hawley, L. (2010). Psychological strengths and cognitive vulnerabilities: Are they two ends of the same continuum or do they have independent relationships with well-being and ill-being? Journal of Happiness Studies, *11*(1), 71–93.

Hutcherson, C. A., Seppala, E. M., & Gross, J. J. (2008, October). Loving-kindness meditation increases social connectedness. *Emotion, 8*(5), 720–724.

Immordino-Yang, M. H., McColl, A., Damasio, H., & Damasio, A. (2009). Neural correlates of admiration and compassion. *Proceedings of the National Academy of Sciences of the United States of America, 106*(19), 8021–8026. doi: 10.1073/pnas.0810363106

Impett, E. A., Sorsoli, L., Schooler, D., Henson, J. M., & Tolman, D. L. (2008). Girls' relationship authenticity and self-esteem across adolescence. *Developmental Psychology, 44*(3), 722–733. doi: 10.1037/0012-1649.44.3.722

Ingersoll, R. E. (2007). Perspectives and psychotherapy: Applying integral theory to psychotherapy practice. *Journal of Transpersonal Psychology, 39*(2), 175–198.

Inglehart, R. (1990). *Culture's shift in advanced industrial society.* Princeton, NJ: Princeton University Press.

Inglehart, R., Foa, R., Peterson, C., & Welzel, C. (2008). Development, Freedom, and Rising Happiness A Global Perspective (1981–2007). *Perspectives on Psychological Science, 3*(4), 264–285.

Inglehart, R., & Rabier, J. R. (1986). Aspirations adapt to situations—but why are the Belgians so much happier than the French? In F. M. Andrews (Ed.), *Research on the quality of life* (pp. 1–56). Ann Arbor: Institute for Social Research, University of Michigan.

International Positive Psychology Association. (2009, October 15). Welcome to the IPPA network online. Retrieved from http://www.ippanetwork. org/Home/

Ironson, G., & Powell, L. (2005). An exploration of the health benefits of factors that help us thrive. *International Journal of Behavioral Medicine*, *12*(2), 47–49.

Irving, L. M., Snyder, C. R., & Crowson, J. J., Jr. (1998). Hope and coping with cancer by college women. *Journal of Personality*, *66*(2), 195–214.

Isaacowitz, D. M., Vaillant, G. E., & Seligman, M. E. P. (2003). Strengths and satisfaction across the adult lifespan. *The International Journal of Aging and Human Development*, *57*(2), 181–201.

Isen, A. (1987). Positive affect, cognitive processes and social behavior. *Advances in Experimental Social Psychology*, *20*, 203–253.

Isen, A. M. (2001). An influence of positive affect on decision making in complex situations: Theoretical issues with practical implications. *Journal of Consumer Psychology*, *11*(2), 75–85.

Isen, A. M. (2008). Positive affect and decision processes: Some recent theoretical developments with practical implications. In C. F. R. Haugdvedt, P. H. Kerr, & Kardes, F. R. (Eds.), *Handbook of consumer psychology*. New York: Erlbaum.

Isen, A. (2009). A role for neuropsychology in understanding the facilitating influence of positive affect on social behavior and cognitive processes. In C. R. Snyder & S. Lopez (Eds.), *Oxford handbook of positive psychology* (2nd ed., pp. 503–518). New York: Oxford University Press.

Issacowitz, D. M., Vaillant, G. E., & Seligman, M. E. (2003). Strengths and satisfaction across the adult lifespan. *International Journal of Aging and Human Development*, *57*(2), 181–201.

Ito, M., & Kodama, M. (2005). Sense of authenticity, self-esteem, and subjective and psychological well-being. *Japanese Journal of Educational Psychology*, *53*(1), 74–85. Retrieved from http://ci.nii.ac.jp/ vol_issue/nels/AN00345837_en.html

Izzo, J. B. (2004). *Second innocence: A choice to see goodness*. San Francisco: Berrett-Koehler.

Jackson, S., & Csikszentmihalyi, M. (1999). *Flow in sports: The keys to optimal experiences and performance*. NY: Human Kinetics.

Jackson, S. A., Kimiecik, J. C., & Ford, S. K. (1998). Psychological correlates of flow in sport. *Journal of Sport & Exercise Psychology*, *20*(4), 358–378.

Jacob, J. C., & Brinkerhoff, M. B. (1999). Mindfulness and subjective well-being in the sustainability movement: A further elaboration of multiple discrepancies theory. *Social Indicators Research*, *46*, 641–368.

Jahoda, M. (1958). *Current concepts of positive mental health*. New York: Basic Books.

James, B. J., & Samuels, C. A. (1999). High stress life events and spiritual development. *Journal of Psychology and Theology*, *27*(3), 250–260.

James, J., & Zarrett, N. (2006). Ego integrity in the lives of older women. *Journal of Adult Development*, *13*(2), 61–75.

James, W. (1892). *Psychology: Briefer course*. Cambridge, MA: Harvard University Press.

James, W. (1907). The energies of men. Retrieved from: http://psychclassics.yorku.ca/index.htm

James, W. (1919). *The will to believe, and other essays in popular philosophy*. New York: Longmans, Green. (Original work published 1896)

James, W. (1920). *The letters of William James* (Vol. 2, H. James, Ed.). Boston: Atlantic Monthly Press.

James, W. (1958). *The varieties of religious experience*. New York: Mentor. (Original work published 1902)

Jamison, K. (1989). Mood disorders and patterns of creativity in British writers and artists. *Psychiatry*, *52*(2), 125–134.

Jeges, S., & Varga, K. (2006). Unraveling the mystery of sense of coherence. *European Journal of Mental Health*, *1*(2), 45–71.

Jenke, W. (2008, October 7). Balance and health: How do positive emotions lead to good health? *Positive Psychology News*. Retrieved from http://positivepsychologynews.com/news/wayne-jenke/200810071062

Jetten, J., & Haslam, C. (2011). *The social cure*. NY: Taylor & Francis.

Jha, A. P., Stanley, E. A., Kiyonaga, A., Wong, L., & Gelfand, L. (2010) Examining the protective effects of mindfulness training on working memory capacity and affective experience. *Emotion*, *1*, 54–64.

Johnson, D. J., & Rusbult, C. E. (1989). Resisting temptation: Devaluation of alternative partners as a means of maintaining commitment in close relationships. *Journal of Personality and Social Psychology*, *57*, 967–980.

Johnson, D. P., Penn, D. L., Fredrickson, B. L., Meyer, P. S., Kring, A. M., & Brantley, M. (2009, May). Loving-kindness meditation to enhance recovery from negative symptoms of schizophrenia. *Journal of Clinical Psychology*, *65*(5), 499–509.

Johnson, K. J., & Fredrickson, B. L. (2005). 'We All Look the Same to Me': Positive Emotions Eliminate the Own-Race Bias in Face Recognition. *Psychological Science*, *16*(11), 875–881.

Johnson, M. W., Richards, W. A., & Griffiths, R. R. (2008, August). Human hallucinogen research: Guidelines for safety. *Journal of Psychopharmacology*, *22*(6), 603–620.

Johnson, S. M. (1991). Marital therapy: Issues and challenges. *Journal of Psychiatry and Neuroscience*, *16*(3), 176–181.

Jokisaari, M. (2003). Regret appraisals, age, and subjective well-being. *Journal of Research in Personality*, *37*(6), 487–503.

Jones, A., & Crandall, R. (Eds.). (1991). Handbook of self-actualization. [Special issue]. *Journal of Social Behavior and Personality*, *6*(5).

Jopp, D., & Rott, C. (2006, June). Adaptation in very old age: Exploring the role of resources, beliefs, and attitudes for centenarians' happiness. *Psychology and Aging*, *21*(2), 266–280.

Joseph, Stephen, & Wood, Alex (2010, November). Assessment of positive functioning in clinical psychology: Theoretical and practical issues. *Clinical Psychology Review*, *30*(7), 830–838.

Jourard, S. (1959). Healthy personality and self-disclosure. *Mental Hygiene*, *43*(4), 499–507.

Jourard, S. (1967). To be or not to be transparent. In S. M. Jourard (Ed.), *Existential-psychological perspectives on the self* (Vol. *34*, pp. 27–36). Gainesville: University of Florida Monographs.

Jourard, S. (1968). *Disclosing man to himself*. Princeton, NJ: Van Nostrand Reinhold.

Jourard, S. (1971a). *Self-disclosure: An experimental analysis of the transparent self*. New York: Wiley.

Jourard, S. (1971b). *The transparent self* (Rev. edition). New York: Van Nostrand Reinhold.

Julkunen, J., & Ahlström, R. (2006). Hostility, anger, and sense of coherence as predictors of health-related quality of life: Results of an ASCOT substudy. *Journal of Psychosomatic Research*, *61*(1), 33–39.

Jung, C. G. (Ed.). (1964). *Man and his symbols*. New York: Doubleday.

Jung, C. G. (1965). *Memories, dreams, and reflections*. New York: Vintage.

Jung, C. G. (1976). *The collected letters of Carl Jung* (Vol. *2*, G. Adler, Ed., J. Hulen, Trans.). Princeton: Princeton University Press.

Jung, C. G. (2006). The undiscovered self. NY: Signet. (work originally published 1957).

Kabanoff, B. (1982, July). Occupational and sex differences in leisure needs and leisure satisfaction. *Journal of Occupational Behaviour*, *3*(3), 233–245.

Kabat-Zinn, J. (1990). *Full catastrophe living*. New York: Dell.

Kabat-Zinn, J. (1993). Mindfulness meditation: Health benefits of an ancient Buddhist practice. In D. Goleman & J. Gurin (Eds.), *Mind/body medicine: How to use your mind for better health* (pp. 259–275). Yonkers, NY: Consumer Reports Books.

Kabat-Zinn, J. (2011). Some reflections on the origins of MSBR, skillful means, and the trouble with maps. *Contemporary Buddhism*, *12*(1), 281–306.

Kabat-Zinn, J., Lipworth, L., & Burney, R. (1985). The clinical use of mindfulness meditation for the self-regulation of chronic pain. *Journal of Behavioral Medicine*, *8*, 163–190.

Kabat-Zinn, J., Lipworth, L., Burney, R., & Sellers, W. (1986). Four year follow-up of a meditation-based program for the self-regulation of chronic pain: Treatment outcomes and compliance. *Clinical Journal of Pain*, *2*, 159–173.

Kabat-Zinn, J., Massion, A, Kristeller, J., Peterson, L. G., Fletcher, K. E., Pbert, L., Lenderking, W. R., & Santorelli, S.F. (1992). Effectiveness of a Meditation-Based Stress Reduction Program in the Treatment of Anxiety Disorders. *American Journal of Psychiatry*, *149*(7), 936–943.

Kahneman, D. (1995). Varieties of counterfactual thinking. In N. J. Roese & J. M. Olson (Eds.), What might have been: The social psychology of counterfactual thinking (pp. 375–396). Mahwah, NJ: Erlbaum.

Kahneman, D., Diener, E., & Schwarz, N. (Eds.). (1999). *Well-being: The foundations of hedonic psychology.* New York: Russell Sage Foundation.

Kahneman, D., & Deaton, A. (2010, September 21). High income improves evaluation of life but not emotional well-being. *PNAS, 107*(38), 16489–16493.

Kaiser, R. (Ed.). (2009). *The perils of accentuating the positive.* Oklahoma City, OK: Hogan.

Kakanen, J., Feldt, T., & Leskinen, E. (2007). Change and stability of sense of coherence in adulthood: Longitudinal evidence from the healthy child study. *Journal of Research in Personality, 41*(3), 602–617.

Kamp Dush, C. M., & Amato, P. R. (2005). Consequences of relationship status and quality for subjective well-being. *Journal of Social and Personal Relationship, 22,* 607–637. doi: 10.1177/0265407505056438

Kamvar, S., Mogilner, C., & Aaker, J. (2009). The meaning of happiness. Research paper No. 2026, Research Paper Series: Stanford Graduate School of Business. Retrieved from: http://ssrn.com/abstact=1418195.

Kaplan, R., & Kronick, R. (2006). Marital status and longevity in the United States population. *Journal of Epidemiology and Community Health, 60*(9), 760–765.

Kaplan, S. (1992). Environmental preferences in a knowledge-seeking, knowledge-using organism. In: J. H. Barkow, L. Cosmides, & J. Tooby, Eds., *The adapted mind: Evolutionary psychology and the generation of culture* (pp. 581–598). New York: Oxford University Press.

Kark, R., Shamir, B., & Chen, G. (2003). The two faces of transformational leadership: Empowerment and dependency. *Journal of Applied Psychology, 88*(2), 246–255.

Kashdan, T. B. (2009). *Curious? Discovering the missing ingredient to a fulfilling life.* New York: William Morrow.

Kashdan, T. B., Breen, W. E., & Julian, T. (2010). Everyday strivings in combat veterans with post-traumatic stress disorder: Problems arise when avoidance and emotion regulation dominate. *Behavior Therapy, 41,* 350–363.

Kashdan, T., & McKnight, P. (2009). Origins of purpose in life: Refining our understanding of a life well-lived. *Psychological Topics, 18*(20), 303–313.

Kashdan, T. B., Rose, P., & Fincham, F. D. (2004). Curiosity and exploration: Facilitating positive subjective experiences and personal growth opportunities. *Journal of Personality, 82*(3), 291–305.

Kashdan, T., & Rottenberg, J. (2010). Psychological flexibility as a fundamental aspect of health. *Clinical Psychology Review, 30*(4), 467–480.

Kashdan, T., & Steger, M. (2007). Curiosity and pathways to well-being and meaning in life: Traits, states, and everyday behaviors. *Motivation and Emotion, 31*(3), 159–173.

Kashdan, T. B., & Steger, M. F. (2011). Challenges, aspirations, and pitfalls for positive psychology. In K. M. Sheldon, T. B. Kashdan, & M. F. Steger (Eds.). *Designing positive psychology: Taking stock and moving forward.* (pp. 293–312). New York: Oxford University Press.

Kasser, T., & Ryan, R. M. (1993). A dark side of the American dream: Correlates of financial success as a life aspiration. *Journal of Personality and Social Psychology, 65,* 410–422.

Kasser, T., & Ryan, R. (1999). The relations of psychological needs for autonomy and relatedness to vitality, well-being, and mortality in a nursing home. *Journal of Applied Social Psychology, 29*(5), 935–954.

Kasser, T., & Sheldon, K. (2000). Of wealth and death: Materialism, mortality salience, and consumption behavior. *Psychological Science 11*(4), 348–351.

Kasser, T., & Sheldon, K. M. (2009). Time affluence as a path towards personal happiness and ethical business practice: Empirical evidence from four studies. *Journal of Business ethics, 84*(2), 243–255.

Katz, P., & Zigler, E. (1967). Self-image disparity: A developmental approach. *Journal of Personality and Social Psychology, 5*(2), 186–195.

Kaufman, C. (2009). Everyday creativity. Retrieved from: http://www.psychologytoday.com/print/34044?page=5

Kaufman, J. C. (2001). The Sylvia Plath effect: Mental illness in eminent creative writers. *Journal of Creative Behavior, 35*(1), 37–50.

Keating, Thomas, Fr. (2009). *Intimacy with God: An introduction to centering prayer (3rd ed.).* Crossroads.

Keller, M. C., Fredrickson, B. L., Ybarra, O., Cata, S., Johnson, K., et al. (2005, September). A Warm Heart and a Clear Head: The Contingent Effects of Weather on Mood and Cognition. *Psychological Science, 16*(9), 724–731.

Kelly, H. H., & Thibaut, J. W. (1978). *Interpersonal relations: A theory of interdependence.* New York: Wiley.

Kelly, J. R., & Ross, J. E. (1989). Later-life leisure: Beginning a new agenda. *Leisure Sciences, 11*(1), 47–59.

Keltner, D. (2009). *Born to be Good: The Science of a Meaningful Life.* NY: W. W. Norton.

Keltner, D. (2000, October). *Laughter, smiling, and the sublime.* Paper presented at the Positive Psychology Summit. Washington, DC.

Keltner, D., & Haidt, J. (2003). Approaching awe, a moral, spiritual, and aesthetic emotion. *Cogniton and Emotion, 17*(2), 297–314.

Kendall-Tackett, K. (2009). Psychological trauma and physical health: A psychoneuroimmunology approach to etiology of negative health effects and possible interventions. *Psychological Trauma: therapy, Research, Practice, and Policy, 1*(1) 35–48.

Kenrick, D. T., Groth, G. E., Trost, M. R., & Sadalla, E. K. (1993). Integrating evolutionary and social exchange perspectives on relationships: Effects of gender, self-appraisal, and involvement level on mate selection criteria. *Journal of Personality and Social Psychology, 64*(6), 951–969.

Kennedy, J. E., Kanthamani, H., & Palmer, J. (1994). Psychic and spiritual experiences, health, well-being, and meaning in life. *Journal of Parapsychology, 58*(4), 353–383.

Kernis, M. H. (2003, January). Toward a Conceptualization of Optimal Self-Esteem. *Psychological Inquiry, 14*(1), pp. 1–26.

Kernis, M. H., & Goldman, B. M. (2005). From thought and experience to behavior and interpersonal relationships: A multicomponent conceptualization of authenticity. In A. Tesser, J. Wood, & D. Stapel, *Building, defending, and regulating the self: A psychological perspective* (pp. 31–52). NY: Psychology Press.

Keyes, C. L. M. (1998). Social well-being. *Social Psychology Quarterly, 61*(2), 121–140.

Keyes, C. L. M. (2005). Mental illness and/or mental health? Investigating axioms of the complete state model of health. *Journal of Consulting and Clinical Psychology, 73*(3), 539–548.

Keyes, C. (2009). Toward a science of mental health. In C. R. Snyder & S. Lopez (Eds.), *Oxford handbook of positive psychology* (2nd ed., pp. 89–98). New York: Oxford University Press.

Keyes, C. L. M., & Lopez, S. J. (2002). Toward a science of mental health: Positive directions in diagnosis and interventions. In C. R. Snyder & S. J. Lopez (Eds.), *Handbook of positive psychology* (pp. 45–59). London: Oxford University Press.

Keyes, C. L. M., Shmotkin, D., & Ryff, C. D. (2002). Optimizing well-being: The empirical encounter of two traditions. *Journal of Personality and Social Psychology, 82*(6), 1007–1022.

Kiecolt-Glaser, J. K., Fisher, L., Ogrocki, P., Stout, J. C., Speicher, C. E., & Glaser, R. (1987). Marital quality, marital disruption, and immune function. *Psychosomatic Medicine, 49*, 13–35.

Kiecolt-Glaser, J. K., Garner, W., Speicher, C., Penn, G. M., Holliday, J., & Glaser, R. (1984). Psychosocial modifiers of immunocompetence in medical students. *Psychosomatic Medicine, 46*, 7–14.

Kiecolt-Glaser, J. K., Newton, T., Cacioppo, J. T., MacCallum, R. C., Glaser, R., & Malarkey, W. B. (1997). Marital conflict and endocrine function: Are men really more physiologically affected than women? *Journal of Consulting and Clinical Psychology, 64*, 324–332.

Kiefer, C. S. (1988). *The mantle of maturity: A history of ideas about character development.* Albany, New York: State University of New York Press.

Kierkegaard, S. (1843, trans. 1987). *Diapsalmata* (Vol. 1), *Either/Or.* Retrieved March 1, 2004, from http://www.barleby.com/66/62/32562.html

Killingsworth, M., & Gilbert, D. (2010, November 12). A wandering mind is an unhappy mind. *Science, 3306006*, 932.

Kimiecik, J. C., & Stein, G. L. (1992). Examining flow in sports contexts: Conceptual issues and methodological concerns. *Journal of Applied Sport Psychology, 4*, 144–160.

King, L. A. (2001). The health benefits of writing about life goals. *Personality and Social Psychology Bulletin*, 27(7), 798–807.

King, L. (2011). Are we there yet? What happened on the way to the demise of positive psychology. In K. M. Sheldon, T. B. Kashdan, & M. F. Steger (Eds.), *Designing positive psychology: Taking stock and moving forward* (pp. 439–446). New York: Oxford University Press.

King, L. A., & Hicks, J. A. (2006). Narrating the self in the past and the future: Implications for maturity. *Research in Human Development*, 3(2–3), 121–138.

King, L. A., Hicks, J. A., Krull, J. L., & Del Gaiso, A. K. (2006). Positive affect and the experience of meaning in life. *Journal of Personality and Social Psychology*, 90(1), 179–196. doi: 10.1037/0022-3514.90.1.179

King, L. A., & Miner, K. N. (2000). Writing about the perceived benefits of traumatic events: Implications for physical health. *Personality and Social Psychology Bulletin*, 26(2), 220–230.

King, L. A., & Napa, C. K. (1998). What makes life good? *Journal of Personality and Social Psychology*, 75(1), 156–165.

Kingston, T., Chadwick, P., Meron, D., & Skinner, T. C. (2007). A pilot randomized control trial investigating the effect of mindfulness practice on pain tolerance, psychological well-being, and physiological activity. *Journal of Psychosomatic Research*, 62(3), 297–300.

Kirschman, K., Johnson, R., Bender, J., & Roberts, M. (2009). Positive psychology for children and adolescents: Development, preventions, and promotion. In C. R. Snyder & S. Lopez (Eds.), *Oxford handbook of positive psychology* (2nd ed., pp. 133–148). New York: Oxford University Press.

Kisley, M. A., Wood, S., & Burrows, C. L. (2007). Looking at the sunny side of life: Age-related change in an event-related potential measure of the negativity bias. *Psychological Science*, 18(9), 838–843.

Kitayma, S., Markus, H., Matsumoto, H., & Norasak-kunkit, V. (1997). Individual and collective processes in the construction of the self: Self-enhancement in the United States and Self-criticism in Japan. *Journal of Personality and Social Psychology*, 72(6), 1245–1267.

Klar, M., & Kasser, T. (2009). Some benefits of being an activist: Measuring activism and its role in psychological well-being. *Political Psychology*, 30(5), 755–777.

Klonoff, E. A., & Landrine, H. (1996). Belief in the healing power of prayer: Prevalence and health correlates for African-Americans. *Western Journal of Black Studies* 20(4), 204–210.

Knabb, J. J. (2010). Centering prayer as an alternative to mindfulness-based cognitive therapy for depression relapse prevention. *Journal of Religion and Health*. doi 10.11007s10943-010-9494-1

Knapp, R. R. (1990). *Handbook for the personal orientation inventory* (2nd ed.). San Diego, CA: EDITS.

Knee, C. R., & Zuckerman, M. (1996). Causality orientations and the disappearance of the self-serving bias. *Journal of Research in Personality*, 30(1), 76–87.

Knee, C. R., & Zuckerman, M. (1998). A nondefensive personality: Autonomy and control as moderators of defensive coping and self-handicapping. *Journal of Research in Personality*, 32(2), 115–130.

Kobasa, S. C. (1979). Stressful life events, personality, and health: An inquiry into hardiness. *Journal of Personality and Social Psychology*, 37, 1–11.

Kobasa, S. C., Maddi, S. R., & Kahn, S. (1982). Hardiness and health: A prospective study. *Journal of Personality and Social Psychology*, 42, 168–177.

Kobasa, S. C., Maddi, S. R., Puccetti, M. C., & Zola, M. A. (1994). Effectiveness of hardiness, exercise and social support as resources against illness. In A. Steptoe & J. Wardle (Eds.), *Psychosocial processes and health: A reader* (pp. 247–260). Cambridge: Cambridge University Press.

Koch, B. J., & Koch, P. T. (2007). Collectivism, individualism, and outgroup cooperation in segmented China. *Asia Pacific Journal of Management*, 24, 207–225.

Koenig, H. G., George, L. K., & Siegler, I. C. (1988). The use of religion and other emotion-regulating coping strategies among older adults. *Gerontologist*, 28(3), 303–310.

Koenig, H. G., McCullough, M. E., & Larson, D. B. (2001). *Handbook of religion and health*. London: Oxford University Press.

Kohlberg, L. (1984). *Essays on moral development, Vol. 2: The nature and validity of moral stages*. San Francisco: Harper & Row.

Kok, B. E., & Fredrickson, B. L. (2010). Upward spirals of the heart: Autonomic flexibility as indexed by vagal tone, reciprocally and prospectively predicts positive emotions and social connectedness. *Biological Psychology, 85*(3), 432–436. doi: 10.1016/j.biopsycho.2010.09.005

Koller, S. H., & Lisboa, C. (2007). Brazilian approaches to understanding and building resilience in at-risk populations. *Child and Adolescent Psychiatric Clinics of North America, 16,* 341–356.

Kolt, L., Slawsby, E. A., & Domar, A. D. (1999). Infertility: Clinical, treatment, and practice development issues. In L. VandeCreek & T. L. Jackson (Eds.), *Innovations in clinical practice: A sourcebook* (Vol. 17, pp. 185–203). Sarasota, FL: Professional Resource Press/Professional Resource Exchange.

Konrath, S. H., O'Brien, E. H., & Hsing, C. (2011). Changes in dispositional empathy in American college students over time: a meta-analysis. *Personality and Social Psychology Review, 15*(2), 180–198. doi: 10.1177/1088868310377395

Kovacs, A. (2007). The leisure personality: Relationships between personality, leisure Satisfaction, and life satisfaction. *Dissertation Abstracts International Section A:Humanities and Social Sciences, 68*(5-A), 2168.

Kramer, D. A. (2000). Wisdom as a classical source of human strength: Conceptualization and empirical inquiry. *Journal of Social & Clinical Psychology, 19*(1), 83–101.

Kraus, M. W., Huang, Ca., & Keltner, D. (2010). Tactile communication, cooperation, and performance: An ethological study of the NBA. *Emotion, 10*(5), 745–749.

Kringelbach, M. L., & Berridge, K. C. (2009). Towards a functional neuroanatomy of pleasure and happiness. *Trends in Cognitive Sciences, 13*(11), 479–487.

Krippner, S. (Ed.). (1972). The plateau experience: A. H. Maslow and others. *Journal of Transpersonal Psychology, 4*(2), 107–120.

Kris, E. (1952). *Psychoanalytic explorations in art.* New York: International Universities.

Kristjansson, K. (2010). Positive psychology, happiness, and virtue: The troublesome conceptual issues. *Review of General Psychology, 4,* 296–310. doi: 10.1037/a0020781

Kruger, J., & Dunning, D. (2009). Unskilled and unaware of it: How difficulties in recognizing one's own incompetence lead to inflated self-assessments. *Psychology, 1,* 30–46.

Kryla-Lighthall, N. (2009). The role of cognitive control in older adults' emotional well-being. In V. Bengston, D. Gans, & N. Pulney (Eds.), *Handbook of theories of aging* (2nd ed., pp. 323–344). NY: Springer.

Kubie, L. S. (1958). *Neurotic distortion of the creative process.* Lawrence: University of Kansas Press.

Kuhlmeier, V., & Dunfield, K. (2010, April 7). Toddlers appreciate good intentions, Queen's study finds. *Psychological Science,* Retrieved from http://www.eurekalert.org/pub_releases/2010-04/qu-tag 040710.php

Kulik, J., & Mahler, H. (2006). Marital quality predicts hospital stay following coronary artery surgery for women but not men. *Social Science and Medicine, 63*(8), 2031–2040.

Kunzmann, U. (2004). Approaches to a Good Life: The Emotional-Motivational Side to Wisdom. In: Positive psychology in practice. Linley, P. Alex (Ed.); Joseph, Stephen (Ed.); Hoboken, NJ, US: John Wiley & Sons Inc, pp. 504–517.

Kupperman, J. (2006). Six myths about the good life: Thinking about what has value. Indianapolis, IN: Hackett.

Kurtines, W. M., Azmitia, M., & Alvarez, M. (1990). Science and morality: The role of values in science and the scientific study or moral phenomena. *Psychological Bulletin, 107*(3), 283–295.

Kuyken, W., Watkins, E., Holden, E., White, K., Taylor, R. S., Byford, S., ... Dalgeish, T. (2010). How does mindfulness-based cognitive therapy work? *Behaviour Research and Therapy, 48*(11), 1105–1112.

Kwan, Y. K. (2010). Life satisfaction and self-assessed health among adolescents in Hong Kong. *Journal of Happiness Studies, 11*(3), 383–393.

Labouvie-Vief, G. (1990). Wisdom as integrated thought: Historical and developmental perspectives. In R. J. Sternberg (Ed.), *Wisdom: Its nature, origins, and development* (pp. 52–86). Cambridge, NY: Cambridge University Press.

Labouvie-Vief, G., & Medler, M. (2002). Affect optimization and affect complexity: Modes and styles of regulation in adulthood. *Psychology and Aging, 17,* 571–587.

Lachman, M., & Agrigoroaei, S. (2010). Promoting functional health in midlife and old age: Long-term protective effects of control beliefs, social support, and physical exercise. *PLos One, 5*(10): Retrieved from http://www.midus.wisc.edu/findings/pdfs/845.pdf

Lachman, M. E., Rocke, C., Rosnick, C., & Ryff, C. D. (2008). Realism and illusion in Americans' temporal views of their life satisfaction: Age differences in reconstructing the past and anticipating the future. *Psychological Science, 19*, 889–897.

Lachs, M. (2011, April 11). *Want to live to be 100? Try to bounce back from stress.* NPR: National Public Radio. Washington, DC.

Lakens, D., & Schubert, T. (2009). Weight as an embodiment of importance. *Psychological Science, 20*(9), 1169–1174.

Lambert, N., Fincham, F., Gwinn, A. M., & Ajayi, C. (2011). Positive relationship science: A new frontier for positive psychology. In K. M. Sheldon, T. B. Kashdan, & M. F. Steger (Eds.). *Designing positive psychology: Taking stock and moving forward.* (pp. 280–292). New York: Oxford University Press.

Lambert, N. M., Fincham, F. D., Braithwaite, S. R., Graham, S. M., & Beach, S. R. H. (2009). Can prayer increase gratitude? *Psychology of Religion and Spirituality, 1*(3), 139–149.

Lambert, N. M., Fincham, F. D., Stillman, T. F., Graham, S. M., & Beach, R. H. (2010). Motivating change in relationships: Can prayer increase forgiveness? *Psychological Science, 20*(10), 1–7.

Lambert, M. J., & Erekson, D. M. (2008). Positive psychology and the humanistic tradition. *Journal of Psychotherapy Integration, 18*(2), 222–232.

Landers, D. M., Han, M., Salazar, W., & Petruzzello, S. J. (1994). Effects of learning on electroencephalographic and electrocardiographic patterns in novice archers. *International Journal of Sport Psychology, 25*(3), 313–330.

Landman, J. (1987). Regret and elation following action and in action: Affective responses to positive versus negative outcomes. *Personality and Social Psychology Bulletin, 13*(4), 524–536.

Lane, R. E. (2000). Diminishing returns to income, companionship and happiness. *Journal of Happiness Studies, 1*(3), 103–119.

Langer, E. (2006). *On becoming an artist: Reinventing yourself through mindful creativity.* New York: Ballantine.

Langer, E. (2009). Mindfulness versus positive evaluation. In: Lopez, Shane J. (Ed.), Snyder, C. R. (Ed.) Oxford handbook of positive psychology (2nd ed.) (pp. 279–293), New York, NY, US: Oxford University Press.

Langer, E., Russell, T., Eisenkraft, N. (2009). Orchestral performance and the footprint of mindfulness. *Psychology of Music, 37*(2), 125–136.

Langer, E., Pirson, M., Delizonna, L. (2010). The mindlessness of social comparisons. *Psychology of Aesthetics, Creativity, and the Arts, 4*(2), 68–74.

Langer, E. J. (1989). *Mindfulness.* Reading MA: Perseus.

Langer, E. J., & Rodin, J. (1976). The effects of choice and enhanced personal responsibility for the aged: A field experiment in an institutional setting. *Journal of Personality and Social Psychology, 34*(2), 191–198.

Larsen, J. T., Hemenover, S. H., Norris, C. J., & Cacioppo, J. T. (2003). Turning adversity to advantage: On the virtues of the coactivation of positive and negative emotions. In L. Aspinwall & U. Staudinger (Eds.). A psychology of human strengths: Fundamental questions and future directions for a positive psychology. (pp. 211–225). Washington, DC, US: American Psychological Association.

Larsen, R. (2009). The contributions of positive and negative affect to emotional well-being. *Psychological Topics, 18*(20), 247–284.

Larsen, R. J., & Kasimatis, M. (1990). Individual differences in entrainment of mood to the weekly calendar. *Journal of Personality and Social Psychology, 58*(1), 164–171.

Larsen, R. J., & Ketelaar, T. (1991). Personality and susceptibility to positive and negative emotional states. *Journal of Personality and Social Psychology, 61*, 132–140.

Larsen, R. J., & Prizmic, Z. (2008). Regulation of emotional well-being: Overcoming the hedonic treadmill. In: The science of subjective well-being. (pp. 258–289). M. Eid & R. J. Larsen (Ed.), New York, NY, US: Guilford Press, 2008.

Larson, J. T., & McKibban, A. R. (2008). Is happiness having what you want, wanting what you have, or both? *Psychological Science, 19*(4), 371–377.

Lauer, R. H., Lauer, J. C., & Kerr, S. T. (1990). The long-term marriage: Perceptions of stability and satisfaction. *International Journal of Aging and Human Development, 31*(3), 189–195.

Lazar, A. (2009). The relation between a multidimensional measure of spirituality and measures of psychological functioning among secular Israeli Jews. *Journal of Transpersonal Psychology, 41*(2), 161–181.

Lazar, S., Kerr, C., Wasserman, R., Gray, J., Greve, D., Treadway, M., McGarvey, M.m Quinn, B., Dusek, J., Benson, H., Rauch, S., Moore, C., & Fischl, B. (2005). Meditation experience is associated with increased cortical thickness. *Neuroreport For Rapid Communication of Neuroscience Research, 16*(17), 1893–1897.

Lazarus, R. S., & Folkman, S. (1984). Coping and adaptation. In W. D. Gentry (Ed.), *Handbook of behavioral medicine.* New York: Guilford Press.

Lazarus, R. S. (2007). Stress and emotion: A new synthesis. In: A. Monat, R. S. Lazarus, G. Reevy, (Eds.), *The Praeger handbook on stress and coping (vol. 1).* (pp. 33–51). Westport, CT, US: Praeger Publishers/ Greenwood Publishing Group.

Leak, G. K., DeNeve, K. M., & Greteman, A. J. (2007). The relationship between spirituality, assessed through self-transcendent goal strivings, and positive psychological attributes. *Research in the Social Scientific Study of Religion, 18*, 263–279. doi: 10.1163/ ej.9789004158511.i-301.102

Leary, M., & Guadagno, J. (2011). The role of hypoegoic self-processes in optimal functioning and subjective well-being. In K. M. Sheldon, T. B. Kashdan, & M. F. Steger (Eds.), *Designing positive psychology: Taking stock and moving forward* (pp. 135–146). New York: Oxford University Press.

Lechner, S., Tennen, H., & Affleck, G. (2009). Benefit-finding and growth. In C. R. Snyder & S. Lopez (Eds.), *Oxford handbook of positive psychology* (2nd ed., pp. 633–640). New York: Oxford University Press.

Lee, G. R., Seccombe, K., & Shehan, C. L. (1991). Marital status and personal happiness: An analysis of trend data. *Journal of Marriage and the Family, 53*, 839–844.

Lefcourt, H. M. (1981). *Research with the locus of control construct.* New York: Academic Press.

Lefcourt, H. M. (2002). Humor. In C. R. Snyder, & S. J. Lopez (Eds.), *Handbook of positive psychology* (pp. 619–631). New York.: Oxford University Press.

LeFevre, J. (1988). Flow and the quality of experience during work and leisure. In M. Csikszentmihalyi &

I. Csikszentmihalyi (Eds.), *Optimal experience* (pp. 307–318). Cambridge: Cambridge University Press.

Leitschuh, G. A., & Rawlins, M. E. (1991). Personal orientation inventory correlated with physical health. *Psychological Reports, 69*(2), 687–690.

Lent, R. W., Singley, D., Sheu, H., Gainor, K. A., Brenner, B. R., Treistman, D., & Ades, L. (2005). Social cognitive predictors of domain and life satisfaction: Exploring the theoretical precursors of subjective well-being. *Journal of Counseling Psychology, 52*(3), 429–442.

Lerner, R. (2009). The positive youth development perspective: Theoretical and empirical bases of a strengths-based approach to adolescent development. In C. R. Snyder & S. Lopez (Eds.), *Oxford handbook of positive psychology* (2nd ed., pp. 149–164). New York: Oxford University Press.

Leu, J., Wang, J., & Koo, K. (2011). Are positive emotions just as "positive" across cultures? *Emotion, 11*(4), 994–999.

Levine, M. (2000). *The positive psychology of Buddhism and yoga: Paths to a mature happiness. With special applications to handling anger.* Mahwah, NJ: Lawrence Erlbaum.

Levinger, G. (1976). A social-psychological perspective on marital dissolution. *Journal of Social Issues, 32*(1), 21–47.

Levy, B., & Myers, L. (2005). Relationship between respiratory mortality and self-perceptions of aging. *Psychology and Health, 20*(5), 553–564.

Lewin, K. (1946). Action research and minority problems. *Journal of Social Issues, 2*(4), 34–46.

Lewis, C. A., & Maltby, J. (1995). Religiosity and personality among U.S. adults. *Personality and Individual Differences, 18*(2), 293–295.

Lewis, M. L. (2002). *Multicultural health psychology: Special topics acknowledging diversity.* Boston: Allyn & Bacon.

Lichter, S., Haye, K., & Kammann, R. (1980). Increasing happiness through cognitive training. *New Zealand Psychologist, 9*, 57–64.

Light, K., Grewen, K., & Amico, J. (2005). More frequent partner hugs and higher oxytocin levels are linked to lower blood pressure and heart rate in premenopausal women. *Biological Psychology, 69*(1), 5–21.

Liljenquist, K., Zhong, C-B., & Galinsky, A. (2010). The smell of virtue: Clean scents promote reciprocity and charity. *Psychological Science, 21*(3), 381–383.

Linehan, M. (1993). *Cognitive-behavioral Treatment of Borderline Personality Disorder.* NY: Guilford.

Linehan, M. M. (1993). *Skills training manual for borderline personality disorder.* New York: Guilford.

Ling, T. O. (1972). *A dictionary of Buddhism: A guide to thought and tradition.* New York: Charles Scribner & Sons.

Linley, P. A., Joseph, S., Maltby, J., Harrington, S., & Wood, A. (2009). Positive psychology applications. In C. R. Snyder & S. Lopez (Eds.). *Oxford handbook of positive psychology (2nd ed.).* (pp. 35–48). New York: Oxford University Press.

Little, B. R. (1989). Personal projects analysis: Trivial pursuits, magnificent obsessions, and the search for coherence. In D. Buss & N. Cantor (Eds.), *Personality psychology: Recent trends and emerging directions* (pp. 15–31). New York: Springer-Verlag.

Lloyd, D. (2011). Mind as music. *Frontiers of Psychology, 2,* 63. doi: 10.3389/fpsyg.2011.00063

Loerbroks, A., Apfelbacher, C. J., Bosch, J. A., & Sturmer, T. (2010). Depressive symptoms, social support, and risk of adult asthma in a population-based cohort study. *Psychosomatic Medicine, 72*(3), 309–315.

Loevinger, J. (1966). The meaning and measurement of ego development. *American Psychologist, 21,* 195–206.

Loevinger, J. (1976). *Ego development.* San Francisco: Jossey-Bass.

Logan, R. D. (1985). The "flow experience" in solitary ordeals. *Journal of Humanistic Psychology, 25*(4), 79–89.

London, E. C. J., & Strumpf, S. A. (1986). Individual and organizational career development in changing times. In D. T. Hall & Associates (Eds.), *Career development in organizations.* San Francisco, CA: Jossey-Bass.

Longhi, E., & Pickett, N. (2008). Music and well-being in long-term hospitalized children. *Psychology of Music, 36*(2), 247–256.

Longmore, R. J., & Worrell, M. (2006). Do we need to challenge thoughts in cognitive behavior therapy? *Clinical Psychology Review, 27,* 173–187. doi: 10.1016/j.cpr.2006.08.001

Lopes, M., & Cunha, M. (2008). Who is more proactive, the optimist or the pessimist? Exploring the role of hope as a moderator. *The Journal of Positive Psychology, 3*(2), 100–109.

Lopez, S. (2009). The future of positive psychology: Pursuing three big goals. In C. R. Snyder & S. Lopez (Eds.). *Oxford handbook of positive psychology (2nd ed.).* (pp. 89–98). New York: Oxford University Press.

Lopez, S. J., Floyd, R. K., Ulven, J. C., & Snyder, C. R. (2000). Hope therapy: Building a house of hope. In C. R. Snyder (Ed.), *The handbook of hope: Theory, measures, and applications* (pp. 123–148). New York: Academic Press.

Lount, R. (2010, March). Study: People sometimes less trusting when in a good mood. *Journal of Personality and Social Psychology,* Retrieved from http://www.sciencedaily.com/releases/2010/03/100302111916.htm.

Lovas, D. A., & Barsky, A. J. (2010). Mindfulness-based cognitive therapy for hypochrondriasis, or severe health anxiety: A pilot study. *Journal of Anxiety Disorders, 24*(8), 931–935.

Lowry, R. (1982). *The evolution of psychological theory.* New York: Aldine.

Lubart, T. I. (1994). Creativity. In R. J. Sternberg (Ed.), *Thinking and problem solving* (pp. 289–332). New York: Academic Press.

Lucas, D., Lloyd, J., & Magaloni, I. (2005). *In spite of content, activity begets happiness.* Poster session presented at the annual meeting of the Southwestern Psychological Association, Memphis.

Lucas, R. (2007). Adaptation and the set-point model of subjective well-being: Does happiness change after major life events? *Current Directions in Psychological Science, 16*(2), 75–79.

Lucas, R. (2008). Personality and subjective well-being. In M. Eid & R. Larsen (Eds.). *The science of subjective well-being.* (pp. 171–194). New York: Guilford Press.

Lucas, R. E., Diener, E., Grob, A., Suh, E. M., & Shao, L. (2000). Cross-cultural evidence for the fundamental features of extraversion. *Journal of Personality and Social Psychology, 79,* 452–468.

Lucas, R. E., & Gohm, C. L. (2000). Age and sex differences in subjective well-being across cultures. In: Culture and subjective well-being. Diener,

Suh, Eunkook M. (Ed.) Cambridge, MA, US: The MIT Press, 2000, pp. 291–317.

Lucas, R. E., Le, K., & Dyrenforth, P. S. (2008, June). Explaining the extraversion/positive affect relation: Sociability cannot account for extraverts' greater happiness. *Journal of Personality, 76*(3), 385–414.

Ludden, J. (2010, August 23). 'Villages' help neighbors age at home. *NPR: National Public Radio.* Washington, DC.

Luders, E., Toga, A., Lepore, N., & Gaser, C. (2009, April 15). The underlying anatomical correlates of long-term meditation: Larger hippocampal and frontal volumes of grey matter. *NeuroImage,* Vol *45*(3), 672–678.

Ludwig, A. M. (1995). *The price of greatness: Resolving the creativity and madness controversy.* New York: Guilford Press.

Luo, L. (2005). In pursuit of happiness: The cultural psychological study of SWB. *Chinese Journal of Psychology, 47*(2), 99–112.

Luo, L., & Klohnen, E. C. (2005). Assortative mating and marital quality in newlyweds: A couple-centered approach. *Journal of Personality and Social Psychology, 88*(2), 304–326. doi: 10.1037/0022-3514.88.2.304

Luthans, C., & Youssef, F. (2007). Emerging positive organizational behavior. *Journal of Management, 33,* 321–349.

Luthans, F., & Youseff, C. (2009). Positive workplaces. In C. R. Snyder & S. Lopez (Eds.). *Oxford handbook of positive psychology (2nd ed.).*(pp. 579–588). New York: Oxford University Press.

Luthans, F., Youssef, C. M., & Avolio, B. J. (2007). *Psychological capital.* New York: Oxford University Press.

Luthar, S., & Latendresse, S. (2005). Children of the affluent: Challenges to well-being. *Current Directions in Psychological Science, 14*(1), 49–53.

Lutz, A., Brefczynski-Lewis, Johnstone, T., & Davidson, R. (2008). Regulation of the neural circuitry of emotion by compassion meditation: Effects of meditative expertise. *PLoS ONE, 3*(3), e1897.

Lutz, A., Dunne, J., & Davidson, R. (2007). Meditation and the neuroscience of consciousness. In P. Zelazo, M. Moscovitch, & E. Thompson (Eds.). *Cambridge Handbook of Consciousness.* Cambridge University Press.

Lutz, A., Greischar, L. L., Rawlings, N. B., Ricard, M., & Davidson, R. J. (2004). Long-term meditators self-induce high-amplitude gamma synchrony during mental practice. *PNAS, 101*(46), 16369–16373.

Lykins, E. L., & Baer, R. A. (2009). Psychological functioning in a sample of long-term practitioners of mindfulness meditation. *Journal of Cognitive Psychotherapy: An International Quarterly, 23*(3), 226–241.

Lykken, D. (2000). *Happiness: The nature and nurture of joy and contentment.* New York: St. Martin's Griffin.

Lykken, D., & Tellegen, A. (1996). Happiness is a stochastic phenomenon. *Psychological Science, 7*(3), 186–189.

Lyubomirsky, S. (2001). Why are some people happier than others? The role of cognitive and motivational processes in well-being. *American Psychologist, 54*(3), 239–249.

Lyubomirsky, S. (2007). *The how of happiness: A scientific approach to getting he life you want.* NY: Penguin Press.

Lyubomirsky, S. (2010, August 10). Can money buy happiness? New research reveals that reminders of wealth impair our capacity to savor life's little pleasures. *Scientific American,* 36. Retrieved June 10, 2011 from http://scientificamerican.com/article.cfm?id=can-money-buy-happiness

Lyubomirsky, S., Diener, E., & King, L. (2005). The benefits of frequent positive affect: Does happiness lead to success? *Psychological Bulletin, 131*(6), 803–855. doi: 10.1037/0033-2909.131.6.803

Lyubomirsky, S., & Lepper, H. S. (1999). A measure of subjective happiness: Preliminary reliability and construct validation. *Social Indicators Research, 46,* 137–155.

Lyubomirsky, S., & Ross, L. (1997). Hedonic consequences of social comparison: A contrast of happy and unhappy people. *Journal of Personality and Social Psychology, 73,* 1141–1157.

Lyubomirsky, S., Sheldon, K. M., & Schkade, D. (2005). Pursuing happiness: The architecture of sustainable change. *Review of General Psychology, 9*(2), 111–131. doi: 10.1037/1089-2680.9.2.111

Lyubomirsky, S., Tkach, C., & DiMatteo, M. R. (2006). What are the differences between happiness and self-esteem? *Social Indicators Research, 78,* 363–404. doi: 10.1007/s11205-005-0213-y

Lyubomirsky, S., Tkach, C., & Sheldon, K. M. (2004). *Pursuing sustained happiness through random acts of kindness and counting one's blessings: Tests of two six-week interventions* [unpublished manuscript]. University of California at Riverside.

Lyubomirsky, S., Tucker, K. L., & Kasri, F. (2001). Responses to hedonically conflicting social comparisons: Comparing happy and unhappy people. *European Journal of Social Psychology, 31*, 511–535.

Ma, S. H., & Teasdale, J. D. (2004). Mindfulness-based cognitive therapy for depression: Replication and exploration of differential relapse prevention effects. *Journal and Clinical Psychology, 72*, 31–40.

MaClean, R. (2005). For young Mexican men, having a confidant raises the odds of condom use. *International Family Planning Perspectives, 31*(1), 43–44.

MacCrae, F. (2009, April 2). Who gets the girl? Funny guys have the last laugh. http://www.dailymail.co.uk/femail/article-1166610/Who-gets-girl-Funny-men-laugh-.html

Madaus, J. W. (2002). Employment self-disclosure rates and rationales of university graduates with learning disabilities. *Journal of Learning Disabilities, 41*(4), 291–299.

Maddi, S. R. (1972). *Personality theories: A comparative analysis.* Homewood, IL: Dorsey.

Maddux, J. E. (2009). Stopping the 'madness': Positive psychology and deconstructing the illness ideology and the DSM. In: Oxford handbook of positive psychology (2nd ed.). Lopez, Shane J. (Ed.) Snyder, C. R. (Ed.) New York, NY, US: Oxford University Press, 2009. pp. 61–69.

Magai, C. (2008). Long-lived emotions: A life course perspective. In M. Lewis, J. Haviland-Jones, & L. Feldman Barrett (Eds.). *Handbook of emotions (3rd edition).* (pp. 376–394). New York: Guilford Press.

Magnusson, D., & Mahoney, J. L. (2003). A holistic person approach for research on positive development. In L. G. Aspinall & U. M. Staudinger (Eds.), *A psychology of human strengths: fundamental questions and future directions for a positive psychology* (pp. 227–244). Washington, DC: American Psychological Association.

Mahoney, M. J. (2002). Constructivism and positive psychology. In C. R. Snyder and S. J. Lopez (Ed.), Handbook of positive psychology. New York: Oxford University Press, 745–750.

Maisel, N., & Gable, S. (2009). For richer … in good times … and in health: Positive processes in relationships. In C. R. Snyder & S. Lopez (Eds.), *Oxford handbook of positive psychology* (2nd ed., pp. 455–462). New York: Oxford University Press.

Maltby, J., Lewis, C. A., & Day, I. (1999). Religious orientation and psychological well-being: The role of the frequency of personal prayer. *British Journal of Health Psychology, 3*, 363–378.

Maltby, J., McCutcheon, L. E., Ashe, D. D., & Houran, J. (2001). The self-reported psychological well-being of celebrity worshippers. *North American Journal of Psychology, 3*(3), 441–452.

Mann, J. H. (1979). Human potential. In R. J. Corsini (Ed.), *Current psychotherapies* (2nd ed., pp. 500–535). Itasca, IL: F. E. Peacock.

Mannes, E. (Producer). (1990). *Amazing Grace with Bill Moyers* [video recording]. Beverly Hills, CA: PBS Video.

Mansfield, E. D., & McAdams, D. P. (1996). Generativity and themes of agency and communion in adult autobiography. *Personality & Social Psychology Bulletin, 22*(7), 721–731.

Marsa, L. (2008, June). Could an acid trip cure your OCD? Researchers are again using mind-bending drugs as a means of treating mental disorders. *Discover*, 24–25, 41–42.

Martens, D., Gutscher, H., & Bauer, N. (2011). Walking in wild and tended urban forests: The impact on psychological well-being. *Journal of Environmental Psychology, 31*(1), 36–44. doi: 10.1016/j.jenvp.2010.11.001

Martin, A. J., & Jackson, S. A. (2008). Brief approaches to assessing task absorption and enhanced subjective experience: Examining "short" and "core" flow in diverse performance domains. *Motivation and Emotion, 32*(3), 141–157.

Martin, A. J., & Marsh, H. W. (2008). Academic buoyancy: Towards an understanding of students' everyday academic resilience. *Journal of School Psychology, 46*(1), 53–83. doi: 10.1016/j.jsp.2007.01.002

Marwick, C. (1995). Should physicians prescribe prayer for health? Spiritual aspects of well-being considered. *Journal of the American Medical Association, 273*(20), 1561–1562.

Maslach, C., Schaufeli, W. B., & Leiter, M. P. (2001). Job burnout. *Annual Review of Psychology, 52,* 397–422.

Maslow, A. H. (1954). *Motivation & personality.* New York: Harper & Row.

Maslow, A. H. (1959). Cognition of being in the peak experiences. *Journal of Genetic Psychology, 94,* 43–66.

Maslow, A. H. (1961). Eupsychia—the good society. *Journal of Humanistic Psychology, 1*(2), 1–11.

Maslow, A. H. (1968). *Toward a psychology of being* (2nd ed.). Princeton, NJ: Van Nostrand Reinhold.

Maslow, A. H. (1970). *Religions, values, and peak-experiences.* New York: Viking.

Maslow, A. H. (1971). *Farther reaches of human nature.* New York: Viking.

Maslow, A. H. (1987). *Motivation and personality* (3rd ed. Rev.). New York: Harper Collins.

Maslow, A. H. (1996). The psychology of happiness. In E. Hoffman (Ed.), *Future visions: The unpublished papers of Abraham Maslow* (pp. 21–25). Thousand Oaks, CA: Sage.

Maslow, A., Honigmann, J., & Mead, M. (1970). Synergy: some notes from Ruth Benedict. *American Anthropologist, 72*(2), 320–330.

Mast, J. F., & McAndrew, F. T. (2011). Violent lyrics in heavy metal music can increase aggression in males. *North American Journal of Psychology, 13*(1), 63–64. Retrieved from http://najp.8m.com/

Masten, A., Cutuli, J., Herbers, J., & Reed, M-G. (2009). Resilience in development. In C. R. Snyder & S. Lopez (Eds.), *Oxford handbook of positive psychology* (2nd ed., pp. 117–132). New York: Oxford University Press.

Masten, A. S. (1994). Resilience in individual development: Successful adaptation despite risk and adversity. In M. Wang & E. Gordon (Eds.), *Risk and resilience in inner city America: Challenges and prospects,* (pp. 3–25). Hillsdale, NJ: Erlbaum.

Masten, A. S., & Reed, M. G. J. (2002). Resilience in development. In C. R. Snyder, & S. J. Lopez (Eds.), *Handbook of positive psychology* (pp. 74–88). London: Oxford University Press.

Mathews-Treadway, K. (1996, July). Religion and optimism: Models of the relationship. *Der Zeitgeist: The Student Journal of Psychology,* 1–13.

Matousek, R. H., & Dobkin, P. L. (2010). Weathering storms: A cohort study of how participation in a mindfulness-based stress reduction program benefits women after breast cancer treatment. *Current Oncology, 17*(4), 62–70.

Matsui, M., & Kodama, M. (2004). Multiphasic aspects of fantasy and mental health. *Japanese Journal of Health Psychology, 17*(1), 38–46.

Matsumoto, D. (1994). *People: Psychology from a cultural perspective.* Pacific Grove, CA: Brooks/Cole.

May, R. (1969). *Existential psychology.* New York,: Crown Publishing Group/Random House.

May, R. (1975). *The courage to create.* London: Collins.

May, R. (1977). *The meaning of anxiety.* New York: W. W. Norton. (Originally published 1950)

May, R., Angel, E., & Ellenberger, H. F. (Eds.). (1958). *Existence: A new dimension in psychiatry and psychology.* New York: Basic Books.

Mayer, J. D., Caruso, D. R., & Salovey, P. (2000). Emotional intelligence meets traditional standards for an intelligence. *Intelligence, 27*(4), 267–298.

Mayo Clinic (2010, January). *Massage: Get in touch with its many benefits.* Retrieved from: http://www.mayo-clinic.com/health/massage/SA00082

McAdams, D. P. (1993). *The stories we live by: Personal myths and the making of the self.* New York: William Morrow.

McAdams, D., & Albaugh, M. (2008). What if there were no God? Politically conservative and liberal Christians imagine their lives without faith. *Journal of Research in Personality, 42*(6), 1668–1672.

McAdams, D. P., Diamond, A., de St. Aubin, E., & Mansfield, E. (1997). Stories of commitment: The psychosocial construction of generative lives. *Journal of Personality and Social Psychology, 72*(3), 678–694.

McAdams, D. P., & de St. Aubin, E. (Eds.). (1998). *Generativity and adult development: How and why we care for the next generation.* Washington, DC: American Psychological Association.

McAdams, D. P., de St. Aubin, E., & Logan, R. (1993). Generativity among young, midlife, and older adults. *Psychology and Aging, 8,* 221–230.

McAuley, E., White, S., Rogers, L., Motl, R., & Courneya, K. (2010). Mastery of physical goals lessens disease-related depression and fatigue

Psychosomatic Medicine, 72(1). Retreived from http://www.news.illinois.edu/news/09/1215physical.html

McClelland, D. C. (1985). *Human motivation.* Glenview, IL: Scott, Foresman.

McClelland, D. C., & Kirshnit, D. (1982). *Effects of motivational arousal on immune functions* [Unpublished manuscript]. Harvard University, Department of Psychology and Social Relations.

McCoy, C. W. (1996). Reexamining models of healthy families. *Contemporary Family Therapy, 18*(2), 243–256.

McCrae, R. (2011). Personality traits and the potential of positive psychology. In K. M. Sheldon, T. B. Kashdan, & M. F. Steger (Eds.), *Designing positive psychology: Taking stock and moving forward* (pp. 193–206). New York: Oxford University Press.

McCrae, R., & John, O. (1992). An introduction to the five-factor model and its applications. *Journal of Personality, 60,* 175–210.

McCraty, R., Barrios-Choplin, B., Atkinson, M., & Tomasino, D. (1998). The effects of different types of music on mood, tension, and mental clarity. *Alternative Therapies, 4*(1), 75–84.

McCraty, R., & Rees, R. (2009). The central role of the heart in generating and sustaining positive emotions. In C. R. Snyder & S. Lopez (Eds.), *Oxford handbook of positive psychology* (2nd ed., pp. 527–548). New York: Oxford University Press.

McCullough, M. E. (1995). Prayer and health: Conceptual issues, research review, and research agenda. *Journal of Psychology and Theology, 23*(1), 15–29.

McCullough, M. E. (2000). Forgiveness as human strength: Theory, measurement, and links to well-being. *Journal of Social and Clinical Psychology, 19*(1), 43–55.

McCullough, M. E., Bono, G., Root, & L. M. (2005). Religion and Forgiveness. In: Handbook of the psychology of religion and spirituality. Paloutzian, Raymond F. (Ed.), Park, Crystal L. (Ed.), New York, NY, US: Guilford Press, 2005. pp. 394–411.

McCullough, M., Root, L., Tabak, B., & van Oyen Witvliet, C. (2009). Forgiveness. In C. R. Snyder & S. Lopez (Eds.), *Oxford handbook of positive psychology* (2nd ed., pp. 427–436). New York: Oxford University Press.

McFadden, S. H. (2005). Points of Connection: Gerontology and the Psychology of Religion. In: Handbook of the psychology of religion and spirituality. Paloutzian, Raymond F., Park, Crystal L. (Ed.), New York, NY, US: Guilford Press, 2005. pp. 162–176.

McGregor, I., & Little, B. R. (1998). Personal projects, happiness, and meaning: On doing well and being yourself. *Journal of Personality and Social Psychology, 74,* 494–512.

McKnight, P., & Kashdan, T. (2009). Purpose in life as a system that creates and sustains health and well-being: An integrative testable theory. *Review of General Psychology, 13*(3), 242–251.

McLean, K. C., & Pratt, M. W. (2006). Life's little (and big) lessons: Identity statuses and meaning-making in the turning point narratives of emerging adults. *Developmental Psychology, 42*(4), 714–722.

McLean, K. C., Pasupathi, M., & Pals, J. L. (2007). Selves creating stories creating selves: A process model of narrative self-development in adolescence and adulthood. *Personality and Social Psychology Review, 11*(3), 262–278.

McMahon, F., Lytle, D., & Sutton-Smith, B. (Eds.). (2005). Play: An interdisciplinary synthesis. *Play and Culture Studies* (Vol. 6). Lanham, MD: University Press of America.

McNamara, W. (1975). Psychology and the Christian mystical tradition. In C. T. Tart (Ed.). *Transpersonal Psychologies.* (pp. 395–436). NY, Harper & Row.

McQuillan, J., & Conde, G. (1996). The conditions of flow in reading: Two studies of optimal experience. *Reading Psychology: An International Quarterly, 17,* 109–135.

Medalie, J. H., & Goldbourt, U. (1976). Angina pectoris among 10,000 men, II: Psychosocial and other risk factors. *American Journal of Medicine, 60,* 910–921.

Medalie, J. H., Strange, K. C., Zyzanski, S. J., & Goldbourt, U. (1992). The importance of biopsychosocial factors in the development of duodenal ulcer in a cohort of middle-aged men. *American Journal of Epidemiology, 10,* 1280–1287.

Mehl, M., Vazire, S., Holleran, S., & Clark, C. S. (2010). Eavesdropping on happiness: Well-eing is related to having less small talk and more substantive conversations. *Psychological Science, 21*(4), 539–541.

Meisenhelder, J. B., & Chandler, E. N. (2001). Frequency of prayer and functional health in Presbyterian pastors. *Journal for the Scientific Study of Religion, 40*(2), 323–330.

Menard, V. (2003). *Latinas in love: A modern guide to love and relationships.* New York: Marlowe.

Merton, T. (2000). In C. Bochen, Ed., *Thomas Merton: Essential writings* [Modern Spiritual Masters Series]. New York: Orbis.

Meyer, B., Enström, M., Harstveit, M., Bowles, D., & Beevers, C. (2007). Happiness and despair on the catwalk: Need satisfaction, well-being, and personality adjustment among fashion models. *Journal of Positive Psychology, 2*(1), 2–17.

Michalos, A. C. (1985). Multiple discrepancies theory (MDT). *Social Indicators Research, 16,* 347–413.

Middlebrook, P. N. (1980). *Social psychology and modern life.* New York: Alfred Knopf.

Mikolajczak, M., Petrides, K. V., Coumans, N., & Luminet, O. (2009, September). The moderating effect of trait emotional intelligence on mood deterioration following laboratory-induced stress. *International Journal of Clinical and Health Psychology, 9*(3), 455–477.

Mikulas, W. (2002). *The Integrative Helper: Convergence of Eastern and Western Traditions.* Pacific Grove, CA: Brooks/Cole.

Miller, D., & Nickerson, A. (2007). Changing past, present, and future: Potential applications of positive psychology in school-based psychotherapy with children and youth. *Journal of Applied School Psychology, 24*(1), 147–162.

Miller, J. S. (2007). *Mystical experiences, neuroscience, and the nature of reality* [Doctoral dissertation]. Bowling Green State University. Permalink: http://rave. ohiolink./edu/etdc/view? Acc__num= bgsu1174405835

Miller, J. J., Fletcher, K., Kabat-Zinn, J. (1995). Three-year follow-up and clinical implications of a mindfulness-based stress reduction intervention in the treatment of anxiety disorders. *General Hospital Psychiatry, 17*(3), 192–200.

Miller, L., & Kelley, B. S. (2005). Relationships of Religiosity and Spirituality with Mental Health and Psychopathology. In: Handbook of the psychology of religion and spirituality. Paloutzian, Raymond F. (Ed.), Park, Crystal L. (Ed.), New York, NY, US: Guilford Press, 2005, pp. 460–478.

Miller, W. R., & C'deBaca, J. (1994). Quantum change: Toward a psychology of transformation. In T. F. Heatherton and J. L. Weinberger (Eds.), *Can personality change?* (pp. 253–280). Washington, DC: American Psychological Association.

Miller, W. R., & C'de Baca, J. (2001). *Quantum change: When epiphanies and sudden insights transform ordinary lives.* New York: Guilford Press.

Mixter, A. (2009). An exploration of adult playfulness in relationship to personality: A correlational study. *Dissertation Abstracts International: Section B: The Sciences and Engineering 70*(5-B), p. 3215).

Mogilner, C. (2010). The pursuit of happiness; Time, money, and social connection. *Psychological Science, 21*(9), 1348–1354.

Mohan, A., Sharma, R., & Bijlani, R. L. (2011) Effect of meditation on stress-induced changes in cognitive functions. *The Journal of Alternative and Complementary Medicine, 17*(3), 207–212.

Molden, D. C. & Dweck, C. S. (2006). Finding 'meaning' in psychology: A lay theories approach to self-regulation, social perception, and social development. *American Psychologist, 61*(3), 192–203. doi: 10.1037/0003-066X.61.3.192

Moneta, G. B. (2004). The flow experience across cultures. *Journal of Happiness Studies, 5,* 115–121.

Montagne, R. (2007, November 18). Human intelligence imitates artificial. *National Public Radio: Morning Edition.* Washington, DC.

Montagne, R. (2010, November 8). Stepping up exercise could help beat the cold virus. *National Public Radio: Morning Edition.* Washington, DC.

Moon, Y.-L. (2009, June). *Frames of meaning for life: A Korean perspective on positive psychology.* Paper presented at the First World Congress of the International Positive Psychology Association. Philadelphia, Pennsylvania.

Morretti, M. M., & Higgins, E. T. (1990). Relating self-discrepancy to self-esteem: The contribution of discrepancies beyond actual-self ratings. *Journal of Experimental Social Psychology, 26,* 108–123.

Morris, W. N. (1999). The mood system. In D. Kahneman, E. Diener, & N. Schwarz (Eds.), *Well-being: The foundations of hedonic psychology* (pp. 169–189). New York: Russell Sage Foundation.

Mount, M. K. (2005). *Exploring the role of self-disclosure and playfulness in adult attachment relationships* [Doctoral dissertation]. Department of Counseling and Personnel Services. College Park: University of Maryland.

Mroczek, D. K., & Kolarz, C. M. (1998). The effect of age on a positive and negative affect: A development perspective on happiness. *Journal of Personality and Social Psychology, 75*, 1333–1349.

Murphy, M., & Donovan, S. (1997). *The Physical and Psychological Effects of Meditation: A Review of Contemporary Research with aCcomprehensive Bibliography 1931–1996.* Sausalito, CA: Institute of Noetic Sciences.

Murray, S., Holmes, J., & Collins, N. (2006). Optimizing assurances: The risk regulation system in relationships. *Psychological Bulletin, 132*(5), 641–666.

Murray, S. L., & Holmes, J. G. (1997). A leap of faith? Positive illusions in romantic relationships. *Personality and Social Psychology Bulletin, 23*(6), 586–604.

Myers, A. (2007). *A study of the differences between appropriate and inappropriate interpersonal self-disclosure in a work environment* [M.A. thesis]. College of Liberal Arts and Sciences, The Elliott School of Communication. Wichita: Wichita State University.

Myers, D. G. (1992). *The pursuit of happiness.* New York: Avon Books.

Myers, D. G. (2000). The funds, friends, and faith of happy people. *American Psychologist, 55*(1), 56–67.

Myers, David G. (2008). Religion and human flourishing. In: The science of subjective well-being. Eid, Michael (Ed.), Larsen, Randy J. (Ed.), New York, NY, US: Guilford Press, 2008. pp. 323–343.

Myers, D. G., & Diener, E. (1995). Who is happy? *Psychological Science, 6*, 10–19.

Nadler, R. T., Rabi, R., & Minda, J. P. (2010). Better mood and better performance: Learning rule-described categories is enhanced by positive mood. *Psychological Science, 21*, 1770–1776.

Nakamura, J., & Csikszentmihalyi, M. (2002). The concept of flow. In C. R. Snyder & S. J. Lopez (Eds.), *Handbook of Positive Psychology* (pp. 89–105). New York: Oxford University Press.

Nakamura, J. & Csikszentmihalyi, M. (2009). Flow theory and research. In C. R. Snyder & S. Lopez (Eds.). *Oxford handbook of positive psychology (2nd ed.).* (pp. 195–206). New York: Oxford University Press.

Narvaez, D. (2010). Moral complexity: The fatal attraction of truthiness and the importance of mature moral functioning. *Perspectives on Psychological Science, 5*(2), 163–181.

Narvaez, D., & Lapsley, D. (Eds.). (2009). *Personality, identity, and character: Explorations in moral psychology.* Cambridge: Cambridge University Press.

Nawijn, J., Marchand, M., Veenhoven, R., & Vingerhoets, Ad J. (2010). Vactioners happier, but most not happier after a holiday. *Applied Research in Quality of Life, 5*(1), 35–47.

Neff, K. (2003). Self-compassion: An alternative conceptualization of a healthy attitude toward oneself. *Self and Identity, 2*, 85–101. doi: 10.1080/15298860390129863

Neff, Kristin D. (2011). Self-compassion, self-esteem, and well-being. *Social and Personality Psychology Compass, 5*(1), 1–12.

Neff, L. D., Rude, S. S., & Kirkpatrick, K. L. (2007). An examination of self-compassion in relation to positive psychological functioning and personality traits. *Journal of Research in Personality, 41*, 908–916. doi: 10.1016/j.jrp.2006.08.002

Nelis, D., Quoidbach, J., Mikolajczak, M., & Hansenne, M. (2009). Increasing emotional intelligence: (How) is it possible? *Personality and Individual Differences, 47*, 36–41.

Neuhoff, C. F., & Schaefer, C. (2002). Effects of laughing: Smiling and howling on mood. *Psychological Reports, 91*, 1079–1080.

Neulinger, J. (1974). *The psychology of leisure.* Springfield, IL: Charles C. Thomas.

Newberg, A., D'Aquilli, E., & Rause, V. (2002). *Why God Won't Go Away: Brain Science and the Biology of Belief.* NY: Ballantine.

Newburg, D., Kimieck, J., Durand-Bush, N., & Doell, K. (2002). The role of resonance in performance excellence and life engagement. *Journal of Applied Sport Psychology, 14*, 249–267.

Ng, W., & Diener, E. (2009). Feeling bad? The power of positive thinking may not apply to everyone. *Journal of Research in Personality, 43*(3), 455–463. doi: 10.1016/j.jrp.2009.01.020

Nicholls, J. G. (1972). Creativity in the person who will never produce anything original and useful: The concept of creativity as a normally distributed trait. *American Psychologist, 27*(8), 717–727.

Nielsen, I., Smyth, R., & Zhai, Q. (2010). Subjective well-being of China's off-farm migrants. *Journal of Happiness Studies, 11*(3), 315–333.

Niemiec, C. P., Brown, K. W., Kashdan, T. B., Cozzolino, P. J., Breen, W. E., Levesque-Bristol, C., & Ryan, R. M. (2010). Being present in the face of existential threat: The role of trait mindfulness in reducing defensive responses to mortality salience. *Journal of Personality and Social Psychology, 99*(2), 344–365. doi: 10.1037/a0019388

Niemiec, C., Ryan, R., & Deci, E. (2009). The path taken: Consequences of attaining intrinsic and extrinsic aspiration in post-college life. *Journal of Research in Personality, 43*(3), 291–306.

Nishimura, M., & Hoffman, E. (2011). Youthful peak-experiences in Brazil, Norway and the United States: New cross-cultural light on motivation. Fourth annual meeting of the Society for the Scientific Study of Motivation. Washington, DC.

Nissen, E., Gustavsson, P., Widström, A. M., Uvnäs-Moberg, K. (1998). Oxytocin, prolactin, milk production and their relationship with personality traits in women after vaginal delivery or Cesarean section. *Journal of Psychosomatic Obstetrics and Gynaecology, Mar19*(1), 49–58.

Nix, G. A., Ryan, R. M., Manly, J. B., & Deci, E. L. (1999). Revitalization through self-regulation: The effects of autonomous and controlled motivation on happiness and vitality. *Journal of Experimental Social Psychology, 35*(3), 266–284. doi: 10.1006/jesp.1999.1382

Noble, K. D. (1987). Psychological health and the experience of transference. *The Counseling Psychologist, 15*(4), 601–614.

Noftle, Erik E., Schnitker, Sarah A., Robins, & Richard W. (2011). Character and personality: Connections between positive psychology and personality psychology. In: Designing positive psychology: Taking stock and moving forward. Sheldon, Kennon M. (Ed.), Kashdan, Todd B. (Ed.), Steger, Michael F. (Ed.), New York, NY, US: Oxford University Press, pp. 207–227.

Nolen-Hoeksema, S., & Rusting, C. L. (1999). Gender differences in well-being. In D. Kahneman, E. Diener, & N. Schwarz (Eds.), *Well-being: The foundations of hedonic psychology* (pp. 330–352). New York: Russell Sage Foundation.

Norris, K. *Hands full of living.* New York: Doubleday, Doran.

Norwich, J. J. (Ed.). (1975). *Great architecture of the world.* New York: Random House.

Novaco, R. (1975). *Anger control.* New York: Rowman & Littlefield.

Nuckolls, K., Cassel, J., & Kaplan, B. (1972). Psychosocial assets, life crisis and the prognosis of pregnancy. *American Journal of Epidemiology, 95*, 431–441.

Nussbaum, A. D., & Dweck, C. S. (2008). Defensiveness versus remediation: Self-theories and modes of self-esteem maintenance. *Personality and Social Psychology Bulletin, 34*, 599–612. doi: 10.1177/0146167207312960

Nyanaponika, T. (1973). *The heart of Buddhist meditation.* San Francisco, CA: Weiser.

Ogilvie, D. M. (1987). Life satisfaction and identity structure in late middle-aged men and women. *Psychology & Aging, 2*(3), 217–224.

Oishi, S., & Diener, E. (2001). Re-examining the general positivity model of subjective well-being: The discrepancy between specific and global domain satisfaction. *Journal of Personality, 69*(4), 641–666.

Oishi, S., Diener, E., & Lucas, R. E. (1999). Cross-cultural variations in predictors of life satisfaction: Perspectives from needs and values. *Personality & Social Psychology Bulletin, 25*(8), 980–990.

Oishi, S., Diener, E., & Lucas, R. (2007). The optimum level of well-being: Can people be too happy? *Perspectives on Psychological Science, 2*, 246–360.

Oishi, S., Diener, E., Suh, E., & Lucas, R. E. (1999). Value as a moderator in subjective well-being. *Journal of Personality, 67*(1), 157–184.

Oishi, S., & Kurtz, J. (2011). The positive psychology of positive emotion: An avuncular view. In K. M. Sheldon, T. B. Kashdan, & M. F. Steger (Eds.), *Designing positive psychology: Taking stock and moving forward* (pp. 101–114). New York: Oxford University Press.

Oishi, S., Whitchurch, E., Miao, F. F., Kurtz, J., & Park, J. (2009). Would I be happier if I moved?

Retirement status and cultural variations in the anticipated and actual levels of happiness. *The Journal of Positive Psychology, 4*, 437–446. doi: 10.1080/17439760903271033

Okun, M. A., & Stock, W. A. (1987). Correlates and components of subjective well-being among the elderly. *Journal of Applied Gerontology, 6*, 95–112.

Okun, M. A., Stock, W. A., Haring, M. J., & Witter, R. A. (1984). Health and subjective well-being: A meta-analysis, *International Journal of Aging and Human Development, 19*, 111–132.

O'Leary, V., & Ickovics, J. (1995). Resilience and thriving in response to challenge: An opportunity for a paradigm shift in women's health. *Women's Health, 1*(2), 121–142.

Oliviero, H. (2005, April 24). Value of more frequent sex: $50. Reorted in the *San Diego Union-Tribune*. Retreived from: http://www.signonsandiego.com/uniontrib/20050424/news_1c24sex.html

Oman, D., & Thoresen, C. E. (2005). Do Religion and Spirituality Influence Health? In: Handbook of the psychology of religion and spirituality. Paloutzian, Raymond F. (Ed.), Park, Crystal L. (Ed.), New York, NY, US: Guilford Press, 2005. pp. 435–459.

Ong, A. (2010). Pathways linking positive emotion and health in later life. *Current Directions in Psychological Science, 19*, 358–362.

Ong, A., Bergeman, C., Biscotti, T., & Wallace, K. (2006). Psychological resilience, positive emotions, and successful adaptation to stress later in life. *Journal of Personality and Social Psychology, 91*(4), 730–749.

Ong, A., & Zautra, A. (2009). Modeling positive human health: From covariance structures to dynamic systems. In C. R. Snyder & S. Lopez (Eds.), *Oxford handbook of positive psychology* (2nd ed., pp. 97–104). New York: Oxford University Press.

Osswald, S., Greitemeyer, T., Fisher, P., & Frey, D. (2006, October). *Moral exemplary and prosocial behavior*. Poster presented at the 5th Annual Positive Psychology Summit, Washington DC.

Ostir, G., Markides, K., Black, S., & Goodwin, J. (2000). Emotional well-being predicts subsequent functional independence and survival. *Journal of the American Geriatric Society, 48*, 473–478.

Otto, M. W., Church, T. S., Craft, L. L., & Smits, J. A. J., Trivedi, M. H., & Greer, T. L., (2007). Exercise for mood and anxiety disorders. *Journal of Clinical Psychiatry, Vol. 68*(5), pp. 669–676.

Otto, R. (1958). *The idea of the holy*. New York: Oxford Press.

Paloma, M. M., & Gallup, G. H., Jr. (1991). *Varieties of prayer: A survey report*. Philadelphia: Trinity Press International.

Paloutzian, R. (1981). Purpose in life and value changes following conversion. *Journal of Personality and Social Psychology, 41*(6), 1153–1160.

Paloutzian, R. F. (2005). Religious Conversion and Spiritual Transformation: A Meaning-System Analysis. In: Handbook of the psychology of religion and spirituality. Paloutzian, Raymond F. (Ed.), Park, Crystal L. (Ed.), New York, NY, US: Guilford Press, 2005. pp. 331–347.

Paloutzian, R. F., & Park, C. L. (Eds.). (2005). Handbook of the psychology of religion and spirituality. New York, NY, US: Guilford Press.

Paloutzian, R. F., Richardson, J. T., & Rambo, L. R. (1999). Religious conversion and personality change. *Journal of Personality, 67*, 1047–1079.

Pals, J. L. (2006). Narrative identity processing of difficult life experiences: Pathways of personality development and positive self-transformation in adulthood. *Journal of Personality, 74*, 1079–1110.

Pals, J. L. (2006a). Narrative identity processing of difficult life experiences: Pathways of personality development and positive self-transformation in adulthood. *Journal of Personality, 74*(4), 1079–1110.

Pals, J. L. (2006b). Constructing the 'springboard effect': Causal connections, self-making, and growth within the life story. In D. P. McAdams, R. Josselson, & A. Lieblich, (Eds.), *Identity and story: Creating self in narrative* (pp. 175–199). Washington, DC: American Psychological Association.

Paluska, S., & Schwenk, T. (2000). Physical activity and mental health: Current concepts. *Sports Medicine, 29*(3), 167–180.

Panksepp, J. (2009, May). Primary process affects and brain oxytocin. *Biological Psychiatry, 65*(9), 725–727.

Panshin, A., & Panshin, C (1990). *The world beyond the hill*. Los Angeles: Tarcher.

Panzarella, R. (1980). Aesthetic peak experiences. *Journal of Humanistic Psychology, 20*, 69–85.

Pargament, K. I., Ano, G. G., & Wachholtz, A. B. (2005). The Religious Dimension of Coping: Advances in Theory, Research, and Practice. In: Handbook of the psychology of religion and spirituality. Paloutzian, Raymond F. (Ed.), Park, Crystal L. (Ed.), New York, NY, US: Guilford Press, 2005, pp. 479–495.

Pargament, K. I., Smith, B. W., Koenig, H. G., & Perez, L. M. (1998). Patterns of positive and negative religious coping with major life stressors. *Journal for the Scientific Study of Religion*, *37*(4), 710–724.

Parish, T. S., & Parish, J. G. (2005). Comparing students' classroom-related behaviors across grade levels and happiness levels. *International Journal of Reality Therapy*, *25*(1), 24–25.

Park, C. (2011). Meaning and growth within positive psychology: Toward a more complete understanding. In K. M. Sheldon, T. B. Kashdan, & M. F. Steger (Eds.), *Designing positive psychology: Taking stock and moving forward* (pp. 324–334). New York: Oxford University Press.

Park, C. L., & Folkman, S. (1997). Meaning in the context of stress and coping. *Review of General Psychology*, *1*(2), 115–144.

Parlee, M. B. (1979, October). The friendship bond. *Psychology Today*, pp. 43–54, 113.

Parrott, W. G. (1993). Beyond hedonism: Motives for inhibiting good moods and for maintaining bad moods. In D. M. Wegner & J. W. Pennebaker (Eds.), *Century Psychology Series. Handbook of mental control* (pp. 278–305). Upper Saddle River, NJ: Prentice-Hall.

Pascual-Leone, J. (1990). An essay on wisdom: Toward organismic processes that make it possible. In R. J. Sternberg (Ed.), *Wisdom: Its nature, origins, and development* (pp. 244–278). Cambridge, NY: Cambridge University Press.

Patterson, J. M. (2002). Understanding family resilience. *Journal of Clinical Psychology*, *58*(3), 233–246.

Peacock, J. R., & Poloma, M. M. (1999). Religiosity and life satisfaction across the life course. *Social Indicators Research 48*, 321–345.

Peng, C. K., Havlin, S., Stanley, H. E., & Goldberger, A. L. (1995). Quantification of scaling exponents and crossover phenomena in nonstationary heartbeat time series. *Chaos*, *5*, 582–87.

Peng, C. K., Mietus, J., Hausdorff, J. M., Havlin, S., Stanley, H. E., & Goldberger, A. L. (1993). Long-range anticorrelations and non-Gaussian behavior of the heartbeat. *Physicians Review Letters*, *70*, 1343–1346.

Pennebaker, J. W. (1993). Putting stress into words: Health, linguistic, and therapeutic implications. *Behavior Research and Therapy*, *31*, 539–548.

Pennebaker, J. W. (1997). *Opening up: The healing power of expressing emotions* (Rev. ed). New York, Guilford Press.

Pennebaker, J. W., Kiecolt-Glaser, J. K., & Glaser, R. (1988). Disclosure of trauma and immune function: Health implications for psychotherapy. *Journal of Consulting and Clinical Psychology*, *56*, 239–245.

Pennebaker, J. W., & Seagal, J. D. (1999). Forming a story: The health benefits of narrative. *Journal of Clinical Psychology*, *55*, 1243–1254.

Pennington, M. B. (1980). *Centering prayer: Renewing an ancient Christian prayer form*. New York: Doubleday.

Persinger, M. A. (2001). The neuropsychiatry of paranormal experiences. *Journal of Neuropsychiatry and Clinical Neurosciences*, *13*, 515–524.

Pert, C. B. (1997). *Molecules of emotion: Why you feel the way you feel*. New York: Scribner.

Peseschkian, N. (1997). *Positive psychotherapy: Theory and practice of a new method*. Berlin: Springer-Verlag.

Peseschkian, N., & Tritt, K. (1998). Positive psychotherapy: Effectiveness study and quality assurance. *European Journal of Psychotherapy, Counseling, and Health*, *1*, 93–104.

Peters, E., Wissing, M. P., & Steyn, F. (2006). Attentional switching and psychosocial well-being. In Correspondence to Prof. M. P. Wissing (pp. 1–3). Potchefstroom: North-West University.

Peterson, C. (1999). Personal control and well-being. In D. Kahneman, D. Diener, & Schwarz (Eds.), *Well-being: The foundations of hedonic psychology* (pp. 288–301). New York: Russell Sage Foundation.

Peterson, C. (2000). The future of optimism. *American Psychologist*, *55*(1), 44–55.

Peterson, C. (2006). Strengths of character and happiness: Introduction to the special edition. *Journal of Happiness Studies*, *7*(3), 289–291.

Peterson, C., & Chang, E. C. (2003). Optimism and flourishing. In C. L. M. Keyes and J. Haidt (Eds.), *Flourishing: Positive psychology and the life well-lived.* Washington, DC: American Psychological Association, 55–79.

Peterson, C., & Park, N. (2009). Classifying and measuring strengths of character. In C. R. Snyder & S. Lopez (Eds.). *Oxford handbook of positive psychology (2nd ed.).* (pp. 25–34). New York: Oxford University Press.

Peterson, C., Park, N., Hall, N., & Seligman, M. E. P. (2009). Zest and work. *Journal of Organizational Behavior, 30,* 161–172.

Peterson, C., & Seligman, M. E. P. (2004). *Character strengths and virtues: A handbook and classification.* New York: Oxford University Press/Washington, DC: American Psychological Association.

Peterson, C., Seligman, M. E., & Vaillant, G. E. (1988). Pessimistic explanatory style is a risk factor for physical illness: A thirty-five-year longitudinal study. *Journal of Personality & Social Psychology, 55*(1), 23–27.

Peterson, C., & Steen, T. A. (2002). Optimistic explanatory style. In C. R. Snyder & S. J. Lopez (Eds.), *Handbook of positive psychology* (pp. 244–256). New York: Oxford University Press.

Peterson, C., & Steen, T. (2009). Optimistic explanatory style. In C. R. Snyder & S. Lopez (Eds.), *Oxford handbook of positive psychology* (2nd ed., pp. 313–322). New York: Oxford University Press.

Peterson, C., & Stunkard, A. J. (1989). Personal control and health promotion. *Social Science and Medicine, 28,* 819–828.

Peterson, G. (2000). *Making healthy families.* Berkeley: Shadow & Light.

Petrides, K. V., & Furnham, A. (2001). Trait emotional intelligence: Psychometric investigation with reference to established trait taxonomies. *European Journal of Personality, 15*(6), 425–448.

Pfeffer, J. (1998). *The human equation: Building profits by putting people first.* Boston: Harvard Business School Press.

Phelps, A., Maciejewski, P., Nilsson, M., Balboni, T., Wright, A. et. al. (2009). Religious coping and use of intensive life-prolonging care near death in patients with advanced cancer. *Journal of the American Medical Association, 301*(11), 1140–1147.

Philippot, P, Chapelle, G., & Blairy, S. (2002). Respiratory feedback in the generation of emotion. *Cognition and Emotion, 16*(5), 605–627.

Pilisuk, M., & Parks, S. H. (1986). *The healing web: Social networks and human survival.* Hanover, NH: University Press of New England.

Pinder, C. (1998). *Work motivation in organizational behavior.* Upper Saddle River, NJ: Prentice-Hall.

Plagnol, A., & Easterlin, R. (2008). Aspiration, attainments, and satisfaction: Life cycle differences between American women and men. *Journal of Happiness Studies.* doi: 10.1007/s10902-008-9106-5

Plante, T. G., & Sherman, C. (2001). Research on faith and health: New approach to old questions. In T. G. Plante & C. Sherman (Eds.), *Faith and health: Psychological perspectives.* New York: Guilford.

Plaut, V. C., Adams, G., & Anderson, S. L. (2009). Does attractiveness buy happiness? It depends on where you're from. *Personal Relationships, 16,* 619–630.

Plutchik, R. (1980). *Emotion: A psychoevolutionary synthesis.* New York: Harper & Row.

Polivy, J., & Peter, H. (2000). The false-hope syndrome: Unfulfilled expectations of self-change. *Current Directions in Psychological Science, 9*(4), 128–131. doi: 10.111/1467-8721.00076

Poloma, M. M., & Pendleton, B. F. (1990). Religious domains and general well-being. *Social Indicators Research, 22*(3), 255–276.

Poortinga, W. (2006). Social relations or social capital? Individual and community health effects of bonding social capital. *Social Science & Medicine, 63*(1), 255–270. doi: 10.1016/j.socscimed.2005.11.039

Post, S. (2005). Altruism, happiness, and health: It's good to be good. *International Journal of Behavioral Medicine, 12*(2), 66–77.

Porges, S. W. (2001). The polyvagal theory: Phylogenetic substrates of a social nervous system. *The International Journal of Psychophysiology, 42*(2), 123–146. doi: 10.1016/S0167-8760(01)00162-3

Porges, S. W. (2007). The polyvagal perspective. *Biological Psychology, 72*(2), 116–143. doi: 10.1016/j.biopsycho.2006.06.009

Powdthavee, N. (2005). Mental risk-sharing in marriage. Retrieved from: http://www.nottingham.ac.uk/economics/res/media/powdthavee.pdf

Powdthavee, N. (2009). Think having children will make you happy? *The Psychologists, 22*(4), 308–311.

Powdthavee, N., & Wilkinson, C. (2010, August 28). The seven secrets of a happy life. *The Financial Times of London.* http://www.ft.com/cms/s/2/9a4d4a64-b0b9-11df-8c04-00144feabdc0.html#axzz1YbYeFG7A.

Pratt, M. W., Norris, J. E., Arnold, M. L., & Filyer, R. (1999). Generativity and moral development as predictors of value-socialization narratives for young persons across the adult life span: From lessons learned to stories shared. *Psychology & Aging, 14*(3), 414–426.

Pratt, M. W., Pancer, M., Hunsberger, B., & Manchester, J. (1990). Reasoning about the self and relationships in maturity: An integrative complexity analysis of individual differences. *Journal of Personality and Social Psychology, 59*(3), 575–581.

Pressman, S. D., Matthews, K. A., Cohen, S., Martire, L. M., Scheier, M., Baum, A., & Schulz, R. (2009). Association of enjoyable leisure activities with psychological and physical well-being. *Psychosomatic Medicine, 71*(7), 725–732.

Price, W. F., & Crapo, R. H. (2002). *Cross-cultural perspectives in introductory psychology* (4th ed.). Pacific Grove, CA: Wadsworth.

Privette, G. (1965, May). Transcendent functioning. *Teachers College Record,* 733–739.

Privette, G. (1981). Dynamics of peak performance. *J. Humanistic Psychology, 21*(1), 57–67.

Privette, G. (1983). Peak experience, peak performance, and flow: A comparative analysis of positive human experiences. *Journal of Personality and Social Psychology, 45*(6), 1361–1368.

Privette, G., & Landsman, T. (1983). Factor analysis of peak performance: The full use of potential. *Journal of Personality and Social Psychology, 44*(1), 195–200.

Progoff, I. (1983). *Life-study: Experiencing creative lives by the intensive journal method.* New York: Dialogue House.

Progoff, I. (1992). *At a journal workshop* (Rev. ed.). Los Angeles: J. P. Tarcher.

Pulkkinen, L., & Caspi, A. (2002). Personality and paths to successful development: An overview. In L. Pulkkinen & A. Caspi (Eds), *Paths to successful development: Personality in the life course* (pp. 1–18). Cambridge: Cambridge University Press.

Pury, C., & Lopez, S. (2009). Courage. In C. R. Snyder & S. Lopez (Eds.), *Oxford handbook of positive psychology* (2nd ed., pp. 375–382). New York: Oxford University Press.

Pyszczynski, T., Greenberg, J., & Solomon, S. (1999). A dual-process model of defense against conscious and unconscious death-related thoughts: An extension of terror management theory. *Psychological Review, 106,* 835–845.

Pyszczynski, T., Greenberg, J., Solomon, S., & Hamilton, J. (1991). A terror management analysis of self-awareness and anxiety: The hierarchy of terror. In R. Schwarzer & R. A. Wicklund, (Eds.), *Anxiety and self-focused attention* (pp. 67–85). Amsterdam, Netherlands: Harwood Academic.

Pytlik Zillig, L., Maul, A., & Dienstbier, R. (2001, October). *What evokes integrity? (Part of) The rest of the story.* Poster presented at the Positive Psychology Summit. Washington DC.

Quick, J. D., Nelson, D. L., Matuszek, P., Whittington, A. C. Quick, J. L., & Campbell, J. (1996). Social support, secure attachments, and health. In C. L. Cooper (Ed.), *Handbook of stress, medicine, and health* (pp. 269–287). Boca Raton, FL: CRC Press.

Quoidbach, J., Dunn, E., Petrides, K., & Mikolajczak, M. (2010). Money giveth, money taketh away: the dual effect of wealth on happiness. *Psychological Science, 21*(6), 759–763.

Rahula, W. (1974). *What the Buddha taught.* New York: Grove Press.

Rama, S., Ballentine, R., Ajaya, S. (1976). *Yoga and psychotherapy: The evolution of consciousness.* Honesdale, PA: The Himalayan International Institute of Yoga Science and Phiosophy.

Rampell, C. (2011, March 5). Discovered: The happiest man in America. Retrieved June 3, 2011 from http://www.newyorktimes.com/2011/03/06/weekinreview/06happy.html

Rand, Kevin L., & Cheavens, Jennifer S. (2009). Hope theory. In: Oxford handbook of positive psychology (2nd ed.). Lopez, Shane J. (Ed.), Snyder, C. R. (Ed.), New York, NY, US: Oxford University Press, . pp. 323–333.

Randall, G., Bhattacharyya, M., & Steptoe, A. (2009). Marital status and heart rate variability in patients with suspected coronary artery disease. *Annals of Behavioral Medicine, 38*(2), 115, 123.

Rappaport, J. (1977). *Community psychology: Values, research, and action.* New York: Holt, Rinehart, & Winston.

Rappaport, J., & Seidman, E. (Eds.). (2000). *Handbook of Community Psychology.* New York: Kluwer/Plenum.

Rashid, T. (2009). Positive interventions in clinical practice. *Journal of Clinical Psychology: In Session, 65*(5), 461–466.

Rasmussen, H., Scheier, M., & Greenhouse, J. (2009). Optimism and physical health: A meta-analytic review. *Annals of Behavioral Medicine, 37*(3), 239–256.

Rasulo, D., Christensen, K., & Tomassini, C. (2005). The influence of social relations on mortality in later life: A study of elderly Danish twins. *The Gerontologist, 45*(5), 601–608.

Rathunde, K. (1988). Optimal experience and the family context. In M. Csikszentmihalyi & I. S. Csikszentmihalyi (Eds.), *Optimal Experience* (pp. 342–363). Cambridge: Cambridge University Press.

Rathunde, K. (2001). Toward a psychology of optimal human functioning: What positive psychology can learn from the "experiential turns" of James, Dewey, and Maslow. *Journal of Humanistic Psychology, 41*(1), 135–153.

Readers Digest. (2001, November). Getting better all the time: Face to face with Paul McCartney (pp. 78–87; 157–160).

Reid, A. (2004). Gender and sources of subjective well-being. *Sex Roles, 51*(11/12), 617–629. doi: 10.1007/s11199-004-0714-1

Reid, K., Baron, K., Lu, B., Naylor, E., Wolfe, L., & Zee, P. (2010). Aerobic exercise improves self-reported sleep and quality of life in older adults. *Sleep Medicine, 11*(9), 934–940.

Reis, H. T., Wilson, I. M., Monestere, C., Bernstein, S., Clark, K., Seidl, E., & Radoane, K. (1990). What is smiling is beautiful and good. *European Journal of Social Psychology, 20*(3), 259–267.

Reynolds F., & Prior S. (2003). 'A lifestyle coat-hanger': A phenomenological study of the meanings of artwork for women coping with chronic illness and disability. *Disability and Rehabilitation, 25,* 785–794.

Reznitskaya, A., & Sternberg, R. J. (2004). Teaching Students to Make Wise Judgments: The 'Teaching for Wisdom' Program. In: Positive psychology in practice. Linley, P. Alex (Ed.); Joseph, Stephen (Ed.); Hoboken, NJ, US: John Wiley & Sons Inc, pp. 181–196.

Ricard, M. (2007). *Happiness: A guide to developing life's most important skill.* NY: Little, Brown & Co.

Rich, G. J. (2002). *Massage therapy: The evidence for practice.* New York: Mosby Harcourt Health Sciences.

Richards, R., Kinney, D. K., Lunde, I., & Benet, M. (1988). Creativity in manic-depressives, cyclothymes, their normal relatives, and control subjects. *Journal of Abnormal Psychology, 97*(3), 281–288.

Richardson, F. C., & Guignon, C. B. (2008). Positive psychology and philosophy of social science. *Theory & Psychology, 18*(5), 605–627. doi: 10.1177/0959354308093398

Richman, L., Kubansky, L., Maselko, J., Kawachi, I., Choo, P., et al., (2005). Positive emotion and health: Going beyond the negative. *Health Psychology, 24*(4), 422–429.

Riley, J., Best, S., & Charlton, B. (2005). Religious believers and strong atheists may both be less depressed than existentially uncertain people. *QJM: Monthly Journal of the Association of Physicians, 98,* 840.

Ritchart, R., & Perkins, D. N. (2002). Life in the mindful classroom: Nurturing the disposition of mindfulness. *Journal of Social Issues, 56*(1), 27–47.

Robb, K. A., Simon, A. E., & Wardle, J. (2009). Socioeconomic disparities in optimism and pessimism. *International Journal of Behavioral Medicine, 16*(4), 331–338.

Roberts, T. B. (2006). *Psychedelic Horizons.* Charlottesville, VA: Imprint Academic.

Robinson, D. N. (1990). Wisdom through the ages. In R. J. Sternberg (Ed.), *Wisdom: Its nature, origins, and development* (pp. 13–24). Cambridge, UK: Cambridge University Press.

Robinson, D. (1997). *The great ideas of philosophy* [CD]. Chantilly, VA: The Teaching Company.

Robinson, D., & Groves, J. (1998). *Introducing philosophy.* New York: Totem Books.

Robinson, J., & Martin, S. (2008). What do happy people do? *Social Indicators Research.* doi: 10.10007/s11205-208-9296-6

Robinson, M., & Compton, R. (2008). The happy mind in action: The cognitive bias of subjective well-being. In M. Eid & R. Larsen (Eds.). *The science of subjective well-being.* (pp. 220–238). New York: Guilford Press.

Robinson, M. D., & Kirkeby, B. S. (2005). Happiness as a belief system: Individual differences and priming in emotion judgments. *Personality and Social Psychology Bulletin, 31*(8), 1134–1144. doi: 10.1177/0146167204274081

Robinson, M. D., & Ryff, C. D. (1999). The role of self-deception in perceptions of past, present, and future happiness. *Personality & Social Psychology Bulletin, 25*(5), 595–606.

Robinson, M. D., & Tamir, M. (2011). A task-focused mind is a happy and productive mind: A processing perspective. In: Sheldon, Kennon M. (Ed.), Kashdan, Todd B. (Ed.), Steger, Michael F. (Ed.), Designing positive psychology: Taking stock and moving forward. (pp. 160–174). New York, NY, US: Oxford University Press.

Robitschek, C. (1998). Personal growth initiative: The construct and its measure. *Measurement & Evaluation in Counseling & Development, 30*(4), 183–198.

Robitschek, C., & Cook, S. W. (1999). The influence of personal growth initiative and coping styles on career exploration and vocational identity. *Journal of Vocational Behavior, 54*(1), 127–141.

Robitschek, C., & Kashubeck, S. (1999). A structural model of parental alcoholism, family functioning, and psychological health: The mediating effects of hardiness and personal growth orientation. *Journal of Counseling Psychology, 46,* 159–172.

Roese, N. J., & Summerville, A. (2005). What we regret most … and why. *Personality and Social Psychology Bulletin, 31*(9), 1273–1285.

Rogers, C. R. (1959). A theory of therapy, personality, and interpersonal relationships as developed in the client-centered framework. In S. Koch (Ed.), *Psychology: A study of a science* (p. 3). New York: McGraw-Hill.

Rogers, C. R. (1961). *On becoming a person.* Boston: Houghton Mifflin.

Rojas, M. (2010). Intra-household arrangements and economic satisfaction. *Journal of Happiness Studies, 11*(2), 225–241.

Ross, C. E., & Jang, S. J. (2000). Neighborhood disorder, fear, and mistrust: The buffering role of social ties with neighbors. *American Journal of Community Psychology, 28,* 401–420.

Rothenberg, A. (1990). *Creativity and madness: New findings and old stereotypes.* Baltimore, MD: Johns Hopkins University Press.

Rottenberg, R., Bylsma, L. M., & Vingerhoets, J. J. M. (2008). Is crying beneficial? *Current Directions in Psychological Science, 17*(6), 401–404.

Rotter, J. B. (1966). Generalized expectancies for internal versus external control of reinforcement. *Psychological Monographs: General and Applied, 81*(1), 1–28.

Rowatt, W. C., Powers, C., Targhetta, V., Comer, J., Kennedy, S., & Labouff, J. (2006). Development and initial validation of an implicit measure of humility relative to arrogance. *The Journal of Positive Psychology, 1*(4), 198–211.

Ruini, C., Belaise, C., Brombin, C., Caffo, E., & Fava, G. (2006). Well-being therapy in school settings: A pilot study. *Psychotherapy and Psychosomatics, 75*(6), 331–336.

Ruini, C., & Fava, G. (2004). Clinical applications of well- being therapy. In A. Linley & S. Joseph (Eds.). *Positive psychology in practice.* (pp. 371–387). Hoboken, NJ: J. Wiley & Sons.

Rusbult, C. E. (1991). Commentary on Johnson's "Commitment to personal relationships": What's interesting, and what's new? In W. H. Jones & D. Perlman (Eds.), *Advances in personal relationships Vol. 3* (pp. 151–169). London: Jessica Kingsley.

Russek, L. G., & Schwartz, G. E. (1997). Perceptions of parental caring predict health status in midlife: A 35-year follow-up of the Harvard mastery of stress study. *Psychosomatic Medicine, 59*(2), 144–149.

Russell, J. A., & Barrett, L. (1999). Core affect, prototypical emotional episodes, and other things called emotion: Dissecting the elephant. *Journal of Personality and Social Psychology, 76*(5), 805–819.

Rust, T., Diessner, R., & Reade, L. (2009). Strengths only or strengths and relative weaknesses? A preliminary study. *The Journal of Psychology, 143,* 465–476.

Rusting, C. L., & Larsen, R. J. (1998). Personality and cognitive processing of affective information. *Personality and Social Psychology Bulletin, 24*(2), 200–213.

Ruzek, N. (2007). Transpersonal psychology in context: Perspectives from its founders and historians of American psychology. *Journal of Transpersonal Psychology*, *39*, 153–174.

Ryan, R. M., Bernstein, J. H., & Warren Brown, K. (2010). Weekends, work, and well-being: Psychological need satisfactions and day of the week effects on mood, vitality, and physical symptoms. *Journal of Social and Clinical Psychology*, *29*(1), 95–122.

Ryan, R. M., & Deci, E. L. (2000). Self-determination theory and the facilitation of intrinsic motivation, social development, and well-being. *American Psychologist*, *55*(1), 68–78.

Ryan, R. M., & Deci, E. L. (2001). On happiness and human potentials: A review of research on hedonic and eudaimonic well-being. *Annual Review of Psychology*, *52*, 141–166.

Ryan, R., & Deci. E. (2008). From ego depletion to vitality: Theory and findings concerning the facilitation of energy available to the self. *Social and Personality Psychology Compass*, *2*(2), 702–717.

Ryan, R. M., & Frederick, C. (1997). On energy, personality, and health: Subjective vitality as a dynamic reflection of well-being. *Journal of Personality*, *65*, 530–565. doi: 10.1111/j.1467-6494.1997.tb00326.x

Ryan, R. M., LaGuardia, J. G., & Rawsthorne, L. J. (2005). Self-complexity and the authenticity of self-aspects: Effects on well-being and resilience to stressful events. *North American Journal of Psychology*, *7*(3), 431–448.

Ryff, C. D. (1985). Adult personality development and the motivation for personal growth. In D. Kleimer & M. Maehr (Eds.), *Advances in motivation and achievement: Motivation and adulthood* (Vol. 4, pp. 55–92). Greenwich, CT: JAI Press.

Ryff, C. D. (1989a). Beyond Ponce de Leon and life satisfaction: New directions in quest of successful ageing. *International Journal of Behavioral Development*, *12*(1), 35–55.

Ryff, C. D. (1989b). Happiness is everything, or is it? Explorations on the meaning of psychological well-being. *Journal of Personality and Social Psychology*, *57*(6), 1069–1081.

Ryff, C. D. (1995). Psychological well-being in adult life. *Current Direction in Psychological Science*, *4*(4), 99–104.

Ryff, C. D., & Heidrich, S. M. (1997). Experience and well-being: Explorations on domains of life and how they matter. *International Journal of Behavioral Development*, *20*(2), 193–206.

Ryff, C. D., & Keyes, C. L. M. (1995). The structure of psychological well-being revised. *Journal of Personality and Social Psychology*, *69*(4), 719–727.

Ryff, C. D., Love, G. D., Urry, H. L., Muller, D., Rosenkranz, M. A., Freedman, E. M., Davidson, R. J., & Singer, B. (2006). Psychological well-being and ill-being: Do they distinct or mirrored biological correlates? *Psychotherapy and Psychosomatics*, *75*(2), 85–95.

Ryff, C. D., & Singer, B. (1998). The contours of positive human health. *Psychological Inquiry*, *9*(1), 1–28.

Ryff, C. D., Singer, B., & Seltzer, M. M. (2002). Pathways through challenge: Implications for health and well-being. In L. Pulkkinen & A. Caspi (Eds.), *Pathways to successful development: Personality in the life course* (pp. 302–328). Location: Cambridge University Press.

Ryff, C. D., & Singer, B. H. (2006). Best news yet on the six-factor model of well-being. *Social Science Research*, *35*(4), 1102–1118.

Ryff, C. D., & Singer, B. H. (2008). Know thyself and become what you are: A eudaimonic approach to psychological well-being. *Journal of Happiness Studies*, *9*(1), 13–39. doi: 10.1007/s10902-006-9019-0

Saks, A. M. (2006). Antecedents and consequences of employee engagement. *Journal of Managerial Psychology*, *21*(7), 600–619.

Salovey, Peter, Caruso, David, & Mayer, John D. (2004). Emotional Intelligence in Practice. In: Positive psychology in practice. Linley, P. Alex (Ed.), Joseph, Stephen (Ed.), Hoboken, NJ, US: John Wiley & Sons Inc, 2004. pp. 447–463.

Salovey, P., & Mayer, J. D. (1990). Emotional intelligence. *Imagination, Cognition and Personality*, *9*, 185–211.

Salovey, P., Mayer, J. D., & Caruso, D. (2002). The positive psychology of emotional intelligence. In C. R. Snyder and S. J. Lopez (Eds.), *Handbook of positive psychology* (pp. 159–171). New York: Oxford University Press.

Salovey, P., Mayer, J., Caruso, D., & Yoo, S. H. (2009). The positive psychology of emotional intelligence. In C. R. Snyder & S. Lopez (Eds.). *Oxford handbook of positive psychology (2nd ed.).* (pp. 237–248). New York: Oxford University Press.

Salovey, P., Rothman, A., Detweiller, J., & Steward, W. (2000). Emotional states and physical health. *American Psychologist, 55*(1), 110–121.

Sampson, E. E. (1988). The debate on individualism: Indigenous psychologies of the individual and their role in personal and societal functioning. *43:* 15–22.

Sampson, R. J. (2001). How do communities undergird or undermine human development? Relevant contexts and social mechanisms. In A. Booth, & A. C. Crouter (Eds.), *Does it take a village? Community effects on children, adolescents, and families* (pp. 3–30). Mahwah, NJ: Lawrence Erlbaum.

Sandage, S. J., & Hill, P. C. (2001). The virtues of positive psychology: The rapprochement and challenges of an affirmative postmodern perspective. *Journal of the Theory of Social Behavior, 31,* 241–260.

Sandvik, E., Diener, E., & Seidlitz, L. (1993). Subjective well-being: The convergence and stability of self-report and nonself-report measures. *Journal of Personality, 61,* 317–342.

Sarason, S. B. (1990). *The challenge of art to psychology.* New Haven, CT: Yale University Press.

Saroglou, V., Buxant, C., & Tilquin, J. (2008). Positive emotions as leading to religion and spirituality. *The Journal of Positive Psychology, 3*(3), 165–173. doi: 10.1080/17439760801998737

Sattah, M. V., Supawiktul, S., Dondero, T. J., Kilmarx, P., Young, N. L., Mastro, T. D., & Grinsven, F. V. (2002). Prevalence and risk factors for methamphetamine use in Northern Thai youth: Results of an audio-computer-assisted self-interviewing survey with urine testing. *Addiction, 97*(7), 801–808.

Sattler, D. N., & Shabatay, V. (1997). *Psychology in context: Voices and perspectives.* New York: Houghton-Mifflin.

Sautter, U. (2010, March). Take two concertos and call me in the morning. *Ode Magazine,* 56–58.

Schafer, M., & Shippee, T. (2010). Age identity, gender, and pessimistic dispositions about cognitive aging? *The Journals of Gerontology: Psychological Sciences, 65B* (1), 91. doi: 10.1093/geronb/gbp046

Schachter, Z., & Hoffman, E. (1983). *Sparks of light: Counseling in the Hasidic tradition.* Boulder: Shambhala.

Schachter-Shalomi, Z., & Gropman, D. (2003). *The first steps to a new Jewish spirit: Reb Zalman's guide to recapturing intimacy and ecstasy in your relationship with God.* Woodstock, VT: Jewish Lights.

Schaufeli, W. B., Bakker, A. B., & Salanova, M. (2002). The measurement of work engagement with a short questionnaire: A cross-national study. *Educational and Psychological Measurement, 66*(4), 701–716.

Schwartz, S. H. (1994). Are there universal aspects in the structure and contents of human values? *Journal of Social Issues, 50*(4), 19–45.

Shapiro, S., Brown, K., Thoreson, C., & Plante, T. (2010). The moderation of mindfulness-based stress reduction effects by trait mindfulness: Results from a randomized controlled trail. *Journal of Clinical Psychology, 67*(3), 267–277.

Scheibe, S., & Carstensen, L. (2010). Emotional aging: Recent findings and future trends. *The Journals of Gerontology: Psychological Sciences, 65B*(2), 135–144.

Scheibe, S., Kunzmann, U., & Baltes, P. (2009). New territories of positive life-span development: Wisdom and life longings. In C. R. Snyder & S. Lopez (Eds.), *Oxford handbook of positive psychology* (2nd ed., pp. 171–184). New York: Oxford University Press.

Scheier, M., & Carver, C. (1985). Optimism, coping, and health: Assessment and implications of generalized outcome expectancies. *Health Psychology, 4*(3), 219–247.

Scheier, M., & Carver, C. (1987). Dispositional optimism and physical well-being: The influence of generalized outcome expectancies on health. *Journal of Personality, 55*(2), 169–210.

Scheier, M. F., & Carver, C. S. (1992). Effects of optimism on psychological and physical well-being: Theoretical overview and empirical update. *Cognitive Therapy and Research, 16,* 201–228.

Schwartz, B., & Sharpe, (2010). *Practical Wisdom: The Right Way to Do the Right Thing.* NY: Riverhead.

Sheridan, S., & Burt, J. (2009). Family-centered positive psychology. In C. R. Snyder & S. Lopez (Eds.), *Oxford handbook of positive psychology* (2nd ed., pp. 551–560). New York: Oxford University Press.

Schiffrin, H., Edelman, A., Falkenstern, M., & Stewart, C. (2010). The associations between computer-mediated communication, relationships, and well-being. *Cyberpsychology, Behavior, and Social Networking, 13*(3), 299–306.

Schimmack, U. (2008). The structure of subjective well-being. In M. Eid & R. Larsen (Eds.) The science of subjective well-being. New York, NY, US: Guilford Press, pp. 97–123.

Schimmack, U., Oishi, S., Furr, M. R., & Funder, D. C. (2004). Personality and life satisfaction: A facet-level analysis. *Personality and Social Psychology Bulletin, 30*(8), 1062–1075. doi: 10.1177/0146167204264292

Schimmel, S. (2000). Vices, virtues and sources of human strength in historical perspective. *Journal of Social and Clinical Psychology, 19*(1), 137–150.

Schlaug, G. (2001). The brain of musicians: A model for functional and structural adaptation. In R. J. Zatorre, & I. Peretz (Eds.), *The biological foundations of music. Annals of the New York Academy of Science* (Vol. *930*, pp. 281–299). New York: New York Academy of Science.

Schlaug, G., Jancke, L., Huang, Y., Staiger, J. F., & Steinmetz, H. (1995). Increased corpus callosum size in musicians. *Neuropsychologia, 33*, 1047–1055.

Schlegel, R. J., Hicks, J. A., Arndt, J., & King, L. A. (2009). Thine own self: True self-concept accessibility and meaning in life. *Journal of Personality and Social Psychology, 96*(2), 473–490. doi: 10.1037/a0014060

Schlesinger, J. (2009). Creative mythconceptions: A closer look at the evidence for the "mad genius" hypothesis. *Psychological of Aesthetics, Creativity, and the Arts, 3*(2), 62–72.

Schneider, K. (2005, September–November). Awe-based learning. *Shift: At the Frontiers of Consciousness, 8*, 16–19.

Schneider, K. (2009). *Awakening to Awe.* NY: Aronson.

Schneider, K., Bugental, J., & Pierson, F. (1991). *The handbook of humanistic psychology.* Thousand Oaks, CA.: Sage.

Schneider, S. (2001). In search of realistic optimism: Meaning, knowledge, and warm fuzziness. *Journal of American Psychologist, 54*(3), 250–263.

Schor, J. B. (1999). *The overspent American: Why we want what we don't need.* NY: Harper.

Schreiner, L., Hulme, E., Hetzel, R., & Lopez, S. (2009). Positive psychology on campus. In C. R. Snyder & S. Lopez (Eds.), *Oxford handbook of positive psychology* (2nd ed., pp. 569–578). New York: Oxford University Press.

Schuler, J., & Brunner, S. (2009). A rewarding effect of flow experience on performance in a marathon race. *Psychology of Sport and Exercise, 10*(1), 168–174.

Schultz, D. (1977). *Growth psychology: Models of the healthy personality.* Pacific Grove, CA: Brooks Cole.

Scioli, A. (2010). The hopes of world religions: Profiles in attachment, mastery, and survival. *Research in the Social Scientific Study of Religion, 21*, 101–135.

Scott, C. (Executive Producer). (1999, June 10). The cellist of Sarajevo. *All things considered* [radio broadcast]. New York and Washington, DC: National Public Radio.

Scott, K. (2009, August 12). Psychologist's science of happiness project announces results of survey and experiment. Retrieved June 16, 2010 from http://www.wired.co.uk/news/archive/2009-08/12/the-science-of-happiness-what-makes-britain-smile

Scott, T. M., Gagnon, J. C., & Nelson, C. M. (2008). School-wide systems of positive behavior support: A framework for reducing school crime and violence. *Journal of Behavior Analysis of Offender and Victim: Treatment and Prevention, 1*, 259–272.

Seery, M., Holman, A., & Silver, R. (2010). Whatever does not kill us: Cumulative lifetime adversity, vulnerability, & resilience. *Journal of Personality & Social Psychology, 99*(6), 1025–1041.

Seeman, J. (1959). Toward a concept of personality integration. *American Psychologist, 14*, 794–797.

Seeman, J. (1983). *Personality integration: Studies and reflections.* New York: Human Sciences Press.

Seeman, J. (1988). Self-actualization: A reformulation. *Person-Centered Review, 3*(3), 304–315.

Seeman, J. (1989). Toward a model of positive health. *American Psychologist, 44*(8), 1099–1109.

Seeman, J. (2008). *Psychotherapy and the fully functioning person.* New York: AuthorHouse.

Segal, Z. V., Williams, J., Mark, G., & Teasdale, J. D. (2002). *Mindfulness-based cognitive therapy for depression: A new approach to preventing relapse.* New York,: Guilford Press.

Segaller, S. (producer) (1989). *Wisdom of the Dream (Vol. 1): A life of dreams (video).* New York: Home Vision/RM Associates.

Segerstrom, S. (2005). Optimism and immunity: Do positive thoughts always lead to positive effects? *Brain, Behavior and Immunity, 19*(3), 195–200.

Segerstrom, S., Smith, T., & Eisenlohr-Moul, T. (2011). Positive psychophysiology: The body and self-regulation. In K. M. Sheldon, T. B. Kashdan, & M. F. Steger (Eds.), *Designing positive psychology: Taking stock and moving forward* (pp. 25–40). New York: Oxford University Press.

Seidlitz, L., & Diener, E. (1993). Memory for positive versus negative events: Theories for the differences between happy and unhappy persons. *Journal of Personality and Social Psychology, 64,* 654–664.

Seligman, M., Peterson, C. (2003). Positive clinical psychology. In L. Aspinwall & U. Staudinger (Eds.) *A psychology of human strengths*. Washington, DC: American Psychological Association.

Seligman, M. E. P. (1998). *Learned optimism* (2nd ed.). New York: Pocket Books.

Seligman, M. E. P. (2002). *Authentic happiness*. New York: Free Press.

Seligman, M. E. P. (2008). Positive health. *Applied Psychology: An International Review, 57,* 3–18. doi: 10.1111/j.1464-0597.2008.00351.x

Seligman, M. E. P. (2011). *Flourish: A visionary new understanding of happiness and well-being*. New York: Free Press.

Seligman, M. E. P., & Csikszentmihalyi, M. (2000). Positive psychology: An introduction. *American Psychologist, 55*(1), 5–14.

Seligman, M. E. P., Rashid, T., & Parks, A. C. (2006). Positive psychotherapy. *American Psychologist, 61*(8), 774–788.

Seligman, M. E. P., Steen, T., Park, N., & Peterson, C. (2005). Positive psychology progress: Empirical validation of interventions. *American Psychologist, 60*(5), 410–421. doi: 10.1037/0003-066X.60.5.410

Seligman, M. E. P., & Peterson, C. (2003). Positive clinical psychology. In L. G. Aspinwall and U. M. Staudinger (Eds.), *A psychology of human strengths: Fundamental questions and future directions for a positive psychology* (pp. 305–317). Washington, DC: American Psychological Association.

Seligman, M. E. P., Reivich, K., Jaycox, L., & Gillham, J. (1995). *The optimistic child*. New York: Houghton Mifflin.

Sethi, M. L. (2009, winter). Does art heal? *Greater Good: Magazine of the Greater Good Science Center at UC Berkeley, V*(3), 27–29.

Shackelford, T. K., & Buss, D. M. (1997). Satisfaction in evolutionary psychological perspective. In R. J. Sternberg & M. Hojjatt (Eds.), *Satisfaction in close relationships* (pp. 7–25). New York: Guilford Press.

Shapiro, A. F., Gottman, J. M., & Carrere, S. (2000). The baby and the marriage: Identifying factors that buffer against decline in marital satisfaction after the first baby arrives. *Journal of Family Psychology, 14*(1), 59–70.

Shapiro, S. L., Brown, K. W., Thoresen, C., & Plante, T. G. (2011). The moderation of mindfulness-based stress reduction effects by trait mindfulness: Results from a randomized control trial. *Journal of Clinical Psychology, 67*(3), 267–277.

Shapiro, S. L., & Carlson, L. E. (2009). *The art and science of mindfulness: Integrating mindfulness into psychology and the helping professions*. Washington, DC: American Psychological Association Publications.

Sharma, V., & Rosha, J. (1992). Altruism as a function of self-actualization and locus of control of benefactor. *Psychological Studies, 37*(1), 26–30.

Shepela, S. T., Cook, J., Horlitz, E., Leal, R., Luciano, S., Lutfy, E., et al. (1999). Courageous resistance: A special case of altruism. *Theory & Psychology, 9*(6), 787–805.

Shedler, J., Mayman, M., & Manis, M. (1993). The illusion of mental health. *American Psychologist, 48*(11), 1117–1131.

Sheldon, K. (2011). What's positive about positive psychology? Reducing value-bias and enhancing integration within the field. In K. M. Sheldon, T. B. Kashdan, & M. F. Steger (Eds.), *Designing positive psychology: Taking stock and moving forward* (pp. 421–429). New York: Oxford University Press.

Sheldon, K., Abad, N., Ferguson, Y., Gunz, A., Houser-Marko, L., et al. (2010). Persistent pursuit of need-satisfying goals leads to increased happiness: A 6-month experimental longitudinal study. *Motivation and Emotion, 34*(1), 39–48.

Sheldon, K. M. (2002). The self-concordance model of healthy goal-striving: When personal goals correctly represent the person. In E. L. Deci & R. M. Ryan (Eds.), *Handbook of self-determination research* (pp. 65–86). Rochester, NY: University Of Rochester Press.

Sheldon, K. M. (2004). *Optimal human being: An integrated multi-level perspective.* Mahwah, NJ: Lawrence Erlbaum.

Sheldon, K. M. (2008). Assessing the sustainability of goal-based changes in adjustment over a four-year period. *Journal of Research in Personality, 42*(1), 223–229.

Sheldon, K. M. (2009). Providing the scientific backbone for positive psychology: A multi-level conception of human thriving. *Psychological Topics, 18*(2), 267–284.

Sheldon, K. M., & Hoon, T. H. (2007). The multiple determination of well-being: Independent effects of positive traits, needs, goals, selves, social supports, and cultural contexts. *Journal of Happiness Studies, 8*(4), 565–592. doi: 10.1007/s10902-006-9031-4

Sheldon, K. M., & Kasser, T. (1998). Pursuing personal goals: Skills enable progress, but not all progress is beneficial. *Personality and Social Psychology Bulletin, 24*(12), 1319–1331.

Sheldon, K. M., & Kasser, T. (2001). Getting older, getter better: Personal strivings and psychological maturity across the life span. *Developmental Psychology, 37*(4), 491–501.
doi: 10.1037//0012-1649.37.4.491

Sheldon, K. M., Kasser, T., Houser-Marko, L., Jones, T., & Turban, D. (2005, March). Doing One's Duty: Chronological Age, Felt Autonomy, and Subjective Well-Being. *European Journal of Personality, 19*(2), 97–115.

Sheldon, K. M., Kasser, T., Smith, K., & Share, T. (2002). Personal goals and psychological growth: Testing and intervention to enhance goal attainment and personality integration. *Journal of Personality, 70*(1), 5–31.

Sheldon, K. M., & King, L. (2001). Why positive psychology is necessary. *American Psychologist, 54*(3), 216–217.

Sheldon, K. M. & Lyubomirsky, S. (2006a). Achieving sustainable happiness: Change your actions, not your circumstances. *Journal of Happiness Studies, 7,* 55–86. doi: 10.1007/s10902-005-0868-8

Sheldon, K. M., & Lyubomirsky, S. (2006b). How to increase and sustain positive emotion: The effects of expressing gratitude and visualizing best possible selves. *The Journal of Positive Psychology, 1*(2), 73–82. doi: 10.1080/17439760500510676

Sheldon, K. M., Ryan, R. M., Deci, E. L., & Kasser, T. (2004). The independent effects of goal contents and motives on well-being: It's both what you pursue and why you pursue it. *Personality and Social Psychology Bulletin, 30*(4), 475–486. doi: 10.1177/014616720326188

Sheldon, K. M., Ryan, R. M., Rawsthorne, L. J., & Ilardi, B. (1997). Trait self and true self: Cross-role variation in the big-five personality traits and its relations with psychological authenticity and subjective well-being. *Journal of Personality and Social Psychology, 73,* 1380–1393.

Sheldon, K., Schmuck, P., & Kasser, T. (2000). Is value-free science possible? *American Psychologist, 55*(10), 1152–1153. doi: 10.1037/0003-066X.55.10.1152

Sheler, J. L. (2001, July 2). Drugs, scalpel … and faith? Doctors are noticing the power of prayer. *U.S. News and World Report,* 46–47.

Shimmel, S. (1997). *The seven deadly sins.* NY: Oxford University Press.

Shin, N. (2006). Online learner's "flow" experience: An empirical study. *British Journal of Education Technology, 37*(5), 705–720.

Shinn, M., & Toohey, S. M. (2003). Community contexts of human welfare. *Annual Review of Psychology, 54,* 427–459.

Shirai, K., Iso, H., Ohira, T., Ikeda, A., Noda, H., et al. (2009). Perceived level of life enjoyment and risks of cardiovascular disease incidence and mortality: The Japan public health center-based study. *Circulation, 120,* 956–963.

Shmotkin, D. (2005). Happiness in the face of adversity: Reformulating the dynamic and modular bases of subjective well-being. *Review of General Psychology, 9*(4), 291–325.

Siegal, J. M. (1990). Stressful life events and use of physician services among the elderly: The moderating role of pet ownership. *Journal of Personality and Social Psychology, 58,* 1081–1086.

Silvia, P. J., & Kashdan, T. B. (2009, September). Interesting things and curious people: Exploration and engagement as transient states and enduring strengths. *Social and Personality Psychology Compass, 3*(5), 785–797.

Simeon, D., Yehuda, R., Cunill, R., Knutelska, M., Putnam, F. W., & Smith, L. M. (2007). Factors associated with resilience in healthy adults. *Psychoneuroendocrinology*, *32*(8–10), 1149–1152.

Simonton, D. K. (1988). Age and outstanding achievement: What do we know after a century of research? *Psychological Bulletin*, *104*, 251–267.

Simonton, D. K. (1999). *Origins of genius: Darwinian perspectives on creativity*. New York: Oxford University Press.

Simonton, D. K. (2002). Creativity. In C. R. Snyder & S. J. Lopez (Eds.), *Handbook of positive psychology* (pp. 189–201). New York: Oxford University Press.

Simonton, D. K. (2010, May/June). Are mad and genius peas in the same pod? *The National Psychologist*, 10.

Simpson, J. A., Ickes, W., & Blackstone, T. (1995). When the head protects the heart: Empathic accuracy in dating relationships. *Journal of Personality and Social Psychology*, *69*(4), 629–641.

Sin, N., & Lyubomirsky, S. (2009). Enhancing well-being and alleviating depressive symptoms with positive psychology interventions: A practice-friendly meta-analysis. *Clinical Psychology*, *65*(5), 467–487.

Singer, I. (1987). *The nature of love: The modern world* (Vol. 3). Chicago, IL: University of Chicago Press.

Sirgy, M. J. (1998). Materialism and quality of life. *Social Indicators Research*, *43*, 227–260.

Skolnick, A. (1981). Married lives: Longitudinal perspectives on marriage. In D. H. Eichorn, J. A. Clausen, N. Haan, M. P. Honzik, & P. H. Mussen (Eds.), *Present and past in middle life: Married life* (pp. 270–300). New York: Academic Press.

Smith, D., Loewenstein, G., Rozin, P., Sheriff, R., & Ubel, P. (2007). Sensitivity to disgust, stigma, and adjustment to life with a colostomy. *Journal of Research in personality*, *41*, 787–803.

Smith, K., & Christakis, N. (2008). Social networks and health. *Annual Review of Sociology*, *34*, 405–429.

Smith, M. B. (1969). *Social psychology and human values*. Chicago, IL: Aldine.

Smith, W. (2001). *Hope Meadows: Real-life stories of healing and caring from an inspiring community*. New York: Berkley.

Smith, W., Compton, W., & West, B. (1995). Meditation as an adjunct to a happiness enhancement program. *Journal of Clinical Psychology*, *51*(2), 269–273.

Smith, K. D., Smith, S. T., & Christopher, J. C. (2007). What defines the good person? Cross-cultural comparisons of experts' models with lay prototypes. *Journal of Cross-Cultural Psychology*, *38*, 333–360.

Smyth, J. M., & Pennebaker, J. W. (1999). Sharing one's story: Translating emotional experiences into words as a coping tool. In C. R. Snyder (Ed.), *Coping: The psychology of what works* (pp. 70–89). New York: Oxford Press.

Snyder, C. R. (1994). *The psychology of hope: You can get there from here*. New York: Free Press.

Snyder, C. R. (Ed.). (1999). *Coping: The psychology of what works*. New York: Oxford University Press.

Snyder, C. R., & Dinoff, B. L. (1999). Coping: Where have you been? In C. R. Snyder (Ed.), *Coping: The psychology of what works* (pp. 3–19). New York: Oxford University Press.

Snyder, C. R., & Lopez, S. (Eds.). *Oxford handbook of positive psychology* (2nd ed.). New York: Oxford University Press.

Snyder, C. R., Rand, K. L., & Sigmon, D. R. (2002). Hope theory: A member of the positive psychology family. In C. R. Snyder & S. J. Lopez (Eds.), *Handbook of positive psychology* (pp. 257–276). London: Oxford University Press.

Snyder, M. (2011). Working for the common good: Individuals and groups address the challenges facing the world. In D. R. Forsyth & C. L. Hoyt (Eds.), *For the greater good of all: Perspectives on individualism, society, and leadership* (pp. 167–182). New York: Palgrave Macmillan.

Snyder, M., Clary, E. G., & Stukas, A. A. (2000). The functional approach to volunteerism. In G. R. Maio & J. M. Olson (Eds.), *Why we evaluate: Functions of attitudes* (pp. 365–393). Mahwah, NJ: Lawrence Erlbaum.

Sosa, R., Kennell, J., Klaus, M., Robertson, S., & Urrutia, J. (1980). The effect of a supportive companion on perinatal problems, length of labor and mother-infant interaction. *New England Journal of Medicine*, *303*, 597–600.

Spiegel, A. (2008, February 25). *Old-fashioned play builds serious skills*. Retrieved from http://www.npr.org/templates/story/story.php?storyId=19212514

Spiegel, D., Kraemer, H. C., Bloom, J. R., & Gottheil, E. (1989, October 14). Effect of psychosocial treatment on survival of patients with metastatic breast cancer. *Lancet, 2*(8668), 888–891.

Stack, S., & Gundlach, J. (1992). The effect of country music on suicide. *Social Forces, 71*(1), 211–218.

Stafford, L. D., Ng, W., Moore, R. A., & Bard, K. A. (2010). Bolder, happier, smarter: The role of extraversion in positive mood and cognition. *Personality and Individual Differences, 48,* 827–832.

Stalikas, A., & Fitzpatrick, M. R. (2008). Positive emotions in psychotherapy theory, research, and practice: New kid on the block? *Journal of Psychotherapy Integration, 18*(2), 155–166.

Stanton, A. L., Kirk, S. B., Cameron, C. L., & Danoff-Burg, S. (2000). Coping through emotional approach: Scale construction and validation. *Journal of Personality and Social Psychology, 78,* 1150–1169.

Stanton, A. L., Parsa, A., & Austenfield, J. L. (2002).The adaptive potential of coping through emotional approach. In C. R. Snyder & S. J. Lopez (Eds.), *Handbook of positive psychology* (pp. 148–158). Oxford: Oxford University Press.

Staudinger, U. M. (2001). Life reflection: A social-cognitive analysis of life review. *Review of General Psychology, 5*(2), 148–160. doi: 10.1037//1089-2680.5.2.148

Stavrou, N. A., Jackson, S. A., Zervas, Y., & Karteroliotis, K. (2007). Flow experience and athletes' performance with reference to the orthogonal model of flow. *The Sport Psychologist, 21*(4), 438–457.

Staw, B. (2000, October). The role of dispositional affect in job satisfaction and performance. Paper presented at the Positive Psychology Summit. Washington, DC.

Staw, B. M., Sutton, R. I., & Pelled, L. H. (1994). Employee positive emotion and favorable outcomes at the workplace. *Organizational Science, 5*(1), 51–71.

Steger, M. (2009). Meaning in Life. In C. R. Snyder & S. Lopez (Eds.), *Oxford handbook of positive psychology* (2nd ed., pp.679–688). New York: Oxford University Press.

Steger, M., Kashdan, T., & Oishi, S. (2008). Being good by doing good: Daily eudaimonic activity and well-being. *Journal of Research in Personality, 42*(1), 22–42.

Steger, M., Kashdan, T., & Sullivan, B., & Lorenz, D. (2008). Understanding the search for meaning in life: Personality, cognitive style, and the dynamic between seeking and experiencing meaning. *Journal of Personality, 76*(2), 199–228.

Steger, M., Oishi, S., & Kashdan, T. (2009). Meaning in life across the lifespan: Levels and correlates of meaning in life from emerging adulthood to older adulthood. *Journal of Positive Psychology, 4*(1), 43–52.

Steinitz, L. Y. (1980). Religiosity, well-being, and Weltanschauung among the elderly. *Journal for the Scientific Study of Religion, 19,* 60–67.

Stephan, Y. (2009). Openness to experience and active older adults life satisfaction: A trait and facet-level analysis. *Personality and Individual Differences, 47*(6), 637–641.

Steptoe, A., Dockray, S., & Wardle, J. (2009). Positive affect and psychobiological processes relevant to health. *Journal of Personality, 77*(6), 1747–1775.

Sternberg, R. J. (1986a). A triangular theory of love. *Psychological Review, 93,* 119–135.

Sternberg, R. J. (1986b). Intelligence, wisdom, and creativity: Three is better than one. *Educational Psychologist, 21*(3), 175–190.

Sternberg, R. J. (1998). A balance theory of wisdom. *Review of General Psychology, 2*(4), 347–365.

Sternberg, R. J. (Ed.). (1990). *Wisdom: Its nature, origins, and development.* Cambridge: Cambridge University Press.

Sternberg, R. J. (Ed.). (1999). *Handbook of creativity.* New York: Cambridge University Press.

Sternberg, R. J., & Hojjat, M. (1997). *Satisfaction in close relationships.* New York: Guilford Press.

Sternberg, R. J., & Lubart, T. I. (1995). *Defying the crowd: Cultivating creativity in a culture of conformity.* New York: Free Press.

Stessman, J., Hammerman-Rozenberg, R., Cohen, A., Ein-Mor, E., & Jacobs, J. (2009). Physical activity, function, and longevity among the very old. *Archives of Internal Medicine, 169*(16), 1476–1483.

Stets, Jan E., & Turner, Jonathan H. (2008). The sociology of emotions. In: Handbook of emotions (3rd ed.). Lewis, Michael (Ed.), Haviland-Jones, Jeannette M. (Ed.), Barrett, Lisa Feldman (Ed.), New York, NY, US: Guilford Press, 2008. pp. 32–46.

Stevenson, B., & Wolfers, J. (2008, June). Happiness inequality in the United States. *The Journal of Legal Studies, 37*(s2). doi: 10.1086/592004

Stevenson, B., & Wolfers, J. (2009). The paradox of declining female happiness. *American Economic Journal: Economic Policy*. Retrieved June 5, 2011 from http://bpp.wharton.upenn.edu/betseys/papers/Paradox%20of%20declining%20female%20happiness.pdf

Stewart, A. J., & Vandewater, E. (1999) "If I had it to do over again …": Midlife review, midcourse corrections, and women's well-being in midlife. *Journal of Personality and Social Psychology, 76*, 270–283.

Stinnett, N. (1979). In search of strong families. In N. Stinnett, Chesser, B., & DeFrain, J. (Eds.), *Building family strengths: Blueprints for action* (pp. 23–30). Lincoln: University of Nebraska Press.

Stokols, D. (2003). The ecology of human strengths. In L. G. Aspinall & U. M. Staudinger (Eds.), *A psychology of human strengths: Fundamental questions and future directions for a positive psychology* (pp. 311–344). Washington, DC: American Psychological Association.

Stolberg, T. L. (2008). W(h)ither the sense of wonder of pre-service primary teachers' when teaching science? A preliminary study of their personal experiences. *Teaching and Teacher Education, 24*, 1958–1964.

Stone-McCown, K., Jensen, A. L., Freedman, J. M., & Rideout, M. C. (1998). *Self-science: The emotional intelligence curriculum* (2nd ed.). San Mateo, CA: Six Seconds.

Strauch, B. (2010). *The Secret Life of the Grown-up Brain: The Surprising Talents of the Middle-Aged Mind*. NY: Viking.

Strauss, G. P., & Allen, D. N. (2006). The experience of positive emotion is associated with the automatic processing of positive emotional words. *The Journal of Positive Psychology, 1*(3), 150–159

Strickland, B. R. (1978). Internal-external expectancies and health-related behaviors. *Journal of Consulting and Clinical Psychology, 46*(6), 1192–1211.

Stroebe, W., & Stroebe, M. (1996). The social psychology of social support. In E. T. Higgins & A. W. Kruglanski (Eds.), *Social psychology: Handbook of basic principles* (pp. 597–621). New York: Guilford Press.

Strümpfer, D. J. W., & Mlonzi, E. N. (2001). Antonovsky's Sense of Coherence Scale and job attitudes: Three studies. *South African Journal of Psychology, 31*(2), 30–37.

Stubbe, J. H., de Moor, M. H. M., Boomsma, D. I., de Geus, E. J. C. (2007). The association between exercise participation and well-being: A co-twin study. *Preventive Medicine: An International Journal Devoted to Practice and Theory, 44*(2), 148–152.

Subkoviak, M. J., Enright, R. D., Wu, C., Gassin, E. A., Freedman, S., Olson, L. M., & Sarinopoulos, I. (1995). Measuring interpersonal forgiveness in late adolescence and middle adulthood. *Journal of Adolescence, 18*, 641–655.

Sugarman, J. (2007). Practical rationality and the questionable promise of positive psychology. *Journal of Humanistic Psychology, 47*(2), 175–197. doi: 10.1177/0022167806297061

Sugarman, K. (1998, November 9). Cohesion. [Online]. Available: http://www.psywww.com/sports/cohesion.htm.

Suh, E. M. (1999). Culture, identity, consistency, and subjective well-being. *Dissertation Abstracts International* (60-09, Sect B, p. 4950).

Suh, E. M., Diener, E., & Fujita, F. (1996). Events and subjective well-being: Only recent events matter. *Journal of Personality and Social Psychology, 70*, 1091–1102.

Suh, E. M., Diener, E., Oishi, S., & Triandis, H. (1998). The shifting basis of life satisfaction judgments across cultures: Emotions versus norms. *Journal of Personality and Social Psychology, 74*(2), 482–493.

Suh, E. M., & Koo, J. (2008). Comparing subjective well- being across cultures and nations: The "what" and "why" questions. In M. Eid & R. Larsen (Eds.). *The science of subjective well-being.* (pp. 414–430). New York: Guilford Press.

Sumerlin, J. R., & Bundrick, C. M. (1996). Brief index of self-actualization: A measure of Maslow's model. *Journal of Social Behavior and Personality, 11*(2), 253–271. Retrieved from http://www.sbp-journal.com/

Sumerlin, J. R., Berretta, S. A., Privette, G., & Bundrick, C. M. (1994). Subjective biological self and self-actualization. *Perceptual and Motor Skills, 79*(3, Pt 1), 1327–1337.

Sumerlin, J. R., Privette, G., Bundrick, C. M., & Berretta, S. A. (1994). Factor structure of the short index of self-actualization in racially, culturally, and socioeconomically diverse samples. *Journal of Social Behavior and Personality, 9*(1), 27–42. Retrieved from http://www.sbp-journal.com/

Surtees, P. G., Wainwright, N. W. J., & Khaw, K. T. (2004). Obesity, confidant support and functional health: Cross-Sectional evidence from the EPIC= Norfolk cohort. *International Journal of Obesity and Related Metabolic Disorders, 28,* 748–758.

Sutich, A. (1969). Introduction. *Journal of Transpersonal Psychology, 1*(1), iv.

Suzuki, D. T., Fromm, E., & De Martino, R. (1960). *Zen Buddhism and psychoanalysis.* New York: Harper & Row.

Suzuki, N. (2005, March). Psycho-physiological approach to emotion: Undoing effect of positive emotions. *Japanese Journal of Psychonomic Science, 23*(2), 202–206.

Tan, H. B., & Forgas, J. P. (2010). When happiness makes us selfish, but sadness makes us fair: Affective influences on interpersonal strategies in the dictator game. *Journal of Experimental Social Psychology, 46,* 571–576. doi: 10.1016/j.jesp.2010.01.007

Tangney, J. (2009). Humility. In C. R. Snyder & S. Lopez (Eds.), *Oxford handbook of positive psychology* (2nd ed., pp. 483–490). New York: Oxford University Press.

Tannen, D. (2010, October 25). Why sisterly chats make people happier. *The New York Times.* http://www.nytimes.com/2010/10/26/health/26essay.html

Tamir, Maya, & Gross, James J. (2011). Beyond pleasure and pain? Emotion regulation and positive psychology. In K. M. Sheldon, T. B. Kashdan, M. F. Steger (Eds.), *Designing positive psychology: Taking stock and moving forward*, (pp. 89–100). New York, NY, US: Oxford University Press.

Tardif, T. Z., & Sternberg, R. J. (1988). What do we know about creativity? In R. J. Sternberg (Ed.), *The nature of creativity,* (pp. 429–440). New York: Cambridge University Press.

Tarnas, R. (1991). *The passion of the western mind: Understanding the ideas that have shaped our world view.* New York: Ballantine.

Tart, C. (Ed.). (1975). *Transpersonal Psychologies.* New York: Harper & Row.

Tashiro, T., Frazier, P., Humbert, R., & Smith, J. (2001, October). *Personal growth following romantic relationship breakups.* Poster presented at the 2001 Positive Psychology Summit, Washington, DC.

Tatarkiewicz, W. (1976). *Analysis of happiness.* The Hague: Martinus Nijhoff.

Tay, L., & Diener, E. (2011). Needs and subjective well-being around the world. *Journal of Personality and Social Psychology, 101*(2), 354–365. doi: 10.1037/a0023779

Taylor, C. (1989). *Sources of the self: The making of the modern identity.* Cambridge, MA: Harvard University Press.

Taylor. D. G., & Mireault, G. C. (2008). Mindfulness and self-regulation: A comparison of long-term to short-term meditators. *Journal of Transpersonal Psychology, 40*(1), 88–99.

Taylor, R. J., Chatters, L. M., Hardison, C. B., & Riley, A. (2001). Informal social support networks and subjective well-being among African Americans. *Journal of Black Psychology, 27*(4), 439–463. doi: 10.1177/0095798401027004004

Taylor, S. (2009). Beyond the pre/trans fallacy. *Journal of Transpersonal Psychology, 41*(1), 22–43.

Taylor, S., & Brown, J. (1988). Illusion and well-being: A social-psychological perspective on mental health. *Psychological Bulletin, 103*(2), 193–210.

Taylor, S., Kemeny, M., Reed, G., Bower, J., & Gruenewald, T. (2000). Psychological resources, positive illusions, and health. *American Psychologist, 55*(1), 99–109.

Teasdale, J. D., Segal, Z. V., Williams, J. M. G., Ridgeway, V. A., Soulsby, J. M., & Lau, M. A. (2000). Prevention of relapse/recurrence in major depression by mindfulness-based cognitive therapy. *Journal of Consulting and Clinical Psychology, 68*(4), 615–623.

Tedeschi, R. G., & Calhoun, L. G. (1995). *Trauma and transformation: Growing in the aftermath of suffering.* Thousand Oaks, CA: Sage Publications.

Telfer, E. (1980), *Happiness.* New York: St. Martin's Press.

Tellegen, A., & Atkinson, G. (1974). Openness to absorbing and self-altering experiences ("absorption"), a trait related to hypnotic susceptibility. *Journal of Abnormal Psychology, 83,* 268–277.

Tellegen, A., Lykken, D. T., Bouchard, T. J., Wilcox, K. J., Segal, N. L., & Rich, S. (1988). Personality similarity in twins reared apart and together. *Journal of Personality and Social Psychology, 54,* 1031–1039.

Tennov, D. (1998). *Love and Limerence: The experience of being in love.* NY: Scarboriough House.

Terkel, S. (1974). *Working: People talk about what they do all day and how they feel about what they do.* New York: Pantheon.

Terman, L. M., Buttenweiser, P., Ferguson, L. W., Johnson, W. B., & Wilson, D. P. (1938). *Psychological factors in marital happiness.* New York: McGraw-Hill.

Thayer, R. E., Newman, J. R., & McClain, T. M. (1994). Self-regulation of mood: Strategies for changing in a bad mood, raising energy, and reducing tension. *Journal of Personality and Social Psychology, 67,* 910–25.

Thomas, S. P. (1997). Distressing aspects of women's roles, vicarious stress, and health consequences. *Issues in Mental Health Nursing, 18*(6), 539–557. doi: 10.3109/01612849709010339

Thompson, S. (2009). The role of personal control in adaptive functioning. In C. R. Snyder & S. Lopez (Eds.). *Oxford handbook of positive psychology* (2nd ed.). (pp. 271–278). New York: Oxford University Press.

Thoreau, H. D. (1980). *Walden or, life in the woods and On the duty of civil disobedience.* New York: New American Library. (Original work published in 1854)

Thorne, A., McLean, K. C., & Lawrence, A. M. (2004). When remembering is not enough: Reflecting on self-defining memories in late adolescence. *Journal of Personality, 72*(3), 513–541.

Thorson, J. A., Powell, F. C., Sarmany-Schuller, I., & Hampes, W. P. (1997). Psychological health and sense of humor. *Journal of Clinical Psychology, 53*(6), 605–619.

Tindle, H., Chang, Y.-F., Kuller, L., Manson, J., Robinson, J., et al. (2009, August 10). Optimism, cynical hostility, and incident coronary heart disease and mortality in the women's health initiative. *Circulation, 120,* 656–662. doi: 10.1161/ CIRCULATIONAHA.108.827642

Tkach, C., & Lyubomirsky, S. (2006). How do people pursue happiness?: Relating personality, happiness-increasing strategies, and well-being. *Journal of Happiness Studies, 7,* 183–225. doi: 10.1007/s10902-005-4754-1

Togari, T., Yamazaki, Y., Takayama, T., Yamaki, C., & Nakayama, K. (2008). Follow-up study on the effects of sense of coherence on well-being after two years in Japanese university undergraduate students. *Personality and Individual Differences, 44*(6), 1335–1347.

Tomasello, M. (2009). Why we cooperate. Cambridge, MA, US: MIT Press, 2009.

Tov, W., Diener, E., Ng, W., Kesebir, P., & Harter, J. (2009). The social and economic context of peace and happiness. In R. S. Wyer, C-y. Chiu, & Y-y. Hong (Eds.), Understanding culture: Theory, research, and application (pp. 239–258). New York: Psychology Press.

Trappe, H.-J. (2010). The effects of music on the cardiovascular system and cardiovascular health. *Heart, 96,* 1868–1871.

Tricomi, E., Rangel, A., Camerer, C. & O'Doherty (2010, February 25). Neural evidence for inequity-averse social preferences. *Nature, 463,* 1089–1092.

Trotter, R. J. (1986, July). The mystery of mastery. *Psychology Today,* 32–38.

Trudeau, M. (2010, March 1). The aging brain is less quick, but more shrewed. NPR: National Public Radio, Washington, DC.

Tsai, Jeanne L. (2007, September). Ideal affect: Cultural causes and behavioral consequences. *Perspectives on Psychological Science, 2*(3), 242–259.

Tsai, Jeanne L., Knutson, Brian, & Fung, Helene H. (2006, February). Cultural variation in affect valuation. *Journal of Personality and Social Psychology, 90*(2), 288–307.

Tsapelas, I., Aron, A., & Orbuch, T. (2009). Marital boredom now predicts less satisfaction 9 years later. *Psychological Science, 20,* 543–545. doi: 10.1111/j.1467-9280.2009.02332.x

Tucak, I., & Nekic, M. (2007). Uloga Eriksonovih komponenti ličnosti u psihičkoj dobrobiti osoba srednje i starije dobi. The role of Erikson's personality components in the psychological well-being of midlife and older adults. *Suvremena Psihologija, 10*(1), 23–36.

Tugade, M., & Fredrickson, B. (2007). Regulation of positive emotions: Emotion regulation strategies that promote resilience. *Journal of Happiness Studies, 8*(3), 311–333.

Tugade, M., Fredrickson, B., & Barrett, L. (2005). Psychological resilience and positive emotional granularity: Examining the benfits of positive emotions on coping and health. *Journal of Personality: Special Issue: Emotions, Personality, and Health, 72*(6), 1161–1190.

Turner, N., Barling, J., & Zacharatos, A. (2002). *Positive psychology at work*. In C. R. Snyder & S. J. Lopez (Eds.), *Handbook of positive psychology* (pp. 715–728). New York: Oxford University Press.

Twenge, J. M., Zhang, L., & Im, C. (2004). It's beyond my control: A cross-temporal meta-analysis of increasing externality in locus of control. *Personality and Social Psychology Review, 8*(3), 308–319. doi: 10.1207/s15327957pspr0803_5

University of Michigan News Service. (2008). In sickness and in health: Caring for ailing spouse may prolong your life. Retrieved from http://ns.umich.edu/htdocs/releases/story.php?id=6859

Updegraff, J. A., & Suh, E. M. (2007). Happiness is a warm abstract thought: Self-construal abstractness and subjective well-being. *The Journal of Positive Psychology, 2*(1), 18–28. doi: 10.1080/17439760601069150

Urry, H. L., Nitschke, J. B., Dolski, I., Jackson, D. C., Dalton, K. M., Mueller, C. J., Rosenkranz, M. A., Ryff, C. D., Singer, B. H., & Davidson, R. J. (2004). Making a life worth living: Neural correlates of well-being. *Psychological Science, 15*(6), 367–372.

U.S. Department of Health and Human Services. (2000). *Healthy people 2000: National health promotion and disease prevention objectives* [DHHS Publication No. (PHS), 91–50213]. Washington, DC: U.S. Government Printing Office.

U.S. Religious Landscape Survey. (2008). Washington, DC: Pew Forum on Religion and Public Life.

United Way of America. (1992). *What lies ahead: A decade of decision*. Alexandria, VA: United Way Strategic Institute.

Vaillant, G. E. (1977). *Adaptation to life*. Boston: Little Brown.

Vaillant, G. E. (2000). Adaptive mental mechanisms: Their role in a positive psychology. *American Psychologist, 55*(1), 89–98.

Vaitl, D., Birbaumer, N., Gruzelier, J., Jamieson, G. A., Kotchoubey, B., et al. (2005, January). Psychobiology of Altered States of Consciousness. *Psychological Bulletin, 131*(1), 98–127.

Vallerand, Robert J. (2008, Febuary). On the psychology of passion: In search of what makes people's lives most worth living. *Canadian Psychology/Psychologie canadienne, 49*(1), 1–13.

Vallerand, R., Carbonneau, N., & Lafrenière, M.-A. (2010). On living life to the fullest: The role of passion. In R. Schwarzer & P. Frensch (Eds.), *Personality, human development, and culture: International perspectives on psychological science*. New York: Psychology Press.

Van Boven, L., & Gilovich, T. (2003, December). To Do or to Have? That Is the Question. *Journal of Personality and Social Psychology, 85*(6), 1193–1202.

Vandewater, E., Ostrove, J., & Stewart, A. (1997). Predicting women's well-being in midlife: The importance of personality development and social role involvements. *Journal of Personality and Social Psychology, 72*(5), 1147–1160.

Van Dierendonck, D. (2011). Servant Leadership: A review and synthesis. *Journal of Management, 37*(4), 1228–1261.

Van Horn, K. R., & Marques, J. C. (2000). Interpersonal relationships in Brazilian adolescents. *International Journal of Behavioral Development, 24*(2), 199–203.

Vecchio, G. M., Gerbino, M., Pastorelli, C., Giannetta, D. B., & Caprara, G. V. (2007). Multi-faceted self-efficacy beliefs as predictors of life satisfaction in late adolescence. *Personality and Individual Differences, 43*, 1807–1818.

Veenhoven, R. (1999). World database of happiness. Erasmus University, Rotterdam, Netherlands. Website: http://www.eur.nl/fsw/research/happiness

Veenhoven, R. (2008). Healthy happiness: Effects of happiness on physical health and the consequences for preventive health care. *Journal of Happiness Studies, 9*(3), 449–469. doi: 10.1007/s10902-006-9042-1

Viney, W., & King, D. B. (1998). *A history of psychology: Ideas and context* (2nd. ed.). Boston: Allyn & Bacon.

Vingerhoets, A. J. J. M., Cornelius, R. R., Van Heck, G. L., & Becht, M. C. (2000). Adult crying: A model and review of the literature. *Review of General Psychology 4*(4), 354–377.

Vitterso, J. (2004). Subjective well-being versus self-actualization: Using the flow-simplex to promote a conceptual clarification of subjective well-being. *Social Indicators Research, 65*(3), 299–331.

Vohs, K. D., Mead, N., & Goode, M. (2006, November). The psychological consequences of money. *Science, 314*(5802), 1154–1156.

Vohs, K. D., Mead, N., & Goode, M. (2008). Merely activating the concept of money changes personal and interpersonal behavior. *Current Directions in Psychological Science, 17*(3), 208–212.

Voss, M., Prakash, R., Erikson, K., Basak, C., & Chaddock, L., et al. (2010). Plasticity of brain networks in a randomized intervention trail of exercise training in older adults. *Frontiers in Aging Neuroscience, 2,* 32. doi: 10.3389/fnagi.2010.00032

Wagner, U., Gais, S., Haider, H., Verlanger, R., & Born, J. (2004, January 22). Sleep inspires insight. *Nature, 427,* 352–355.

Wahba, M. A., & Bridwell, L. G. (1976). Maslow reconsidered: A review of research on the need hierarchy theory. *Organizational Behavior and Human Performance, 15,* 212–240.

Wainwright, N. W. J., Surtees, P. G., Wareham, N. J., & Harrison, B. D. W. (2007). Psychosocial factors and asthma in a community sample of older adults. *Journal of Psychosomatic Research, 62*(3), 357–361.

Walker, C. J. (2010). Experiencing flow: Is doing it together better than doing it alone? *The Journal of Positive Psychology, 5*(1), 3–11.

Walker, C. P. (2003). Life is pleasant and memory helps to keep it that way! *Review of General Psychology, 7*(2), 203–210. doi: 10.1037/1089-2680.7.2.203

Walker, L. J., & Hennig, K. H. (2004). Differing conceptions of moral exemplarity: Just, brave, and caring. *Journal of Personality and Social Psychology, 86*(4), 629–647. doi: 10.1037/0022-3514.86.4.629

Walker, W. R., Skowronski, J. J., & Thompson, C. P. (2003). *Life is pleasant—and memory helps to keep it that way! Review of General Psychology, 7*(2), 203–210.

Wallace, B. A., & Shapiro, S. L. (2006). Mental Balance and Well-Being: Building Bridges Between Buddhism and Western Psychology. *American Psychologist, 61*(7), 690–701.

Wallas, G. (1926). *The art of thought.* New York: Harcourt, Brace.

Wang, W.-Z., Tao, R., Niu, Y.-J., Chen, Q., Jia, J.-P. et al. (2010). Preliminary proposed diagnostic criteria of pathological Internet use. *Chinese Mental Health Journal, 23*(12), 890–894.

Wapnick, K. (1980). Mysticism and schizophrenia. In R. Woods (Ed.), *Understanding mysticism.* Garden City, NY: Image Books.

Warr, P. (1999). Well-being and the workplace. In D. Kahneman, E. Diener, & N. Schwarz (Eds.), *Well-being: The foundations of hedonic psychology* (pp. 392–412). New York: Russell Sage.

Washburn, M. (2003). *Embodied spirituality in a sacred world.* Albany: SUNY Press.

Waterman, A. S. (1993). Two concepts of happiness: Contrasts of personal expressiveness (Eudaimonia) and hedonic enjoyment. *Journal of Personality and Social Psychology, 64*(4), 678–691.

Waterman, A. S. (2008, October). Reconsidering happiness: A eudaimonist's perspective. *The Journal of Positive Psychology, 3*(4), 234–252.

Watkins, P., Van Gelder, M., & Frias, A. (2009). Furthering the science of gratitude. In C. R. Snyder & S. Lopez (Eds.), *Oxford handbook of positive psychology* (2nd ed., pp. 437–446). New York: Oxford University Press.

Watson, D., & Clark, L. A. (1984). Negative affectivity: The disposition to experience aversive emotional states. *Psychological Bulletin, 96,* 465–490.

Watson, D., & Naragon, K. (2009). Positive affectivity: The disposition to experience positive affective states. In C. R. Snyder & S. Lopez (Eds.), *Oxford handbook of positive psychology* (2nd ed., pp. 207–216). New York: Oxford University Press.

Watson, D., & Pennebaker, J. W. (1989). Health complaints, stress, and distress: Exploring the central role of negative affectivity. *Psychological Review, 96,* 234–254.

Waugh, C. E., & Fredrickson, B. L. (2006). Nice to know you: Positive emotional, self-other overlap, and complex understanding in the formation of a new relationship. *The Journal of Positive Psychology, 1*(2), 93–106. doi: 10.1080/17439760500510569

Webster, J. D. (2003). An exploratory analysis of a self-assessed wisdom scale. *Journal of Adult Development, 10*(1), 13–22.

Webster, J., Trevino, L. K., & Ryan, L. (1993). The dimensionality and correlates of flow in human computer interactions. *Computers in Human Behavior 9*(4), 411–426.

Wehmeyer, M. L. (1996). Self-determination as an educational outcome: Why is it important to children, youth and adults with disabilities? In D. J. Sands & M. L. Wehmeyer (Eds.), *Self-determination across the life span: Independence and choice for people with disabilities* (pp. 17–36). Baltimore: Paul H. Brookes.

Wehmeyer, M., Little, T., & Sergent, J. (2009). Self-determination. In S. Lopez & C. R. Snyder (Eds.) Oxford handbook of positive psychology (pp. 357–366). NY: Oxford University Press.

Weinstein, N. D. (1980). Unrealistic optimism about future life events. *Journal of Personality and Social Psychology, 39*(5), 806–820.

Weitan, W. (2005). *Psychology: Themes and variations* (6th ed.). Belmont, CA.: Wadsworth.

Welch, I. D., Tate, G. A., & Medeiros, D. C. (1987). *Self-actualization: An annotated bibliography of theory and research.* New York: Garland Publishing.

Wells, A. (1988). Self-esteem and optimal experience. In M. Csikszentmihalyi & I. Csikszentmihalyi (Eds.), *Optimal experience* (pp. 327–341). Cambridge: Cambridge University Press.

Welwood, J. (1997). *Love and awakening: Discovering the sacred path of intimate relationship.* New York: Harper Collins.

Welzel, C., & Inglehart, R. (2010). Agency, values, and well-being: A developmental model. *Social Indicators Research, 97*(1), 43–63.

Werner, E. E. (1995). Resilience in development. *Current Directions in Psychological Science, 4*(3), 81–85.

Westerhof, G., & Barrett, A. (2005). Age identity and subjective well-being: A comparison of the United States and Germany. *The Journals of Gerontology, 60B,* S129–S136.

Whalen, S. P., & Csikszentmihalyi, M. (1991, May). Putting flow theory into educational practice: The key schools' flow activities room. *Report to the Benton Center for Curriculum and Instruction, University of Chicago,* 1–39.

White, M., & Epston, D. (1990). *Narrative means to therapeutic ends.* New York: W. W. Norton.

White, R. (1959). Motivation reconsidered: The concept of competence. *Psychological Review, 66,* 297–323.

Whitfield, K., Markham, H., Stanley, S., & Blumberg, S. (2001). *Fighting for your African-American marriage.* San Francisco: Jossey-Bass.

Whitman, D. S. (2009). Emotional intelligence and leadership in organizations: A meta-analytic test of process mechanisms. *FIU Electronic Theses and Dissertations. Paper 113.*http://digitalcommons.fiu.edu/etd/113

Whittaker, A. E., & Robitschek, C. (2001). Multidimensional family functioning: Predicting personal growth initiative. *Journal of Counseling Psychology, 48*(4), 420–427.

Whittington, B. L., & Scher, S. J. (2010). Prayer and subjective well-being: An examination of six different types of prayer. *International Journal for the Psychology of Religion, 20*(1), 59–68.

Wierzbicka, A. (1986). Human emotions: Universal or culture-specific? *American Anthropologist, 88,* 584–594.

Wilkinson, R., & Pickett, K. (2009). *The Spirit Level: Why Greater Equality Makes Societies Stronger.* NY: Bloomsbury.

Wilson, S. R., & Spencer, R. C. (1990). Intense personal experiences: Subjective effects, interpretations, and after-effects. *Journal of Clinical Psychology, 46*(5), 565–573.

Wirtz, D., Chiu, C., Diener, E., & Oishi, S. (2009). What constitutes a good life? Cultural differences in the role of positive and negative affect in subjective well-being. *Journal of Personality, 77*(4), 1167–1193. doi: 10.111/j.1467-6494.2009.00578.x

Wirtz, D., Kruger, J., Scollon, C. N., & Deiner, E. (2003). What to do on spring break? The role of predicted, on-line, and remembered experience in future choice. *Psychological Science, 14*(5), 520–524.

Wisner, B. L., Jones, B., & Gwin, D. (2010). School-based meditation practices for adolescents: A resource for strengthening self-regulation, emotional coping, and self-esteem. *Children and Schools, 32*(3), 150–159.

Williams, D., Spencer, M., Jackson, J., & Ashmore, R. (1999). Race, stress, and physical health: The role of group identity. In R. Contrada & R. Ashmore (Eds.), *Self, social identity and physical health* (pp. 71–100). New York: Oxford University Press.

Williams, J. M. (Ed.). (1993). *Applied sport psychology: Personal growth to peak performance.* Mountain View, CA: Mayfield.

Williams, J. M., & Krane, V. (1993). Psychological characteristics of peak performance. In J. M. Williams (Ed.), *Applied sport psychology: Personal growth to peak performance* (pp. 137–147). Mountain View, CA: Mayfield.

Williamson, G., & Christie, J. (2009). Aging well in the 21st Century: Challenges and opportunities. In C. R. Snyder & S. Lopez (Eds.), *Oxford handbook of positive psychology* (2nd ed., pp. 165–170). New York: Oxford University Press.

Wink, P., & Helson, R. (1997). Practical and transcendental wisdom: Their nature and some longitudinal findings. *Journal of Adult Development, 4,* 1–15.

Witter, R., Stock, W. A., Okun, M. A., & Haring, M. J. (1985). Religion and subjective well-being in adulthood: A quantitative synthesis. *Review of Religious Research, 26,* 332–42.

Witters, D. (2011, January 4). Americans happier, less stressed in 2010. Retrieved from http://www.gallup.com.

Wohl, M., DeShea, J. A., Wahkinney, L., & L., R. (2008). Looking within: Measuring state self-forgiveness and its relationship to psychological well-being. *Canadian Journal of Behavioural Science/Revue canadienne des sciences du comportement, 40*(1), 1–10.

Wong, P. (1998). Implicit theories of meaningful life and the development of the Personal Meaning Profile (PMP). In P. T. P. Wong & P. Fry (Eds.), *The human quest for meaning: A handbook of psychological research and clinical applications* (pp. 111–140). Mahwah, NJ: Lawrence Erlbaum Associates, Inc., Publishers.

Wong, P. T. P. (2009). Meaning therapy: An integrative and positive existential psychotherapy. *Journal of Contemporary Psychotherapy, 40*(2), 85–93.

Wong, P. (2009b). Chinese positive psychology: What is the ancient Chinese secret to resilience and happiness? *International Network on Personal Meaning.* Retrieved April 15, 2011 from http://meaning.ca/archives/archive/art_Chinese-PP_P_Wong.htm

Wong. P. (2011). Toward a dual-system model of what makes life worth living. Retrieved April 20, 2011 from http://www.drpaulwong.com/index.php?option=com_content&view=article&id=140: towards-a-dual-system-model-of-what-makes-life-worth-living&catid=36:articles&Itemid=66

Wood, A., Froh, J., & Geraghty, A. (2010). Gratitude and well-being: A review and theoretical integration. *Clinical Psychology Review, 30*(7), 890–905.

Wood, A. M., Linley, A. P., Malthy, J., Baliousis, M., & Joseph, S. (2008). The authentic personality: A theoretical and empirical conceptualization and the development of the authenticity scale. *Journal of Counseling Psychology, 55*(3), 385–399. doi: 10.1037/0022-0167.55.3.385

Wood, A. M., Maltby, J., Gillett, R., Linley, P. A., & Joseph, S. (2008). The role of gratitude in the development of social support, stress, and depression: Two longitudinal studies. *Journal of Research in Personality, 42,* 854–871.

Wood, A., & Terrier, N. (2010). Positive clinical psychology: A new vision and strategy for integrating research and practice. *Clinical Psychology Review.* doi: 10.1016/j.cpr.2010.06.003

Wood, J. V., Perunovic, W. Q. E., & Lee, J. W. (2009). Positive self-statements: Power for some, peril for others. *Psychological Science, 20,* 860–866.

Wood, W., Rhodes, N., & Whelan, M. (1989). Sex differences in positive well-being. A consideration of emotional style and marital status. *Psychological Bulletin, 106,* 249–264.

Woods, R. (Ed.). (1980). *Understanding mysticism.* NY: Image Books.

Woolfolk, R. L. (2002). The power of negative thinking: Truth, melancholia, and the tragic sense of life. *Journal of Theoretical & Philosophical Psychology, 22*(1), 19–27.

Wordsworth, W. (1988). In S. Gill (Ed.), *William Wordsworth.* New York: Oxford University Press. (Original published in 1798)

World Health Organization. (1948). *Constitution of the World Health Organization.* Geneva, Switzerland: Author.

Wright, J. J., Sadlo, G., & Stew, G. (2007). Further explorations into the conundrum of flow process. *Journal of Occupational Science, 14*(3), 136–144.

Wrosch, C., Bauer, I., & Schier, M. F. (2005). Regret and quality of life across the adult life span: The influence of disengagement and available future goals. *Psychology and Aging, 20,* 657–670.

Wrosch, C., Bauer, I., Miller, G. E., & Lupien, S. (2007). Regret intensity, diurnal cortisol secretion, and physical health in older individuals: Evidence for directional effects and protective factors. *Psychology and Aging*, *22*, 319–330.

Wrzesniewski, A., McCauley, C., Rozin, P., & Schwartz, B. (1997). Jobs, careers, and callings: People's relations to their work. *Journal of Research in Personality*, *31*(1), 21–33.

Wulff, D. (2004). Mystical experience. In L. Cardena, & S. Krippner (Eds.) *Varieties of Anomalous Experience: Examining the Scientific Evidence*. Washington, DC: American Psychological Association.

Wynd, C., & Ryan-Wegner, N. (2004). Factors predicting health behaviors among army reserve, active duty army, and civilian hospital employees. *Military Medicine*, *169*(12), 942–947.

Xu, A., Xie, X., Liu, W., Xia, Y., & Dalin, L. (2007). Chinese family strengths and resiliency. *Marriage & Family Review*, *41*, 143–156.

Xu, J. (2006). Subjective well-being as predictor of mortality, heart disease, and obesity: Prospective evidence from the Alameda Country study (California). *Dissertation Abstracts International: Section B: The Sciences and Engineering* (66, 7–B, p. 3671).

Yalom, I. D. (1980). *Existential psychotherapy*. New York: Basic Books.

Yang, K. S. (1982). Causal attributions of academic success and failure and their affective consequences. *Chinese Journal of Psychology (Taiwan)*, *24*, 65–83. (Abstract only in English)

Yang, Y. (2008). Social inequalities in happiness in the United States, 1972 to 2004: An age-period-cohort analysis. *American Sociological Review*, *73*(2), 204–227.

Yip, W., Subramanian, S. V., Mitchell, A. D., Lee, D. T., Wang, J., & Kawachi, I. (2007). Does social capital enhance health and well-being?: Evidence from rural China. *Social Science & Medicine*, *64*, 35–49. doi: 10.1016/j.socscimed.2006.08.027

Yong, E. (2009, September 7). Secrets of the centenarians: Life begins at 100. *New Scientist*, Issue 2724. Retrieved from http://www.newscientist.com/article/mg20327241.300-secrets-of-the-centenarians-life-begins-at-100

Youssef, C., & Luthans, F. (2011). Positive psychological capital in the workplace: Where we are and where we need to go. In K. M. Sheldon, T. B. Kashdan, & M. F. Steger (Eds.), *Designing positive psychology: Taking stock and moving forward* (pp. 351–364). New York: Oxford University Press.

Zagorski, N. (2008, Spring/Summer). Music on the mind. *Hopkins Medicine*. Retrived from http://hopkinsmedicine.org/hmn/s08/feature4.cfm

Zammit, C. (2001). The art of healing: A journey through cancer. Implications for art therapy. *Art Therapy: Journal of the American Art Therapy Association*, *18*(1), 27–36.

Zatorre, R. J., & Peretz, I. (Eds.). (2001). *The biological foundations of music*. New York: New York Academy of Science.

Zeidan, F., Gordon, N. S., Merchant, J., & Goolkasian, P. (2010). The effects of brief mindfulness meditation training on experimentally induced pain. *The Journal of Pain*, *11*(3), 199–209.

Zell, Anne L. (2008). Pride and humility: Possible mediators of the motivating effect of praise. *Dissertation Abstracts International: Section B: The Sciences and Engineering*, *68*(9-B), 63–96.

Zenter, M. (2005). Ideal mate personality concepts and compatibility in close relationships: A longitudinal analysis. *Journal of Personality and Social Psychology*, *89*(2), 242–256.

Zhong, C.-B., & Liljenquist, K. (2006, September). Washing away your sins: Threatened morality and physical cleansing. *Science*, *313*, 1451–1452.

Zhong, C.-B., Strejcek, B., & Sivanathan, N. (2010). A clean self can render harsh moral judement. *Journal of Experimental Social Psychology*, *46*(5), 859–862.

Zhou, X., Sedikides, C., Wilschut, T., & Ding Guo, G. (2008). Counteracting loneliness: On the restorative function of nostalgia. *Psychological Science*, *19*(10), 1023–1029.

Zimmer, M. R., Little, S. K., & Griffths, J. S. (1999). The impact of nostalgic proneness and need for uniqueness on consumer perception of historical branding strategies. *American Marketing Association Conference Proceedings*, *10*, 259–267.

Name Index

Aaker, J., 184
Abdel-Khalek, A., 75
Acevedo, B. P., 112
Ackerman, S., 179
Adams, A., 168
Adams, C. E, 240
Adams, G., 66
Adány, R., 195
Ader, R., 130
Adler, A., 6, 18, 118, 132, 172, 206, 219, 256, 267
Adler, J. M., 189
Adler, M., 237
Adler, N. L., 105
Affleck, G., 193
Agrigoroaei, S., 141
Ahlström, R., 195
Ahmad, N., 240
Ai, A. L., 232
Albaugh, M., 68
Alfermann, D., 80
Algoe, S., 9, 32, 115, 237, 284
Allemand, M., 238
Allen, D. N., 38
Allen, J., 88
Allen, L., 80
Allport, G., 255, 284
Alper, M., 253
Altenmüller, E., 162
Alvarez, M., 292
Alvarez, S., 85
Amabile, T. M., 166
Amato, P. R., 103
Ambady, N., 278
Amico, J., 135
An, J., 179
Anderson, A., 54
Anderson, E., 29
Anderson, N. D., 92
Anderson, R., 140, 247

Anderson, S. L., 66
Andreasen, N. C., 172
Andrews, F. M., 52
Andrews, P., 75
Angel, E., 210
Angeles, L., 118
Anglin, L. P., 91
Ano, G. G., 233
Ansbacher, H. L., 206
Anthony, E. J., 190
Antonovsky, A., 194, 195, 287
Arch, J., 144
Ardelt, M., 180, 201, 206
Argyle, M., 8, 67, 80, 81, 102, 182, 183, 230, 245
Arieti, S., 166
Aristotle, 11–12, 29, 43
Arndt, J., 43, 213
Arnold, M. L., 179
Aron, A., 102, 112, 115
Arora, R., 66, 275
Asakawa, K., 21
Ashby, F. G., 25
Ashe, D. D., 88
Ashmore, R., 131
Askegaard, S., 66
Aspinwall, L., 57
Assad, K., 114
Assagioli, R., 256
Asser, S. M., 231
Astaire, F., 81
Atkinson, G., 88
Atkinson, M., 162
Aubin, E., 179
Austenfield, J. L., 148
Austin, J. H., 252, 253
Averill, J., 41, 159, 171
Avolio, B., 266
Aziz, R., 246
Azmitia, M., 292

Bacon, F., 15
Baer, R. A., 92, 144, 251
Bailey, T. C., 57
Baker, K., 136
Balajti, I., 195
Baltes, P., 140, 184, 201, 202, 203, 206
Bandura, A., 58, 142
Banning, J. H., 262
Bard, K. A., 170
Barefoot, J., 141
Bargh, J. A., 24, 196
Barling, J., 263
Barnes, L., 131
Barnes, M. L., 104, 106
Barnes, S., 113
Barrett, A., 189
Barrett, L. F., 24, 193
Barrett, W., 209
Barrios-Choplin, B., 162
Barron, F., 165, 167, 170, 196
Barsky, A. J., 144
Bass, B., 266
Bassett, C., 202
Batcho, K. I., 75
Batson, C. D., 240
Bauer, I., 139
Bauer, N., 68
Baumeister, R. F., 15, 37, 56, 69, 128
Bauminger, N., 111
Baumrind, D., 118
Beach, S., 115
Beals, K. P., 111
Beard, K., 85
Beattie, R., 80
Becht, M. C., 140
Becker, D., 294
Bedard, J., 154
Behrens, B., 124

Belsky, J., 106
Bender, J., 181
Benedict, R., 271
Benet, M., 173
Bennett, D., 131
Bennett, H. Z., 97
Bennis, W., 266
Benson, H., 142, 144, 232
Benson, P. L., 31, 229
Bentham, J., 15
Berg, I. K., 268
Bergan, A., 233
Berking, M., 42
Berkman, L. F., 131
Bernstein, J. H., 80
Berry, D. S., 137
Berscheid, E., 111
Best, S., 230
Beuys, J. Z., 170
Bhattacharyya, M., 103
Bijlani, R. L., 143
Birmingham, W., 104, 133
Bíró, E., 195
Bishop, A. J., 184
Bishop, S. R., 92
Biswas-Diener, R., 62, 269, 291
Black, S., 146
Blackstone, T., 114
Blanchflower, D., 182
Blane, D., 193
Bleil, M., 132
Blizinsky, K., 279
Block, J. H., 178
Block, J., 59, 178
Bloom, J. R., 131
Blumenthal, J., 272
Bock, A. V., 196
Boden, J. M., 69
Boehm, J. K., 261
Bohart, A. C., 223
Bok. S., 32, 276
Bolling, S. F., 232
Bonaparte, N., 265
Bond, F., 291
Boniwell, I., 28
Bonnefon, J. F., 139
Boomsma, D. I., 80
Boorstein, S., 246–247
Booth, A., 111
Bouchard, T. J., 26

Boyle, P., 131
Bradbury, T. N., 108, 114
Brancaccio, D., 279
Brandtstader, J., 181, 184
Brannon, L., 129, 142
Bratslavsky, E., 37
Braud, W. G., 140, 247
Braun, A., 161
Brdar, I., 31
Breen, W. E., 193
Brennan, M., 85
Brenner, B. R., 35
Breznitz, S., 149
Bridwell, L. G., 220, 221
Brief, A. P., 260
Brinkerhoff, M. B., 93
Briñol, P., 129
Brinthaupt, T. M., 85
Brockmann, H., 183
Brockway, W., 160
Brown, J., 58
Brown, K. W., 9, 64, 80, 92,
    144, 285
Brown, S., 81, 146
Brunell, A., 113
Brunhart, S. M., 57, 69
Brunner, S., 95
Bryant, F., 94, 187
Buchman, A., 131
Buchowski, M., 137
Buckingham, M., 29, 263
Buettner, D., 146, 147
Bugental, J., 222
Bunderson, J. S., 262
Bundrick, C. M., 218
Burns, G., 291
Burpee, L., 91, 113
Burri, A., 41
Burrows, C. L., 183
Burt, J., 119
Buss, D. M., 6, 101, 108
Buttenweiser, P., 107
Buxant, C., 230
Byrom, T., 28

Cacioppo, J. T., 10, 134
Cain, D. J., 19, 222, 223, 267
Calhoun, L. G., 235
Calvin, J., 262
Cameron, C. L., 149

Cameron, D., 279
Campbell, A., 56, 80
Campbell, J., 189
Campbell-Sills, L., 193
Campos, B., 108
Cantor, N., 35, 43, 235
Caprara, G. V., 28
Carbonneau, N., 157
Carey, M. P., 195
Carlo, G., 122
Carlson, L. E., 92, 143, 144
Carlyle, T., 265
Carmody, J., 144
Carrere, S., 121
Carroll, J., 67
Carstensen, L. L., 67, 112, 183,
    184, 185
Carton, J. S., 118
Caruso, D., 40, 41, 42
Carver, C., 28, 56, 57, 141
Carver, G. W., 216
Caspi, A., 108, 178
Cassel, J., 131
Cassell, E., 239
Cassem, N. H., 149
Castenada, C., 177
Cather, W., 288
Cavanagh, M., 269
C'deBaca, J., 247
Ceja, L., 90
Chamberlain, T. J., 229
Chambers, D., 130
Chamorro-Premuzic, T., 224
Chan, M., 145, 146
Chandler, E. N., 232
Chang, B. H., 144
Chang, E. C., 67, 119
Change, R., 293
Charlton, B., 230
Charness, N., 153–156
Chartrand, T. L., 196
Chaudieu, I., 189, 190
Cheavens, J. S., 36, 56, 57, 73
Cheng, S-T., 66
Chenier, T., 40
Chenot, D., 44
Cherkas, L., 41
Chesney, M., 130
Cheung, F. M., 122
Cheung, S. F., 122

Chi, M. T., 154
Chiao, J., 278, 279
Chirban, 1986, 248
Choo, P., 130
Chow, S., 9, 32, 284
Christakis, N., 271
Christensen, K., 146
Christie, J., 183
Christopher, J. C., 292, 294
Churchill, W., 265
Ciarrocchi, J. W., 230
Cicoria, T., 171
Clark, A. E., 265
Clark, M. P., 47
Clarke, S. G., 89
Clary, E. G., 273
Clayton, V., 200, 201
Cleary, T. S., 245
Clifton, D., 29, 30, 263–264
Cloninger, C. R., 31
Coan, R. W., 46, 47
Cocteau, J., 160
Coffman, C., 29, 263
Cohan, S., 193
Cohen, A., 146
Cohen, N., 130
Cohen, R., 279
Cohen, S., 80, 131
Cohler, B. J., 190
Cohn, M., 37, 38, 39, 73
Coleman, M., 119
Coleridge, S., 17, 243
Collins, A. L., 89
Collins, J., 69
Collins, N., 108
Colvin, C. R., 59
Compton, R., 56
Compton, W. C., 43, 58, 72, 80,
    143, 221, 246, 292, 293, 295
Conde, G., 85, 88
Conger, K. J., 119
Conger, R. D., 114, 119
Connor, K., 193
Converse, P. E., 80
Cook, S. W., 222
Cook-Greuter, S. R., 202
Cooney, T., 179
Cooper, A., 83
Corbin, J. M., 128
Cornelius, R. R., 140

Cornish, K., 43
Cosma, J. B., 85
Costa, P. T., 53
Coumans, N., 41
Cousins, N., 136
Cowen, E. L., 287
Coyne, J. C., 104, 131
Cramer, P., 196
Crandall, R., 221
Crapo, R. H., 278
Craske, M., 144
Creswell, J. D., 144
Crooker, K. J., 51
Crowson, J. J., Jr., 141
Crumpler, C., 29
Csikszentmihalyi, I. S., 84, 86
Csikszentmihalyi, M., 2, 9, 20, 67,
    82–87, 88, 89, 90, 94, 97, 170,
    208, 221, 262, 269
Cummings, E. E., 244
Cunha, M., 141
Cunningham, M. H., 111
Cupitt, D., 256

Dahlsgaard, K., 292
Dalai Lama, 229
Dalbert, C., 66
Dalin, L., 122
Dalla-Bella, S., 161
Daly, M., 279
Danner, D., 145
Danoff-Burg, S., 149
d'Aquili, E. G., 253
Darbes, L., 130
Dautovich, N. D., 144
Davidson, J., 25
Davidson, R., 25, 143, 253, 293
DaVinci, L., 154, 172, 265
Davis, C., 189, 193
Davis, F., 75
Davis, M., 148
Davydov, D. M., 189, 190
Day, I., 232
de Botton, A., 169
De Fruyt, F., 140
de Geus, E. J. C., 80
de Groot, A., 154
De Martino, R., 209
de Moor, M. H. M., 80
de Pree, M., 216

de Shazer, S., 268
de Silva, P., 250
de St. Aubin, E., 179, 180
de Vries, M., 40
Deaton, A., 66
DeCaprio, L., 163
Deci, E., 33, 34, 43, 44, 57, 128,
    213, 214, 215
DeJong, T., 257
Delega, V. J., 111
Delizonna, L. L., 91
Deneke, E., 230
Depp, C., 183
DeShea, J. A., 239
Deshpande, S. P., 85
Dewey, J., 159, 269, 288
Diamond, A., 179, 180
Diaz-Loving, R., 122
Dickens, C. M., 133
Dickerhoof, R., 138
Dickerson, S. S., 25, 102
Diehl, M., 7
Diener McGavran, M. B., 102, 118
Diener, C., 275, 278
Diener, E., 4, 9, 27, 33, 34, 42, 51,
    52, 53, 54, 55, 56, 58, 62, 66,
    67, 68, 69, 70, 71, 72, 80, 102,
    103, 107, 130, 145, 146, 185,
    261, 269, 275, 276, 278, 279,
    284, 288, 291
Diener, M., 118, 278
Dienstbier, R., 225
Diessner, R., 31, 291
Dietrich, A., 129
Dik, B. J., 262
Dillbeck, M. C., 252
Dillon, K., 136
DiMatteo, M. R., 56
Ding Guo, G., 75
Dinoff, B. L., 147
Dippel, A., 42
Dissanayake, E., 163
Djikic, M., 91
Dobkin, P. L., 144
Doell, K., 156
Dolski, I., 25, 43
Domar, A. D., 131
Dominguez, M. M., 118
Donahue, M. J., 229, 255
Donne, J., 259

Donnellan, M., 114
Doyle, W. J., 130
Draguns, J. G., 122
Drakopoulos, S. A., 220
Drigotas, S. M., 115
Du Pre, A., 137
Dua, J., 131
Duckworth, A. L., 4, 157, 158, 268
Dunfield, K., 7
Dunkle, R. E., 232
Dunn, D., 190
Dunn, H., 127
Dunne, J., 25
Dunning, D., 69
Durand-Bush, N., 156
Dusek, J. A., 144
Dweck, C., 192, 195, 214, 289
Dy-Liaacco, G. S., 230
Dyrenforth, P. S., 61
Dzuka, J., 66

Easterlin, R., 65
Ebersole, P., 245
Edmonson, W., 165
Eid, M., 26
Ein-Mor, E., 146
Einstein, A., 156, 172, 216, 284
Eisenkraft, N., 91
Eisenlohr-Moul, T., 129
Elangovan, A. R., 262
Eliot, T. S., 156
Ellenberger, H. F., 210
Elliot, T., 190
Elliott-Moskwa, E. S., 107, 214
Emerson, R. W., 17, 288
Emmons, R. A., 29, 34, 35, 36, 52, 67, 233, 235, 236, 237, 238, 241, 242, 243, 246, 284
Engler, B., 210
Enright, R. D., 237, 238
Epel, E. S., 128
Epstein, R. M., 143
Epston, D., 268
Erasmus, D., 15
Erber, M. W., 31
Erber, R., 31
Erickson, J., 80
Ericson, M., 162
Ericsson, K. A., 153–156

Erikson, E., 145, 178, 179, 180, 201–202
Erikson, J. M., 179
Eshelman, E. R., 148
Evans, A., 74
Evans, D. R., 92
Exline, J. J., 238, 240
Eyre, R. N., 37

Fackelman, K., 25
Fagan-Jones, S., 224
Fagley, N., 237
Fan, J., 88
Farrell, P. A., 25, 80
Fava, G. A., 268
Fave, A. D., 86, 90
Fefer, M., 105
Fehr, B., 106
Feingold, A., 66
Feist, J., 129, 142
Feldt, T., 195
Feltz, D. E., 97
Fenchel, G. H., 98
Ferrer, J. N., 246
Feshbach, N., 132
Field, T. M., 134
Filyer, R., 179
Fincham, F., 58, 114, 115, 224
Finkel, E. J., 115
Finkenauer, C., 37
Fisher, L., 134
Fitzpatrick, M. R., 4
Fitzpatrick, S. M., 162
Flaxman, P., 291
Fletcher, K., 143
Florida, R., 169, 274
Flory, J., 132
Floyd, R. K., 73
Folkman, S., 148, 234
Fordyce, M. W., 52, 71–72
Forgas, J. P., 69
Fowers, B. J., 7, 29, 117, 205, 285, 292, 294
Fowler, R., 255
Fowler, S., 271
Frank, J. B., 268
Frank, J. D., 268
Frank, R. H., 64
Frankl, V. E., 210–211, 235, 287
Frazier, P., 117

Frederick, C., 128
Fredrickson, B. L., 9, 19, 23, 32, 37, 38, 39, 40, 54, 70, 73, 129, 193, 240, 284
Freedman, J. M., 270
Freedman, S., 238, 239
Frenz, A. W., 195
Freud, S., 6, 14, 18, 104, 132, 156, 160, 167, 172, 196, 206, 216
Frey, B. S., 276
Frias, A., 237
Friedler, S., 137
Friesen, W., 145
Frijda, N., 23, 38
Frisch, M. B., 47
Froese, A., 149
Froh, J., 88, 237
Fromm, E., 207–208, 209, 210, 212, 256
Fuchs, E., 67
Fujita, F., 59, 66, 107
Fullagar, C. J., 85
Fung, H. H., 32
Furnham, A., 41, 224
Furr, M. R., 56

Gable, S., 103, 110, 115, 117, 196, 237
Gagnon, J. C., 269
Gainor, K. A., 35
Gallagher, M. W., 58, 88, 224
Gallois, P., 252
Galway, W. T., 86, 98
Gandhi, M. K., 156, 266
Ganong, L. H., 119
Gardner, H., 166, 172
Garfield, C. A., 97
Garland, E. L., 38
Garmezy, N., 119, 190
Gates, B., 265
Gay, V. P., 4
Gaynor, M. P., 137
Gentry, W. D., 143
George, J. M., 260
George, L. K., 229, 230, 231, 233, 236
Geraghty, A., 237
Gergen, K. J., 187, 288
Gergen, M. M., 187, 288
Gernsback, H., 243
Gerstorf, D., 66
Gertsen, M. C., 66

Gestwicki, R., 139
Ghani, J. A., 85
Gianaros, P., 132
Gilbert, D., 36, 37, 56
Gilbert, P., 75
Gillham, J., 181
Gilovich, T. D., 64, 139
Girard, M., 238
Glancy, M., 80
Glaser, R., 134, 138
Glasser, W., 269
Glenn, N. D., 103
Glock, C., 245
Gohm, C. L., 66
Goldberger, A. L., 137
Goldbourt, U., 134
Goldman, B., 213, 214
Goldstein, E., 245
Goleman, D., 250
Gonzaga, G. C., 108
Gonzales-Molina, G., 263
Gonzales-Roma, V., 259
Goode, M., 64
Goodwin, J., 146
Goolkasian, P., 144
Gorchoff, S. M., 121
Gordon, N. S., 144
Gore, A., 272
Goretzki, M., 246
Gorman, M. O., 103
Gorman, R. M., 129
Gosnell, C., 115
Gottheil, E., 131
Gottlieb, M., 225
Gottman, J. M., 103, 105, 109, 112,
    113, 121, 122, 123–124
Gottman, J. S., 112, 113, 123–124
Grafanaki, S., 85
Graham, M., 156
Grant, A. M., 7
Grant, A., 269
Grant, W. T., 196
Grape, C., 162
Greeley, A. M., 241
Green, A., 251
Green, E., 251
Greenberg, L. S., 223
Greene, K., 111
Greenhouse, J., 141
Greenspan, M. J., 97

Greitmeyer, T., 224
Greve, W., 189, 192
Grewen, K., 135
Griffin, S., 52
Griffiths, R. R., 254
Griffiths, J. S., 75
Gropman, D., 249
Gross, J. J., 240
Gross, J., 32, 42, 43
Grossman, P., 143
Groth, G. E., 108
Groves, J., 13
Grühn, D., 7, 240
Guadagno, J., 88, 205, 241
Guignon, C. B., 212, 294
Guilford, J. P., 166, 170
Gundlach, J., 71
Gustafson, A. B., 25
Gutscher, H., 68
Gwaltney, J. M., Jr., 130
Gwin, D., 144

Hackett T. P., 149
Hackman, J. R., 267
Hagemann, D., 129
Hagerty, M. R., 220, 276
Hahlweg, K., 109
Haidt, J., 19, 31, 115, 237, 241,
    242, 256
Halford, W. K., 124
Hall, C. A., 229
Hall, J., 115
Halpern, S., 137
Hammerman-Rozenberg, R., 146
Hampes, W. P., 137
Han, S., 85
Handelsman, M., 225
Hansenne, M., 42
Hansson, L., 162
Harada, T., 278
Harari, Y. N., 85
Harding, S. R., 230
Haring, M. J., 230
Harker, L., 53, 146
Harrington, A., 293
Harrington, D. M., 165, 167
Harris, P. R., 56
Harter, J. K., 30
Harter, J., 275
Harter, S., 212, 213

Harvey, J. H., 113, 124
Haslam, A., 131
Hatfield, E., 104
Havinghurst, R., 67
Havlena, W., 75
Havlin, S., 137
Hawkins, D. N., 111
Hawley, L., 4, 31
Haworth, J. T., 89
Hayes, S. C., 92, 268, 293
Headey, B., 27, 28, 70
Heath, D. H., 288
Heatherton, T. F., 69
Heidegger, M., 212
Heidrich, S. M., 181, 182, 288
Helgeson, V. S., 193
Helson, R., 121, 185, 186, 201
Hemenover, S. H., 10
Hendrick, C., 104, 105
Hendrick, S. S., 104, 105, 111
Hendricks, G., 144
Henning, K., 225
Heo, J., 80
Heppner, P. P., 142
Herbener, E. S., 108
Hergenhahn, B. R., 171
Herrbach, O., 261
Herrigel, E., 98
Herzog, A. R., 66, 182
Hewitt, J., 56
Hickinbottom, S., 294
Hicks, J. A., 43, 188, 213
Hickson, J., 162
Higgins, E. T., 35
Higgins, R. L., 140
Hildon, Z., 193
Hill, C. E., 110
Hill, G., 44
Hill, P. C., 29
Hill, S., 262
Hitlin, S., 273
Hjelle, L. A., 221
Ho, M. Y., 122
Hoare, C. H., 145
Hodges, T. D., 30
Hoerster, K., 130
Hofer, J., 75
Hoffman, E., 14, 118, 122, 132,
    237, 243, 244, 245, 246, 248,
    249, 251, 263

Hojat, M., 41
Hojjat, M., 108, 113, 114, 122
Holak, S., 75
Holbrook, M. B., 75
Holland, R. W., 40
Holliday, J., 134
Holman, A., 192, 196
Holmes, J. G., 108, 114
Holmes, S., 85
Holt, M., 9, 285
Holt-Lundstad, J., 103, 133, 146
Hölzel, B. K., 144
Honderich, T., 3, 10, 12, 15
Honigmann, J., 288
Hood, R. W., Jr., 229, 241,
    245, 247
Hooley, J. M., 109
Hoon, T. H., 276, 290
Horney, K., 226
Houran, J., 88
Housley, W., 162
Howell, A. J., 144
Howell, C. J., 44
Howell, R. T., 44
Hsing, C., 240
Huang, C., 133
Huang, P., 272
Huang, Y., 133
Huebner, E. S., 269
Hughes, R., 160
Humbert, R., 117
Hunt, M., 16, 122
Hunter, I., 262
Huppert, F., 28
Huta, V., 4, 31, 43
Hutcherson, C. A., 240

Ickes, W., 114
Ickovics, J. R., 128
Ilardi, B., 213
Im, C., 58
Immordino-Yang, M. H., 256
Impett, E., 213
Ingersoll, R. E., 246
Inglehart, R., 276
Ironson, G., 130
Irving, L. M., 141
Isaacowitz, D. M., 181
Isen, A. M., 25, 131, 260
Ito, M., 213

Iversen, V., 244
Izzo, J. B., 243

Jackson, J., 131
Jackson, S. A., 85, 89, 94, 95, 97
Jacob, J. C., 93
Jacobs, J., 146
Jacobs, S., 206
Jahoda, M., 223
James, B. J., 229
James, J., 179
James, W., 17, 18, 181, 200, 231,
    243, 247, 288
Jamison, K., 172
Jang, S. J., 272
Janoff-Bulman, R., 193
Jaycox, L., 181
Jefferson, T., 16, 216
Jeges, S., 195
Jencke, W., 130
Jennings, J., 132
Jensen, A. L., 270
Jesse, R., 254
Jeste, D., 183
Jha, A. P., 144
Jobin, J., 139
Jobs, S., 265
John, O. P., 31, 121
Johnson, D. J., 116
Johnson, D. P., 38, 240
Johnson, K. J., 54
Johnson, M. W., 254
Johnson, R., 181
Jones, A., 221
Jones, B., 103, 133, 144
Jopp, D., 66
Jorgensen, R. S., 195
Jourard, S., 110–111
Julian, T., 193
Julkunen, J., 195
Jung, C. G., 6, 18, 163, 172,
    206–207, 248, 256, 267

Kabanoff, B., 81
Kabat-Zinn, J., 92, 143, 250, 293
Kahn, S., 143
Kahneman, D., 42, 139
Kaiser, R., 291
Kakanen, J., 195
Kamp Dush, C. M., 103

Kamvar, S., 184
Kanthamani, H., 241
Kaplan, B., 131
Kaplan, R., 104
Kaplan, S., 159, 163
Kark, R., 266
Karteroliotis, K., 85, 95
Kashdan, T. B., 28, 31, 58, 88, 142,
    154, 193, 224, 288, 291
Kashubeck, S., 222
Kasser, T., 35, 64, 66, 128, 146, 179,
    215, 272, 291
Kaufman, J. C., 170, 173
Kawachi, I., 130
Keller, M. C., 68
Kelley, B. S., 255
Kelloway, E. K., 85
Kelly, D., 157
Kelly, H. H., 116
Kelly, J. R., 80
Keltner, D., 7, 53, 135, 146, 242
Kennedy, J. E., 241
Kennell, J., 131
Kenrick, D. T., 108
Kernis, M. H., 69, 213
Kerr, S. T., 111
Keyes, C. L. M., 5, 6, 8, 46, 179,
    180, 182, 267, 270
Kiecolt-Glaser, J. K., 134, 138
Kiefer, C. S., 11, 13
Kierkegaard, S., 288
Killingsworth, M., 37, 56
Kilmer, R. P., 287
Kimiecik, J. C., 83, 156
King, B. J., 84
King, D. B., 16, 136
King, L. A., 1, 4, 5, 33, 36, 43, 54,
    58, 69, 130, 138, 181, 188,
    213, 261, 285
King, M. L., Jr., 266
King, S. P., 187
Kingston, T., 144
Kinney, D. K., 173
Kinnunen, U., 195
Kirk, S. B., 149
Kirkeby, B. S., 55
Kirkpatrick, K. L., 240
Kirschman, K., 181
Kisley, M. A., 183
Kitayama, S., 278

Kivnick, H. Q., 179
Klar, M., 272
Klaus, M., 131
Klohnen, E. C., 108
Klonoff, E. A., 231
Knabb, J. J., 248
Knapp, R. R., 221
Knapp, S., 225
Knee, C. R., 44, 214
Knutson, B., 32
Kobasa, S. C., 143, 194
Koch, B. J., 122
Koch, P. T., 122
Kodama, M., 88, 213
Koenig, H. G., 229, 233, 236
Kohlberg, L., 256, 271
Kok, B. E., 129
Kolarz, C. M., 183
Koller, S. H., 122
Kolt, L., 131
Konrath, S. H., 240
Koo, J., 57, 279
Koo, K., 292
Kósa, K., 195
Kovacs, A., 81
Kraemer, H. C., 131
Kramer, D. A., 200, 201
Krampe, R. T., 155
Krane, V., 96, 97
Kraus, M. W., 135
Kring, A. M., 38
Krippner, S., 245
Kris, E., 167
Kristjánsson, K., 291
Kronick, R., 104
Kruger, J., 69, 80
Kryla-Lighthall, N., 28, 184
Kubansky, L., 130
Kubie, L. S., 167
Kuhlmeier, V., 7
Kulik, J., 134
Kunzmann, U., 140, 201, 202, 206
Kupperman, J., 19, 20
Kurtines, W. M., 292
Kuyken, W., 143, 240
Kwan, Y. K., 21

Labouvie-Vief, G., 186, 200, 202
Lachman, M. E., 66, 141, 184
Lachs, M., 146

Lafrenière, M.-A., 157
LaGuardia, J. G., 212, 213
Lakens, D., 128
Lambert, M. J., 9
Lambert, N. M., 232, 288
Landers, D., 86
Landes, S., 180
Landrine, H., 231
Landsman, T., 95, 96, 139
Lang, A., 294
Langer, E. J., 90, 91, 93, 113, 146, 170
Langer, R., 66
Larsen, J. T., 10
Larsen, R. J., 26, 40, 52, 53, 55, 61, 67, 70, 183
Larson, D. B., 229, 236
Larson, R., 67
Lau, M., 92
Lauer, R. H., 111
Lawrence, A. M., 187
Layton, B., 146
Lazar, A., 246
Lazarus, R. S., 141, 147, 148
Le, K., 61
Leary, M., 88, 205, 240, 241
Lechner, S., 193
Lee, Dong-Gwi, 142
Lee, G. R., 103
Lee, J. A., 104
Lee, J. W., 28, 69
Lee, Y., 80
Lefcourt, H. M., 58, 137
LeFevre, J., 87, 262
Leibowitz, R., 140
Leitschuh, G. A., 130
Lemaire, A., 154
Lennon, J., 91, 168, 169
Lent, R. W., 35
Lepper, H. S., 52
Lerner, R., 180, 181
Leskinen, E., 195
Leu, J., 292
Levenson, R. W., 123
Levine, M., 293
Levine, S., 67
Levinger, G., 116
Levy, B., 146
Lewin, K., 289
Lewis, C. A., 230, 232
Lewis, C. S., 221

Lewis, M. L., 67, 131, 275
Li, Z., 278
Light, K., 135
Lightsey, O. R., 56
Liljenquist, K., 257
Limb, C., 161
Lincoln, A., 216, 265, 266
Linehan, M. M., 92, 144
Ling, T. O., 249
Linley, P. A., 267
Lisboa, C., 122
Lishner, D., 240
Little, B. R., 35, 234
Little, S. K., 75
Little, T., 35, 215
Liu, W., 122
Lloyd, D., 137
Lloyd, J., 72
Loerbroks, A., 133
Loevinger, J., 226
Logan, R. D., 85, 179
London, E. C. J., 265
Longhi, E., 162
Lopes, J., 111
Lopes, M., 141
Lopez, S. J., 5, 58, 73, 88, 119, 224, 267, 270
Losada, M. F., 19, 39, 40
Louis, D. Z., 41
Lount, R., 40
Lovas, D. A., 144
Love, G. D., 8, 24
Lowry, R., 14, 15
Lubart, T. I., 164, 165, 170
Lucas, D., 72
Lucas, R. E., 26, 34, 51, 52, 53, 54, 55, 56, 58, 61, 66, 68, 70, 72, 185, 273, 275, 284
Ludden, 2010, 273
Ludwig, A. M., 172
Luminet, O., 41
Lumley, M, 7
Lunde, I., 173
Luo, L., 108
Luthans, C., 260, 261
Luthans, F., 261
Luthar, S., 191
Luther, M., 262
Lutz, A., 25, 240
Lykins, E., 251

Lykken, D., 26, 27
Lytle, D., 81
Lyubomirsky, S., 4, 33, 34, 52, 54, 56, 66, 69, 72, 74, 130, 138, 139, 199, 237, 261, 268

Ma, S. H., 144
MacCallum, R. C., 134
MacCrae, F., 108
MacDonald, M., 184
Maclean, R., 133
Madaus, J. W., 111
Maddi, S. R., 143, 206
Maddux, J. E., 58
Magaloni, I., 72
Magnusson, D., 288, 289
Mahler, H., 134
Mahoney, J. L., 288, 289
Mahoney, M. J., 295
Maimonides, M., 14, 132, 248
Maisel, N., 103, 110, 117
Malarkey, W. B., 134
Maltby, J., 88, 230, 232
Manis, M., 59, 213
Manly, J. B., 128
Mann, J. H., 222, 223, 267
Mannes, E., 89
Mansfield, E. D., 179, 180
Manuck, S., 132
Marchand, M., 80
Marecek, J., 294
Markham, F. W., 41
Markides, K., 146
Markus, H., 278
Marques, J. C., 122
Marsa, 2008, 254
Marsh, H. W., 269
Martens, D., 68
Martin, A. J., 89, 269
Martin, G., 169
Martin, J., 92
Martin, P., 184
Martin, S., 80
Martire, L. M., 80
Marwick, C., 232
Maselko, J., 130
Maslach, C., 259
Maslow, A. H., 7, 18, 72, 80, 171, 184, 215–221, 243, 244, 245, 263, 269, 271, 288

Massimini, F., 86
Mast, J. F., 71
Masten, A. S., 119, 190
Master, A., 192
Mathews-Treadway, K., 230
Matousek, R. H., 144
Matsui, M., 88
Matsumoto, D., 7, 32, 107, 113, 122, 273, 276, 277
Matsumoto, H., 278
Matthews, A., 111
Matthews, K. A., 80
Matthews, M., 157
Matuszek, P., 233
Maul, A., 225
May, R., 167, 210
Mayer, J. D., 40, 41, 42
Mayman, M., 59, 213
Mayr, U., 185
McAdams, D. P., 68, 179, 180, 187
McAndrew, F. T., 71
McAuley, E., 128
McCann, U., 254
McCartney, P., 168
McCauley, C., 262
McClain, T. M., 71
McClelland, D. C., 135
McConatha, J. T., 233
McCormick, B. P., 80
McCrae, R. R., 31, 53
McCraty, R., 129, 162
McCready, W. C., 241
McCullough, M. E., 229, 232, 236, 237, 238, 239
McCutcheon, L. E., 88
McDaniel, W. F., 129
McEwen, B. S., 128
McFadden, S. H., 230, 231
McGavran, M. B. D., 118
McGregor, I., 43, 234
McKay, M., 148
McKnight, P., 28, 288
McLean, K. C., 187, 188
McMahon, F., 81
McNamara, W., 248
McQuillan, J., 85, 88
Mead, M., 288
Mead, N., 64
Medalie, J. H., 134

Medeiros, D. C., 221
Medler, M., 186
Medvec, V., 139
Mehl, M., 110
Meisenhelder, J. B., 232
Menard, V., 122
Merchant, J., 144
Merton, T., 248
Metsäpelto, R.-L., 195
Meyer, B., 107
Michalos, A. C., 54
Midlarsky, E., 224
Mikolajczak, M., 41, 42
Mill, J. S., 15, 16
Miller, D., 269
Miller, J. J., 143
Miller, J. S., 253
Miller, L., 255
Miller, S., 268
Miller, W. R., 247
Minchoff, B., 136
Minda, J. P., 170
Miner, K. N., 138
Mireault, G. C., 246
Mishra, A., 237
Mixter, A., 81, 224
Mlonzi, E. N., 195
Mogilner, C., 184
Mohan, A., 143
Molden, D., 289
Moneta, G. B., 86
Montagne, R., 128, 154
Montaigne, M., 15
Moon, Y-L., 278, 292
Moore, R. A., 170
More, T. A., 159
More, Thomas, 15
Morgan, W. P., 25
Morris, W. N., 33
Moskowitz, D. S., 179
Mount, M. K., 111
Moyers, B., 89
Mroczek, D. K., 183
Muffels, R., 28, 70
Muller, D., 24
Mullett, E., 238
Muramoto, S., 244
Murray, S. L., 108, 114
Myer, P. S., 38
Myers, A., 111

Myers, D. G., 51, 53, 54, 55, 58, 102, 230, 233
Myers, L., 146

Nadler, R. T., 170
Nakamura, J., 20, 83, 85, 87, 89, 90
Nakayama, K., 195
Nanrei Kobori-Roshi, 253
Nanus, B., 266
Narvaez, D., 256
Navarro, J., 90
Nawijn, J., 80
Near, J. P., 51
Neff, K. D., 240
Neff, L. D., 240
Nekic, M., 179
Nelis, D., 42
Nelson, C. M., 269
Nelson, D. L., 233
Nesselroade, J. R., 185
Netuveli, G., 193
Neuhoff, C. F., 137
Neulinger, J., 81
Newberg, A. B., 253
Newburg, D., 156
Newman, J. R., 71
Newton, T., 134
Ng, W., 69, 170, 275
Nicholls, J. G., 164
Nickerson, A., 269
Niebuhr, R., 13
Nielsen, I., 21
Niemiec, C. P., 210
Nietzsche, F., 167, 171
Nishimura, M., 244
Nissen, E., 102
Nitschke, J. B., 25, 43
Nix, G. A., 128
Noftle, E. E., 31
Nolen-Hoeksema, S., 189, 193
Norasakkunkit, V., 278
Norris, C. J., 10
Norris, J. E., 179
Norris, K., 132
Norris, R. C., 143
Norwich, J. J., 156
Notarius, C. I., 103
Novaco, R., 132
Nuckolls, K., 131

Nussbaum, A. D., 214
Nyanaponika, T., 293

O'Brian, E. H., 240
Ogrocki, P., 134
Oishi, S., 28, 52, 53, 54, 55, 58, 66, 67, 68, 72, 185, 273, 275, 278, 284
Okun, M. A., 230
O'Leary, V., 128
Oliviero, H., 65
Oman, D., 230, 231, 232, 233
Omarzu, J., 112
Ong, A., 146, 288
Orbuch, T., 112
Ortiz, F., 122, 244, 263
Osswald, S., 226
Ostir, G., 146
Ostrove, J., 179
Oswald, A., 65, 182, 265, 274
Otto, R., 242
Ouellette-Kobasa, S. C., 143
Ozer, D. J., 108

Page, R., 293
Pahnke, W., 254
Palmer, J., 241
Palmer, S., 131
Paloma, M. M., 230
Paloutzian, R. F., 29, 229, 233, 234, 245, 246
Pals, J. L., 178, 187, 188
Paluska, S., 129
Panksepp, J., 102
Panshin, A., 243
Panshin, C., 243
Panzarella, R., 244
Pargament, K. I., 233
Parish, J. G., 54
Parish, T. S., 54
Park, C. L., 58, 229, 233, 234, 287
Park, N., 30, 31, 73, 268
Parks, A. C., 4
Parks, S. H., 131
Parlee, M. B., 60
Parrott, W. G., 10
Parsa, A., 148
Pascual-Leone, J., 200, 202
Pasupathi, M., 185, 187, 188
Patterson, J. M., 119

Pauwels, B., 113, 124
Pavot, W., 71
Paweleck, J. K., 47
Peacock, J. R., 230
Pedersen, P. M., 80
Pejic, T., 42
Pelled, L. H., 261
Pendleton, B. F., 230
Peng, C. K., 137
Pennebaker, J. W., 137, 138, 140, 142
Pennington, M. B., 248
Peretz, I., 161
Perez, L. M., 233
Perkins, D. N., 91
Perls, T., 145
Persinger, M. A., 253
Pert, C. B., 25
Perunovic, W. Q. E., 28, 69
Peseschkian, N., 268
Peters, E., 86
Peterson, C., 7, 8, 30, 31, 57, 58, 73, 119, 141, 157, 232, 237, 260, 268, 292
Petrarch, F., 15
Petrides, K. V., 41
Petty, R., 129
Phelps, A., 233
Picasso, P., 154, 156, 171, 172
Pickett, N., 162
Pierson, F., 222
Pilisuk, M., 131
Pinder, C., 260, 267
Pirson, M., 91
Plagnol, A., 65
Plante, T. G., 229, 232
Plato, 11, 15
Plaut, V. C., 66
Plutchick, R., 24
Polivy, J., 73
Poloma, M. M., 230, 231
Poon, L., 184
Poortinga, W., 271
Porges, S. W., 129
Post, S., 136, 273
Poulin, M. J., 189
Powdthavee, N., 65, 103, 117
Powell, F. C., 137
Powell, L., 130
Pratt, M. W., 179, 187

Pressman, S. D., 80
Price, W. F., 278
Prior, S., 162
Privette, G., 95, 96, 97
Prizmic, Z., 61, 183
Progoff, I., 139
Pulkkinen, L., 178, 195
Pury, C., 224
Pytlik Zillig, L., 225

Qualls, D., 43
Quick, J. D., 233
Quick, J. L., 233
Quinn, P., 158
Quoidbach, J., 42, 64

Rabi, R., 170
Rabier, J. R., 276
Rabin, B. S., 130
Rabinowitz, C., 41
Rahula, W., 249, 251
Rampell, C., 68
Rand, K. L., 36, 56, 57, 73, 295
Randall, G., 103
Rappaport, J., 272
Rashid, T., 4
Rasmussen, H., 141
Rasulo, D., 146
Rathunde, K., 85, 87, 89, 167, 200, 288
Rawlins, M. E., 130
Rawsthorne, L. J., 212, 213
Reade, L., 31, 291
Reed, M. G. J., 190
Rees, R., 129
Reid, A., 66
Reid, K., 129
Reis, H. T., 66
Reivich, K., 181
Rentfrow, P., 274
Reynolds, F., 162
Reynolds, K. A., 193
Reznitskaya, A., 205
Rhodes, N., 65
Ricard, M., 285
Rice, L. N., 223
Rich, G. J., 134
Rich, S., 26
Richards, R., 173
Richards, W. A., 254

Richardson, F. C., 294
Richardt, A., 42
Richman, L., 130
Rideout, M. C., 270
Riley, J., 230
Rique, J., 238, 239
Ritchart, R., 91
Ritchie, K., 189, 190
Roberts, M., 181
Roberts, T. B., 254
Robertson, S., 131
Robinson, D. N., 11, 12, 13, 200
Robinson, J., 80, 136
Robinson, M. D., 55, 56, 88
Robitschek, C., 222
Rochberg-Halton, E., 75
Rocke, C., 184
Rodgers, W. L., 66, 80, 182
Rodin, J., 90
Roese, N. J., 139
Rogers, C. R., 110, 167, 213, 214–215, 222
Rogers, G., 81
Rogers, N., 167
Rojas, M., 21
Roosevelt, E., 216, 218
Roosevelt, F. D., 266
Rose, P., 58, 224
Rosenkranz, M. A., 24
Rosha, J., 221
Rosnick, C., 184
Ross, C. E., 272
Ross, J. E., 80
Ross, J. M., 255
Rothenberg, A., 172
Rott, C., 66
Rottenberg, J., 142
Rottenberg, R., 140
Rotter, J. B., 57, 141
Rouse, S. V., 47
Rowat, W. C., 241
Rozin, P., 262
Rubinstein, A., 155, 184
Rudd, M. D., 47
Rude, S. S., 240
Ruini, C., 268
Runco, M., 165
Rusbult, C. E., 115, 116
Russek, L. G., 134
Russell, J. A., 24

Russell, T., 91
Rust, T., 31, 291
Rusting, C. L., 61
Ruzek, N., 246, 247
Ryan, L., 88
Ryan, R. M., 33, 34, 35, 43, 44, 57, 80, 92, 128, 144, 146, 212, 213, 214, 215
Ryan-Wegner, N., 131
Ryff, C. D., 8, 24, 46, 178, 179, 180, 181, 182, 184, 268, 288

Sacks, O., 25
Sadalla, E. K., 108
Sadlo, G., 89
Saks, A. M., 260
Salovey, P., 40, 41, 42, 131, 132, 270
Sampson, R., 272, 294
Samuels, C. A., 229
Sandage, S. J., 29
Sanderson, C. A., 35, 43, 235
Sandgren, M., 162
Sandvik, E., 71
Sarason, S. B., 159
Sarkisian, N., 89
Sarkozy, N., 279
Sarmany-Schuller, I., 137
Saroglou, V., 230
Sattah, M. V., 133
Sattler, D. N., 138
Sautter, U., 162
Savary, L., 137
Scales, P. C., 31
Schachtel, R. H., 65
Schachter, Z., 249
Schachter-Shalomi, Z., 249
Schafer, M., 137, 189
Schaufeli, W. B., 259
Scheibe, S., 140, 183, 185, 201, 206
Scheier, M., 28, 57, 80, 141
Scher, S. J., 231, 232
Schiffrin, H., 133
Schimmack, U., 8, 24, 54, 55, 61
Schimmel, S., 12, 14
Schkade, D., 72
Schlaug, G., 161, 162
Schlegel, R. J., 43, 199, 213
Schlesinger, J., 172
Schmuck, P., 291

Schneider, K., 222, 242, 267, 269
Schneider, S., 57
Schnitker, S. A., 31
Schreiner, L., 29
Schubert, T., 128
Schuler, J., 95
Schultz, D., 226
Schumann, R., 178
Schwartz, B., 205, 262
Schwartz, G. E., 134
Schwartz, S. H., 31
Schwarz, N., 42
Schweitzer, A., 216
Schwenk, T., 129
Scioli, A., 141
Scollon, C. N., 70, 80
Scott, C., 286
Scott, K., 74
Scott, T. M., 269
Seagal, J. D., 138
Seccombe, K., 103
Sedikides, C., 75
Seeman, J., 19, 143, 221, 222, 223, 267, 290
Seery, M., 192, 196
Segal, Z. V., 92
Segaller, S. 256
Segerstrom, S., 28, 57, 92, 129, 141
Seidlitz, L., 55
Seidman, E., 272
Seligman, M. E. P., 1, 2, 3, 4, 5, 9, 28, 30, 31, 45, 46, 54, 57, 60, 73, 128, 141, 181, 195, 203–205, 230, 237, 267, 268, 284, 292
Seltzer, M. M., 178
Seppela, E. M., 240
Sergent, J., 35, 215
Sethi, M. L., 162
Shabatay, V., 138
Shackelford, T. K., 101
Shapiro, A. F., 121
Shapiro, S. L., 92, 143, 144, 245
Sharma, R., 143
Sharma, V., 221
Sharpe, K., 205
Shedler, J., 59, 213
Shehan, C. L., 103
Sheldon, K. M., 1, 5, 19, 32, 35, 66, 72, 74, 80, 179, 184, 199,

213, 215, 237, 268, 273, 276, 290, 291
Sheldon, L., 64
Sheler, J. L., 232
Shelton, C. S., 236
Shepela, S. T., 285
Sheridan, S., 119
Sherman, C., 229, 232
Sheu, H., 35
Shin, C. M., 85
Shin, N., 85
Shinn, M., 273
Shippee, T., 189
Shirai, K., 145
Shmotkin, D., 9, 182, 286–287
Siegal, J. M., 134
Sigmon, D. R., 36, 295
Silanathan, N., 257
Silver, N., 112, 123–124
Silver, R., 192, 196
Silverberg, E. L., 149
Silvia, P. J., 88
Simeon, D., 193
Simon, A. E., 141
Simonton, D. K., 156, 164, 173
Simpson, J. A., 114
Sin, N., 268
Singer, B. H., 178, 182
Singer, I., 17
Singley, D., 35
Sirgy, M. J., 64
Skolnick, A., 112
Skoner, D. P., 130
Skowronski, J. J., 56
Slawsby, E. A., 131
Smajlovic, V., 285–286
Smart, C. M., 187
Smart, L., 69
Smith, A. P., 130
Smith, B. W., 233
Smith, D., 141
Smith, G., 193
Smith, H. L., 68
Smith, J., 117
Smith, K., 292
Smith, M. B., 7
Smith, M., 43
Smith, S., 268, 292, 293
Smith, T., 129, 146
Smith, W., 72, 272

Smyth, J. M., 138
Smyth, R., 21
Snowdon, D., 145
Snyder, C. R., 36, 57, 73, 141, 147, 295
Snyder, M., 273
Socrates, 11, 15
Solgian, F., 263
Solomon, S., 64
Sonnentag, S., 7
Sosa, R., 131
Sousa, L., 138
Spector, T., 41
Speicher, C. E., 134
Spencer, M., 131
Spiegel, A., 81
Spiegel, D., 131
Srivastava, S., 185, 186
Stace, W. T., 247
Stack, S., 71
Stafford, L. D., 170
Stalikas, A., 4
Stanat, P., 159
Stanley, H. E., 137
Stansberry, H., 85
Stanton, A. L., 148, 149
Stapleton, S. F., 91
Stark, M., 232
Stark, R., 245
Starr, M. J., 40
Staudinger, U. M., 187, 189, 192, 201, 202, 203
Stavrou, N. A., 85, 95
Staw, B. M., 261
Steca, P., 28
Steen, T. A., 4, 8, 31, 57, 268
Stefanek, M., 131
Steger, M., 28, 58, 88, 224, 234, 287, 288, 291
Stein, G. L., 83
Stein, M., 193
Steinitz, L. Y., 230
Stephan, Y., 224
Steptoe, A., 103
Sternberg, R. J., 104, 105–106, 108, 122, 164, 165, 166, 167, 203–205
Stessman, J., 146
Stets, J. E., 32
Stevenson, B., 63, 65

Stew, G., 89
Stewart, A. J., 139, 179
Stewart, R., 189, 190
Steyn, F., 86
Stock, W. A., 230
Stokols, D., 285
Stolberg, T. L., 243
Stoll, O., 80
Stone-McCown, K., 270
Storm, L., 246
Stout, J. C., 134
Strange, K. C., 134
Strauch, B., 183
Strauss, G. P., 38
Stravinsky, I. F., 156, 160, 161
Strejcek, B., 257
Strickland, B. R., 141
Stroebe, M., 131
Stroebe, W., 131
Strosahl, K., 92, 268
Strumpf, S. A., 265
Strümpfer, D. J. W., 195
Stubbe, J. H., 80
Stukas, A. A., 273
Stunkard, A. J., 58
Stutzer, A., 276
Subkoviak, M. J., 238
Sugarman, J., 294
Suh, E. M., 34, 56, 57, 68, 102,
    275, 278
Sumerlin, J. R., 218
Summerville, A., 139
Surtees, P. G., 133
Sutich, A., 246
Sutton, R. I., 261
Sutton-Smith, B., 81
Suzuki, D. T., 207, 208–209
Suzuki, N., 39
Swan, R., 231
Syme, S. L., 131

Takayama, T., 195
Tamir, M., 32, 43, 88
Tan, H. B., 69
Tang, K., 85
Tangney, J., 240
Tannen, D., 65
Tardif, T. Z., 165, 166
Tarnas, R., 247
Tart, C., 246

Tashiro, T., 117
Tate, G. A., 221
Tay, L., 62, 72
Taylor, C., 17
Taylor, D. G., 246
Taylor, J. B., 254
Taylor, J., 130
Taylor, R. J., 67
Taylor, S., 58, 60, 102, 246
Taylor. D. G., 68
Teasdale, J. D., 92, 144
Tedeschi, R. G., 235
Telfer, E., 12
Tellegen, A., 26, 27, 88
Tennen, H., 193
Terman, L. M., 146, 107
Tesch-Roemer, C., 155
Thalbourne, M. A., 246
Thayer, J., 129
Thayer, R. E., 71
Theorell, T., 162
Thibaut, J. W., 116
Thomas, S. P., 132
Thompson, C. P., 56
Thompson, J. A., 262
Thompson, S., 57, 58, 279
Thomson, J., 75
Thoreau, H. D., 17, 127, 209
Thoresen, C. E., 230, 231,
    232, 233
Thorne, A., 187
Thornton, A., 111
Thorson, J. A., 137
Tice, D. M., 69
Tilquin, J., 230
Tindle, H., 146
Tkach, C., 56, 66, 72, 237
Togari, T., 195
Tomasello, M., 7
Tomasino, D., 162
Tomassini, C., 146
Tomich, P. L., 193
Toohey, S. M., 272, 273
Tov, W., 276
Trappe, H.-J., 162
Trevino, L. K., 88
Triandis, H., 278
Tricomi, E., 276
Tritt, K., 268
Trost, M. R., 108

Trotter, R. J., 167
Trudeau, M., 183
Tsai, J. L., 32
Tsapelas, I., 112
Tucak, I., 179
Tugade, M., 193
Turken, A. U., 25
Turner, J. H., 32
Turner, N., 263
Twenge, J. M., 58
Tyrrell, D. A. J., 130

Ulven, J. C., 73
Underhill, E., 247
Updegraff, J. A., 56
Urrutia, J., 131
Urry, H. L., 8, 24, 25, 43
Uswatte, G., 190

Vahia, I. V., 183
Vaillant, G. E., 136, 141, 193, 196,
    197, 214
Vallerand, R. J., 47, 157
Van Boven, L., 64
Van Dierendonck, D., 266
Van Gelder, M., 237
Van Heck, G. L., 140
Van Horn, K. R., 122
Vandewater, E., 139, 179
Varga, K., 195
Vaughn, C., 81
Vecchio, G. M., 58
Veenhoven, R., 62, 80, 146
Veroff, J., 94
Viney, W., 16, 136
Vingerhoets, A. J. J. M., 140
Vitterso, J., 221
Vohs, K. D., 37, 64, 128
Voss, M., 128

Wachholtz, A. B., 233
Wagner, B., 129
Wagner, G., 28, 70
Wagner, U., 168
Wahba, M. A., 220, 221
Wahkinney, L., 239
Wainwright, N. W. J., 133
Waldstein, S., 129
Walker, C. J., 85
Walker, L., 225

Walker, W. R., 56
Wallas, J., 167
Walumbwa, F., 266
Wang, J., 292
Wapnick, K., 245
Wardle, J., 141
Warhol, A., 165
Warr, P., 260, 264
Washburn, M., 246
Watkins, P., 237, 255
Watson, D., 142
Wayne, K., 85
Weaver, C. N., 103
Weber, T. J., 266
Webster, J. D., 88, 201
Wehmeyer, M., 35, 215, 269
Weinstein, N. D., 57, 69
Weinstock, H., 160
Weitan, W., 23
Welch, I. D., 221
Welles, O., 160
Wells, A., 87
Welwood, J., 117
Welzel, C., 276
Wender, R., 41
Werner, E. E., 190, 191
West, B., 72
Westerhof, G., 189
Whalen, S., 88, 269
Whelan, M., 65
White, M., 268
White, R. W., 33
Whitman, D. S., 265
Whittington, A. C., 233
Whittington, B. L., 231, 232
Whitton, S. W., 115
Wierzbicka, A., 273
Wieselquist, J., 115
Wilbourne, P., 247
Wilcox, K. J., 26
Wilkinson, C., 65

Wilkinson, R., 276
Williams, D., 131, 224
Williams, J. M., 92, 96, 97
Williams, L. E., 24
Williams, R. P., 91
Williamson, G., 183
Willits, F. W., 80
Wilschut, T., 75
Wilson, K., 92, 268
Wilson, T. D., 37
Wink, P., 201
Winkielman, P., 40
Winner, E., 89
Winslet, K., 163
Wirtz, D., 80, 277
Wiseman, R., 74
Wisner, B. L., 144
Wissing, M. P., 86
Withey, S. B., 52
Witter, R., 230
Witters, D., 53
Wohl, M., 239
Wolfers, J., 63, 65
Wolsic, B., 66, 107
Wong, A., 68
Wong, P., 276, 285, 286–287, 288
Wood, A. M., 65, 212, 213, 237
Wood, J. V., 28, 69
Wood, S., 183
Wood, W., 65
Woods, R., 246
Woodworth, J., 66, 182
Woolfolk, R. L., 9, 285
Wordsworth, W., 17, 243
Wright, F. L., 156, 172
Wright, J. J., 89
Wrosch, C., 139
Wrzesniewski, A., 262
Wulff, D., 247
Wupperman, P., 42
Wynd, C., 131

Xia, Y., 122
Xie, X., 122
Xu, A., 122

Yalom, I. D., 234, 235
Yamaki, C., 195
Yamazaki, Y., 195
Yang, Y., 62, 65, 66, 67, 68
Yip, W., 270, 271
Yong, E., 145
Yoo, S. H., 41
Yurkewicz, C., 88
Yussef, F., 260, 261
Yves-Simon, J. Y., 263

Zacharatos, A., 263
Zagorski, N., 161
Zammit, C., 162
Zarrett, N., 179
Zatorre, R. J., 161
Zautra, A., 288
Zeidan, F., 144
Zell, Anne L., 241
Zenter, M., 106
Zervas, Y., 85, 95
Zhai, Q., 21
Zhang, J., 139
Zhang, L., 58
Zhang, W., 193
Zhong, C–B., 257
Zhou, X., 75
Zimbardo, P., 28, 225
Zimmer, M. R., 75
Znoj, H., 42
Zoccola, P. M., 25, 102
Zonderman, A. B., 53
Zou, X., 64
Zuckerman, M., 44, 214
Zuroff, D. C., 179
Zyzanski, S. J., 134

Subject Index

Absorbed attention, 86
Absorption, 88, 94, 159, 224
Acceptance, 218–219
Acceptance and commitment therapy (ACT), 268
Accommodation, 178
Achievers, 186
ACT. *See* Acceptance and commitment therapy
Action orientation, 262
Active-destructive response, 110
Activity theory, 43–44
Adaptive competence, 146
Adler, Alfred, 206
Adolescents. *See* Youth
Adults: playfulness, 81; posttraumatic growth, 193–194; resiliency in, 192–196; sense of coherence, 194–195; well-being in, 181–185
Aesthetics, 158–163; attributes of, 159–161; definition of, 159; importance of, 159; origins of, 163
Affect: complexity, 186; forecasting, 36–37; optimization, 186
Affectionate attention, 92
Affective forecasting, 36–37
Agape, 105
Age: identity, 189; subjective well-being and, 66–67
Age of Enlightenment, 15–16
Aging: positive, 145–147, 183–185; successful, 80, 183–185
Agreeableness, 61–62
Altruism, 136. *See also* Volunteerism; religion and, 233
Angst, 209
Anhedonia, 140

Appreciation, 219, 236–238
Aristotle, 11
Art, 161–162
Art therapy, 162
Assimilation, 178
Athletes, 94–95, 97, 162–163
Attention: absorbed, 86; affectionate, 92; bare, 92; bids for, 109–110, 117; interested, 86; paying, 86
Attentional switching, 86
Attitude, 92; elements in mindfulness meditation, 93
Authenticity: defenses and, 213–214; existentialism and, 209–214; well-being and, 213
Authoritative parenting style, 118–119
Autonomous motivation, 33–34
Awe, 241–242

Balance theory, 116, 203–205
Bare attention, 92
Basking, 94
Beauty, 162–163
Behavior, 28–31; positive organizational, 267; spontaneous, 260
Behavioral medicine, 133
Benefit finding, 189
Bids for attention, 109–110, 117
Big Five, 31
"Billiard ball" model of causality, 289
"Blue zones," 146–147
Bottom-up theory, 54–55
Brain: "happy," 25; left brain/right brain, 168; middle-aged, 183; music and, 161; mysticism and, 251–253

Brainstorming, 171. *See also* Creativity
Broaden-and-build model, 37–39, 73
Buddhism, 240, 249–250; approach to mindfulness, 91–93; comparison between Ellen Langer's and Buddhist styles of mindfulness, 93–94; healthy and unhealthy mental factors of, 250

Capitalization, 110
Careers, 267–270
CASIO model of assessment, 47
Challenges, 160
Character, 29
Character Education, 270
Children. *See also* Youth: experience of, 17; family and, 118; forgiveness and, 238; protective factors for resilience in, 191; resiliency in, 190–192
Christianity, 13–14, 248
Climate, subjective well-being and, 67–68
Cognition, 28; health and, 140–142; models of, 98; predictors, 58–60; stages of religious, 255–256; subjective well-being and, 55–60; wisdom and, 202
Coherent positive resolution, 188
Collective efficacy, 272–273
Commitment, 106; motivation and, 155; script, 180
Communication, 109–111
Community interventions, 273
Community psychology, 272–273
Compassion, 6–7, 239–240; health and, 135–136; self-compassion, 240
Competence, 146

Complete mental health, 5–6; model of, 6
Conflict, 122–123
Conscientiousness, 61–62
Conservers, 186
Construals, 55–56
Consummate love, 106
Contemplative spirituality, 246–248
Control, 57–58; personal, 58
Controlled motivation, 33–34
Conversion, 245
Coping, positive, 147–149; comments on, 149; definition of, 147; dimensions of, 148; emotion-focused, 148; importance of daily hassles, 147–148; problem-focused, 148–149; religion and, 233; styles, 148–149
Cosmic meaning, 234
Counseling, 124
Couples, 116
Courage, 224
Creativity, 164–171, 219; comparisons between excellence and creativity, 166; confluence approach to, 170; creative environments, 168; creative person, 165–166; creative process, 166–168; description of, 164; emotional, 171; left brain/right brain and, 168; meaning of life and, 235; personal growth and, 171; potential of, 170–171; product approach to, 170; research perspectives of, 164–170; role of the unconscious in, 167; stages of the creative process, 167–168
Crying, 140
Culture: of appreciation, 112; collectivist, 278–279; community psychology and, 272; conceptualizations of self, 278; cultural conceptualization of emotions, 276–278; definition of, 273; individualistic, 278; influences on relationships, 121–122; positive psychology and, 32;

subjective well-being and, 67–68, 275–279
Curiosity, 88, 224

Daimonic, 210
Dalai Lama, 249
Dance therapy, 161–162
Defense mechanisms, 196–197; adaptive, 197; authenticity and, 213–214; mature, 196–197
Deliberate practice, 155
Demand-withdraw pattern, 123
Democracy, 16; equality and, 276
Depression, as an opportunity, 75–76
Developmental assets, 181
Dewey, John, 269
Dispositional authenticity, 113
Dispositional optimism, 57
Divine command theory, 10
Drugs. *See* Entheogens
"Duchenne" smile, 53

Eastern psychology, 293
Education: positive psychology in schools, 269–270; subjective well-being and, 67–68
Effectance motivation, 33
Ego, development of, 226
EI. *See* Emotional intelligence
Elation, 241–242
Emotional creativity, 41–42
Emotional expression, 137–140
Emotional intelligence (EI), 40–42
Emotions: as antidotes to stress, 39; basic, 23–24; biology of, 25–28; broaden-and-build model, 37–39, 73; components of, 24; core affects, 24; cultural conceptualization of, 276–278; genetics of, 25–27, 27–28; independence of positive and negative, 8; intensity and frequency of positive, 70–71; negative, 8–9, 285–287; positive, 3–5, 285–287; regulation of, 42; romantics and, 16–17; sacred, 236–241; social and cultural influences on, 31–32; well-being and positive emotion, 37–42

Empathy, 6–7, 239–240
Empiricism, 15
Employee engagement, 259–267; definition of, 259–260; in flow at work, 262–263; focus on strengths, 263–264; job versus calling, 262; leadership, 265–266; myths of career satisfaction and success, 263; positive emotions and work, 260–261; positive work environment, 264–265; self-actualizing at work, 263
Empowerment: community psychology and, 272; learned, 272
Empty nest syndrome, 121
Engaged living, 88
Engagement theory, 43–44, 263; strength-based approach, 263–264
Enlightenment, 249–250
Entheogens, 254–255
Epicureans, 12–13
Epiphany, 241
Equality, democracy and, 276
Erikson's model of life stages, 178–180
Eros, 105
Ethics, 220, 256–257
Eudaimonia, 12, 43
Evaluation theory, 56
Evolution, love and, 101–102
Excellence, pursuit of, 153–158; comparisons between excellence and creativity, 166; definition of, 153; development of, 154–156; foundations of, 153–154; grit, 157–158; passion, 157; passion and performance model, 158; practice and, 155; resonance, 156–157; ten-year rule, 156; wisdom and, 202–203
Exercise, 128–129
Existentialism: authenticity and, 209–214; positive psychology and, 286–287; Rollo May and, 210; Viktor Frankl and, 210–211

Experience sampling method, 40
Exploratory narrative processing, 188
Extraversion, 60–61

Facebook, 271
Family, 42; empty nest syndrome, 121; flourishing, 118–119; life cycle of, 120–121; positive, 117–122; resilient, 119–120; social and cultural influences, 121–122
Family-centered positive psychology, 119–120
Fight-or-flight response, 37, 102
Fixed mindset, 192
Flooding, 123
Flourishing, 5, 43, 45
Flow and optimal experience, 82–90, 97–98; absorption and curiosity, 88; characteristics of, 83–85; comments on, 89–90; contexts and situations of, 85–86; definition of, 82; microflow, 85–96; model of, 85; nature of the experience, 84; skills and, 84–85; subjective well-being and, 86–88; unique qualities of, 86; at work, 262–263
Forgiveness, 238–239; phases of, 239; self-forgiveness, 239
Four Cardinal Virtues, 14
Four Horsemen of the Apocalypse, 123
Frankl, Viktor, 210–211, 287
Freud, Sigmund, 206
Friendship, health and, 132–133
Fromm, Erich, 207–209
Fulfillment, 46–47
Fully functioning person, 214–215
Fundamental attribution error, 113

Gemeinschaftsgefühl, 206
Gender, 91; happiest man in America, 68–69; subjective well-being and, 65–66, 103
Generativity, 179–180
Genetics: emotions and, 25–28; influences on well-being, 26
Genius, 172–173; madness and, 172–173

Global meaning, 234
Goals: abstract, 35; approach, 35; avoidance, 35; balance with life, 36; concrete, 35; goal-achievement gap, 98; motivation and, 34–37; short-term, 35
Good life: Greek ideas on, 13; qualities of, 3
Gore, Vice President Al, 272
Gratitude, 236–238
Grit, 157–158
Growth mindset, 192

Happiness, 9, 51. *See also* Subjective well-being; age and, 66–67; alternatives to, 287–288; authentic, 45–46; definitions, 42–47; five happiest countries in surveys of well-being, 274; gender and, 65–66; happiest man in America, 68–69; importance of, 53–54; income and, 63; increasing, 74–76; maintenance of, 74; sustainable, 72–73
Happiness set point, *See* Set point, happiness
Happiness Training Program (Fordyce), 71–72
Hardiness, 143, 194
Harmonious passion, 157
Health, 127–151; cognition and, 140–142; comments on, 149; compassion and, 135–136; emotional expression and, 137–140; emotionality, 130–131; exercise and, 128–129; friendship, confidant relationships and, 132–133; hardiness and, 143; humor and, 136–137; Internet use and positive relationships, 133; longevity, 145–147; love and, 134–136; marriage and, 103–104; music and, 137; positive, 128–130; positive aging, 145–147; positive coping, 147–149; psychological factors important to, 130–142; psychoneuroimmunology and,

129–130; regret and, 139–140; religion and, 230–231; social support and, 131–132; social support and the immune system, 134; social support from pets, 134; vagal tone and heart rate variability, 129; vitality and, 128; wellness, 127–128
Heart rate variability (HRV), 129
Hedonic adaptation, 70
Hedonic calculus, 16
Hedonic perspectives, 42–43
Hedonic treadmill theory, 64, 70
Hedonism, 10, 42–43
The Hero Project, 225–226
Homogamy, 107–108
Hope theory, 36, 56–57, 140–141. *See also* Optimism; training, 73
Horizontal transcendence, 229
HRV. *See* Heart rate variability
Humanistic psychology, 18–19
Humility, 240–241
Humor, health and, 136–137
Hypnosis, 98
Hypoegoic state, 88

Immune system, social support and, 134
Immunoglobulin A, 135
Income, subjective well-being and, 62–65, 275
Individuation, 207
Intelligence: emotional, 40–42; IQ, 158, 165, 168–169
Intention, 92
Interested attention, 86
Internet, 133
Intimacy, 105
Intrinsic interest, 159–160
IQ, 158, 165, 168–169

Jahoda, Marie, 223–224
JCM. *See* Job characteristics model
Job characteristics model (JCM), 263
Jonah complex, 218
Joy, 38, 162
Jung, Carl G., 206–207; on religion and spirituality, 256

Kabbalah, 248–249
Knight Foundation, 170–171
Knowledge base, 154

Laugh clubs, 137
Leadership, 265–266
Learned empowerment, 272
Learned optimism, 28, 57, 141, 181
Learned powerlessness, 272
Leisure, 79–82; activity into, 81–82;
    definition of, 80; vacations, 80;
    well-being and, 79–81
Leisure worlds, 81–82
Life. *See also* Well-being: adjusting to
    difficult events, 189–197;
    differences in lifespan
    development, 185–189; good,
    158–163; harmony in, 234;
    midlife crisis, 182–183; models,
    178–185; normative events in,
    178; numinous experiences,
    245; peak experiences,
    244–245; purpose in, 288;
    recognizing a life well-lived,
    284–285; satisfaction with, 51,
    87; sense of meaning in, 58,
    234–241, 287–288; themes,
    188; well-being across the
    lifespan, 177–198; wisdom as a
    stage of, 201–202
Life coaching, 268–269
Life longing, 140
Limerence, 105
Livability theory, 62
Longevity, 145–147
Love, 17; biochemistry of, 102;
    communication, 109–111;
    companionate, 104;
    consummate, 106; demand-
    withdraw pattern, 123;
    evolution and, 101–102; health
    and, 134–136; hierarchy of,
    106–107; maps, 113;
    passionate, 104; as a prototype
    or an ideal, 106; romance and,
    88, 107–108, 112; Sternberg's
    love triangle, 105–106;
    stonewalling, 123; styles of,
    104–105; two-factor theory of,
    104; varieties of, 104–107;
    well-being and, 101–126

"Love hormone" (oxytocin), 25, 102
Loving kindness meditation, 73
Ludus, 105
Luxuriating, 94

Mania, 105
Marriage. *See also* Relationships:
    counseling, 124; health and,
    134; nurturing, 123–124;
    physical health and, 103–104;
    positive, 104; quality of,
    102–103; satisfaction, 120;
    well-being and, 102–104, 117
Marveling, 94
Maslow, Abraham, 215–221
Maturity, development of, 185–189
May, Rollo, 210
MBSR. *See* Mindfulness-based stress
    reduction program
Meaning. *See also* Purpose: 20, 211
    (will to meaning), 234–236, 286
    (meaning mindset), 287–288
Meditation. Buddhist, 91–93;
    elements in mindfulness, 93;
    loving kindness, 73; mindfulness
    and, 143–144, 250–251
Memory-building, 94
Men, subjective well-being and,
    65–66
Mental health, two-continua model
    of, 8
Merging, 86
Michelangelo phenomenon, 115
Microflow, 85–86
Middle Ages, 13–14
Midlife crisis, 182–183
Mindfulness, 90–94, 97–98;
    acceptance and respect, 115;
    Buddhist approach to, 91–93;
    comparison between Ellen
    Langer's and Buddhist styles of,
    93–94; definition of, 90;
    elements in meditation, 93;
    Ellen Langer's approach to,
    90–91; intense experiences, 93;
    meditation and, 143–144,
    250–251
Mindfulness-based stress reduction
    (MBSR) program, 144
Minding, 112–117; attributions,
    113–115; balance theory, 116;

continuity, 116–117; felt
    security, 117; knowing and
    being known, 113;
    Michelangelo phenomenon,
    115; reciprocity, 115–116;
    romantic illusions and,
    114–115; social exchange
    theory, 116
Model of meaning making, 235
Models: "billiard ball" model of
    causality, 289; broaden-and-
    build, 37–39, 73; CASIO model
    of assessment, 47; of cognition,
    98; of complete mental health,
    6; of Dov Shmotkin, 286;
    Erikson's model of life stages,
    178–180; of flow, 85; of goal-
    achievement gap, 98; job
    characteristics model, 263; life,
    178–185; model of meaning
    making, 235; passion and
    performance model, 158; of
    Paul Wong, 286–287;
    Resonance Performance
    Model, 157; selective
    optimization with
    compensation, 184–185;
    self-expansion model, 115; of
    social constraints, 31–32;
    sustainable happiness, 72–73;
    systems perspective model,
    290–291; value-as-moderator
    model, 185; of well-being,
    178–185
Modes of fulfillment, 46–47
Monastic Christianity, 248
Money, subjective well-being and,
    62–65, 275
Moods: strategies for creating a good
    mood, 71; well-being and,
    32–33
Morality, 256–257
Moses Maimonides, 14
Mother Teresa, 239
Motivation, 33–37; autonomous,
    33–34; controlled, 33–34;
    early theories of, 33; effectance,
    33; intrinsic and extrinsic, 33–34;
    pursuit of goals and, 34–37
Music, 161–162, 285–286; brain
    and, 161; health and, 137

Mysticism, 15, 219, 247–248. *See also* Religion; Spirituality; the brain and, 251–253
"Myth of the hero," 189

Narrative therapy, 268
National Institute of Play, 81
Need fulfillment, 275
Needs (Maslow), 216–221; being (B-needs), 217; deficiency (D-needs), 217; security versus growth, 217–218
Negative reciprocity, 123
Negative sentiment override, 123
Neuromysticism, 251–253
Neuroplasticity, 25
Neurotheology, 253–254
Neuroticism, 51, 62
Nirvana, 249–250
Nostalgia, 75
Numinous experiences, 245
Nun study, 145–146

Obsessive passion, 157
Openness to Experience, 81, 92, 214, 218, 224
Optimal experiencing, 89
Optimism, 56–57, 141, 146. *See also* Hope theory; dispositional, 57; future of positive psychology and, 295; learned, 28, 57, 141, 181; realistic, 57; unrealistic, 69
Oxytocin, 25, 102

Parents, authoritative style, 118–119
Passion, 105, 107, 157; definition of, 157; harmonious, 157; obsessive, 157
Passive-destructive response, 110
Paying attention, 86
PBS. *See* Positive Behavior Support
Peak experiences, 244–245
Peak performance, 94–98; in sports, 94–95, 96–97; training for, 97
Penn Resiliency Program, 181
Perceived control, 141–142
PERMA theory, 45–46
Personal control, 58
Personal growth: creativity and, 171; human potential and, 222–223; initiative, 222

Personality integration, 221–222; religion and, 233
Personality traits, 60–62, 165–166; agreeableness, 61–62; Alfred Adler and, 206; attributions and, 114; Carl Jung and, 206–207; conscientiousness, 61–62; Erich Fromm and, 207–209; extraversion, 60–61; neuroticism, 62; optimal, 223–226; psychodynamic ideas of optimal, 206–209; relationships and, 108–109; of self-actualizing people, 218–220
Pets, social support, health and, 134
Plateau experience, 245
Plato, 11
Pleasure, 25, 159
PNI. *See* Psychoneuroimmunology
POB. *See* Positive organizational behavior
Politics, subjective well-being and, 67–68
Positive Behavior Support (PBS), 269
Positive clinical psychology, 268
Positive communities, 270–273; flourishing, 270–271; social networks and, 271
Positive emotions, 3–5, 130–131, 145–146
Positive ethics, 225
Positive Growth Initiative, 223
Positive illusions, 69
Positive mental health, 223–224
Positive organizational behavior (POB), 267
Positive psychology, 1–22; basic themes of, 3–9; careers and, 267–270; cross-cultural considerations, 292–295; culture and, 32; description of, 1–2; dimensions of, 2; existentialism and, 286–287; family-centered, 119–120; foundations of, 23–49; future of, 283–296; integration with general psychology, 291; interventions, 73–74; motivation and, 33–37; optimism and, 295; positive and negative emotions, 285–287; in

schools, 269–270; scope of, 2–3; systems perspective, 290–291; in the twenty-first century, 20–21; values and, 291–292
Positive psychotherapy, 267–268
Positivity effect, 183
Positivity ratio, 40
Post-modern psychology, 293–294
Posttraumatic growth, 189
Pragma, 105
Prayer, 248; well-being and, 231–232
Productive orientation, 208–209
Productive personality, 208–209
Prosocial intention, 262
Prosperity, types of, 277
PsyCap. *See* Psychological capital
Psychological capital (PsyCap), 261
Psychological flexibility, 142
Psychological immunity, 190
Psychological well-being (PWB), 182
Psychological Well-Being Scale, 182
Psychoneuroimmunology (PNI), 129–130
Psychosocial development, 179
Purpose in life. *See also* Meaning, 28, 46, 288
PWB. *See* Psychological well-being

QOLT. *See* Quality of life therapy
Quality of life, 47
Quality of life therapy (QOLT), 47

Race, subjective well-being and, 67–68
Realistic optimism, 57
Redemptive sequence, 188–189
Regret, 139–140
Relationships. *See also* Marriage; Social relationships: autonomy and, 219; compatibility, 107; conflict and, 122–123; felt security, 117; friendship and confidant relationships, 132–133; Internet use and positive relationships, 133; minding, 112–117; nonregulated couples, 116; nurturing, 123–124; personality traits and, 108–109; positive, 146, 219–220; regulated couples, 116; repair attempts, 123; respect, 115; satisfaction, 108–111;

Relationships (*continued*)
self-expansion model, 115; social and cultural influences, 121–122; stability of, 111–112; validating couples, 116; as a vehicle for personal growth, 116–117

Religion, 229–258. *See also* Mysticism; altruism and, 233; conversion, 245–246; definition of, 229; entheogens and, 254–255; extrinsic, 255; gender and, 230; health and, 230–231; intrinsic, 255; numinous experiences, 245; personality integration and, 233; positive coping strategies and, 233; prayer and, 231–232, 248; psychodynamic perspectives on, 256; psychological theories of religious maturity, 255–257; religious experiences, 236, 241–246; social support and, 233; stages of religious cognition, 255–256; subjective well-being and, 229–230; traditions, 248–251

Renaissance, 15–16

Resacralization, 245

Resiliency, 178, 189–190; in adulthood, 192–196; in children, 190–192; training, 195–196

Resonance, 156–157

Resonance Performance Model (RPM), 157

Respect, 115

Rogers, Carl, 214–215

Romanticism, 16–17

RPM. *See* Resonance Performance Model

Sadness, 163

Salutogenic orientation, 194

Savoring, 94, 97–98; types of, 94

Science: history of, 15; values in, 291–292

"Science of Happiness Project," 74

Search Institute's Developmental Assets Scale, 31

Seekers, 186

Seeman, Julius, 221–222

SEL. *See* Social and Emotional Learning programs

Selective optimization with compensation, 184–185

Self, cultural conceptualizations of, 278–279

Self-actualization, 214–221, 215–216; research on, 220–221; at work, 263

Self-compassion, 240

Self-concordance, 35, 215

Self-congratulation, 94

Self-determination theory, 44

Self-disclosure, 110–111

Self-efficacy, 57–58, 142

Self-esteem, 56

Self-expansion model of relationships, 115

Self-forgiveness, 239

Self-realization, 207

Self-regulation, 92

Self-transcendent person, 211

Self Science curriculum, 269–270

Senses, sharpening, 94

Set point, happiness, 27, 28, 69, 70, 72

Seven Deadly Sins, 14

Sharing, 94

SHM. *See* Sustainable happiness model

Shmotkin, Dov, 286

Skill variety, 263

Smajlovic, Vedran, 285–286

Social and Emotional Learning (SEL) programs, 270

Social capital, 270–271

Social comparison processes, 59–60

Social constraints model, 31–32

Social contagion, 271

Social equality, 276

Social exchange theory, 116

Social interest, 206

Social networks, 271

Social relationships: importance of, 15–16; positive, 7, 60

Social support: health and, 131–132; immune system and, 134; from pets, 134; religion and, 233

Social well-being, 270

Socioemotional selectivity, 185

Socrates, 11

Solution-focused therapy, 268

Spirituality, 229–258. *See also* Mysticism; contemplative, 246–248; definition of, 229; entheogens and, 254–255; transcendent experiences, 254; transpersonal psychology, 246–247

Spontaneity, 219

Sternberg's love triangle, 105–106

"Stockdale paradox," 69

Stoics, 13

Stonewalling, 123

Storge, 105

Strengths, 29–31; signature, 30

StrengthsFinder (Clifton), 29–30

StrengthsQuest Program, 30, 269

Stress, positive emotions as antidotes to, 39

Strivings, well-being and, 36

Subjective well-being (SWB), 51–77, 182. *See also* Happiness; Well-being; age and, 66–67; bottom-up predictors of, 62–69; climate and, 67–68; cognition and, 55–60; down side of feeling up, 69; education and, 67–68; gender and, 65–66; increasing happiness and life satisfaction, 69–76; measurement of, 51–55; money and, 64–65; politics and, 67–68; race and, 67–68; self-report measures of, 52–53; stability of, 53; top-down and bottom-up theories of, 54–55; top-down predictors of, 55–62

Suffering, 235

Supplication, 231. *See also* Prayer

Sustainable happiness model (SHM), 72–73

Suzuki, D. T., 207, 208–209

SWB. *See* Subjective well-being

"Sylvia Plath effect," 173

Systems theory, 289–291

Tao, 229, 294

Tasks: identity, 263; significance, 263

Temperament and Character Inventory, 31
Templeton Prize in Positive Psychology, 20
Temporal realism, 184
Tend-and-befriend response, 102
Ten-year rule, 156
Tetrahydrocannabinols (THC), 25
Thanksgiving, 94, 231, 232
THC. *See* Tetrahydrocannabinols
Thought-action tendencies, 38
Thriving, 128
Time: affluence, 79–80; passage of, 84; poverty, 79–80
Top-down theory, 55
Touch, 134–135
Tragedy, 163
Transcendent experiences, 241
Transformational leadership, 266
Transformation processing, 188
Transpersonal psychology, 246–247
Transcendent functioning, 96
Twins, 146

Undoing hypothesis, 39
Unrealistic optimism, 69
Utilitarianism, 16

Vacations, 80
Vagal tone, 129
Value-as-moderator model, 185
Values, in science, 291–292
Values in Action (VIA) Project, 30–31, 292; classification of character strengths and virtues, 30
Vertical transcendence, 229
VIA. *See* Values in Action Project

Virtues, 7–8, 29–31; marital well-being and, 117; wisdom and, 205
Virtue theory, 12; in the Middle Ages, 14
Vitality, 128
Volunteerism, 273. *See also* Altruism

Wealth, subjective well-being and, 62–65, 275
Well-being. *See also* Life; Subjective well-being: Abraham Maslow and, 215–221; across the lifespan, 177–198; in adults, 181–185; authentic happiness and, 45–46; authenticity and, 209–214; Carl Rogers and, 214–215; cross-cultural subjective, 273–279, 292–295; definitions, 42–47; engagement perspectives, 43–44; eudaimonic perspectives, 43; finding one's true self and, 211–214; five happiest countries in surveys of well-being, 274; flow and, 86–88; gender and, 103; genetic influences on, 26; history of, 9–20, 19–20; humanistic perspectives, 214–223; job characteristics and, 264; Julius Seeman and, 221–222; leisure and, 79–81; love and, 101–126; marriage and, 102–104, 117; modules, 286; money, income, wealth and, 62–65; moods and, 32–33; optimal, 199–227; personal growth and, 222–223; personal traits for optimal, 224–225; positive

communities, 270–273; positive emotion and, 37–42; positive institutions and cultural, 259–281; prayer and, 231–232; psychological, 46; religion and, 229–258; Rollo May and, 210; science of, 9; self-determination theory, 44; spirituality and, 229–258; strivings and, 36; subjective, 51–77; therapy, 268; Viktor Frankl and, 210–211; wisdom and, 201; in youth, 180–181
Wellness. *See* Health
Western psychology, 294–295
Wisdom, 200–206; about, 200–201; balance theory of, 203–205; cultivating, 205–206; as a form of excellence, 202–203; as the "master" virtue, 205; as post-formal cognitive development, 202; practical, 205; predictors of, 203; as a stage of life, 201–202; well-being and, 201
Women: crying and, 140; religion and, 230; social support and, 131–132; subjective well-being and, 65–66
Wonder, 242–244
Wong, Paul, 286–287
Work engagement, 85
World Database on Happiness, 63
Writing, 137–139

Youth. *See also* Children: forgiveness and, 238; positive development, 180–181

Zen meditation, 2–3